Physical
Education for
Elementary
School Children

Physical Education for Elementary School Children

Second Edition

*An Illustrated Program of
Activities for Kindergarten to Grade Six*

Glenn Kirchner
Simon Fraser University

WM. C. BROWN COMPANY
PUBLISHERS
Dubuque, Iowa

PHYSICAL EDUCATION

Consulting Editor
Aileene Lockhart
University of Southern California

HEALTH

Consulting Editor
Robert Kaplan
The Ohio State University

PARKS AND RECREATION

Consulting Editor
David Gray
California State College, Long Beach

Dedicated to elementary school teachers who hold the key to making physical education a truly educational experience.

Acknowledgments

In the first edition I indicated it was the result of a pooling of ideas developed by teachers and students in several schools throughout the United States. Because of this extensive collaborative and cooperative effort it was difficult to single out one or two individuals for special acknowledgment.

The changes and additions which have been included in this second edition are again the result of experimental programs involving numerous teachers and, of course, hundreds of children. The writer would like to express his sincere appreciation to the Coquitlam School District, and particularly to Mr. R. McBay and his staff of the Porter Street School, for their assistance in several experimental programs. Many of the ideas developed in these programs are contained in this text. Also, the numerous suggestions provided by Mr. David Turkington, Mrs. Jean Cunningham, and Miss Eileen Warrell were most helpful in the preparation of this material.

Many of the ideas set out in Chapter 15 (Educational Gymnastics) were obtained from observations and discussions with numerous classroom teachers and supervisors while in England during my sabbatical year. To these teachers, and particularly to the children who really provided the majority of the movement ideas, my deepest gratitude.

I would like to express my appreciation also to the teachers and supervisors who have sent me suggestions relating to various parts of this book. They will recognize that many of their ideas have been incorporated herein.

I would also like to express my sincere gratitude to Mrs. Doris Muzzlewhite, my patient secretary, for her enduring efforts in the typing of this manuscript.

Preface

The material in this second edition has been written and extensively illustrated to meet the unique and changing needs of classroom teachers. Since the first edition, the writer has had the good fortune to participate in several experimental projects and to visit numerous innovative programs in Canada, England, and the United States. Many of the ideas and activities observed in these programs are incorporated in this text.

Changes in the structure and content of contemporary elementary school physical education have necessitated a major reorganization of the material in this edition. This new format coupled with the addition of several new chapters will provide classroom teachers and supervisors of elementary school physical education with a basic reference to the content and methods used in this subject. The major purpose of this text is to aid elementary school majors who are required in their major curricula to take a course in physical education. Many teaching suggestions are provided as well as hundreds of illustrations to assist these beginning teachers to acquire skills, knowledge, and understanding of this very important, meaningful, and enjoyable subject in the elementary school curriculum.

In Part I, the meaning and purpose of elementary school physical education is presented. Also included in this section is a discussion of the characteristics of children and how they learn motor skills.

Part II provides the necessary information to plan, organize, and evaluate a physical education program. Although there are many "how-to" suggestions contained in this important part of the text, each respective chapter provides a format or basis whereby each classroom teacher can choose methods, techniques, and organizational procedures that best fit her *own* teaching style.

Parts III, IV, and V may be considered the resource areas. Part II contains individual and team game activities and includes illustrations of skills and suggested lessons and unit organization for Kindergarten through Grade Six. A new chapter, entitled "Games from Other Countries," has been included to provide a new source of extremely interesting and enjoyable games.

One of the most significant changes occurring in the elementary school physical education program is within the self-testing area. In Part IV a distinction is first made between our contemporary approach to teaching these activities and what is known as Educational Gymnastics. This is followed by three chapters which contain the basic stunts, tumbling, and apparatus activities currently being taught in the majority of elementary schools. Chapter 15, and being the last chapter in Part IV, describes the Educational Gymnastics approach and illustrates how it can be incorporated in the self-testing program of any grade. Once teachers develop sufficient understanding of this new and exciting approach, there will undoubtedly be a gradual adoption of its creative and exploratory methods and techniques.

Part V includes the fundamental skills of dance, descriptions of numerous folk dances and singing games, and an introduction to creative movements.

Due to the continuing importance given to physical fitness, Part VI has been included to provide the basic information relating to fitness testing and follow-up procedures.

General information pertaining to diagrams of inexpensive equipment is provided in the Appendix. The latter section should be extremely useful to teachers with limited equipment and facilities. The cost of these items is negligible; most teachers could make them for a few dollars and in a short period of time.

G. K.

Contents

PART III

Game Activities

PART IV

Self-Testing Activities

PART V

Dance Activities

PART VI

Physical Fitness Evaluation

APPENDIXES

Foundation
of Physical Education

P
A
R
T
I

Part I is designed to provide teachers with a basic history and philosophy of physical education and an understanding of the characteristics of children and how they learn motor skills. The first chapter covers the objectives of physical education and presents the trend and contemporary meaning of this activity in the elementary school curriculum. In Chapter 2 the basic considerations relating to the growth and development of each age group are discussed and their implications to the program of instruction are outlined. Chapter 3 is concerned with the theories and principles of teaching and how these should direct the learning of various tasks in physical education.

Meaning and Purpose of Physical Education

T HE nature of physical education and the contributions it can make to the educational process is the subject of this introductory chapter. A simple statement of the objectives of a well-conceived program tells very little of the transition in content and method that has occurred in this subject area. Hence, a very brief historical review of physical education is first presented to provide some perspective of the past, the present, and the future role of this subject in the elementary school curriculum. The objectives of physical education are stated in relationship to the broad purposes of all education since physical education is but one important part of the total program. Finally, since the ultimate success of any program rests with classroom teachers, a few important comments are made with respect to the qualifications of a successful teacher of physical education.

HISTORICAL DEVELOPMENT OF PHYSICAL EDUCATION

The history of education reveals that physical education has always been present but as a subject it has been regarded with varying degrees of importance. In the age of the classical Greeks the idea of a harmony of body and mind was emphasized in the education of its citizens. This concept of unity and balance involved the harmonious development of the mental, physical, and spiritual aspects of the human personality. Consequently, physical education was considered an integral component of the educational program with similar purposes but unique contributions. Plato expressed this idea in his writings and by personal exemplifications of his participation in physical exercise.[1] During this period in the history of man such balance of mind and body produced men of genius and a culture rarely equaled in the generations which followed.[2] The warlike Spartans, however, emphasized the physical training of the body for military purposes. Repetition of the latter emphasis has been recorded in virtually every civilization which followed. One major exception was the aesthetic which, throughout the Middle Ages, stressed the spiritual to the complete neglect of the physical and social aspects of man and society.

From the Period of Enlightenment to the Twentieth Century, education primarly emphasized the intellectual development of man. Physical Education, expressed in terms of natural play or organized activities such as gymnastics and games, was emphasized by such writers as Locke, Rousseau, and Spencer. The purposes of such programs, however, were conceived in terms of "training" the body to enhance optimum intellectual development. It has only been

---

1. Plato, *Republic*, trans. F. M. Cromford (New York: Clarendon Press, Oxford University Press, Inc., 1941).

2. P. J. Arnold, *Education Physical Education and Personality Development* (London: Heinemann Educational Books Ltd., 1968), p. 3.

during the Twentieth Century that the Greek ideal of balance and harmony has returned to the philosophy education.

Since the beginning of the Twentieth Century there have been profound changes in the philosophy, content, and methods of teaching at all levels in the public school. These changes toward "education for democratic living" were not brought into existence by chance. New theories of learning, such as those presented by Thorndike and Gestalt psychology, have produced significant changes in the way children are taught.[3] Dewey and his disciples made their interpretations of the nature of learning chiefly in terms of social and philosophical rationale. The combined influences of philosophers, economists, and educators provided the impetus and rationale for the transition toward a liberal or general education for all citizens.

Physical education too has undergone profound changes in the nature of its activities and methods of teaching. At the turn of the Twentieth Century rigid gymnastic programs were still strongly emphasized although games were beginning to be accepted as a valid part of elementary and secondary school physical education programs. The influence of Dewey, particularly during the period between 1930-40, created major changes in the philosophy and thereby in content of physical education. Gymnastics were almost eliminated from the program while games were given a predominant role. Because the educational emphasis was on "learning by doing" with children allowed to determine their own needs and interests, play through games was considered to contribute strongly to social adjustment and only minor emphasis was placed on skill and physical development.

During the early 1940's and until the latter part of the 1960's physical education programs were changed substantially. Increased attention has been given to the professional preparation of specialists in physical education as well as for classroom teachers. State laws requiring physical education, coupled with certification requirements, have also upgraded the caliber of teaching this subject. Extensive research in such areas as growth and development, motor learning, and physical performance has brought back the rationale for a balanced program of physical activities for all levels of public and private education. International conflicts have, for reasons of national survival, required a special emphasis on physical fitness. Trends in automation and urbanization throughout the western world now present physical educators with possibly their greatest challenge: a program, in harmony with the contemporary philosophy of education, to develop within each child sufficient skill, knowledge, health, and fitness, and a positive attitude toward continuous participation in wholesome recreational activities throughout life.

The majority of elementary school physical education programs today are virtually at the crossroads. Traditional "group-paced" instructional pro-

---

3. E. L. Thorndike, *Principles of Teaching* (New York: A. G. Seiler Co., 1906).

grams are giving way to "individualized" programs and this requires major changes in the physical environment of the school (open area plans and flexible scheduling) as well as the adoption of methods and techniques that emphasize self-direction through exploratory and problem-solving methods. Games, dance, and self-testing activities are important parts of a modern program of physical education. What must change, however, is the *way* in which we teach these activities. We appear to be moving toward this type of program with more enthusiasm than has ever been shown with our previous programs. Major emphasis on individualized instruction and creative teaching is an exciting and challenging task for all specialists and classroom teachers of Physical Education.

OBJECTIVES OF PHYSICAL EDUCATION

Many elementary school teachers think of physical education as a daily period devoted to games or other physical activities, while others think of it as the major sports program or just athletics. Neither impression is correct, for physical education in its modern connotation includes all the physical activities from the simplest classroom game to the more vigorous and highly organized competitive sports. Physical education is that part of the educational process which contributes to the mental, physical, social, and emotional growth and development of *each* child through the medium of physical activity.[4]

To enable the elementary school teacher to better understand the contemporary role of physical education it is helpful to state the generally accepted purposes of elementary education. Once these purposes are understood, the aims of physical education can be seen as unique, yet in harmony with the broad purposes of the total curriculum.

Purpose of Elementary Education

Numerous statements developed by many leading educational organizations over the past five decades represent the general goals of elementary education. For example, the 1938 Educational Policies Commission outlined four broad objectives which were subsequently used as a basis upon which many state and local organizations structured their educational programs. These were:[5] (1) objectives of self-realization; (2) objectives of human relationships; (3) objectives of economic efficiency; and (4) objectives of civic responsibility. In mid-century, another comprehensive study was undertaken to determine what changes in the fundamental objectives of elementary education have developed since the 1938 Educational Policies Commission's four-

---

4. Charles A. Bucher, *Foundations of Physical Education* (St. Louis: C. V. Mosby Co., 1952), p. 30.

5. Education Policies Commission, "The Purpose of Education in American Democracy," (Washington, D.C.: 1938).

point statement. This was done in the early 1950's by focusing attention on those objectives most often presented to the elementary school.[6]

The following recommended areas were identified at that time as being the most often allocated to the elementary school.[7]

1. Physical development and body care. This objective is interpreted to include an individual's health and safety, physical education, and an understanding of human growth and development.
2. Individual social and emotional development. This category includes knowledge and understanding relating to mental health, emotional stability, and growth of personality. The emphasis should be on understanding and evaluating oneself.
3. Ethical behavior, standards, and values. This area involves the development and fostering of such qualities as sportsmanship, kindliness, helpfulness, and the problems involved in living in a society with other people.
4. The social world. The child in this category is considered in a broader social setting. The behavior of the child is seen in relationship to the community, state, and nation. Civics, elementary geography, economics, and the traditional way of life are included in this broad area.
5. Social relations. This area is devoted to the individual as a person; his personal-social relations with others when he has to consider their needs, interests, motives, and ideals.
6. The physical world (the natural environment). Attention is centered on an enlarged concept of science with reference being made to many aspects of a child's environment. Physical science problems as well as the science that deals with plants and animals are emphasized. Stress is on learning to think scientifically.
7. Aesthetic development. In this area emphasis is placed on aesthetic appreciation and expression. Although primary emphasis is given to art, music, and crafts, other types of creative expression are also encouraged.
8. Communication. This area emphasizes the mechanical and skill aspect of reading, writing, composition, speaking, and listening. It also includes group skills such as conducting a meeting.
9. Quantitative relationships. This involves the ability to analyze and solve problems on the basis of the particular type of problem, the information needed to solve it, and how to get information. Emphasis is on giving a child an understanding of how our number system works and why, so he will have greater competence in using numbers.

Other statements could be quoted; however, in the main they are all very similar in purpose. Note the specific reference to "physical development, health, body care" as a major objective for elementary education.

---

6. G. W. Sowards and M. M. Soobey, *The Changing Curriculum and the Elementary Teacher* (Belmont: Wadsworth Publishing Co. Inc., 1962), p. 46.

7. N. C. Kearney, *Elementary School Objectives* (New York: Russell Sage Foundation, 1953), p. 52.

It should be clearly evident that the philosophy which underlies the entire elementary school curriculum must, in a very direct manner, prescribe the objectives of elementary school physical education.

Purpose of Physical Education

The basic aim of physical education is to contribute to optimum physical, mental, social, and emotional growth of each individual in order that he may take his place as an active member in a democratic society. Translating this broad purpose into meaningful objectives is no mean task for the teacher. It is, however, generally agreed by most supervisors and teachers of physical education that the basic objectives of physical education are (1) to develop and maintain maximum physical efficiency; (2) to develop useful physical skills; (3) to act in socially useful ways; and (4) to enjoy wholesome physical recreation.[8] These objectives should assist each teacher in developing her program of instruction. Each activity, method, or technique used in the physical education program should be selected on the basis of its potential contribution to one or more of the following objectives:

1. To develop and maintain maximum physical efficiency.

FIG. 1.1

This statement refers to the "physical training" or physical development of children. Since the publication of the Kraus-Hirshland report which showed a dramatically low level of physical fitness among our younger generation, there has been a continuing interest in the physical development objective.[9]

---

8. Joint Committee of AAHPER and the Society of State Directors for Health, Physical Education and Recreation Education, *Physical Education, An Interpretation for Superintendents, Supervisors, Principals, Directors of Physical Education, Teachers and Parents,* AAHPER, Washington, D.C.: 1951, p. 3.

9. Hans Kraus and Ruth P. Hirshland, "Minimum Muscular Fitness Tests in School Children," *Research Quarterly,* Volume 25, No. 2. May, 1954, p. 178.

More stress has been and will continue to be given to vigorous physical activities. Although there is a very justifiable need to improve and maintain the physical fitness of elementary school children, nevertheless this objective must not be given exclusive attention to the neglect of other important contributions of physical education.

2. To develop useful physical skills.

FIG. 1.2

All movements that are used in everyday activities, such as walking, dodging, or climbing as well as the highly complex skills used in sports, gymnastics, and dance activities, may be classified as "useful physical skills." Other names, such as neuromuscular or motor skills, are also used to designate this type of physical performance. The one thing that all the aforementioned skills have in common is that they have to be learned. To develop useful physical skills would, therefore, imply that our task is to assist each child in developing and perfecting a wide variety of motor skills that will be used in everyday activities and in future leisure time pursuits. The values of efficient and skillful movements, particularly in sports and dance, are many. A child who demonstrates ease and grace of movement is usually physically fit and well adjusted within his peer group. Furthermore, if a child is skillful in an activity, such as basketball or swimming, he will not only experience a great deal of enjoyment through participation, but in addition will usually continue participating in the same activity for many years. This particular lesson should be well understood by adults for we participate in those activities in which we demonstrate a reasonable degree of skill; rarely do we enjoy or actively pursue a sport that we cannot master in part or whole.

3. To act in socially useful ways.

According to the platform statement of the AAHPER, a socially mature person is one who works for the common good, respects personalities of his

FIG. 1.3

fellow peers, and acts in a sportsmanlike manner. Implicit in this statement is the fundamental principle that we must, as democratic citizens, possess a deep sense of group consciousness and cooperative living.[10] Physical education, through its team games and other group activities, can foster desirable social behavior, but game situations which require loyalty, honesty, and fair play can promote these behavior patterns only if they are intelligently organized and directed experiences. A physically fit and well-coordinated child is a valuable asset; however, the individual who does not possess desirable social traits cannot realize or contribute to the broader ideals of a democratic community.

4. To enjoy wholesome physical recreation.

During the past sixty years we have witnessed unbelievable changes in the social and economic structure of this country. The average work week has been reduced from sixty to forty hours and there are strong indications

FIG. 1.4

---

10. Bucher, *op. cit.*, 151.

of an even shorter work week within the next few years. Rapid transportation, urbanization, and automation in the home and industry have given us leisure never before experienced in a modern society, but these changes have also created a vital challenge to use leisure for the betterment and well-being of self and community.

The objective "to enjoy wholesome physical recreation" is an expressed need of our contemporary society, a need to educate children in their formative years so they have a knowledge and appreciation of skills that can be used in their daily life activities. Skills that will contribute to a sense of creativity and relaxation and provide a means of filling the ensuing years with wholesome physical activity are implicit in this objective. To elementary school teachers the task may appear to be overwhelming; however, it is their job to lay the foundation for the development of many skills which may be perfected in later years.

The contemporary philosophy of physical education, as expressed by the four broad objectives, indicates what the goals of a modern physical education program should be. Perhaps the most unique contributions of physical education are physical fitness and motor skill development. The need for a physically fit nation from childhood through adulthood has been emphasized by Presidents of the United States, by members of the medical profession, and by countless leaders in business and education. The inherent values of motor skill development, both from the standpoint of worthy use of leisure time and the positive contributions of physical activity to long term mental health, must also be considered of equal importance. Physical education, as a subject in the elementary school curriculum, thus must not be considered merely as a means of "training the body"; it must be thought of as an integral part of the total curriculum with similar goals and contributions.

THE TEACHER AND PHYSICAL EDUCATION

Current research relating to how and why children learn indicates that learning, regardless of subject area, occurs more effectively and efficiently when guidance and direction are provided. Such guidance and direction, however, do not consist of simply presenting knowledge or skill, allowing time for practice, then applying corrective and evaluative techniques. Teaching, as all teachers recognize, is both an art and a science. It is a process of guiding the learner toward desirable change. From the point of view of society, there are certain skills, knowledges, and understandings that we believe all children should learn. This, in a very direct sense, is a necessary form of indoctrination in order to perpetuate the democratic tenets of our society. On the other hand, we consider self-direction, expressed in terms of individuality of thought and action, as being equally important. *A teacher, therefore, must not only provide an environment which affords the necessary direction and substance of learning, but also gives children an opportunity to develop self-direction commensurate with their experience and potential ability.*

The general qualities of "good" teaching have been presented by numerous authorities and apply equally to teaching physical education as to any other subject. It is the writer's personal feeling that a genuine enthusiasm toward the value of physical education is the most critical factor in making this area a truly educational experience. A great deal of space has been given to the advantages and disadvantages of specialist teachers in handling all physical education in the elementary school. The fundamental truth is, however, that for the foreseeable future classroom teachers will and must assume the responsibility for this subject area. Currently, in excess of eighty percent of all elementary schools, physical education is handled in this manner.[11] If classroom teachers are convinced of its value, they will seek ways and means of implementing a well-conceived program. In many ways the classroom teacher is the ideal person to conduct physical education.

Many other qualities and qualifications can be listed to indicate what are desirable and sometimes necessary characteristics for teaching physical education. Though the list here is incomplete, if a teacher possesses the following, there is more than a reasonable chance that children will experience an enjoyable and truly educational experience through the medium of physical education.

1. A teacher should possess a genuine enthusiasm toward physical education.
2. A teacher should possess a positive attitude toward acquiring more competence in teaching physical education.

FIG. 1.5

11. E. Shurr, *Movement Experiences for Children: Curriculum and Methods for Elementary School Physical Education* (New York: Appleton-Century-Crofts, 1967), p. 18.

In the main, classroom teachers are normally required to take one or two professional courses in physical education. This, of course, is an inadequate preparation to teach all the content areas of this subject. It is, therefore, necessary for teachers to actively gain new skills and insights through additional courses, texts, films, and other inservice media. Probably of equal importance is the personal quality "to have the courage to be imperfect and enjoy it." No teacher can be an expert in every subject in the curriculum. What is more important for successful teaching is the courage to try new ideas and methods of teaching, however insecure one might feel. A child's attitude toward a teacher is not based entirely on the teacher's overall competence; it is based on the very simple premise that both he and the teacher are jointly engaged in the search for knowledge and understanding. It is, in essence, a mutual respect for the abilities and efforts of each. When a child knows the teacher is trying something new for his benefit, he, in turn, will respond in a mature and understanding way.

3. A teacher should possess a sense of humor.

The writer is often tempted to place this quality at the top of the list. Teaching is very hard work; it is also a very rewarding profession. In the day-to-day task of teaching, the ability to laugh at one's own inadequacies and "gentle" errors is vitally important for the maintenance of sanity and perspective. This quality is particularly important to classroom teachers who work long hours, in confined quarters with children who are extremely demanding on one's patience and understanding. The need for a sense of humor is equally, if not more important, to the teacher of physical education.

4. A teacher should possess an optimum level of health.

Obviously, teachers are fully aware of the need to maintain good physical and mental health. Without it, the pressure of teaching becomes too demanding with serious consequences to both teacher and student. Because physical education is physically demanding, a teacher who lacks strength and stamina will tend to neglect this area of the curriculum. This is a loss both to the teacher and to her class. New teaching methods do not require a high level of motor skill on the part of the teacher. They do, however, require physical effort and enthusiasm.

THE USE OF THIS BOOK

The fundamental purpose of contemporary education is to provide opportunity for every child to develop his maximum mental, physical, and social potentialities so that he can take his place as an active member of a democratic society. Our task in physical education is to translate this purpose into a program of instruction that will develop within each individual the capacity to meet the physical and psychological tasks that are ever present in a dynamic and challenging society. Today and in the foreseeable future we need individuals who possess a diversity of knowledge, a capacity to think critically, an ability to meet emotional stresses, and the physical fitness to meet the requirements of work, personal and national emergencies, and leisure time pursuits. Obviously, the foundations of each of these qualities begin in the home; however, it soon becomes the responsibility of elementary school teachers to continue teaching them. From Kindergarten on, teachers must make a judgment as to the place, importance and emphasis of academic, physical, and social experiences that will aid them in assisting each child to meet these stated aims of education.

Thus, it becomes necessary for each elementary school teacher to make a judgment about the value and eventual emphasis of physical education in her program. In order to make this value judgment she must know what contributions physical education can make to the stated aims of elementary education. The aims have been stated and the obvious outcomes of a well-conceived program indicated. Other important considerations which directly affect the type of activities and the way they are taught are the characteristics of children and how they can and should learn motor skills. These are discussed in the next two chapters.

Part II provides information relating to planning, organizing, teaching, and evaluating student and program progress. The remaining parts of this text may be considered a resource from which activities may be selected. Although there are numerous "how to" suggestions within each of the subsequent chapters, these are included as guidelines. The manner in which any program is conceived and taught ultimately depends on the enthusiasm and ability of the classroom teacher, his values and convictions.

SELECTED REFERENCES

ARNOLD, P. J. *Education Physical Education and Personality Development.* London: Heinemann Educational Books Ltd., 1968.

BUCHER, CHARLES A. *Foundations of Physical Education.* St. Louis: C. V. Mosby Co., 1952.

CUBBERLY, ELLWOOD P. *Public Education in the United States.* Cambridge, Mass.: Houghton Mifflin Co., 1947.

DALEN, DEOBOLD B.; MITCHELL, ELMER D.; and BENNETT, BRUCE L. *A World History of Physical Education.* New York: Prentice-Hall, Inc., 1953.

EDUCATION POLICIES COMMISSION, "The Purpose of Education in American Democracy." Washington, D.C.: N.E.A., 1958.

HALSEY, E. *Inquiry and Invention in Physical Education.* Philadelphia: Lea and Febiger, 1964.

Joint Committee of AAHPER and the Society of State Directors for Health, Physical Education and Recreation Education, *Physical Education, An Interpretation for Superintendents, Supervisors, Principals, Directors of Physical Education, Teachers and Parents,* AAHPER. Washington, D.C.: 1951.

KEARNEY, N. C. *Elementary School Objectives.* New York: Russell Sage Foundation, 1953.

LEONARD, FRED EUGENE and AFFLECK, GEORGE B. *A Guide to the History of Physical Education.* Philadelphia: Lea and Febiger, 1952.

MOSTON, M. *Teaching Physical Education.* Columbus: Charles E. Merrill Publishing Co., 1966.

Plato, *Republic,* trans. F. M. Cromford. New York: Clarendon Press, Oxford University Press, Inc., 1941.

Report of Ninth Conference on Elementary Education. Washington, D.C.: U.S. Department of Health, Education and Welfare, Office of Education, 1956.

SHURR, E. *Movement Experiences for Children: Curriculum and Methods for Elementary School Physical Education.* New York: Appleton-Century-Crofts, 1967.

SOWARDS, G. W., and SCOBEY, M. M. *The Changing Curriculum and the Elementary Teacher.* Belmont: Wadsworth Publishing Co., Inc., 1962.

THORNDIKE, L. E. *Principles of Teaching.* New York: A. G. Seiler Co., 1906.

VANNIER, M., and FOSTER, M. *Teaching Physical Education in Elementary Schools,* Fourth Edition. Philadelphia: W. B. Saunders Co., 1968.

SUGGESTED FILMS

Title:	"Readiness: The Fourth R"
Details:	16 mm., color, sound, 27½ minutes
Distributor:	The Athletic Institute
Description:	Interprets role of physical education in modern school curriculum. Designed for lay audiences
Purchase Price:	$170.00 Rental $4.00

Title:	"Children's Play"
Details:	16 mm., sound, black and white
Distributor:	McGraw-Hill Test Films
Description:	Illustrates play as a factor in a child's development
Purchase Price:	$260.00

Title:	"Physical Education in Elementary Schools"
Details:	16 mm., color, 20 minutes
Distributor:	Stuart Finley, 3428 Mansfield Road, Falls Church, Virginia
Description:	Illustrates physical education from Kindergarten through the elementary grades
Purchase Price:	$200.00

Title:	"They Grow Up So Fast"
Details:	16 mm., color, sound, 28 minutes
Distributor:	The Athletic Institute
Description:	Interprets physical education to the public
Purchase Price:	$135.00

The Child
and Physical Education

Growth and Development Characteristics
The Exceptional Child

T HE aims and objectives of the physical education program must be based not only on the needs of society but also on a most adequate consideration of the physical, mental, and social characteristics and needs of children. This chapter will discuss the physiological and psychological characteristics of primary and intermediate school-age children. A brief coverage of the exceptional child is also provided to show how provisions can be made to integrate him into the regular physical education program. When these basic considerations are seen in perspective, they become vital guidelines for the planning and instructional phase of the physical education program.

GROWTH AND DEVELOPMENT CHARACTERISTICS

The choice of an activity as well as the manner in which children are motivated to learn must be based upon their growth and developmental characteristics. Although individual variations exist in virtually all phases of growth, there are certain characteristics which are quite dominant in primary and intermediate school children. These physical, mental, and social traits are discussed in relation to their participation in the physical education program.

Primary School Children (5-8 years)

Generally speaking, this is a period of relatively stable and regular structural growth and physical maturation. Children gradually lose their baby fat and show proportionate gains in muscular tissue. The resulting increase in muscle tissue gives rise to a general increase in strength, particularly in the arms and legs. Muscular control, specifically that relating to hand-eye movements and reaction time, is relatively poor during the early years, but shows steady improvement with increased age. There is an increase in the incidence of fractures which is due to the peculiar "accident prone" characteristic of this age group, with the greatest number occurring in boys. The heart and lungs are small in proportion to body weight, causing early fatigue in strenuous activity. However, rapid and almost unbelievable recovery from acute fatigue will take place after short rest periods. Throughout this age group no major physiological differences exist between boys and girls.

This might well be classified as the age of conflict. At times the child is still quite individualistic, self-assertive, and independent; then, without reason or warning, he may reveal a willingness of sharing and to cooperate. By seven years of age, adult approval is more important that that of his classmates; by eight, there is a shift to the participation in and importance of "gang life." The latter characteristic is quite obvious in the child's interest in group games, team spirit, and team loyalty. Although there is a dominant interest in organized games, children also develop a sense of personal achievement which becomes quite evident with their increased attention span and

FIG. 2.1

their desire to practice specific skills. These children are still very mobile, imaginative, and keenly interested in rhythmical sounds, and enjoy expressive movements of all kinds. They are, however, easily excited, sensitive to criticism, and strongly in need of approval and close supervision.[1]

There are several implications that apply to the way children of this age range should be taught as well as what types of activities are most suitable. Although the summary provided in the accompanying chart is far from complete, it will provide important guidelines for the development of any physical education program involving this age group. Additional information may be found in the selected references.

CHARACTERISTICS AND IMPLICATIONS TO PROGRAM DEVELOPMENT PRIMARY SCHOOL CHILDREN (5-8 YEARS)	
Characteristics	Implications To Physical Education Program
PHYSICAL AND MOTOR CHARACTERISTICS	
1. Height and weight gains moderate and steady. Boys Height Weight 5 years 41.9 –45.9″ 37.7 –48.7 lbs. Girls 5 years 41.6 –45.6″ 36.1 –47.9 lbs. Boys 6 years 44 –48.2″ 41.3 –53.9 lbs. Girls 6 years 43.7 –47.9″ 39.6 –53.2 lbs.	1. Continuous provision for gross motor activities such as running, jumping, and climbing, same type of activities for boys and girls. General concern for postural development, need for early detection of structural anomalies. Children of this age have relatively small bodies, hence consideration should be given in relative size of supplies and equipment.

1. Charles C. Cowell and Helen W. Hazleton, *Curriculum Designs in Physical Education* (Englewood Cliffs, New Jersey: Prentice-Hall, Inc., 1955), p. 166.

Boys
7 years   46   –50.4"   45.4 –59.6 lbs.
Girls
7 years   45.7 –50.1"   43.7 –58.7 lbs.
Boys
8 years   48.1 –52.7"   49.5 –66.9 lbs.
Girls
8 years   47.7 –52.3"   47.5 –66.3 lbs.
Average gain in height = 2"
Average gain in weight = 6 lbs.

2. Proportional gains in weight are primarily attributable to growth in bone and muscular tissue and a reduced rate of increase in fatty tissue.

2. Continuous vigorous exercise throughout age range with special attention to developing strength and endurance.

3. Heart and lungs are not fully developed. Pulse and breathing rates show a gradual decline. By age 9, pulse rate is rarely above 90 beats per minute. Respiration rate is approximately 20. Easily fatigued and rapid recovery is a particular characteristic of this age range.

3. Vigorous activity, particularly running, climbing, and swimming, with provision for frequent rest intervals. Long periods of inactivity should be discouraged. Recess and periodic breaks throughout the school day should be encouraged and be characterized by vigorous and total body movement.

4. Eye-hand coordination not fully developed. Lack precise focus (tendency to farsightedness) and spatial judgment.

4. Provision for manipulation (catching, throwing, kicking, etc.) of various size balls. Initial instruction should include relatively slow speeds of throwing, etc. with short distances. Gradually increase speed, use of small objects, and increase distance as skill develops.

5. Reaction time slow but shows a persistent increase throughout this age range.

5. Participation in numerous activities involving a quick change of speed and direction. Games and stunts involving speed, dodging, and changing direction should be provided for all children throughout this age range.

MENTAL AND EMOTIONAL CHARACTERISTICS

1. Gradual and sustained increase in attention span. Periods of restlessness in early grades and present throughout age range.

1. Provide large variety of activities within any instructional period. Games should be simple in purpose, rules, and directions.

2. Extremely creative.

2. Provide method and content that fosters creative interests and movements (creative dance and educational gymnastics).

3. Enjoys rhythm and music.

3. Provide various forms of dance experiences, including singing games, folk and creative dance. Musical accompaniment to self-testing activities is also strongly suggested. (e.g. with rope skipping and other types of activities).

4. Keen desire to repeat activities they know and perform quite well.

4. Allow children to choose activities, such as playing one game "over-and-over" each recess period. In dance and self-testing activities, chronic interest in one activity is a characteristic. With patience, children will soon "run the course" and move on to other challenges. The challenge to teachers is to provide activities which are more interesting and challenging.

5. Individualistic as well as showing a need for peer and adult approval.

5. In one respect, children are basically individualistic. Hence, provision should be made for numerous individual activities in which immediate success is possible for all children regardless of ability. Children of this age level are also in need of peer acceptance as well as adult approval. There should be planned experience which involves sharing, team play, and group cooperation.

6. General lack of fear and an extremely high spirit of adventure.

6. The spirit of adventure (climbing, testing one's own ability with other children), should obviously be encouraged. At the same time teachers must develop within each child the concern for personal safety as well as the general awareness and concern for the safety of others. Extensive use of Educational Gymnastic approach with self-testing activities.

SOCIAL CHARACTERISTICS

1. Little concern for opposite sex during early grades with gradual trend toward "mutual" antagonism.

1. Throughout the primary grades both sexes have no difficulty in playing together. In the third grade some provision should be made to allow boys and girls to choose their own games. Boys will normally show a higher skill level in team games and a keener interest in "team spirit" and competition. Some provision should therefore be made for this difference in the sexes.

2. No concern for discrimination either on the basis of race, color, or religion.

2. Although teachers show no preference with respect to these factors, care should be taken in the methods and techniques used to choose teams, leaders, and various social groupings. The essential teaching characteristic should be fairness to all children.

3. Will accept just punishment for self and total group.

3. With respect to administering punishment, a whole group should not be punished for the "wrong doings" of one child. Children recognize inconsistencies in "degrees" of punishment, hence, teachers should be consistent and fair with the type and amount of discipline and punishment. Because of the "social awareness" and inherent fairness of children, stress should be on group control through self-discipline.

Intermediate School Children (9-12 years)

This is a transition period from childhood to early adolescence. It is characterized by periods of normal and rapid changes in growth and maturation. Girls, on the average, are two years ahead of boys in physiological maturation. The appearance of secondary sex characteristics as early as nine and ten years of age for girls is not uncommon for this age level. The growth process becomes quite peculiar to each child's time and growth cycle. Heart and lungs are, in size capacity, proportionate to height and weight; however endurance may show a slight decrease. Muscle strength continues to increase with boys showing a significant improvement over the girls. This may be due to the more vigorous activities boys participate in rather than a structural or physiological change. Girls, however, are more flexible and graceful in self-testing and rhythmic activities. Coordination and reaction time continue to improve with both sexes.

The influence of physical maturation on psychological development of this age group creates a period of transition and differentiation in the interest and behavior patterns of both boys and girls.[2] Generally speaking, both sexes are becoming quite conscious of their bodies, each however for different reasons. In terms of physical appearance, boys tend to be sloppy in dress

---

2. P. J. Arnold, *Education Physical Education and Personality Development* (London: Heinemann Educational Books Ltd., 1968), Chapter 2.

FIG. 2.2

with more concern about their physical fitness and skill development. They are keenly interested in vigorous competitive sports, show a strong concern about their peers, and a great deal of confidence in adults. Hero worship, particularly for well-known basketball and football players, is the rule rather than the exception. On the other hand, girls become concerned with their own personal femininity. Activities such as general body mechanics and social dance are now more important than "vigorous" and "rough" team sports. There may be early signs of "tomboyishness"; however, after the beginning of puberty this gives way to the previous trend. Both sexes are easily excitable, demanding, enthusiastic, and constantly seeking peer loyalty and independence.

There is no magic line separating one age level from another. Teachers of Grades Four to Six are aware of the tremendous diversity of psychological characteristics of these children. The nine to twelve age range produces a variety of growth patterns, as well as changing psychological needs of boys and girls. However, like the previous age range, there are still more basic implications applicable to both sexes. These implications, coupled with the needs produced by the marked differences in growth patterns of these upper elementary school-age children, indicate a definite need for a modification in the organization and content of the physical education program. These are indicated in the accompanying chart.

CHARACTERISTICS AND IMPLICATIONS TO PROGRAM DEVELOPMENT
INTERMEDIATE SCHOOL CHILDREN (9-12 YEARS)

Characteristics	Implications To Physical Education Program

PHYSICAL AND MOTOR CHARACTERISTICS

1. Height and weight gains moderate and gradual prior to the beginning of puberty.

Height	Weight
Boys 9 years	
50 –54.8″	54.6 – 74.2 lbs.
Girls 9 years	
49.6 –54.4″	51.9 – 74.1 lbs.
Boys 10 years	
51.8 –56.8″	59.2 – 82.2 lbs.
Girls 10 years	
51.6 –56.8″	57.1 – 83.5 lbs.
Boys 11 years	
53.6 –58.8″	64.5 – 90.7 lbs.
Girls 11 years	
53.7 –59.3″	63.5 – 94.5 lbs.
Boys 12 years	
55.3 –61.1″	69.8 –101.4 lbs.
Girls 12 years	
56.1 –61.9″	71.9 –107.5 lbs.

Average gain in height = 2″
Average gain in weight = 7 lbs.

Girls normally reach puberty between 10 and 11 years, while boys begin approximately two years later. Marked differences in height and weight gains will therefore show in Grades Five and Six.

1. Continue to provide vigorous activities, emphasizing strength and endurance for longer periods of time. Although girls, particularly those who have reached the early stages of puberty, may show a general disinterest in vigorous activities, normal growth and development is dependent upon vigorous and continuous activity.

Postural development for this age group is a particular problem. The problem has been intensified in the past two decades by excessive television viewing and general sedentary living. Classroom teachers should observe in the classroom the sitting and walking postures, and plan activities in the physical education program for general posture development. Again, special attention should be given to girls who have reached puberty and tend toward sloping shoulders to compensate for height and chest development.

2. Heart and lungs are in size and capacity proportionate to height and weight gains. By 12, heart rate is between 80-90 beats per minute. Respiration rate is between 15-20. Longer periods of endurance are possible for this age group; however, girls who reveal early signs of puberty will show early signs of fatigue.

2. Continue to provide vigorous activities for longer periods of time. It is also wise to provide frequent rest periods for both sexes. Special concern should also be given to girls who show early signs of fatigue. In the upper two grades make provision for separate classes for different activities of the program.

3. Muscle strength continues to increase with boys gaining more than girls. The difference in strength increases is not consistent with propor-

3. Provision for strength development of both sexes. Although all muscles of the body need consistent exercise of an overload nature, special attention should

tionate height and weight, and general maturation of each sex. Differences in strength between boys and girls during this age level may be due to the type of activities participated in rather than inherent structural or physiological changes within each sex.

4. Muscle coordination and reaction time continue to improve with boys revealing a noticeable superiority in skills involving hand-eye coordination.

5. Flexibility decrease with boys showing greater losses than girls.

be given to activities involving the arms and shoulder girdle, back and abdominal area. The latter indicates provision for more self-testing activities which develop strength in these regions of the body. Team games and dance activities are low contributors to developing strength of these muscle groups.

4. Provision for more highly organized and competitive individual and team sports. Girls and boys should be separated in team games to allow both sexes to develop according to their own level of skill and interest. Both sexes, however, require extensive practice in the refinement of throwing, catching, and kicking skills. Separate and solid unit construction is appropriate particularly in the upper grades.

5. Lack of flexibility appears to be due to the type of activity rather than structural or growth reasons. Hence, more provision for movements which enhance flexibility should be noted. Self-testing activities, particularly those involving stretching and the use of apparatus such as stall bars and agility equipment, should be encouraged.

MENTAL AND EMOTIONAL CHARACTERISTICS

1. Marked increase in length of attention span.

2. General increase in intellectual curiosity.

1. Provision for activities which are more complex and challenging. This applies to individual and team games where allowance is made for extensive practice in learning skills, rules, and complex team strategy. Similarly with dance and self-testing activities, time should be allowed for developing complex and creative movements.

2. Children should not only be taught physical and motor skills but, in addition, an understanding of other related concepts and principles of movement. Provision should also be made, through the application of the problem-solving method, to test and challenge a child's intellectual ability through movement tasks.

3. Increased control of emotions in individual and group situations.

3. Careful selection of activities commensurate with emotional development of each age group. Outbreaks of emotions in tense game situations are normal and, in some situations, desirable. More provision for each child to experience leadership roles is necessary for this age group.

4. General increase toward independence and peer group identity.

4. The essence of good teaching should be the development of self-direction on the part of each child. Independence is a natural tendency for this age group and must be provided for both in methods and appropriate activities. Teacher-directed approaches should not be completely abandoned but should be blended with other approaches which call for greater freedom and responsibility on the part of the learner. Special attention should be given to the kind of groupings that will provide for identification as well as to foster team cooperation and loyalty.

SOCIAL CHARACTERISTICS

1. Major difference in attitudes toward opposite sex as well as toward different types of activities. Boys and girls alike, particularly during upper grades, show a lack of sympathy and understanding toward each other. Boys tend toward more "rough" team sports, increased concern for physique and skill, and a dominant interest in competition. Girls begin to show concern for personal appearance, activities involving graceful and creative movements, and a general distaste for "rough" and vigorous sports.

1. Separation of sexes with a class for various activities, specifically team games. Self-testing activities when taught through the educational gymnastics approach can cope with major interest and skill differences of both sexes. Dance, particularly folk, square, and social, should be coeducational. Creative dance activities are normally restricted to girls in the upper grades, not because this activity is undesirable for boys; it is because boys normally lack the necessary background and attitude toward this activity.

2. Social acceptance is more peer-centered than adult-centered.

2. Provisions should be made within the instructional and extra-class program for children to participate in both individual sex and mixed group activities. Extensive opportunities should be available for boys and girls to plan and direct activities. The latter not only contributes to the development of cooperation, leadership, and team loyalty, but also provides for children to develop

other important social traits and personal friendships.

3. Girls tend to be more self-conscious in the presence of boys as well as when performing within their own sex grouping.

3. If children, particularly in the fifth and sixth grades, are mixed, special attention should be given when asking girls to demonstrate skills or movements. Although girls are normally more graceful than boys in gymnastic type movements, they tend to be embarrassed when asked to demonstrate. The reverse, however, is generally true with ball skills where girls are much less proficient than boys. The essential task for teachers is to develop an understanding and appreciation for the differences which exist between boys and girls of this age level.

THE EXCEPTIONAL CHILD

The exceptional child in contemporary education is defined as a child who, in various ways, deviates from the "normal" intelligence, physical health, and behavioral characteristics of the "average" or "typical" child. Such a definition includes the intellectually gifted, the physically gifted, the physically handicapped, the slow learner, and the social deviant. This total category includes approximately twelve percent of the school population, with each requiring some form of special attention.[3]

In physical education, as in all other subjects, it is first necessary to distinguish the various types of "gifted" individuals before planned experiences can be provided. A few of the more important special program areas will be discussed in the accompanying paragraphs.

The Physically Gifted Child

Few writers in the general field of physical education have attempted to define what is meant by a physically gifted child. Yet, by observation of performance as well as analysis of programs, its contemporary meaning is quite clear. A child who possesses a unique talent or ability in sports, dance, or gymnastics may be described as being physically gifted. In individual and team sports, the gifted child is recognizable as a member of the school team. The gifted dancer, gymnast, or swimmer is in a school or community club.

3. O. T. Jarvis and L. R. Wootton, *The Transitional Elementary School and its Curriculum* (Dubuque: Wm. C. Brown Company Publishers, 1966), p. 167.

FIG. 2.3

Within the physical education program of an elementary school these special talents are also recognized and provided for in both instructional and extra-class programs. Providing all children are given a well-rounded program, special activities for the physically gifted appear to be in harmony with the education philosophy and principles of contemporary elementary school programs. The following factors should be considered when providing special programs for the physically gifted child:

1. All phases of the physical education program should be given fair consideration and emphasis.
2. Gifted children should be expected to do a great deal of planning, executing, and evaluating relative to classroom activities.[4]
3. Higher standards of achievement are established for gifted children.
4. Gifted children should be encouraged to expand their interests and enrich their experiences through participation in special interest clubs within the school or within the community.
5. Specialists in various sports, dance, and gymnastic activities should be used within the organized physical education program. A specialist is defined as a qualified person recognized by the school and capable of teaching his special talent. Example: a parent who possesses special talent and qualifications in folk dance would meet this criteria.

The Physically Handicapped

A normal healthy child may be defined as one who is free of disease and physical handicaps. Conversely, a handicapped child is one who may

---

4. W. B. Ragan, *Teaching America's Children* (New York: Holt, Rinehart & Winston, Inc., 1961), p. 91.

be suffering from an acute or chronic disease such as rheumatic fever or may be handicapped because of birth or hereditary malformations. The latter type of handicap includes hearing loss, cerebral palsy, and diabetes, as well as an extensive list of orthopedic malformations that impair a child's physical performance.[5]

Contemporary educational philosophy adheres to the fundamental principle that a child in school is educable. Hence, whenever physically and psychologically feasible, provisions should be made within the physical education program to provide desirable experiences for the physically handicapped child. Obviously the handicapped child's limitations and needs must be determined by experts such as physicians, corrective therapists, and psychiatrists. Furthermore, specific recommendations pertaining to the type of physical experiences these children should participate in must be clearly determined by such competent authorities. For example, a cerebral palsied child with limited impairment may be permitted to participate in physical activities involving gross motor movement such as simple games and certain dance experiences. Movements involving rapid hand-eye coordination such as throwing and catching skills may be too great a task for the spastic child.

In virtually all learning experiences involving the handicapped child, teachers have demonstrated a keen insight into the problem. Within the regular classroom situation, children with sight and hearing loss are placed in a more advantageous seating arrangement. The epileptic child is no longer kept at home nor is his condition concealed from his peers. Within the physical education program the physically handicapped child must be integrated to the limits of his own capacity into the daily physical activities. The scope of the child's program must be based, to some degree, on the following implications and suggestions:

1. The type of exercise should be indicated by a competent medical adviser.
2. The type of activities selected should be appropriate to the child's capabilities and needs.
3. A physical education specialist should be consulted for assistance in developing corrective and remedial programs.
4. The program should be designed to allow the child to experience immediate success and enjoyment.
5. Whenever wise and feasible, the extent of a child's handicap should be explained to his peers.
6. The program should include activities that are of long range recreational value.

---

5. Donald K. Mathews, Roland Krause, and Virginia Shaw, *The Science of Physical Education for Handicapped Children* (New York: Harper and Brothers, 1962), p. 1.

The Slow Learner

In the majority of instances, a slow learner is classified according to scores received on one or more intelligence tests. Generally speaking, children who possess I.Q.'s between 70 and 90 are classified as slow learners. These children are usually placed in regular classes, hence become part of the normal problems when planning and teaching physical education. With respect to this type of heterogeneous grouping the suggestions presented by Ragan are as applicable to physical education as to any other subject.[6] These are:

1. Standards of achievement for slow-learning children should be set up in terms of their ability.
2. Short, frequent drill periods are essential for slow learners.
3. Materials should be divided into short, definite learning units.
4. Visual appeal should be used extensively to stimulate interest.
5. Opportunities to succeed in small undertakings should be provided.
6. Slow learning children frequently need help in making adjustments to group living as well as to school subjects.

The above definition and suggestions relating to the slow learner have been based primarily upon the criterion of inherent intellectual ability. In recent years there has been a growing awareness of the importance of perceptual motor development and academic achievement. Inadequate preschool motor development can lead to serious perceptual motor problems. The latter, in turn, may seriously retard the normal academic achievement of children. Although space does not permit an extensive discussion of this topic, its importance nevertheless cannot be overemphasized. There are several outstanding books on this subject and references are provided in the list of suggested readings.

SELECTED REFERENCES

ARNOLD, P. J. *Educational Physical Education and Personality Development.* London: Heinemann Educational Books Ltd., 1968.

BUCHER, CHARLES A., KOENIG, CONSTANCE, and BARNHARD, MILTON. *Methods and Materials for Secondary School Physical Education.* St. Louis: C. V. Mosby Co., 1961.

COWELL, CHARLES B., and HAZELTON, HELEN W. *Curriculum Designs in Physical Education.* Englewood Cliffs, New Jersey: Prentice-Hall, Inc., 1955.

CRATTY, B. J. *Motor Behavior and Motor Learning,* 2nd Edition. Philadelphia: Lea and Febiger, 1967.

DAY, R. H. *Perception.* Dubuque: Wm. C. Brown Company Publishers, 1966.

ESPENSCHADE, A., and ECKHART, H. M. *Motor Development.* Columbus: C. E. Merrill Books Inc., 1967.

ESPENSCHADE, A. "Physical Education in the Elementary Schools. What Research Says to the Teacher," No. 27. Washington, D.C.: Department of Classroom Teachers N.E.A., 1963.

---

6. Ragan, *op. cit.,* p. 91.

FAIT, H. F. *Special Physical Education.* Philadelphia: W. B. Saunders Company, 1966.

HUMPHREY, J. H. *Child Learning.* Dubuque: Wm. C. Brown Company Publishers, 1965.

JARVIS, O. T. and WOOTTON, L. R. *The Transitional Elementary School and its Curriculum.* Dubuque: Wm. C. Brown Company Publishers, 1966.

KEPHART, N. C. *The Slow Learner in the Classroom.* Columbus: C. E. Merrill Books, Inc., 1960.

MATHEWS, DONALD K.; KRAUSE, RONALD; and SHAW, VIRGINIA. *The Science of Physical Education for Handicapped Children.* New York: Harper & Row, Publishers, 1962.

RADLER, C. H. with KEPHART, N. C. *Success Through Play.* New York: Harper & Row, Publishers, 1960.

RAGAN, W. B. Teaching America's Children. New York: Holt, Rinehart & Winston, Inc., 1961.

TANNER, J. M. *Growth At Adolescence,* Second Edition. Oxford: Blackwell Scientific Publications Ltd., 1962.

SUGGESTED FILMS

Title:	"If Those Were Your Children"
Details:	16 mm., sound, black and white
Distributor:	Metropolitan Life Insurance Co., 1 Madison Avenue, New York
Description:	A child study with emphasis on the detection of early signs of emotional disturbance in day-to-day behavior patterns
Purchase Price:	Free loan

Nature of Learning
and Physical Education

A Theory of Instruction in Physical Education
A Theory of Learning in Physical Education
An Application of Principles of Learning

A discussion of learning usually begins with a definition of learning, as expressed in accordance with a particular psychological theory; then follows an application of certain principles relating to how and what we teach. This procedure has some merit in attempting to understand how children learn, but it does not give full perspective to other factors such as educational philosophy, growth and development, or the specific medium through which children learn. What appears to be required is a clarification of a theory of INSTRUCTION, which includes a consideration of philosophy, growth and development, as well as an understanding of several contemporary theories of learning. This should be followed with a discussion of the application of a theory of learning which one can accept; this becomes the basis of selecting, arranging, and presenting learning experiences which will accomplish the goals of the program.

In this chapter an attempt is made to follow the above procedure, beginning with a theory of instruction with particular reference to physical education; this is then followed by a discussion of appropriate theories of learning. Selected principles of learning are also included to provide a guideline for the selection of methods and techniques of instruction.

A THEORY OF INSTRUCTION IN PHYSICAL EDUCATION

According to Gage[1] there is a basic distinction between THEORIES OF LEARNING that interest psychologists and THEORIES OF INSTRUCTION that are of primary interest to teachers. The former deals with the ways in which an organism learns. A THEORY OF INSTRUCTION deals with the ways in which a person influences an organism to learn. The latter, therefore, is "prescriptive" since it provides guidelines and rules with respect to the most effective way of achieving knowledge or skill. It is concerned with the best way to learn "how one wishes to teach," with improving rather than describing learning. Bruner states there are four major features which must be present in any theory of instruction.[2] These are listed below with reference to the subject of physical education.

● *A theory of instruction should specify the experiences which most effectively implant in the individual a predisposition toward learning—learning in general or a particular type of learning.*

This statement infers that the PREDISPOSITION to learning is dependent upon the prior experience of the child before he enters school as well as

1. N. L. Gage, "Theories of Teaching," in *Theories of Learning and Instruction*, 63rd. Yearbook of the National Society for the Study of Education, Part I. edited by E. Hilgard (Chicago: University of Chicago Press, 1964), p. 268.

2. J. S. Bruner, *Towards a Theory of Instruction* (Cambridge: Harvard University Press, Belknap Press, 1966), p. 40.

the on-going provision on the part of the teacher to provide a teaching situation which is conducive to learning. In physical education, as stated in Chapter 1, we set our goals as (1) to develop and maintain maximum physical efficiency; (2) to develop useful physical skills; (3) to act in socially useful ways; and (4) to enjoy wholesome physical recreation. Achievement of each of these goals, individually and collectively, requires an atmosphere which will enhance learning. Regardless of the theory of learning one eventually adheres to, the following general considerations must be taken into account:

1. The teacher must create a positive relationship between herself and the pupils. In essence, the teacher's relationship must be seen as a guider of the learning experience rather than that of a director.
2. The teaching atmosphere should be characterized by informality, with responsibility for learning considered a dual function between the teacher possessing the knowledge, skill, and understanding of the learning process as well as what should be learned, and the child who possesses the ability and interest to learn. A child learns new skills and insights when he is capable of exploring alternatives. This means he must have a goal, some uncertainty as to how to reach it, and the ability and motivation to attempt to reach the goal. The essential task for every teacher of physical education, as with all subjects, is to set a learning task which is within the reach of each child and to provide continuous encouragement and assistance throughout.

The many different knowledges, motor skills, and understandings of physical education cannot be learned through one approach or method. Each new learning situation must be organized to meet age, skills, and ability needs. Consequently, there is no single formula or method which will guarantee a positive predisposition toward each new learning task. The function of each

FIG. 3.1

teacher is to attempt to create a favorable learning setting and a reasonable and challenging learning task for each child. To do this, numerous approaches, methods, and techniques must be exploited.

• *A theory of instruction should specify the ways in which a body of knowledge should be structured so that it can be most readily grasped by the learner.*

The way knowledge, understanding, and physical skills are organized depends upon the age, background, and ability of the learners. With respect to learning and particularly motor skill, the nature of the activity must also be taken into consideration. Hence, for primary school children, games are normally organized and taught with a minimum number of rules and regulations. Older children with a repertoire of skills and knowledge can be presented with extended units of instruction, including complex skills, rules, and strategy.

Generally speaking, the content of physical education is organized on the basis of similar activities (Games, Dance, or Gymnastics). With respect to creative dance and educational gymnastics, content is still organized on the basis of meaningful areas ("shape" as in educational gymnastics) but the progression in skill development becomes an individual matter of progressing from the simple to the more complex.

• *A theory of instruction should specify the most effective sequences in which to present the materials to be learned.*

In physical education, the manner in which knowledge, understanding, and physical skills are presented to the learners, is based primarily upon the criterion of "simple to complex." The ability of teachers to assemble learning tasks in games, dance, or self-testing activities on the basis of simple to complex is not a simple linear arrangement. Children are placed in physical education classes primarily upon the basis of chronological age. Levels of ability, previous experience, and readiness to learn will, however, vary immensely with each class. The important consideration is the awareness of the complexity of the skill and a conscious recognition that individual differences exist in every learning situation.

• *A theory of instruction should specify the nature and placing of rewards and punishments in the process of learning and teaching.*

Ideally, every teacher would prefer all learning to be intrinsically motivated. Such is not the case with any group, regardless of age or task to be learned. In physical education, it is essential to attempt to provide learning tasks in such a way that the task itself, rather than the end result, becomes intrinsically valuable to the learner. Through direct teaching we can set goals such as performing a certain number of exercises, executing a number of gymnastic skills, or running a certain distance within a set period of time. We can provide rewards or penalties for success or failing to perform these acts, but their very nature is extrinsic. When removed there is no guarantee and probably reasonable certainty that whatever was learned in this manner will not be participated in when the reward-punishment factor is removed.

The acquisition of motor skill requires ability, concentration, and repetition. Initially, extrinsic rewards may be necessary to initiate the learning process. At every maturational level and within each movement task, the transition to intrinsic motivation should begin. The exact moment in any learning task when this should occur is unpredictable. It depends on the ability of the teacher to sense when and how to structure the learning task in order that the child sees *its* value *from his own* intrinsic point of view.

If the latter is accomplished, participation in physical activities will be continuous and for values other than those conceived by adults and experts in physiological functions of the human body. Participation in physical activities, whatever the medium, must be based upon a fundamental joy of movement and social companionship. Fitness, in terms of strength, cardiorespiratory efficiency, is important, but must be seen by the learner as a means rather than an end.

The above four features or criteria of a THEORY OF INSTRUCTION are concerned with two basic factors. First there is concern with the way materials (knowledge, understandings, and skills) to be learned should be organized. Secondly, there is concern with the ways in which a teacher can structure and facilitate the learning of material. A theory of instruction is, therefore, concerned with both content and method.

A THEORY OF LEARNING IN PHYSICAL EDUCATION

A theory of learning is a theoretical assumption of how an organism learns. As such it should provide reason and direction for one's theory of instruction, which deals with the way in which a teacher can structure and facilitate learning. In terms of physical education, the theory selected must provide a reasonable basis for understanding motor learning and a list of principles of learning that are compatible with the theory of instruction. A brief description of two major theories of learning is presented in the following paragraphs in order to provide a framework for understanding the meaning of motor learning and the important principles that should be considered in the process of teaching physical education. It is impossible to include an extensive coverage of each theory of learning in the pages which follow. Such treatment may be found in Hilgard[3] and Hill,[4] and others listed in the selected references.

---

3. Hilgard, *op. cit*. Theories of Learning and Instruction.
4. W. Hill, *Learning: A Survey of Psychological Interpretations* (San Francisco: Chandler Publishing Co., 1963).

Stimulus-Response Theory

The Stimulus-Response Theory developed by Thorndike in 1906 was an attempt to describe how an individual learns and adjusts to his world. His hypothesis was that learning consists of a strengthening of the connection (called a "bond") between a stimulus and a response.[5] Accordingly his conception of learning was that an individual is acted upon and then initiates an act as a responding mechanism. His "laws" of learning, still greatly influential in teaching today, are very briefly described below:

1. Law of Readiness: Learning depends upon readiness to act which, in turn, facilitates the response.
2. Law of Effect: Learning is facilitated or retarded according to the degree of satisfaction or annoyance that accompanies the act.
3. Law of Exercise: The more often a connection between bonds is repeated the more firmly the connection (pairing of bonds) becomes fixed (learned).

In later years Thorndike modified his laws on the basis of additional findings. He found that greater effects result from satisfaction than displeasure. Since his research was concerned with human learning, the importance and obvious implications of reward rather than punishment have greatly affected the nature of teaching.

Principles of teaching physical education based on Stimulus-Response Theory appear to be helpful but incomplete. They are helpful from the point of view of recognizing the importance of repetition of motor skills and the need to make the learning task satisfying to the learner. One can visualize the partial application of this theory to learning such skills as throwing, kicking, swimming, and traditional gymnastic movements. Since the theory fails to recognize the fundamental concept (from a Gestalt viewpoint) that a

FIG. 3.2

---

5. E. L. Thorndike, *Principles of Teaching* (New York: A. G. Seiler Co., 1906), p. 3.

learner is a purposeful and holistic organism capable of thinking, it has major limitations in providing a basis for understanding other types of learning and behavior. For example, when this theory is used to explain social behavior, individual and team strategy or creative movement in dance or gymnastics, it falls immeasurably short.

Field Theory

The Field Theory, developed by Wertheimer and others, assumes that the learner has a personality and reacts from the very beginning as a whole. It maintains that the human organism possesses a certain order from the beginning. All attributes are considered to be integral and indivisible parts of the whole personality; they may be differentiated but cannot be separated from the organization of the whole being.[6] Learning proceeds from comprehension of the whole to the identification of smaller parts. Learning, therefore, is not considered, as with Stimulus-Response Theories, to be an additive process; it consists of a continuous reorganization of new learnings with previous learnings, resulting in new insights.

The Field Theory appears to be more compatible with the features of the previously stated Theory of Instruction. This theory stresses that the fundamental importance any learning experience may have on the learner depends upon his own unique perception of the experience in relationship to his previous experiences, abilities, and personal desires. Learning from this point of view is an individualized process, thus the teacher's role is viewed as being a guider of the learning experience. Inherent in this concept is the belief that each child learns according to his own unique style.

FIG. 3.3   FIG. 3.4   FIG. 3.5

6. B. Knapp, *Skill in Sport* (London: Routledge and Kegan Paul, 1967), p. 148.

AN APPLICATION OF PRINCIPLES OF LEARNING

Continuous experimentation has produced principles of learning which provide a reasonable guideline for teachers as they organize learning experiences and select methods and techniques of instruction. Some of the accompanying list of principles are derived from the Stimulus-Response Theory while others are the direct application of the Field Theory. This represents an eclectic point of view since the following principles are based upon several theoretical frameworks. Since our knowledge of the learning process is still incomplete, we should use these principles only as guidelines and apply our own "common sense" to each and every learning situation.

Principle of Interest

The acquisition of any skill, whether it be climbing a rope or throwing a softball, will take place most efficiently when the child has a personal motive for wanting to learn.[7] A teacher may establish a goal such as the overhand catch for a six-year-old child. The attitude of the child toward the learning of the skill, however, will determine, for the most part, the amount and kind of learning. It is possible that learning may occur out of fear or because of some extrinsic reward such as a star or check put beside his name. Inherent in this principle is the concept that teachers must foster in the child a desire to learn motor skills. Learning will take place if the child experiences immediate personal satisfaction, if he perceives the necessity of building a strong healthy body, or if he values the skill as something he wishes to use during his leisure time.

Implications for Physical Education.

1. Select activities that are appropriate to a child's interests, needs, and capacities.
2. Stress the intrinsic value of the activity.

Principle of Practice

Research in the field of motor learning substantially indicates that practice is a necessary ingredient in the acquisition of a motor skill. It must, however, be practice of the correct pattern until the skill becomes overlearned or automatic. Once a child has learned to swim, several months may elapse without practice, yet he will still be able to swim. In general, the greater the skill is "overlearned," the longer the time interval before it is lost. Another important point regarding practice is that if undertaken badly it will not lead to improvement but may even lead to retrogression.[8]

---

7. P. J. Arnold, *Education Physical Education and Personality Development* (London: Heinemann Educational Books, Ltd. 1968), p. 60.
8. Arnold, *op. cit.*, p. 61.

FIG. 3.6

Implications for Physical Education.
1. Select skills that are appropriate to the interest and maturation level.
2. Stress proper form as skills are first learned. After the skill has been learned, stress other factors such as speed and distance.
3. Repeat drill activities after several months to insure retention.

Principle of Distributed Practice

A motor skill is learned more effectively with distributed practice periods rather than with massed practice periods. The length of each practice period as well as the length between each practice depends upon the difficulty of the skill, the level of ability, and previous background of the learner. One can, however, generalize that a short period of intense effort and attention is better than a half-hearted longer period.[9]

This principle applies "generally" to all age levels and to virtually all skills. There are certain situations in learning motor skills that may shorten or extend the practice period beyond what is normally considered wise. For example, the amount of interest shown by the children and the required amount of effort may influence the length of the practice period. To illustrate, if a class is practicing the forward roll and is permitted to repeat the movement to the extent that dizziness and fatigue result from the activity, this would indicate that regardless of student interest the practice period was too long and too strenuous. Self-testing activities for any age group should require variation in physical performance so that one part of the body is not overworked.

---

9. Knapp, *op. cit.*, p. 62.

A teacher working with fifth and sixth grade children in an activity such as volleyball lead-up games may find that interest and enthusiasm may continue for ten or fifteen minutes or even longer. As long as interest is high and skill development is fostered, it is not only permissible but desirable to extend the practice period. On the other hand, when indifference is shown and skill is not being attained, a change in the lead-up activity or a shorter practice period is advocated.

Implications for Physical Education,

1. Adjust the length of the practice period and the spacing of rest periods to the class and to the material being taught.
2. Change an activity whenever fatigue, boredom, and poor skill development is indicated.

Principle of Skill Specificity

The ability of a child to acquire a particular skill depends upon his own unique characteristics. A child, therefore, may excel in one particular skill and be retarded in other skills requiring approximately the same maturational level and physical effort.[10] To illustrate, a nine-year-old boy may demonstrate skill in softball activities—he can throw, catch, and hit a ball with ease and accuracy. In volleyball activities, although requiring approximately the same effort and physical attributes, he may demonstrate a sub-par performance. This principle also applies to children who have reached the same psychological and physiological maturity level. After one demonstration of a particular skill, one child may be able to perform it in its entirety, while another child may require more demonstration and additional practice to perform even one part of the skill. This is dramatically illustrated in such sports as swimming, basketball, and track and field.

Implications for Physical Education

1. Provide a varied program of activities at all grade levels.
2. Allow for individual difference in standards of performance for the same skill.
3. Allow for variation in the speed of acquiring the same skill.
4. Develop standards based upon an individual's level and rate of development rather than the class average.

Principle of Whole—Part Learning

According to Knapp,[11] in the whole method, material is learned by going through it completely time after time. In the part method, the material is divided into portions, then practiced, and eventually joined together as a whole. In physical education, and within any skill area, it is difficult to

---

10. B. J. Cratty, *Movement Behavior and Motor Learning*, 2nd Edition (Philadelphia: Lea and Febiger, 1967), p. 225.

11. Knapp, *op. cit.*, p. 59.

define what is whole and what is a part of the skill or game. Recognizing the difficulty in distinguishing whole or part learning, the available evidence indicates that the "whole" method is superior to the "part" method in teaching motor skills.[12]

To apply this principle a teacher must first decide whether to teach a movement in its entirety or break it down into parts. The choice of the "whole" or "part" methods first depends upon the complexity of the skill and second upon the demonstrated amount and speed of skill development of the learner. To illustrate, a teacher has demonstrated to a third grade class a one foot hop skipping skill using a single rope. The children are then allowed to attempt the skill in its entirety. This is practice through the "whole" method. If only a few children learn the skill after repeated attempts, the "part" method using a breakdown into simpler movements is indicated. The teacher would require a one foot hop over a long rope turned by two people to assist the child in learning the hop. Once this is accomplished, each child would attempt the one foot hop with a single rope using a one-half swing of the rope. Finally the full turn of the rope with the hopping movement is integrated into the rhythmic turning of the rope.

Implications for Physical Education.

1. Attempt to teach, using the "whole" method whenever the skill represents a single functional movement.
2. With more complex skills it may be desirable to break them down into smaller component parts. Complexity depends upon the skill as well as upon the ability of the learner.
3. Generally, the rate and amount of learning will indicate the effectiveness of the method used.

Principle of Transfer

Transfer in physical education may be defined as the effect that practice of one motor task has upon the learning or performance of a second and closely related task.[13] Underlying this principle of transfer is the assumption that in a new situation a learner will take advantage of what the new situation has in common with previous experience.[14] For example, the underhand throwing motion is similar, but not identical to the motion required to serve a volleyball. Although it has been contended that transfer will occur particularly between identical skills or movements, there is no conclusive evidence to support this statement. This evidence seems to support the previous principle of specificity.

Implications for Physical Education.

12. G. B. Johnson, *Motor Learning* in W. R. Johnson, *Science and Exercise of Medicine and Sports,* (New York: Harper & Row, Publishers, 1960).
13. Cratty, *op. cit.,* p. 283.
14. Arnold, *op. cit.,* p. 67.

During the past few years Educational Gymnastics (Movement Education) has been incorporated into numerous elementary school physical education programs. Proponents of this approach to teaching, including its originator (Rudolf Laban), have stated that Educational Gymnastics has a strong carry-over to other skill learning. Since there is no evidence to indicate there is a common motor skill factor, this is a dubious statement. Current research indicates transfer depends upon the degree of resemblance between the respective skills.

There are, however, many other reasons for adopting Educational Gymnastics. These will be discussed in detail in Part IV of this text. What may be stated here is that a carry-over does occur in Educational Gymnastics in the form of a positive attitude toward other activities. The latter is extremely important with reference to the amount of emphasis that should be given to this approach throughout the elementary school program.

Principle of Skill Improvement

The manner in which a child learns physical skills does not always follow the same pattern from one skill to another. There are too many factors affecting the learning curve. One must understand the complexity of the skill, then consider such pertinent learning factors as motivation and physical ability, as well as the adequacy of instruction. Generally speaking, however, the initial phase of learning is usually quite rapid. This may be due to enthusiasm for a new activity, learning the easy parts first, and utilizing previously acquired skills. Gradually, even as practice continues, progress slows down almost to a period of no overt improvement. There are numerous explanations for these "plateaus" of learning, such as lack of motivation, failure to learn a prerequisite skill, and improper instruction. With proper analysis and correction an increase in skill attainment should result and an end brought to the current plateau.

Implications for Physical Education.

1. Teachers should recognize individual differences in the learning curve for the same activity.
2. After the introduction of a new skill allow sufficient practice time for mastery.
3. Be aware of physiological limitations that hinder or prevent additional improvement.

Older concepts of teaching methods were based upon the premise that the teacher was the sole authority of what was correct and desirable for children. Children were expected to learn regardless of their own limitations, of their own interests, or the inadequacies of the learning situation. Contemporary education has replaced these older concepts with principles of learning that are based upon tested thinking and controlled experimentation.

All principles of learning are applicable to the field of physical education. Those stated in this chapter, however, are extremely important with respect to the selection of physical activities, the choice of appropriate methods, as well as to an understanding of how motor skills are learned. When these principles of learning are considered in relationship to the goals of the program and the characteristics of the learner, the scope and direction of the total program becomes meaningful.

Selected References

Arnold, P. J. *Education Physical Education and Personality Development.* London: Heinemann Educational Books Ltd., 1968.

Bruner, J. S. *Towards a Theory of Instruction.* Cambridge: Harvard University Press, Belknap Press, 1966.

Cratty, B. J. *Movement Behavior and Motor Learning,* 2nd Edition. Philadelphia: Lea and Febiger, 1967.

Davis, E. C. and Wallis, E. L. *Towards Better Teaching in Physical Education.* Englewood Cliffs: Prentice-Hall Inc., 1961.

Gage, N. L. "Theories of Teaching," in *Theories of Learning and Instruction,* 63rd Yearbook of the National Society for the Study of Education, Part I, edited by E. Hilgard (Chicago: University of Chicago Press, 1964).

Hill, W. *Learning: A Survey of Psychological Interpretations.* San Francisco: Chandler Publishing Co., 1963.

Humphrey, J. *Child Learning Through Elementary School Physical Education.* Dubuque: Wm. C. Brown Company Publishers, 1965.

Johnson, G. B. *Motor Learning in W. R. Johnson, Science and Exercise of Medicine and Sports.* New York: Harper & Row, Publishers, 1960.

Knapp, B. *Skill in Sport.* London: Routledge and Kegan Paul, 1967.

Laban, Rudolf von and Lawrence, F. C. *Effort.* London: Macdonald and Evans, 1947.

Shurr, E. L. *Movement Experiences for Children: Curriculum and Methods for Elementary School Physical Education.* New York: Appleton-Century-Crofts, 1967.

Thorndike, E. L. *Principles of Teaching.* New York: A. G. Seiler Co., 1906.

Physical Education
Curriculum

P
A
R
T

II

The curriculum in physical education includes all of the organized and directed experiences provided for within the instructional and extra-class program. Chapter 4 includes basic information relating to planning a comprehensive program of activities for each grade level. In Chapter 5 consideration is given to such factors as equipment and supplies, "organizing" tournaments, and developing safe instructional and playing areas. Chapter 6 provides a clarification of the methods and techniques used to teach physical education as well as pertinent information relating to routine procedures and class organization. Chapter 7 includes a general discussion of evaluation, grading, and reporting pupil progress.

Planning a Physical Education Program

The Instructional Program
The Extra-Class Program

T HE physical education program for elementary school children is divided into two closely related areas. The first and more important is the instructional program which consists of the regular activities carried on during the daily physical education period. Broadly speaking, the extra-class program includes all other supervised physical education activities that are under the direct supervision of teachers. The latter includes organized competition between classes, all school track meets, and limited competition between schools in the form of play days and sports days.

Obviously, the most important part of the physical education program in the elementary school is the regular instruction carried on during the daily physical education period. The average time allotment for physical education may vary from fifteen minutes in the primary grades to a full hour in the intermediate grades. Most authorities, however, recommend a minimum instructional period of thirty minutes for all grades in the elementary school. Also, the scope of the program for Kindergarten through Grade Six should be primarily instructional in nature with provisions for supervised free play activities during recess, noon hour, and after school. Organized intramural activities, such as competition between classes in one or more sports, annual school track meets, and play days with other schools, should be provided for fifth and sixth grade children. These extra-class activities should, however, be considered an important supplement to and not a replacement for the instructional program.

The first part of this chapter is applicable to all grades since it shows how to organize a yearly instructional program. The information contained in the latter section applies only to the upper grades. Here the extra-class program will be discussed with respect to its scope of activities and the methods of organizing groups for competition.

THE INSTRUCTIONAL PROGRAM

The main task is to choose activities and methods which will most effectively realize the objectives of physical education. This, of course, is no mean task, since the teacher must be able to distinguish among the various types of activities and know where to place the greatest emphasis, and be able to plan a program in a logical and sequential pattern. To provide a basic framework for each teacher to develop a physical education program, the activities are arranged in three broad categories, namely games, dance, and self-testing activities. Each grade level is also provided with a guide showing the percentage of time that should be devoted to each type of activity. Also included are three types of instructional units that can be used as basic formats in planning a specific program of activities.

Type of Activities

The content of the physical education program includes all of the physical activities children participate in through planned instruction and extra-class activities. Just how these activities should be classified, however, has not been agreed upon by members of the physical education profession. Because of this confusion, the relative degree of emphasis given each type of activity by grade level seems to depend upon "author's preference" and geographical location. This problem of classification has been further complicated by the development of new types of programs such as "Movement Education" or "Educational Gymnastics" which are, in essence, approaches to teaching involving both activities and methods of instruction. It is quite obvious that a classification system should be as simple as possible to allow classroom teachers to select and emphasize appropriate activities.

In this text, all activities are classified as Games, Self-Testing and Dance activities. The types of specific activities contained in these broad categories will be listed in the accompanying chart. In addition, a clarification of "Educational Gymnastics" (or Movement Education) will be provided to show the relationship of types of activities to methods and general approaches to teaching.

PHYSICAL EDUCATION ACTIVITIES

GAMES	SELF-TESTING	DANCE
Games of Low Organization	Warm-up exercises	Fundamental movements
–simple team games	stunts and tumbling	singing games
–relay and tag games	small apparatus activities	pantomime activities
–classroom games	–partner activities	creative activities
–individual and dual games	–hoop activities	folk dances
	–cane activities	
Individual and Team games		
–basketball	–beanbag activities	
–soccer	–Indian Club activities	
–softball	–individual rope activities	
–touch football	Large Apparatus activities	
–volleyball	–balance beam and benches	
	–horizontal ladder	
–track and field	–stall (wall) bars	
–rounders	–overhead ladder	
	–climbing ropes	
	–box and springboard	
	–trampoline	
	–agility apparatus	

Aquatic Activities have not been included in the foregoing chart as an appropriate activity for elementary school children simply because of the general lack of facilities available to the vast majority of elementary schools. There are strong indications that swimming will and should become a popular activity as facilities become available. Several school districts have experimented with the "portable" pools and found them to be inexpensive and extremely useful, particularly for "beginner" programs. The writer has recently surveyed a number of elementary school facilities in Great Britain and found aquatics to be a very popular activity in many programs. Virtually all schools utilized the portable pool with instruction given by classroom teachers. The latter were given special in-service courses prior to the inauguration of instructional programs in swimming for the children.

Educational Gymnastics and Movement Exploration

The difficulty in defining Educational Gymnastics (Movement Education) lies in the fact that it is a comprehensive approach to teaching one part of the physical education program rather than a specific method or a specific activity such as "basketball" or "singing games." This "approach" is recommended by many leading authorities in education and it has been incorporated in Part IV of this text. The latter, however, has been modified to meet the unique conditions in our public schools as well as to "blend into"

FIG. 4.1

FIG. 4.2

rather than "replace" other well-established and educationally sound approaches to teaching physical education. A clarification of its meaning is provided to allow teachers to see its relationship to other activities in the physical education program.

Definition of Educational Gymnastics

Educational Gymnastics, as an approach to teaching physical education, may be broadly defined as "that part of the self-testing program in which emphasis is placed on helping the child to understand and control the many ways in which his body may move."[1]

The foregoing definition becomes quite meaningful only when the unique aspects of Educational Gymnastics are understood. This is best explained by comparing Educational Gymnastics with our contemporary approaches to teaching physical education.

COMPARISON OF THE CONTEMPORARY AND EDUCATIONAL GYMNASTIC APPROACHES

Contemporary Approach to Teaching Self-Testing Activities	Educational Gymnastics Approach to Teaching Self-Testing Activities
Classification of Activities	
Introductory or Warm-up Exercises Small Apparatus Large Apparatus	Introductory Activities Small Apparatus Large Apparatus
Classification and Analysis of Skill	
Standardized skills and stunts (example: "Forward roll," "front vault," and "head stand." Skills are defined and arranged from simple to complex.	All movement is classified and analyzed according to three basic elements of movement. These are body shape, body position, and body action. These elements or principles of movement may be applied to all movements including self-testing, dance, or game skills.
Methods of Instruction	
Emphasis on direct method of instruction with some application of limitation and indirect methods.[2]	Emphasis on limitation and indirect method of instruction.

In the foregoing chart there are minor differences in the classification of activities between the contemporary and the Educational Gymnastic approaches. The first major difference, however, is centered in the Classifica-

---

1. Board of Education "Movement Education for the Teacher and his Staff," (DeKalb: DeKalb Community Unit District 428), p. 1.

2. See Chapter 6 for a definition of each method of instruction.

tion and Analysis of Skill. Contemporary programs, with the exception of "creative or interpretive" dance, utilize a standardized classification of skills. For example, in individual and team sport activities there are certain basic skills of kicking, throwing, or catching that are performed in much the same way by all participants. Similarly, rules and regulations for many games provide the "form" for participating in the activity. As such, they are taught primarily through a teacher-directed approach.

Methods of instruction, (see Chapter 6), present the greatest area of misunderstanding. Although teaching standardized skills requires more of a teacher-directed approach, it is also quite possible and desirable to use limitation or problem-solving methods in teaching team skills as well as other important intellectual and social understandings. On the other hand, the combined use of a new system of analyzing movement skills, coupled with an informal atmosphere which emphasizes the use of limitation and problem-solving methods in the Educational Gymnastics Approach, permits children to learn skills and understanding according to their own abilities and personal interests. This approach is, therefore, extremely effective in the self-testing area since a child no longer has to learn a "set number of skills" which are performed in the same way by all students. It is the freedom of interpretation provided by the extensive use of the limitation and indirect methods of instruction, plus the new format for analyzing skills, that makes Educational Gymnastics unique as an Approach.

Educational Gymnastics programs began in Great Britain as a direct result of Rudolf Laban's[3] writings and personal influence. However, these programs have undergone extensive revisions. Today, the majority of programs of this nature are primarily restricted to self-testing activities. To verify this statement, the writer visited numerous elementary schools in Great Britain and discussed this subject with recognized experts in England and Scotland. There is a predominately Educational Gymnastic emphasis in the primary, intermediate, and even in several secondary schools. There is equal emphasis, however, in the team games and dance activities which are still taught chiefly with a teacher-directed approach, thus providing a balance between the type of activities taught and the approaches and methods used in the total physical education program.

Educational Gymnastics should find its place in our self-testing area of instruction and complement rather than replace other approaches and methods of teaching games and dance activities.

Definition of "Movement Exploration"

There are a number of "interpretations" or definitions of Movement Exploration. According to Halsey and Porter this term means "planned problem-

---

3. R. Laban, *The Mastery of Movement,* Second Edition, (reviewed and enlarged by Lisa Ullmann) (London: Macdonald and Evans, 1960).

solving experiences, progressing in difficulty, through which the child learns to understand and control the many ways in which his body may move and thus improve many skills."[4] Others simply define it as a basic problem-solving method applied to teaching fundamental skills of movement but not according to the unique structure originally provided by Rudolph Laban. There are, therefore, strong indications both in published literature and observed programs that "educational gymnastics," "movement education," and "movement exploration" can be taken as being synonymous.

The writer may appear to be over-emphasizing this particular point of clarification. It is important since the essence of Part IV is to provide the reader with a means of understanding and gradually adopting the "Educational Gymnastics" approach to teaching self-testing activities. On the other hand, the use of the teacher-directed approach with provisions for problem-solving methods and student participation in planning is recommended in the teaching of other activities in the program.

Planning a Yearly Program

A brief review of the objectives of the elementary school physical education program indicates that teachers should provide experiences that will (1) develop and maintain maximum physical efficiency; (2) develop useful physical skills; (3) provide opportunities to foster socially acceptable traits; and (4) provide opportunities to enjoy wholesome physical recreation. We know, however, that each of the foregoing broad categories of activities is more effective in accomplishing one or more of the stated objectives. For example, the activities listed under Games can assist in developing useful physical skills, wholesome physical recreation, and social traits such as team loyalty and sportsmanship. It is, however, quite debatable if Games per se are as effective as the activities listed under Self-Testing Activities in raising and maintaining an optimum level of physical fitness. Furthermore, Games and Self-Testing Activities are not as effective as Dance in accomplishing certain social, creative, and physical skills. When these factors are considered, as well as the characteristics and needs of children, the following general estimate of time devoted to these activities will be of assistance in planning an appropriate physical education program for each grade level.

PERCENTAGE OF TIME FOR EACH ACTIVITY							
Type of Activity	Percentage of time per grade						
	K	1	2	3	4	5	6
Games	20%	30%	40%	40%	50%	50%	50%
Dance	20%	20%	20%	20%	20%	20%	20%
Self-testing	60%	50%	40%	40%	30%	30%	30%

4. E. Halsey and L. Porter, *Physical Education for Children* (New York: Holt, Rinehart & Winston, Inc., 1967), p. 172.

Teachers should also refer to local and state physical education guides to see how activities are organized and should note the recommended time allotments. In certain areas, climate and available facilities will affect the amount of emphasis each teacher can devote to Games, Dance, or Self-Testing Activities.

Suggested Activities

Selecting appropriate games, dance, or self-testing activities from within each of these broad categories is a difficult task for the classroom teacher. In the first place, classes are usually organized by age rather than ability. Ability in physical education, as with other subject areas, varies immensely within any age level. For example, a class of second graders will range from late six to early eight in chronological years. In terms of physiological maturity, there may be as much as five years' difference existing within this age range. In addition to these important factors there is the problem of varying prior physical education experiences and different levels of physical and motor ability. Consequently, each teacher normally has to experiment, more or less on a trial-and-error basis, with various games, dance, and self-testing activities to find the appropriate level of difficulty to suit her class.

Within Parts IV, V and VI, there are suggested grade levels for each specific activity. The following chart will indicate the chapter and page where each type of activity is located. Teachers should first decide the type of instructional unit (see next section) they will adopt, then utilize this chart as a quick reference to finding the appropriate page where activities are located. Each chapter in the next three parts also contains information relating to the planning of various types of teaching units.

			SUGGESTED ACTIVITIES							
Activity	Chapter	Page	Suggested Grade Levels							
			K	1	2	3	4	5	6	
GAME ACTIVITIES										
Games of Low Organization	8	117								
Simple Team Games	8	118	X	X	X	X	X	X	X
Relays	8	142	X	X	X	X	X	X	X
Tag Games	8/9	153	X	X	X	X	X	X	X
Active and Quiet Classroom										
Games	8	164	X	X	X	X	X	X	X
Individual and Dual										
Activities	8/9	178	X	X	X	X	X	X	X
Individual and Team Games	9	189								
Basketball	9	190					X	X	X
Soccer	9	215					X	X	X
Softball	9	238					X	X	X
Volleyball	9	256				X	X	X	X

Activity	Chapter	Page	Suggested Grade Levels						
			K	1	2	3	4	5	6
Touch Football	9	273					X	X	X
Track and Field	9	288					X	X	X
Rounders	10	317				X	X	X	X
Goodminton	10	326						X	X
SELF-TESTING ACTIVITIES									
General Information	11	336	X	X	X	X	X	X	X
Introductory Activities	12	351	X	X	X	X	X	X	X
General Warm-up Activities	12	357	X	X	X	X	X	X	X
Rubber-band Activities	12	359	X	X	X	X	X	X	X
Mimetics	12	358	X	X	X	X	X	X	X
"Who can" . . .	12	358	X	X	X	X	X	X	X
Circuit Training	12	363						X	X
Rope Skipping	12	366	X	X	X	X	X	X	X
Tag Games	12	367	X	X	X	X	X	X	X
Floor and Small Apparatus Activities									
Stunts and Tumbling	13	371	X	X	X	X	X	X	X
Partner Activities	13	380	X	X	X	X	X	X	X
Hoops	13	384	X	X	X	X	X	X	X
Beanbags, Braids and Indian Clubs	13	387	X	X	X	X	X	X	X
Blocks, Chairs, and Wands	13	389	X	X	X	X	X	X	X
Rope Activities	13	394	X	X	X	X	X	X	X
Large Apparatus Activities	14	415	X	X	X	X	X	X	X
Balance Beam and Benches	14	416	X	X	X	X	X	X	X
Springboards, Mini-tramp, Vaulting Box	14	423	X	X	X	X	X	X	X
Horizontal Bar, Ladder and Stall Bars	14	428	X	X	X	X	X	X	X
Climbing Ropes	14	436	X	X	X	X	X	X	X
Boxes, Sawhorse, Planks	14	438	X	X	X	X	X	X	X
Agility Apparatus	14	439	X	X	X	X	X	X	X
DANCE ACTIVITIES									
Fundamental Rhythm Skills	16	525	X	X	X	X			
Traditional and Contemporary Dances	17	549							
Singing Games	17	550	X	X	X				
Folk Dances	17	562		X	X	X	X	X	X
Square Dances	17	572				X	X	X	X
Creative Rhythms	18	581	X	X	X	X	X	X	X

Planning Instructional Units

Once a teacher has decided what types of activities she will include in the yearly physical education program there remains the task of planning smaller units of instruction. Factors, such as available time, interest, and ability levels, and available equipment and facilities, must be considered when deciding what type of teaching unit will be the most desirable. There are three basic types of teaching units that can be used with varying degrees of success, each with some inherent limitations. Each will be described in the accompanying paragraphs with advantages and disadvantages indicated. Each teacher should select the instructional unit that most readily meets the needs of her grade level and which is in harmony with the basic approach she adopts to teach the selected activity.

MULTIPLE TEACHING UNIT

The multiple unit is actually three units taught concurrently throughout the year. In other words, games, dance, and self-testing activities may be taught on alternate days for an indefinite time period. To illustrate, the following week of activities for kindergarten includes games on Mondays, self-testing on Tuesday, and dance on Wednesday. On Thursday, singing games, representing dance, would start the second rotation of activities. Hence the rotation system can be modified by the repetition of similar activities within a two day period.

SAMPLE WEEKLY PLAN FOR KINDERGARTEN

Monday	Tuesday	Wednesday	Thursday	Friday
Game Skills	Floor Stunts	Rhythmic activities	Singing Games	Classroom Games
Bouncing practice activities 1. bounce and catch. 2. bounce several times 3. bounce to partner	Camel walk, elevator, tight rope walk	Pantomime animal walks such as bears, lions, dogs, and horses	"London Bridge"	"Ring-master"

Generally speaking, this approach provides for a variation of activities during any week, month, or throughout the school year. The main advantage of this method is its flexibility, hence it can be used for Kindergarten and Grade One to cope with the short attention span of five and six-year-olds. Available facilities and equipment may determine whether or not to adopt this method of unit organization. Regardless of the reasons for selecting the multiple unit, care should be taken to insure that games, dance, and self-testing activities are given the appropriate amount of emphasis suggested for each grade.

Modified Teaching Unit

The modified unit is a set block of time allocated primarily for the instruction of one type of activity. In other words, during three or four weeks one activity such as dance is emphasized approximately ninety percent of the time while the remaining ten percent could be devoted to games and self-testing activities. To further illustrate this method, let us assume a third grade class has a thirty minute physical education period each day in the gymnasium.

In the first week of such a unit dance activities are taught on Monday, Tuesday, Thursday, and Friday. Wednesday is set aside for gymnasium or outdoor games. This method of organization provides continuity and variety in learning numerous skills. For example, on Monday "Paw Paw Patch" is introduced for the first time and is repeated on Tuesday so that the basic skills and dance patterns are learned. Later in the same lesson, "Bleking" is introduced. To provide a variation, Wednesday is set aside for vigorous running and tag games. Depending on the weather, these games could be played in the gymnasium or out-of-doors. The remaining two days, however, would be devoted to dance activities. This pattern is continued throughout the second and third weeks.

DANCE UNIT
(Grade 3)

Week	Monday	Tuesday	Wednesday	Thursday	Friday
1st week	Introduce: "Paw Paw Patch"	Review: "Paw Paw Patch" Introduce: "Bleking"	Games Stunt Relay Pinch-oh	Review: "Bleking" Introduce: "Skip to My Lou"	Review: "Paw Paw Patch" "Bleking" "Skip to My Lou"
2nd week	Review: "Skip to My Lou" Introduce: "Pease Porridge Hot"	Review: "Pease Porridge Hot" "Skip to My Lou"	Self-testing - stunts - balance beam - rope skipping	Review: "Bleking" "Pease Porridge Hot"	Review: "Skip to My Lou" Introduce: "Heel and Toe"
3rd week	Review: "Heel and Toe" Introduce: "Shoo-Fly"	Games	Review: "Heel and Toe" "Shoo Fly"	Review: "Paw Paw Patch" "Bleking" "Skip to My Lou"	Review: "Pease Porridge Hot," "Skip to My Lou," and "Heel and Toe"

The modified block appears to take into consideration the general weakness of the multiple unit approach since it provides for a continuity in learning skills. It also has certain desirable instructional features for it permits the teacher to plan one type of activity for an extended period of time rather than three different types for each week. Furthermore, it is much easier to plan a one year program using the modified unit rather than the multiple approach.

SOLID TEACHING UNIT

A solid unit may be defined as an extended period of instruction that is devoted exclusively to one type of activity. No other activities are taught during this unit. The length of this type of unit may vary from one to several weeks. Its value lies in its continuity since there is no variation in the type of skill development. Perhaps the solid unit has its greatest application in team teaching where the most qualified teacher is used to maximum effectiveness. However, fifth and sixth grade teachers who are responsible for their own physical education programs may find this type of unit applicable in teaching activities which hold a high degree of interest and motivation for their students. To illustrate this method a solid four week unit on softball has been organized for a sixth grade class.

EXAMPLE SOFTBALL UNIT FOR GRADE SIX USING THE SOLID BLOCK APPROACH

	Monday (40 min)	Tuesday (15 min)	Wednesday (40 min)	Thursday (15 min)	Friday (40 min)
First week	Explain: Underhand throw (pitching) Practice: Zigzag passing Lead-up: Center ball	Practice: Throwing Lead-up: Shuttle throw	Explain: Bunting Practice: Swing at four Lead-up: Twenty-one softball	Review: Shuttle throw and twenty-one	Explain: Grounders Practice: Zigzag passing Lead-up: Bat ball

Note: Continue the above pattern with 2nd, 3rd, and 4th weeks.

It should be noted in the illustration that on Monday, Wednesday, and Friday the physical education period is forty minutes long, while on Tuesday and Thursday there is only a fifteen minute period. The longer periods of instruction are used to explain and demonstrate new skills as well as for various practice drills and lead-up games. The shorter periods on Tuesday and Thursday are just long enough for a short drill and possible one lead-up game. A similar pattern is followed during the second, third, and fourth weeks. As a suggestion, plan the first week in detail. After four or five days of instruction it may be noted that certain skills will require additional concentration or possibly more advanced skills, and lead-up games may also be indicated. The remaining three weeks should be planned in relationship to the level of skills and expressed interests of the class. There are possibilities of utilizing both the modified and solid units throughout the year. Early fall and spring activities are particularly adaptable to the solid unit while activities requiring indoor facilities may, on the basis of available facilities, indicate the modified unit as being the only feasible approach. Additional samples of instructional units are provided in Parts III and IV to illustrate how different types of units are planned and organized to cope with various approaches to teaching physical education.

THE EXTRA-CLASS PROGRAM

The extra-class program includes a variety of activities such as competition between classes in one or more sports, all-school track meets, and limited or extramural competition with other schools. In essence, the program should be an outgrowth or supplemental to the instructional program. Furthermore, to be truly intramural in principle, it should be a voluntary program with a major emphasis on participation and minor emphasis on winning. These fundamental principles are contained in a platform statement issued by the National Conference on Physical Education for Children of Elementary School Age. The following points should act as guidelines in the development of any extra-class physical program.[5]

1. First, as a foundation, all children should have a broad, varied, and graded physical education under competent instruction through all grades. In many of the activities in this program the competitive element is an important factor. The element of competition provides enjoyment and, under good leadership, leads to desirable social and emotional as well as physical growth.
2. Based upon a sound, comprehensive instructional program in Grades Five through Eight, children should have opportunity to play in supervised intramural games and contests with others who are of corresponding maturity and ability within their own school. In grades below the fifth, the competitive elements found in the usual activities will satisfy the needs of children.
3. As a further opportunity to play with others beyond the confines of their own school or neighborhood, play or sports day programs may be planned

---

5. National Conference on Physical Education for Children of Elementary School Age: Physical Education for Children of Elementary School Age (Chicago: The Athletic Institute, Inc., 1951), p. 22.

with emphasis on constructive social, emotional, and health outcomes. Teams may be formed of participants coming from more than a single school or agency, thus making playing together important.

In order to develop a comprehensive program of extra-class activities, teachers must understand the scope of the program, that is, just what type of organization and activities are appropriate for upper elementary school-age children. The next problem is to establish an equitable method of organizing children for competition. Finally, there are various types of tournaments (see next chapter) that should be used for different age levels and for specific sports.

Scope of the Program

The extra-class program for the upper elementary grades is basically intramural in nature; however, some extramural activities may be organized between schools. Intramural activities are conducted within the boundaries of a particular school, which would include competition between classes in one or more sports, noon hour or after school gymnastic or sports clubs, as well as all school swimming or track meets. Extramural activities include play days and sports days. In the context of extramural competition, play days involve children from two or more schools playing together on the same team; for example, a basketball play day involving five schools would require each team be composed of one player from each school. Sports days, on the other hand, are virtually the same as play days except that teams represent their own school. Using the latter illustration, the basketball sports day would involve a tournament among the five school teams with one school eventually declared the winner.

Methods of Organizing for Competition

Since extra-class activities should be organized on a voluntary basis, the procedure used to group children for competition is of paramount importance. Perhaps the ultimate success of most competitive programs depends upon equal competition and adequate provision for all children to participate. The method of organization selected for upper elementary grades must depend in part upon the foregoing, but also must consider the number of participants, type of activities, and available facilities and supervisors. Several methods will be presented, each with its own advantages and disadvantages.

GRADE AND HOMEROOMS

Of the numerous methods of organizing teams for competition probably homerooms appear the most popular.[6] It is fair competition when sixth

6. Louis E. Means, *The Organization and Administration of Intramural Sports* (St. Louis: C. V. Mosby Co., 1952), p. 62.

graders compete against sixth graders; it is unfair competition to match sixth graders with fifth graders. Therefore, in competitive team sports such as track and swimming, use homerooms when it is possible to match them from within the same grade. If this policy is violated, competition may be unequal and distinterest will become quite apparent with both grade levels.

CLASSIFICATION INDEX

By the time children reach the fifth and sixth grade level, age alone is not a fair assessment of physical growth and maturation. Some other method, therefore, should be used to arrange players so they are competing with others of approximate physical maturation and ability. A classification index may be used to arrange children into groups whereby the taller and older players are in the top section and the shorter and lighter players are in the lower section. To illustrate the use of this index, let us suppose there are sixty boys from the fifth and sixth grades registered for an after school intramural basketball tournament. Theoretically this would represent six teams of ten members each. Apply the formula ten times age (in years) plus weight (in pounds) to every boy. The four examples will provide us with an idea of how to divide the sixty players into two leagues of three teams each. Assuming ap-

Score
Player No. 1: 10 × 10 (age) plus 70 (weight) equals 170
Player No. 20: 10 × 11 (age) plus 86 (weight) equals 196
Player No. 35: 10 × 11 (age) plus 92 (weight) equals 202
Player No. 48: 10 × 12 (age) plus 123 (weight) equals 243

proximately one-half of the boys had a score of 196 or less, arbitrarily use this score as the dividing line between the two leagues. The actual dividing line will obviously depend upon the maturity levels of the group of children within your school. The method, however, is quite simple and may be used to equate players for competition in team and individual sports.

SKILL LEVELS

Competition in team and individual sports is often more dependent upon such factors as level of skill and desire than upon age, height, and weight. Since the level of skill for each child will vary from one sport to another, the actual level of skill for each intramural activity can be used as a method of organizing teams and leagues. However, this method is dependent primarily upon the teacher's assessment of each child's performance in the intramural activity. To illustrate the application of this method, let us assume that at the end of a four week instructional unit in volleyball three sixth grade classes wish to have a coeducational volleyball tournament after school. Eleven boys and girls from each class register for the tournament, a total of sixty-six players. Since the children are not playing for their homeroom, the intramural director has asked each homeroom teacher to rate his class members as either "A" or "B" players, and to divide the class into two approximately equal groups. The intramural director could then arbitrarily place all "A" players in one league and all "B" players in another. If one league is desired, the director would place an equal number of each type of player on each respective team.

If extra-class activities are organized on the basis of equitable competition and are well supervised, desirable physical and social experiences will result. It is wise to initiate an extra-class program on a limited basis such as a round robin volleyball tournament between three fifth or sixth grade classes. With demonstrated active participation and adequate supervision, then expand the program to meet the needs and interests of the fifth and sixth grade children.

SELECTED REFERENCES

American Association for Health, Physical Education and Recreation, After-School Games and Sports, Grades 4, 5, 6, Washington, D.C.: 1964.

American Association for Health, Physical Education and Recreation, Desirable Athletics Competition for Children, Washington, D.C.: 1966.

BEEMAN, H. F. and HUMPHERY, J. H. *Intramural Sports A Text and Study Guide*, Dubuque: Wm. C. Brown Company Publishers, 1960.

Board of Education, "Movement Education for the Teacher and His Staff, DeKalb: South Dakota Community Unit, School District 428 (mimeographed materials).

COWELL, CHARLES C., and HAZELTON, HELEN W. *Curriculum Designs in Physical Education*, Englewood Cliffs, New Jersey: Prentice-Hall, Inc., 1955.

HALSEY, E., and PORTER, L. *Physical Education for Children*, Revised Edition, New York: Holt, Rinehart & Winston, Inc., 1967.

IRWIN, LESLIE W. *The Curriculum in Health and Physical Education*, 3rd ed., Dubuque, Iowa: Wm. C. Brown Company Publishers, 1960.

KIRCHNER, G.; CUNNINGHAM, J.; and WARRELL, E. *Introduction to Movement Education*, Dubuque: Wm. C. Brown Company Publishers, 1969.

LABAN, R. VON. *The Mastery of Movement*, Second Edition, (revised and enlarged by Lisa Ullman) London: Macdonald and Evans, 1960.

MEANS, LOUIS E. *The Organization and Administration of Intramural Sports*, St. Louis: C. V. Mosby Co., 1952.

National Conference on Physical Education for Children of Elementary School Age: Physical Education for Children of Elementary School Age, Chicago: The Athletic Institute, Inc., 1951.

Physical Education for the Elementary School, Bulletin No. 73, South Dakota State Department of Education, South Dakota: 1958.

Physical Education: Grades One Through Seven, State Board of Education, Commonwealth of Virginia, Vol. 35, No. 9, 1960.

Physical Education, Grade Two, Physical Education Advisory Committee, San Diego City Schools, San Diego: 1962.

Physical Education Teachers Guide: Kindergarten, Grade One, Grade Two, Publication No. 472, Los Angeles, California, 1957.

Physical Education: Third-Eighth Grade, Oak Park Elementary Schools, Oak Park, Illinois: 1958.

SHURR, E. L. *Movement Experiences for Children: Curriculum and Methods for Elementary School Physical Education*, New York: Appleton-Century-Crofts, 1967.

VANNIER, M., and FOSTER, M. *Teaching Physical Education in Elementary Schools*, Fourth Edition, Philadelphia: W. B. Saunders Co., 1968.

Organizing for Physical Education

Responsibility for Physical Education
The Playground, Gymnasium, and Classroom
Basic Equipment and Supplies
Types of Tournaments
Accidents and Preventative Safeguards

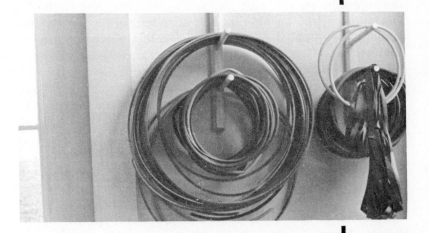

T HE quality of any physical education program primarily depends upon the interest and competence of the teacher and the available time and facilities. Although each school will vary in the amount and quality of these basic components, there are common organizational problems which confront every school. In this chapter how teachers can be effectively utilized in the physical education program is discussed as well as information about pertinent organizational problems relating to equipment, supplies, and the safety of the instructional area.

RESPONSIBILITY FOR PHYSICAL EDUCATION

There are several methods used in assigning the responsibility for teaching physical education. The first and most ideal method is to employ a trained physical education specialist to handle virtually all phases of the physical education program. The next is to employ rotating specialists or consultants to assist classroom teachers in such areas as program development, equipment and facility planning, and general instruction. The third and certainly the most common approach is to assign all the responsibility for physical education to the classroom teacher. The last method may become "team teaching" when there is a pooling of talent among classroom teachers in order to provide a well-rounded physical education program. The merits and undesirable features of each of these methods will be discussed in the following paragraphs.

Full-Time Physical Education Teachers

The employment of a full–time physical education teacher in the elementary school has, until the past few years, been the exception rather than the rule. During the past few years, however, more school districts have moved toward hiring physical education specialists, particularly in the upper grades. The essential reason underlying this trend is the recognition of the value of a well-rounded physical education program and the obvious need for a trained specialist. The latter will permit specialists in physical education to develop individual programs for children with perceptual motor or low fitness problems as well as to provide enriched programs for all children in such areas as dance, gymnastics, and individual and team sports.

Consulting Specialists

Due to the increased demands on the classroom teacher in all areas of the curriculum, administrators have attempted to alleviate their teaching load by employing consultant or teaching specialists. Examples of this trend, particularly in the larger school systems, are music, speech, and physical education teaching specialists whose main task is to provide the classroom teacher with up-to-date materials, new methods, and techniques, and conducting classroom demonstrations and general in-service sessions. The responsibility for each of these subject areas, however, still remains with the classroom teacher.

A classic example of how a "teaching specialist" is used in a large school is illustrated in the Blair Elementary School near Spokane, Washington. This is the largest elementary school in the State of Washington with nearly twelve hundred students representing Kindergarten through Grade Eight. Recognizing the need for a qualified physical education instructor, the administration hired one teaching specialist to provide general assistance to the classroom teachers in this school. Since it was virtually impossible for the specialist to meet with every teacher on a daily basis a modified approach was taken. During the first three months of the school year, the specialist and each teacher jointly developed units of instruction and daily lesson plans. This procedure gave the specialist an opportunity to evaluate the ability of each teacher to use her physical education guide, as well as to evaluate the teacher's general competence in handling the physical education program. At the end of the three month experimental period, a policy was established by the school administration which required any teacher needing help to submit a lesson plan three days before the scheduled lesson. This policy not only stimulated the teacher to develop a lesson plan but, in addition, assisted the specialist in his own preparation for the classroom teacher. Within a period of several months he was able to put many teachers "on their own." Generally speaking, the mutually developed program provided the assistance each teacher needed to develop her own program. With additional "free" time, the specialist was able to enrich the program by providing in-service sessions for specific grades in such activities as basketball skills, gymnastics, and track and field activities.

Self-Contained Classroom

Although administrators and teachers alike recognize the need for physical education specialists, the fact remains that elementary schools are organized predominantly on a self-contained basis. This implies that a classroom teacher, regardless of grade level, is competent to teach as many as eight or nine subject areas. In terms of physical education, the majority of classroom teachers have had approximately one general course in physical education during their college preparation. Obviously, this type of preparation is inadequate and indicates a definite need for in-service workshops, better teaching guides, additional audiovisual aids, and summer school courses. The latter should be designed to provide general assistance in content, organization, methods, and evaluative devices for all levels in the elementary school.

To say the current situation is hopeless or to consider physical education as a period of free play is both unjust to the intelligence of the classroom teacher and unfair to the needs of growing children. The implications of research, educational philosophy, and automation in its broadest meaning, indicate a need for a daily physical education program.[1] The program must include a variety of activities to enhance normal growth and development as well as to provide opportunities that will foster emotional growth, social adjustment, and permanent leisure time pursuits.

There are numerous examples of how school districts, large and small alike, have attempted to provide a physical education program without the assistance of physical education specialists. In Holt, Michigan, for example, the school board had no official policy with regard to physical education in their four elementary schools, yet a program was initiated. According to the director of elementary education, teachers were encouraged to attend workshops, summer sessions, and other in-service sessions to obtain information pertaining to the elementary physical education program. Their efforts led to the writing of a guide for Kindergarten through Grade Six which included physical education, health, and safety. Since most schools in this district were equipped with all-purpose rooms, each teacher was scheduled for one forty-five minute physical education period each week in this facility. In addition, all teachers could devote thirty minutes a day to classroom or out-of-door activities. As a follow-up to this program, the administration hired adults to supervise noon hour activities on the play field and indoors during inclement weather.[2]

Team Teaching

Team teaching is the organization of teachers and students into instructional groups which permit maximum utilization of staff abilities and enhances optimum growth of students.[3] The extent of team teaching may vary from two teachers exchanging classrooms for one subject to a pooling of all teachers into a single unified effort. The latter may involve regrouping of children, major curricula changes, and extensive utilization of outside experts. Obviously, the application of some form of team effort in handling physical education in the elementary school is worthy of consideration.[4] As we are aware, the self-contained classroom organizational structure, particularly for the inter-

---

1. President's Council on Youth Fitness, Youth Physical Fitness, Suggested Elements of a School-Centered Program, Washington, D.C.

2. "Elementary Schools Make Progress in PE Without Services of Qualified Instructor," Physical Education Newsletter, (New London, Connecticut: Letter 12, Vol. 7; Arthur C. Croft Publications, Feb. 1963), p. 3.

3. Arthur G. Miller and Virginia Whitcomb, Physical Education in the Elementary School Curriculum (Englewood Cliffs, New Jersey: Prentice-Hall, Inc., 1963), p. 17.

4. "Team Teaching: An Aid to Planning and Presenting a Vitalized PE Program Geared to Individual Needs," Physical Education Newsletter (New London, Connecticut: Letter 14, March 12, 1963), p. 2.

mediate grades, is not flexible enough to permit or encourage utilization of the special abilities of all teachers.

Since there are many forms of team teaching, it is difficult to present a list of advantages that will be applicable to every situation. However, the following advantages will apply to the simplest form of team teaching:

1. Provides a means whereby the most effective use of teacher skill and talent is utilized.
2. Encourage more complete and detailed lesson preparation and presentation.
3. Provides an opportunity for students to be exposed to a larger number of capable teachers.
4. Provides an opportunity for more flexible grouping of students.
5. Provides a means of in-service experiences for all teachers.
6. Provides an opportunity for teachers to investigate the effectiveness or new methods, materials, and techniques.
7. Provides an opportunity for teachers to experience greater personal and professional satisfaction.[5]

The simplest form of teaching is where one or more teachers exchange their classes for an assigned subject. The reason for such an exchange is obvious: to draw upon the greatest competencies of each teacher. With respect to physical education, the most common example of this is found in the fifth and sixth grades. Providing there are adequate facilities, the boys from both classes are taught by the male teacher and the girls by the female teacher. This is especially desirable for the fall and spring seasons where sex preferences in activities differ and where skill levels in sports such as soccer, volleyball, and softball are decidedly higher in boys.

When there are limited facilities, such as one available gymnasium, and two or more teachers have strong backgrounds in different subject areas, another approach is taken. To illustrate the latter situation, a fourth grade teacher who is extremely well qualified in music may exchange classrooms with a fifth grade teacher who may be equally competent in physical education. This type of exchange allows children to receive optimum instruction in both areas as well as encourages teachers to utilize their greatest talents.

Another type of team teaching consists of two or more teachers pooling their talents for the instruction of several classes in one subject area. Applied to physical education, this would mean dividing two or more classrooms into different groups based upon a criterion other than their grade or classroom identity. The criterion used may be skill performance, physical fitness levels, or a classification index based upon age, height, and weight. The writer visited and studied the program in the Eastern Elementary School located near

---

5. Luvern L. Cunningham, "Team Teaching; Where Do We Stand?" Administrator's Notebook, Vol. 18, No. 8, April 1960, p. 2.

San Juan, California. The school was experimenting with this type team teaching in physical education, using a classification index as a means of grouping children from Grades Three to Six. The merits of this experiment deserve further explanation.

Four teachers in the Eastern School representing Grades Three through Six formed the instructional staff for the team approach to physical education. In their planning sessions, it was found that one teacher was strong in gymnastics, one in the dance, and one in track and field. The fourth teacher, not too strong in any particular area, was hestitant to teach any of the previously mentioned activities. She was assigned games as an area of emphasis. Since the climate permitted outdoor activities virtually every day of the school year and there were sufficient teaching stations in the playground area, one-half hour from two to two-thirty in the afternoon was set aside for physical education for Grades Three through Six. All children within these grades were then assigned to one of four groups based upon a classification index.

A three week instructional schedule for the four classified groups was next established. To illustrate, the gymnastics teacher was assigned Group One in the gymnasium for a three week block of stunts and tumbling activities. The other teachers were assigned one of the remaining groups for a similar period, each emphasizing her own speciality. At the completion of the three week period, each group rotated to a different instructor who in turn taught his own speciality to the new group.

This type of team effort encourages each teacher to develop more complete detailed lesson plans. Throughout the rotation system, better understanding of student performance was obtained coupled with a greater effort on the part of the equated groups. With a limited area of preparation, each teacher found time to experiment with new methods and techniques of learning. Because of the equalizing classification system students also could compete realistically for the same goals and hence found more satisfaction and enjoyment in physical activities.

THE PLAYGROUND, GYMNASIUM, AND CLASSROOM

Another important consideration relating to the scope and success of the physical education program is the adequacy of indoor and outdoor facilities. Without minimum playing space, teaching procedures are ineffective, activity offerings are limited, and optimum growth and development of children are usually restricted. Important considerations relating to placement, size, and safety precautions will be discussed under the "playground," "gymnasium," and "classroom." Further, the suggestions and recommendations listed under each of these facilities should be helpful in establishing important guidelines and operating policies for existing as well as potential physical education facilities.

Playground

The size of the school facility, including gymnasium and outdoor space, is first dependent upon the number of children in the school. National standards recommend a minimum of five acres for any elementary school plus one acre for every one hundred pupils.[6] Hence a school with two hundred children would require seven acres. Beyond this minimum standard the dimensions of a school site will depend upon other pertinent considerations such as climate, economic conditions, and the philosophy of the school and community toward physical education.

FIG. 5.1

The primary consideration, however, of any play area is its safety. School playgrounds situated within an urban area should be surrounded by a fence of heavy wire construction; entrance areas should have double fences rather than gates. If the playground is used by primary and intermediate children, separate areas should be designated for various age groups. With limited space, a fence around the kindergarten-primary area may be indicated. Part of the playground should be set aside for permanent equipment such as jungle gyms, climbing cubes, horizontal ladders, swings and slides. This type of apparatus should be permanently anchored in cement casings. The area immediately under and around each apparatus should be loose dirt, sawdust, or sand. A portion of the playground, preferably the area close to the school, should be blacktop and large enough for activities such as running and tag games. The remaining playground area should be, when water supply permits, grass turf. Other types of surfaces used are oil treated dirt, mixed sand, dirt and sawdust, and asphalt.

6. Athletic Institute, A Guide for Planning Facilities for Health, Physical Education and Recreation, Washington, D.C.: American Association for Health, Physical Education and Recreation, 1965.

FIG. 5.2

Basic recommendations pertinent to the playground are:
1. Remove any physical hazard.
2. Restrict children to specific play areas.
3. Choose play equipment on the basis of proven safety and practical value.
4. Provide adequate room within each area for additional equipment.
5. Establish a list of safety rules and make sure it is followed by every child.
6. Teach children to think in terms of safety for themselves and for their classmates.
7. Make periodical inspections of all equipment.
8. Provide competent supervision within the playground area during regular class, recess, and noon hour periods.

Gymnasium

The location, size, and special features of a gymnasium should be determined by the philosophy and planned activities of the physical education program. All too often, however, this is not the case, with incorrect planning resulting in such undesirable features as inadequate court dimensions, low ceilings, and, in many cases, avoidable hazards or obstructions. To assist in eliminating mistakes in the planning and construction of future elementary school gymnasiums, a guide to planning facilities has been developed by national leaders in the field of health and physical education.[7] Included in this guide are standard recommendations for floor construction, playing space, storage facilities, and numerous other related features of a well-planned gymnasium. Hence, when planning new facilities it is advisable to use this publication as a basic reference for nationally acceptable standards of gymnasium construction.

---

7. Planning Facilities for Health, Physical Education, and Recreation, p. 56.

There are, however, basic recommendations relating to floor dimensions, placement of equipment, and general safety standards that apply to any gymnasium or multipurpose room that is used for physical education. The following suggestions will assist teachers in organizing the indoor physical education facility so that maximum use and optimum safety are obtained.

1. Maintain gymnasium temperature between sixty and sixty-five degrees.
2. Paint on permanent boundary lines for those activities used most often in the program. Use different colored lines for each game activity. For example, use black for basketball, red for volleyball, and green for a large center circle.
3. Provide adequate safety margins for all games. The standard basketball dimensions for elementary school children is seventy-four by forty-two feet. If the existing facility is only seventy by forty feet then the actual court dimensions should be sixty-seven by thirty-seven to provide a minimum three foot safety zone around the outside of the court.
4. Remove all equipment that is not being used during the physical education class.
5. Request that any hazardous fixtures such as floor level heating ducts and lighting fixtures be covered with protective screens.
6. Establish a standard procedure for obtaining and returning equipment to the storage room.

Classroom

There are many elementary schools throughout the country in which the only available indoor space for physical education is in the classroom. Granted this is inadequate; however, with some minor furniture adjustments the classroom can be used for many different physical activities. It is possible to shift movable desks and tables in order to provide one area of the classroom that is free of obstructions. Since most lighting and window fixtures in the classroom are not screened, do not permit activities that will in any way create a potentially hazardous situation. Adjustable and movable bars may be placed in doorways, mats can be used for tumbling activities, and short four-by-four beams and chairs may be used for various balance activities.

BASIC EQUIPMENT AND SUPPLIES[8]

Physical education equipment refers to the more permanent apparatus and materials such as balance beams and outdoor play apparatus. Generally speaking, these materials will last, even with repeated use, from five to twenty years. Supplies, on the other hand, are expendable items such as

---

8. See Appendix A for diagrams of inexpensive equipment. See Appendix B for a list of commercial manufacturers and distributors of equipment and supplies.

balls, whistles, and records. These items will last one to two years and will then need to be replaced. These two types of materials should be distinguished; each teacher must be able to list the proper equipment for her respective grade level and, where budgets are limited, she should be able to suggest how to make various types of homemade equipment.

There are many factors such as the type of physical education program, the geographical area, and the economic conditions, which will determine the type of equipment a school will purchase. The following suggested lists will assist in ordering the proper type and size of gymnasium and outdoor equipment.

Recommended Playground Equipment

Climbing apparatus: (climbing cubes, Swedish gyms, etc.)
Horizontal bar: ("chinning" or "turning bar"), three levels, 48", 54", and 64"; 5' wide for each level
Monkey rings
Horizontal ladder: 6½ ft. high, length optional.
Slide: 8 ft. high with safety platform.
Balance Beam: 8 ft. to 12 ft. long, three levels 18", 24", or 48".
Tether ball standard (see Appendix A), minimum 3.
Basketball standards (minimum of two; height 8 ft.)
Volleyball standards (minimum of two)
Softball backboards (minimum of two)
Soccer goal posts (minimum of two)
Swings (with canvas seats)
Creative play apparatus
Sandbox (6 ft. × 10 ft. with cover)
Track and Field equipment (see Chapter 8)
Long jump pit
High jump pit and standards
Hurdles
Optional and "Home-made" equipment
—Automobile tires suspended on rope or chain bottom of line 12" to 14" off ground
—Moveable barrows and kegs
—Moveable planks (8 ft. to 12 ft. long with planed edges)
—Sawhorses of different heights (see Appendix A)
—Concrete sewer pipes arranged in units of three or four
—Jumping boxes (see Appendix A)
—Obstacle courses—permanent or portable (type and construction should complement the climate and geographical area)

Recommended Indoor Equipment

Tumbling mats: (light synthetic material) minimum number 4; sizes optional, 4 ft. × 6 ft. are easy to handle and store.
Individual Mats: 18" × 36" × ¾", minimum number 40 or one per child. See Chapter 15 for use in program.
Record player: (3 speeds)
Dance drum

Balance beam: 12″ to 4 ft. high, depending upon general use, and approx.
    12 ft. long. (See Appendix A)
Balance benches: reversible for optional use plus hook attachment on one
    end. (See Appendix A)
Horizontal Bar (see Appendix A)
Scooters: 12″ × 12″ with four castors (see Appendix A)
Volleyball net and standards with adjustable heights
Basketball standards: Rim 8 ft. from floor
Climbing ropes: 15 ft. to 20 ft. high, diameter 1½″ to 2″
Vaulting box (see Appendix A)
Set of Jumping Boxes (see Appendix A)
Springboard or Mini-tramp
Sawhorses: minimum of 6 (see Appendix A)
Agility Apparatus; One set; see Chapter 15 for illustrations and recom-
    mended apparatus
Optional Equipment
Trampoline and spotting apparatus
Peg boards
Parallel bars

Recommended Supplies for Gymnasium and Playground

Supplies are materials that are expendable within a reasonably short period of time. In physical education, such items as balls, bats, beanbags, wands, and records are supplies. The number of items listed below is a suggested minimum number based upon a maximum of thirty children who will use these supplies during one physical education period. If two or more classes meet at the same time, multiply the total supply for each item by two or more.

Supplies	Minimum Number
Long skipping ropes[9] ⅝″ sash, nylon or plastic (13′, 14′ and 15′)	2 of each length
Individual skipping ropes, ⅜″ sash, nylon or plastic (10 at 6′; 10 at 7′; 10 at 7½′; 10 at 8′)	1 set or 40 ropes
Utility Balls	6 each size
Soccer balls (rubber cover)	5 to 6
Volleyball (rubber cover)	5 to 6
Softballs	10 to 15
Softball bats	10 to 12
Beanbags (6″ × 6″)	30
Wands[10] (10 at 3′; 10 at 3½′; 10 at 4′; 10 at 4½′)	1 set of 40 wands
Indian clubs or bowling pins	24 to 30
Measuring tape (50 ft.)	1
Ball inflater with gauge	1
Rhythm drums	1
Records (see Chapters 16-18)	

---

9. See Appendix A for method of estimating the length of rope needed, procedure of cutting and taping ends and storage of ropes.
10. See Appendix A for methods of cutting, marking, and storing wands.

Colored arm bands	2 sets of 15
Rubber bands[11] (from old tire inner tubes)	1 set of 50
Whistles	10 to 12
Stop watch	6
Hoops	30
Jacks	60
Softball bases	4 sets
Softball catcher's mask, mit, and body protector	2 each
Softball batting tee	2
Footballs (junior size)	6 to 8
Basketballs (junior size)	6 to 8
Plastic tape (1″, 1½″ and 2″ assorted colors)	2 rolls of each
Clip boards	4
Braids (cloth)	30
Blocks (4″ × 4″ × 1′)	30
Deck tennis rings	10
Paddles (paddle tennis)	24
Dance supplies (castanets, tambourines, bells, etc.)	4 of each

TYPES OF TOURNAMENTS

Within the instructional and extra class program there should be opportunities for children, particularly those in the intermediate grades, to test their abilities in organized competition. Such competition, however, should be well organized and, wherever possible, provide for maximum participation of all children.

There are numerous ways teams or individuals can compete with one another. The type of tournament that is selected will, however, depend upon the activity, available space, time, and number of competitors. An "Olympic Meet" plan is the only feasible type of tournament for track, swimming, and gymnastic activities. Single or double elimination and round robin tournaments may be used for a variety of team and individual sports. Ladder tournaments are very useful for individual activities which can be played during instruction time, noon hour, or after school. Before selecting the type of tournament, careful consideration should be given to the strengths and weaknesses of each in relation to the available time, space, and number of competitors.

Olympic Meet Plan

This type of tournament is used for contests which include a number of separate events such as track and field activities. The winners of each event are awarded points with a total aggregate individual and team champion determined on the basis of accumulated points. To adhere to the principle of mass participation, first to sixth or seventh place winners are awarded an arbitrary number of points. To illustrate, in an all-school track meet, the

---

11. See Appendix A for a method of cutting old inner tubes.

first six places in a fifty yard dash are awarded 10, 9, 8, 7, 6 and 5 points, respectively. To encourage participation, relay and tug-of-war teams may be awarded a higher number of points than individual events. A high aggregate winner can be determined by adding each performer's points won in the individual and team events. Team points are calculated on the same basis as the individual aggregate winners.

Single Elimination

The elimination tournament is the easiest to organize and the quickest way to declare the winner. Its use will, therefore, depend upon a large number of teams, limited facilities, and minimum number of days to complete the tournament. Two examples of a single elimination are shown below.

In the first round of tournament A, the odd played the even numbers with teams 2, 3, 6 and 8 eliminated from competition. In the second round team 4 beat team 1 and team 7 beat team 5. Only teams 4 and 7 remain in the last round with team 4 winning the tournament. The same procedure is followed with the five team single elimination shown in tournament B except that three teams are given a "bye" in the first round.

TOURNAMENT A
(For even number of teams)

Round 1   Round 2   Round 3

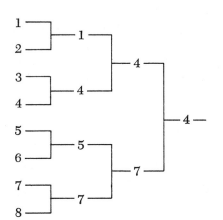

TOURNAMENT B
(For odd number of teams)

Round 1   Round 2   Round 3

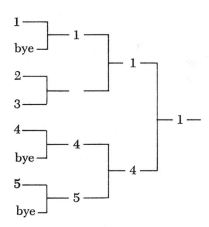

The single elimination tournament does not require any "byes" with even number teams, providing they equal any power of two (2, 3, 8, 16, etc.). All other even number teams must provide the "bye" in the first round. With odd number of teams such as 3, 5, or 7, it is necessary to give one or more teams a "bye" in the first round. The number of "byes" required for such odd number of teams is provided in the chart following.

Number of teams	Number of byes	Number of teams	Number of byes	Number of teams	Number of byes
3	1	11	5	19	13
5	3	13	3	21	11
7	1	15	1	23	9
9	7	17	15	25	7

Round Robin

A round-robin tournament requires each team to play every other team in the league. Hence, if time and facilities permit, this is the most desirable type of competition for team and individual sports. The winner is determined on the basis of the largest number of wins in the tournament. To organize this type of tournament follow the procedure outline following.

1. Determine the number of games to be played by applying the formula $\frac{n\,(n-1)}{2}$ (n equals the number of teams).

   For example, six teams would require $\frac{6\,(6-1)}{2}$ or 15 games to complete the tournament.

2. Give each team a number and arrange in two columns.
   Round No. 1.
   1 plays 6
   2 plays 5
   3 plays 4

3. Keep team number 1 constant and rotate all other teams one place in a counterclockwise direction until fifteen games have been scheduled.

Round No. I	Round No. II	Round No. III	Round No. IV	Round No. V
1 vs 6	1 vs 5	1 vs 4	1 vs 3	1 vs 2
2 vs 5	6 vs 4	5 vs 3	4 vs 2	3 vs 6
3 vs 4	2 vs 3	6 vs 2	5 vs 6	4 vs 5

4. With odd number of teams use "bye" in place of a number and follow the foregoing procedure. The example below is for five teams with each "bye" indicating the team will not play.

1 vs bye	1 vs 5	1 vs 4	1 vs 3	1 vs 2
2 vs 5	bye vs 4	5 vs 3	4 vs 2	3 vs bye
3 vs 4	2 vs 3	bye vs 2	5 vs bye	4 vs 5

Ladder Tournament

A ladder tournament is a continuous type of competition which is limited only by space and time available. Each player or team is placed (arbitrarily, by chance, or by the results of prior competition) on a ladder as shown in the accompanying chart. The object is to climb to the top of the ladder and remain there until the end of the tournament. This type of competition is primarily used in individual activities during instructional, noon hour, or after school. Its limitation is the number of students that can participate. Its main advantage is that students, once orientated to the general rules, can run their own tournaments as time and space permit.

To organize this type of tournament the following procedure is suggested.

1. Construct a ladder chart in which names may be written (grease pencil) or placed. (tagged names or cards)
2. Place all players on the ladder. The simplest procedure is to place all names in a hat and record them on the ladder (from top down) on the basis of a "chance" drawing.

Free Throw Tournament
Bill
Mary
Jim
Susan
Jane
Don
Mike
Jack

3. Establish rules and post near tournament chart. Rules should include:
   a. A player may challenge only the first or second player immediately above his own name.
   b. Winners of each game remain, if originally on higher rung or exchange positions if originally on lower rung.
   c. Once a challenge has been made, set a deadline when the game must be played before it is cancelled (e.g. within two or three days).
   d. Set a completion date for the tournament.
   e. Other rules: This will depend upon the nature of the tournament as well as what the teacher and class would like included. Allow players to add any legitimate rule.

ACCIDENTS AND PREVENTATIVE SAFEGUARDS

In virtually every school situation the teacher acts in loco parentis, that is, in place of the parent. This implies that in any situation, whether it be in the classroom, on the playground, or on a class visitation, the teacher is responsible for the welfare and safety of her pupils. The teacher of physical activities must plan and supervise in such a manner that any accident that may occur is not the result of negligence. Since teachers may be held legally liable for acts of negligence, an understanding of this problem and its implication for the physical education program is extremely important.[12]

Negligence

According to the National Education Association, negligence is any act —or its absence—which falls below the standard established by law for the protection of others against unreasonable risk or harm. Negligence, therefore, may be (1) an act which a reasonable man would have realized involved an unreasonable risk of injury to others, or (2) failure to do an act which is necessary for the protection or assistance of another and which one is under duty to do.[13] According to this definition, teachers may be held liable if they are proved negligent in the following circumstances:

1. If a pupil incurs injuries on the school premises (playground, buildings, or equipment) which are judged to be defective.

This statement implies there is a safety standard for all facilities and equipment. The standard is usually set by the school district and must be maintained. Consequently, for the protection of the childen, any facility or piece of equipment that does not meet this standard (excessive damage to field such as large rocks showing; extensive holes caused by flooding; or broken gymnastic equipment) should be reported and *NOT used* until competent authorities have certified it meets all safety requirements.

2. If a teacher leaves an assigned instructional or supervisory group for any period of time and an injury occurs.

In virtually every teaching situation in the public schools, only a qualified teacher (usually defined as one holding a teacher's credential and under contract with a school district) can asume the responsibility for the instruction and safety of the pupils. Classroom teachers should, therefore, seek clarification with respect to student teachers and various forms of "paraprofessional" assistance (part-time helpers, parents, etc.) with respect to delegated authority. Certainly, there is no question of negligence if a teacher

---

12. Three states, namely California, New York, and Washington, no longer have a state immunity law. This means the school district or its employees may be sued without the consent of the state.

13. National Education Research Division for the National Commission on Safety Education: "Who is Liable for Pupil Injuries?" Washington, D.C.: National Education Association, Oct., 1950, p. 6.

leaves a student in charge while she leaves the instructional area, regardless of the reason or duration of time.
3. If a pupil incurs injury while attempting to perform an exercise or movement which is beyond his ability.

This area of concern is probably the most difficult for a teacher. It is within the self-testing area, particularly with stunts that are potentially hazardous, that a teacher may be vulnerable. If a child has been taught according to a normal progression of skill and is given adequate instruction with respect to form and safety, an accident will probably not occur. When adequate teaching has been provided and safety precautions taken, then if an accident occurs, the teacher is usually not considered liable. The important point is for teachers to follow the recommended programs and provide adequate instruction and safety for all participants. It is important to note that the suggested self-testing program recommended in this book adheres to the principle that each child should progress according to his demonstrated ability, and not according to some arbitrary standard set up for all participants.
4. If a pupil incurs an injury as the direct result of the negligence of another pupil.

The fundamental consideration with respect to this situation is that a teacher should be able to foresee and prevent malicious conduct on the part of any child under her care. This would appear to be axiomatic for all reasonable and prudent teachers. Any teaching situation requires the class to adhere to a standard of conduct which includes the respect and consideration for the safety of every member of the class. The latter is usually stated by the teacher (and better, agreed upon by the pupils) in the form of "rules of conduct" to which every child must adhere. When malicious behavior of one child causes injury to another, the "case" would depend upon an evaluation of the teacher's general ability, the situation, and a thorough investigation of the incident.

Accidents and Preventative Safeguards

An accident is an unforseen event occurring without the will or design of the person whose act caused it; it is an event which occurs without fault, carelessness, or want of proper circumspection for the person affected, or which could not have been avoided under the existing circumstances.[14] An accident, therefore, excludes negligence.

There are general implications relating to accident prevention that are applicable to all grades. If the following basic standards are adhered to, optimum safety will be guaranteed.

---

14. Charles A. Bucher, *Administration of School Health and Physical Education Programs,* 3rd Edition, (St. Louis: C. V. Mosby Co., 1963), p. 146.

1. Maintain playground and gymnasium equipment in proper working order. Immediately repair defective equipment or remove it from the play area.
2. Introduce activities that are appropriate to the skill level of the child. This has two implications: first, follow educationally acceptable textbooks or physical education guides; and second, never require a child to perform a stunt or skill beyond his capabilities.
3. Provide continuous supervision for any scheduled physical education activity. This implies that recess and noon hour activities are adequately supervised according to a desirable pupil-teacher ratio. This ratio should be in the form of a policy written and agreed to by the school board, principal, and teachers.
4. Provide safe instructional play areas. The size of the instructional area should meet the standards established by national, state, or local authorities, and be free of physical hazards and known nuisances. When it is virtually impossible to remove potential hazards, safety rules should be established and adhered to in order to eliminate any potential accident.
5. Provide competent[15] periodic health and physical examinations to determine whether a child should participate in regular or remedial physical education activities. Adequate follow-up procedures for allowing children to return to physical activities after illness, and provision for detected physical deficiencies should be established.
6. Employ only certified personnel for teaching or supervising physical education activities.

Physical education by its very nature is susceptible to accidents. Because activity is vital to the normal growth and development of every child, teachers should not eliminate vigorous activities from their program because of fear of accidents. They should, however, use wisdom and prudence in the selection, instructions, and supervision of the physical education program.

SELECTED REFERENCES

Athletic Institute, Planning Facilities for Health, Physical Education and Recreation, Washington, D.C.: American Association for Health, Physical Education and Recreation, 1965.

BUCHER, CHARLES A. Administration of School Health and Physical Education Programs, 3rd Edition. St. Louis: C. V. Mosby Co., 1963.

"Elementary Schools Make Progress in P.E. Without Service of Qualified Instructor," Physical Education Newsletter, New London, Connecticut: Arthur C. Croft Publications, Letter 12, Vol. 7., Feb. 1963.

GABRIELSEN, M. ALEXANDER and CASWELL, MILES M. Sports and Recreation Facilities for School and Community. Englewood Cliffs, New Jersey: Prentice-Hall, Inc., 1958.

---

15. The interpretation of "competent" should be made by the principal or superintendent. Generally speaking, a competent health and physical examination is one that is given by a licensed medical practitioner.

MILLER, ARTHUR G., and WHITCOMB, VIRGINIA. *Physical Education in the Elementary School Curriculum,* 2nd Edition. Englewood Cliffs, New Jersey: Prentice-Hall, Inc., 1963.

NERBER, JOHN. "Elementary School Physical Education in Chicago Public Schools," *Physical Education Newsletter,* Arthur C. Croft Publications, Letter 19, Vol. 14, June 1960.

Physical Education for Boys and Girls, Curriculum Department, Elementary School Division, Modesto City Schools, Modesto, California.

Physical Education: Grade Two, San Diego City Schools, San Diego, California: President's Council on Youth Fitness, Youth Physical Fitness. Suggested Elements of a School Centered Program, Washington, D.C.: U.S. Government Printing Office.

VANNIER, M. and FOSTER M. *Teaching Physical Education in Elementary Schools,* Fourth Edition. Philadelphia: W. B. Saunders Co., 1968.

SUGGESTED FILMS

Title:	"Lifetime Sports in Education"
Details:	16 mm., sound, color, 17 minutes
Distributor:	N.E.A., Washington, D.C.
Description:	Demonstrates methods and techniques of organizing and teaching for large group instruction
Purchase Price:	$80.00

Selecting Methods and Techniques

Methods of Teaching
Routine Procedures
Techniques of Class Organization
Techniques of Teaching

E VERY teacher, regardless of grade level or subject area, will develop various methods and techniques for taking attendance, grouping children, and planning lessons. Organizing for physical education instruction follows the same pattern as that in other academic subjects; however, certain aspects require a slightly different approach and procedure.

How a classroom teacher utilizes the various methods and techniques in her physical education period will depend upon several prior factors. The first consideration, and sometimes a limiting one, is the qualifications and experience of the teacher. To illustrate, a teacher with an adequate background in physical education and several years' experience will permit a more permissive and informal atmosphere in appropriate situations. On the other hand, the inexperienced teacher may tend to be more strict and formal about routine procedures and general class management. Other factors such as the activity, age of children, available equipment, and size of play area also have a bearing on the type of method and technique a teacher will select.

There are, however, certain procedures in the planning, organizing, and managing a physical education class that must be solved by all teachers. This chapter provides information relating to the types of methods and techniques that are used in contemporary physical education programs.

METHODS OF TEACHING

In a previous chapter, an approach to teaching was defined as a comprehensive way of utilizing both content and method in the teaching of physical education. A "teacher-directed" approach is not simply utilizing the direct method of instruction; it emphasizes the latter but also includes other methods and a unique arrangement and emphasis of content. Similarly, such terms as "Individualized," "Student-Orientated," "Movement Exploration," and "Educational Gymnastics," are approaches because they too involve a unique arrangement of content and a special use of one or more methods and techniques of instruction.

Within each approach, a teacher may select one or more basic methods of teaching which she considers to be the most suitable for the learning task. A method, as distinct from an approach or technique, may be defined as a general way of guiding and controlling learning experiences.[1] There are in turn various ways of classifying methods such as "lecture," "tutorial," or "problem-solving." Each of these, however, may be subdivided into more specific methods. The latter procedure more often leads to confusion rather than to clarification. Recognizing the limitation of any definition the following will provide a basis for understanding and applying one or more "methods" of instruction in the teaching of physical education. The following clas-

---

1. E. C. Davis and E. L. Wallis, *Towards Better Teaching in Physical Education* (Englewood Cliffs: Prentice-Hall, Inc., 1961), p. 249.

sification of methods is based upon the amount of freedom or choice given to the children in the particular learning task.

Direct Method

A direct method is when the choice of the activity and how it is to be performed is entirely that of the teacher's.[2] The teacher structures the physical arrangement of the class, (in lines or circle formation), chooses the type of activity to be performed, (practicing the chest-pass in basketball), and prescribes how and where each child is to practice the movement. Although this is a restrictive method, in that the possibilities for student participation in choosing the activity as well as how it should be practiced are limited, there are situations when this method is extremely useful and educationally defensible. For example, when teaching a specific movement skill, safety procedure or rules of a game, the direct method is the most effective and efficient way of teaching. In cases where the general level of skill is low, such as heading in soccer or headstands in gymnastics, this method is appropriate to use to illustrate, clarify, and practice various aspects of a skill or movement. Also, when the general class discipline is low, the teacher can use this method to regain control and direction both from the teacher's and class' point of view.

FIG. 6.1

Limitation Method

The limitation method is actually a compromise between the direct and indirect methods of instruction.[3] Limitation simply means the choice of the activity or how it is performed is limited in some way by the teacher. Since it possesses the best aspects of direct and indirect teaching it has the greatest

---

2. A. Bilbrough and P. Jones, *Physical Education in the Primary Schools,* London: University of London Press, 1965), p. 30.

3. G. Kirchner; J. Cunningham; and E. Warrell, *Introduction to Movement Education* (Dubuque: Wm. C. Brown Company Publishers, 1970).

application and obvious value in virtually all areas of the physical education program. For example, when teaching Dance, a primary teacher may initially use the direct method to teach a "skip" or "gallop" step. Once the step has been learned she may apply the limitation method by providing a musical accompaniment and allowing the children to move in any direction, create individual or dual patterns with the single limitation of requiring all to move using a skip. When teaching Educational Gymnastics (see Chapter 12) the limitation method is predominately used since it allows for some direction to be given by the teacher while at the same time permits each child to progress according to his level of interest and inherent ability. Numerous examples of this method will be found in the latter sections of this book and particularly within Self-Testing Activities.

FIG. 6.2

A few of the more obvious advantages of this method are:
1. It allows some direction and guidance to be given by the teacher without restricting the free or creative expressions of children.
2. It allows for individual differences in physical and personal interests of each child.
3. It allows the teacher, through a careful choice of activities, to develop all aspects of movement rather than what might become a "one-sided" development if left solely to each child.
4. The analysis and correction of movements by the teacher is simplified because one type of movement is to be practiced.

Indirect Method

The indirect method allows children, individually or collectively, to choose the activity as well as the opportunity to decide how they wish to utilize their time. Obviously, when this method is defined without reference to a particular activity or age level, its meaning and application appear quite ridiculous. To allow six or seven-year-olds the complete freedom of choice in a well-equipped gymnasium room, without prior instruction in skill and safety, is unjust to students and teacher. However, when children have been taught a basic movement "vocabulary," as well as to progress according to their own level of ability, the application of the indirect method has meaning and value. Once children have developed the ability to work independently and have developed respect for the safety and interests of other children, freedom should be given so that children have maximum opportunity to develop leadership, creative movements, and group cooperation without the "direct" assistance of the teacher. On this basis, the indirect method may be used in game, dance, or self-testing activities to develop and foster these skills and personal characteristics.

FIG. 6.3

These methods of instruction should not be considered as separate entities even within the framework of a single lesson. The selection and emphasis of any method should depend upon what and how a particular movement skill or understanding can best be learned by the children. Other factors relating to the teacher's philosophy and ability, facilities and ability grouping of students are also important considerations when selecting any method of instruction. The following factors will assist a teacher in determining which methods should be selected and emphasized in various parts of the physical education program:[4]

4. Davis, et al., *op. cit.*, p. 252.

1. The teacher's skill in using a particular method.
2. The nature of the activity.
3. The backgrounds of the students.
4. The student's growth, development, and maturity levels.
5. The objectives set up for accomplishment.
6. The nature of the local school.
7. The makeup and type of community.
8. Possible department policies.
9. The theory or theories of learning used by the teacher.
10. Previous experience with the students.
11. The type of evaluation to be used.
12. The teacher's personality.
13. The availability of human and other aids.
14. The welfare of the students.
15. The teacher's philosophy of education and physical education.
16. The types of techniques in which the teacher is most expert.

ROUTINE PROCEDURES

The success of any physical education program will depend to a large extent upon the simple routine a class follows in going to, participating in, and returning from a physical education activity. Normally, primary teachers are not confronted with the problems of showering; however, they are concerned with problems relating to changing attire, class excuses, and class control. On the intermediate level where classes may be segregated the problems of costume changing, showering, and individual excuses from physical education must be solved. Basic considerations pertinent to each of these areas will be discussed in the accompanying paragraphs.

Physical Education Apparel

Children in the primary grades usually are not required to wear a special uniform for physical education. The time required to change in relation to the time available for physical education, particularly for five, six and seven-year-olds, does not justify a complete change. However, for games and some dance activities, tennis shoes should be worn. This, of course, applies to all grades. With respect to the self-testing area a suggestion will be made later about the type of clothing and how teachers can "speed-up" the changing time.

The recommended costumes for girls in Grades Three through Six is a one piece suit with a skirt or short-type bottom. Dark shorts and white blouses are also acceptable gymnasium wear. The boy's uniform should be dark shorts and a white T-shirt. In areas where the initial cost of a standard uniform may be an economic burden to parents, allow multicolored shorts and blouses, and strongly recommend to parents that new purchases should meet recommended standards.

The following considerations may assist teachers in the general care and management of gymnasium costumes:

1. All uniforms, including shoes and socks, should have the owner's name clearly marked with a nonerasable ink.
2. All uniforms should be kept clean and free of rips and tears. Establish one day, for example Friday, when uniforms must be taken home and washed.
3. Establish a list of rules and regulations for the locker and shower rooms. Include rules relating to horseplay, running, place of drying, place for street clothes and books, and amount of time to dress and shower.
4. Establish some form of incentive system to encourage children to remember to bring their costumes on the days physical education is taught. Points to squads on a monthly neatness award is far more acceptable than not allowing a child to participate because he forgot his uniform or his mother did not wash it in time for class.

Roll Call

Since the length of physical education periods are usually all too short, little time should be lost in the routine procedure of checking attendance. In most cases, "roll call" for physical education is not necessary in primary grades. Also, when any classroom teacher, regardless of grade, is responsible for her own physical education program, she will know if any child is absent. However, in situations where specialist teachers or team teaching requires a roll call procedure, the following methods may be used:

1. Line formation based upon alphabetical list in roll book.
2. Line formation based upon tallest to shortest child, each child assigned a number.
3. Squads, with one member assigned the responsibility for roll taking.

Class Excuses

The problems relating to excuses for physical education may range from permanent waiver due to a chronic condition to temporary excuses of colds or other illnesses. It is imperative for the principal, the school nurse, and the teacher to establish a list of policies covering the various problems encountered in this area. The following situations should be included in the list of policies:

1. Temporary excuse from physical education should be authorized by the school nurse.
2. Children returning to physical activity after any illness should be authorized by the school nurse.
3. Children with physical handicaps should be encouraged to participate in physical education classes. The amount and type of participation should be indicated by the parents and/or family physician.

4. On recommendation by the teacher, a child may be excused from participation in a physical education class because of a detectable illness or injury.

TECHNIQUES OF CLASS ORGANIZATION

Classroom teachers often attempt to apply the same techniques and standards of a classroom situation to the gymnasium or playground. In other words, children are required to be reasonably quiet, orderly, and generally speaking, emotionally calm in both situations. Participation in physical activities obviously should be well supervised; it should be structured to foster enjoyment which may be expressed in terms of vocal encouragement of the team's effort, and maximum body movement. When the activities are challenging and satisfying to each student, there is little chance of boredom or "attention-getters" from the children.

FIG. 6.4

There are several aspects of class organization where effective techniques and procedures should be developed to assist the teacher and class in utilizing every minute of the period. Several of the more important areas are discussed under the following paragraphs.

Effective Use of Teaching Formations

Basic formations which teachers can use in organizing physical education activities are line, circle, or shuttle patterns. These patterns are used to divide a class into smaller groups for relays, team games, or drill exercises. Once learned by the student, they can be formed quickly and in an orderly manner at a simple command of the teacher and will save valuable practice and play time, eliminate class confusion, and minimize potential accidents.

In many cases the selection of a particular formation is governed by the activity itself. For example, running and tag games require a specific formation and many folk dances begin with a circle or line position. Other activities such as warm-up exercises, apparatus, and low organization games may be performed from a variety of different formations. Two principles, however, apply to all formations. First, each squad should be aligned in such a position that all members may view the performer. Second, the activities of one squad should not interfere with those of another. These principles should be remembered when selecting the following formations:

Formation	Explanation	Uses

Circle
 	
    X
  X   X
X   X
X   X
  X   X
    X
	Children may form a circle by following the teacher as she walks around in a circle. Other methods include all join hands and form a circle, or have the class take a position on a circle printed on the floor or play area.	—simple games
		—warm-up exercises
		—circle relays
		—teaching simple stunts
		—teaching basic dance steps
		—teaching throwing and kicking skills
		—marching
		—mimetics

Line X X Teacher X or X Leader X	Place one child for each line desired equal distance apart, then signal the class to line up behind these children. The first child in each line may move out in front of his line or shift to the side as illustrated.	—relays —simple games —marching —teaching stunts on floor or mats —roll taking —teaching basic skills

Fan
    X
   X
X
X   X
   Teacher
X or
  X Leader
    X
	The fan formation is used for small group activities. First, arrange children in a line facing their leader, then join hands and form a half circle.	—throwing and kicking drills
		—relays
		—mimetics
		—simple floor stunts
		—teaching dance skills

Formations	Explanation	Uses
Shuttle 6 X 4 X 2 X 1 X 3 X 5 X	Arrange children in two, three, or more equal lines, then separate lines the desired distance required for the activity. Number one performs his skill then shifts to the rear of the opposite line; number two performs and shifts to the rear of the opposite line, etc.	—throwing and kicking drills —relays —tumbling activities from opposite ends of mat —activities requiring close observation by teacher
Zigzag 1X X2 3X X4 5X X6	Arrange class or squads into two equal lines with partners facing each other. Player 1 passes to 2; 2 passes to 3; 3 passes to 4; until the last player is reached.	—throwing, catching, and kicking skills

Scattered
   X
X   X
   X
X   X
   X
X   X
   X
   X
	Allow children to find a spot in the play area. Have each child reach out with arms to see if he can touch another person. Require the children who can touch others to shift until they are free of obstructions.	—warm-up exercises
		—mimetics
		—tag games
		—simple floor stunts
		—creative activities

Effective Grouping Procedures

Grouping children in physical education classes is arranging them in squads according to age, height, or ability levels. The type of grouping technique a teacher selects will depend upon the activity and the various levels of performance of her class. To illustrate, a third grade teacher wishes to organize her class into four teams for a relay. She could arrange them according to teams of two boys and two girls, by numbering children from one to four or by allowing four team captains to choose their own teams. Since the latter is a common method for organizing into equal teams as well as fostering leadership and team loyalty, it will be explained in detail.

The teacher or the class first selects four captains. In order to preclude favoritism, sex preferences, and emotional-social problems in the last one selected, have the captains meet with the teacher away from the class where the actual selection of teams is made. This prevents members of the class from knowing the order each was chosen. In the chart following, squad leader A is awarded first choice; B, second; C, third; and D, fourth. At this point indicate to each squad leader that if his first choice is a boy, the next choice must be a girl, alternating a boy then a girl, until the last member is chosen. In the chart, let us assume Captain D selected a boy in round number one, Captain D also has the next selection which must be a girl. Continue this procedure until the last player is chosen.

Round No.	SQUAD LEADERS			
	A	B	C	D
1	1st	2nd	3rd	4th
2	8th	7th	6th	5th
3	9th	10th	11th	12th
4	16th	15th	14th	13th
5	17th	etc.		

Other methods of organizing children into squads should be used throughout the year to provide opportunities for each child to work with different groups in both a leadership and followership capacity. The choice of the following methods of grouping will depend upon the activity, space, and age of children.
1. Skill tests or observation of skill ability.
2. Numbering off in twos, fives, or whatever number of teams desired.
3. Arrange the class in a circle, then divide it into the desired number or squads.
4. Select teams on the basis of their birth dates. For example:
   Team 1: Children born between January and March.
   Team 2: Children born between April and June.
   Team 3: Children born between July and September.
   Team 4: Children born between October and December.
5. Administer a classification test such as McCloy's Index, which places the heavier and older children in the top group and the lighter and younger children in the lower group. The formula, 10 times age plus weight, may be used for ages fifteen and below.[5]

---

5. Charles H. McCloy, *The Measurement of Athletic Power* (New York: A. S. Barnes & Co., Inc., 1932), p. 95.

Effective Use of Squads

Once children can effectively move into squads (or "teams," "groups," "section places," or "units"), its use to the teacher and children can be highly profitable. From the point of view of the teacher, children can be organized in a short period of time and according to a particular criterion either selected by the teacher or jointly with the class. Regardless of the reason for organizing squads, the duties of each elected or assigned leader should include the following:

1. Maintaining order and general control of one's squad.
2. Checking routine procedures such as attendance, uniforms, and tardiness.
3. Assisting the teacher in daily planning and lesson organizing.
4. Setting an example of leadership.

The inherent value of squads from a purely organizational point of view cannot be overemphasized. Our purpose as teachers, however, should be to provide maximum opportunity for every child to experience a leadership role. We recognize that some students seem to develop this ability in the early primary grades, others need encouragement and subtly planned experiences as leaders. Consequently, squad leaders should be considered temporary appointments so that each child is given an opportunity to test his ability as the "squad captain." There will always be moments of frustration when young children are given leadership roles. Teachers as well as children must develop tolerance, understanding, and patience in this enterprise. The value of the latter to the individual and to the group is immense and worth the time and effort.

TECHNIQUES OF TEACHING

Previously, a "method" was defined as a general way of guiding and controlling the learning experiences of children. Three methods were described to illustrate how teachers could select one or more when teaching physical education. A "technique" may be defined in two ways. In a restricted sense, it may be described as a small part of a method. For example, a demonstration of a throwing or kicking skill by the teacher is clearly part of the direct teaching method. A carefully worded question or a unique movement challenge is one technique used within the limitation method. There are other types of techniques, such as variations in voice inflections, ways of using equipment and apparatus, and unique applications of audiovisual materials. The latter do not belong to any particular method but are used in varying ways and degrees by each teacher. It is the manner and emphasis each teacher gives to various techniques that produce her "style" of teaching. Hence, there is no set number of techniques that one must master to be an effective teacher. Each teacher will take years to develop her "style of teaching" and will retain or discard each technique on the basis of its efficiency in the learning process.

Teaching Motor Skills

There are many ways to teach motor skills, each with advantages and disadvantages to the teacher or to the child. The technique that is best usually is the one that works. To learn any skill, however, a child must have the inherent ability, a clear understanding of the movements involved, a reason for learning it, and an opportunity to repeat the skill until it is learned. Generally speaking, a skill is learned through a process of explaining, demonstrating, discovering, and perfecting. This is in no way a simple progression from a demonstration of a skill to practice and analysis. Each child will acquire a skill in his own unique way. To assist children in learning "standardized" skills, which are those which are performed in much the same way by all children, we usually follow a pattern of explaining and demonstrating, then allow time for individual practice and analysis. There are several important factors relating to how each of these techniques should be used. The accompanying list will provide several basic suggestions to assist each teacher in developing her own effective techniques.

FIG. 6.5

1. Arrange the class in a teaching formation that permits every student to have a clear view of your demonstration. Also, eliminate unnecessary interference such as equipment, poor lighting, and excessive noise.
2. Explain the skill in a clear and concise manner. Allow time for the class to digest each important part of the skill.
3. Pause repeatedly throughout the explanation and check to see if the class understands; where necessary, repeat a particular part of the demonstration.
4. Speak in a vocabulary that is appropriate to the group.

5. Provide an accurate demonstration of the skill. If the teacher is unable to demonstrate, do not hesitate to use a pupil or visual aids.
6. Provide a demonstration that is clearly visible to all students and execute the skill in a slower speed than normally performed.
7. Repeat the demonstration several times, including key explanation of one or more parts of the skill.
8. Keep demonstration short and to the point.
9. Be patient and sympathetic; children acquire skills according to their own degree of readiness and inherent capacity.
10. If a child is not learning a skill in its entirety, break it down into simpler parts.
11. Give encouragement and praise rather than scorn and punishment, regardless of how small or large the task.

Planning and Presenting Lessons

A lesson plan should be a flexible guideline and not a rigid and unalterable plan of presenting facts, skills, and ideas to children. There are simply too many variables such as time allotment, maturity levels, type of method, and available equipment and facilities which necessitate a variety of lesson plans.

Each part of the physical education program such as teaching games or self-testing activities will require a different approach to teaching and in the format of a lesson. When teaching game activities a rather standard format is suggested particularly for older children. The education justification for the latter is that children can effectively and efficiently learn skills required in individual and team sports primarily through a teacher-directed approach. Lessons are prepared to introduce the skills and rules of a game in a progressive and sequential order, beginning from the simple and finishing with the complex skills and team strategies. The following is an example of this type of lesson plan.

EXAMPLE LESSON PLAN
Grade 3—Two-hand Chest Pass
1. Routine procedures (5-6 minutes)
   Changing into tennis shoes and roll call.

2. Warm-up (5-6 minutes)
   Arrange class in circle formation. Begin with everyone running in place, then hopping on right and left foot. After a few minutes of total body movement, lead the class through a series of vigorous exercises involving the head and neck, arm and shoulder girdle, trunk and legs. (Appropriate exercises for each grade are described in Parts III, IV, and V.)

3. Explanation—Demonstration (3-4 minutes)
   Keep children in the circle formation for the initial explanation and demonstration of the two-hand pass. Stand on the edge of the circle and without a ball demonstrate the throw. Move to the center of the

circle with a ball then pass the ball around circle, requiring each child in turn to pass ball back to you, using the two-hand chest pass.

4. Practice—Analysis (4-5 minutes)
   Arrange children in small circles of six to eight children. Place one child in the center of each circle. The center player, using a two-hand chest pass, throws the ball to each circle player. Player in the circle catches the ball and returns it to center player with same pass. As children are practicing, move from one circle to another to evaluate and correct skills.

5. Activity (10-12 minutes)
   Select a lead-up game that involves the two-hand chest pass. Since the children are in small circles, "Call Ball" could be selected as an example lead-up game. The game is played by having the center player throw the ball into the air, and at the same time call a circle player's name. The circle player must catch the ball before it touches the floor, or one bounce may be allowed. If the circle player catches the ball he becomes the center player. Require the throw to be a high two-hand chest pass, thus continually emphasizing the skill.

6. Routine procedures (2-3 minutes)
   Collect balls and return to storage bin.
   Follow routine procedure for returning to classroom.

There are numerous examples of this type of lesson construction in Part III. It must be emphasized, however, that all suggested lesson plans are included to illustrate a basic way of planning a lesson. Each teacher, in turn, will develop her own type of lesson format and presentation to cope with the ability, interest, and previous background of her class. Other factors, such as the length of instructional period and available facilities, will drastically affect the general format of any lesson.

In Part IV an Educational Gymnastic (Movement Education) approach to teaching Self-Testing activities is suggested for all grades in the elementary school. In this type of program there is a different format for learning movement skills which, in turn, necessitate a unique structure of a lesson plan. Since children are encouraged to develop their own movement patterns, without any reference to standardized skills as in formal gymnastics, rigid lesson plans are clearly out of place. Furthermore, in this approach, each child progresses according to his own ability and interest. As a consequence the type of lesson plan used in this approach is characterized by general flexibility. Since this is a relatively new approach to teaching self-testing activities, numerous lesson plans and suggestions are provided throughout Part IV.

SELECTED REFERENCES

BILBROUGH, A. and JONES P. *Physical Education in the Primary Schools*, London: University of London Press, 1965.

DAVIS, E. C. and WALLIS, E. L. *Towards Better Teaching in Physical Education*, Englewood Cliffs: Prentice-Hall Inc., 1961.

HALSEY, E., and PORTER, L. *Physical Education for Children,* Revised Edition, New York: Holt, Rinehart & Winston, Inc., 1967.

KIRCHNER, G.; CUNNINGHAM, J.; and WARRELL, E. *Introduction to Movement Education,* Dubuque: Wm. C. Brown Company Publishers, 1970.

KOZMAN, H. C.; CASSIDY, R.; and JACKSON, C. O. *Methods in Physical Education,* Fourth Edition, Dubuque: Wm. C. Brown Company Publishers, 1967.

McCLOY, C. H. *The Measurement of Athletic Power,* New York: A. S. Barnes & Co., Inc., 1932.

SHURR, E. L. *Movement Experiences for Children: Curriculum and Methods for Elementary School Physical Education,* New York: Appleton-Century-Crofts, 1967.

VANNIER, M. and FOSTER, M. *Teaching Physical Education in Elementary Schools,* Fourth Edition, Philadelphia: W. B. Saunders Co., 1968.

SUGGESTED FILMS

Title:	"Profiles of Elementary Physical Education." 3 reels, 16 mm., color and black and white, 32 minutes
Distributor:	Coronet Films
Description:	Stresses successful methods of teaching physical education to elementary school children
Purchase Price:	$360.00

Evaluating Program
and Student Progress

E VALUATION is essential to all phases of the physical education program. When a teacher assesses the effectiveness of the program of activities or the methods and techniques, she is able to detect various strengths and weaknesses and make appropriate changes. Test results can also be sent to the parents and other interested members of the community. This type of communication assists others to understand the scope of the program and, in addition, directly helps to support or supplement the program with needed facilities and equipment.

Teachers must first consider the very practical uses of testing within such areas as physical fitness, skill development, knowledge, and social adjustment. Perhaps the widest use of testing is for grading purposes; it is not, however, the most important. The more salient value of testing is to determine an individual's current level of performance in order to establish realistic goals for him. Furthermore, when testing is used continuously throughout the school year, additional changes can be made to meet the revealed needs and potentials of every child. Numerous other practical values for a testing program could be mentioned. However, it would be remiss not to stress the importance of testing as a motivational device. When a child can see his own test results and realize his possibilities for improvement, greater personal effort and satisfaction usually result. This is well illustrated when children are given a ball handling skill test such as throwing for distance. Once a child can see how far he can throw he will usually set a higher goal and continue to practice so long as there is improvement. The important point to keep in mind when measuring a pupil's performance is to judge the child's score in relationship to his *own* performance, not in relationship to the norms of the whole class. The latter are useful as guidelines; they are not established goals for all children to reach.

EVALUATING STUDENT PROGRESS

The subjective and objective measuring devices that are used to evaluate student progress in physical education must be based upon their ability to accurately measure the extent to which the objectives of the program are being realized. As previously stated, the objectives of the program relate to health and physical development, motor skills, knowledge, and social adjustment. All of the factors pertinent to each of these objectives can, to some degree, be measured by subjective judgment or by use of objective tests. Most teachers rely heavily upon subjective ratings of student progress in such areas as skill and social development. However, within all grade levels, there are various aspects of the child's performance that can be measured by objective tests. Hence, all teachers should be cognizant of both subjective and objective measuring devices available under each of the following areas.

Health and Physical Development

A general and continuous concern for the health and physical development of each child is the responsibility of school health officials as well as teachers. Physical education provides a special avenue to observe, detect, and refer possible anomalies to more competent authorities. A teacher who has an understanding of posture, nutrition, and physical fitness can in certain situations correct or prevent remedial problems. It is also the responsibility of each teacher to be able to detect early signs of illness and to refer these problems to the school nurse or physician.

In most school districts, a physical examination is usually required on an annual basis or other scheduled times throughout the elementary school program. The results of this examination should be made known to the classroom teacher, particularly for children who may require special limitations (rheumatic fever, birth anomalies, etc.) in the physical education program. There are other evaluations which a teacher can make which will help her understand and plan for the various growth and development needs of each child. Several of the more important evaluative techniques are described in the accompanying paragraphs.

AGE, HEIGHT, AND WEIGHT

A periodic record of age, height, and weight can be of tremendous help in assessing the normal growth of each child. It should be recognized, however, that available height-weight tables are based upon age and therefore do not take into consideration such factors as physiological maturity, bone density, and other important physiological traits. Hence, the height-weight tables should be used as a general guideline. The important factor in height-weight assessments is the ability to detect radical changes in height or weight periodically throughout the year. Hence, it is wise to take such measurements at least two and preferably three times a year.

PHYSICAL FITNESS

Since the publication of the Kraus-Hirshland report which showed American youth to be extremely below par in minimum muscular fitness, greater emphasis has been devoted in physical education to raising the level of physical fitness of elementary school children.[1] As a follow-up to this problem numerous tests have been developed to measure the basic components of physical fitness. Although there is a diversity of opinion with respect to which basic components of physical fitness should be measured, the majority of the published test batteries include strength, endurance, flexibility, agility, power, and speed. The child who registers a high score in the test items is

---

1. Hans Kraus and Ruth P. Hirshland, "Muscular Fitness and Health," *Journal for the American Association for Health, Physical Education and Recreation*, Vol. 24. Dec., 1953, p. 17.

considered to be physically fit. Conversely, a low score indicates the child does not possess the strength and vitality to carry out his everyday experiences or unexpected emergencies. A low score on any physical fitness test may reveal not only a lack of exercise but also possible nutritional, congenital, and other temporary illnesses that may be the cause of low fitness.

Various states throughout this country have already adopted standardized physical fitness tests. Some of the more widely used test batteries currently being used are mentioned below with the appropriate age or grade level that can be tested.

Name of Test	Appropriate Age or Grade Level	Source
President's Council's Youth Physical Fitness Screening Test	Age 10-17	U.S. Government Printing Office, Washington, D.C.
AAHPER Youth Fitness Test	Age 10-17	AAHPER, 1201 16th Street, Washington, D.C.
Kraas-Weber Test of Minimum Muscular Fitness	Age 6-13	Journal of AAHPER. Vol. 24. Dec. 1953, p. 17
New York State Physical Fitness Test	Grade 4-12	New York State, Department of Education, Albany, N.Y.
Oregon Motor Fitness Test	Grades 4-6	Oregon State Department of Education, Salem, Oregon
Elementary School Physical Fitness Test	Age 2-12	See Chapter 19

The Elementary School Physical Fitness Test mentioned above was designed by the writer to be used by self-contained classroom teachers.[2] There are five test items which measure strength, endurance, power, and speed. The test battery is valid, reliable, inexpensive, and easy to administer. There are separate norms for boys and girls, ages six through twelve years, which are based upon thirty thousand cases representing urban and rural school children in six states. To assist classroom teachers in initiating a physical fitness testing and follow-up program, a complete description of the test items, as well as additional follow-up material, will be found in Chapter 19.

POSTURE

Parents, teachers, and school health officials have always been concerned about a child's posture. The adoption of slanting desks, variable blackboards,

---

2. The Elementary School Physical Fitness Test has been adopted by the State of Washington as well as many other districts, such as Houston, Texas; Holyoke, Massachusetts; and Glenview, Illinois.

and improved lighting are all directly related to enhancing and maintaining correct posture. Since there is a strong relationship between posture and such factors as perceptual acquity, emotional health, and general physical fitness, teachers are becoming increasingly aware of correct sitting, standing, and dynamic posture of each child. The problem of chronic television viewing coupled with inadequate exercise for many children has produced numerous postural problems that are readily detectable and correctable by vigorous exercise.

An experienced teacher will normally detect chronic postural problems in the classroom. There are, however, simple screening postural tests that can assist in this evaluation. Teachers should analyze these tests in consultation with competent school health officials to select the most suitable one for use in their particular program. Chronic problems should be referred to the school nurse or parent for immediate follow-up.

The following screening tests can be used in the elementary school program with the minimum expenditure of time and financial investment.

Name of Test	Appropriate Age or Grade Level	Source
New York State Physical Fitness Test (contains a standardized posture test item)	4-12	New York State Education Department, Albany, New York
Postural Evaluation Charts —Static and Movement patterns	Age 6-13	Anderson, Elliot and La-Berge, Play with a Purpose, Chapter 7

Skill Development

There are two basic types of motor skills that should be measured to indicate student progress or achievement. The first is classified as fundamental or basic skills which include the locomotor skills of walking, running, and skipping, as well as the non-locomotor skills such as dodging, pushing, and pulling.[3] The second types are specific sport, dance, and self-testing skills. An example of how each type of skill can be measured is illustrated following.

FUNDAMENTAL SKILLS

In the accompanying table, each of the fundamental skills used in dance activities is listed under the first column. A subjective rating of "good, fair, and poor" could be made at the beginning of the school year to assess the level of performance a child has for each of these skills. Under "correction indicated," various comments can be made to assist the teacher in planning

---

3. See Chapter 16 for a description of the locomotor and non-locomotor skills.

for activities that will correct individual weaknesses. This type of evaluation sheet can also be developed for specific sports skills and self-testing activities. They are especially useful in explaining to parents the child's level of performance and in pointing out certain corrective measures that can be done at home.

TABLE I

Subjective Rating for Fundamental Skills

Name: Jim Adams Date: September, 1969	Performance in Fundamental Skills			
	Rating			Correction
Name of Skill	Good	Fair	Poor	Indicated
Walking			X	Toes inward
Running			X	Toes inward
Skipping	X			
Leaping	X			
Jumping		X		
Sliding		X		
Galloping			X	Changes lead foot
Hopping	X			
Swing and swaying		X		
Rising and falling		X		
Pushing and pulling		X		
Bending and stretching		X		
Striking and dodging		X		

MOTOR SKILLS

An objective skill test should be designed so that it measures one or more skills that are used within a specific area of physical activity. The example shown following is a skill test for throwing and catching skills. Each of the five test items is designed to measure skill performance in throwing and catching. The first four test items are concerned with accuracy while the latter is a measure of distance.

Test No. 1: Underhand catch: The teacher stands twenty feet away from each child and throws him ten balls. The ball must be caught with an underhand catch. One point is awarded for each successful catch.

Test No. 2: Overhand Catch: Repeat Test No. 1 only require an overhand catch.

Test No. 3: One-hand Underhand Throw: Each child stands fifteen feet away from a wastepaper basket and attempts to throw ten softballs into the basket. The underhand throw must be used. One point is awarded for each successful throw.

Test No. 4: Two-hand Chest Throw: Repeat Test No. 3 only require a two-hand chest throw.

Test No. 5: Throw for Distance: Each child is given three throws with a softball. The total score is divided by three and recorded in the appropriate column of the chart below.

			TABLE 2				
			Objective Skill Test				
	Throwing and Catching Skills					Total Grade	
Name of Student	Test No. 1 Under-hand Catch	Test No. 2 Over-hand Catch	Test No. 3 One hand Over-hand Catch	Test No. 4 Chest Throw	Test No. 5 Throw for Dis-tance	Score	Grade
1. John Smith	7	5	6	5	38′	61	B
2. Mary Able	6	4	5	5	26′	46	C
3.							
4.							

There are several examples of "teacher-made" skill tests in Part III. The following tests are described on the pages indicated. Teachers should use these sample test batteries as a basic guideline and develop their own tests. Other examples may be found in list of suggested readings.

When developing a teacher-made skill test, it should be devised so that it is possible to add individual scores into one composite score. This provides a means of ranking children as well as indicating where additional emphasis should be placed in the selection of practice activities and lead-up games.

KNOWLEDGE

One of the objectives of the physical education is to acquire knowledge and understanding of physical activities and their contribution to physical and mental health. When children know the names of team positions, rules, and the strategy of a game, there is less chance of misunderstandings and fighting. Furthermore, a knowledge of the rules of a team sport, the verses in a singing game, or the parts to a complex gymnastic skill will enhance motor learning.

In the primary grades, verbal questions are used to teach simple rules, verses in singing games, and to stimulate creative thought through interpretive movements. Written tests may be used in the upper grades in all phases of the physical education program. The choice of true or false, multiple choice, or short answer tests will depend upon the teacher and the capabilities of her students. Regardless of the type of test chosen, care should be taken to pose questions that are clear and appropriate to the physical activity.

Social Development

The qualities or traits represented in the term "social adjustment" do not readily lend themselves to either subjective or objective measurement. For example, "the ability to get along with others," "team loyalty," and "sportsmanship" are not accurately measurable by a rating scale, anecdotal record, or even an expert's judgment. Nevertheless, they are extremely important qualities that we profess to develop within the scope of the physical education program. Consequently, there should be some attempt, however meager, to evaluate the development of the various traits and qualities represented in this general area. Some of the more practical techniques and tests are described below.

TEACHER OBSERVATION

Probably the most commonly used technique to assess individual growth in this area is the daily observations a teacher makes while a child is playing in a structure situation or during free play activities. Through observation, behavioral problems such as cheating and poor sportsmanship may be noted by the teacher. The manner in which the teacher copes with the various adjustment problems may vary from a change in the method of instruction to a complete change in the activities.

INTERVIEW

A personal interview between the teacher and the child or parent is another technique that is used to gain a better understanding of the general behavior of a child. Usually, specific adjustment problems are discussed with the child or where appropriate with the parent, to determine the reasons

FIG. 7.1

behind certain behavioral problems. Care should be taken, however, not to lecture but to develop confidence and a feeling of genuine concern for the child. When a child has respect and trust in the teacher there is a good chance that he, in turn, will be able to come to understand his problem and make appropriate changes.

SOCIOGRAM

The sociogram is a technique used to study the relationships within a group. By posing key questions such as "With whom would you like to practice catching skills during recess?" or "Who would you like to have on your team?" it is possible to identify children who appear to be well adjusted within the group as well as the isolates and rejected individuals. To obtain the best results from this technique it is wise to keep the following procedures in mind when asking students various questions:[4]

1. Be sure the situation is real for which students are asked to make choices.
2. Make use of the choices to group students according to their preferences.
3. Have confidence that the atmosphere is informal and friendly.
4. Let the students understand that their answers will be confidential.
5. Give no cues to the students about how to choose.

---

4. Hilda C. Kozman; Rosalind Cassidy; and Chester O. Jackson, *Methods in Physical Education*, 4th edition, (Dubuque: Wm. C. Brown Company Publishers, 1967).

The results of the sociogram can be very helpful in identifying children who need assistance. By drawing circles on a sheet to represent each child, then drawing lines to each child as the question dictates, it becomes quite clear who are the popular and rejected children in a particular social group. By a simple regrouping of children, the shy and retiring child can be brought into a more favorable group without making the reasons for such a change obvious to the children concerned. Furthermore, undesirable group situations may also indicate possible variations in methods of class organization, selection of team captains, and changes in the type of group activities.

GRADING AND REPORTING PUPIL PROGRESS

The purpose of grading in physical education is identical to that in all other subjects in the curriculum—to report the progress a child has made. Although the majority of elementary school report cards require only an "S" or "U" or "P" or "F," additional information relating to skill performance, physical fitness, and social adjustment should be available in the form of a cumulative record. When the answer to the parent's question "How is my child doing in physical education?" is something like "He is well adjusted in his group" or "He is doing fairly well in physical skills," very little insight has been gained and probably an unfavorable impression of the program has been created.

To overcome the weakness of the "P" or "F" grading and reporting system, many schools are now requiring a cumulative record in physical education (see Chapter 19). This is particularly true in districts where children are given a physical fitness test in the fall and spring. After the latter test has been given, the physical fitness scores are reported to parents or passed on to the next grade to assist the new teacher in setting reasonable limits for each child to teach. Within the cumulative record of each child, additional information relating to skill performance in rhythmic, games, and self-testing activities should be recorded. The child's grade should then be based on his own improvement rather than how he ranks with others in his class.

EVALUATING PROGRAM PROGRESS

The physical education program in its broadest meaning includes all the organized experiences, facilities, and teachers involved in teaching and supervisory roles. Evaluative techniques to measure all these factors are simply not available. If they were available, the time element alone would prohibit extensive assessments in any one of these areas. There are, however, various periodical evaluations teachers should make about the effectiveness of the content and methods used, as well as to allocation and use of time and space for physical education. A few of the more important areas will be discussed in the accompanying paragraphs.

Teaching Staff

Every teacher should make a self-appraisal of her teaching in order to determine what steps should be taken to improve her effectiveness in the classroom and gymnasium. Since the physical education program is undergoing extensive changes, both in content and methods of instruction, teachers should assess whether they are as "up-to-date" in this area as they are with current changes in other subjects of the elementary school curriculum. Some consideration should be given to each of the following areas:

1. New developments in Educational Gymnastics (Movement Elucation) and Movement Exploration.
2. New textbooks in the general field of physical education as well as specialized texts in games, dance, and self-testing activities.
3. New developments in audiovisual materials for physical education (films, film-strips, and video-tapes).
4. New developments in equipment and apparatus, particularly the new agility apparatus.
5. Related research in perceptual-motor development and physical education.
6. New program developments, particularly the programs supported by federal and state funds.

Information and general assistance in the above areas can be secured from state and local district supervisors of physical education. In addition, numerous national organizations, such as AAHPER, Office of Education, and the Athletic Institute will provide information concerning the above developments upon request.

Facilities and Equipment

In the majority of school districts there are established policies relating to the allocation of funds for physical education. Normally, each school receives an annual equipment and supplies grant based upon the number of children in the school. Teachers should refer to the suggested list of equipment and supplies in Chapter 5 and use this as a basic guideline for her own program. It is extremely valuable for each school district to establish their own "recommended list" in order to provide teachers with a reasonable idea of the quantity and quality of equipment she can expect to receive for use in her program.

Although the above policy and recommended list of equipment and supplies will be of some help in evaluating each teaching situation, there are other questions that every teacher should ask herself. These are:

1. Are the facilities and equipment maintained in safe working order?
2. Is there equipment in the gymnasium or outdoor playing area that is not recommended for use in the elementary school program. Serious consideration should be given to such apparatus as "merry-go-round," swings with steel or wooden seats, and certain gymnastic equipment such as the

trampoline and mini-tramp. The latter two pieces of equipment are desirable for upper elementary provided there are competent teachers to teach the skills on this type of equipment.
3. What kinds of improvized equipment and supplies can be secured with limited funds? In this respect Appendix A will provide information about "how to" construct inexpensive equipment.

Program

Evaluation should be considered an on-going process of assessing whether one's goals are being achieved. Much that has been said in the previous sections applies to the program in general. Adequate program evaluation primarily involves the day-to-day assessment of each lesson in order to make modifications and changes in activities and methods of instruction. Contemporary programs also include student participation in evaluating the program. Although the latter cannot see the value and reason for all activities, they can provide valuable assistance with respect to their needs and unique interests. Provision should be made for children to actively participate in program evaluation. When children are respected for their contributions, they will in turn provide the effort and enthusiasm to make the program a success.

SELECTED REFERENCES

ANDERSON, M. H.; ELLIOT, M. E.; and LaBERGE, J. J. *Play with a Purpose,* New York: Harper & Row, Publishers, 1966.
ARNOLD, P. J. *Education Physical Education and Personality Development,* London: Heinemann Educational Books Ltd., 1968.
BUCHER, CHARLES A.; KOENING, CONSTANCE; and BARNHARD, MILTON. *Methods and Materials for Secondary School Physical Education,* St. Louis: C. V. Mosby Co., 1961.
CLARKE, H. H. *Application of Measurement to Health and Physical Education,* 4th Edition, Englewood Cliffs, New Jersey: Prentice-Hall, Inc., 1967.
KAZMAN, HILDA; CASSIDY, ROSALIND; and JACKSON, CHESTER O. *Methods in Physical Education,* 4th Edition, Dubuque: Wm. C. Brown Company Publishers, 1967.
KRAUS, HANS, and HIRSHLAND, RUTH P. "Muscular Fitness and Health," *Journal for the American Association for Health, Physical Education and Recreation,* Vol. 24, December, 1953.
LIEN, A. J. *Measurement and Evaluation of Learning,* Dubuque: Wm. C. Brown Company Publishers, 1967.
MILLER, ARTHUR G. and WHITCOMB, VIRGINIA. *Physical Education in the Elementary School Curriculum,* Englewood Cliffs: Prentice-Hall, Inc., 1963.
PEARSON, C. ERIC. *A Classroom Teacher's Guide to Physical Education,* New York: Bureau of Publications, Teachers College, Columbia University, 1958.
VANNIER, MARYHELEN, and FOSTER, MILDRED. *Teaching Physical Education in Elementary Schools,* 4th Edition, Philadelphia: W. B. Saunders Co., 1968.
WILLGOOSE, C. E. *Evaluation of Health Education and Physical Education,* New York: McGraw-Hill Book Co., Inc.

Game Activities

P
A
R
T

III

Game activities constitute a major portion of the elementary school physical education program. There is, in fact, a proportionate increase in the amount of time and emphasis given to game activities and a decrease in time given to gymnastics and dance as children progress through the various grades. Consequently, there should be a clear understanding of the organization of games to assist each teacher in selecting and emphasizing appropriate skills as well as preventing unnecessary repetition.

In this section, games are arranged on the basis of three broad categories. Games of Low Organization include simple team games, relay and tag games, classroom and individual activities. These activities are given major emphasis in the primary grades with a gradual decrease in emphasis as children develop skills and interest in the more organized and competitive Individual and Team games. The accompanying chart illustrates the reverse trend of importance of these activities at the different levels in the elementary school. Games from Other Countries are essentially a mixture of Low Organization, Individual and Team Games, and have been given a separate chapter on the basis of identification rather than on the basis of skill required of each game.

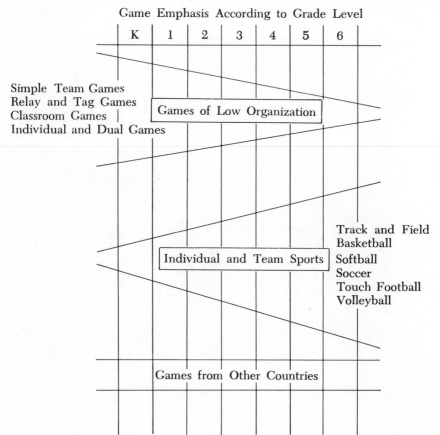

Game Emphasis According to Grade Level

Games
of Low Organization

CHAPTER

8

T HERE are four different types of game activities that are appropriate for elementary school-age children. The first type includes *all games that require a specific ball handling skill* such as throwing, catching, or kicking. In the first part of this chapter these basic game skills are described and accompanied by suggested games for each grade.

The second type of game activity includes *all the relay and tag games* played in the gymnasium or on the play field. These games contribute indirectly to the development of sports skills by improving speed and agility. Their purpose, however, should be to provide vigorous physical activity and enjoyment as well as to foster desirable social traits such as team loyalty and sportsmanship.

The third type of game activity is known as *active and quiet classroom games*. These are often called "rainy day activities," and may involve running, tagging, small manipulation, or an element of surprise. Their purpose, however, is fun and relaxation rather than the development of basic sport skills.

The fourth type of game activities appropriate for both primary and intermediate level children is classified as *"Individual and Dual"* games. In the main, these latter activities are played before school, at recess and lunch, and after school.

SIMPLE TEAM GAMES

All games require some degree of motor skill such as in running, dodging or throwing. This section, however, includes those activities which require specific ball handling skills of rolling or bouncing, throwing or catching, kicking or dribbling, and batting or hitting. Since these latter skills are the fundamentals of all major sport activities it is imperative that they be learned correctly and in an orderly manner. This section is, therefore, of major importance to primary teachers since they hold the key, not only to proper skill development but also to the beginning of a positive attitude toward team sports in general.

Teachers in the intermediate grades will use these games in a different fashion than primary teachers. Since a major emphasis in the intermediate grades is devoted to developing skill and knowledge of the major team sports (see Chapter 9), the simple team game activities included in this section are usually selected for recess or as warm-up activities for regular physical education classes.

SIMPLE TEAM GAMES

No.	Name of Game	Page	Skills	K	1	2	3	4	5	6
				Suggested Grade Level						

A. ROLLING AND BOUNCING GAMES

No.	Name of Game	Page	Skills	K	1	2	3	4	5	6
1.	Teacher and Class	122	roll, bounce, throw, catch.	X	X	X				
2.	Tunnel Ball	122	roll, catch	X	X	X				
3.	Ball Race	122	bounce			X	X			
4.	Two Squares	123	bounce, catch		X	X	X			

B. THROWING AND CATCHING GAMES

No.	Name of Game	Page	Skills	K	1	2	3	4	5	6
5.	Keep Away	127	catch, throw				X	X	X	X	X
6.	Circle Ball	128	catch, throw				X	X	X	
7.	Beanbag Basket	128	throw	X	X	X	X			
8.	Duck on the Rock	128	throw	X	X	X				
9.	Dodge Ball	129	catch, throw				X	X	X	X	X
10.	Borden Ball	130	catch, throw				X	X	X	X
11.	Progressive Dodge Ball	130	catch, throw				X	X	X	X
12.	Scooter Basketball	131	catch, throw				X	X	X	X

C. KICKING AND DRIBBLING GAMES

No.	Name of Game	Page	Skills	K	1	2	3	4	5	6
13.	Boundary Ball	133	kick, trap				X	X	X	X	X
14.	Place Kick Ball	133	kick				X	X	X	X	X
15.	Battle Ball	134	kick, trap				X	X	X	X
16.	Crab Soccer	134	kick				X	X	X	X	X
17.	Scooter Soccer	135	kick				X	X	X	X	X

D. HITTING GAMES

No.	Name of Game	Page	Skills	K	1	2	3	4	5	6
18.	High Ball	138	throw, catch, volley				X	X	X	X
19.	Shower Ball	138	volley			X	X	X	X	X
20.	Bounce Net Ball	138	volley				X	X	X	X
21.	Swing at Five	139	throw, catch, fielding				X	X	X	X
22.	Long Ball	139	catch, throw, bat				X	X	X	X
23.	Bat Ball	140	catch, throw, bat				X	X	X	X
24.	Scooter Softball	141	throw, catch					X	X	X

A. ROLLING AND BOUNCING GAMES

Rolling: This skill involves a push of the hands against the back and sides of the ball causing it to roll along the floor toward the desired object or player. Important fundamentals are:

1. Start with hands behind the ball.
2. Push the ball; do not slap or hit it forward.
3. Push with both hands and follow through in the direction of the ball.

TWO-HAND ROLL

FIG. 8.1	**FIG. 8.2**	**FIG. 8.3**
Sit with back straight, elbows slightly bent, and legs spread sideways. Spread hands around the back and sides of ball. Only fingertips and thumbs should be in contact with the ball.	Extend elbows and push the ball forward.	Continue forward movement of arms to assist in the accuracy of the roll. This latter follow-through movement is very important as most children will favor their "strong" hand, causing the ball to roll to one side rather than straight ahead.

Simple practice activities:
1. Roll ball in a forward direction, run after and stop it.
2. While seated with legs spread sideways, roll a ball to partner seated in same position.
3. While standing, turn back to partner and roll ball through legs to him.
4. Roll ball into box or cardboard carton.
5. Roll a ball along a painted line on the floor.
6. Stand six feet away and roll ball at wooden pins or milk cartons.

Bouncing: This is controlled bouncing with one or two hands while standing or moving in any direction. Basic to controlled bouncing are:
1. Use peripheral vision while dribbling. This means a child should look at his target and not directly at the ball while dribbling; he will see it without looking directly at it.
2. Do not slap ball downward; push it "into the floor."
3. Learn to dribble with either hand.

One-Hand Bounce

FIG. 8.4	FIG. 8.5	FIG. 8.6
Begin with body leaning forward, knees slightly bent and weight evenly distributed on both feet. Hold the ball in left hand with fingers of right hand spread over top of ball.	Extend forearm downward and forward and "push" the ball toward the floor with fingertips.	Hold hand down and wait for the ball to rebound back. Let fingers, wrist and arm "ride" back with the ball.

Simple practice activities:
1. Bounce a ball with two hands and catch it with two hands.
2. Bounce a ball to a partner.
3. Bounce a ball several times with one or two hands.
4. Bounce a ball while walking.
5. Bounce a ball while running.
6. Teacher bounces ball to children. Use circle or line formation.
7. Bounce ball and clap hands before catching it.
8. Bounce ball to a rhythm, "bounce, bounce, and clap"; repeat.
9. Bounce ball, turn around and catch it after one bounce.
10. Bounce ball successively in squares of hopscotch or ladder.
11. O'Leary bounce ball several times, swing leg over ball and continue bouncing.

No. 1: Teacher and Class (K - 2)

Formation:	Large semicircle with approximately five feet between each player.
Equipment:	Utility ball (6, 9, or 13 inch).
No. of Players:	6 - 12.
Skills:	Rolling, bouncing, throwing, and catching.
How to Play:	Note: Change rules according to the skill you wish to emphasize.

1. Children stand in a semicircle with about five feet between each player. The teacher or "leader" stands six to ten feet away and faces the group.
2. The "leader" bounces the ball to the player at the head of the line, who catches it and repeats a bounce pass to the leader.
3. Continue pattern to the last player.
4. After the last person has had his turn, the "leader" goes to the end of the line and the first player in the line becomes the "new leader."

Teaching Suggestions:
1. Lengthen the distance between "leader" and circle players as the skill level increases.
2. Use various size balls.

No. 2: Tunnel Ball (K - 2)

Formation:	Single circle with children facing the center. One player stands in the middle of the circle.
Equipment:	Utility ball (9 or 13 inch).
No. of Players:	10 to 12.
Skills:	Rolling and catching.

How to Play:
1. Children form a circle with each player in a "stride" position (legs apart).
2. One child is chosen to be "it" and stands in the center of the circle with the ball.
3. "It" attempts to roll the ball between the legs of any circle player or between any two players.
4. Circle players may use their hands to stop the ball; however, they cannot move their feet.
5. If the circle player prevents the ball from rolling out of the circle he becomes "it."

Teaching Suggestions:
For an element of surprise, have all circle players turn around. The ball must be rolled through the legs. If a circle player can catch the ball before it rolls away, he becomes "it."

No. 3: Ball Race (2 - 3)

Formation:	File formation behind a starting line with about five to six feet between each team. Draw a two foot circle about ten feet in front of each team.

Equipment: One soccer ball for each team.

No. of Players: 6 to 8 on each team.

Skills: Dribbling (hands or feet).

How to Play:

1. Lead players start at the same time and dribble the ball around the circle and back to starting line.
2. The first child back is the winner, or the first team to complete the relay is the winner.

Teaching Suggestions:

Place circles far enough apart to prevent interference between players.

No. 4: Two Squares (1 - 3)

Formation: Draw two five foot squares side by side and place one player in each square.

Equipment: Utility ball (9 or 13 inch).

No. of Players: 2 to 8.

Skills: Bouncing.

How to Play:

1. Two players stand in opposite squares while the remaining players stand just outside one square.
2. To start, one player bounce-serves the ball into the square of the other player. (It may be wise to allow players to throw the ball instead of bounce-serving it; as skill increases, require a bounce-serve.)
3. After the ball bounces in the opposing player's square, he returns it by batting it in an upward direction with one or both hands back into the square of the server.
4. Continue play until one of the following violations occurs:
    a. Ball lands out of square (liners are good).
    b. Ball hit with fist.
    c. Holding the ball (catching it).
    d. Hitting the ball downward.

When a violation occurs, the player committing it leaves the game and the next waiting player takes his place.

B. THROWING AND CATCHING GAMES

Thowing: Passing a ball from one player to another or toward a target may be done from a stationary position or while in motion. The ball may also be thrown with one or both hands and in a variety of ways. Common to all throwing movements, however, are the following fundamentals:

1. Learn the proper foot and hand positions before attempting to throw.
2. Keep "eyes on the target" and not on the ball.
3. Learn to throw with accuracy, then acquire speed and distance.
4. Follow through with hands and arms with every throw.

Two-Hand Side Throw

FIG. 8.7

Stand with left foot forward, weight evenly distributed on both feet. The ball should be held in front of the body, elbows slightly bent and fingers spread around sides of ball.

FIG. 8.8

Swings arms back to right side until the ball is opposite the right hip, and shift weight to right foot. At this point, the right hand is behind the ball, left elbow bent and left hand on the front of the ball.

FIG. 8.9

Simultaneously swing the arms forward, shift body weight to left foot and rotate towards the left. Note: the ball should leave both hands at the moment of release.

Underhand Throw (Pitching)

FIG. 8.10

Stand facing target (batter) with legs slightly apart and weight evenly distributed on both feet. Hold ball in front of body with both hands slightly under the ball.

FIG. 8.11

Simultaneously swing right hand downward and backward, twist body to the right and shift weight to right foot.

FIG. 8.12

Swing right arm forward, rotate shoulders toward the left and step forward on the left foot. Release ball and follow through with the right hand and step forward on the right foot.

OVERHAND THROW

FIG. 8.13	**FIG. 8.14**	**FIG. 8.15**
Stand with left foot forward and weight evenly distributed on both feet. Hold ball with both hands in front of body.	Twist body toward the right as ball is brought upward above shoulder and behind the ear and shift body weight to right foot.	Swing right arm forward, rotate shoulders to left, and shift weight to left foot. Continue forward and release ball off fingertips.

Catching: A ball may be caught with one or two hands and virtually from all angles. In the primary grades, however, stress should be placed on two main catches, namely, the two-hand underhand and the two-hand overhand catch. The following fundamentals are common to both types of catches:

1. Keep "eyes on the ball" until it is caught.
2. Arms and hands should "go out" to meet the ball, then recoil back toward the body.
3. After catching the ball, never hold it with the palms of the hand—hold it with the fingertips and thumbs.
4. After catching the ball, get it into proper throwing position for the next play.

Simple practice activities:

1. Throw beanbag using underhand toss to partner.
2. Throw beanbag into air and catch it.
3. Throw beanbag into box or cardboard carton.
4. Throw beanbag into air, clap hands and catch it.

TWO-HAND UNDERHAND CATCH

FIG. 8.16	**FIG. 8.17**	**FIG. 8.18**
Stand with feet about twelve inches apart, elbows bent, hands pointing forward, with fingers and thumbs spread apart.	Simultaneously step forward with the left (or right) foot, extend arms forward and downward, and bring hands closer together. The ball should be caught with the tips of the thumb and fingers. Baby fingers should be close together with the remaining fingers and thumb spread around the sides of the ball.	As the ball is caught bend elbows, shift weight to back foot and bring left foot back to starting position. The body weight should now be evenly distributed on both feet.

5. Two beanbags—throw beanbag to partner and catch the beanbag partner has tossed.
6. Throw beanbag using underhand toss to knock off another beanbag placed on top of pin six or more feet away.
7. Throw ball to partner five or more feet away using underhand toss, and catch returned ball.
8. Throw ball into box six or more feet away using underhand toss.
9. Throw ball into air, let it bounce and catch it.
10. Throw utility ball at target on wall six feet to fifteen feet away.
11. Throw a ball into the air and clap hands or turn around before catching it.

OVERHAND CATCH

FIG. 8.19	**FIG. 8.20**	**FIG. 8.21**
Stand with feet about twelve inches apart, elbows bent, hands pointing forward with fingers and thumbs spread apart.	Extend arms forward and upward, and bring hands closer together. The ball should be caught with the tips of fingers and thumbs. Thumbs are close together and fingers are spread apart.	Bend elbows allowing the ball to be brought close to the chest. The recoil action should bring body weight back to an even distribution on both feet.

No. 5: Keep Away (2 - 6)

Formation: Scattered formation within a designated playing area.

Equipment: One utility ball or basketball.

No. of Players: 8 to 10 on each team.

Skills: Passing, catching, and guarding.

How to Play:

1. On signal, the teacher gives the ball to a player on one of the teams, who then passes the ball to another teammate.
2. The opposing players attempt to intercept or to break up the pass. If they are successful, then they may pass to each other.
3. Fouls are called whenever a defensive player grabs or holds on to an offensive player.

Teaching Suggestions:
1. Players who are waiting their turns must be kept out of the playing area.
2. Do not allow players to run with the ball.
3. If adequate space is available, divide class into four teams and play two games at the same time.
4. If teams are large and there is a limited playing area, rotate in fours or fives every few minutes.

No. 6: Circle Ball (3 - 5)

Formation:	Single circle with six to eight feet between each player.
Equipment:	Basketball or utility ball.
No. of Players:	10 to 15 on each team.
Skills:	Passing and catching.

How to Play:
1. The ball is passed to each player in turn around the circle.
2. Once the ball is started, introduce a second ball to be passed in the same direction.

Teaching Suggestions:
1. Use stopwatch to time speed.
2. Change direction frequently to keep children's interest.

No. 7: Beanbag Basket (K - 3)

Formation:	File formation behind a starting line with about five to six feet between each team. Place a wastebasket five feet in front of each team.
Equipment:	Three beanbags and one wastebasket for each team.
No. of Players:	5 to 6 on each team.
Skills:	Throwing.

How to Play:
1. Each child is given three consecutive throws at the basket.
2. After each player completes his third throw he collects the bags and gives them to the next player then goes to the rear of the line.
3. The player with the highest number of successful baskets wins, or count up the total number for each team.

Teaching Suggestions:
As skill improves, use smaller baskets or increase the throwing distance.

No. 8: Duck on the Rock (K - 2)

Formation:	Arrange children in a line formation ten feet away from a milk carton.
Equipment:	One milk carton for each game and one beanbag for each player.

No. of Players: 6 to 10.

Skills: Throwing.

How to Play:

1. Place a beanbag (duck) on top of a milk carton (rock). One player, the guard, stands three feet to one side of the "duck." The guard cannot stand in front of the "duck."
2. The first player throws his beanbag and tries to knock the "duck" off the "rock."
3. If he succeeds in knocking the "duck" off (including the "rock" over), he runs to retrieve his beanbag and returns to his place behind the line.
4. The "guard" must stand the "rock" up, place the "duck" on top and try to tag the "thrower" before he retrieves his beanbag and runs back over his throwing line. If tagged, the thrower and guard change positions.
5. If any thrower is unsuccessful in knocking the "duck" off, he must leave his beanbag on the ground until another player knocks the "duck" off. When this occurs, all players whose beanbags are on the ground run and attempt to retrieve them and return to their positions. The guard, however, may then tag any one of these players.

Teaching Suggestions:

If the guard is too successful, move him four or five feet away from the "rock."

No. 9: Dodge Ball (2 - 6)

Formation: Circle.

Equipment: Volleyball or utility ball.

No. of Players: Class.

Skills: Throwing, catching.

How to Play:

1. Divide players into two teams; one team remains on the circle while the other stands in the center.
2. On signal, players in the outside circle try to hit any player below the waist in the circle.
3. Inside players, to avoid being hit, may move anywhere within the boundaries of the circle.
4. Outside players may enter the circle to retrieve the ball; however, they may not throw at an opponent while inside the circle.
5. Any player hit below the waist immediately joins the outside circle.
6. Last person remaining in circle is the winner.

Teaching Suggestions:

1. To start, allow any player hit by a bouncing ball to be eliminated. Later allow only a "fly" hit to count. (Fly hit is one in which the ball travels from the thrower directly to a circle player.)
2. Use two or more balls.

No. 10: Borden Ball (3 - 6)

Formation:	Divide playing area in two equal sections and place one team on each.
Equipment:	Football.
No. of Players:	Divide class into two equal teams.
Skills:	Throwing, catching.

How to Play:
1. Place one goalie from each team in an eight foot goal drawn in the center of each end line.
2. Players take any position they desire in the playing area.
3. The game is started with a jump ball between two opposing players.
4. The object is to throw the ball through the goal.

Basic Rules:
1. The ball may be thrown in any direction.
2. The ball may not be hit or kicked.
3. A player may hold the ball for three seconds or less.
4. A player may take a maximum of three steps, (five if playing on a field).
Penalty: The ball is given to the nearest opponent.
5. Opponents who do not have possession of the ball may check the player with the ball but may not touch, hold, or push him.
6. One point for each goal.
7. After a point, half time, or any official stopping of play, start play with a jump ball at center.
8. If ball goes over sidelines, non-offending player throws it into the field of play.

No. 11: Progressive Dodge Ball (3 - 6)

Formation:	Draw three parallel twenty foot squares and designate each square as "A," "B," and "C," respectively.
Equipment:	Ball.
No. of Players:	Class.
Skills:	Throwing,

How to Play:
1. This game is played in three periods of three to five minutes each.
2 Teams rotate playing areas (A, B, and C) after each period.
3. On signal, a player in one section tries to hit players (below the waist) in the other sections. Players may throw from any section to any other section.
4. No player is eliminated. Scores are made by hitting players of another team. The teacher or leader keeps the score for each team.
5. Since no player is eliminated, as soon as he is hit he should try to get the ball and throw it at an opponent.
6. Players may not cross boundary lines.
7. Team with highest score after three periods wins.

No. 12: Scooter Basketball (3 - 6)

Formation: Arrange teams as shown in the diagram.

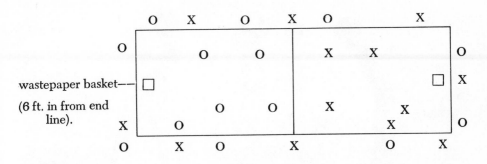

Equipment: 12 scooters, 2 wastepaper baskets, and a volleyball.
No. of Players: 6 on each team.
How to Play:
1. All players assume a sitting position.
2. Players sitting on scooters may advance the ball by throwing or dribbling it.
3. Players on the side and end lines must not move more than three feet to secure a loose ball and must throw it to a player on a scooter.
4. Scooter players may throw the ball to side or end line players.
5. A jump ball is used to start game, after held balls, and after ball goes over end or side lines.
6. Free throws are awarded for infractions such as charging, kicking, or any unnecessary rough play.
7. One point for each basket, including free throws.
Teaching Suggestions:
1. Vary the basic positions such as one hand and one foot or kneeling, etc.
2. Substitute side and end line players every two to three minutes.

C. KICKING AND DRIBBLING GAMES

Kicking: The majority of kicking games played in the primary grades involve three closely related kicking skills. These are kicking a stationary or moving ball, dribbling a ball with both feet and trapping and stopping a ball with one foot or shins. Important points to remember will be listed under the description of each skill.

Basic fundamentals to stress in kicking skills are:
1. Keep your "eyes on the ball" as it approaches you or as you approach it.
2. Kick the ball with the instep (top or side of instep), never with the toe.
3. The knee of the kicking foot should be bent prior to the kick.
4. After the ball has been kicked, follow through with the "kicking foot" for a short distance.

INSTEP KICK

FIG. 8.22	**FIG. 8.23**	**FIG. 8.24**
Stand with left foot even with ball, head well in front of ball, and right toe pointing down. The arms are sideways for balance.	Swing right leg downward and forward and contact ball with top of instep.	Continue kicking leg forward and slightly upward.

DRIBBLING

FIG. 8.25	**FIG. 8.26**	**FIG. 8.27**
Begin with weight evenly distributed on both feet, trunk bent slightly forward and arms extended sideward.	Move right foot forward and push ball forward and slightly to the left with inside of right foot.	Place right foot down transferring weight to this foot, and shift flexed left leg forward to repeat action.

Important fundamentals to stress in dribbling skills are:
1. Push the ball; do not kick it.
2. Begin with a very slow (walking speed) but controlled dribble.
3. Increase speed as control increases.
4. Do not allow the ball to get more than five or six feet away from the feet.

Simple Practice Activities:
1. Kick a ball toward a boundary line, run after it and stop it with hands.
2. Stand fifteen to twenty feet away from a primary circle, kick ball from a stationary position so it rolls into circle.
3. Stand six to eight feet away from wall, roll ball to wall and kick rebound ball back to wall.
4. Partner rolls ball to other partner standing six to ten feet away who, in turn, kicks the ball back.
5. Dribble to a line ten feet away, stop ball with hands, and dribble back.
6. Dribble around a chair six to ten feet away.

No. 13: Boundary Ball (2 - 6)

Formation: Draw three lines with twenty to thirty feet between each line. Arrange each team in a scattered formation on each side of the center line.
Equipment: Two soccer balls.
No. of Players: 10 to 15 players on each team.
Skills: Kicking and trapping.

How to Play:
1. Each team is given one ball.
2. Play is started by each team kicking a ball toward the opponents' goal line.
3. Players on both teams may move freely about in their own half of the field and try to prevent the opponents' ball from crossing the goal.
4. Players cannot touch the ball with their hands.
5. One point is scored each time the ball crosses the opponents' goal line.

Teaching Suggestions:
Require only "left foot" or "right foot" kicking.

No. 14: Place Kick Ball (2 - 6)

Formation: Draw a softball diamond with thirty feet between each base. Place one team in the field and one in a line formation behind the home base.
Equipment: Utility or soccer ball.
No. of Players: 10 to 12 on each team.
Skills: Kicking.

How to Play:
1. Place one team (fielding team) in the playing area outside the base lines.
2. Each player on the "kicking team" is given one stationary kick.
3. If the kick is fair (inside boundary line), the kicker tries to run around the bases before any member of the fielding team can get the ball and run to home base before the kicker.
4. Any fly ball that is caught puts the kicker out.

Teaching Suggestions:
1. After the stationary kick is learned, introduce a "dribble and kick." Draw a line ten to fifteen feet behind the home base and require the kicker to dribble to the base, then kick the ball.
2. The second time "up to bat," require the kick to be made with the opposite foot.
3. If only a few players are successful in running around the bases, have players run to first base and back rather than around all four bases.

No. 15: Battle Ball (3 - 6)

Formation:	Draw two parallel lines twenty feet apart. Place one team on each line and require players to hold hands.
Equipment:	A slightly deflated soccer ball.
No. of Players:	10 to 12 on each team.
Skills:	Kicking and trapping.

How to Play:
1. Side "A" tries to kick the soccer ball over side of "B's" goal line.
2. Side "B" tries to stop the ball and kick it back over side of "A's" line, and so on.
3. The team which kicks the ball over the opponents' line receives two points.
4. The first side to reach a score decided by the teacher wins the game.

Rules:
1. If a player touches the ball with his hands, his team loses a point.
2. If the ball is kicked too high (over the heads of the other team), one point is deducted from the score of the kicking team.

Teaching Suggestions:
1. Have players pass the ball from teammate to teammate before kicking it toward the opponents' line.
2. Allow children to use their hands to prevent the ball from hitting their faces.

No. 16: Crab Soccer (2 - 6)

Formation:	Divide playing area into two equal sections and place one team in each section. Place goals on end lines.

Equipment: Utility ball or soccer ball.
No. of Players: 15 to 17 on each team.
Skills: Kicking.
How to Play:
1. Players from either team may start from any position within the playing area.
2. All players, except one goalie for each team, must remain in the "crab walk" position. They may move anywhere in the court area.
3. The goalies may use their hands; however, all other players move the ball with their feet.
4. A foul occurs when a player catches the ball or strikes it with his hands. The teacher should stop the game when a foul occurs and give the ball to the nearest opponent.
5. Award one point for each goal scored.
Teaching Suggestions:
1. Practice the crab walk first.
2. After the game is well understood, introduce striking with hands only or a combination of hands and feet.

No. 17: Scooter Soccer (2 - 6)

Formation: Arrange teams as shown in the diagram.

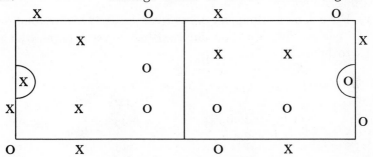

Equipment: Soccer or volleyball, and 12 or more scooters.
No. of Players: 6 on each team.
Skills: Kicking.
How to Play:
1. All scooter players must assume a sitting position.
2. Side and end line players must assume a sitting position.
3. Scooter players may start from any position within the playing area.
4. The game is started with a jump ball between two opposing players.
5. Once the game is started, each team must use feet only and attempt to kick the ball to teammates or through the goal.
6. Side and end line players may stop the ball with their feet and kick it to teammates on scooters. However, side and end line players may not score goals.

7. A foul occurs when a player catches the ball, strikes it with his hands, or commits unnecessary roughness. The teacher should stop the game when a foul occurs and give the ball to the nearest opponent.
8. One point for each goal.

Teaching Suggestions:
1. Rotate side line players every three to four minutes.
2. After the game is well understood, introduce other positions, such as lying, kneeling, or one foot on scooter.

D. HITTING GAMES

There are two types of hitting skills that should be stressed in the second and third grades. The first is batting a ball thrown from an underhand pitch. The second skill is the two-hand underhand and the two-hand overhand hit used in volleyball-type games. Basic fundamentals pertinent to each skill will be listed under each respective description.

The following fundamentals are common to all types of batting:
1. Keep "eyes on the ball" until it has been hit.
2. Maintain a firm grip on the bat.
3. Follow through on every hit with the exception of bunting.

Simple Practice Activities:
   a. Batting Activities
      (1) Hit ball off batting tee. Allow five to six hits before rotating player.
      (2) Teacher throws twelve inch softball to each pupil who attempts to hit it.

BATTING

FIG. 8.28	**FIG. 8.29**	**FIG. 8.30**
Stand with the left side toward the pitcher and spread legs comfortably apart with weight on both feet. Elbows are bent and away from the body. Grip the handle with the left hand touching the right.	At the moment the ball is pitched, shift weight to rear foot, then, simultaneously swing bat downward and forward and shift weight to front foot.	After contacting the ball, continue twisting body to the left as bat swings around in a wide arc ending over left shoulder.

UNDERHAND AND OVERHAND HIT (*Volleying*)

In volleyball activities, the ball may be hit by an underhand or overhand striking motion. Furthermore, one or two hands may be used in an open hand or closed fist position. Teachers should stress the following fundamentals for both types of hitting skills:

1. Keep "eyes on the ball" as it approaches and until it is hit.
2. Body weight should be evenly distributed on both feet prior to the ball reaching the player. This is the "set" position.
3. After the ball has been hit follow through with hands and arms.
   b. Hitting or Volleyball Activities
   (1) One player bounces the ball then hits it to his partner ten to fifteen feet away.
   (2) Stand four to five feet away from wall. Throw ball against wall and hit the rebound with an underhand or overhand hit.
   (3) With net, one player throws ball over net to partner, who in turn attempts to hit it back over net.

OVERHAND HIT OR VOLLEY

| FIG. 8.31 | FIG. 8.32 | FIG. 8.33 |

As the ball approaches, the player should be able to see it through the "window" created by his thumbs and fingers.

Begin with knees slightly flexed back straight, elbows bent and sideward. The fingers should be slightly spread apart with thumbs facing each other.

As the ball drops, extend the body upward and slightly forward. Hit the ball with "stiff" fingers. Do not allow the fingers to relax as this will lead to catching the ball then throwing it. Follow through with an upward and forward motion in the direction of the ball.

No. 18: High Ball (3 - 6)

Formation:	Drop the volleyball net down to about six feet or string a rope between two standards. Place one team on each side of the net in a scattered formation.
Equipment:	Volleyball, net, court.
No. of Players:	10 to 15 players on each team.
Skills:	Throwing, catching, and volleying.

How to Play:

1. One team throws the ball over the net and the other team must catch it before it hits the ground, and return it over the net.
2. When a team drops the ball the other team gets a point.

Teaching Suggestions:

1. Use the same rules and add the following: As soon as a player catches the ball he must throw it to one of his own teammates, who, in turn, must hit it over the net.
2. Keep children in their assigned areas—no wandering.

No. 19: Shower Ball (2 - 6)

Formation:	Drop the volleyball net down to about six feet or string a rope between two standards. Place one team on each side of the net in a scattered formation.
Equipment:	Volleyball, net, court.
No. of Players:	10 to 12 on each team.
Skills:	Volleying.

How to Play:

1. Place two equal teams on each side of the net.
2. Action is started by one player hitting the ball over the net.
3. Any player on the opposite team attempts to catch the ball.
4. The player who catches it is allowed one step, then he must hit it back over the net.
5. One point for the serving team if the receiving team does not catch the ball. One point for receiving team if they catch the ball before it bounces.

Teaching Suggestions:

As skill improves, have each child throw the ball up—then hit it over the net.

No. 20: Bounce Net Ball (3 - 6)

Formation:	Drop the volleyball net down to about six feet or string a rope between two standards. Place one team on each side of the net in rows or in scattered formation.
Equipment:	Volleyball, volleyball court.

No. of Players: 6 to 9 on each team.
Skills: Volleying.
How to Play:
1. Play is started by one player hitting the ball over the net.
2. The ball must bounce before being returned.
3. Any number of players can hit ball any number of times; however, the ball must bounce between each player.
4. The team that loses the point starts ball next time.
5. Fouls: (a) throwing ball; (b) ball caught and held; (c) ball bouncing more than once; (d) ball hit; or (e) out of bounds ball.
6. When a team commits a foul, the opposite team gets one point.
Teaching suggestions:
Instead of allowing one bounce between players, make them hit it directly from a volley pass.

No. 21: Swing at Five (3 - 6)

Formation: Draw a softball diamond with thirty feet between each base. Place one team in the field and one in a line formation behind a restraining line drawn ten feet back and to the right of home plate.
Equipment: One bat, one softball, four bases.
No. of Players: 18 to 24.
Skills: Throwing, catching, and fielding.
How to Play:
1. The pitcher, using an underhand throw, pitches the ball to the batter.
2. A ball landing in the infield scores one point while a ball landing in the outfield scores two points.
3. Fouls—no score, but count as swings.
4. If the player throws the bat after a hit, he is out.
Teaching Suggestions:
1. Alternate pitcher.
2. Waiting batters should stand at least ten feet away from the batter.

No. 22: Long Ball (3 - 6)

Formation: Draw a softball diamond with thirty to thirty-five feet between each base. Place one team in the field and the other in a file formation behind a restraining line drawn ten feet back and to the right of home plate.
Equipment: Softball, softball bat, two bases.
No. of Players: 9 on each team.
Skills: Running, pitching, catching, and batting

How to Play:
1. Players are divided into two teams (number each player).
2. Each team selects a pitcher and catcher. Other players are fielders or batters.
3. When a ball is hit the batter runs to the first base and, if possible, returns home.
4. Any hit is good; there are no fouls in the game.
5. Base runner may stop on first base.
6. Any number of runners may be on base at the same time.
7. Runners may not steal home.
8. Batter is out when he strikes out, is touched off base, steals base, throws bat, fly ball caught.
9. One point for each run to the base and back.

Teaching Suggestions:
1. Alternate pitchers and catchers.
2. Keep children away from batters.
3. Move pitcher closer as skill indicates.

No. 23: Bat Ball (3 - 6)

Formation:	Draw a softball diamond with thirty to thirty-five feet between each base. Place one team in the field and the other in a file formation behind a restraining line drawn ten feet back and to the right of home plate.
Equipment:	Softball, bat, and two bases.
No. of Players:	9 on each team.
Skills:	Batting, running, and throwing.

How to Play:
1. Divide players into two teams of nine each. One team in field and one at bat.
2. First player of team at bat hits ball into field and runs to first base and home in one complete trip. He may not stop on base.
3. If he makes complete trip without being put out, he scores one run for his team.
4. Runner is out if: (a) fielder catches fly ball, or (b) fielder touches runner with ball before he reaches home.
5. When a team at bat makes three outs it goes into field and the team in field comes to bat.
6. Winner is team with most scores at the end of the playing period. (Teams must have same number of times at bat.)

Teaching Suggestions:
1. Alternate pitchers and catchers. Alternate boy and girl in batting order.
2. Try two outs if one team stays up too long.
3. Vary distance according to level of skill.

No. 24: Scooter Softball (4 - 6)

Formation: Arrange teams as shown in the diagram.

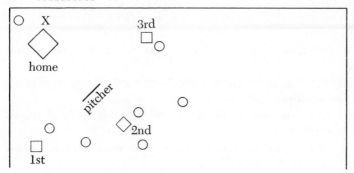

Equipment:	Scooters, volleyball, or utility ball.
No. of Players:	12 on each team.
Skills:	Pitching and catching,

How to Play:
1. Regular softball rules are used with the following modifications:
    a. Ball is batted with arm.
    b. Pitcher kneels on scooter about fifteen feet away from batter.

Teaching Suggestions:
Shorten or lengthen bases according to level of skill.

RELAY AND TAG GAMES

Relay and tag games included in this section may be played in the gymnasium or on any suitable outdoor playground area. These activities require a minimum of class organization, skill development, and playing facilities. Generally speaking, games of this nature will develop such skills as running, jumping, dodging and stopping. Indirectly, they will assist in developing such sports skills as throwing and kicking by improving a child's speed, reaction time, and general body coordination. It would be fair to say, however, that the greatest contribution of these activities are twofold: just plain fun and vigorous physical activity.

The first section contains relay activities which are basically running in nature. The second section includes games which involve tagging a player by one or more players designated to be "it." First, decide what type of activity you want, that is, whether it should be tag or relay activity. Second, check to see if you have available space and equipment. Note the improvizations that can be made on the page where the game is described. Finally, check the basic rules of the game. A slight variation in the rules injected by the teacher may make the difference between what might be an extremely boring or a very exciting activity.

Relays

Most of the relays listed in the accompanying chart are running type activities. Each teacher, regardless of grade level, should establish a standard procedure for teaching this type of activity. The following suggestions may assist in developing a procedure applicable to the grade and available facilities:

1. Divide the class into as many equal teams as space and equipment permit.
2. Arrange the teams in the correct formation before explaining the rules.
3. Tell the children the name of the relay.
4. Explain and demonstrate the basic rules. Allow several pupils to demonstrate the relay.
5. Start the relay with a definite signal such as a whistle, verbal command, or loud beat of the drum.
6. Always pick a certain number of winners and give them credit for their success.
7. Encourage student participation in rule changes and general modifications of the game.

Relay Formations

There are four basic formations used to organize relays. Although the file formation is the most common one used in the elementary school, line, circle, and shuttle relays are also appropriate for this age level. The formation a teacher selects is governed by the type of relay, available space, and the skill required of the children. Each of the formations are described below along with several teaching suggestions.

FILE FORMATION:

A number of teams are selected and arranged one behind the other as shown in the diagram. Each player runs to the turning line and back.

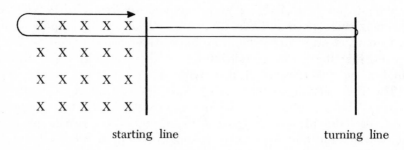

starting line   turning line

Variations may be (1) run through obstacles (chairs, beanbags) to the turning line; (2) run around an obstacle at the turning line; or (3) run to turning line and stop. The latter usually involves throwing something back to the next player.

Teaching Suggestions:
1. To prevent cheating, require each player upon returning to run around his team and back to the front of the line.
2. To prevent accidents, all runners should, at the turning line, run around the left side of the obstacle, and, upon returning, around the left side of his team.

LINE FORMATION:
    This formation is quite similar to the File Formation with the exception that all players face one player positioned in front.

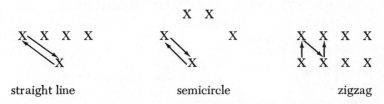

straight line   semicircle   zigzag

SHUTTLE FORMATION:
    The shuttle formation is basically a file formation with one-half of each team placed on an opposite line. As soon as player number one reaches player number two he walks back to the end of his line, then

5	3	1			2	4	6
X	X	X			X	X	X
X	X	X			X	X	X
X	X	X			X	X	X

each player moves forward one place.

CIRCLE FORMATION:
    Players are placed equal distance apart on a circle.

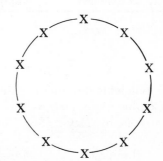

Teaching Suggestions:
1. Use available painters' circles or draw with chalk (inside) or stick (ground). Tie chalk or stick on end of string to make circles.
2. Provide adequate space between each circle.

Types of Relays

As previously indicated, most relays are run from a file or parallel line formation. The type of relay is usually described under one of the following categories. Several relays representing each type are described, as well as a chart indicating their appropriate grade level.

No.	Name of Relay	Skills	Page	Suggested Grade Level						
				K	1	2	3	4	5	6
A. RELAYS USING LOCOMOTOR SKILLS.										
1.	Walk, Run, or Hop Relay	optional locomotor	145	X	X	X	X			
2.	Leapfrog Relay	leap + run	145	X	X	X	X	X	X	X
3.	Rescue Relay	run	145	X	X	X	X	X		
4.	Shuttle Relay	run	146				X	X	X	X
5.	Zigzag Relay	run, dodging	146				X	X	X	X
B. RELAYS USING STUNTS										
6.	Animal Walk Relay	optional	146	X	X	X	X			
7.	Stunt Relay	optional	147	X	X	X	X	X	X	
8.	Skipping Rope Relay	skipping	147		X	X	X	X	X	X
9.	Wheelbarrow Relay	hand walking	147			X	X	X	X	X
10.	Skin the Snake Relay	sit + stand	148				X	X	X	X
C. RELAYS USING EQUIPMENT OR OBSTACLES										
11.	Circle Post Relay	run, turn	148	X	X	X	X	X	X	X
12.	Stick and Ball	run, manipulate	148		X	X	X	X	X	X
13.	Obstacle Relay	optional	149				X	X	X	X
14.	Scooter Relays	optional	149	X	X	X	X	X	X	X
D. RELAYS USING SPORTS SKILLS										
15.	Sport Skill Relays	optional	151	X	X	X	X	X	X	X

A. RELAYS USING LOCOMOTOR SKILLS

The following locomotor skills may be used in file, circle, and shuttle relays. Combinations such as run to turning line and skip back add interest and enjoyment to relays. (See Chapter 16 for a description of all locomotor skills.)

Running	Galloping
Walking	Hopping (one-foot)
Skipping	Sliding
Jumping (two-foot)	

No. 1: Walk, Run, or Hop Relay (K - 3)

Formation: File
Equipment: None
No. of Players: 6 to 8 on each team.
How to Play:
1. Draw a turning line twenty to forty feet away from starting line, distance depending upon age and ability.
2. Each player, in turn, performs any specified locomotor movement (run, walk, hop, leap, skip, slide, or gallop) to the turning line and back.

No. 2: Leapfrog Relay (K - 6)

Formation: File
Equipment: None
No. of Players: 6 to 8 on each team.
How to Play:
1. Place teams in a line formation with enough space between each player so that each player can reach the player's hips in front of him.
2. Player number one bends over, places hands on knees, and ducks his head.
3. Player number two places his hands on number one's hips, jumps over him and assumes the same position as number one.
Teaching Suggestions:
1. Make sure all keep their heads ducked until players have leaped over.
2. Vary relay by having players crawl under legs.

No. 3: Rescue Relay (K - 4)

Formation: File.
Equipment: None.
No. of Players: 6 to 8 on each team.
How to Play:
1. Each team stands in a file formation behind the starting line.
2. The captain stands behind a second line drawn twenty feet in front of the first line.
3. On signal, the captain runs to the first member of his team, grasps his hand, and runs back with the player to his turning line.
4. The player, whom the captain brought over, returns and brings the next player back.
5. Continue relay until the last man has been brought over the captain's line.
Teaching Suggestions:
Vary the way players are brought back. Other ways may include holding both hands, locking elbows back to back, and piggyback.

No. 4: Shuttle Relay (3 - 6)

Formation:	One-half of each team on each side of two restraining lines, spaced approximately twenty feet apart.
Equipment:	None.
No. of Players:	6 to 8 on each team.

How to Play:

1. Place one-half of each team behind each of the two restraining lines. Number the players 1, 3, 5, and 7, on one side, and 2, 4, 6, and 8 on the other side.
2. Player number one runs across around the left side of his team and tags number two.
3. Number two runs back around opposite side and tags number three, etc., until all have had a turn.

No. 5: Zigzag Relay (3 - 6)

Formation:	Line formation with players spaced six to eight feet apart.
Equipment:	None.
No. of Players:	8 to 12 on each team.

How to Play:

1. Number one runs in and out in a zigzag pattern to the last man on his team, encircles him, then repeats back to his original position.
2. Number two starts zigzagging backward around the last man, continues zigzag pattern up the line around first player, then back to his original position.
3. First team back in original position wins relay.

B. RELAYS USING STUNTS

Many of the stunts that are learned in self-testing activities such as crab walk, monkey run, and rope skipping can be incorporated into most relays. Some of the most enjoyable stunt relays are listed below. Other novelty stunts such as "egg-and-spoon," "orange under chin," and "thread the needle," all lend themselves to enjoyable relays. (See Chapter 13.)

Crab walk	Rabbit jump
Bear walk	Kangaroo hop
Seal walk	

No. 6: Animal Walk Relay (K - 3)

Formation:	File.
Equipment:	None.
No. of Players:	6 to 8 on each team.

How to Play:

This is a basic line relay with the movement imitating a specific animal walk. Some variations would be donkey, seal, crab, lame puppy, or bear.

No. 7: Stunt Relay (K - 5)

Formation: File.
Equipment: None.
No. of Players: 6 to 8 on each team.
How to Play:
1. Teams stand in a line formation behind the starting line.
2. A turning line is drawn about thirty to forty feet away.
3. On signal, the first player runs to the turning line and on his way back performs a stunt.

Teaching Suggestions:
Teacher may require the stunt to be performed from different positions, that is, from front lying position, from a sitting position, etc.

No. 8: Skipping Rope Relay (1 - 6)

Formation: File.
Equipment: One skipping rope for each team.
No. of Players: 5 to 6 on each team.
How to Play:
1. Teams line up behind the starting line with the first player holding a skipping rope. Draw a turning line about twenty feet away.
2. On signal, the first player skips to the turning line and back.
3. Continue relay until last player has had his turn.

Teaching Suggestions:
1. Same relay but skip backwards.
2. Same relay but have each player stop on turning line and do stationary skip ten, fifteen, or twenty times before returning to his line.

No. 9: Wheelbarrow Relay (2 - 6)

Formation: Partners in a file formation.
Equipment: None.
No. of Players: 10 to 12 on each team.
How to Play:
1. Divide players into equal teams and each team into couples of equal size and weight.
2. On signal, one partner places his hands on the floor and raises legs to other partner's hips. The standing partner holds his partner's feet close to his sides. Both walk to a turning line (twenty to twenty-five feet away).
3. When both have crossed the turning line, they exchange positions and return to the starting line.

Teaching Suggestions:
1. Instruct standing partner not to push the "walking" partner—hold feet only and walk.
2. Increase distance as strength increases.

No. 10: Skin the Snake Relay (3 - 6)

Formation: File.   Equipment: None.
No. of Players: 5 to 6 on each team.
How to Play:
1. Each player extends his left hand backward between his legs and grasps the right hand of the player behind him. Each succeeding player does the same.
2. On signal, every member of the file, except the last player, starts moving backward.
3. As the backward movement commences, the last player lies down on his back but holds on to the player in front.
4. The second rear player, after passing over the last player, lies down but still maintains grasp with his two hands.
5. Continue this pattern until everyone is lying down.
6. As soon as all are lying on their backs, the one at the rear stands, moves forward pulling the second player to his feet.
7. Continue this pattern until everyone is standing up.

C. RELAYS USING EQUIPMENT OR OBSTACLES

There are two types of relays involved in this section. The first uses an obstacle to maneuver around or through while the second type requires the player to carry or manipulate it as part of the relay.

No. 11: Circle Post Relay (K - 6)

Formation: Arrange each team in a file formation behind a starting line. Draw a second "turning line" twenty feet in front of the starting line. Place a chair or pin on the turning line and directly in front of each team.
Equipment: Post, pins, or chairs.
No. of Players: 6 to 8 on each team.
How to Play:
1. Player number one runs forward, makes a complete circle moving to the left around the post, then runs back around his own team and tags player number two.
2. Continue pattern until each player has circled the post.

No. 12: Stick and Ball Relay (1 - 6)

Formation: File.
Equipment: One stick and one ball for each team.
No. of Players: 6 to 8 on each team.
How to Play:
1. Draw a turning line about twenty to fifty feet in front of the starting line.
2. The first player holding the stick in contact with the ball must guide it while running to the turning line and back.
3. Continue relay until the last player has had a turn.

No. 13: Obstacle Relay (3 - 6)

Formation:	File.
Equipment:	Utility balls or Soccer balls, chairs.
No. of Players:	6 to 8 on each team.

How to Play:

1. Place chairs (or Indian clubs) six to ten feet apart and directly in front of each team.
2. The first player runs "in and out" around the chairs and back around team to the starting position.
3. Continue relay until last player has had a turn.

Teaching Suggestions:

If sufficient chairs, beanbags, wands, etc., are available, create a variety of obstacles to go around, under, or through.

No. 14: Scooter Relays*

Formation:	File or circle.
Equipment:	12 to 24 scooters.
No. of Players:	Variable.

How to Play:

Scooters provide an additional reservoir of file and circle relays played on or with scooters. Since this may be a new activity to many teachers a list of possible relay positions is provided along with several illustrations.

Names of Scooter Relays	Suggested Grade Level						
	K	1	2	3	4	5	6
Two Hand Relay	X	X	X	X	X	X	X
One Hand Relay	X	X	X	X	X	X	X
One Hand, One Foot Relay				X	X	X	X
Two Hand, One Foot Relay				X	X	X	X
One Foot Relay				X	X	X	X
Sitting Relay	X	X	X	X	X	X	X
Kneeling Relay			X	X	X	X	X
Lying Relay	X	X	X	X	X	X	X
Two Foot Relay			X	X	X	X	X
Scooter Position Relay	X	X	X	X	X	X	X
Seat and Feet Relay			X	X	X	X	X
Knees and Hands Relay				X	X	X	X
Feet and Hands Relay				X	X	X	X
Lying on Two Scooters	X	X	X	X	X	X	X
Partners—Elbows Locked Relay		X	X	X	X	X	X
Partners—Back to Back Relay			X	X	X	X	X
Partners—Push Cart Relay		X	X	X	X	X	X
Partners—Wheelbarrow Relay				X	X	X	X
Partners—Legs Crossed Relay				X	X	X	X
Partners—Chariot Relay				X	X	X	X

*See Appendix A for a diagram of floor scooters and a simple method of storing this equipment.

TWO HANDS   ONE HAND

FIG. 8.34

FIG. 8.35

ONE HAND AND ONE FOOT   TWO HANDS AND ONE FOOT

FIG. 8.36

FIG. 8.37

KNEELING   LYING

FIG. 8.38

FIG. 8.39

CHARIOT RACE

FIG. 8.40

DOUBLES—BACK TO BACK

FIG. 8.41

DOUBLES—PUSH CART

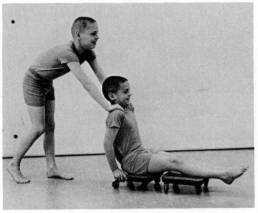

FIG. 8.42

DOUBLES—WHEEL-
BARROW

FIG. 8.43

D. RELAYS USING SPORTS SKILLS

In most physical education programs sports skill relays are usually taught as part of a team sport such as soccer, volleyball, or basketball. Further, emphasis in the form of a four or five week unit covering one sport should begin in the intermediate grades. Primary children, particularly second and third graders, should, however, participate in sports skill relays to develop the basic skill of the team and individual sports. Hence, the following relays should be used by primary teachers who, in turn, should modify any part of each relay to meet the level of skill of her class.

Sports Skills	Name of Relay	Page	Suggested Grade Level						
			K	1	2	3	4	5	6
Soccer Skills	Line Dribbling	227		X	X	X	X	X	X
	Shuttle Dribbling	228		X	X	X	X	X	X
	Around the Square	228				X	X	X	X
Volleyball Skills	Shuttle Volleying	264			X	X	X	X	X
	Zigzag Volleying	265			X	X	X	X	X
	Wall Volleying	264			X	X	X	X	X
Basketball Skills	Circle Passing	201		X	X	X	X	X	
	Line Dribble	203			X	X	X	X	
	Wall Passing	200			X	X	X	X	
Softball Skills	Overtake	246		X	X	X	X	X	
	Zigzag Throwing	246				X	X	X	
	Softball Throw Relay	250				X	X	X	
Track and Field Skill	Call Race	308		X	X				
	Potato Race	309	X	X	X				
	Double Shuttle Relay	307		X	X				

Tag Games

Tag games, like traditional folk dances, are found in virtually all countries. Although climates and geographical conditions vary from country to country, similar type games involving running, tagging, fleeing, and hunting seem to be common to all children. Their purpose too appears to be the same in each country. Children use play as illustrated in tag games for a variety of uncomplicated reasons. They enjoy movement for its own sake, thrill to any delightful surprise, copy their adults in hunting games, and test their own abilities through running, dodging, fleeing, and guessing.

There are several factors to be taken into consideration before any tag game is selected from the accompanying chart. Since this type of game usually involves tagging, slapping, or holding another player, plus one or more obstacles, certain safety rules should be established. Also, tag games are usually very active for the "tagger" and the one being chased, while the rest of the class is inactive. Boredom and inactivity can be overcome and unnecessary accidents eliminated by adhering to the following suggestions:

1. Make sure all unnecessary hazards are eliminated from the playing area.
2. Provide adequate safety margins beyond a designated "home base" line.
3. Teach children to tag easily rather than to push or strike another player.[1]
4. If the tag game involves competition between two or more teams, it is better to have the teacher select teams rather than by "Captain's Choice."
5. Encourage everyone to participate in the game. This can be accomplished by: (a) requiring every player to keep moving—if a child stops he becomes "it" or is eliminated; (b) reducing the size of the playing area; (c) dividing the class into two or more separate games; and (d) increasing the number of "it" as the game permits.
6. Insist on fair play, with all players abiding by the rules of the game.
7. Insist on immediate response to the blow of your whistle.

TYPES OF TAG GAMES

Since there is no common method of arranging tag games, the teacher is usually left to her ingenuity to select, organize, and present this type of activity. This, however, should not be considered a hindrance since each teacher may select what she considers to be appropriate and to modify the game to meet the interests and abilities of her class.

The accompanying chart contains tag activities that have proven to be popular with elementary school-age children. Information relating to formation, skills, and suggested grade level should assist each teacher in selecting the most appropriate activity. The latter "suggested grade level" should be considered as a rough guide line; do not hesitate to try any tag game listed even though it is not suggested for your grade. It is the children who really decide and make these activities appropriate.

---

1. Arthur G. Miller and Virginia Whitcomb, *Physical Education in the Elementary School Curriculum* (Englewood Cliffs, New Jersey: Prentice-Hall, Inc., 1963), p 74.

TAG GAMES

No.	Name of Game	Formation	Page	Skills	K	1	2	3	4	5	6
					Grade Level						
1	Beefsteak	3 lines	154	run, tag, dodge	X	X	X	X	X		
2	Brownies & Fairies	2 lines	155	run, turn, dodge	X	X	X				
3	Old Mother Witch	scattered	155	run, dodge, turn	X	X	X				
4	Simple Tag	scattered	155	run, dodge	X	X	X	X	X		
5	Snake Catch	scattered	156	run, catch	X	X	X	X	X		
6	Poison Tag	scattered	156	run, dodge, turn		X	X	X	X	X	
7	Elimination Tag	scattered	156	run, dodge, turn	X	X	X	X	X		
8	Uncle Sam	2 lines	157	run, dodge, turn		X	X	X			
9	Gardener & Scamp	circle	157	optional stunts		X	X	X			
10	Back to Back	scattered	158	run, dodge, turn	X	X	X	X	X		
11	Crab Tag	scattered	158	crab walk		X	X	X	X	X	
12	Dumbbell Tag	scattered	158	run, dodge, pass		X	X	X	X		
13	Broncho Tag	scattered	158	run, dodge, catching			X	X	X	X	X
14	Red Rover	3 lines	159	run, dodge, turn		X	X	X	X	X	
15	Midnight	2 lines	159	run, dodge, turn		X	X	X			
16	Partner Tag	scattered	160	run, dodge, catching			X	X	X		
17	Circle Tag	circle	160	run			X	X	X	X	
18	Snatch Club	2 lines	160	run, catch, dodge			X	X	X	X	
19	Posture Tag	scattered	161	run, balance		X	X	X	X	X	X
20	Commando	circle	161	run, push, pull			X	X	X	X	
21	Hip Tag	scattered	161	run, dodge, turn			X	X	X	X	
22	Chain Tag	scattered	161	run, dodge, turn				X	X	X	
23	Poor Pussy Cat	circle	162	run			X	X	X	X	X
24	Squirrel in the Tree	scattered	162	run, catch		X	X	X	X		

No. 1: Beefsteak (K - 4)

Formation: Draw three lines approximately 20 to 25 feet apart.
Equipment: None.
No. of Players: Class.
How to Play:

1. One child is chosen to be "it" and stands on the finish line twenty to twenty-five feet away from a starting line. "It" should have his back facing the starting line.
2. All other players stand on the starting line.
3. "It" begins to count aloud to ten and then calls "Beefsteak" and turns around to face the other players.

4. As "it" is counting, all other players are running forward trying to cross the finish line.
5. Any player caught stepping or running after "Beefsteak" is sent back.
6. First player over finish line becomes "it."

No. 2: Brownies and Fairies (K - 2)

Formation:	Draw two lines approximately thirty feet apart. One team lines up along each line.
Equipment:	None.
No. of Players:	Class.

How to Play:
1. Divide the class into two groups known as the "Brownies" and the "Fairies."
2. The "Fairies" face away from the "Brownies."
3. The "Brownies" creep up as quietly and as close as possible to the "Fairies."
4. The teacher calls out "Brownies are here," whereupon the "Fairies" try to tag the "Brownies" before they can run back over their own line.

No. 3: Old Mother Witch (K - 2)

Formation:	Scattered around small circle.
Equipment:	None.
No. of Players:	Class.

How to Play:
1. One player is selected to be the "Old Witch" and stands in the middle of the circle. The circle is drawn near one end of the play area.
2. Draw a line across opposite end of play area. This is the "safe line."
3. Players approach circle and tease the "Old Witch" by chanting:
    "Old Mother Witch
    Fell in a ditch,
    Picked up a penny,
    And thought she was rich."
4. The witch keeps asking "Whose children are you?"
5. The children answer with any name they wish.
6. When a child says "Yours," it is a signal for the witch to chase and tag a player before he crosses the safe line.
7. Whoever is caught becomes the "Old Witch."

No. 4: Simple Tag (K - 4)

Formation:	Scattered.
Equipment:	None.
No. of Players:	Class.

How to Play:
1. One child is chosen to be "it."
2. All players are scattered within a designated play area.
3. "It" tries to tag another player.
4. When a player is tagged, he must call out "I'm it" and the game continues.

Teaching Suggestions:
1. Use the following variations with tag games:
   a. Shadow tag—when "it" crosses a runner's shadow, he becomes "it."
   b. Stoop tag—when a player stoops, he cannot be tagged.

No. 5: Snake Catch (K - 4)

Formation: Scattered.
Equipment: Short Skipping Rope.
No. of Players: Class.

How to Play:
1. Scatter players over playing area.
2. One player is chosen to be the "snake catcher" and is given a skipping rope.
3. On signal, the "snake catcher" runs around the playing area dragging the free end of the rope on the ground.
4. All other players try to catch the free end with their hands. As soon as a player catches it, he becomes the "snake catcher."
5. Players may not step on the rope in an attempt to catch it.

Teaching Suggestions:
Enforce the ruling that once a player catches the free end of the rope, the "snake catcher" must immediately release the rope.

No. 6: Poison Tag (1 - 5)

Formation: Scattered.
Equipment: None.
No. of Players: Class.

How to Play:
The game is played the same as simple tag except that "it" must place one hand on the spot where he was tagged and hold it there while attempting to tag another player.

No. 7: Elimination Tag (K - 4)

Formation: Scattered.
Equipment: None.
No. of Players: Class.

How to Play:
1. One player is chosen to be "it."
2. "It" attempts to tag any player. As soon as player is tagged, he becomes "it" and the "tagger" sits on the floor to become an obstacle.

3. Continue game until last person is tagged.
4. Players sitting on floor cannot interfere with runners.

No. 8: Uncle Sam (1 - 4)

Formation: Draw two lines thirty to forty feet apart. Place
                               children along one line. The other line is known
                               as the "river."
Equipment: None.
No. of Players: Class.
How to Play:
1. One player is chosen to be Uncle Sam and stands in center of play area.
2. Other players stand behind one line and call "Uncle Sam, may we cross
   your river?"
3. Uncle Sam says, "Yes, if you have on . . . blue" (or any color).
4. All children wearing that color must run to opposite side.
5. Uncle Sam tries to tag as many as he can before they cross the opposite
   end line.
6. Those caught must help Uncle Sam.
7. Last person to be caught wins game.

No. 9: Gardener and Scamp (1 - 3)

Formation: Circle.
Equipment: None.
No. of Players: Class.
How to Play:
1. One player is chosen to be "scamp" and stands in the middle of the circle.
2. A second player is chosen to be the "gardener" and stands outside the circle.
3. "Scamp" and "gardener" talk and act out the following:
   Gardener: "Who let you into my garden?"
   Scamp: "No one."
   Gardener: "I'll chase you out."
   Scamp: "Try and catch me."
4. The "scamp" leaves the circle with the "gardener" following exact
   path through the circle.
5. The "scamp" may perform any stunt he wishes, such as crawling on all
   fours, and the "gardener" must copy his movements.
6. The "scamp" must make it back into the circle through the same place
   he left, before the "gardener" tags him.
7. If the "gardener" fails to perform all stunts demonstrated by the "scamp,"
   the "scamp" wins.
8. Change both players after every turn.

No. 10: Back to Back Tag (K - 4)

Formation: Scattered.
Equipment: None.
No. of Players: Class.
How to Play:

1. This game is played the same way as simple tag except that when any two players stand back to back, they are safe.
2. As soon as back to back players feel they are safe, they separate to find new partners.
3. Any player tagged becomes "it" and the game continues.

No. 11: Crab Tag (1 - 5)

Formation: Scattered.
Equipment: None.
No. of Players: Class.
How to Play:

1. This game is played the same way as simple tag, however, when a player is in the crab-walk position he is safe.

Teaching Suggestions:

1. Change the "safe" position to seal walk, elephant walk, etc.
2. Change "safe" position to a continuous exercise movement such as push-ups, etc. This could become a "fun" approach to the warm-up period.

No. 12: Dumbell Tag (1 - 4)

Formation: Scattered.
Equipment: Dumbbell (beanbag or towel).
No. of Players: Class.
How to Play:

1. One player is selected to be the "runner" and is given the "dumbbell."
2. One player is selected to be "it."
3. To start the game, "it" begins to chase the "dumbbell."
4. The player who has the "dumbbell" may, at any time, give it to any player.
5. The player to whom he gives the "dumbbell" must take it.
6. If "it" tags the player with the "dumbbell," that player becomes "it."
7. The new "it" must count to three before chasing anyone.

No. 13: Broncho Tag (2 - 6)

Formation: Groups of three in scattered formation.
Equipment: None.
No. of Players: Class.

How to Play:
1. One player is chosen to be "it."
2. All other players form groups of three. Each group forms a "broncho" by standing with the second and third players placing their arms around the waist of the player in front of him.
3. "It" tries to attach himself to the rear player of any "broncho." If he succeeds, the front player becomes "it."

No. 14: Red Rover (1 - 5)

Formation: Draw three lines each twenty feet apart. Place children on one end line and facing the center line.
Equipment: None.
No. of Players: Class.
How to Play:
1. One player is chosen to be "it" and stands on the center line.
2. All other players stand on one end line.
3. "It" calls "Red Rover, let Jim and Mary and Joe and Sue (4 or 5 players) go."
4. Players who were called run to opposite end line while "it" attempts to tag as many as possible before they reach the line.
5. Allow "It" three or four turns then choose a new "it."
6. Player with most caught wins the game.

No. 15: Midnight (1 - 4)

Formation: Draw two lines twenty-five to thirty feet apart. Place class behind one line known as the "home" line. In the middle of the opposite line draw a five foot square. The square is the "fox's" den.
Equipment: None.
No. of Players: Class.
How to Play:
1. One player is chosen to be the "fox."
2. The "fox" stands in his den marked off at one end of play area.
3. The "chickens" approach the "fox's" den and ask, "What time is it?"
4. The "fox" may answer any time.
5. When the "fox" answers "Midnight," this signals the "chickens" to run across their home line.
6. After saying "Midnight," the "fox" tries to tag as many "chickens" as he can before they cross the home line.
7. Any "chickens" tagged must go to the "fox's" den and assist the "fox" in catching the remaining "chickens."

No. 16: Partner Tag (2 - 5)

Formation: Partners scattered about the play area.
Equipment: None.
No. of Players: Class.
How to Play:
1. One child is chosen to be "it" and another to be the "chaser."
2. Other children select partners and link elbows.
3. The "chaser" tries to tag "it" who may run anywhere in the play area.
4. Whenever "it" links elbows with a player, he is safe.
5. The partner at the opposite side where "it" linked on becomes the new "it."
6. If the "chaser" tags "it," they change positions and the game continues.

No. 17: Circle Tag (3 - 6)

Formation: Circle.
Equipment: None.
No. of Players: 10 to 12.
How to Play:
1. Begin with players standing in circle formation with about six feet between each player.
2. On signal, every player runs in a clockwise direction around the circle.
3. Each player attempts to tag the player directly in front of him.
4. When a player is tagged, he takes two steps toward the center of the circle and sits down until the last player is tagged.
5. Last player left is the winner.

No. 18: Snatch Club (3 - 6)

Formation: Draw two goal lines spaced thirty feet apart. Arrange each team along each line and number players from one to the last player. Place a bowling pin or small object in the center of the playing area.
Equipment: Club or pin.
No. of Players: 10 to 12 per team.
How to Play:
1. Number each team from "one" to last player.
2. Teacher calls a number and players from each team run out to get the club.
3. If the player from Team A grabs the club and runs back to his baseline without being tagged by his opponent, his team receives one point. However, if he is tagged before reaching his baseline, the opposing team receives one point.
4. The game is continued with the teacher calling various numbers at random.

No. 19: Posture Tag (1 - 6)

Formation: Scattered.
Equipment: Two beanbags.
No. of Players: Class.
How to Play:
1. One player is chosen to be "it" and another to be the "runner."
2. The "runner" and "it" have beanbags on their heads. No hands are used to hold beanbag.
3. "It" chases the "runner" and tries to tag him.
4. The "runner" may transfer his beanbag to any player's head with that player becoming the new "runner."

No. 20: Commando (3 - 6)

Formation: Circle.
Equipment: None.
No. of Players: 8 to 10 in each circle.
How to Play:
1. One player is selected to be "it" and stands in the middle of the circle.
2. Circle players join hands.
3. On signal "it" tries to break through the circle by crawling under or over joined hands, or by breaking the handholds of the players.
4. If "it" breaks through, the two circle players chase him and the one who tags him becomes the new "it."
Teaching Suggestions:
Separate boys from girls.

No. 21: Hip Tag (3 - 6)

Formation: Scattered.
Equipment: Towel.
No. of Players: Class.
How to Play:
1. One player is selected to be "it" and is given a towel to tag other players. He must hit below the waist.
2. On signal, "it" tries to tag other players.
3. Any player tagged may assist "it" by holding other players and calling "it."
4. Last one tagged is the winner.

No. 22: Chain Tag (4 - 6)

Formation: Scattered.
Equipment: None.
No. of Players: Class.

How to Play:

1. One player is chosen to be "it" and tries to tag another player.
2. The first player tagged joins hands with "it" and helps tag other players. Both may use their free hand.
3. Each player tagged joins hands with the one who tagged him.
4. Continue game until last man is tagged.
5. No tag is fair if the line is broken.

No. 23: Poor Pussy Cat (2 - 6)

Formation: Circle, facing center.
Equipment: None.
No. of Players: Class.
How to Play:

1. Draw two circles with approximately three feet between each circle.
2. One child is chosen to be in the center of the circles.
3. Players stand on outer circle, facing, arms outstretched, and palms up.
4. The center player walks around the inside of the circle and strokes the hands of each player saying "Poor Pussy."
5. When the center player taps the hand of a player and says "Scat," that child attempts to catch the center player before he runs between the two circles and around and back to the vacated spot.
6. Whoever wins is safe and the other player continues the game.

No. 24: Squirrel in the Tree (1 - 4)

Formation: Scattered in groups of three.
Equipment: None.
No. of Players: Class.
How to Play:

1. Arrange class in groups of three and scattered about the play area.
2. Of the group, two join hands forming a hollow tree and the third player takes the part of the squirrel.
3. There should be two or three extra squirrels who are placed randomly throughout the play area.
4. On signal from the teacher, all squirrels must find a new tree.
5. After four turns, have children return to original positions and repeat game.

CLASSROOM GAMES

Classroom games or what are commonly known as "rainy day activities" are simply games, relays, or contests that can be played within the classroom. Usually these games require little or no furniture adjustment or elaborate equipment. For purposes of classification, these activities are usually designated as being "active" or "quiet"; however, the dividing line between the two is rather vague. One class with a great deal of enthusiasm may turn a quiet game into an active one and, of course, vice versa. For ease of selection, however, the more "vigorous" games will be listed under "active," and the less active under "quiet" activities.

When to Use Classroom Games

There is no season or time of day that should be set aside for quiet or active classroom games. Their use will depend upon such factors as the weather, amount of time and available space. Perhaps the most important criterion is the "mood" of the class. To illustrate, there are times during the day, especially after long periods of mental concentration, that a short classroom game will provide the needed relaxation for both teacher and student. However, the judgment of the teacher should determine when to, what to, and how to present a classroom activity.

Teaching Suggestions and Safety Precautions

If the classroom is to be used for quiet or active games, the teacher must survey the situation with respect to potential hazards, noise, and adequate playing space. The following suggestions, particularly those relating to safety and noise, should be carefully considered before introducing any classroom game.

1. Provide an opportunity for every member of the class to participate in the game.
2. Permit running only when there is adequate space between the aisles and around the circumference of the classroom.
3. Remove all materials such as books, pencils, and rulers from the tops of desks.
4. Require all children who are seated to keep their feet under their desks.
5. Avoid unnecessary noise by modifying verbal commands and require hand clapping rather than team or class yells.
6. Use beanbags or balloons rather than the regulation balls in games involving throwing. If a ball is necessary it may be wise to partially deflate it as well as limit the type of throw to an underhand or side toss.
7. Have players shake hands with each other as well as stipulate the side of the aisle each must be on in games involving passing of players in the aisles.

How to Select the Appropriate Game

The accompanying pages contain active and quiet games for elementary school children. First, decide on the type you want to use. Second, check the columns on the right to see whether you want a game involving guessing, tagging, imitating, manipulating, or an element of surprise. Finally, check to see if you have the necessary equipment.

Active and Quiet Classroom Games

No.	Name of Game	K	1	2	3	4	5	6	Page	Guessing	Relay	Imitation	Tag	Surprise	Small Manipulation
ACTIVE CLASSROOM GAMES															
1.	Do This, Do That	X	X	X	X				165	X		X		X	X
2.	Fox and Rabbit	X	X						165					X	X
3.	Beanbag Basket Relay	X	X	X	X				165		X				X
4.	I'm Tall, I'm Small	X	X						166	X		X		X	X
5.	Forty Ways to Get There	X	X	X	X	X			166			X			
6.	Ringmaster	X	X	X	X				166			X			
7.	Follow the Leader	X	X	X	X				167			X			
8.	Go Go Stop	X	X	X	X				167	X				X	
9.	Animal Trap	X	X	X					167	X		X		X	
10.	Duck, Duck, Goose	X	X	X	X				168	X			X	X	
11.	A-Tisket, A-Tasket	X	X						168				X	X	
12.	Circle Spot	X	X	X	X	X			168				X	X	
13.	Musical Chairs	X	X	X	X	X	X	X	169				X	X	
14.	Steal the Bacon				X	X	X	X	169				X	X	X
15.	Seat Tag			X	X	X	X	X	169				X	X	
16.	Beanbag Pile			X	X	X	X	X	170		X			X	
17.	Vis-a-vis			X	X	X	X	X	170	X				X	
18.	Simon Says		X	X	X	X	X	X	171			X		X	
19.	Poor House			X	X	X	X		171					X	
20.	Who's Leading			X	X	X	X	X	171	X				X	
21.	Balloon Base			X	X	X	X	X	172						X
QUIET CLASSROOM GAMES															
22.	My Ship Is Loaded	X	X	X					172			X		X	
23.	Crumple and Toss		X	X	X				172		X				X
24.	I Saw		X	X	X				173	X		X			X
25.	Hens and Chickens	X	X						173	X		X		X	
26.	Ring, Bell, Ring	X	X						173	X				X	X
27.	Who Moves?	X	X	X					174	X				X	
28.	Hide the Thimble	X	X	X	X				174	X				X	
29.	Crambo		X	X	X				174	X				X	
30.	Clothespin Drop				X	X	X	X	175		X				X
31.	Hat Race		X	X	X	X	X	X	175		X				X
32.	Tick-Tack-Toe				X	X	X	X	175		X			X	X
33.	Rattlesnake and Bumble Bee				X	X	X	X	176	X		X		X	
34.	Human Checkers					X	X	X	176		X			X	
35.	Puzzled Words					X	X	X	176	X				X	X
36.	Spell Act				X	X	X	X	177	X		X		X	X
37.	Charades						X	X	177	X				X	X

ACTIVE CLASSROOM GAMES

No. 1: Do This, Do That (K - 3)

Formation: Sitting or standing with leader facing class.
Equipment: None.
No. of Players: Class.
How to Play:

1. The leader stands at the front of the class and calls out "Do this," and moves in any way he desires. Everyone must imitate his movement.
2. When the leader calls "Do that" and moves into a new position, everyone must stand still.
3. Children who fail to move on "Do this" or "Do that" are eliminated from the game.
4. After one-half of the class are eliminated the teacher chooses another leader.

No. 2: Fox and Rabbit (K - 1)

Formation: Single circle or children seated.
Equipment: Two beanbags.
No. of Players: Class.
How to Play:

1. One beanbag called the "rabbit" is passed around the circle.
2. A second beanbag known as the "fox" is started around the circle.
3. When the "fox" catches the "rabbit," the game ends.
4. Start each game with a new player.

No. 3: Beanbag Basket Relay (K - 3)

Formation: Lines facing a basket about six to eight feet in front of first player.
Equipment: Beanbags, wastepaper baskets, or hoops.
No. of Players: Class.
How to Play:

1. Arrange pupils in rows facing the baskets.
2. Draw a line across the front of the rows.
3. On command, the first pupil attempts to throw beanbag into basket. (One point for each basket)
4. After shooting, each player retrieves his beanbag, returns it to the next player and tells the teacher his score.
5. Continue until last player has had his turn.
6. Team with highest score wins.

No. 4: I'm Tall, I'm Small (K - 1)

Formation: Single circle with one child in center.
Equipment: None.
No. of Players: Class.
How to Play:
1. One child stands in the center of the circle with his eyes closed.
2. Circle players walk slowly around singing the following verse:
    > I'm tall, I'm very small,
    > I'm small, I'm very tall
    > Sometimes I'm tall
    > Sometimes I'm small
    > Guess what I am now.
3. As children walk and sing "tall," "very tall," or "small," or "very small," they stretch up or stoop down depending on the words.
4. At the end of the singing, the teacher signals circle players to assume a stretching or stooping position.
5. The center player then guesses which position they have taken.
6. If the center player guesses correctly, he remains; if unsuccessful, a new player is selected.

No. 5: Forty Ways to Get There (K - 4)

Formation: Seated.
Equipment: None.
No. of Players: Class.
How to Play:
1. Each child is given a chance to move across the front of the room in any manner he wishes.
2. Once a child has used a "walk," "hop," or whatever movement, no one following may copy that movement.
3. Any novel way of moving is acceptable.

No. 6: Ringmaster (K - 3)

Formation: Single circle with one child in center.
Equipment: None.
No. of Players: Class.
How to Play:
1. One child is selected to be "Ringmaster" and stands in the center of the circle.
2. The "Ringmaster" moves about the center of circle pretending to crack his whip and calls out the names of various animals.
3. The circle players then imitate the animals.
4. If the "Ringmaster" calls out "All join the parade," the children may imitate any animal they wish.

No. 7: Follow the Leader (K - 3)

Formation: Single lines.
Equipment: None.
No. of Players: Class.
How to Play:
1. Arrange the class in two or three lines of ten to twelve players.
2. The leader walks and begins to perform any kind of movement such as hands on head, arms sideward, or leaping from one spot to another.
3. All other players in his line must copy the movement.
4. If anyone fails to perform the feat, he goes to the back of the line.
Teaching Suggestions:
Play the game in a circle formation with the leader standing in the center.

No. 8: Go Go Stop (K - 3)

Formation: Single line with children facing sideways.
Equipment: None.
No. of Players: Class.
How to Play:
1. The teacher says "Go, Go, Go," and all must run straight ahead.
2. When the teacher says "Stop," all must stop.
3. If a child fails to stop, he must return to starting line and begin again.
Teaching Suggestions:
1. Use other locomotor movements such as skip, slide, hop, etc.
2. Turn back to students when calling "Go, go, go," then turn around and call "Stop." This will increase the element of surprise.

No. 9: Animal Trap (K - 2)

Formation: One-half of the class form a circle; the other half scatter outside the circle.
Equipment: None.
No. of Players: Class.
How to Play:
1. Circle players join hands.
2. All other players decide on what kind of animal they want to be and stand outside the circle.
3. On signal from the teacher, the "animals" run in and out of the "trap."
4. When the teacher claps her hand the trap is closed.
5. All animals caught inside join the circle.
6. After all animals have been caught, change positions and start a new game.

No. 10: Duck, Duck, Goose (K - 3)

Formation:	Single circle with one child standing outside of the circle.
Equipment:	None.
No. of Players:	Class.

How to Play:

1. One child is selected to be "it" and stands outside the circle.
2. "It" runs around the circle, touches one child and says "duck," touches another and says "duck," and touches a third and says "goose."
3. The "goose" chases "it" who now runs around the circle back to the "goose's" place before the "goose" can tag him.
4. If the "goose" tags "it" before he gets into place, he continues to be "it."
5. If "it" is successful, the "goose" becomes "it" and the game continues.

No. 11: A-Tisket, A-Tasket (K - 1)

Formation:	Circle facing center with one child outside of circle.
Equipment:	Beanbag.
No. of Players:	12 to 20.

How to Play:

1. One player is chosen to be "it" and walks around outside of circle with a beanbag in his hand.
2. While "it" is walking around the outside, the circle players sing the following:

> A-Tisket, A-Tasket,
> A green and yellow basket,
> I sent a letter to my love,
> and on the way I dropped it,
> I dropped it, I dropped it.
> And on the way I dropped it.

3. As soon as the circle players sing "I dropped it," "it" drops the beanbag immediately behind a circle player and begins to run around the circle.
4. The circle player immediately in front of the beanbag must pick it up and run after "it" and tag him before he returns to the vacant spot.
5. If "it" makes it back before being tagged he stays in the circle and the chaser becomes "it." If "it" is tagged before reaching the spot, he remains "it."

No. 12: Circle Spot (K - 4)

Formation:	Circle formation with four feet between each player.
Equipment:	Beanbags and blocks.
No. of Players:	10 to 20.

How to Play:
1. One child is chosen to be "it" and stands in the center of the circle. Circle players stand with at least four feet between each player with a beanbag on the floor immediately in front of them.
2. On signal from teacher, everyone "walks," "skips," etc., around outside of circle of beanbags.
3. On second signal everyone, including "it," tries to place one foot on a beanbag.
4. The "extra" child becomes "it" and takes his place in the center of the circle.

No. 13: Musical Chairs (K-6)

Formation: Circle formation with two to three feet between each chair.
Equipment: Chairs.
No. of Players: Class.

How to Play:
1. Arrange chairs in a circle pattern around room. There should be one less chair than number of children.
2. Use musical accompaniment such as a record, percussion instruments, or clapping for marching or skipping around chairs.
3. When music begins, all march around chairs; when it stops all try to sit on a chair.
4. The "extra" player who remains standing must take a chair from the circle and sit away from the players.
5. Last player remaining is the winner.

No. 14: Steal the Bacon (3 - 6)

Formation: Lines facing each other.
Equipment: Stick or eraser.
No. of Players: 2 to 15 on each team.

How to Play:
1. Each team is numbered from one to fifteen.
2. Place a stick in the center between the two lines.
3. A number is called and players with that number try to retrieve the stick without being tagged by the opposing player.
4. If number two from team A picks the stick up first, number two from team B tries to tag him before he crosses his line.

No. 15: Seat Tag (2 - 6)

Formation: Seated in rows.
Equipment: None.
No. of Players: Class.

How to Play:

1. Two players are selected; one is "it" and the other is the runner.
2. Other players remain seated.
3. "It" begins to chase the "runner" who may avoid being tagged by sitting with any player.
4. The player with whom the "runner" sits immediately becomes the new runner.
5. If the "runner" is tagged, he becomes "it" and the game continues.

Teaching Suggestions:

For safety, stipulate that if the runner touches a desk or chair while he is running, he automatically becomes "it."

No. 16: Beanbag Pile (2 - 6)

Formation: Sitting on floor in rows.
Equipment: One beanbag for each member.
No. of Players: 5 or 6 in each row.

How to Play:

1. Players are seated in a single line formation with beanbags placed in a pile in front of the first player.
2. On signal "go," the first player takes a bag and passes it to the second player.
3. The remaining beanbags are passed back one at a time.
4. The last player lays the first beanbag on the floor.
5. Each succeeding bag must be placed one on top of the other with ONLY the first beanbag touching the floor.
6. The stack must stand without any assistance from the stacker.
7. If the stack falls, it must be restacked.
8. The first team to pile the bags correctly wins the relay.

No. 17: Vis-a-Vis (2 - 6)

Formation: Scattered with partners.
Equipment: None.
No. of Players: Class.

How to Play:

1. One child is chosen to stand among partners.
2. If the teacher calls "back to back" or "face to face," the children do as directed.
3. If the teacher calls "busy bee," everyone, including the extra child, must find a new partner.
4. The child who fails to get a new partner becomes the extra player.

Teaching Suggestions:

After the children have learned the game, allow the extra player to call the directions.

No. 18: Simon Says (1 - 6)

Formation: Seated in rows, one player in front of class.
Equipment: None.
No. of Players: Class.
How to Play:
1. One player is chosen as leader and comes to the front of the class.
2. Other players remain at their seats.
3. Players at seats follow the leader's action when he prefaces his instructions with "Simon says." For example: "Simon says hands on head place." All should follow this movement. If the leader says "Hands on hips place," no one should move.
4. Any player who commits an error must pay a forfeit or be dropped from the game.
Teaching Suggestions:
Teams can be organized and count number of errors to make it a contest.

No. 19: Poor House (3 - 6)

Formation: Semicircle or horseshoe formation.
Equipment: None.
No. of Players: Class.
How to Play:
1. Players choose partners and sit in chairs placed in a horseshoe pattern.
2. Two chairs representing the poorhouse are placed at the open end of the horseshoe formation.
3. Each couple has a number, for example, 1, 2, 3, and must keep their hands joined throughout the game.
4. Game begins with one couple in the poorhouse calling out two numbers.
5. The couples whose numbers were called must change places.
6. During the change-over the poorhouse couple attempts to reach the chairs vacated by one of the couples.

No. 20: Who's Leading (2 - 6)

Formation: Circle formation.
Equipment: None.
No. of Players: Class.
How to Play:
1. One player is chosen to be "it" and stands outside of the circle with hands over his eyes.
2. The teacher then selects a player in the circle to be a "leader." The leader starts any motion he chooses (blinking eyes, waving arms over head, etc.).
3. "It" opens his eyes and tries to guess who the leader is.
4. As the game progresses, the leader slyly switches to other movements and it is the task of "it" to find this person.
5. Allow two or three guesses, then change "leader" and "it."

No. 21: Balloon Base (2 - 6)

Formation:	Move desks and chairs back against wall.
Equipment:	Balloons.
No. of Players:	Class—2 teams.

How to Play:
1. Batter starts game by hitting balloon with an open hand into the "field."
2. Fielders, with "open-hand hitting," attempt to hit balloon across the home base line before the batter walks to first base and home.
3. If the fielders catch the ball the batter is safe.
4. Batter is out if the balloon does not get into the air on the first try.
5. Three outs and teams exchange position.
6. One point is awarded for each run.

QUIET CLASSROOM GAMES

No. 22: My Ship Is Loaded (K - 2)

Formation:	Seated in circle.
Equipment:	Utility Ball (9" or 13").
No. of Players:	Class.

How to Play:
1. One child starts rolling a ball to another player and says, "My ship is loaded with cars." (Any cargo he wishes.)
2. The player receives the ball ("2 cars"), and repeats what the first child said and adds a new item. He would say "My ship is loaded with cars and hats," as he rolls the ball to another player.
3. Each player, in turn, adds a new item.
4. When a child fails to repeat all the "cargo," the ball is given to a player on his right who starts a new game.

No. 23: Crumple and Toss (K - 3)

Formation:	Line facing baskets with front player about ten feet from the basket.
Equipment:	Newspapers, wastebaskets, or cardboard boxes.
No. of Players:	Class.

How to Play:
1. Each player is given a piece of newspaper which he must crumple with one hand.
2. The first player attempts to throw his crumpled paper into the wastepaper basket.
3. After each child takes his turn, he goes to the back of the line and the next player moves up to the line and takes a turn.
4. The team with the largest number of papers in the basket wins.

No. 24: I Saw (1 - 3)

Formation: One child stands facing others seated at desks.
Equipment: None.
No. of Players: Class.
How to Play:

1. The child standing is "it" and says "On my way to school I saw . . . . . ,"
   and pantomimes what he saw.
2. The child who correctly guesses what he saw becomes "it."
3. If no one guesses correctly in five tries, "it" tells what he saw.
4. If the class decides that his imitation was too poor, he must choose
   a new "it."
5. If the class decides the imitation was a good one and they did not guess
   it within five tries, "it" continues for another time.

No. 25: Hens and Chickens (K - 1)

Formation: Seated.
Equipment: None.
No. of Players: Class.
How to Play:

1. One child is chosen to be the "hen" and walks to cloakroom or hall.
2. While "hen" is out of room, the teacher walks around room tapping
   several children who become chickens.
3. All children now place their heads on their desks, hiding their faces
   in their arms.
4. The "hen" comes in and moves about the room saying "cluck, cluck."
5. All children keep their heads down and the "chickens" answer with
   "peep, peep."
6. The "hen" listens and taps any child on the head she believes is a chicken.
7. If the "hen" is correct, the "chicken" must sit up straight; if incorrect,
   he continues to hide his head.
8. After the "hen" has selected all the chickens, she or the teacher selects
   a new "hen."

No. 26: Ring, Bell, Ring (K - 1)

Formation: Seated.
Equipment: Small bell.
No. of Players: Class.
How to Play:

1. One child is chosen to be "it" and closes his eyes while another child
   hides the bell.
2. The child with the bell holds it so that no sound is heard and runs to
   another part of the room.

3. The teacher, after seeing the child with the bell is located and ready, turns to the child with eyes covered and tells him to call.
4. The child with eyes still covered calls "ring, bell, ring."
5. The child with the bell rings it a few short times.
6. The first child must now guess the place where the bell is.
7. If he points in right direction, he becomes the bell ringer.
8. Change "guesser" after each turn.

No. 27: Who Moves? (K - 2)

Formation: Line formation in front of class.
Equipment: None.
No. of Players: Class.
How to Play:
1. Five children are selected by the teacher to stand in front of class.
2. Children who are seated look at the line, then lay their heads on their arms.
3. While the children have their heads down, the teacher changes the positions of two or three children in the line.
4. On a signal from the teacher, the seated children look at the line in front of the class.
5. One child is selected to arrange the line as it was in the first place.

No. 28: Hide the Thimble (K - 3)

Formation: None.
Equipment: Small object.
No. of Players: Class.
How to Play:
1. Class decides on an object to be hidden. It should be a small object such as an eraser or small toy.
2. The teacher chooses one player to be the "hunter" and sends him out of the room while the class hides the "object."
3. As the "hunter" enters the room and approaches or moves away from the object, the class may hum or clap, loudly or softly, depending upon the position of the "hunter" to the object.
4. When the "hunter" finds the object, he chooses another hunter.
Teaching Suggestions:
Use various means of "hinting" such as raising or lowering hands, hissing, etc.

No. 29: Crambo (1 - 3)

Formation: Seated.
Equipment: None.
No. of Players: Class.

How to Play:
1. One child is chosen to be "it."
2. "It" starts game by saying, "I am thinking of something (inside or outside the room) that rhymes with "rain."
3. Other players ask "Is it a train?" "Is it a drain?" etc.
4. The child who guesses the correct answer has the next turn.

No. 30: Clothespin Drop (3 - 6)

Formation: Rows.
Equipment: Milk bottle or container and five clothespins for each row.
No. of Players: Class.
How to Play:
1. Each row represents one team.
2. Place a milk bottle in front of each row.
3. Players take turns standing erect and above the bottle and drop the clothespins, one at a time, into the bottle.
4. Each clothespin counts one point.

No. 31: Hat Race (1 - 6)

Formation: Rows.
Equipment: Ruler and Hat.
No. of Players: Class.
How to Play:
1. Every other row participates.
2. Each player stands in the aisle with a ruler in his right hand.
3. The first player has a hat which he places on his ruler.
4. On the signal "go," the front player passes the hat over his right shoulder to number two player.
5. Number two takes the hat with his ruler and passes it over his shoulder to number three.
6. The last player in the row walks down the empty aisle to the front of his line.
7. If a player drops the hat, he must pick it up with the ruler; no hands are allowed.
8. Everyone shifts back one position and the relay continues until all players are back in their original positions.
Teaching Suggestions:
Try same sitting down.

No. 32: Tick-Tack-Toe (3 - 6)

Formation: Seated in rows.
Equipment: Chalk.

No. of Players: Class.

How to Play:

1. Number each row and draw a tick-tack-toe diagram on the board between the two competing teams.
2. Only two teams play at one time.
3. The teacher chooses the starting team.
4. The first player from one team makes an "X" in one of the spaces.
5. The first player from the other team marks an "O" in one of the remaining spaces.
6. Continue alternating until one team gets three marks in a row.

No. 33: Rattlesnake and Bumble Bee (3 - 6)

Formation: Seated at desks or tables.
Equipment: 2 small unlike objects.
No. of Players: 2 equal teams.

How to Play:

1. One player is chosen from each team and is sent out of the room.
2. While the two players are out, team captains hide the two articles. (Team A hides for Team B and vice versa.)
3. The two players return and begin looking for their article.
4. Members of either team "buzz" or "hiss" according to the nearness each player is to his object.
5. Repeat with two new "finders."
6. One point for player and his team who first find the object.

No. 34: Human Checkers (4-6)

Formation: On chairs in a row.
Equipment: 7 chairs.
No. of Players: 6 on each team.

How to Play:

1. Place seven chairs in a row.
2. Place three girls on three chairs at one end; three boys at the other end.
3. The object is to move the girls to the boys' chairs and the boys to the girls' chairs in fifteen moves.
4. Only one move can be made at one time. For example: Girl number three moves to the spare chair; second move, boy number four jumps girl number three who is now in the spare position, etc.
5. Moves are made by sliding into an open chair or "jumping" over one person.
6. Players cannot move backwards.

No. 35: Puzzled Words (4 - 6)

Formation: Groups of 5 to 8 players.
Equipment: Pieces of paper.

No. of Players: Class.
How to Play:
1. Organize the class into groups of five to six children.
2. The teacher has previously printed several words on separate pieces of paper. She has cut the words and shuffled them into piles of letters.
3. Each group receives a "pile of letters" which, after reshuffling, will form a word.
4. On a signal from the teacher, each group tries to put their word together.
5. First team to assemble their word wins the game.
Teaching Suggestions:
After the group puts the word together, allow them to act out the word for the other children to guess.

No. 36: Spell Act (3 - 6)

Formation: Two teams on opposite sides of room.
Equipment: None.
No. of Players: Class.
How to Play:
1. Play this game as in regular spelling match.
2. Add the following:
   The letters "A" and "T" must not be spoken but must be indicated as follows:
   "A" scratch right ear and raise left hand.
   "T" scratch left ear and raise right hand.

No. 37: Charades (5 - 6)

Formation: Small groups.
Equipment: None.
No. of Players: Class.
How to Play:
1. Five or six groups are selected and allowed sufficient time to work out a charade together.
2. A captain is elected from each group.
3. The word or object chosen by a group should have syllables to make it easier to act out.
4. All dramatizations must be in pantomime.
5. One group acts out its charade in front of the class.
6. The captain of the group asks the class to guess the syllable or complete word.
7. If the word has not been guessed within a certain time, the captain tells the class and the next group has its turn.
Teaching Suggestions:
Ask class to decide on a specific category from which all words must be chosen. Example: Books, cities, famous names, songs, etc.

INDIVIDUAL AND DUAL ACTIVITIES

There are a few games for elementary school-age children that can be played by one, two (singles), three, or four (doubles) players. These are generally referred to as individual or dual activities and are usually played before school, at recess, lunch, and after school. The majority of these games are recreational in nature. However, games such as paddle tennis and one-wall handball can be used to teach the basic skills and rules of the more advanced games.

With the trend toward open area schools and individualized teaching, individual and dual games will become more important and popular, particularly with upper elementary school-age children.

INDIVIDUAL AND DUAL SPORTS

No.	Name of Game	Page	Skills	Suggested Grade Level						
				K	1	2	3	4	5	6
1.	American Hopscotch	178	throw, hop		X	X	X			
2.	French Hopscotch	179	throw, hop		X	X	X			
3.	Italian Hopscotch	180	throw, hop		X	X	X			
4.	Marbles	181	shoot		X	X	X	X	X	X
5.	Jacks	181	throw, catch, balance		X	X	X	X		
6.	Four Square	181	bounce			X	X	X	X	
7.	Tether Ball	182	hit			X	X	X	X	
8.	Paddle Ball	183	run, hit, serve			X	X	X	X	
9.	One Wall Handball	184	run, hit, serve						X	X
10.	Deck Tennis	185	run, throw, catch				X	X	X	X
11.	Paddle Tennis	186	run, serve, hit						X	X

No. 1: American Hopscotch (1 - 3)

Formation: Draw the pattern as shown in the diagram below.

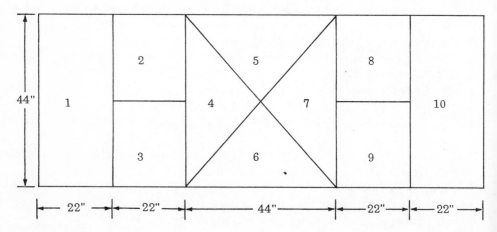

Equipment: Beanbags, buttons, beads, or other small objects.

No. of Players: 6 to 8 on each team.

How to Play:

1. Arrange teams in a file formation with player number one facing square number one.
2. Player number one stands on one foot outside area one and holds a "puck" in his hand.
3. Player number one tosses the "puck" into area one then hops over this area and lands with left foot in area two and right foot in area three.[2]
4. Hop and land on one foot in area four.
5. Hop and land with left foot in area five and right foot in area six.
6. Continue pattern, hopping and landing with one foot in single spaces and two feet in adjacent areas.
7. Two hops are permitted in area ten in order to turn and be in a ready position for the return movements.
8. Upon landing in areas two and three, lean forward, pick up "puck" and hop out.
9. Player number one now tosses the puck into area two and repeats pattern. She must, however, modify her hopping to avoid landing in area two.
10. On the return movement, player one must land on one foot in area three, pick up "puck," hop over to area two then to area one and out.
11. Player one continues pattern through area ten and back.
12. A player is out if he steps on a line, tosses the "puck" on a line or in the wrong area, changes feet on single hops, or touches hand or other foot during any hopping or retrieving movement.
13. When a child commits an error, he goes to the back of the line.

No. 2: French Hopscotch (1 - 3)

Formation: Draw the pattern as shown in the diagram below.

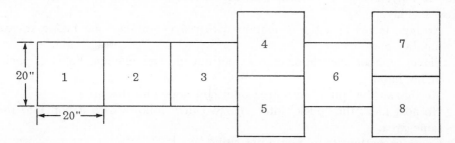

Equipment: Beanbags, beads, buttons, or other small objects.

No. of Players: 6 to 8 on each team.

---

2. Landing with each foot in adjacent areas is known as "spread eagle."

How to Play:

The game follows the same basic rules as American Hopscotch (No. 1), the player hopping on one foot in each single square and two feet in adjacent squares. When a player lands with one foot in area seven and the other in area eight, he must jump up and turn around in the air and land with feet in the same areas.

No. 3: Italian Hopscotch (1 - 3)

Formation: Draw the pattern as shown in the diagram.

8	7	6	5
1	2	3	4

12"

12"

Equipment: Beanbags, buttons, beads, or other small objects.

No. of Players: 6 to 8 on each team.

How to Play:

1. Arrange teams in a file formation with player number one facing square number one.
2. Player number one stands on one foot outside area one and holds a "puck" in his hand.
3. He throws the "puck" into area one then hops into this area.
4. He next kicks the "puck" into area two then follows with a hop into the same area.
5. Continue pattern to area number eight.
6. When he reaches area eight, he may place both feet on the ground, pick-up "puck" and hop backwards through all squares to the starting position.
7. A player is out if he steps on a line; if his puck stops on a line; if both feet are put down in any area except eight; or if he changes feet.
8. When a child commits an error he goes to the back of the line.

No. 4: Marbles (1 - 6)

Formation: Circle (five to six feet in diameter)
Equipment: Marbles—various sizes.
No. of Players: 2 - 6 players.

How to Play:
1. Each player places one or two marbles in the center of the circle.
2. Playing order is determined by each player throwing his shooting marble (shooter is called "taw") toward a line drawn 6 to 10 feet away. Players shoot in the order of the nearest marble to the line.
3. A player may shoot from anywhere outside of the circle. He tries to knock the marbles outside of the large circle. His "taw" must remain inside the circle. If successful he continues from where his taw stopped.
4. After each player has had his turn, he removes his "taw" from the circle.
5. At the end of the game all marbles "should" be returned to their owners. (The author still remembers his boyhood days when he would come home with more marbles than he started with, and too, when the reverse was the case.)

No. 5: Jacks (1 - 4)

Formation: Circle on a hard surface.
Equipment: 6 jacks and a small rubber ball.
No. of Players: 2 - 6.

How to Play:
1. The first player tosses the jacks on the ground.
2. The first player throws the ball into the air, picks up one jack, and catches the ball before it lands on the ground.
3. If successful, the jack is held in the other hand and the player continues until all jacks are picked up. If unsuccessful, the next player takes his turn.
4. After a player has successfully picked up all jacks one at a time, he repeats the game picking up two at a time. Continue with "3's," "4's," "5's" and "6's."

Variations:
1. Pigs in the Pen: Jacks are brushed into other hand (held in cupped position).
2. Eggs in the Basket: Jacks are picked up and transferred to opposite hand before the ball is caught.
3. Lazy Susan: The ball is allowed to bounce twice before the jacks are picked up.

No. 6: Four Square (3 - 6)

Formation: Draw a sixteen foot square, then divide it into four equal four foot squares. Designate each square as A, B, C, and D, respectively.

Equipment: Large utility ball.
Number of Players: 5 - 7 players per group.
How to Play:

1. One player stands in each square (A, B, C, and D).
2. Player D starts the game by bouncing the ball, then he hits it with one or two hands so it bounces in one of the other three squares.
3. Player who receives the ball must hit it after one bounce to any of the other three squares.
4. Game proceeds until one player fails to return the ball properly or a foul is committed.
5. When a foul or failed return is committed, the offending player is eliminated and goes to the end of the waiting line. All players move one square toward D.
6. Waiting player always moves to Square A.

Basic Rules:

1. The ball must arch before landing; it cannot be struck downward.
2. Service always begins from Square D.
3. A player may go anywhere to return a fair ball (out of his own court, if necessary).
4. Ball may not be held.

Fouls:

1. A ball that hits any line.
2. A ball struck with closed fists.
3. A ball that hits a player who is standing in his own square.

No. 7: Tether Ball (3 - 6)

Formation: Draw the tether court area as shown in the diagram.

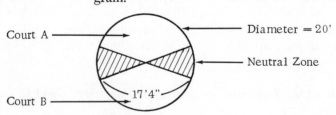

Court A ——
                                            —— Diameter = 20'

                                            —— Neutral Zone

Court B ——   17'4"

Equipment: Tether ball.
Number of Players: 2.
How to Play:

1. One player stands in each court.
2. One player starts the game by throwing the ball into the air and hitting it with the hand or fist in the direction he chooses.
3. The opposing player may not strike the ball until it passes him on the second swing around the pole. He must also strike it in the opposite direction.

4. The player who first winds the ball around the pole is the winner. (A five foot foul line may be drawn around the pole. In this case the players must wind it around the pole and above the foul line.)

Fouls:

1. Hitting ball with any part of the body other than hands.
2. Touching the pole.
3. Catching the ball.
4. Hitting the rope.
5. Playing the ball while standing outside the playing area.
6. Stepping in the neutral zone.
7. Throwing the ball.
8. Winding ball below five foot foul mark.

Penalty for fouls: forfeits game to opponent.

No. 8: Paddle Ball (3 - 6)

Formation: Draw a court outline as shown in the diagram below. Note: any available wall and floor space can be used. Use chalk or plastic tape to mark court dimensions.

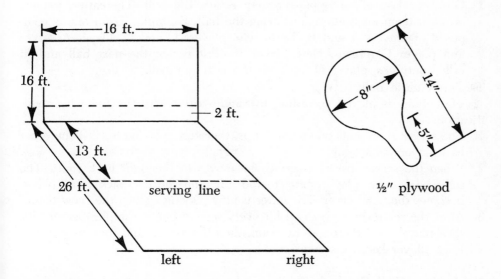

Equipment: Tennis ball and bat.

Number of Players: Singles (2 players), doubles (4 players), and triples (3 players)

How to Play:

Singles: Paddle Ball.

1. The server may stand anywhere between the wall and the serving line.

2. The server must bounce the ball, then hit it toward the front wall. The ball must hit the wall above the two foot line, land behind the serving line and inside the court. He is allowed one serve.

3. The receiver must wait until the ball has bounced once then hit it back to the wall.

4. After the serve, all returned balls by either player must hit above the two foot line but may land anywhere inside the full court area (13 ft. × 26 ft.).

5. If the server hits the ball above the line and back over the serving line, and the receiver fails to return the ball, the server receives one point. He continues serving until he faults or misses the ball.

6. Any player may go outside the court to return a ball.

7. Game may be played to 11, 15, or 21 points.

Doubles: Paddle Ball.

The game is played according to Singles Rules with the following modifications:

1. On the serve, the server's teammate should stand outside the court when the serve is being made. This prevents any hindrance to the opponent who is trying to return the service.

2. After the server loses his serve his teammate takes his turn. Each team, therefore, has two serves in succession.

3. On the serve, either opponent may return the ball. Thereafter, players on each team must alternate hitting the ball. Example: Team one is composed of players A and B. Team two, players C and D. Player A serves and player C returns. Now player B must return the next ball and, if rally continues, player D must hit the next fair ball.

Triples: Paddle Ball.

The game is played according to Singles rules with the following modifications:

1. The server represents one team. He is, therefore, playing against the other two players as a team.

2. When the server loses his service he moves to the right back court. The right back court player shifts to the left, and the left back court player becomes the new server. The latter is now playing against the "new team."

3. After the serve the server will hit every second ball. Example: Server hits, then player A of the opposing team, then the server, and then player B.

4. Each player keeps his own score.

No. 9: One Wall Handball (5 - 6)

Formation: Same court size as Paddle Ball, however the two-foot wall line is not used in Handball.

Equipment: Tennis ball, sponge rubber ball, or Oregon size regulation handball.

No. of Players: Two, three, or four.

How to Play:

This game is played according to Paddle Ball rules with the following modifications:

1. On the serve, the ball may hit anywhere on the front wall (two foot line not used) then back over serving line.
2. The receiver may hit the ball "on the fly" (before it bounces) or after the bounce.
3. All players must hit the ball with their hand. Players may not catch the ball then hit it. Two hand hits are not permitted.

No. 10: Deck Tennis (3 - 6)

Formation: Draw a court outline as shown in the diagram below, or use any existing court—volleyball, badminton, etc.

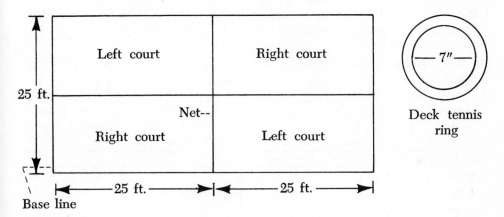

Deck tennis ring

Equipment: Deck tennis ring. These can be purchased through local sports stores or made from 2″ diameter rope or plastic tubing. (see Appendix A)

No. of Players: Singles (2 players) or Doubles (4 players)

How to Play:

Singles.

1. The server must stand behind the base line and on the right half of the court. He must deliver the ring in a forehand fashion with the ring rising to an arch before it begins to descend into the opponent's right court. The server must alternate courts on each serve.
2. The receiver must catch the ring with one hand and immediately return the ring with a forehand upward toss to any part of the opponent's court.
3. The server scores a point if the receiver fails to return the ring or commits one of the following fouls:

a. Catches ring with two hands.
b. Changes ring to other hand before returning it.
c. Holds ring too long before returning. (Count three seconds)
d. Steps over net line.
e. Fails to cause the ring to arc before it begins to descend into opponent's court.
4. If the server faults or misses the return throw, there is a change in the server. However, no point is scored by the opposing team.
5. Game may be played to 11, 15, or 21 points.
Doubles.

The game is played according to singles rules with the following modifications:
1. Each team has two serves in succession.
2. After the receiver has returned the server's toss, any player may return each alternate toss. Example: Player A from Team one serves. Player C of Team two catches and returns right back to player A. It is legal for player A to catch and return.

No. 11: Paddle Tennis (5 - 6)

Formation: Draw a court outline as shown in the diagram below. Use existing badminton court if available.

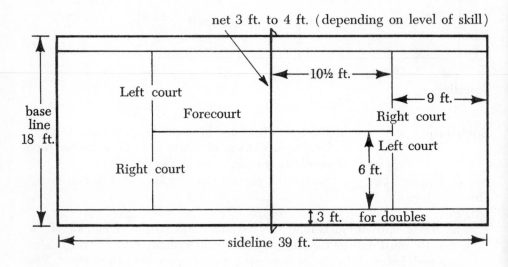

Equipment: Four paddles (see diagram under paddle ball), tennis or sponge rubber ball.
No. of Players: Singles (2 players) or Doubles (4 players).

How to Play:

Singles.

1. The server must stand behind the baseline and on the right-hand side of the court.
2. The server must bounce the ball then hit it over the net into the opponent's right forecourt.
3. The receiver must hit the ball back again after it has bounced once.
4. After the receiver returns the serve the ball may be hit "on the volley" or after one bounce. For singles, it must land inside the small court.
5. Simple scoring may be used with each player serving until he loses by fault or fails to return a ball. Score may be 11, 15, or 21 points. Paddle tennis may be played and scored according to proper tennis rules. In tennis, a player serves for one full game, then his opponent serves, with each, in turn, alternating until a set (6 games) is completed. A single game is scored 15 points (1st point), 30 points (2nd point) 40 points (3rd point), and game (4th point). If both players have 40 points, this is called DEUCE. When this occurs one player must win two successive points. After DEUCE, the next point is called ADVANTAGE, and followed by GAME. If the server has the ADVANTAGE, it is called "ADVANTAGE-IN." If the receiver has the ADVANTAGE it is called "ADVANTAGE-OUT."

Doubles.

The game is played according to singles with the following modifications:

1. One player serves the full game. On each point, however, he alternates serving from right to left side and vice-versa.
2. Service changes after each game.
3. After the receiver returns the service the ball may be hit by any member of the team.
4. The additional 3 foot alley is used for doubles.

Selected References

ANDERSON, M. H.; ELLIOT, M. E.; and LaBERGE, J. *Play with a Purpose.* New York: Harper & Row, Publishers, 1966.

DAUER, VICTOR, P. *Fitness for Elementary School Children through Physical Education.* Minneapolis: Burgess Publishing Co., 1962.

FAIT, HOLLIS E. *Physical Education for the Elementary School Child.* Philadelphia: W. B. Saunders Co., 1964.

Games, Stunts, Relays for Titus Scooters, R. E. Titus Gym Scooter Co., Winfield, Kansas, 1956.

Guide for Teaching Physical Education: Grades 1-6, State Department of Education, Columbia, S.C.: 1961.

HALSEY, E., and PORTER, L. *Physical Education for Children,* Revised Edition. New York: Holt, Rinehart & Winston, Inc., 1967.

How We Do It Game Book, 3rd Edition, Washington, D.C.: American Association for Health, Physical Education and Recreation, 1964.

Kindergarten Guidebook, Colorado Department of Education, Denver: 1960.

LATCHAW, MARJORIE. *A Pocket Guide of Games and Rhythms for the Elementary School.* Englewood-Cliffs, New Jersey: Prentice-Hall, Inc., 1958.

MEYER, HENRY O. *Rainy Day Activities,* Modesto City Schools, Modesto, California, 1962.

MILLER, ARTHUR G., and WHITCOMB, VIRGINIA. *Physical Education in the Elementary School Curriculum,* 2nd Edition. Englewood Cliffs, New Jersey: Prentice-Hall Inc., 1963.

Physical Education Grade One, San Diego City Schools, San Diego, 1962.

RICHARDSON, HAZEL A. *Games for the Elementary Schools Grades.* Minneapolis: Burgess Publishing Co., 1961.

SHURR, E. *Movement Experiences for Children.* New York: Appleton-Century-Crofts, 1966.

STUART, FRANCES R. *Classroom Activities.* Washington, D.C.: AAHPER, 1963.

VANNIER, MARYHELEN, and FOSTER, MILDRED. *Teaching Physical Education in Elementary Schools,* 4th Edition. Philadelphia: W. B. Saunders Co., 1968.

Individual and Team Games

Basketball (winter)
Soccer (fall or spring)
Softball (spring or summer)
Volleyball (fall, winter, or spring)
Touch Football (fall)
Track and Field (spring or summer)

T HIS second category of games contains the major individual and team sports activities that are appropriate for upper elementary school-age children. In the main these are seasonal sports with Soccer, Touch Football, and Volleyball normally played in the fall. Winter is definitely the Basketball season. As soon as the weather permits, Softball will be the first spring activity, followed very closely by Track and Field activities. Climate and local interest will, in turn, dictate when and how long these activities will be taught.

Although these are basically intermediate level activities, primary teachers will find an excellent supplement of low organization games and relays as well as several suggestions for teaching track and field activities to primary level children.

BASKETBALL

Description of Skills
Suggested Sequence of Presenting Skills and Rules
How to Develop a Unit
Practice Activities and Lead-up Games
Basketball: Basic Rules and Regulations
Evaluative Techniques

The history of basketball is very similar to volleyball in that it was originated in the United States and has since become a sport that is played in nearly every country in the world. There is no single reason for its popularity as a participant and a spectator sport. Children, youth, and adults enjoy the game because it is fun, challenging, and contributes to many important components of physical fitness. Since the game can be modified to meet the limitations of available court size and varying levels of skill proficiency, it should be considered as a basic activity for the upper elementary school physical education program.

The first part of this section includes a description of the basic skills of the game and a suggested sequence of presenting skills and rules for Grades Four through Six. To help organize the various practice activities and lead-up games, a sample unit is provided, then followed by two sections containing practice activities and lead-up games with appropriate grade levels indicated. The latter part of this section includes a simplified version of the basic rules and regulations of basketball, and suggestions relating evaluation of student progress.

Description of Skills*

Basketball skills can be broadly classified as passing, catching, dribbling, and shooting. Each skill in turn can be further subdivided, such as the passing skill broken down into a chest, a two-hand underhand, or a baseball pass. The following illustrated skills, once learned, will provide the basis for playing a well-organized and skillful game of basketball.

PASSING

Passing is exchanging the ball from one player to another from a stationary position or while in motion. A player may pass the ball with one or both hands and from a variety of positions. Basic fundamentals to all passes are: (1) be accurate, avoid "wild throws"; (2) follow through with every pass; and (3) shift the ball as quickly as possible from the receiving position to the passing position.

Two-hand Chest Pass

The two-hand chest pass is one of the most useful and effective passes used in basketball. Since its main advantage is ease and speed of delivery, it is the most often used pass, particularly for short distances.

Two-hand Bounce Pass

This pass is performed in the same manner as the two-hand chest pass with one exception. Instead of the ball traveling directly from chest height of the passer to approximately chest height of the receiver, the ball is bounced on the floor then rebounds to the receiver. The main advantage of this pass is to permit a player to pass the ball past an opponent before the latter is able to bend down and block the pass.

---

*All skills are described for the right-handed child. Descriptions relating to hand, arm, leg, and foot positions must be reversed for the left-handed child.

FIG. 9.1

FIG. 9.2

Stand with both feet together. Hold ball chest high, hands behind center of ball with fingers spread around surface of ball. The thumbs should be close together.

Simultaneously extend the arms forward and take one step forward shifting the weight to the front foot. Continue the forward "pushing" movement. Do not snap the wrists and fingers to the side.

One Hand Overhand Pass (Baseball Pass)

This pass is used when a player wishes to throw the ball a long distance. Care must be exercised, particularly with beginners, in using this pass as it may often lead to inaccurate passing.

FIG. 9.3

FIG. 9.4

Begin with left foot forward, and weight evenly distributed on both feet. The ball should be held in front of the body, elbows bent, and fingers spread around the sides of the ball.

Bring arms back, transferring the ball to the right hand when it is above the shoulder and behind the ear. The body weight should shift to the right foot simultaneously with the backward shift of the hands. Extend right arm forward, rotate body toward the left and shift body weight to forward foot. Release ball with a final snap of wrists and fingers.

Two-hand Overhead Pass

This pass is extremely effective when a player wishes to throw the ball above the reach of an opponent to one of his teammates. Also, when the ball is held in the overhead position it is very easy to "fake" or pretend to pass, thus causing the opponent to be off guard before actually releasing the ball.

DRIBBLING

Dribbling is controlled bouncing in any direction and at varying speeds. Basic fundamentals to stress in teaching this skill are: (1) do not slap the ball downward—push it toward the floor; (2) learn to dribble with both hands; and (3) when a player is not being checked, he should bring the ball in front of his body and raise the height of the dribble in order to increase forward running speed.

FIG. 9.5

Begin with body slightly forward, knees partially bent, with weight evenly distributed on both feet. Hold the ball in left hand with fingers of right hand spread over top of ball, then extend forearm downward and forward and "push" toward the floor with the fingertips.

FIG. 9.6

Hold hand down and wait for the ball to rebound back. Let fingers, wrist and arm "ride" back with the ball.

When a player is being checked, he must place his body between his opponent and the ball. The player, when dribbling, must learn to keep his eye on his opponent in order to watch for sudden moves and shift the ball to a more advantageous position. Also, when a player is being checked he should keep the ball near his hip and lower the bounce to approximately waist high.

SHOOTING

It is quite obvious that all the skills of basketball are important; none, however, are as important as shooting. When teaching the following basic shooting skills stress the fundamental principle of watching the target and not the ball and follow through after every shot at the basket.

There is a very important teaching consideration that is currently of concern in the majority of elementary schools. This, of course, is the height of the basket rim which is usually placed at the official ten foot height. If elementary school-age children are to learn shooting skills correctly and efficiently, the height of the basket rim should be lowered to a height which allows children to shoot without undue strain. For upper elementary school children the appropriate height should be between eight and nine feet depending upon the age and ability of the children.

Lay-in

The lay-in shot should be the first shooting skill to be learned. Although this skill involves dribbling, leaping, and the ability to judge distance, it can be learned by boys and girls in the intermediate grades. In fact, most children become more successful in this skill than in other types of shooting skills, such as the one or two-hand set shot. The reason for this factor is the short distance between the hand release and the rim of the basket in the lay-in shot.

FIG. 9.7

Approach the basket at a forty-five degree angle and simultaneously shift weight to left foot, raise ball upward as far as possible with both hands, then release left hand and carry the ball upward with the right hand.

FIG. 9.8

Continue upward with the right hand and lay the ball against the backboard about eighteen inches above the rim. The ball should rebound into the basket.

One-hand Set Shot

This shot may be performed by either keeping both feet on the floor with the same foot as the shooting hand in a slightly forward position, or taking a step with the opposite foot of the shooting hand. Both types are essentially the same since the same foot as the shooting hand finishes in a forward position.

ONE-HAND SET SHOT

FIG. 9.9

FIG. 9.10

Place the same foot as the shooting hand slightly in front. Hold the ball with both hands opposite the chin and above the lead foot. Keep the back straight and bend the knees to a comfortable position as illustrated.

Simultaneously, straighten the knees and extend forward and upward pushing the ball toward the basket. Release the ball with a slight snap of the wrist and fingers. Continue the follow-through of the shooting arm.

Two-hand Set Shot

This shot is the same as the one-hand set shot with the only difference being the use of two hands.

FIG. 9.11

FIG. 9.12

Begin with one foot slightly in front of the other, and weight evenly distributed on both feet. Hold the ball between spread fingers, in front of the chest and elbows close to side.

Bend the knees slightly to aid in the upward motion, then simultaneously straighten knees and extend forward and upward pushing the ball toward the basket. Release the ball with a slight snap of the wrist and fingers. Continue the follow-through with extended arms and palms toward the basket.

Two-hand Underhand Shot

This shot should only be used for foul shooting.

FIG. 9.13

FIG. 9.14

Stand with feet comfortably spread apart with weight evenly distributed on both feet and back straight. Hold the ball with spread fingers, both hands slightly under the ball and elbows close to the body. Keep the back and arms straight, bend the knees slightly and bring the ball downward to about knee high.

Swing the ball forward and upward with the arms in a wide extended arc, and at the same time, extend the knees. Follow through in the direction of the ball.

PIVOTING

Footwork in basketball involves stopping, starting, pivoting, and turning in all directions and at varying speeds. When teaching the pivot and turn, stress the importance of gaining body control before attempting a pivot or

FIG. 9.15

FIG. 9.16

Stand with the right foot in front of the left and weight evenly distributed on both feet. Hold ball between spread fingers of both hands and elbows bent and close to body.

Pivot Left: The right foot has been declared the pivot foot, hence it must remain on the floor. The left foot is the only foot free to move toward the right or left side. In this case, the player has pivoted toward the left on his right foot.

turn. Also, teach pupils not to change the pivot foot once it is declared, otherwise traveling will be charged. Finally, emphasize the need to maintain fingertip control of the ball for quick release after the pivot is made.

DEFENSIVE SKILLS

In the elementary school it is essential that children first learn to move the ball by dribbling and passing, then learn the basic skills of the defensive. It is important to stress the fact that to legally stop an opponent from scoring is just as important as scoring itself.[1] The following basic techniques of defense should be emphasized particularly in the sixth and seventh grades:

1. Never cross the feet when checking an opponent—use a sliding step.
2. Keep the buttocks low and the back in an upright position.
3. When checking, keep one hand up at all times.
4. Do not reach across for a lead—move the body to a position in front of the offensive player, then attempt to take the ball.
5. Always try to get your chest in front of the offensive player.
6. Check with one hand toward the ball and the other hand toward your check.
7. Position yourself between your check and your own basket.

FIG. 9.17

1. D. Turkington and G. Kirchner, *Basketball for Intermediate Grades*. Audio-Visual Centre, Simon Fraser University, Burnaby 2, British Columbia, Canada, 1970, page 2.

Suggested Sequence of Presenting Skills and Rules

Many skills used in basketball have been learned in prior grades or during out-of-school hours. The large number of "back-yard basketball" courts not only attest to the popularity of this sport, but also provide the opportunity for elementary school-age children to learn basketball skills from older brothers and parents. Consequently, in virtually every intermediate grade in the elementary school there is a wide variation in the level of basketball skill. Since boys in the intermediate grades are very keen on basketball they usually show greater interest and ability than girls of a similar age range. This must be taken into consideration when planning a unit for mixed classes.

With the above considerations in mind, the following suggested sequence of skills and rules is provided as a guide line. All teachers should pretest children with the evaluative techniques provided in the latter part of this section to determine what skills should be given the greatest emphasis.

Suggested Sequence of Presenting Skills and Rules of Basketball					
	Grade				Rule Presentation
Skill	4	5	6	7	
1. Passing					
Two-hand chest pass	X	X	X	X	Out of bounds
Two-hand bounce pass	X	X	X	X	
Baseball pass		X	X	X	Line violations
Two-hand overhand pass		X	X	X	Holding ball more than five seconds
					Positions
2. Dribbling					
Standing	X	X	X	X	
Running	X	X	X	X	Traveling (double dribble)
Changing hands	X	X	X	X	
Weaving	X	X	X	X	
3. Shooting					
Lay-in	X	X	X	X	Scoring
One-hand set	X	X	X	X	
Two-hand set	X	X	X	X	Key positions
Two-hand underhand	X	X	X	X	
4. Pivoting					
With both feet on floor	X	X	X	X	Dragging pivot foot
While on one foot		X	X	X	
After receiving ball with both feet in air				X	Changing pivot foot Excessive use of elbows
5. Defense					
One on one without ball			X	X	Holding
One on one with ball			X	X	Blocking
One on one drive to the basket				X	Offensive charging

How to Develop a Unit

Basketball activities should be taught during the months of January, February, and March. Factors such as size of class, previous background, available space, as well as time allotments for physical education (daily or alternate days for physical education), will determine the length of time that will be devoted to basketball. Furthermore, teachers may wish to intersperse dance and self-testing activities throughout a major unit on basketball. A comprehensive unit on basketball, therefore, will not be outlined. Instead a modified format for unit construction is provided as a guide to illustrate how to use the "Practice Activities" and "Lead-up Games." Also, the unit is based upon the premise that each thirty minute lesson on Monday, Wednesday, and Friday is composed of three parts. The first is the explanation and demonstration of a skill. The second phase is devoted to practicing the skill previously demonstrated. The latter part is participation in one or more lead-up games.

See "Description of Skills" (page 191 to 197)

See "Practice Activities and Lead-up Games" (page 199 to 210)

	MONDAY 30 minutes	TUESDAY 15 minutes	WEDNESDAY 30 minutes	THURSDAY 15 minutes	FRIDAY 30 minutes
First week	Explain: Chest pass Practice: shuttle Passing Lead-up: Bombardment	Practice: Shuttle Passing Lead-up: Five passes	Explain: One lay-in shot Practice: Dribble and shoot. Lead-up: Side line basketball	Sideline Basketball	Explain: One-hand set shot Practice: Basket Shooting Lead-up: Twenty-one

Note: Continue above pattern in the second and third and fourth weeks or modify as illustrated in this week.

Second week	Basketball Activities	Dance Activities	Basketball Activities	Self-testing Activities	Basketball Activities
Third week	Repeat according to the pattern you select.				
Fourth week	Repeat according to the pattern you select.				

Practice Activities and Lead-up Games

The following practice activities and lead-up games will assist in developing passing, shooting, dribbling, and pivoting skills. Modify any activity to meet unique limitations of the playing area and to cope with variations in the level of skill and interest of your class.

All suggested activities described in this section are designed to give each student the maximum amount of practice. If sufficient numbers of basketballs are not available, use soccer, volleyball, or utility balls. Also, it is important for the teacher to circulate among students during these practice activities in order to correct errors or to provide encouragement and praise where needed.

PRACTICE ACTIVITIES AND LEAD-UP GAMES

Activity	Page	Catching	Passing	Shooting	Dribbling	Pivoting	Suggested Grade Level 4	5	6
A. PRACTICE ACTIVITIES									
1. Wall Passing	200	X	X	X			X	X	X
2. Pig in the Middle	201	X	X			X	X	X	X
3. Circle Passing	201	X	X			X	X	X	X
4. Shuttle Passing	202	X	X		X	X	X	X	X
5. One Knee Dribble	202				X		X	X	X
6. Movement Drill	203				X		X	X	X
7. Line Dribble	203				X		X	X	X
8. Weave Dribble	204				X			X	X
9. Whistle Dribble	204				X			X	X
10. Dribble and Shoot	204			X	X		X	X	X
11. Line Shooting	205	X		X	X		X	X	X
12. Basket Shooting	205			X	X		X	X	X
13. One on One	206				X	X		X	X
B. LEAD-UP GAMES									
14. Bombardment	206	X	X	X			X	X	
15. Arch Goal Ball Relay	207			X			X	X	X
16. Keep Away	207	X	X		X	X	X	X	X
17. Side Line Basketball	208	X	X	X	X	X	X	X	X
18. Five Passes	208	X	X				X	X	X
19. Twenty-one	209	X	X	X			X	X	X
20. Basketball Snatch Ball	209	X		X	X			X	X
21. In and Out Basketball	210	X	X	X	X	X		X	X
22. Nine Court Basketball	210	X	X	X	X	X		X	X

No. 1: Wall Passing (4 - 6)

Formation: Line formation around available wall surface.

Basic Drill: Players should stand approximately five feet away from wall and gradually move farther away as skill

increases. This wall drill can be used to practice
all types of passing and catching skills.

Variations: a. Add lines or targets on wall to increase accuracy.
b. Add timing contests (Number of hits in 10
seconds, etc.)

No. 2: Pig in the Middle (4 - 6)

Formation: Arrange three players in a line with approximately
six feet between each player. The two outside
players are end players while the middle player
is designated as "pig."

Basic Drill: Do not allow the end players to move to the right
or left. End players attempt to pass the ball between each other without the middle player
("pig") touching the ball. If "pig" touches the
ball he replaces the person who threw the ball.
The ball may not be thrown above the reach of
the middle player and the "pig" must always advance toward the ball.

Variations: Allow the end player who is receiving the ball to
move into an open space.

No. 3: Circle Passing (4 - 6)

Formation: Divide class into squads of five to six players.
Arrange children in circles with approximately six
feet between each player.

Basic Drill: The first player turns toward the second player
and passes the ball to him; second player catches,
turns toward the third and passes to him, etc. If
the ball is dropped, it is retrieved by the "receiver" who returns to his place in the circle and
continues the drill.

Variations: a. "Five Against One": One player goes to the
center of the circle. The five outside players
pass the ball to each other, always skipping
a man, while the center player attempts to
intercept the pass. When the center player
intercepts the pass, he takes the position of
the player who threw the ball.
b. One player goes to the center of the circle
with the ball. Center player now passes to
each player in the circle.

c. Double Passing: This is similar to b. with the addition of one more ball. Require center player to make a bounce pass while circle players make a direct pass.

No. 4: Shuttle Passing (4 - 6)

Formation:

Divide class into squads of six to eight players. Arrange each squad in a shuttle formation with about fifteen feet between the two center players.

Basic Drill:

The first player throws across to the second player. Each player in turn catches, throws, and goes to the back of his line.

Variations:

a. Repeat the basic drill and require one bounce before it reaches the receiver.

c. Repeat the basic drill with the first player passing across to the second player, then the first player continues forward and goes to the back of the opposite line. Continue pattern from both sides.

c. Move lines twenty-five feet apart. The first player now dribbles twice, stops, passes, and goes to the back of the opposite line. Another skill may be added by requiring each player to dribble twice then pivot left, then back and pass to the next player. Vary the direction of the pivot.

No. 5: One Knee Dribble (4 - 6)

Formation: Scattered.

Basic Drill: All players kneel on one knee and begin bouncing the ball with the same hand as the kneeling knee.

FIG. 9.18

This drill will eliminate unnecessary arm action. Players should also keep their eyes on the teacher and "feel" for the ball.

Variations:
    a. Dribble ball with elbow at side.
    b. Move ball backward and forward.
    c. Move ball around the front of the opposite leg and change hands.
    d. Move ball under leg to the other hand.
    e. Bounce the ball in rhythm set by the teacher.
    f. Play follow the leader. This makes everyone look at the leader and not the ball.
    g. Repeat above drills from a standing position.

No. 6: Movement Drill (4 - 6)

Formation: Scattered with each player in possession of a ball.

Basic Drill: The teacher or a leader stands in front of the group then shifts to the right, left, forward, or any direction. All players move in the same direction as the

FIG. 9.19

leader. When players shift to the left they should be bouncing the ball with their right hand and vice versa.

Variation: The leader may use hand directions instead of actually shifting positions.

No. 7: Line Dribble (4 - 6)

Formation: Divide class into three or four squads of about eight to ten players. Arrange each squad in a line formation and place one pin (or chair) twenty feet in front of each line.

| Basic Drill: | The first player dribbles around the pin and back around his squad and passes the ball to the next player. The first player goes to the end of the line and the second player continues the relay. |

No. 8: Weave Dribble (5 - 6)

Formation:	Divide the class into three or five squads of about six to eight players. Arrange each squad in a straight line formation with about ten feet between each player.
Basic Drill:	The first player starts the dribble around the second, back and around opposite side of each successive player until he is back in his original position. Every one moves up one position and the first player goes to rear of the line.
Variation:	Use chairs or pins instead of players for obstacles.

No. 9: Whistle Dribble (5 - 6)

Formation:	Divide class into three or four squads of about six to eight players. Line squads up at one end of floor. The teacher stands in the center of the playing area.
Basic Drill:	When the whistle blows, the first player from each squad dribbles forward. At your discretion, blow the whistle and all players must stop immediately and hold the ball ready for the next move. As soon as any player reaches a line parallel to you, he turns and dribbles back to his team.
Variations:	a. Use hand signals rather than the whistle for stopping and starting. (This encourages the "head-up" dribble.) Hand over head means dribble; hand straight down means stop.
	b. Introduce arms extended sideward (right or left) as a signal to pivot right or left. Hence, it would be hand over head (dribble forward), hand down (stop), arm out to right (pivot right, then back ready for next command).

No. 10: Dribble and Shoot (4 - 6)

| Formation: | This drill should follow three stages with the last stage arranged as shown in the diagram. |
| Basic Drill: | a. Each player stands three to four feet away from the basket, takes one step with left foot (when shooting with right hand) and shoots. |

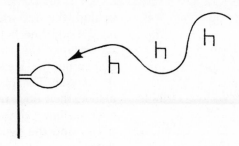

b. Same as a. and being with right foot.
c. Place chairs in a line and approximately at an angle of 45°. Chairs should be about three to four feet apart. Players now dribble around chairs and shoot.

No. 11: Line Shooting (4 - 6)

Formation:	Divide class into as many squads as you have baskets. Line one-half of each squad on each side of the key.
Basic Drill:	The first player on the left side of the key shoots at the basket and the first player on the right side of the key retrieves the ball. Both players then go to the rear of their lines. When the first players return to their original positions, right player shoots and left player retrieves. At the start of the third cycle, exchange lines in order to allow all players to shoot from the right and left sides of the basket.
Variations:	a. Place one player on the free throw line. Now "free throw player" shoots and right side player retrieves the ball and everyone moves one position to the right. In this type of rotation the first player would cross over and take the first position on the right.
	b. Move both lines back and to a forty-five degree angle to the backboard. First player on the right side dribbles toward backboard and attempts a lay-in shot while first player on the left retrieves the ball. Repeat pattern described under basic drill.

No. 12: Basket Shooting (4 - 6)

Formation:	Divide class into as many squads as you have baskets. Arrange each squad in a file formation

	behind the free-throw line. One player remains on the end line behind the basket.
Basic Drill:	As soon as the first player dribbles forward the player on the base line comes forward to guard the basket. The player with the ball must attempt a shot, then both try to recover the rebound. Whoever retrieves the rebound passes it on to the next player and the two rebound players exchange positions.
Variations:	a. Have one guard with two offensive players teaming up and trying to get by the guard and shoot.
	b. Have two guards and two offensive players and repeat a.
	c. Have two guards and three offensive players and repeat a.

No. 13: One on One (5 - 6)

Formation:	Partners facing each other and scatter around gymnasium.
Basic Drill:	Without a ball, one player attempts to run past the other. The defensive player must move his body into position to stop the offensive player. Arms and feet may not be used to stop the player —only the trunk. Do not allow the defensive player to lean into his opponent.
Variations:	a. Repeat above drill with a ball.
	b. Repeat a. and dribble toward a basket.

No. 14: Bombardment (4 - 5)

Formation:	Arrange teams in a scattered formation on each side of the center line. Place five to ten bowling pins across the end line of each team.
Equipment:	10 to 20 Indian clubs or bowling pins, 2 basketballs.
No. of Players:	10 to 30.
Skills:	Passing, shooting, and catching.

How to Play:
1. One ball is given to each team.
2. On signal, each team tries to knock down other team's clubs.
3. One point is scored for each pin that is knocked down, either by opponent's ball or when the defensive team accidentally kicks one over.
4. Each team must stay on their side. If a player reaches over midline, one point is awarded to other team.
5. Time limit or total points may be used.

Teaching Suggestions:
1. Make sure playing area is kept free of pins.
2. Use inactive students as scorekeepers or timekeepers.
3. Emphasize teamwork and proper throwing technique.

No. 15: Arch Goal Ball Relay (4 - 6)

Formation: Arrange each team in a line formation facing the basket.
Equipment: 1 basketball for each team.
No. of Players: 6 to 10 on each team.
Skills: Shooting.

How to Play:
1. On signal, the rear player on each team, using both hands, starts the ball forward by passing it over the head of the player in front of him.
2. Other players do likewise, using both hands.
3. When ball reaches the front player he stands and shoots for a basket, without going over the restraining line.
4. After shooting, the player recovers ball, returns to the rear of the line and starts the ball again.
5. This procedure continues until all have shot.
6. Each successful shot scores one point. The team with the highest number wins.

Teaching Suggestions:
1. Set the restraining line according to ability.
2. Go through it once or twice before counting scores.

No. 16: Keep Away (4 - 6)

Formation: Arrange two teams in a scattered formation within a designated play area.
Equipment: 1 basketball for each team.
No. of Players: 8 to 10 on each team.
Skills: Passing, catching, pivoting, and dribbling.

How to Play:
1. If teams are large and space limited, rotate in fours or fives every few minutes.
2. On signal, the teacher gives the ball to one of the teams, which passes it among themselves trying to keep the ball away from the other team.
3. Players on the opposing team must check as in regular basketball.

Teaching Suggestions:
1. Inactive players must be kept out of the playing area.
2. Players may be allowed two dribbles.

No. 17: Side Line Basketball (4 - 6)

Formation:	Five players from each team play in the court area while remaining players from both teams are alternately placed along the side and end lines.
Equipment:	Basketball—1 for each game.
No. of Players:	5 to 7 per team.
Skills:	Catching, passing, shooting, dribbling, and pivoting.

How to Play:
1. Basketball rules are followed, except that the ball may be passed to a sideline player.
2. Start game with a jump ball in center of playing area. Team who gains possession is designated as offensive team.
3. If defensive team intercepts the ball, they must pass to one of their sideline players before they become the offensive team.
4. Stepping over the sideline gives the ball to opponents on their sideline.
5. Players on the sidelines rotate with players on the floor.
6. Field goals score two points and free throws score one point.

Teaching Suggestions:
1. Assign numbers before the game and use these in the rotation sequence.
2. More players may be used on the court.

No. 18: Five Passes (4 - 6)

Formation:	Arrange two teams in a scattered formation on one side of playing court or within a designated playing area.
Equipment:	2 basketballs.
No. of Players:	4 or 5 on a team.
Skills:	Passing and catching.

How to Play:
1. Play is started with a jump ball between any two opposing players.
2. Basketball rules are followed with respect to traveling, fouling, and ball handling.
3. Passes must be counted out loud by the passer.
4. Ball cannot be passed back to person from whom it was received and no dribbling is allowed.
5. Whenever a series of passes is interrupted by a bad pass or fumble, a new count is started.
6. A free throw from one teammate to another is awarded to the team who did not commit the foul.
7. One point whenever a team completes five passes in a row.

Teaching Suggestions:
1. Call fouls closely.
2. Encourage quick passes.

3. After a point, ball may be awarded to the other team or a jump ball may be used.
4. By using half-court, two games can be played simultaneously.

No. 19: Twenty-One (4 - 6)

Formation:	Arrange players in a scattered formation around one basket.
Equipment:	One basket for each goal.
No. of Players:	6 or 7 on each team.
Skills:	Shooting and catching.

How to Play:
1. Player number one shoots from the free-throw line while other players stand wherever they wish in the playing area.
2. Player number one continues shooting from free-throw line until he misses, with each successful basket counting one point.
3. When number one misses, any player who can get possession of the ball may try for a field goal which counts two points.
4. If the try for a field goal fails, any player who can get the ball may try for a field goal. This procedure is continued until a field goal is made.
5. After a field goal is made the ball is given to number two player, who takes his turn at the free-throw line.
6. Continue foregoing rotation until one player has twenty-one points.

No. 20: Basketball Snatch Ball (5 - 6)

Formation:	Divide class into two equal groups and place one team on each sideline. Place two balls in the center of the court.
Equipment:	2 basketballs.
No. of Players:	10 to 15 per team.
Skills:	Catching, shooting, and dribbling.

How to Play:
1. Players are numbered consecutively and must stand in this order on the sideline of basketball court.
2. Two balls are placed in the center of the court.
3. When the teacher calls a number, that player from each team runs to the ball, dribbles to the basket on his right, and makes a basket.
4. When a basket is made, he dribbles back and replaces ball.
5. The first player to make a basket and return the ball scores one point for his team.

Teaching suggestions:
Players may run by pairs with two players from each team having the same number. In this case, the ball must be passed between the players three times before and after the shot is made.

No. 21: In and Out Basketball (5 - 6)

Formation:	Two teams play in one-half of the basketball court. A third "waiting" team stands on the sideline.
Equipment:	2 basketballs.
No. of Players:	6 teams of 4 players each.
Skills:	Shooting, catching, dribbling, and pivoting.

How to Play:

Regular basketball rules apply with the following modifications:
1. Three teams play in one-half of the court.
2. Two teams play while the third team remains on the sidelines.
3. When a field goal or free throw is made, the third team takes the loser's place.
4. Each player is allowed two dribbles.

Teaching suggestions:
1. Keep third team players off the playing floor.
2. Use this game to explain rules and strategy as well as skills.
3. If goals are not being scored, use a time limit as a substitute.
4. If there is enough room, have passing or dribbling drills for the inactive team.

No. 22: Nine Court Basketball (5 - 6)

Formation:	Divide the basketball court into nine equal areas and place one guard and one opposing forward in the three end squares. Place one guard from each team in the remaining squares.
Equipment:	Basketball.
No. of Players:	9 on each team.
Skills:	Passing, catching, shooting, dribbling, and pivoting.

How to Play:

Regular basketball rules apply with the following modifications:
1. Each player is assigned an area and must stay in it.
2. Players advance ball by passing and/or one dribble.
3. Only forwards may shoot at the goal.
4. Jump ball is used to start the game.
5. Free shots are awarded for fouls.
6. Ball is taken out of bounds for crossing line, traveling, double dribble, etc.

Teaching suggestions:
1. After each goal, players may rotate to the next higher position.
2. Encourage students to keep on the move in their area.
3. Use chalk or tape to designate areas.

Basketball: Basic Rules and Regulations

Basketball is probably the most popular team sport in the upper elementary grades. This, of course, is true particularly of boys. Although skill development, especially ball handling and shooting skills, necessitates the majority of the time being spent on drills and lead-up games, the full game should be played several times during a unit of instruction. Modifications in the rules, such as lowering the height of the basket and limiting the number of dribbles, can be made to encourage the development of specific skills. Care should be taken, however, not to play the full game too often to the neglect of needed skill development.

1. Field of Play:

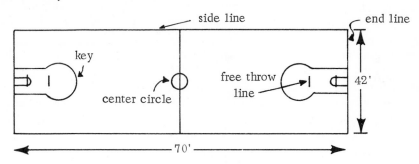

2. Positions:

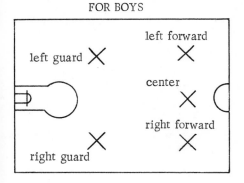

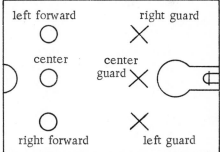

For boys: All five players may play in both halves of the court.

Three guards must play only on their half of the court. The three forwards must play in their opponent's half of the court. The three guards on one team, therefore, are actually against the three opposing forwards on the other team.

3. To Start Game: The game is started at the center circle. The referee tosses the ball in the air between the two opposing centers. The centers attempt to tap the ball to one of their own players. This "jump ball" is also used in the following cases: (a) when the ball is held by two opposing players (the jump will be taken at the nearest key or center circle); (b) when the ball goes out of bounds and the referee is uncertain as to which team caused it to go out; and (c) to start the second half of the game.

4. After a successful free throw: The ball is put into play at the end of the court by the defending team.

5. After a ball goes out of bounds: The ball is put into play from behind the line and immediately in front of the place where it went out. Any player from the team who did not cause it to go out may put it into play.

6. Game Time: The game is divided into four quarters of six minutes each.

7. Points: Two points are awarded for every field goal. One point is awarded for every successful free throw.

8. Substitution: One or all substitutes may enter the game whenever the ball is not in play (out of bounds, before a jump ball, etc.).

9. Violations: A violation is charged against a player if he commits the following:
   a. Travels—takes more than one step with the ball without dribbling.
   b. Double dribble—dribbles the ball, stops, then dribbles again without another player handling the ball or palming, that is, not clearly dribbling, or dribbling the ball with two hands.
   c. Steps on or over the boundary line while he is in possession of the ball.
   d. Kicks the ball.
   e. Stays longer than three seconds in the key area under the offensive basket. The penalty: The play is stopped and the referee awards a free throw from the sideline to the other team nearest the point where the infraction occurred.

10. Fouls: A foul is charged against a player if he commits the following:
   a. Kicks, trips, or pushes another player.
   b. Holds or charges another player.
   c. Commits unsportsmanlike conduct.

The penalty: The play is stopped and the referee awards one or two free throws to the nonoffending team from the free-throw line. The number of free throws awarded is based upon the following:
   a. One free throw for a player who is fouled when he is participating in an activity other than shooting. After a successful free throw, the defending team puts the ball into play from behind the end line. If the free throw is unsuccessful, the ball continues to be in play.

   b. Two free throws for a player who is fouled when he is in the act of shooting a goal. After the second successful free throw, the defending team puts the ball into play from behind the end line. If the second free throw is unsuccessful, the ball continues to be in play.

Evaluative Techniques

There are several tests that can be used to measure the basic skills of passing, dribbling, and shooting. The following test items are reliable and quite easy to administer. Modify any test item to meet your own teaching situation and add additional items if desired. Also, keep scores from each year in order to build appropriate norms for your school.

	Basketball Skill Test					
Name	Passing (total pts)	Dribbling (total pts)	Shooting (50 pts)	Subjective Evaluation (50 pts)	Total Score	Grade
1. 2. 3.	Rank all total scores → for the class then convert to letter grades or to ratings (superior, good, etc.)					

Test No. 1. Passing: Place a target on the wall as shown in the accompanying diagram:

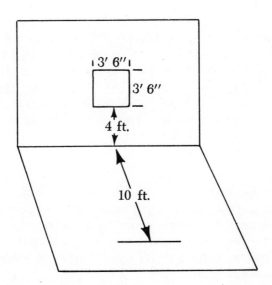

Each player must stand and shoot from behind the ten foot line. He has 30 seconds to hit the target as many times as possible. If a player drops the ball within the thirty second period, he may pick up the ball, return to the ten foot line and continue adding to his cumulative score. One point is scored for each pass that lands on the target area. Allow two trials and record the highest score.

Test No. 2. Dribbling: Arrange four chairs as shown in the accompanying diagram.

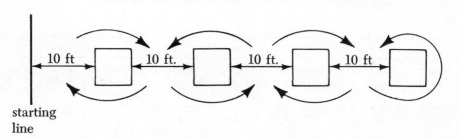

A ball is placed on the starting line. Each player must stand behind the starting line with both hands resting on his knees. On signal "go," he picks up the ball and dribbles around the chairs in a zigzag pattern. One point is awarded each time he passes a chair. Allow twenty seconds for the test. Two trials are also allowed with the highest score recorded.

Test No. 3. Shooting: Draw a line at a 45° angle and thirty feet away from the basket. Each student attempts ten lay-in shots. He must begin dribbling from the thirty foot line and attempt each shot when he reaches the basket. Improper footwork and poor timing causing a miss should be so counted. Award five points for each successful basket.
Other shooting tests, such as free throws, one or two-hand sets, may be substituted for the lay-in test.

Test No. 4. Subjective Evaluation: Establish a criteria which represents the skills and playing ability required in basketball. For example, using such skills and abilities as shooting ability, dribbling, defensive skill, and passing, the teacher would award each player a total point score from zero to fifty points. Three players can be used as judges with the average score recorded.

SOCCER

Description of Skills
Suggested Sequence of Presenting Skills and Rules
How to Develop a Unit
Practice Activities and Lead-up Games
Soccer: Basic Rules and Regulations
Evaluative Techniques

The game of soccer is usually thought to be an English pastime; however, this is far from true. Of all the major sports, soccer is played in more countries and probably by more people than any other sport in the world. It is a sport requiring a great deal of skill in kicking, running, and dribbling. Because of the limited expense (a ball and two goalposts), mass participation, and total body involvement, it is an excellent activity for an upper elementary school physical education program. Furthermore, to enjoy the game only a few skills and rules need to be learned; later, with additional skill other rules and strategy can be introduced.

In the first part of this section all pertinent skills are illustrated, along with basic teaching hints. Following the description of skills is a suggested format for presenting the basic skills and rules of soccer. The latter part of this section contains a sample outline of an instructional unit, practice activities, lead-up games, a simplified version of the basic rules and regulations of soccer, and evaluative techniques.

Description of Skills

Soccer is basically a kicking and running game; however, when played correctly, other skills such as dribbling, trapping, heading, and throwing are necessary for maximum success and enjoyment. Each of these skills will be described and illustrated and accompanied by a list of important fundamentals.*

KICKING

In soccer, the ball may be kicked from a stationary, running, or from a volley position (while in the air). Although each type of kick can be performed with either foot, there are certain fundamentals common to both that should be stressed in every practice and game situation. First, the player should watch or "keep his eye" on the ball as it approaches him or as he approaches the ball. Second, kick the ball with the instep (top side of instep); never kick it with the toe. Finally, after the ball has been kicked, follow through with the "kicking foot" for a short distance in the direction of the kick. Each of these fundamental points applies to the following five basic kicking skills.

INSTEP KICK — TOP OF FOOT

FIG. 9.20	**FIG. 9.21**

Just before the ball is kicked, the left foot should be even with the ball, head and trunk leaning slightly forward, and right knee bent. The arms are extended sidewards for balance.

Swing right foot downward and forward, contacting the ball with top of the instep. Continue forward and upward with kicking leg.

---

*All skills will be described for the right-handed child. Descriptions relating to hand, arm, leg, and foot positions must be reversed for the left-handed child.

INSTEP KICK — INSIDE OF FOOT

FIG. 9.22

FIG. 9.23

The body is bent slightly forward with weight evenly distributed on both feet and ball approximately six inches in front of feet. Shift weight to right foot and swing left leg sideward and slightly forward.

Swing left leg downward and toward the right, contacting the ball with inside of left foot. Follow through with left leg crossing in front of right toe.

INSTEP KICK — OUTSIDE OF FOOT

FIG. 9.24

FIG. 9.25

The body is bent slightly forward with weight evenly distributed on both feet and ball approximately six inches in front of feet. Shift weight to left foot, bend right knee and swing right leg across left foot.

Swing right foot downward and toward the right, contacting the ball with outside of foot. Follow through with right leg until the knee is nearly extended.

VOLLEY KICK — BALL IN THE AIR

FIG. 9.26

FIG. 9.27

Stand with the nonkicking foot in front of kicking foot. Head and body facing ball and a slight forward tilt of body. The weight should be evenly distributed on both feet.

As the ball approaches, shift weight to the nonkicking foot and raise the kicking leg with knee slightly bent and toe pointing down. Contact ball with instep and follow through in a forward and upward direction.

PUNTING

FIG. 9.28

FIG. 9.29

Stand with left foot approximately twelve inches in front of right foot and hold ball in front of body about chest high.

Swing right leg forward and upward and shift weight to left foot. Release ball as right leg is swinging forward. Contact ball with the instep on the forward and upward swing. Follow through into an extended leg position.

DRIBBLING

Dribbling, as used in soccer, is moving the ball with short pushes by either foot. These short "pushes" permit the player to control the ball whether he is dribbling forward, sideward, or even backward. Because the ball must be in constant control, do not let it get more than five or six feet away from the feet. Hence, to develop this skill, begin with a very slow walking speed and increase the speed of the dribble in proportion to the amount of control demonstrated.

FIG. 9.30

Begin with trunk bent slightly forward, arms sideward for balance and weight on left foot. Move right foot forward and push ball forward and slightly to the left with inside of right foot.

FIG. 9.31

Place right foot down, transferring weight to this foot and shift the left leg forward to repeat action.

TRAPPING

This is stopping the ball while it is moving through the air or rolling on the ground. Any part of the body, with the exception of the hands and arms,

FOOT TRAP

FIG. 9.32

As the ball rolls toward the player, raise right foot approximately eight inches off ground, toes up to form a "V" between ground and sole of foot. When the ball makes contact with sole of foot relax foot thus allowing ball to lose its recoil action and remain beneath the foot.

SHIN TRAP

FIG. 9.33

As the ball rolls toward the player, flex both knees, bend trunk forward, and arms extended sideward. At the moment the ball makes contact, extend legs slightly and shift weight to nonkicking foot.

may be used to trap a ball. The type of trap one uses will depend upon the flight of the ball, the position of opponents, and the amount of time the trapper has available.

INSIDE LEG TRAP	CHEST TRAP

FIG. 9.34	FIG. 9.35

This trap is used when ball is approaching from a low bounce. As the ball approaches, shift body weight to the foot closest to ball, flex far knee and raise forward. As the ball makes contact, allow the leg to "give" a little thus preventing the ball from recoiling too far forward.

This type of trap is used when the ball is descending from a high volley, or when a player wants to attempt to prevent a high rising ball from getting past him. In this type of trap, the player brings his extended arms forward, but does not touch the ball with hands or arms. The arm position aids in creating a "hollow" chest or pocket for the ball. However, the player's chest is held in a normal position, that is, up to the moment the ball makes contact. Upon contact, the player relaxes his chest muscles, thus creating a pocket for the ball to stop and drop directly below.

HEADING

Heading the soccer ball is actually hitting or bunting it with the front or side of the forehead. By leaning back and then moving toward ball, hitting it with a forward motion of the head, the player has greater accuracy than simply allowing the ball to rebound off the head. The main points to stress when teaching this skill are (1) watch or keep "eyes on ball" as it approaches; (2) lean back prior to hitting the ball; and (3) contact the ball with the forehead, not the top of the head.

FIG. 9.36

As the ball approaches, drop head backward and raise one or both arms to the side and shift weight to back foot.

FIG. 9.37

Begin from the back foot, shifting body weight forward and upward and bring head forward to meet the ball. Remember, the contact must be made with the forehead. Immediately after hitting the ball, follow through in the direction of the ball.

THROW-IN

Whenever the ball goes over the side lines it is put back into play by a "throw-in." In executing this skill, the ball must begin from behind the head with a two-hand throw. Part of both feet must remain on the ground until the ball leaves the player's hands. However, any position of the feet is permissible as long as part of both are on the ground throughout this movement. The main points to stress when teaching this skill are: (1) hold sides of ball with both hands; (2) bring ball all the way back to top of shoulders and arch body back to gain greater throwing distance; and (3) throw the ball forward with both hands.

FIG. 9.38

Begin with one foot in front of the other or in a parallel position. Bring ball back to top of shoulders and arch back.

FIG. 9.39

Shift body weight forward and upward and bring ball over head extending arms toward the direction of the throw. Release ball and follow through with hands and arms.

TACKLING

In a game of soccer, the players of the team who have possession of the ball are known as the offensive or attacking team. Any player on the defending team may legally tackle the opposing player who has possession of the ball. A legal tackle, however, must be done from the front or side and with the feet and shoulders. The use of the hands or tackling from behind is clearly against the rules.

Important points to remember in tackling an opponent are:[1]

1. Be quick and decisive when you approach an opponent who has possession of the ball.
2. Tackle the opponent when he is in control of the ball but is slightly off balance. This is usually when he pushes the ball forward a little.
3. Be ready to pass the ball as soon as you gain possession.

TACKLING

FIG. 9.40	FIG. 9.41

When tackling, watch the ball and feet of an opponent for "clues" to his possible direction. Keep body weight evenly distributed on both feet in order to shift right or left.

Tackle opponent when he is slightly off balance. Once you gain possession of the ball, be ready to pass it.

Suggested Sequence of Presenting Skills and Rules

The appropriate skill development for any grade is obviously dependent upon previously learned skills and the present level of ability of each class. Taking these factors into consideration, a list of appropriate skills and rules for each grade level, as shown in the accompanying chart, is provided as a general guide for each respective grade level. It should be recognized in a physical activity such as soccer that the progression of skills is not just a

---

1. The Football Association of Great Britain, "Skilful Soccer for Young Players," London, Educational Productions Ltd., 1967, p. 63.

cumulative addition of new skills; it is a sequential addition of skills plus a continuous improvement in accuracy and form of all previously acquired skills.

Skill	Grade				Rule Presentation
	4	5	6	7	
1. Kicking	X	X	X	X	Kick-off, free kick
Instep kick	X	X	X	X	Goal kick, penalty kick
Punting	X	X	X	X	Corner kick
Volley kick		X	X	X	
	X	X	X	X	positions, field markings and scoring
2. Dribbling	X	X	X	X	
		X	X	X	off side
3. Trapping					
foot trap	X	X	X	X	handling the ball
shin trap	X	X	X	X	
inside of leg trap		X	X	X	rules for goalie
chest trap			X	X	
		X	X	X	drop ball
4. Heading		X	X	X	
5. Throwing the ball	X	X	X	X	throw-in rule
6. Tackling	X	X	X	X	charging and pushing

How to Develop a Unit

Soccer is usually classified as a fall activity; however, there is no reason why this activity could not be played in the spring, particularly when the weather is suitable. Regardless of the season chosen for this activity, consideration should be given to such factors as inclement weather, available space, and shared time with other types of activities. The format for developing a soccer unit outlined following may be modified to meet any unique or unusual teaching situation.

The following sample unit on soccer activities is based upon the premise that each lesson contains three main parts. The first part of each lesson should be an explanation and demonstration of a specific soccer skill. All skills have been described under "Description of Skills," hence teachers should review each skill prior to teaching it to the class. After a skill is introduced, children should be placed in a practice situation that will emphasize this skill. This is the second part of the lesson and includes practice activities and lead-up games. A list of appropriate practice activities are provided on page 224. To illustrate the organization of a modified unit and the use of the accompanying chart of practice activities and lead-up games, a three-week-unit is outlined. Use this example as a general guide when constructing a soccer unit.

"See Description of Skills" (page 216 to 222)

See Practice Activities and Lead-up Games (page 224 to 233)

	Monday (30 min)	Tuesday (15 min)	Wednesday (30 min)	Thursday (15 min)	Friday (30 min)
First week	Explain: Kicking with instep	Practice: Circle Kicking	Explain: Trapping with inside of leg	Soccer Dodge Ball	Review: Kicking Practice:
	Practice: Circle Kicking Lead-up Game: Boundary Ball	Lead-up: Boundary Ball	Practice: Circle Dribble Lead-up Game: Circle Soccer Tag		Zigzag Kicking Lead-up Game: Kick Baseball
2nd week	Soccer Activities	Dance Activities	Soccer Activities	Self-testing Activities	Soccer Activities
3rd week	Repeat pattern as shown in Week 1 or Week 2				

Practice Activities and Lead-up Games

The following list of activities is organized according to the various skills they assist in developing. Modify any activity to meet unique limitations of the playing area and to cope with the variations in the level of skill and interest of your class.

No.	Activity	Page	Kicking	Trapping	Dribbling	Heading	Throw in	Tackling	4	5	6
A.	**PRACTICE ACTIVITIES**										
1.	Wall Kicking	225	X	X		X	X		X	X	X
2.	Zigzag Kicking	225	X	X		X			X	X	X
3.	Circle Kicking	226	X	X		X			X	X	X
4.	Kicking for Distance	226	X	X					X	X	X

No.	Activity	Page	SKILLS				Throw in	Tackling	Grade		
			Kick-ing	Trap-ping	Drib-bling	Head-ing			4	5	6
5.	Goal Kicking	227	X	X	X				X	X	X
6.	Line Dribbling	227	X	X	X				X	X	X
7.	Shuttle Dribbling	228		X	X	X	X	X	X	X	X
8.	Around the Square	228			X					X	X
9.	Goal Heading	228		X		X				X	X
	B. LEAD-UP GAMES										
10.	Boundary Ball	229	X	X					X	X	X
11.	Circle Soccer Tag	229	X	X		X			X	X	X
12.	Circle Soccer	230	X	X	X				X	X	X
13.	Soccer Elimination	230	X	X	X				X	X	X
14.	Soccer Dodgeball	231	X	X					X	X	X
15.	Kick Baseball	231	X				X			X	X
16.	Keep Away	231	X	X	X	X	X	X		X	X
17.	Punt Back	232	X	X						X	X

No. 1: Wall Kicking (4 - 6)

Formation:	Line formation around available wall surface. Players should start approximately six feet away from the wall and with at least four feet between each player.
Basic Drill:	Each player kicks the ball to the wall, retrieves the rebound with a foot or shin trap and continues kicking practice.
Variations:	a. Allow each child to kick the ball as it rebounds back to him.
	b. Start each child several yards back from the ball and run up and kick it.
	c. Start child and ball several yards back from kicking line, dribble up to line and kick ball to wall.
	d. Repeat above with opposite foot.
	e. For heading, throw ball and head the rebound.

No. 2: Zigzag Kicking (4 - 6)

Formation:	Divide class into squads of six to ten players. Arrange squads in two lines about fifteen feet apart with partners facing.
Basic Drill:	Player "A" kicks the ball to "B." "B" may use his hands or feet, depending on the level of "trapping" skill, to stop the ball. "B" places ball on ground

	and kicks it to "C." Continue pattern to player "F" or allow players to continue pattern back to player "A."
Variations:	a. "A" rolls ball to "B" who in turn kicks the ball to "C." "C" kicks the ball to "D," etc., until "F" or back to player "A."
	b. "A" bounces the ball to "B" who, in turn, kicks the ball to "C." This time "C" stops the ball, picks it up, and bounces it to "D." Continue pattern.
	c. Repeat above with opposite foot.

No. 3: Circle Kicking (4 - 6)

Formation:	Divide class into three or four squads of eight to twelve players each. Arrange children in a large circle formation with at least fifteen feet between each player.
Basic Drill:	Player "A" turns, faces "B," and kicks the ball to him. "B" traps the ball, (or he may stop it with his hands), turns and kicks the ball to "C." Continue pattern until "A" receives the ball.
Variations:	a. All children remain facing the center of the circle. "A" using the inside of the left foot kicks to "B." "B" traps the ball with his right foot, then kicks it to "C" with his left foot.
	b. Repeat a. in the opposite direction, trapping with the left foot and kicking with the right foot.
	c. Place one child in the center. Center player kicks to "A." "A" traps and kicks back to "center player," who, in turn, traps and kicks to "B." Continue pattern.

No. 4: Kicking for Distance (4 - 6)

| Formation: | Divide class into four squads. One squad lines up to kick while the other scatters in the field to retrieve the ball. The field may be a line every five yards or "retrievers" may simply mark the kick. |
| Basic Drill: | Each child on the kicking squad is given three or four kicks, depnding upon the number of available balls. Mark the ball where it lands, not where it rolls. After each player on the kicking squad has had his turn, change squad positions. |

Variations:	Kicking squad may vary the type of kick, that is, a stationary kick, a punt, or kicking while ball is rolling forward.

No. 5: Goal Kicking (4 - 6)

Formation:	Divide class into four squads, one squad in a semicircle formation on each side of goal area.
Basic Drill:	Player "A" kicks the ball through the goal, then any player on the opposite team traps and returns kick. Caution: Do not allow any player to move more than two yards away from his position to retrieve the ball. If the ball goes "through" the retrieving team, allow the player, who was closest to the ball as it passed by, to retrieve it.
Variations:	a. Vary the type of kick, that is, a stationary kick, kicking a moving ball as well as using the inside and outside of the instep. (Move closer to goal when practicing this type of kick.) b. Place a player in the center of the goalpost to practice "goal tending." c. Volley kicking: Players on team "A" must throw the ball over the goalposts. Any player on team "B" may attempt to kick the ball through the goalposts before it lands.

No. 6: Line Dribbling (4 - 6)

Formation:	Divide class into as many squads of four or five players as you have balls. Arrange squads in a file formation behind a restraining line. Draw a second line approximately twenty feet in front of the restraining line.
Basic Drill:	Each player dribbles the ball to the designated line, stops the ball on the line, turns around, dribbles back and all the way around his squad. He stops the ball opposite the next player, who has moved up one position, then returns to the back of the line. Note: by requiring each player to go around his squad, you develop better control of the ball.
Variations:	a. Dribble around a pin or chair. b. Dribble and stop. Start the first child from each squad at the same time. As they dribble forward, blow your whistle and require each

child to stop the ball as soon as he can. Another variation with the whistle is to blow it and say "left," "right," "back," or "forward." Now the child must first stop the ball, then dribble it in the direction you have designated.

No. 7: Shuttle Dribbling (4 - 6)

Formation:
Divide class into squads of six to eight players. Place three players of one team behind one line and the other three players behind a second line drawn thirty feet away.

Basic Drill:
Player "A" dribbles the ball over and stops it in front of "B." "B" repeats to "C" while "A" moves to the back of "B's' line. Continue pattern.

Variations:
a. "A" must go around "B's" team, then back to "B."
b. For heading, have one player throw while receiver heads ball back.
c. For tackling, have player come out and attempt to tackle player A.

No. 8: Around the Square (5 - 6)

Formation:
Divide class into squads of four players. Arrange squads into square formations with ten feet between each player. Letter each player A, B, C, and D, respectively, around the square.

Basic Drill:
Player "A," using a regulation throw-in, throws the ball to "B." "B" attempts to head the ball to "C." "C" catches the ball and throws to "D." "D" heads to "A," etc., continuing pattern.

Variations:
a. Start with "A" throwing to "B." Now "B" heads to "C" and "C" attempts to head the ball to "D." "D" heads to "A," etc.
b. Introduce throw, trap, and kicking sequence.

No. 9: Goal Heading (5 - 6)

Formation:
Divide the class into as many squads as you have goals. (Wire backstops, or any substitute "goal" area will work for this drill.) Arrange squads in a line formation ten feet in front of and parallel to the goal. The first player in each squad moves fifteen feet in front of his team, turns and faces the second player in the line.

Basic Drill: Player "A" throws to "B" who, in turn, attempts to head the ball through the goal. "B" chases his own ball, throws it to "A," then returns to the end of the line.

Variations: Make two lines facing the goal with "A" standing on the goal line and front players of the two lines standing ten feet away. "A" throws the ball up and between the first two players. Both attempt to head the ball back to "A."

No. 10: Boundary Ball (4 - 6)

Formation and
Playing Area: Divide playing area into two equal halves. Players may take a scattered position on their own side of the center line.

Equipment: 2 soccer balls.

No. of Players: 10-15 players on each team.

Skills: Kicking and trapping.

How to Play:
1. Each team is given a ball.
2. Play is started by each team kicking a ball toward the opponent's goal line; the ball must roll across the goal line.
3. Players on both teams may move freely about in their own half of the field and try to prevent the opponent's ball from crossing the goal.
4. Players cannot touch the ball with their hands.
5. One point is scored each time a ball crosses the goal line.

No. 11: Circle Soccer Tag (4 - 6)

Formation and
Playing Area: Form a large circle with approximately two feet between each player. One child is in the center of the circle.

Equipment: One soccer ball.

No. of Players: 20 or less.

Skills: Kicking, passing, trapping, heading.

How to Play:
1. "It" is placed in the center of the circle.
2. Circle players try to keep "it" from touching the ball (keep away).
3. If the ball goes outside the circle, "it" is replaced by the person who missed the ball or in the case where "it" touches the ball, "it" is replaced by the last person to kick the ball.
4. No score is kept.

Teaching suggestions:
1. If a player misses the ball, have him secure it and return to his position and then proceed to pass the ball.
2. Stress accurate passing and trapping.

No. 12: Circle Soccer (4 - 6)

Formation and Playing Area:	Form a large circle with two feet between each player. Draw a line through the center of the circle, thus creating two teams.
Equipment:	One soccer ball.
No. of Players:	8 to 10 on each team.
Skills:	Kicking and trapping.

How to Play:
1. The ball is put into play by the captain of one team kicking it toward the opponents.
2. Each team attempts to kick the ball past the opposing players, below shoulder height.
3. Opposing players try to prevent the ball from going out of the circle on their own side.
4. While the ball is in play, every player must remain at his place in the circle. Only the captain may move out of the circle.
5. One point for each time the ball is kicked out of the circle.

No. 13: Soccer Elimination (4 - 6)

Formation and Playing Area:	Scattered formation within a designated playing area.
Equipment:	One soccer ball.
No. of Players:	20 or less.
Skills:	Instep kick, trapping, and dribbling.

How to Play:
1. All players are scattered throughout the playing area and one player is chosen to be the "tagger."
2. The "tagger" may dribble anywhere in the playing area in an attempt to kick the ball and hit another player.
3. If the "tagger" hits another player with the ball below the chest, he goes to the side of the field or court.
4. The "tagger" remains "it" until five players are eliminated. The fifth player eliminated becomes "it."
5. No score is kept.

Teaching suggestions:
1. Make sure that players have plenty of room to move around.
2. Stress dribbling the ball close to player's feet before attempting to kick it.

No. 14: Soccer Dodgeball (4 - 6)

Formation and
Playing Area: One-half of players form a large circle while other
                             half scatter inside the boundaries of the circle.

Equipment: One soccer ball.
No. of Players: One-half class on each team.
Skills: Kicking and trapping.

How to Play:
1. The players forming the circle attempt to hit the players inside the circle
    by kicking the ball at them.
2. When a player is hit below the waist he must join the circle.
3. The winner is the last man out.

No. 15: Kick Baseball (5 - 6)

Formation and
Playing Area: Use a softball diamond and arrange teams as in
                             softball.

Equipment: One soccer ball.
No. of Players: 10 to 30.
Skills: Kicking for distance and trapping.

How to Play:
This game is played by the same rules as softball with the following exceptions:
1. The kicker stands with one foot behind the plate.
2. Pitched balls must be below the batter's knees; a ball is called if not over
    the plate or below the knees.
3. A ball hitting the batter above the knees is a dead ball. A base runner
    can't advance on a dead ball.
4. A player hit by a thrown ball is out if he is off base.

Teaching suggestions:
Set a limit to the number of points that can be scored by one team in one
inning.

No. 16: Keep Away (5 - 6)

Formation and
Playing Area: Permit teams to scatter within a designated play
                             area.

Equipment: One soccer ball.
No. of Players: 8-16 on each team.
Skills: Kicking, dribbling, passing, heading, throw in pass,
                             and trapping.

How to Play:

1. This is the same as any keep-away game with the following exceptions:
   a. The ball may be kicked.
   b. The ball may be caught in the air but not picked up off the floor or field.
   c. The team may throw it around (both hands over the head and both feet must remain on the floor at all times).
2. Fouls are any kind of roughness, tripping, hitting, pushing, etc.
3. No score is kept. The object is to see which team can keep the ball the longest.
4. Do not allow any players to hold the ball longer than three seconds.
5. If the ball goes out of bounds have a player from the team not sending it out retrieve it for his team.

Teaching suggestions:

1. Watch for roughness, particularly near the latter stages of the game.
2. Encourage players to look at each other and signal for passes without shouting.

No. 17: Punt Back (5 - 6)

Formation and Playing Area:	Allow players to assume scattered position behind the front players of their own team. Opposing teams must stay at least fifteen feet away from each other throughout the game.
Equipment:	One soccer ball.
No. of Players:	4 to 20.
Skills:	Trapping and kicking.

How to Play:

1. A captain is chosen for each team.
2. A ball is placed in the middle of the field.
3. A captain of the kicking team kicks the ball to start the game.
4. Once the game has started, opposing teams must be at least fifteen feet apart. This prevents any player from either team mingling with opposite team.
5. Any member of the receiving team may trap the ball.
6. The person who traps the ball must kick it toward his opponent's goal and so on.
7. If a player kicks the ball over the opponent's goal, his team receives one point.
8. The team which did not score starts the ball from the center of the field.

Fouls: Any player who contacts another player while the latter is attempting to kick the ball commits a foul.

Penalty: A free kick is awarded to the other team.

Teaching suggestions:
Use only one soccer ball at the start; later two or more may be added.

Soccer: Basic Rules and Regulations

By the time children reach the fifth grade the majority of skills necessary to play soccer should have been learned. This does not imply, however, that time should not be devoted to practice activities and lead-up games. The game of soccer, with some basic modifications, should be played in its entirety periodically during an instructional unit. If this is done, children will understand the reason for practice sessions and lead-up activities designed to improve the speed and accuracy of the required skills of the game.
1. Field of Play:

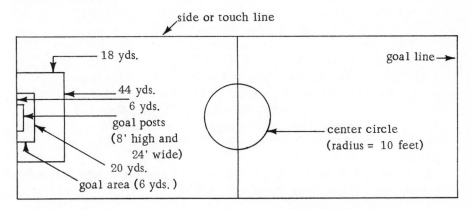

Length of field—not more than 120 feet; not less than 110 feet.
Width of field—not more than 75 feet; not less than 65 feet.

2. Name of players and line up positions. (Positions players take at start of game, after a goal is scored, and after half time.)

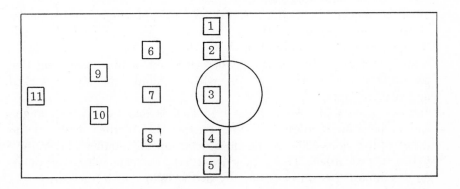

No.	Name of Position	No.	Name of Position
1.	Left wing (outside left)	7.	Center half back
2.	Inside left	8.	Right half back
3.	Center forward	9.	Left full back
4.	Inside right	10.	Right full back
5.	Right wing (outside right)	11.	Goalie
6.	Left half back		

3. Penalty kick: If a defensive player, other than the goalie, touches the ball in the 18 × 44 yard penalty area, a penalty kick is awarded to the offensive team. When this kick is taken from the twelve yard penalty mark by any member of the offensive team, the goalie must stand on the line between the goalposts, and all other players must stand outside the penalty area until the ball has been kicked. After the kick has been taken, any player from either team may enter the penalty area.

4. Free Kicks: There are two types of free kicks, namely, the Direct Free Kick and the Indirect Free Kick. Each type will be explained following.

   a. Direct Free Kick: A direct free kick is one from which a goal may be scored directly. In other words, it can be kicked from the place where the infraction occurred and travel directly through the goal.

      When it is awarded: This kick is awarded to a team when any player on the opposing team commits any of the following infractions while outside the penalty area:

      (Remember, if it occurs inside the penalty area, it would become a penalty kick, taken from the penalty mark.)

      (1) kicking an opponent.

      (2) charging in a violent and dangerous manner.

      (3) tripping an opponent.

      (4) handling the ball, (Note: the goalkeeper may handle the ball only when he is inside the penalty area. If he handles the ball when he is outside the penalty area, a direct free kick, therefore, will be awarded to the opposing team), or

      (5) pushing with hands or arms.

      What happens: The ball is placed on the spot where the infraction occurred. Any player on the team awarded the kick may then take the kick. He lines up behind the ball (three or four yards) and players from both teams may stand anywhere in front of him, providing they are at least ten yards away. The whistle sounds, the ball is kicked, and play resumes.

   b. Indirect Free Kick: An indirect free kick is one from which a goal cannot be scored unless it is first touched by another player before it enters the goal. (The goalie does not count as another player.)

      When it is awarded: This kick is awarded to a team when any player on the opposing team commits any of the following infractions:

(1) a player who kicks the ball a second time before it has been played by another player at the kickoff, a free kick, a goal kick, or a corner kick.

(2) a ball not kicked forward from a penalty kick.

(3) carrying the ball by the goalie more than four steps without bouncing the ball on the ground.

(4) ungentlemanly conduct—improper language, unnecessary arguing, etc.

(5) off side, and

(6) obstruction other than holding.

5. Throw-in: When the ball is pitched, headed, or legally forced over the touch line by a player, the opposing team is awarded a throw-in.
What happens: The ball is put back into play from behind the touch line at a point from which the ball went out. The player who makes the throw-in must have both hands on the ball and throw it from behind his head. He must also have part of both feet in contact with the ground until he has released the ball. If it is not thrown in properly, the opposing team is awarded the second throw-in.

6. Corner Kick: When the ball is kicked, headed, or legally forced over the goal line by a player on the defensive team, the opposing team is awarded a corner kick.
What happens: The ball is placed on the corner of the field (where the side line meets the goal line) on the side the ball went out. Usually the wing player kicks the ball into play. All other players may stand any-where on the field providing they are at least ten yards away from the ball.

7. Goal Kick: When the ball is kicked, headed, or legally forced over the goal line by a player on the attacking team, a goal kick is awarded to the defensive team.
What happens: The ball is placed in the goal area on the side nearest to where the ball crossed the line. Any defensive player may kick the ball back into play; however, it must cross the penalty line to be in play. If not, it is taken over. The offensive team remains outside the penalty area until the ball has crossed the penalty line.

8. Off side: A player is off side if he is nearer his opponent's goal line than the ball at the moment the ball is played. He is not off side, however, under the following circumstances: (a) He is in his own half of the field; (b) there are two opponents nearer their goal than he is at the moment the ball is played; or (c) when he received a ball directly from a corner kick, a throw-in, or a goal kick.

Examples of off side:

Case I: The right winger is off side because he does not have two defensive players in front of him at the moment the ball was kicked.

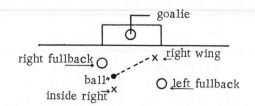

Case II: In this case, "at the moment" the inside right kicked the ball, the right winger had two defensive players in front of him. Now the right winger may dribble in and attempt a shot at the goal.

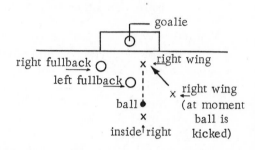

9. Scoring: One point is awarded to the attacking team if any player kicks, heads, or legally causes the ball to cross over the goal line between the goalpost and under the crossbar. A ball accidentally kicked through the goal by a defensive player, therefore, would count for the attacking team.

Evaluative Techniques

Although there are a number of standardized tests to measure the various skills of soccer, in the main they are designed for secondary and college level students. The same tests, however, can be modified to meet the level of ability of upper elementary school-age children. The following test battery is an example of a "teacher-made" test which can be administered without elaborate equipment and in a short period of time. Keep scores from year to year in order to develop appropriate norms for your school.

Soccer Skill Test						
Name	Kick and Trap total score	Dribbling	Shooting	Subjective evaluation	Total score	Grade
1 2 3 4 5		Rank all total scores for the class then convert to letter grades or to ratings (Superior, Good, etc.). ———⟶				

Test No. 1. Kick and Trap: Draw line five feet from the wall. The ball is
placed on the line. Each player attempts to kick the ball and hit the
front wall as many times as possible within thirty seconds. All kicks must
be taken from behind the five foot line. If a player loses control of the
ball, he may retrieve it with his feet and continue kicking. Count the
total number of kicks. One point for each successful hit. Allow two trials
and record the highest score.

Test No. 2. Dribbling: Arrange four chairs as shown in the diagram. Place a
ball on the starting line.

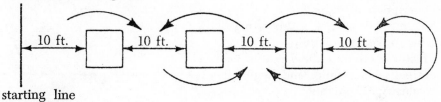

starting line

Each player starts behind the starting line with both hands resting on
his knees. On signal "go," he dribbles the ball around the chairs in a
zigzag pattern. One point is awarded each time he passes a chair. Allow
thirty seconds for the test. Two trials are also allowed with the highest
score recorded.

Test No. 3. Shooting: Arrange the field markings in front of the goalposts as
shown in the diagram. Players may use the right or left approach. Each
player starts to dribble the ball in the approach area and must continue
moving into the "shooting zone." While he is in the shooting zone he
must attempt to kick the ball through the goalposts. Ten trials are given
with five points awarded for each successful goal.

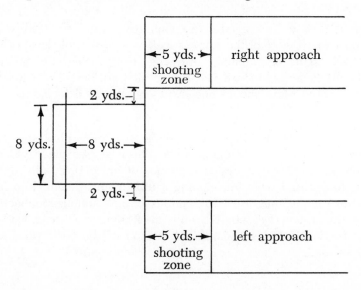

Test No. 4. Subjective Evaluation: Establish a criteria which represents the
    skills and playing ability required in soccer. For example, using such
    skills as passing, dribbling, team play, and defensive ability, the teacher
    would award each player a total point score from zero to fifty points.
    Three players can be used as judges with the average score recorded.

SOFTBALL

Description of Skills
Suggested Sequence of Presenting Skills and Rules
How to Develop a Unit
Practice Activities and Lead-up Games
Softball: Basic Rules and Regulations
Evaluative Techniques

If softball is to be played as a competitive team game every participant
must have a knowledge of the rules as well as a reasonable level of proficiency
in the basic skills of catching, throwing, and hitting. Furthermore, every
child should have experience in playing all positions. The catcher, pitcher,
and first base positions should not always be allocated to the more proficient
players.

In the first section, all pertinent skills have been illustrated and accompanied by a list of basic teaching hints. The next two parts will provide information relating to a suggested sequence of presenting skills and rules and
a format to be used when developing a unit of instruction. Immediately following the sample unit are two sections of low-organization activities: the
first is a list of practice activities and the second is a list of lead-up games.
The last section includes a simplified version of the basic rules and regulations of softball.

Description of Skills

Softball skills for elementary school-age children may be classified as hitting and fielding skills. The first five throwing and catching skills are appropriate for all intermediate grade levels. With reference to the next three hitting or batting skills, all are important, with bunting and fungo hitting probably the most difficult for fourth graders and girls in the fifth and sixth grades.

THROWING

It is permissible in softball to throw the ball from an underhand, side or overhand position. Underhand throwing or pitching, however, is the only legal throw for a pitcher. Basic fundamentals to stress with all types of throws are: (1) Watch or "keep your eye" on the target until the ball is thrown; (2) learn accuracy and form first, speed and distance later; and (3) follow through after every throw.

OVERHAND THROW

FIG. 9.42	**FIG. 9.43**
Stand with left foot forward and weight evenly distributed on both feet. Hold ball with both hands in front of chest. Twist body toward the right as ball is brought upward above shoulder and behind the ear and shift body weight to right foot.	Simultaneously, swing right arm forward, rotate shoulders to left, and shift weight to left foot. Continue forward with right arm and release ball off fingertips. After completing the throw, step forward with the right foot.

UNDERHAND THROW OR PITCH

FIG. 9.44

FIG. 9.45

Stand facing target (batter) with both feet parallel and slightly apart and weight evenly distributed on both feet. Hold ball in front of body with right hand and left hand slightly under the ball. Simultaneously swing right hand downward and backward, twist body to right, raise extended left arm forward and shift weight to right foot.

Simultaneously swing right arm forward and parallel to body, rotate shoulders toward the left, step forward and shift weight to left foot. Release ball, follow through with the right hand and step forward with right foot.

CATCHING

In softball the ball may be caught with one or both hands; however, for elementary school children we should adhere to the saying "two hands for

UNDERHAND CATCH

FIG. 9.46

FIG. 9.47

Stand with feet parallel and approximately twelve inches apart and weight evenly distributed on both feet. Hold arms slightly apart and in front of body with elbows slightly bent. The baby fingers should be close to each other while the other fingers and thumbs are slightly cupped.

Simultaneously extend arms and hands to meet the ball, step forward and shift weight to left (or right) foot. The ball should be caught with cupped hands, palms toward oncoming ball. Draw hands back toward the body and shift weight to the right foot.

Overhand Catch

FIG. 9.48

FIG. 9.49

Stand with one foot slightly in front of the other and weight evenly distributed on both feet. The arms are forward and upward, elbows bent, fingers and thumbs slightly spread, thumbs are inside and touching.

As the ball approaches, simultaneously shift body weight to the front foot and extend hands upward. The palms are slightly cupped, thumbs close together, and fingers pointing upward. At the instant the ball hits the palms, close fingers around ball and relax elbows. Bring ball down in front of body and shift weight to rear foot in preparation for the next throw.

Grounding

FIG. 9.50

FIG. 9.51

Begin with feet parallel and about shoulder distance apart. The body weight should be well forward with hands near or on the bent knees. As the ball approaches, drop downward placing right knee on ground and hands slightly forward, with fingers pointing down and thumbs pointing upward and sideward.

Cup hands around the oncoming ball, draw hands toward chest and raise trunk.

beginners." The two-hand underhand and overhand catch and grounding, therefore, will be described for major emphasis in upper elementary softball activities. As in so many sports the principle of "keeping the eye on the ball" until it is caught deserves continuous attention. Emphasize the idea of the hands "going out" to meet the ball followed by the recoil action toward the body. Finally stress the use of two hands; it's better to be safe than sorry.

BATTING

There are three basic ways of hitting a ball in softball. The first, and most important, is hitting a pitched ball with maximum force and follow-through. Bunting is a form of hitting a pitched ball; however, there are basic differences in grip, force, and follow-through. Fungo batting is simply throwing the ball up with one hand, regrasping the bat, and hitting the ball before it hits the ground. Fundamental to all types of batting are:
1. Keep "your eyes" on the ball until it has been hit.
2. Maintain a firm grip on the bat, and
3. Follow through on every hit with the exception of bunting.

BATTING

FIG. 9.52   FIG. 9.53

Stand with the left side toward the pitcher, head and eyes facing pitcher, spread legs comfortably with weight evenly distributed on both feet. Elbows are bent and away from the body. Grip the handle with the left hand touching the right. The bat should be held over the right shoulder with left elbow at shoulder height.

At the moment the ball is pitched, shift weight to rear foot, then, simultaneously swing bat downward and forward and shift weight to front foot. After contacting the ball, continue twisting body to the left as bat swings around in a wide arc ending over left shoulder.

BUNTING

FIG. 9.54

FIG. 9.55

Stand with left side toward the pitcher, head and eyes facing pitcher, legs spread comfortably with weight evenly distributed on both feet. The bat should be held over the right shoulder with left elbow at shoulder height. As the ball moves toward the strike zone, simultaneously draw the front foot sideward and backward, twist body toward the ball, release right hand and pull bat downward and forward.

The tips of the fingers and thumb of the right hand are behind the bat and near the end. As the ball hits the bat, the fingers and thumb relax allowing the bat to "push" toward the palm of the hand.

FUNGO BATTING

FIG. 9.56

FIG. 9.57

Start with feet parallel and comfortably spread apart, with weight evenly distributed on both feet. The bat is held suspended over the right shoulder while the ball is held in the left hand.

Simultaneously toss the ball upward, swing bat downward and forward grasping it with left hand. Continue forward, transferring weight to front foot and twisting body toward the left. Hit the ball approximately in front of left foot and follow through with swing around left shoulder.

Suggested Sequence of Presenting Skills and Rules

The problems relating to selecting and teaching appropriate skills and rules of softball are very similar to those found in teaching basketball activities. Most children at this age level are acquainted, through the medium of television, organized leagues, and "sand-lot" pick-up games, with the skills and rules of softball. The problem, however, is compounded for teachers of this age level, in that boys begin to develop a keener interest and a higher level of skill in virtually all aspects of the game. This, of course, is exemplified in the large number of "out-of-school" organized leagues and the popular boy's pastime of playing catch. Girls at this level, because of social and other more complex reasons, tend to move away from highly competitive activities.

If a teacher is organizing a unit of softball for a mixed class, it is advisable to separate the sexes, particularly for lead-up games or when playing a competitive game of softball. It must be emphasized that when girls, even those in the sixth and seventh grades, are playing softball together, they will enjoy the activity. There are occasions, however, mainly for social reasons, to play a game of mixed softball. When this occurs, have a boy pitch to the opposing boys and a girl for their opposite numbers.

With the above factors in mind, the following suggested sequence is provided as a rough guideline. The skill tests found in the latter part of this section should be used to pretest the class to determine what skills need to be given the greatest emphasis.

Suggested Sequence of Presenting Skills and Rules of Softball					
	Grade				
Skill	4	5	6	7	Rule Presentation
1. Throwing	X	X	X	X	Team positions
Underhand throw	X	X	X	X	Pitching rule
Overhand throw	X	X	X	X	
2. Catching	X	X	X	X	
Underhand catch	X	X	X	X	Outs (fly and touched out)
Overhand catch	X	X	X	X	
Grounders	X	X	X	X	
3. Batting	X	X	X	X	Strikes and balls, batting order
Batting a pitched ball	X	X	X	X	Runner off base
Bunting a pitched ball		X	X	X	Third strike rule, in field fly
Fungo hitting		X	X	X	
	X	X	X	X	Base running rules

How to Develop a Unit

Softball activities are normally taught during the last two or three months of the school year. As in so many other major sports, factors such as size of class, available field space, and time allotment for physical education (daily or alternate days for physical education) will determine the length of time you wish to devote to softball. Also, you may wish to include other activities such as dance and self-testing activities, hence a comprehensive unit on softball will not be outlined. Instead, a format for unit construction is provided as a guide to show you how to use the Practice Activities and Lead-up Games for softball. Further, the unit is based upon the premise that each thirty minute lesson Monday, Wednesday, and Friday is composed of two parts. The first is the explanation and demonstration of a skill. After the demonstration there should be a period of time for practice activities or one or more lead-up games. Since the time for physical education on Tuesday and Thursday is relatively short, only practice activity or lead-up games are scheduled for these days.

┌── See Description of Skills (page 239 to 243)

┌── See Practice Activities and Lead-up games (page 245 to 252)

	Monday (30 min)	Tuesday (15 min)	Wednesday (30 min)	Thursday (15 min)	Friday (30 min)
First week	Explain Overhand throw Wall Throwing ↓ Lead-up: Overtake	Practice: Overtake Lead-up Softball throw relay	Explain: Overhand Catching Practice: Zigzag Passing Lead-up: Shuttle throw	Review: Softball throw relay Shuttle throw	Explain: Hitting Practice: Swing at four Lead-up Beatball softball
Second week	Note: Continue the above pattern with weeks 2, 3, and 4, or modify as illustrated in this week				
	Softball Activities	Dance Activities	Softball Activities	Self-testing Activities	Softball Activities
Third week	Repeat according to the pattern you select.				
Fourth week	Repeat as above.				

Practice Activities and Lead-up Games

The following practice activities and lead-up games will assist in developing such skills as throwing, catching, grounding, and batting. Modify any of these activities to meet unique limitations of the play area and to cope with variations in the level of skill and interest of your class.

Practice Activities and Lead-up Games

Activity	Page	Throwing	Catching	Batting	Base Running	Grade Level		
						4	5	6
A. PRACTICE ACTIVITIES								
1. Zigzag Throwing	246	X	X			X	X	X
2. Overtake	246	X	X		X	X	X	X
3. Wall Throwing	247	X				X	X	X
4. Fly Ball Catching	247	X	X	X		X	X	X
5. Swing at Four	248	X	X	X	X	X	X	X
B. LEAD-UP GAMES								
6. Bat Ball	248	X	X	X	X	X	X	X
7. Throw for Distance	248	X				X	X	X
8. Overtake	249	X	X			X	X	X
9. Softball Throw Relay	250	X	X			X	X	X
10. Long Ball	250	X	X	X	X	X	X	X
11. Twenty-one Softball	251	X	X	X	X	X	X	X
12. Fungo Softball	251	X	X	X			X	X
13. Beatball Softball	252	X	X	X	X		X	X
14. Seventeen Man Softball	252	X	X	X	X	X	X	X

No. 1: Zigzag Throwing (4 - 6)

Formation:	Divide class into three or four squads of six to eight players. Arrange squads in a zigzag formation with approximately twenty feet between lines.
Basic Drill:	The first player throws across to the second; second throws back to the third; and continue until the end of the line.
Variations:	Optional throwing—The first player begins throwing; however, after the second player receives the ball he may throw to any player on the opposite line, etc.

No. 2: Overtake (4 - 6)

Formation:	Divide class into squads of eight to ten players. Arrange squads around bases with player "A" at

pitcher's line, "B" on home plate, "C" on first, "D" on second, and "E" on third base. Remaining players form a line opposite home plate.

Basic Drill: When the whistle blows, player "A" throws to "B," and at the same time "F" takes off for first base and around bases, attempting to reach home plate before the ball. Two rules apply: (1) base runner must touch all bases, and (2) rotate players after each run. "A" takes "B's" position, "B" goes to the back of line, "F" takes "A's" and everyone shifts one place to the right.

Variations: a. Make two diamonds with the smaller one for runners and larger one for throwers.

b. Add one or more fielders.

No. 3: Wall Throwing (4 - 6)

Formation: Divide class into three or four squads of six to eight players. Arrange squads in a file formation with the first player thirty feet away from the target.

Basic Drill: Use old softballs. The first player throws three to five balls at the target, (strike zone drawn on wall), then retrieves his balls. The first player gives the balls to the next player, then goes to the back of his line.

Variations: a. Increase distance and change size of target for overhand throwing.

b. Place a batter standing next to target. (He does not bat.)

No. 4: Fly Ball Catching (4 - 6)

Formation: Place one batter at home plate and remaining players scattered in the field.

Basic Drill: The batter using "fungo" batting hits fly balls into the field. As soon as the fielder catches a fly ball, he becomes the batter.

Variations: a. Place all fielders in a large semicircle and require the batter to hit two balls to each player in turn. Rotate after last player has received his second fly.

b. Use a pitcher and catcher as part of basic drill.

No. 5: Swing at Four (4 - 6)

Formation:	Divide class into two or three squads of ten to twelve players. Arrange squads according to infield positions with spare players in a line formation behind home plate.
Basic Drill:	The pitcher throws four balls to each hitter. Batter attempts to hit each ball into the infield. Infield players retrieve ball and throw it to first. The first baseman returns ball to pitcher. Rotate players after each player has had four hits. The batter would take the third baseman's position with everyone shifting one place to the left. Catcher goes to the back of the "waiting" line.
Variations:	Add outfielders and allow batters to hit anywhere.

No. 6: Bat Ball (4 - 6)

Formation:	Divide players into two teams of nine each; one in the field and one at bat.
Equipment:	Softball and bat, two bases.
No. of Players:	9 on each team.
Skills:	Throwing, catching, and batting.

How to Play:
1. The first player of team at bat hits the ball into field and runs to first base and home in one complete trip. He may not stop on the base.
2. If he makes complete trip without being put out, he scores one run for his team.
3. Runner is out if (a) fielder catches fly ball; (b) fielder touches runner with ball before he reaches home.
4. When team at bat makes three outs it goes into field, and team in field comes to bat.
5. Winner is team with most scores at end of playing period. (Teams must have same number of times at bat.)

Teaching suggestions:
1. Have waiting batter stand behind a restraining line.
2. Alternate pitchers and catchers. Alternate boy and girl in batting order.
3. Try two outs if one team stays up too long.
4. Vary distance to base according to level of skill.

No. 7: Throw for Distance (4 - 6)

Formation:	Arrange field as illustrated in the diagram.
Equipment:	Tape measure and softballs.
No. of Players:	4 to 5 players on each team.
Skills:	Throwing.

How to Play:
1. Throw must be made from within two restraining lines.
2. After a reasonable warm-up, the pupil throws the ball as far as possible from behind the restraining line.
3. The thrower may take one or more steps providing he remains within the restraining lines.
4. The longest throw wins or total yardage for each line wins.

No. 8: Overtake (4 - 6)

Formation:	Arrange class into large circle formation with five to six feet between each player.
Equipment:	One softball per team.
No. of Players:	10 to 16 per team.
Skills:	Throwing and catching.

How to Play:
1. The players stand in a circle and count off by twos.
2. Those numbered "one" are members of one team and "twos" are the other.
3. Each team selects a captain who stands in the center of the circle of players.
4. Both captains have a ball. On signal, each captain, starting with any team member, tosses his ball to him, who, in turn, tosses it back to the captain.
5. The captain tosses it to the next team member (in a clockwise direction) who also tosses it back to the captain.
6. The ball is tossed in this manner clockwise around the circle by both teams until each ball has been thrown to all members of the team and is back in the captain's hands.
7. One team "overtakes" the other team when its ball passes that of the other team as the balls are tossed around the circle.
8. The team which tosses the ball completely around the circle as described, and finishes first with its ball in the hands of the captain, scores one point.
9. When a team "overtakes" and finishes first, it scores two points. The team first scoring five points wins the game.

Teaching suggestions:
1. Explain and enforce response to the signal used to start the tosses. Use the same signal for each start.
2. Play the game with various kinds of balls, different throws, and passes.
3. Vary distance according to level of skill.

No. 9: Softball Throw Relay (4 - 6)

Formation: Arrange teams in equal lines behind a starting line with approximately six feet between each team. Draw a second throwing line ten feet in front of the starting line. Place a catcher for each team on a third line drawn twenty-five feet in front of the throwing line.

No. of Players: 20 to 30.

Equipment: Chalk or stick to draw line.

Skills: Throwing and catching.

How to Play:

1. Each player runs to the throwing line to receive the ball thrown by the catcher, then throws it back to the catcher.
2. The first thrower returns to his line and tags the next waiting player on the starting line, who, in turn, continues the relay.

Teaching suggestions:

1. Have the children use various throwing skills, underhand, overhand, left handed, and right handed.
2. Alternate catchers each time a team wins; first person in line then becomes catcher.
3. Keep children behind starting line until their turn to throw.

No. 10: Long Ball (4 - 6)

Formation: Divide class into equal teams. Fielding team consists of a pitcher and catcher with remaining players scattered in field.

Equipment: Softball, bat, and 2 bases.

No. of Players: 9 on each team.

Skills: Throwing, catching, and hitting.

How to Play:

1. Players are divided into two teams (number each player).
2. Each team selects a pitcher and catcher. Other players are fielders or batters.
3. When the ball is hit the batter runs to base, and if possible returns home, scoring a point.
4. Any hit is good and there are no fouls in the game.
5. Base runner may stop on base.
6. Any number of runners may be on base at the same time.
7. Runners may not steal home.
8. Batter is out when: Strikes out, touched off base, steals a base, throws bat, or a fly ball caught.
9. One point for each run.

Teaching suggestions:
1. Alternate pitchers and catchers.
2. Draw a line behind batter's box for other children to wait behind.
3. Move pitcher closer as skill indicates.

No. 11: Twenty-one Softball (4 - 6)

Formation:	Arrange teams as in regular softball.
Equipment:	Two bats, one ball, and 4 bases.
No. of Players:	9 to 10 on each team.
Skills:	Throwing, catching, and hitting.

How to Play:
Play according to regular softball rules with the following exceptions:
1. Batter gets three swings to hit the ball.
2. Batter hits the ball and runs the bases in order until he is put out.
3. Runner safe at first scores one point; safe at second, two points; safe at third, three points; and home, four points.
4. After three outs teams exchange places.
5. The first team to score twenty-one points wins.

Teaching suggestions:
1. Teach fielders to throw to the base ahead of the runner to put him out.
2. Keep waiting batters ten to fifteen feet away from batter's box.
3. Change pitcher and batter each time teams change positions.
4. Play same game only use "fungo" hitting instead of pitcher.
5. Change scoring to eleven or fifteen rather than twenty-two.

No. 12: Fungo Softball (5 - 6)

Formation:	Arrange class into groups with one batter and the remaining players scattered in the field of play.
Equipment:	Two bats, two softballs.
No. of Players:	9 to 12 on each team.
Skills:	Throwing, catching, and hitting.

How to Play:
1. Batter stands at home plate and "fungo" hits the ball to the rest of the players in the field.
2. If a fielder catches a fly ball, he changes with the batter.
3. If a fielder fields two grounders, he becomes the batter.
4. If the fielder rolls the ball from the spot where it stopped and hits the bat placed on the ground in front of the batter, the fielder becomes the batter.
5. No score is kept.

Teaching suggestions:
1. Fielders should be at least twenty feet from the batter.
2. Alternate fielding positions.

No. 13: Beatball Softball (5 - 6)

Formation:	Arrange teams as in regular softball.
Equipment:	Bat, softball, and four bases.
No. of Players:	9 on each team.
Skills:	Throwing, catching, and hitting.

How to Play:

Play according to regular softball rules with the following exceptions:

1. Any fielders who get the ball must throw to the first baseman who, in turn, must touch the base with the ball in his hand, then continues throwing from first to second, second to third, and third to home.
2. If the ball gets home ahead of runner, then he is out.
3. If runner beats the ball, he scores a run for his team.
4. Three outs and the teams exchange places.

Teaching suggestions:

1. Teach the fielders to throw around the runner when he is running the bases.
2. Rotate the fielders so they learn to play all positions.
3. Use "fungo" hitting instead of a pitcher.
4. Move bases closer together for girls or separate into boys' and girls' games in separate diamonds.

No. 14: Seventeen Man Softball (4 - 6)

Formation:	Arrange teams as in regular softball with girls on inside bases (forty-five feet between bases) and boys on outside bases (fifty-five feet between bases).
Equipment:	2 bats, 4 bases, 1 softball.
No. of Players:	17 on each team.
Skills:	Throwing, catching, and hitting.

How to Play:

1. There are two diamonds; girls play the forty-five foot bases and the boys play the fifty-five foot bases.
2. The girls pitch to girls and the boys pitch to boys. A boy catches for both pitchers.
3. A boy bats then a girl bats.
4. When a boy bats the ball, the boy fielders must throw to the fifty-five foot bases.
5. When a girl bats the ball, the girl fielders must throw to the forty-five foot bases.
6. One point for each run.

Softball: Basic Rules and Regulations

Although the level of skill development for each grade and class will vary, the complete game of softball should be played periodically throughout a unit of softball. By playing the game according to the basic rules, children learn to appreciate the value of practice and team play. Modifications in the rules may be such as shortening the length between bases, allowing girls to pitch to girls, and reducing the number of strikes to two. While children are playing the full game, the teacher should make a note of the major weaknesses in order to select appropriate drills and lead-up games that can be used to improve these deficiencies.

1. Field of Play and Positions:

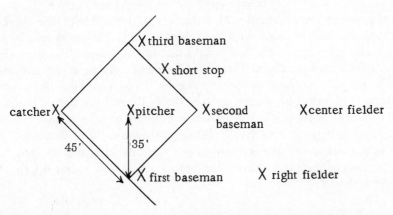

2. Batting Order: Players are permitted to hit in any order; however, it is wise to have players at bat according to their positions. Once order is established, it cannot be changed even if players change their positions.
3. The batter advances to first base when he: (1) hits a fair ball and reaches first base before the ball; (2) is walked, that is, receives four called balls; (3) is hit by a pitched ball; or (4) is interfered with by the catcher when batting.
4. The batter is out when he: (1) has three strikes; (2) is thrown out at first; (3) is tagged before reaching first base; (4) hits a fair or foul ball that is caught on the fly; (5) hits the third strike and the ball is caught by the catcher; (6) bunts a foul on the third strike; (7) throws the bat more than ten feet; (8) steps on home plate when batting; (9) interferes with catcher when he is catching a fly or putting out a runner coming home; or (10) fouls any ball to the catcher that rises above the batter's head and is caught.
5. The base runner when traveling the bases: (1) may advance to the next base after a fly is caught; (2) must advance to the next base when forced to do so by another base runner; (3) may advance one base on an over-

throw at first or third base; (4) may advance two bases when overthrows are in the field of play; (5) may attempt to steal a base as soon as the ball leaves the pitcher's hand; or (6) may advance to the next base on a fair hit that is not caught on the fly.

6. The base runner is out when he: (1) leaves the base before the ball leaves the pitcher's hand; (2) is forced to run to the next base and does not arrive before the fielder touches the base with the ball in his possession; (3) leaves the base before a fly ball is caught and a fielder tags him or that base before he returns; (4) is hit by a batted ball when off base; (5) intentionally interferes with a member of the fielding team; (6) is tagged when off the base; (7) fails to touch a base and the fielder tags him or the base before he returns; (8) passes another base runner; or (9) touches a base that is occupied by another base runner.

7. The pitcher: (1) must stand with both feet on the rubber, face the batter and hold the ball in front with both hands; (2) is allowed one step forward and must deliver the ball while taking that step; (3) must deliver the ball with an underhand throw; (4) cannot fake or make any motion toward the plate without delivering the ball; (5) cannot deliberately roll or bounce the ball; (6) cannot deliver the ball until the batter is ready.

8. If there is an illegal pitch, the batter is entitled to take a base.

9. The game shall be five to seven innings, as agreed by both teams. When there is not sufficient time to complete the game, the score reverts to the even innings score (the score after both squads have been up the same number of times).

Evaluative Techniques

There are several tests that can be used to measure the basic skills of softball. The following tests are quite reliable and can be administered with student help in a short period of time. Modify any test item to meet your own teaching situation and add items if desired. Also, keep scores from year to year in order to build appropriate norms for your school.

Softball Skill Test						
Name	Accuracy throw (total points)	Distance throw (total points)	Fielding (total points)	Subjective Evaluation (50 points)	Total	Grade
1 2 3 4	Rank all total scores for the class ⸻ then convert to letter grades or change to ratings (Superior, Good, etc.).				⟶	

Test No. 1. Accuracy Throw: Place a target on the wall as shown in the accompanying diagram. Use a regulation softball.

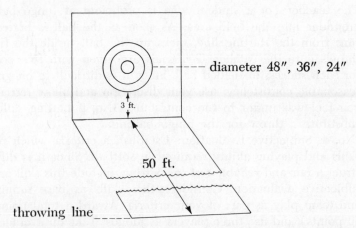

diameter 48″, 36″, 24″

3 ft.

50 ft.

throwing line

A player is given ten consecutive throws from behind the starting line. He must use the overhand throw. Score 6, 4, and 2 for hits within each respective circle. If a ball hits a line, award the higher value. One trial only and record the total score.

Test No. 2. Distance Throw: Place the following lines on the field. Stakes can be used as a substitute for white gypsum lines. Use a regulation softball.

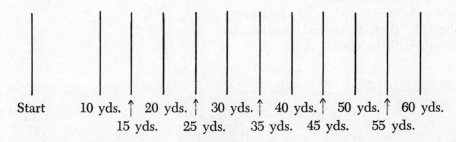

Start   10 yds. ↑ 20 yds. ↑ 30 yds. ↑ 40 yds.↑ 50 yds. ↑ 60 yds.

            15 yds.   25 yds.   35 yds.   45 yds.   55 yds.

Test No. 3. Fielding: Place the following lines on a field. Stakes or other "corner" markers can be substituted for lines.

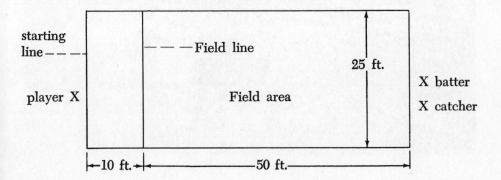

starting
line — — —   — — —Field line

                                                          25 ft.

                                                                    X batter

player X   Field area   X catcher

        |←10 ft.→|←————————50 ft.————————→|

The teacher (or a student who is proficient at fungo batting) bats a grounder into the field area. As soon as the ball is batted, the player runs from the starting line, picks up the ball inside the field area and throws it to the catcher. Ten trials are given with five points awarded for each successful fielded ball. Since it is difficult to hit grounders with reasonable consistency, use your discretion and allow retrials on any ball you feel was unfair to the contestant. Also, if batting skill is too poor, substitute a throw for the fungo batting.

Test No. 4. Subjective Evaluation: Establish a criteria which represents the skills and playing ability required in softball. Since it is difficult to construct a fair and reliable test for batting, include this skill as part of your subjective evaluation. Consider other skills as base running, catching, and team play as part of your criteria. Award a total point score (0 to 50 points) and use three players as judges. Take an average of the three ratings.

VOLLEYBALL

Description of Skills
Suggested Sequence of Presenting Skills and Rules
How to Develop a Unit
Practice Activities and Lead-up Games
Volleyball: Basic Rules and Regulations
Evaluative Techniques

The game of Volleyball was originated by William G. Morgan in 1895 while he was teaching at the Y.M.C.A. in Holyoke, Massachusetts. Although the rules, number of players, and size of ball have changed since the first game, it can be classified as an American contribution to the world of sports. Today, volleyball is played in more than sixty countries and by more than fifty million people each year. The reasons for this phenomenal growth in such a short span of history are probably due to the game's simplicity, enjoyment, and general contributions to physical fitness. Because volleyball can be modified to meet the limitations of available facilities and varying levels of proficiency, it is particularly adaptable to the upper elementary school physical education program.

The first part of this section will include a description of the basic skills and a suggested sequence of presenting skills and rules for each grade level. A sample unit is provided to assist teachers in organizing the various volleyball activities. The following sections contain a list of practice activities and lead-up games with appropriate grade levels indicated. The latter sections include a simplified version of the basic rules and regulations of volleyball as well as suggested evaluative techniques.

Description of Skills

There are two basic skills used in volleyball, namely, serving and passing or volleying a ball. Each of these skills may, however, be modified, such as the two-hand underhand volley requiring the use of forearms. Basic skills for intermediate grades will be described and illustrated below.*

PASSING OR VOLLEYING

In volleyball, the ball may be passed or volleyed to another player or over the net by an underhand or overhand hit. Two hands must be used in the overhand pass while the forearms are normally used for the underhand pass. When teaching both types of skills, children should be taught to watch the ball and not their hands or opponents. The body weight should be evenly distributed on both feet before the ball reaches the player. Finally, after the the ball has been hit, stress the follow-through with hands and arms.

Two-Hand Overhand Pass

This is the most important volleyball skill for elementary school-age children to learn. It is virtually the perquisite to playing the game of volleyball; hence, requires a great deal of practice and constant correction by the teacher. Teachers should thoroughly understand the following description before introducing this skill to the class.[2]

---

*All skills are described for the right-handed child. Descriptions relating to hand, arm, leg, and foot positions must be reversed for the left-handed child.

2. D. Turkington and G. Kirchner, *Volleyball for Intermediate Grades*, (Vancouver: Best Printers, 1968), p. 12.

FIG. 9.58   **FIG. 9.59**   **FIG. 9.60**

Begin with knees slightly bent, back straight, elbows bent and sideward. The fingers should be slightly spread apart with thumbs facing each other. As the ball approaches, the player should be able to see it through the "window" (Fig. 9.58) created by his thumbs and fingers.

As the ball drops, extend the body upward and slightly forward. Hit the ball with "stiff" fingers. Do not allow the fingers to relax as this will lead to catching the ball, then throwing it. Follow through in this upward and forward direction.

Two-Hand Underhand Hit (Bumping)

The forearm bounce pass, known as "bumping" or the two-hand "dig," should be used when the ball must be hit below the waist or when a player's back is toward the net. This skill is performed by allowing the ball to bounce off the flat surface of the clasped hands, wrists, or forearms. There is very little follow-through.

BUMPING

FIG. 9.61   **FIG. 9.62**

Hand position: Place one hand on top of the other, then fold thumbs into the palm of the top hand.

As the ball approaches, keep back straight, bend knees and lower arms in preparation for the underhand hit.

FIG. 9.63

FIG. 9.64

Keep back straight, raise arm slightly upward to allow the ball to contact the arms between wrists and elbows. At moment of contact the arms should be relaxed thus allowing the ball to "rebound" rather than being "hit."

As the ball is contacted, the whole body moves slightly in the direction of the ball and with a very slight follow-through with the arms.

SERVING

It is permissible in volleyball to serve the ball from an underhand or overhand position. The hand may be open or closed. Boys and girls in the intermediate grades are capable of developing a high level of skill in the underhand and overhand "float" serve. Begin with the underhand serve and, after sufficient skill has been developed with this skill, introduce the overhand serve.

Underhand Serve

There are several basic fundamentals to stress when teaching the underhand serve. Children should be taught to watch or "keep their eyes" on the ball until it has been hit. The ball should be hit with the heel of an open hand.

Although the official rule states the ball must be in the air when it is "contacted" by the striking hand, allow students to hit the ball out of the holding hand.

UNDERHAND SERVE

FIG. 9.65

FIG. 9.66

FIG. 9.67

Begin with the left foot slightly in front of the right, weight on the right foot and body bent slightly forward. Hold the ball with the palm of the left hand and toward the right side so ball is held in a "ready" position in front of right knee. The right arm is extended backward and upward.

Swing right arm downward and forward, and at the same time shift the weight to the left foot. The ball should be hit "out of the left hand" with the heel of the right hand.

Continue the follow-through action of the right arm and step forward with the right foot.

OVERHAND FLOAT SERVE

FIG. 9.68

FIG. 9.69

FIG. 9.70

The server stands facing the net with his left foot slightly forward. The right hand is held above the head in a "cocked" or ready position.

The ball is tossed up with the left hand above the right shoulder (2′ to 3′).

As the ball begins to descend, the elbow of the right arm leads as the arm is straightened in preparation for the contact. The contact is made with the heel of the hand and continues in a follow-through motion in the direction of the ball.

Overhand "Float" Serve

This serve should be learned only after a player has developed skill in performing the underhand service. The advantage of the "float" serve is it can be accurately placed and also has an element of deception caused by its floating and wobbling action.

Suggested Sequence of Presenting Skills and Rules

One of the most difficult tasks in teaching physical education is to determine whether the activity one wishes to teach has already been learned or if the children have the potential ability to develop the skills of the activity. Volleyball is no exception to this particular problem. Some children have already acquired, through previous grades, some of the basic skills and an understanding of the rules of this game. Others may not have seen a game of volleyball or even hit the ball in the correct manner. With these factors in mind, the following suggested sequence of presenting skills and rules should be considered as a basic guideline. Teachers of Grades Six and Seven should pretest, with the evaluative techniques provided in the latter part of this section, to determine what skills need the greatest emphasis.

SUGGESTED SEQUENCE OF PRESENTING SKILLS AND RULES

Skill	Grade				Rule Presentation
	4	5	6	7	
1. Two-hand overhand hit	X	X	X	X	The ball must be cleanly hit
		X	X	X	Three hits per side on each volley
2. Two-hand underhand hit (bumping)	X	X	X	X	
		X	X	X	Court dimensions
		X	X	X	Rotation of players
		X	X	X	It is a fault to touch the net
		X	X	X	Player may not hit the ball twice in succession
3. Serving Underhand serve	X	X	X	X	Serve must be taken from behind end line and within ten feet from right side
	X	X	X	X	Players must serve in rotation
		X	X	X	Center line may be stepped on but not over
Overhand serve		X	X	X	
4. Set				X	
5. Spike				X	
6. Block				X	See official rules

How to Develop a Unit

Volleyball activities are normally taught during the late fall or winter months. Since it is basically an indoor sport, factors such as size of class, available floor space, and time allotment will determine the length of time a teacher may wish to devote to it. Also, teachers may prefer to intersperse other activities such as dance or self-testing within a unit of volleyball. A comprehensive unit on volleyball, therefore, will not be outlined. Instead a modified format for unit construction is provided as a guide to show how to use the Practice Activities and Lead-up Games. The unit is based upon the premise that each thirty minute volleyball lesson is composed of two main parts. The first is the explanation and demonstration of a skill. After the demonstration there should be a period of time for practice activities or lead-up games.

The following unit outline is based upon a thirty minute physical education lesson Monday, Wednesday, and Friday. Only fifteen minutes are allotted for physical education on Tuesday and Thursday.

┌─── See Description of Skills (page 257 to 261)
┌─── See Practice Activities and Lead-up Games (page 263 to 270)

	Monday (30 min)	Tuesday (15 min)	Wednesday (30 min)	Thursday (15 min)	Friday (30 min)
First week	Explain Overhand Volley Practice: sitting and standing volley Lead-up: Keep It Up	Practice: Circle Volleying Lead-up: Nebraska Ball	Explain: Serving Practice: Wall Serving Lead-up: Modified Volleyball	Review: Keep It Up and Modified Volleyball	Review: Overhand Volley Practice: Circle Volleying Lead-up: Mass Volleyball

Note: Continue the above pattern with weeks 2, 3 and 4 or modify the unit as illustrated in this week.

Second week	Volleyball Activities	Dance Activities	Volleyball Activities	Self-testing Activities	Volleyball Activities
Third week	Repeat according to the pattern you select				
Fourth week	Repeat as above				

Practice Activities and Lead-up Games

The following practice activities and lead-up games will assist in developing such skills as overhand volleying, bumping, and serving. Modify any of these suggested activities to meet unique limitations of the playing area and to cope with variations in the level of skill and interest of your class.

Practice Activities and Lead-up Games							
Activity	Page	Overhand Volley	Underhand Volley	Serving	Suggested Grade Level		
					4	5	6
A. PRACTICE ACTIVITIES							
1. Sit or Stand Volleying	263	X	X		X	X	X
2. Wall Volleying	264	X	X	X	X	X	X
3. Shuttle Volleying	264	X	X	X	X	X	X
4. Circle Volleying	264	X	X		X	X	X
5. Zigzag Volleying	265	X	X	X		X	X
6. Circuit Volleyball	265	X	X	X		X	X
7. Alley Serving	266			X	X	X	X
8. Baseline Serving	266			X		X	X
B. LEAD-UP GAMES							
9. Nebraska Ball	266	X	X	X	X	X	
10. Bounce Net Ball	267	X	X		X	X	
11. Mass Volleyball	267	X	X	X	X	X	X
12. Keep It Up	267	X	X		X	X	X
13. Newcomb	268	X	X	X	X	X	X
14. Modified Volleyball	268	X	X	X	X	X	X
15. Circle Volley	269	X	X			X	X
16. Keep Away	269	X	X			X	X

No. 1: Sit or Stand Volleying (4 - 6)

Formation: Arrange children in a scattered formation. This drill requires one ball for each child; however, *any* type of inflated ball can be used (utility or soccer balls are excellent substitutes).

Basic Drill: Players begin in a sitting position and attempt to volley the ball as many times as possible.

Variations: a. While sitting volley between partners.

b. While standing volley between partners.

c. While sitting, volley against wall.

No. 2: Wall Volleying (4 - 6)

Formation:	Arrange class in a line formation around gymnasium wall with players about six feet away from the wall.
Basic Drill:	Each player, using an underhand or overhand volley, hits the ball against the wall as long as he can. As skill increases, move farther away from the wall.
Variations:	a. Volley with open hand position.
	b. Volley with closed hand position.
	c. Volley with one hand.
	d. Draw a line, square, or circle on the wall and stipulate that the ball must land within the new boundaries.
	e. Bounce ball on floor and hit the rebound toward the wall.
	f. Use same drill for serving.

No. 3: Shuttle Volleying (4 - 6)

Formation:	Divide class into three or four squads. Arrange squads in a shuttle formation with about six feet between players.
Basic Drill:	The first player throws the ball to the second player who, in turn, volleys the ball back to the third player who has taken the first player's position. Each player goes to the end of his line after he has volleyed the ball. Reverse direction of throw after everyone has had a turn.
Variations:	a. Same formation with net between lines.
	b. Volley with one or two hands.
	c. As proficiency develops, increase the distance between the lines.
	d. Bounce the ball rather than a direct throw.

No. 4: Circle Volleying (4 - 6)

Formation:	Divide class into three or four squads. Arrange class into circle formation with about five feet between each player.
Basic Drill:	The first player throws the ball up and toward the next player who, in turn, volleys the ball back to the first player. The first player throws to the second person and so on until every circle player has volleyed the ball back to the first player.

Variations:

    a. As proficiency increases have the first player throw to the second player; the second player volleys to the third; the third volleys to the fourth, and so on around the circle.

    b. Keep it up—after the first player has started the drill, allow anyone to hit the ball and see how long the squad can keep it up.

No. 5: Zigzag Volleying (5 - 6)

Formation: Divide the class into three or four squads of six to eight players. Arrange squads in a zigzag formation with about ten feet between each line.

Basic Drill: The first player throws the ball across to the second player who, in turn, volleys the ball back to the third player. Continue the zigzag volleying pattern until the last man receives the ball.

No. 6: Circuit Volleyball (5 - 6)

Formation: Divide the class into five teams and arrange as shown in the diagram:

```
X  X  X  X  X                    X  X  X  X  X
(1)  Underhand serve             (2)  Overhand volley
     against wall                      against wall

X ←——————→ X                     X ←——————→ X

X ←——————→ X   (3)  Passing between   X ←——————→ X
                    partners


(4)  Bumping against wall        (5)  Overhand serve
X  X  X  X  X                         against wall
                                 X  X  X  X  X
```

Basic Drill: On command "go" each team practices its respective skill for a set period of time. (This may range from one to several minutes.) At the end of each practice period each team places the ball on the floor and rotates to the next station. Continue rotation.

No. 7: Alley Serving (4-6)

Formation:	Divide class into two squads with the first player on each team behind the base line. Divide the playing area on the opposite side of the net into three equal sections and place one "retriever" in each section. The "retrievers" return each ball to the appropriate line.
Basic Drill:	Each player has three serves in which he attempts to serve one ball into each of the designated areas. The sections are perpendicular to the net.
Variations:	a. Have players serve ball into one area only.
	b. Adjust the serving line to meet the skill level of your students.
	c. Rotate "retrievers" after everyone has had a serve.

No. 8: Baseline Serving (5 - 6)

Formation:	Divide class into two squads, with each evenly distributed along their respective baseline. One player from each team is assigned the retriever position. Use as many balls as you have available.
Basic Drill:	Any child on the baseline may begin by serving the ball over the net. The ball is then served back by the child who receives the ball. No serving order need be kept in this drill. The retriever's job is to catch and pass the ball back to anyone on his team.
	Note: Start with one ball, then bring in the remaining balls one at a time.

No. 9: Nebraska Ball (4 - 5)

Formation:	Arrange players in a scattered formation on each side of the net.
Equipment:	Volleyball court, net, 24 inch ball.
No. of Players:	10 to 15 on each team.
Skills:	Serving and volleying.

How to Play:

1. One player serves the ball over the net from a serving line drawn fifteen feet away from the net.
2. Any number of players may hit the ball to assist it over the net.
3. A point is scored when the ball lands on the floor.

Teaching suggestions:

Shorten serving distance if skill level is too low.

No. 10: Bounce Net Ball (4 - 5)

Formation:	Arrange teams in a scattered formation on each side of the net.
Equipment:	Volleyball and net.
No. of Players:	6 to 9 on each team.
Skills:	Volleying.

How to Play:
1. Any player may hit the ball over the net into the opponent's court.
2. The ball must bounce once before being returned.
3. Any number of players can hit ball any number of times.
4. The team that loses the point starts the ball in the next rally.
5. Fouls are: (1) throwing ball; (2) ball caught and held; (3) ball bouncing more than once; (4) ball hit before one bounce; and (5) ball out of bounds.
6. When a team loses play of the ball, the opposite team gets one point.
7. A time and a point limit may be set by the teacher.

Teaching suggestions:
Instead of the players volleying the ball, require each successive hit to be bounced before it is hit.

No. 11: Mass Volleyball (4 - 6)

Formation:	Arrange players of each team in equal rows on each side of the net.
Equipment:	Volleyball court, net, volleyball, or large utility ball.
No. of Players:	10 to 15 on each team.
Skills:	Serving and volleying.

How to Play:
1. Any player may serve the ball from anywhere in his court.
2. Teams volley the ball back and forth across the net.
3. Fouls are: (1) team fails to return ball; (2) player catches ball; (3) ball out of bounds; (4) ball touches floor; or (5) player touches net.
4. Anyone can hit ball as many times as he wishes. However, only three players may touch the ball before it is returned over net.
5. Change serve after a team fails to return the ball.
6. Serving team scores one point whenever opponents commit one of the foregoing fouls. A game may be played to any predetermined number of points. (Eleven or fifteen is desirable.)

No. 12: Keep It Up (4 - 6)

Formation:	Arrange squads in circle formation with or without a player in the middle.
Equipment:	One volleyball for each circle.
No. of Players:	6 to 8 on each team.
Skills:	Volleying.

How to Play:
1. Each circle tries to keep their ball up the longest by volleying it from one player to another.
2. The ball may be hit to any player in the circle.
3. The team which keeps ball up longest wins.

Teaching suggestions:
1. Hit ball up rather than at a player.
2. Simplify the game by allowing one bounce between each hit.
3. Place a player in the middle of the circle.
4. As skill improves, require only one type of hit—two-hand underhand or one-hand underhand.

No. 13: Newcomb (4 - 6)

Formation:	Arrange teams in equal rows on each side of net.
Equipment:	Volleyball, net, court.
No. of Players:	9 on each team.
Skills:	Serving and volleying.

How to Play:
1. Server serves ball over the net (a second hit from another player may be permitted).
2. Other team tries to return ball after the serve, with any number of players allowed to hit the ball.
3. Server continues until his team loses the ball.
4. Fouls are: (1) hitting ball out of bounds; (2) holding the ball; (3) touching the net; (4) walking with the ball; (5) throwing the ball out of bounds; or (6) ball hitting the floor.
5. Only serving team scores.
6. A predetermined time limit or score is set.

Teaching suggestions:
If skill level is too low, allow players to catch ball, then hit it.

No. 14: Modified Volleyball (4 - 6)

Formation:	Arrange teams in scattered position or in equal rows on each side of net.
Equipment:	Net, volleyball, and volleyball court.
No. of Players:	9 to 12 on each team.
Skills:	Serving and volleying.

How to Play:
1. Regular volleyball rules are used with the following exceptions:
   a. may serve from any position in court,
   b. two or more service trials are allowed,
   c. during rally no limit on number of players that can hit the ball,
   d. position play not be required,

e. same player can hit ball three times, and

f. rotation may be eliminated.

2. The regular volleyball scoring system is used.

Teaching suggestions:

Adjust any or all foregoing rules to meet level of skill or to emphasize a particular skill.

No. 15: Circle Volley (5 - 6)

Formation:	Arrange squads in a circle formation with five to six feet between each player.
Equipment:	Volleyball.
No. of Players:	8 to 10 on each team.
Skills:	Volleying.

How to Play:

1. Form a circle with five to six feet between each player.
2. Volley the ball in the air from player to player in a clockwise pattern.
3. Players count the number of volleys before the ball hits the ground.
4. Team with the highest number of volleys at the end of the playing time is the winner.

Teaching suggestions:

1. All players volley the ball in a clockwise pattern and allow them to miss one or more players.
2. Adjust distance between players according to their ability.
3. When skill level is too low for a satisfactory game, place one or two players in the middle of the circle.

No. 16: Keep Away (5 - 6)

Formation:	Arrange teams in a scattered formation within a designated play area.
Equipment:	Volleyball or large utility ball.
No. of Players:	Any number on each team.
Skills:	Volleying.

How to Play:

1. By volleying the ball from one team member to another, the team with the ball tries to keep the ball away from the other team.
2. Members of the other team try to intercept the ball by catching it.
3. After the ball has been intercepted, the team in possession must pass it by volleying the ball.
4. Interceptions can take place only when the ball is dropping (on the downward arc).
5. The team volleying the ball the highest number of times wins.
6. A time limit may also be used.

Teaching suggestions:
Play the same game in a scattered formation with both teams attempting to keep the ball in their possession. However, no catching is allowed.

Volleyball: Basic Rules and Regulations

Although there are fewer skills to learn in volleyball than the other major sports, it is one of the more difficult games for boys and girls in Grades Four through Six. The difficulty, in most cases, is the result of inadequate arm and shoulder girdle strength coupled with the inaccuracy in serving and volleying. Nevertheless, fifth and sixth graders should be exposed to the complete game of volleyball early in an instructional unit. Modifications can be made in the height of the net and distance of serving line to assist in learning the skills of the game.

1. Field of Play:

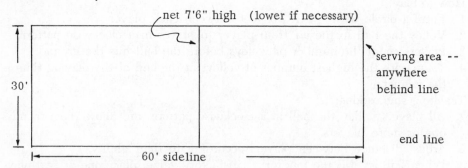

2. Recommended Net Heights:
   Grade 4—6 feet.
   Grade 5—6 feet.
   Grade 6—7 feet.
3. Positions and rotation pattern (after opponents lose their serve):

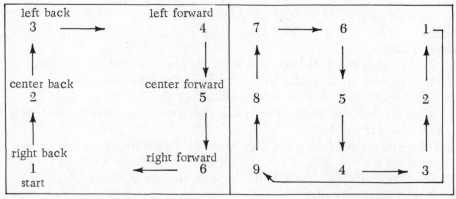

For six players   For nine players

4. To Start Game:
   a. The right back player starts the game by serving the ball from any-where behind the end line. (It is wise to begin the service from the right hand corner—later allow children to serve from various positions along the end line.)
   b. The server must serve with both feet behind the line.
   c. The server is allowed only one serve unless the ball hits the top of the net, then he is given another serve. If the server has made one point and his next serve hits the top of the net, he loses his serve. The net serve applies only on the first serve.
   d. Before serving, the server must call out his score, his opponent's score, and then "service."

5. To Return the Ball: After the ball has been served, players on both sides must abide by the following rules:
   a. Any player who receives the ball is allowed one volley (hit). He may hit the ball back over the net or to another teammate.
   b. The ball may not be volleyed (hit) more than three times before it is sent over the net.
   c. If the ball hits the net on the return volley and falls into the opponent's court, it is a fair ball.
   d. If the ball hits the net on the return volley and falls back into the court from which it was sent, it may be played, provided: (1) it is not volleyed by the player who hit it into the net; and (2) it was not volleyed by more than two different players before the ball hit the net.

6. To Play: The server hits the ball over the net. If the opposing team fails to return the ball over the net, one point is awarded the serving team. However, if the ball is returned back over the net and the serving team fails to return the ball back over the net, they lose the serve. No point is awarded on the loss of serve. Player rotation as shown under rule number three should be made only by the team receiving the serve.

7. Violations: If the following violations are committed by the serving team, the service is lost. This is called "side out." When they are committed by the receiving team, the serving team is awarded one point.
   a. Failure to make a fair or legal serve.
   b. Allowing the ball to hit the court surface.
   c. Returning the ball in any way other than hitting it. Balls may not be caught, then thrown over the net.
   d. Volleying the ball more than three times before going over the net.
   e. If the ball touches the floor outside the court lines.
      Note: a ball may be played from outside the court area providing it has not touched the ground.
   f. Failure to return the ball over the net.
   g. Failure to rotate according to the proper order.

8. Scoring.
   a. The serving team is the only team which can score points.
   b. Eleven, fifteen, or twenty-one points constitute a game. A team must win by two points. Hence, if the score was ten all in an eleven point game, one team must score two successive points to win.

Note: The above rules should be modified to meet the level of skills, available facilities, and number of children. Consideration should be given to modifying the length of game, number of players, height of net, and size of the playing court.

Evaluative Techniques

There are numerous methods of measuring volleyball skill and knowledge.[3] The majority of tests used by classroom teachers are of an objective nature and usually modifications of existing standardized test batteries. Teachers should be encouraged to develop their own test batteries and keep scores of each test in order to develop appropriate norms for their particular teaching situation.

The following test battery is an example of a "teacher made" test which can be administered by the children in a short period of time.

Volleyball Skill Test					
Name	Wall Volley total score	Service over net (50 pts)	Subjective Evaluation (50 pts)	Total Score	Grade
1	Rank all total scores ⟶ for the class then convert to letter gradings or ratings (Superior, Good, etc.)				
2					
3					
4					

Test No. 1. Wall Volley: Draw a line on the wall six feet from the floor and a second line on the floor and three feet from the wall. Each player must stand behind the line, toss the ball in the air and begin to volley the ball against the wall and above the line. One point is awarded for each hit above the line. Score the number of hits performed in twenty seconds. If a player drops the ball within the twenty-second period, he may pick up the ball and continue volleying and adding to his cumulative score. Allow two trials and record the highest score.

Test No. 2. Serving Over the Net: Each player is given ten consecutive serves with each successful serve awarded five points. This test can be modified by dividing the opposite court into zones with each given a dif-

3. W. R. Campbell and N. M. Tucker, *An Introduction to Tests and Measurements*, (London: G. Bell and Sons, Ltd., 1967).

ferent point value. For example, make three equal zones running perpendicular to the net with the zone farthest away from the server equal to five points, next three points, and the nearest zone one point.

Test No. 3. Subject Evaluation of Playing Ability: Establish a criteria which represents the skills and playing ability required in volleyball. For example, using such factors as positional play, alertness, volleying ability, and team play, the teacher would award each player a total point score from zero to fifty points. Three players can be used as judges with the average score recorded.

TOUCH FOOTBALL

Description of Skills
Suggested Sequence of Presenting Skills and Rules
How to Develop a Unit
Practice Activities and Lead-up Games
Touch Football: Basic Rules and Regulations
Evaluative Techniques

When Football is suggested as an appropriate activity for elementary school-age children, parents and teachers usually think of the competitive game involving expensive equipment, elaborate coaching, and, most important, the problems of a contact sport. All of these points are valid and should be taken into consideration. This, however, does not mean that a modified game involving many of the skills used in football should not be taught to boys in the upper intermediate grades. It is not recommended for girls at any age level.

Boys will play numerous versions of football during out-of-school hours wherever there is available space and with whatever type of equipment they may possess. It is the writer's contention, as well as many experts, that the skills of this game should be taught under competent instruction to boys ranging in age from ten to twelve years.[4, 5] Appropriate skills and rules of Football can be taught through modified games such as Flag or Touch Football which do not involve any form of tackling or body contact. Once these skills are correctly learned in school, there is a better chance they will be used in out-of-school games correctly and without injury. These skills also provide the foundation for contact football which will be played by many boys in the Secondary School.

The first part of this section will include a description of the basic skills of Touch Football and a suggested sequence of presentation. A sample unit is also provided along with a list of practice activities and lead-up games. The latter part contains a simplified version of the rules and regulations of Touch Football and suggestions relating to evaluation of student progress.

Description of Skills

Touch or Flag Football require many of the skills of the competitive game of Football with the exception of tackling and blocking. The main emphasis for elementary school-age boys should be in developing passing, catching, and kicking skills along with acquiring a knowledge of team positions and simple play formations.

PASSING

There are three types of passes used in Touch Football. The forward "spiral" pass is similar to the baseball throw, however requires a different hand grip and release in order to cause a small spiral flight of the ball. Lateral passing is a sideward throw of the ball and is used as an effective technique virtually anywhere in the field of play. Hiking or centering the ball is a throw used solely by the Center to start each play from the line of scrimmage.

4. M. H. Anderson; M. E. Elliot; and J. LaBerge, *Play with a Purpose* (New York: Harper & Row, Publishers, 1966), p. 243.

5. A Curriculum Guide in Elementary Physical Education for Boys and Girls, Board of Education, Prince George's County, Upper Marlboro, Maryland, 1965, p. 85.

FORWARD PASS

FIG. 9.71

FIG. 9.72

FIG. 9.73

Stand with the opposite foot to the throwing hand in a forward position with weight evenly distributed on both feet. Hold the ball with fingers gripping the lace slightly behind the center of the ball. The opposite hand holds the front and side of the ball.

Shift the ball back past the ear and rotate the body away from the throw. The elbow of the throwing hand should be kept high; however, young children with proportionately smaller hands will find this difficult and tend to drop the elbow in order to hold the ball in this position.

Rotate body toward the target, thrust forearm and wrist forward and snap wrist to allow the ball to roll off the fingers. The "roll-off" the fingers will give the ball the "spiral" action of the throw.

HIKING OR CENTERING

FIG. 9.74

The body should be in a wide stride position with knees bent and body weight well forward over the shoulders and arms. The ball is grasped in the same way as the forward pass and must not be raised off the ground until the hike.

LATERAL PASS   LATERAL BALL

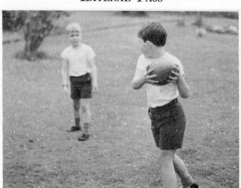

FIG. 9.75   **FIG. 9.76**

Shift the ball from the carrying position   in a backward direction.
and . . . . .

CATCHING

A ball thrown from a hike or lateral pass is normally caught with an underhand catch. Catching or receiving a forward pass is usually done while "on the run" and requires balance, timing, and a cradling action of the hands. This skill requires an accurate pass and lots of practice on the part of the receiver.

CATCHING A FORWARD PASS

FIG. 9.77   **FIG. 9.78**

At the moment the "receiver" is ready to catch the ball he should be slightly turned toward the passer with hands held forward and upward. The elbows should be slightly flexed and fingers spread.

Reach for the ball and immediately pull it toward the body and continue forward running motion.

KICKING

In Touch Football, the ball may be punted or kicked from a stationary or "place kick position." Punting a football is very similar to punting a soccer ball with the former contacting the ball on the top side of the instep and with a more pronounced follow-through of the kicking leg. Since tennis shoes are usually worn in physical education class, the place-kick should be performed with the top of the foot and not the toe. This means the ball should slant toward the kicker.

PUNTING

FIG. 9.79	FIG. 9.80	FIG. 9.81
Stand with left foot slightly forward and weight evenly distributed o v e r both feet. The ball should be held with the right hand on the right side near the back of the ball. The left hand is holding the front and left side of the ball.	Step right then left and simultaneously drop the ball as the kicking leg comes forward. The ball should be contacted with the top and slightly outer side of the foot.	Continue forward and upward movement of kicking leg. Arms should extend sideways to assist balance.

STANCE

The type starting position a player takes will depend upon whether he is in an offensive or defensive situation and whether he is playing on the line or in the backfield. The following illustration is a typical planting position for a lineman and is modified to meet the defensive or offensive playing situation.

THREE POINT STANCE
Assume a wide crouched and stride position with knees slightly bent, seat down and left arm forward. Body weight should be well forward.

FOUR POINT STANCE
Assume a wide crouched and stride position with knees slightly bent, seat down and both arms forward. Body weight should be well forward.

FIG. 9.82

Suggested Sequence of Presenting Skills and Rules

The problems of organizing and teaching touch football skills are very similar to those found in teaching basketball and softball. Teachers will find that many boys, even at the ten and eleven year age range, can throw a spiral pass, punt a ball, and can usually elucidate the advantages of a single or double-wing formation. Other boys who have not had the advantages of an older brother on the high school team may not have thrown or kicked a football. Both situations should be considered when planning a unit of Touch Football.

The following suggested sequence should, therefore, be considered a very rough guideline. If a teacher pretests the boys with the suggested skill tests in the latter part of this section, he can usually determine what skills will need the greatest emphasis.

Suggested Sequence of Presenting Skills and Rules				
Skill	\ 4	Grade \ 5	6	Rule Presentation
1. Passing		X	X	Positions
Forward pass	X	X	X	Line of scrimmage
Lateral pass		X	X	Passers and receivers
Hand off			X	
Hiking		X	X	
		X	X	Field markings
2. Catching		X	X	Number of downs
from a forward pass	X	X	X	
from a lateral pass		X	X	
from a kicked ball		X	X	Scoring
3. Kicking		X	X	Kick-off
Punt	X	X	X	Off side
Place kick			X	
4. Blocking (no hands or		X	X	Penalty
body contact)		X	X	Formations
		X	X	Plays

How to Develop a Unit

Touch Football activities should be taught in the early fall at the same time as the high school and college football season. Boys at this age level will reveal a strong hero-worshipping tendency toward the local high school or college football star. This natural "state of affairs" should be coped with through a well-organized unit of Touch or Flag Football. Provision should be made for proper demonstrations, appropriate practice activities, and time to play the various lead-up games. Consideration should also be given to available facilities and inclement weather by providing other activities such as volleyball or gymnastics whenever such factors necessitate indoor activities.

The following unit is based on a thirty minute physical education lesson on Monday, Wednesday, and Friday. Only fifteen minutes are allocated for physical education on Tuesday and Thursday.

┌─ See Description of Skills (page 274 to 278)
│ ┌─ See Practice Activities and Lead-up Games (page 280 to 284)

	Monday (30 min)	Tuesday (15 min)	Wednesday (30 min)	Thursday (15 min)	Friday (30 min)
First week	Explain: Forward pass. Practice: File Relay Lead-up Game Endball	Practice: Endball	Explain: Punting. Practice: Use Punt and Catch	Punt and catch	Explain: team positions. Practice: Use One-down Football.
Second week	Note: Continue the above pattern with weeks 2, 3, and 4 or modify the unit as illustrated in this week.				
	Touch Football Activities	Volleyball Activities	Touch Football Activities	Gymnastic Activities	Touch Football Activities
Third week	Repeat according to the pattern you select				
Fourth week	Repeat as above				

Practice Activities and Lead-up Games

The following practice activities and lead-up games will assist in developing such skills as throwing, catching, kicking, and blocking. Modify any of these activities to meet unique limitations of the playing area and to cope with variations in skill and interest of your class.

Activities	Page	Throwing	Catching	Kicking	Blocking	Grade 4	Grade 5	Grade 6

A. Practice Activities and Lead-up Games

Activities	Page	Throwing	Catching	Kicking	Blocking	4	5	6
1. File Relay	280	X	X				X	X
2. Blocking Practice	280	X			X		X	X
3. End Ball	281	X	X				X	X
4. Punt and Catch	282		X	X			X	X
5. One-down Football	282	X	X	X			X	X
6. Field Ball	283	X	X	X			X	X

No. 1: File Relay (5 - 6)

Formation:	File formation. Draw a turning line 20 to 25 feet in front of the starting line.
Basic Drill:	The first player on each team runs with the ball to the turning line, turns around and throws the ball to the next player. As soon as he has thrown the ball he runs to the end of his line while other players move forward one position and the drill continues.
Variations:	1. Shorten the distance between the lines and require a hike or lateral pass.
	2. Have one player for each team stand on the starting line. The first player runs out and the "thrower" passes the ball to him.

No. 2: Blocking Practice (5 - 6)

Formation:	Arrange field and players as shown in the diagram.

X
— 8 ft. —   X offense X   X   X
─────   ─────   ─────   ─────
0   0 defense 0   0   0

Basic Drill:	One player is designated as the offense, the other as defense. Both assume a football stance position.

On signal "hike," the offense player attempts to get past the defense player. The offense player must stay within the eight foot line and may feint, dodge, or do any movement to get around the defense player. Neither player is allowed to use his hands or cause body contact.

Variations: Repeat drill with a ball.

No. 3: End Ball (5 - 6)

Formation: Arrange field and team positions as shown in the diagram.

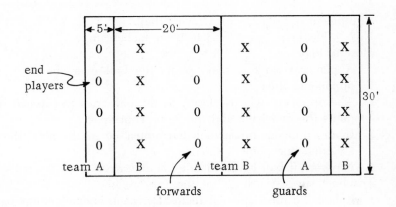

Equipment: One football.
No. of Players: 10 to 12 on each team.
Skills: Passing, catching, guarding.

How to Play:
1. The ball is given to a guard on Team A.
2. The guard may pass the ball to any forward teammate in the other half of the playing area. The forward then attempts to throw the ball over the heads of the opposing guards to one of his end players.
3. If an end player while in his end zone receives a catch from one of his forward teammates, he scores one point for his team.
4. If a guard on the opposing team intercepts or knocks the ball down, the game continues.

Teaching suggestions:
1. Reduce the number of end men to two.
2. Play same game with a lateral pass.

No. 4: Punt and Catch (5 - 6)

Formation: Arrange field and team positions as shown in the
                              diagram.

X X	← 30'-35' →	0 0
X X		0 0
X X	neutral	0 0
X X	zone	0 0

|← ——————————— 80'-90' ——————————— →|

Equipment: One football.
No. of Players: 8 to 9 on each team.
How to Play:
1. A player from one team punts the ball over the neutral zone into his
   opponent's area.
2. The opponent who is closest to the ball tries to catch it. If successful he
   punts the ball back and the game continues.
3. If an opponent misses a catch (must be in the air), the kicking side is
   awarded one point.
4. No score if ball lands outside playing area.
Teaching suggestions:
1. Rotate the lines on each team after a number of points have been scored
   or at set time intervals.
2. Play same game using a forward pass.

No. 5: One-down Football (5 - 6)

Formation: Arrange field and team positions as shown in
                              diagram.

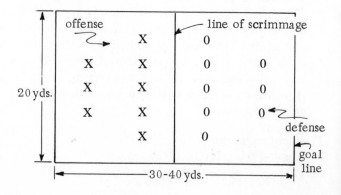

Equipment: One football.
No. of Players: 8 on each team.
How to Play:
1. To start the game both teams line up on opposite sides of the center line. One team is designated as the offense and is given one down to score a touchdown.
2. After the "hike," the ball may be run or passed any number of times in any direction from any position on the field.
3. The defense team attempts to tag the ball carrier below the waist with two hands.
4. If a player is tagged before he reaches the opponent's goal lines, the ball is downed and the other team take their down at this point.
5. If a ball is intercepted the game continues with the defense now becoming the offensive team.

Teaching suggestions:
1. When introducing this game have all players play "man-to-man," that is, linesmen check linesmen and backs check their opposite number. Later, variations can be made to meet the wishes of the defensive team.
2. Play same game using *just* the lateral pass.

No. 6: Field Ball (5 - 6)

Formation: Arrange field and team positions as shown in the diagram. Length and width of field is optional.

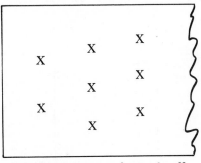

Receiving position for Kick-off   Offensive and defensive Line-up positions

Equipment: One football.
No. of Players: 8 on each team.
How to Play:
1. The game is started with one team kicking the ball into the opponent's half of the field. Kicking team may not advance until the ball is caught or recovered. (Balls kicked out-of-bounds are kicked again.)
2. The receiving team starts their advance by either running with the ball or passing it. Any number of passes are permitted in any direction and from any position on the field.

3. Opponents must tag the ball carrier with two hands and below the waist. When this occurs the opponents take over the down. (See diagram above for offensive and defensive line-up.)
4. The offensive team has one down to score a touchdown (6 points).
5. Any play which starts from returning a kick-off or a run back from an intercepted pass is not counted as a down.
6. Players may not block, trip, hold, or push an opponent. If offensive team fouls, ball is awarded to defensive team. If defensive team fouls, the ball is advanced eight paces from where the foul took place. (Ball may not, however, be placed closer than five paces from the goal line.)

Teaching suggestions:
1. Determine your own length of playing halves.
2. Restrict game to one type of pass, such as a. only forward pass or b. only lateral pass.
3. Play the same game with a soccer ball.

Touch Football: Basic Rules and Regulations

It is recommended that upper elementary school-age boys play seven man Touch or Flag Football. The latter game is essentially the same with removing two tags substituted for the two-hand touch below the waist. Commercial tags may be purchased from local sports stores or improvised tags may be constructed.

1. Field Layout:

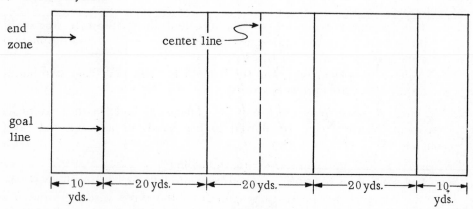

2. Offensive and Defensive Line-up Positions:

3. To Start Game: The game is started with a kick-off (punt or place kick) from the goal line. The ball must be kicked past the center line and land within the field of play. If the first ball is kicked out-of-bounds, it is re-taken. If the second kick goes out-of-bounds, the other team starts play at their 20 yard line. The kick-off team may recover the ball only after the other team touches and fumbles it.

4. Offensive Play:
   a. Once a player who is returning the kick-off is touched, the ball is placed on the spot where the tag took place. The line parallel to the spot is known as the scrimmage line. In all cases the ball must be placed five paces in from the side line.
   b. The offensive team has four downs to move the ball into the next zone or score a touchdown. Always start a new series of downs whenever a team crosses a zone line.
   c. When executing a play, the offensive team must have at least three men on the line when the play begins. The center player must pass the ball backward through his legs. A backfield man who receives the ball may, in turn, hand off, lateral or throw a forward pass from behind the line of scrimmage. On a forward pass, any player, except the center, may receive the pass. The offensive team may punt on any down providing they call for a punt formation. When this occurs, neither team may cross the scrimmage line until the punt receiver has caught the ball.

5. Defensive Play:
   a. The defending team must remain behind the scrimmage line until the ball has left the opposing center's hands. Special rule applies to a punt as previously described.
   b. A defensive player may stop the ball carrier if he can place two hands on or below his opponent's waist.

6. Blocking: A player may block only by placing his body in the way of an opponent. Neither team is allowed to use hands or any form of body contact.

7. Scoring: Points are awarded for the following:
   a. Touchdown: 6 points for a touchdown. Following the touchdown, one play is given to the scoring team from the three yard line and one point is awarded if the team crosses the goal line.
   b. Safety: 2 points.
   A safety is awarded if the team in possession of the ball is tagged behind their own goal line. The defensive team receives two points. Immediately following the safety the ball is put into play by the team scored against by a kick-off from behind the goal line.

8. Touchback: If a defensive player intercepts a ball behind his own goal line and does not run it out or if the ball is kicked over the goal line by

the offensive team, a touchback occurs. The ball is taken to the 20 yard line and given to the defending team.

9. Penalties: Award five yards to the nonoffending team for the following infractions:
   a. Pushing, holding, or tripping.
   b. Unsportsmanlike conduct.
   c. Interfering with the pass receiver.
   d. Off side.
10. Length of Game: Two eight minute periods.

Evaluative Techniques

There are a few standardized tests that are designed to measure the basic skills of Football. The majority of these tests, however, are designed for high school or college level players, hence must be modified to meet the level of skill and ability of elementary school-age players. The example "teacher made" test battery described below can be administered without elaborate equipment and in a short period of time. Use students to assist in testing and keep scores from year to year in order to develop appropriate norms for your school.

				Touch Football Skill Test		
Name	Accuracy Pass (total points)	Punting (total points)	Ball Carrying (total points)	Subjective Evaluation (50 points)	Total Score	Grade
1 2 3 4		Rank all total scores for the class then convert to letter grades or ratings (Superior, Good, etc.) ——————→				

Test No. 1. Accuracy Pass: Place a target on the wall as shown in the diagram. Each player is given ten consecutive throws from behind the

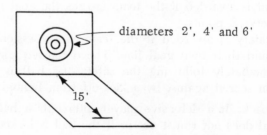

diameters 2', 4' and 6'

15'

starting line. He must use a forward pass. Score 6, 4, and 2 for hits within each respective circle. If a ball hits a line, award the higher value. Record the total score.

Test No. 2. Punting: Place the following lines on the field. Stakes can be used as a substitute for white gypsum lines. Use a regulation size football.

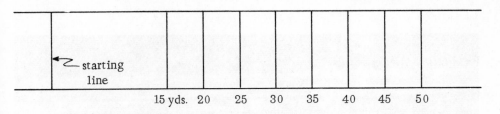

Each player must punt the ball from behind the starting line. Mark the point of landing with a stick or small object. Allow a total of three kicks and record the highest score. Yards are equivalent to points.

Test No. 3. Ball Carrying: Arrange four chairs as shown in the diagram. Place a ball on the starting line.

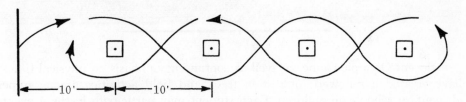

Each player stands behind the starting line with both hands resting on his knees. On signal, he picks up the football, places it in his left hand and runs around the left side of the first chair. He continues the zigzag running pattern and must change the ball to the opposite hand as he passes each chair. Allow 30 seconds for the test. One point is awarded for each chair he passes correctly (must exchange hands). Two trials are allowed with the highest score recorded.

Test No. 4. Subjective Evaluation: Establish a criteria which represents the skills and playing ability required in Touch Football. For example, use such skills as passing, feinting, kicking, and defensive ability. The teacher or a group of three players would award each player a total score ranging from zero to fifty points. When these players are judging, take an average of their scores.

TRACK AND FIELD

Description of Skills
Suggested Sequence of Presenting Skills and Rules
How to Develop a Unit
Practice Activities
Track and Field Meet
Evaluative Techniques

Recent Olympic Games as well as continuing emphasis on physical fitness have created a renewed interest in track and field activities among upper elementary school-age children. Each student may participate in these events at his own level of physical capacity and personal motivation. Furthermore, track and field activities are relatively easy to teach, require little expense, and provide vigorous competitive experience for all children. The inherent values of this activity, coupled with the feasibility of modifying existing facilities, make it one that should be considered a basic requirement in the elementary school physical education program.

The basic skills are described in the first part of this section, followed by a suggested sequence of presenting each skill for each grade level. To assist teachers in developing a unit of track activities, a sample unit provided to show how to organize each lesson and how to use the accompanying list of practice activities and lead-up games section (entitled "Track and Field Meet") will provide information relating to track size, order of events, and required officials for an all-school track meet. Finally, the latter section on evaluative techniques provides several suggestions for evaluating performance and improvement in the various track and field events.

Description of Skills

There are two basic types of events in track and field. The first is the running events which include the sprints and hurdles and longer endurance runs. The second type is field events and includes such activities as high jump, long jump, and the shot put. The following skills should be taught to all students regardless of their inherent ability. Once a child has been exposed to these skills, allow him to select and concentrate on one or more events that are best suited to his potential capabilities.

STARTING

The starting position for running events is determined by the length of the race. For short races, such as twenty and thirty yard dashes, the "kneeling start" is the best type to use. For longer races, the "standing start" is the more acceptable starting position.

STANDING START

FIG. 9.83

Stand with the left toe close to the starting line and the right foot slightly to the rear. The head is up, trunk bent forward, knees slightly flexed and weight on left foot. Right arm is forward with elbow flexed and left arm downward and slightly backward.

The sprint start is important to the success of any beginning sprinter. The correct form and general techniques of this skill are quite easy to master, even for the fourth grader. The skill will be described as it is executed in a race. (See page 290.)

Common Faults.
1. Feet too close to starting line.
2. Buttocks raised too high.
3. Sitting back over the legs on the "set" command instead of the weight being forward over the hands.
4. Head up causing strain—relax the neck muscles.
5. Jerking up into the "set" position. Come up slowly, under control.
6. Standing up before starting to run. The drive should be forward. It should take 15-20 yards to assume a full running position.

FIG. 9.84	**FIG. 9.85**	**FIG. 9.86**

"On your mark": The runner kneels down and places the toe of his front foot behind the starting line. (Front foot is normally determined as being opposite the "kicking foot.") Arms are extended straight down with weight on fingertips. Squeeze fingers together to make a "bridge" with the thumb.

"Set": Raise lower knee and buttocks until the back is straight and parallel to the ground. The weight should be evenly distributed between hands and front foot. The head is not raised as the runner should be looking at a spot on the ground a few feet in front of the starting line.

"Go" (or fire a starting gun): When everyone is motionless, the gun is fired. Drive forward with the lead leg and, at the same instant, bring the rear leg forward.

RUNNING

There are several types of running positions, each with a slightly different body lean, arm action, and foot contact. In the elementary school track program, however, two types, namely sprinting and distance form, are those with which we should be concerned. In the sprinting form the body leans well forward, there is vigorous arm action and the weight of the body is taken on the ball or front of foot (Figure 9.87). In distance running the body is more erect, there is less vigorous arm action, and the weight is first taken on the heel, then a "rock" forward action. (Figure 9.88).

FIG. 9.87

FIG. 9.88

Stress the following in both types of running:
1. Maintain a slight lean forward.
2. Swing slightly bent arms opposite to leg action. In the example shown, (Figure 9.87), the right leg and left arm are forward.
3. Twist shoulders slightly but keep trunk on a straight plane.
4. Land on balls or heels (depending on type of run) but push off from toes.

Relay Running

Many teachers have observed that fast runners will lose a relay race to their slower competitors simply because of poor passing techniques. It is quite possible to teach upper elementary school-age children the correct "upswing" method of passing in a short period of time. This method is perhaps the easiest for the beginner to master.

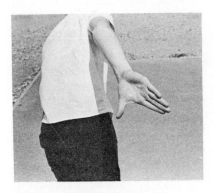

FIG. 9.89

The right hand is drawn straight back toward the approaching runner. Fingers are held together and pointing to the side. The thumb points toward the body. This forms a "V" into which the approaching runner places the baton.

FIG. 9.90

The approaching runner brings the baton upward into the hand of the runner. As soon as the front runner receives the baton she should bring it forward into the left hand in preparation for the next pass.

Check marks: When students are ready to practice baton passing with full speed, it is important that each runner establish his own check mark, that is, when he should start to run. As a general rule, have each runner place a mark on the ground five yards back of his starting point.

```
check mark
   *  ◄────────5 yards─►  X    outgoing runner          passing zone
on ground                       acceleration zone        22 yards
```

The incoming runner starts 50 yards back of the line and runs as fast as possible. When he passes this 50 yard line, the outgoing runner turns and runs as fast as possible. When the latter reaches the Passing Zone he puts his hand back for the baton. He must be inside the Passing Zone before he receives the baton or his team is disqualified. If the incoming runner cannot catch up to the outgoing runner, the check mark is moved closer to the outgoing runner. If the incoming runner runs past the outgoing runner, the check mark is moved farther back from the outgoing runner.

HURDLES

Contrary to popular belief, elementary school children can run the hurdles with speed and efficiency. The main reason they usually do not learn to hurdle properly is because the hurdles are usually set too high and too far apart.

FIG. 9.91	FIG. 9.92	FIG. 9.93
When the runner is approximately seven feet away from the hurdle, the lead leg is lifted and extended forward. The opposite arm to the lead leg should also extend forward.	The lead leg continues forward and upward until it clears the hurdle. The rear leg starts forward with toe turned up. Note the important forward body lean as the runner prepares for the next stage.	Vigorously draw the lead leg down and a forward thrust of the trailing leg. Note, throughout this whole movement, the shoulders should be parallel to the finish line.

The following stages should be followed when introducing hurdles:
1. Begin by having the children sprint the length of the gymnasium or approximately 25 yards.
2. Place an obstacle (cane or old broom handle) on the floor approximately halfway down the gymnasium floor, or between 30-45 feet from the starting line. Again the children sprint the length of the floor; however, no attempt should be made to hurdle the obstacle.

3. Place a second obstacle on the floor so that it is midway between the third and fourth stride. The teacher can check whether runners are taking the correct three strides between hurdles by observing to see if they are taking very short steps (usually five steps) or if they land on a different foot after each hurdle (usually four steps).

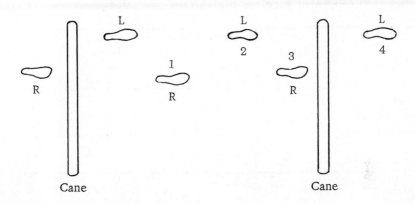

In order to assist the runner in developing the three step sequence between each hurdle, set up numerous courses (see diagram) so that each runner can select the one that fits his step pattern.

4. The obstacles should be raised now nine to twelve inches. This may be accomplished by using shoe boxes, bricks, small stands, or adjustable hurdles. Allow practice and gradually raise the hurdle height to 30".

When the obstacle approaches 24", the children should be taught what to do with the trailing leg. This may be accomplished by having the runners walk down beside the hurdle. As they approach the hurdle, they step in front and slightly to the side of the hurdle with their lead leg and then take their trailing leg over the hurdle. The thigh of the trailing leg should be parallel to the top of the hurdle, then brought through quickly into the next stride. Once the correct technique is acquired the children should jog down beside the hurdles doing the same drill. Finally have them run from the starting position and hurdle in the center of each hurdle.

Teaching Suggestions
1. The take-off must be between five and seven feet from the hurdle. The actual distance will depend upon the size and strength of the child. This seems like a long way when you stand and look at it, but when in motion it is very easy to negotiate the hurdle from this distance (Figure 9.91).
2. Bring the lead leg knee up quickly toward the hurdle.
3. Lean forward into the hurdle to acquire good balance.
4. Bring the lead leg down quickly.

5. Snap the trailing leg through quickly into the next running stride.
6. Always lean forward on the hurdle, *never* backwards.

Recommended Competitive Hurdles

The following chart will indicate the proper height, distance between hurdles, and length of race for the various age levels:

	Height (inches)	No. of Hurdles	Start to First Hurdle	Between Hurdles	Last Hurdle to Finish Line	Total Distance
11 and under						
BOYS	30	6	33′4″	22′3″	35′5″	60 yards
GIRLS	30	6	33′4″	22′3″	35′5″	60 yards
13 and under						
BOYS	30	8	39′4″ (12 m)	26′3″ (8 m)	39′4″ (12 m)	87½ yards (80 metres)
GIRLS	30	6	36′4″	14′3″	22′5″	60 yards
15 and under						
BOYS	36	10	14 yds.	9 yds.	15 yds.	110 yards
GIRLS	30	8	39′4″ (12 m)	26′3″ (8 m)	39′4″ (12 m)	87½ yards (80 metres)

HIGH JUMP

There are two types of jumping styles described here. The "scissors style" is the easier of the two and should be learned first. The "straddle roll," although more difficult to learn, is the better of the two in terms of heights that can be reached. Regardless of the jumping method that will be taught, it is imperative that a good landing surface is provided. Children will not learn to jump correctly if they are afraid to land in the pit. Although foam rubber is the more aceptable, shavings and the following improvised "rubber tube" pit provide a satisfactory landing surface.

A very inexpensive jumping pit can be constructed by using old discarded automobile tire inner tubes. The rubber tubes are placed on the ground, as shown in the illustration, and tied together. A tumbling mat is then placed on the top of the tubes. This provides a safe and comfortable landing surface which can be used indoors and out-of-doors.

FIG. 9.94

Scissors Method

The scissors method of high jumping is the most natural for most children. Unfortunately it is not the most efficient in its traditional form. However, by modifying this method, it is possible to attain greater heights, as was demonstrated by the 1968 Olympic Games, Dick Fosbury who used his now famous "Fosbury Flop." Successful for Fosbury as it has been, it is not recommended that beginning jumpers learn this method.

FIG. 9.95

FIG. 9.96

The jumper approaches from the left at a slight angle to the bar (15 to 20 degrees). She takes a few steps, plants her right "take-off" foot, then swings her left foot high into the air.

The left leg continues over the bar followed by the right in a scissors action. At the same time the arms swing forward and upward assisting the upward lift of the body. The right foot should land first followed by the left completing the scissors action.

Straddle Method

The most popular method used by world ranking high jumpers is the straddle method. The great Russian jumper, Brumel, used this method while setting the world record of 7 ft. 5½ in. It is important that proper technique be stressed while introducing this method of jumping. Poor technique will lead to little or no improvement and a disillusioned jumper.

FIG. 9.97

T h e jumper approaches from the left side at approximately 45° to the bar. He takes a few steps, plants his left "take-off" f o o t, swings his right leg forward and upward and raises arms upward.

FIG. 9.98

Continue upward and forward movement extending body and lifting leg upward.

FIG. 9.99

At the height of this jump, the body should be parallel to the bar. Continue "rolling" movement over the bar landing on hands and "take-off" foot.

Standing Broad Jump

In this event the performer stands behind the starting line, takes a preliminary swing with his arms, then jumps as far as possible. The measurement is made from the take-off board to the nearest point on the ground touched by the jumper.

| FIG. 9.100 | FIG. 9.101 | FIG. 9.102 |

Begin in a squat position, arms extended backward and toes of both feet parallel to and back of starting line. Simultaneously, shift arms forward and upward and extend legs.

As soon as the feet leave the floor, begin to flex the knees but continue to move arms forward and upward.

Land with feet parallel, trunk flexed, and arms extended in a forward direction.

Long Jump

| FIG. 9.103 | FIG. 9.104 | FIG. 9.105 |

Start several yards back from the take-off board, run forward, place take-off foot on the board.

Continue movement, bringing the rear leg forward and upward while extending both arms forward.

The heels land first, then a vigorous backward movement of both arms forcing the body forward. The latter movement is done to prevent the jumper from falling back to a sitting position.

LONG JUMP

A successful long jumper must be able to combine the elements of speed and jumping. Elementary school-age children are capable of sufficient speed for this event and can execute the "hang" or "hitch-kick" flight with a relatively high standard of performance.

The Hitch Kick

This technique involves "Running in the air" (Figure 9.106). As previously stated, the knee of the free leg is driven up into the air. Next, the take-off leg is brought forward and the free leg shifts back. The free leg is then brought forward to join the other leg just before landing.

FIG. 9.106

An effective technique to aid the students in their quest for height is to suspend a hat from a crossbar or on the end of a rope attached to a stick. The height of the hat should be adjusted so that the jumper must jump to maximum height in order to put the hat on his head. In this drill, the distance from the take-off point will vary, but should be a little more than half of the total jump.

FIG. 9.107

TRIPLE JUMP

This event has proven to be a very popular event among boys and girls alike. The appeal seems to be in the distance that is traveled as well as immediate improvement once the proper techniques are learned.

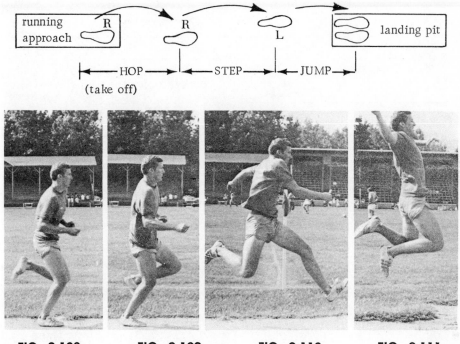

FIG. 9.108	**FIG. 9.109**	**FIG. 9.110**	**FIG. 9.111**
The runner starts thirty to forty yards back to gain maximum speed at the take-off mark. The first stage is a hop from the take-off board. (Hop Right)	To maintain forward speed, the hop is kept low with the opposite leg driving forward followed by the take-off foot and the landing of this foot. (Land Right)	Continue forward with a thrust of the left leg, land on the heel of left foot, and rock forward toward the toe.	Continue forward action by pushing off from the left foot and landing on both feet in the pit.

SHOT PUT

The shot put event has proven to be an extremely safe and enjoyable activity for boys and girls in the upper elementary school. Too often, however, this event is neglected in the upper elementary school track and field program. Various reasons are given, yet, upon close investigation, most of the arguments prove invalid.[6]

---

6. D. Turkington and G. Kirchner, *Track and Field for Intermediate Grades.* Audio-Visual Centre, Simon Fraser University, Burnaby, B. C. Canada, 1970, page 42.

FIG. 9.112

FIG. 9.113

Stand near the back of the circle, weight on the right leg, with the shot cradled on the neck. Left arm is held upward for balance.

Lower trunk over right leg; raise left leg upward and toward the front of the circle.

FIG. 9.114

FIG. 9.115

Simultaneously, the right leg makes a powerful drive toward the board as the left leg shifts toward the toe board. Throughout this shift, the body is kept low.

Continue movement, driving upward from the right leg transmitting the power through the arm and with a final push of the fingertips. Continue movement around to left and resume the foot positions to retake the weight on the right foot.

Recommended Weight for the Shot:

	Boys	Girls
10 to 11 years	6 lbs.	6 lbs.
12 to 13 years	4 Kilograms	6 lbs.
	(8 lbs. 13 oz.)	

Common Faults:
1. Holding the shot behind the head.
2. Raising the body too quickly on the shift across the circle.
3. Trying to put the shot with just the arm.
4. Stepping into the "bucket" with the left leg in front of the circle. (That is, too far to the left side of the toe board.)
5. Reversing before it is necessary.
6. Putting the shot too low. The correct angle is between 40° to 50°.

How to Construct the Throwing Area for Shot Putting
1. Take a piece of rope approximately five feet in length and tape the ends. Drive two nails through the rope exactly 3'6" apart. One nail is held stationary while the other end scribes an arc.
2. The second circle is constructed in the same manner, but seven feet away from the first circle. This is continued until all eight circles have been drawn as shown in the diagram.
3. Draw a 28'6" arc from the *centre* of each 3'6" circle.

Suggested Sequence of Presenting Skills and Rules

Appropriate skill development in any of the official track and field events is dependent upon the potential or inherent ability of each performer, plus the amount and type of previous training. Taking these factors into consideration, the suggested list of appropriate skills shown in the accompanying chart is provided as a rough guideline. In this type of activity, progression or improvement in individual events is not simply an accumulation of new skills; it is a sequential addition of skills plus an improvement in form and general conditioning. Form and condition are equally important in the development and improvement of all track and field events.

EXPECTED PROFICIENCIES

Since proficiency in track and field events is measured in time or distance, the accompanying chart will provide a rough estimate as to what can be expected of elementary school-age children. If teachers are introducing track and field activities similar to those listed in the chart, it is wise to establish their own school records. Use the suggested high and low records shown in the chart as a guide in establishing "expected" records within your school.

Suggested Sequence of Presenting Skills and Rules of Track and Field

Skill		K	1	2	3	4	5	6	Rule Presentation
				Grade*					
1.	Starting		X	X	X	X	X	X	
	For distance runs						X	X	Starting commands
	For sprints					X	X	X	
							X	X	False starts
2.	Running								
	Sprints	X	X	X	X	X	X	X	
	Distance						X	X	Lane positions and violations
	Relay			X	X	X	X	X	passing rule
	Hurdles					X	X	X	
3.	High Jump								
	Scissors method			X	X	X	X	X	number of jumps
	Straddle method					X	X	X	
4.	Standing Broad Jump	X	X	X	X	X	X	X	foot fault and recording
5.	Long Jump			X	X	X	X	X	foot fault and recording
6.	Triple Jump						X	X	foot fault and recording
7.	Shot Put						X	X	foot fault and recording
						X	X	X	General track meet rules

*Numerous track and field type activities can be used in the primary grades to stimulate interest and to lay the foundations for advanced Track and Field activities. Some of the more popular activities are listed below. These activities are normally used for Primary Grade Track and Field Meets.

1. Potato Race.

2. Three-legged Race.

3. Softball Throw.

4. Wheelbarrow Race.

5. Thread the Needle.

6. Sack Race.

7. Obstacle Race.

	Proficiency Levels for Track and Field							
	Minimum to Optimum Records							
	Grade 4		Grade 5		Grade 6		Grade 7	
Name of Event	Low	High	Low	High	Low	High	Low	High
50 yd. dash (boys)	10.	6.	9.5	6.	9.	6.0	5.8	8.9
50 yd. dash (girls)	10.	6.	10.	6.	10.	5.9	6.0	10.2
220 yd. run (boys)	42.0	31.0	40.0	32.5	38.0	30.5	37.0	30.0
150 yd. run (boys)	27.0	22.0	25.0	19.1	23.0	18.2	22.5	18.0
150 yd. run (girls)	28.0	23.0	26.0	21.0	15.0	20.0	24.0	19.5
High jump (boys)	2'11"	3'4"	3'0"	3'10"	3'6"	4'2"	3'8"	4'6"
High jump (girls)	2'10"	3'2"	3'0"	3'4"	3'0"	3'6"	3'3"	4'0"
Standing broad jump (boys)	4'0"	6'4"	4'8"	6'8"	4'10"	6'11"	4'5"	8'9"
Standing broad jump (girls)	3'9"	5'9"	3'11"	6'4"	4'2"	6'10"	7'6"	3'9"
Running broad jump (boys)	11'0"	12'2"	12'0"	13'2"	13'0"	14'2"	13'6"	15'0"
Running broad jump (girls)	10'0"	11'0"	11'0"	12'0"	12'0"	13'6"	12'6"	14'0"
Softball throw (boys)	35'	175'	70'	205'	76'	207'	88'	245'
Softball throw (girls)	21'	167'	32'	141'	37'	159'	36'	150'

How to Develop a Unit

Track and field activities are traditionally scheduled for late spring to cope with climate and possible pre-vacation enthusiasm. Running and field events are highly self-testing, with each child choosing his own events for specialization and extensive practice. Hence, there is an immediate need on the part of the teacher to introduce many different events as soon as possible. This principle has been followed in the sample unit shown following. Although not indicated, each lesson should begin with a comprehensive warm-up or conditioning period involving running, jogging, walking, and a vigorous set of exercises designed to increase strength, endurance, and flexibility. The latter two days of the unit should be devoted to a class or possibly an all-school track and field meet to provide a means of encouraging greater effort, team spirit, and personal satisfaction on the part of every participant. (See the last section for an outline of the schedule of events in a track and field meet.)

See Description of Skills (page 289 to 301)
See Practice Activities (page 305 to 309)

	Monday	Tuesday	Wednesday	Thursday	Friday
First week	Explain: Sprint start	Review: Sprint start	Explain: Standing start	Explain: High jump— Scissors kick	Review: 1. High Jump 2. Sprint start
	Practice: Start and Pass	Practice: Call Race Circle Post Relay	Practice: Walk, Run, and Jog	Practice: Over the Rope	Practice: Optional
Second week	Explain: Standing Broad jump Practice: Number of Jumps Review: Walk, Run and Jog	Explain: Running Broad jump Practice: Individual Practice	Continue pattern ending unit at end of third or fourth week with a class track & field meet.		
Third week	Continue pattern with emphasis on squad practice or previously introduced skills.			Class Track Meet	Class Track Meet

Practice Activities

Track and field skills require a great deal of individual attention by the teacher and extensive practice on the part of the participant. Hence, the following practice activities should be used throughout a track and field unit to supplement individualized instruction and to encourage the competitive spirit among all members of the class.

PRACTICE ACTIVITIES

Activity	Page	General Conditioning	Starting	Running	Standing Broad Jump	Relay	Jumping	1	2	3	4	5	6
1. Continuous Running	306	X		X							X	X	X
2. Interval Training	306	X		X		X						X	X
3. Walk, Run, Jog	306	X		X						X	X	X	X
4. Double Shuttle Relay	307		X	X						X	X	X	X
5. Start and Pass	307		X	X						X	X	X	X
6. Call Race	308		X	X						X	X	X	X
7. Number of Jumps	308				X				X	X	X	X	X
8. Over the Rope	308						X		X	X	X	X	X
9. Potato Race	309		X	X				X	X	X	X	X	
10. Baton Passing	309		X	X		X					X	X	X

Additional Activities: The following relays, described under "Low Organization games," are suitable for track and field activities.

Circle Post Relay	148	X		X		X		X	X	X	X	X	X
Zigzag Relay	146	X		X		X		X	X	X	X	X	X
Rescue Relay	145	X		X		X		X	X	X	X	X	X
Wheelbarrow Relay	147	X		X		X			X	X	X	X	X
Skipping Rope Relay	147	X		X		X			X	X	X	X	X

No. 1: Continuous Running (4 - 6)

Basic Drill: A set distance is established for the runners. For
                                          example, the children could be asked to run one
                                          mile on the track or to run from the school to a
                                          point one mile away. Enjoyable courses can be
                                          set up on the school ground or in a nearby park
                                          or wilderness area. Although young children can
                                          and should run long distances, care must be taken
                                          to insure that each child gradually increases his
                                          distance, day by day.

No. 2: Interval Training (5 - 6)

Basic Drill: This is the most commonly used training method
                                          among track and field athletes. This form of train-
                                          ing has three components, which are: (a) distance
                                          covered on each interval; (b) recovery period
                                          between intervals; and (c) the number of repeti-
                                          tions performed. The following example will illus-
                                          trate this form of training: The class is required
                                          to run 5×220 yards with a three minute rest in-
                                          terval between each 220 yard run. The speed ex-
                                          pected would vary for each of the children. To
                                          illustrate, the children in this situation were train-
                                          ing to run in a future 440 yard race. Their best
                                          time for the 440 yards was 70 seconds. Therefore,
                                          they are asked to run each 220 yards in 35 seconds
                                          (or $70/2$). Once this has been established the
                                          children would try to complete the above workout
                                          as prescribed. When the workout was completed
                                          by each child, it would be made more challenging
                                          by changing one of the components, that is, either
                                          (a) running the fast piece faster; (b) cut down
                                          on recovery period; or (c) doing more repetitions.

No. 3: Walk, Jog, Run (3 - 6)

Formation: Make a small track out of pins, or any type of
                                          marker.
Equipment: Pins, chairs, rags.
No. of Players: All.
Skills: Run and Jog.
How to Play:

1. Teach the children the difference between a "walk," "jog," and "run." A
   "jog" is about half speed and a "run" is "full speed."

2. To start, students are allowed to walk at their own "random" speed around the markers.
3. First blow of the whistle means everyone jog.
4. Second blow of the whistle means everyone runs at top speed.
5. Third blow of the whistle means everyone walks.
6. Fourth blow of the whistle means everyone walks.
7. Continue this sequence (walk, jog, run, jog, walk, etc.)

Teaching suggestions:
At the beginning of unit, allow longer time between the walk and jog phase, and short periods at top speed. Gradually increase the time at full speed.

No. 4: Double Shuttle Relay (3 - 6)

Formation:	Arrange class in file formation with one-half of each team behind two starting lines spaced thirty to fifty feet apart.
Equipment:	Whistle.
No. of Players:	5 or 6 runners on each squad.
Skills:	Start and run.

How to Play:
1. On signal, number one runners jog or run across the field, touch next player, then walk to the rear of the line.
2. Start each new set of runners on a whistle signal.

Teaching suggestions:
Stress at the beginning of this practice activity that it is not a competitive relay. After a sufficient warm-up period, it may be used as a competitive relay.

No. 5: Start and Pass (3 - 6)

Formation:	Arrange class into line formations with one-half of each team behind two starting lines spaced twenty-five feet apart.
Equipment:	Whistle.
No. of Players:	5 to 6 on each squad.
Skills:	Start and sprint.

How to Play:
1. This is essentially a starting drill. The teacher should use the following commands:
   "Take your marks"
   "Set"
   Blow whistle.
2. On the whistle, each runner makes a fast start and runs until each passes the other. At the passing point each player slows down to a walk and goes to the rear of the line.

Teaching suggestions:
1. Repeat as in the foregoing except allow each player to run over the opposite line, then slow down to a walk back to the rear of the line.
2. Use standing and kneeling starts.

No. 6: Call Race (3 - 6)

Formation:	Arrange two teams on a starting line. Draw a turning line thirty feet in front of the starting line.
Equipment:	Whistle.
No. of Players:	5 to 10 on each team.
Skills:	Start and sprint.

How to Play:
1. Line up each team on either side of the dividing line. Number each player.
2. The teacher calls out any number, such as "four."
3. Number 4 from each team runs to the turning line and back across the starting line.
4. Continue random calling until all runners have had a turn.

Teaching suggestions:
Repeat the foregoing procedure but add "take your mark," "set," then call one number. Only players whose numbers were called should run. Remaining players stand up and wait for next turn. This is an excellent starting drill.

No. 7: Number of Jumps (2 - 6)

Formation:	Arrange each team in a long line formation with participants' toes touching the starting line. Draw a finish line twenty to thirty feet in front of the starting line.
Equipment:	None.
No. of Players:	Class.
Skills:	Standing broad jump.

How to Play:
1. This is a standing broad jump activity.
2. Each child begins on the starting line and jumps as far as possible.
3. His second, third, etc., jumps start from where his heels touched.
4. The object is to see who can make it across with the fewest number of jumps.

Teach suggestions:
Use partners to make landing positions.

No. 8: Over the Rope (3 - 6)

Formation:	Arrange each team in a line formation facing a mat.
Equipment:	Tumbling mats, long skipping ropes.
No. of Players:	5 to 8 on each squad.
Skills:	High jump.

How to Play:
1. This is a high jumping activity. It can be used outside on grass or indoors on mats.
2. Two players hold a long skipping rope at various heights while the remainder of the squad practice the scissors or western roll over the rope.

No. 9: Potato Race (1 - 5)

Formation:	Arrange each team in a line formation behind the starting line. Draw four small circles spaced five feet apart in front of each team. Place one "potato" (beanbag) in each circle.
Equipment:	2″ blocks of wood or beanbags, 4 large tin cans, chalk and whistle.
No. of Players:	6 to 7 on each team.

How to Play:
1. On signal, player number one from each team runs to first circle, picks up the "potato," runs back and places it in the container.
2. Player number one repeats procedure until all the "potatoes" are placed in the container.
3. As soon as player number one places the last "potato" in the container, player number two takes one "potato" out and places it in the first circle.
4. Player number two continues this pattern until all "potatoes" are returned to the circle.
5. Player number three repeats number one's task, etc., until all players have had a turn.

No. 10: Baton Passing (4 - 6)

Basic Drill:	The class is divided into groups of 4 - 8 runners and placed in a single line approximately four feet apart.

X Baton ————— X ————— X		X	X	X	X	X	X
X Baton	X	X	X	X	X	X	X
X Baton	X	X	X	X	X	X	X
X Baton	X	X	X	X	X	X	X

From a standing position, the baton starts at the end of each line and is passed with the left hand to the next runner who takes the baton in his right hand. He immediately brings it forward into his left hand in preparation for the next pass. The baton should be brought up into the right hand. When the baton reaches the front of the line everyone turns in the opposite direction and the drill is repeated.

After the students have the "feel" of passing the baton in a standing position, they repeat the drill with a slow jog. The distance between each runner will, therefore, have to be increased. Repeat drill with a gradual increase in speed and a proportionate increase in the distance between each runner.

Track and Field Meet

The organization and general rules and regulations of any elementary school track and field meet will depend upon the general interest and available facilities and time. The following information, although not complete, will assist in developing the facilities, meet rules, and order of events for most elementary school track meets.

Track dimensions: A track with a three hundred yard oval will provide an eighty yard straightaway and a seventy yard curve at each end of the track. The curve should have a sixty-seven foot radius as shown in the diagram.

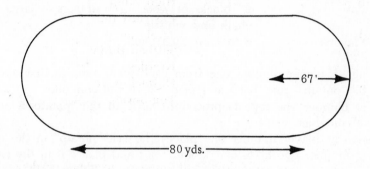

High Jump Pit

The size of the pit should be twelve feet long and ten feet wide. Sawdust or shavings should be used to fill the pit, which should be boarded with straw bales. (Also see improvised pit constructed of rubber tubes, page 295)

Long Jump Pit

The runway to the pit should be approximately thirty yards long with an eight inch take-off mark located five feet from the pit. The pit should be ten feet wide and twenty feet long and filled with fine sand.

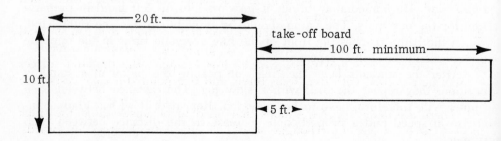

Order and Number of Events

Each school may vary the length of dashes as well as include additional events listed in the following order. This order should provide a format for scheduling all events.

Boys' Events	Girls' Events
50 yard dash	25 yard dash
Shot put	50 yard dash
60 yard dash	Standing broad jump
Standing broad jump	Long jump
Long jump	240 yard relay
240 yard relay	High jump
High jump	150 yard run
220 yard run	Triple jump
Triple jump	Softball throw
Softball throw	**Hurdles**
Hurdles	Obstacle race
Obstacle race	Tug-o-war
Tug-o-war	

Track and Field Officials

The following jobs should be allocated to teachers or dependable students.
1. Meet director.
2. Starters, same for all track events.
3. Finish judges: head finish judge, and first, second, third, and, if desired, additional place judges.
4. Field judges: one judge and one helper for the high jump, standing broad jump, and running broad jump.
5. Recorder and announcer: one head recorder with assistants for running messages and obtaining results of the events.

Meet Requirements

Each school should establish their own eligibility requirements for the following situations:
1. Number of events each participant may enter. For example, each child may enter two track and one field event.
2. Classification of participants. There are several methods that can be used to classify participants; for example, age, grade, or a classification index.
3. Number of places and point awards. For example, the first four places will be recorded with five, four, three, and two points for each respective place.
   There are many other questions that need to be answered if the track meet is to be successful. Thought should be given to the type of awards,

methods of keeping school records, and required practice, before any participant is eligible for the track and field meet. Once the teachers and students have agreed on the basic rules and regulations of the track meet, time should be taken to explain them to the students, and simplified rules should be posted in the classroom and gymnasium.

Evaluative Techniques

Although performance in track and field events appear to be easy to evaluate, quite the contrary is true. Each event is scored on the basis of either distance or time. The problem lies in giving a value for amount of improvement rather than an arbitrary number of points for one's ranked position in each event. This problem is further complicated by the philosophy underlying a track and field unit. At this age level, boys and girls should be free from excessive competitive pressure and should not have to judge themselves against the standards set by the exceptional athlete. The solution to the problem of assessment is to allow each student the choice of selecting a certain number of units and then record his initial and final scores.

The above approach to evaluating performance and improvement becomes a personal assessment. A child who is a low achiever can, in turn, set a realistic goal for himself without worrying about who is the best in each respective event. Similarly, the outstanding performer can set for himself a high standard which, in turn, motivates him to work at his maximum capacity.

SELECTED REFERENCES

ANDERSON, M. H.; ELLIOT, M. E.; and LaBERGE, J. *Play With a Purpose.* New York: Harper & Row, Publishers, 1966.

BLAKE, O. WILLIAM. *Lead-Up Games to Team Sports.* Englewood Cliffs, New Jersey: Prentice-Hall, Inc., 1964.

Basketball Instructors Guide, Chicago: The Athletic Institute, 1961.

BOYER, M. H. *The Teaching of Elementary School Physical Education Games and Related Activities.* New York: J. Lowell Pratt & Co., 1965.

BOYER, M. H. *The Teaching of Elementary School Physical Education.* New York: J. Lowell Pratt & Co., 1965.

BRESNAHAN, G. W.; TUTTLE, W. W.; and CRETZMEYER, F. *Track and Field Athletics.* St. Louis: The C. V. Mosby Co., 1960.

COOKE, DAVID C. *Better Basketball for Boys.* New York: Dodd, Mead & Co., 1960.

DAUER, VICTOR P. *Fitness for Elementary School Children.* Minneapolis: Burgess Publishing Co., 1963.

DiCLEMENTE, FRANK F. Soccer Illustrated. New York: A. S. Barnes & Co. Inc., 1955.

EGSTROM, G. H., and SCHAAFSMA, F. *Volleyball.* Dubuque: Wm. C. Brown Company Publishers, 1966.

FAIT, HOLLIS F. *Physical Education for the Elementary School Child.* Philadelphia: W. B. Saunders Co., 1964.

FOREMAN, K. E., and HUSTED, V. *Track and Field*. Dubuque: Wm. C. Brown Company Publishers, 1965.

HALSEY, ELIZABETH, and PORTER, LORENA. *Physical Education for Children*, Revised Edition. New York: Holt, Rinehart & Winston, Inc., New York, 1963.

How We Do It Games Book, Third Edition. Washington, D.C.: American Association for Health, Physical Education and Recreation, 1964.

KNEER, M.; LIPINSKI, D.; and WALSH, J. *How to Improve your Softball*, Chicago: The Athletic Institute, 1963.

KNEER, M. and McCORD, C. L. *Softball*. Dubuque: Wm. C. Brown Company Publishers, 1966.

LANE, E. C.; OBRECHT, D.; and WIENKE, P. *Track and Field for Elementary School Children and Junior High Girls*. Chicago: The Athletic Institute, 1964.

LAWRENCE, HELEN B. and FOX, GRADE I. *Basketball for Girls and Women*. New York: McGraw-Hill Book Co., 1954.

LOFTUS-TOTTENHAM, T. *Your Book of Soccer*. London: Faber and Faber, Ltd., 1958.

MITLER, K., ed. *Physical Education Activities*. Dubuque: Wm. C. Brown Company Publishers, 1966.

National Collegiate Athletic Association, Official N.C.A.A. Soccer Guide, New York: The National Collegiate Athletic Bureau (publishes annually) Soccer Instruction Guide, The Athletic Institute, 1961.

NELSON, R. L. *Soccer for Men*, Revised Edition. Dubuque: Wm. C. Brown Company Publishers, 1967.

NEWELL, PETE, and BENNINGTON, JOHN. *Basketball Methods*. New York: The Ronald Press Company, 1962.

POWELL, J. T. *Fundamentals for Teacher and Coach*. Champaign, Illinois: Stripes Publishing Co., 1965.

ROBB, G. *Soccer*. London: Weidenfeld and Nicolson, Ltd., 1964.

SHURR, E. L. *Movement Experiences for Children: Curriculum and Methods for Elementary School Physical Education*. New York: Appleton-Century-Crofts, 1967.

TURKINGTON, D. and KIRCHNER, G. *Volleyball for Intermediate Grades*. Burnaby, B.C.: Simon Fraser University, 1968.

TURKINGTON, D. and KIRCHNER, G. *Track and Field for Intermediate Grades*. Burnaby, B.C.: Simon Fraser University, 1969.

TURKINGTON, D. and KIRCHNER, G. *Basketball for Intermediate Grades*. Burnaby, B.C.: Simon Fraser University, 1969.

VANNIER, M. and FOSTER, M. *Teaching Physical Education in Elementary Schools*, Fourth Edition. Philadelphia: W. B. Saunders Co., 1968.

WILEY, ROBERT C. *Soccer: A Syllabus for Teachers*. The University of Oregon Cooperative Store, Eugene, Oregon, 1962.

WINTERBOTTOM, WALTER. *Training for Soccer*. London: William Heinemann Ltd., 1960.

WOODEN, J. R. *Practical Modern Basketball*. New York: The Ronald Press Co., 1966.

SUGGESTED FILMS

Title:	"Hold High the Torch"
Details:	16 mm., color, sound, 29 minutes
Distributor:	(Rental) Association Films
Description:	Story of the Olympics as carried out in the U.S.A. Shows how athletes are selected and trained

INDIVIDUAL AND TEAM SPORT FILMS

Basketball

"Ball Handling in Basketball," 10 minutes, Encyclopaedia Britannica Films

"Basketball for Intermediate Grades," 28 minutes, Audio-Visual Services, Simon Fraser University, Burnaby, B.C., Canada

"Basketball for Girls—Fundamental Techniques," 10 minutes, Cornet Films

Soccer

"Soccer for Girls," 11 minutes, Cornet Films

Softball

"Softball for Boys," 10 minutes, Cornet Films

"Softball for Girls," 11 minutes, Cornet Films

Track and Field

"Fundamentals in Track and Field," 26 minutes, Encyclopaedia Britannica Films

"Track and Field for Intermediate Grades," Audio-Visual Services, Simon Fraser University, Burnaby, B.C., Canada

"Sprinting and Hurdling: Young Athlete," 16 mm., 17 minutes, Educational Foundation for Visual Aids, 33 Queen Anne Street, London, W. 1.

"The High Jump," 16 mm., 12 minutes, Educational Foundation for Visual Aids, 33 Queen Anne Street, London, W. 1.

"Long Jump," 16 mm., 10 minutes, Rank Audio-Visual, Ltd., Woodger Road, Shepherds Bush, London, W. 12.

"Triple Jump," 16 mm., 10 minutes, Rank Audio-Visual, Ltd., Woodger Road, Shepherds Bush, London, W. 12.

"Shot Putting," 16 mm., 10 minutes, Rank Audio-Visual, Ltd., Woodger Road, Shepherds Bush, London, W. 12.

Touch Football

"Ball Handling in Football," 11 minutes, Encyclopaedia Britannica

Volleyball

"Volleyball for Boys," 11 minutes, Cornet Films

"Volleyball Techniques for Girls," 9 minutes, McGraw-Hill Book Company

"Volleyball for Intermediate Grades," 26 minutes, Audio-Visual Services, Simon Fraser University, Burnaby, B.C., Canada

Games
From Other Countries

Rounders from England
Orienteering from Scandinavia
Goodminton from Canada
North Winds and South Winds from Sweden
Tapo-Ae from New Zealand
Eyeglasses Play from Korea
Kuwakha Nchuwa from Malawi
Four Chiefs from Nigeria

DURING the past few years, the writer has had the opportunity to observe many physical education programs in various countries throughout the world. Although there are major differences from one program to another, games appear to be the one universal activity. Many of these games, played in countries separated by oceans and with major variation in climate and customs, are essentially the same. Nigeria's game of "Four Chiefs" has many of the same characteristics of America's "Prisoner's Base." Both have the hunter represented. England's "Jacks" is quite similar to Malawe's "Kuwakha Nchuwa" as both require the simple manipulation of small objects in a similar fashion. The universality of games is not a complicated phenomenon; it is simply a child's way of copying one's elders or of expressing in an acceptable manner the social customs of their society.

Since there is a growing awareness to increase our international understanding of the customs and mores of other people, what better way than through the sharing of games and activities of mutual enjoyment. There is another important justification for the inclusion of certain games in this chapter. It is the writer's opinion that some of these activities are extremely compatible with the changing pattern of elementary education. For example, Orienteering not only provides an enjoyable recreational pursuit for children and youth, it also provides a lifesaving skill for other outdoor recreational activities such as camping and mountaineering. What better place to begin them than in the elementary school. Without treading on anyone's "sacred cow," the English game of "Rounders" requires many of the skills of Softball, yet involves more activity and is less expensive.

The following short list of games is, therefore, an experiment in this edition. If elementary school teachers find these activities are enjoyed by children, others may be found in the additional references provided. Further, the suggested grade level is a reasonable guess on the part of the writer. Teachers should, therefore, experiment with each activity to determine its appropriateness to her particular grade. Also, teachers should boldly experiment with modifying rules and regulations to cope with the needs, interests of her class, as well as with the available equipment and facilities.

Games from Other Countries

Name of Game	Page	Country of Origin	Type of Game	Skills	Suggested Grade						
					K	1	2	3	4	5	6
1. Rounders	000	England	Team Sport	throw, catch, hit, run				X	X	X	X
2. Orienteering	000	Scandinavia	Individual Sport	running, map reading					X	X	X
3. Goodminton	000	Canada	Team Game	run, serve, hit						X	X
4. North Winds and South Winds	000	Sweden	Tag Game	run, tag		X	X	X	X		
5. Tapo-Ae	000	New Zealand	Team Game	run, throw, catch				X	X	X	X
6. Eye glasses Play	000	Korea	Tag Game	run, tag	X	X	X	X			
7. Kuwakha Nchuwa	000	Malawi	Individual Game	throw and catch		X	X	X			
8. Four Chiefs	000	Nigeria	Tag Game	run, tag		X	X	X	X	X	X

ROUNDERS FROM ENGLAND

The Game

In many respects, Rounders is quite similar to Softball, in that it is played with nine players on each team, there are bases, the ball is batted, and players can catch or tag a runner out. There are, however, many unique and enjoyable aspects of Rounders that may give Softball a challenge, particularly for girls in the upper elementary school grades.*

Playing Area and Positions: (See Diagram on following page.)

Object of Game:

The game is played between a batting and a fielding team. The object of the batting team is to hit the ball into the field of play, then run around the four posts before the fielding team can put the batter out.

---

*Rounder bats and balls may be purchased from Educational Consultants Ltd., 1393 Greenbriar Way, North Vancouver, British Columbia, Canada.

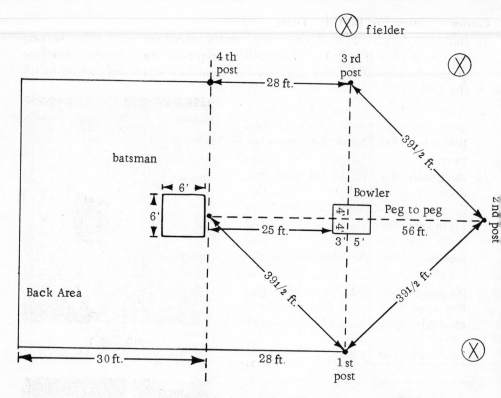

FIELD OF PLAY

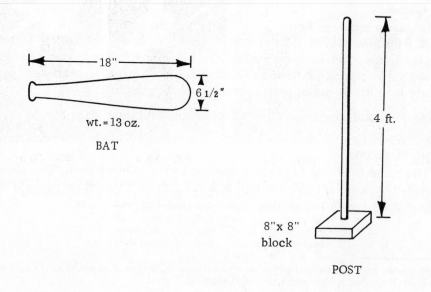

18"

6 1/2"

wt. = 13 oz.

BAT

4 ft.

8" x 8"
block

POST

General Rules for Batting Team

1. Batting Position: The batsman may stand anywhere within the batting square (6 ft. × 6 ft.). He is allowed to step over the side and back line of the serving square but not over the front line when attempting to hit the ball.

2. Number of Hits: Each batsman is given one hit from a fair pitched ball which must pass the batter between his head and knees and within the reach of the bat. Any ball that does not pass the batter within this designated boundary area need not be hit. The latter are called "no hit" balls, and are called "out" by the umpire before the ball reaches the batter. When a fair ball is pitched, the batter must attempt to hit it and run around the four posts. If missed by the batter, he must still attempt to

FIG. 10.1

BATTING

FIG. 10.2	**FIG. 10.3**	**FIG. 10.4**	**FIG. 10.5**
Stand with left shoulder toward the bowler and weight on the left foot. Hold the bat in both hands in front of the body and above the waist.	As the ball approaches, the batter may shift his foot position, raise bat backward and upward in preparation for the bat. The weight should also shift to the rear foot.	Swing bat forward with elbow leading and away from the body. Contact ball and continue strong wrist flick and turn of hand.	Continue forward swing with bat.

run around the posts. If a batter receives three "no balls," he automatically scores a run called a "Rounder" (see later section on scoring).

3. Number of hits per inning: A batting team is allowed three outs before they change places with the fielding team.

4. Number of innings: Depends upon available time, however games of 5, 7, or 9 innings are appropriate for this age level.

5. Where the ball may be hit and how to score. (See previous diagram and next section.)

Skills for the Batting Team

The field of play consists of the open field of play in front of the batter's box, (usually limited to the available space. Recommended minimum size is about one-half acre), and the Back area (recommended size 60 ft. × 30 ft.).

The ball may be hit into the Forward or Back Area. When a ball has been hit into the forward area the Batter must carry his bat and run around the four posts.

1. If a batter hits a ball into the forward area and runs around the four posts without being put out, he scores ONE ROUNDER.

2. If a batter misses a "fair pitch" or it is hit into the Back Area and he still attempts to run around the posts, if he makes it before being put out, he scores a HALF-ROUNDER.

3. If a batter has started his run, either from a forward or backward hit, and cannot make it all the way around, he may stop at any post. When the next player bats, any teammate who is waiting on the first, second, or third post may run as soon as the "bowler" has released the ball.

   Important: No player who is caught at any post and makes it to the fourth post as the result of a hit by another teammate can score a Rounder or a Half-Rounder.

   Important: When a batsman is at a post, he must either hold it with his hand or keep in contact with it with his bat. (See Figure 10.6)

FIG. 10.6

Important: A ball that strikes the ground in the forward area then rolls or bounces into the back area is still counted as a forward hit.

4. Substitute Runner: A batsman may request a substitute runner because of injury or special handicap. The substitute must stand in the assigned position and may run as soon as the batter hits, or after a fair pitch has been missed by the batter.

5. A batter may be put out in any of the following ways:[1]

   a. If he steps over the front line of the square in hitting the ball.
   b. If he is caught out from a "good" ball.
   c. If he is stumped (put out) by a fielder, with the hand holding the ball touching the post to which the batsman is running, before the latter makes contact.
   d. If, after taking a ball, a fielder touches him with the hand holding the ball while the batsman is still in the batting square or running around the track.
   e. If he overtakes another batsman.
   f. If he loses contact with his post, he can be stumped (put) out. (He is assumed to have started toward the next post and it is there that he has to be put out.)
   g. If he obstructs a fielder, unless that fielder is on the batsman's direct route.
   h. If a fielder bounces the ball in the batting square when there are no more batsmen waiting to bat.
   i. If after a warning to the team he leaves a post after the bowler has started his action but before the ball has left the bowler's hand. (N.B. The team will be warned by the umpire for the first offense and the player given "out" for the second offense.)
   j. If he runs on the inside of a post, unless he is prevented from running on his correct path by an obstructing fielder.
   k. If his substitute runner starts to run before the batsman hits the ball or it has passed him.

Skills for the Fielding Team

Fielding skills used in Rounders are very similar to those required to play Softball. Fielders must be able to catch, pick up a grounder, and throw a ball. All appropriate catching, grounding, and throwing skills are described under Softball. The bowling skill used in Rounders is slightly different from the softball pitch, hence will be described in detail.

---

1. National Rounders Association, Rounders, (Halifax, England: Fawcett, Greenwood and Co. Ltd., 1965), p. 9.

FIELDING SKILL

FIG. 10.7   FIG. 10.8

BOWLING

FIG. 10.9	FIG. 10.10	FIG. 10.11	FIG. 10.12
Stand at the back of the b o w l i n g square with left side toward the batter. Hold the ball in the right hand and extend left arm toward the batter.	Step sideways with left foot.	Bring right f o o t forward near left, and . . .	Step forward with left foot, swing right arm d o w n-ward and forward and release the ball.

General Rules for the Fielding Team

1. Bowler (the pitcher). The bowler must deliver the ball with an un-derhand throw. He may, however, stand anywhere in the "bowling square" (8 ft. × 8 ft.) and take any number of steps he desires before releasing the ball. A "fair pitch" is a ball that passes the batter between his head and knees and within reach of the bat. The latter rule applies to the batter at the moment the bowler releases the ball. It is important to remember that the batter may, after the ball has been delivered, move forward, backward, or sideways

to hit the ball. Remember too, a batter may intentionally or unintentionally move away from a good pitch making it appear to be a "no-ball."

2. Fielders: Follow rules as they apply to putting a batter out. The main point to add is that a fielder cannot intentionally obstruct a runner. If he does, the batting team is awarded ONE-HALF ROUNDER.

How to Keep Score

The following scoring chart will be adequate for beginners in the Game of Rounders.

Batting Order	Scores		3rd In.	4th In.	5th In.	6th In.	7th In.	Total
	1st In.	2nd In.						
Team 1								
1. Smith	1, .5							
2. Brown	1, X							
3. Green	X							
4. James	X							
5. Downs	.5							
6. Bates	.5							
7. Jones	1,							
8. Schools	1,							
9. Weeks	1,							
Team 2								
1.								
2.								
3.								
4.								
5.								
6.								
7.								
8.								
9.								

In the first half of the first inning all players were up to bat once with Smith (player No. 1) and Brown having a second turn at bat. Since Brown was put out, the team retires and Team two becomes the batting team. The score at the end of the first half of inning number one is 6½ rounders to 0.

ORIENTEERING FROM SCANDINAVIA

True or official Orienteering may be defined as competitive way-finding on foot, across country, using map and compass.[2]

Since there is no definite proof to substantiate whether Norway or Sweden originated this sport, which incidentally both emphatically claim, we will call it a Scandinavian contribution. The real origin of this sport may be traced to World War II when many Scandinavians were initiated to Orienteering through the Resistance Movement. Accurate navigation by these resistance fighters often meant the difference between life or death since it was necessary to use a compass to find supplies, avoid enemy camps, and seek out hidden installations.

The purpose of Orienteering today is for wholesome outdoor enjoyment and to provide a lifesaving skill for the ever-increasing number of people who are turning to camping and other outdoor recreational activities. These are but a few reasons why Orienteering is taught in many Scandinavian schools and why the writer believes this sport could find its place in many elementary and secondary schools in North America. In fact, several schools in Canada and the United States have incorporated Orienteering in their programs.

Since maps and compasses are expensive, another type of Orienteering called "Score Orienteering" will be described for elementary school programs. The latter has been found to be extremely popular with boys and girls in the intermediate grades.

Score Orienteering:

In Score Orienteering each player is given a map of the area which includes all necessary landmarks such as school buildings, post office, statues, trees, and paths. The following is an example of a school and the immediate

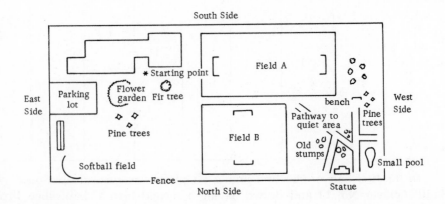

---

2. C. Schaanning, *Hints on Orienteering*. (London: B. J. Ward Ltd., 1965), p. 2.

major landmarks. Each player is also given a "Word Description Chart." Note in the accompanying chart that each description is simple with farthest points awarded the highest point value.

WORD DESCRIPTION CHART

Time Allowed 10 minutes

Name: John Smith   Start Time: 10.00
                           Finish Time: 10.09
                           Penalty Points: 0 (at 5 points a minute)

No.	Description of Landmark	Value	Insert Code Letter
1.	On the east end of softball backstop	15	T
2.	On the north side of flower garden	10	B
3.	On the south goal post of field B	5	C
4.	On the northwest side of an old stump	10	F
5.	At the northeast end of the softball stands	15	R
6.	On the bench near three pine trees	15	U
7.	On the southwest side of field A	10	A
8.	On the west corner of statue	25	Y
	Total points .... Final Score .... Penalty points		

General Procedure and Instructions for Orienteering

1. Each student is given a map and a word description chart. They write their name on the chart, and leave everything else blank.
2. Four or five runners leave from the starting point at the same time (to avoid congestion, allow 30 seconds between groups). The teacher marks on each chart the starting time (0.00, 0.30, 1.00, 1.30, etc.). From the time the runners leave, they have 10 minutes (or whatever time you set) to go to as many points as possible and return to the recorder's desk.
3. Each runner then takes his map up to the wall and marks on it the various points (the teacher has placed the Code letter on each landmark before the Orienteering Lesson) that are shown on the master map. Be careful to place the numbers in the right place.
4. When each runner arrives at a check-point, he places the code letter (of that check-point) in the appropriate space on the recording sheet. Runners may choose which check-point they wish to reach and according to their own order of preference.
5. A runner is penalized five points for each minute he exceeds the ten minute time limit.

Teaching Suggestions:

There are several possibilities for Score Orienteering. Competitions can be developed on the basis of one class of landmark such as trees, flowers, or buildings. If a school is situated near a park or wilderness area, the possibilities in turn become unlimited. Also, the addition of a compass and authentic maps of the geographical area open the door to an enjoyable and constructive recreational pursuit. Finally, if a teacher does not possess the skills of a reading a compass or a geographical map, she will find many people in the community, such as scout leaders and surveyors, more than willing to donate their services.

GOODMINTON FROM CANADA

In terms of antiquity, Goodminton, like Canada, has a very young history. According to two of its main boasters it is not more than twenty-five years old.[3,4] When one analyzes the game, he soon learns it is an offshoot or, more appropriate, a combination of Badminton and Volleyball. The inexpensive equipment, simple and flexible rules, and enjoyment of this game give every promise of it becoming a popular game in any country.

The Game:
Formation and Playing
    Area: Use a regulation volleyball court (60 ft. × 30 ft.; net 8 ft. high).

Equipment: Volleyball net (or rope), bats (see diagram) badminton bird (used are quite suitable) or yarn ball (cover with tape or cloth)

3 ply-grain to run lengthwise

5" to 6 1/2"

8" to 10" diameter

4"

Handle 1 1/4" diameter

14 1/2" to 15"

---

3. J. Farthing, *"Goodminton; A Good Game,"* Saskatchewan Recreation, Fitness and Recreation Division, Government Administration Building. (Regina, Saskatchewan: Winter, 1953), p. 3.

4. W. D. Ross, *"Goodminton,"* Australian Journal of Physical Education, Nov., 1961, p. 18.

No. of Players: 6 or less on each team.
How to Play:
Courts and Service:

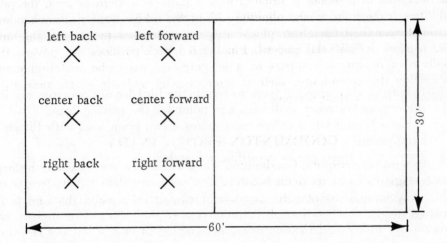

1. The captains shall toss a coin for courts or for service. The winner of the toss may choose either first service or his choice of courts.
2. Each server shall continue to serve until the referee calls *side out*.
3. The team receiving the right to serve shall immediately rotate one position clockwise. (The front row moves to the right, right forward moves to the right back position, back row moves to the left, left back moves to left forward position.)
4. Teams shall change at the end of each game.
5. Server has one serve only. The bird must clear the net entirely.

PLAYING THE BIRD:

1. The bird may be batted in any direction. Scooping, lifting, or any form of holding is not permitted.
2. The bird, other than on the service, may be recovered from the net provided the player avoids touching the net.
3. The bird may be batted only THREE times by one team before being returned over the net. (The same player may not hit the bird twice in succession, but he may give it the FIRST and THIRD hit.)

Points and Service:

If any player of the serving team commits any of the following acts, it shall be *side out*. If any player of the receiving team commits any of the following acts, the serving team shall be awarded a point.

1. Serve illegally.
2. Catch or hold the bird.

3. Touch the net with any part of the body or bat. If two opponents touch the net simultaneously, the bird shall be re-served.
4. Under any circumstances, reach over the net.
5. Play out of position.
6. Touch the floor on the opposite side of the center line or allow hands or bat over the center line.
7. "Spike" or "kill" the bird when playing a back position.

Scoring:
1. Failure of the receiving team to return the bird legally over the net into the opponent's court shall earn one point for the serving team.
2. A game is won when either team scores a two point lead with fifteen or more points.
3. Two out of three games constitute a match.

Substitution:
   Any number of players may be substituted only when the bird is declared dead.

NORTH WINDS AND SOUTH WINDS FROM SWEDEN

Formation and Playing
   Area: Large rectangular area. Scattered formation.
Equipment: Two blue ribbons and one yellow ribbon. Colors
                        are optional.
No. of Players: Class.
How to Play:
   This is essentially a "tag" game with the delightful addition of a player who can *free* any tagged player.[5]
1. Two players are chosen to represent the "North Wind" and are marked with blue ribbons.
2. One child is chosen to represent the "South Wind" and is marked with a yellow ribbon.
3. All other children are scattered in the rectangular playing area.
4. The two "North Wind" players, representing cold and danger, attempt to tag as many players as possible.
5. When a player is tagged by a "North Wind" player, he must squat down on all fours and become stiff and motionless.
6. The "South Wind" player tries to "free" as many tagged players as possible by touching them and shouting "free." As soon as a player is touched he is free and continues to take part in the game.

---

5. ICHPER Book of World Wide Games and Dances. (Washington: ICHPER, 1967), p. 53.

7. The teacher sets a time limit, such as two minutes, and a number of players. For example, the game lasts two minutes and if there are less than
three tagged players the South Wind wins the game. If more than three
tagged players remain, the North Wind wins the game.

TAPO-AE FROM NEW ZEALAND (3 - 6)

Formation and Playing Area:

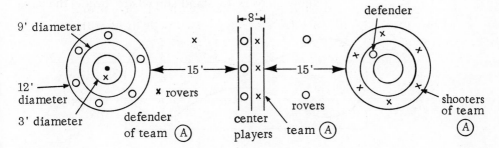

Equipment: Two Indian clubs, one football, and one utility
ball.

No. of Players: 12 players on each team.

How to Play:

The basic object of this game is to knock over the opponent's Indian
club with a ball.[6]

1. Arrange "defenders," "rovers," and "shooters" for each team as shown in
the above diagram.
2. A "center" player from each team is given a ball.
3. On signal, each "center" player attempts to throw the ball to one of his
"shooters" in the outer ring of their opponent's goal area.
4. When a "shooter" receives the ball, he may pass it to any other "shooter"
or try to throw it at the Indian club. "Shooters" may not leave their 3 ft.
playing ring.
5. If a defender gains possession of the ball, he must throw it to a "center"
player.
6. Rovers retrieve any ball that leaves the circle and must throw directly to
a center player.
7. It is permissible and desirable to maneuver both balls into the opponent's
area at the same time.
8. One point is awarded for knocking over an opponent's Indian club.

---

6. ICHPER Book of Worldwide Games and Dances, (Washington: ICHPER, 1967),
p. 43.

Teaching suggestions:
1. Rotate positions after a set time interval.
2. Restrict throwing to one type of throw. Example, one hand underhand or chest pass.

EYEGLASSES PLAY FROM KOREA (K - 3)

Formation and Playing
    Area: Draw a pattern in the shape of eyeglasses and allow players to stand anywhere inside the area.

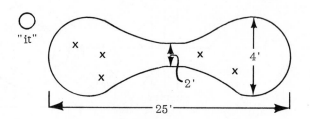

No. of Players: 5 to 10 for each playing area.
How to Play:
1. One player is chosen to be "it" and stands outside the "glasses." Other children scatter inside the area.
2. The tagger tries to tag any player inside the area or to get him to step on or over the line. The tagger may jump across the playing area but may not step inside.
3. Players within the area may move anywhere within the boundaries of the playing area.
4. If one of the circles becomes empty, the tagger can jump into and "conquer" the circle. When this occurs, the teacher chooses a new "tagger."

KUWAKHA NCHUWA FROM MALAWI (1 - 3)

Formation and Playing
    Area: Circle (size depends on the number of players)
Equipment: Approximately 200 small stones and one small pebble.
No. of Players: 2 to 10 players.
How to Play:[7]
1. Players sit around the outer edge of the circle.
2. The stones are placed in a pile in the middle of the circle.

---

7. ICHPER Book of Worldwide Games and Dances. (Washington: ICHPER, 1967), p. 39.

3. The small pebble is given to one player who tosses it into the air, tries to pick up one stone, then catch the pebble in the hand holding the stone.
4. If she catches the pebble before it reaches the ground she places the stone beside her and continues for ten more turns.
5. If she fails to catch the pebble she must return the stone and pass the pebble to the next player.
6. The team with the highest number of stones wins the game.

FOUR CHIEFS FROM NIGERIA (1 - 6)

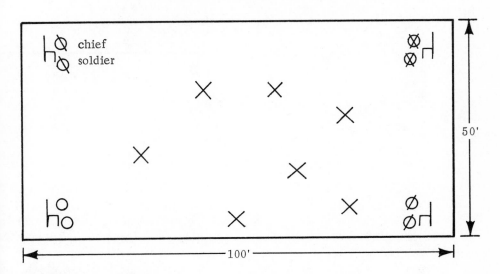

Formation and Playing
   Area:
Equipment: 4 chairs, 4 sets of colored ribbons.
No. of Players: Class.
How to Play:[8]
1. The teacher selects four "chiefs" and four "soldiers."
2. The "Chief" sits on his chair.
3. At the command "Go," all soldiers run with their team's colored ribbons and attempt to tag as many players as possible. As soon as a player is tagged he is given a ribbon and must run and stand behind the chief of that color.
4. At the end of a designated time, the teacher blows the whistle and counts number of prisoners on each team. The chief with the highest number wins.

———————————
   8. ICHPER Book of Worldwide Games and Dances. (Washington: ICHPER, 1967), p. 44.

SELECTED REFERENCES

GAMMA, A. B. *The Traditional Games of England, Scotland and Ireland,* Volume II. New York: 1964.

ICHPER Book of World Wide Games and Dances, Washington, D.C.: ICHPER, 1967.

National Rounders Association, Rounders, Halifax, England: Greenwood and Co. Ltd., 1965.

SCHAANNING, C. *Hints on Orienteering.* London: B. J. Ward Ltd., 1965.

TAYLOR, M. C. *Rounders: Its Play and Coaching Clubs,* London, Central Council of Recreative Physical Training, 1943.

Self-Testing Activities

PART IV

Part IV represents one of the most important changes occuring in elementary school physical education. It is within this area where Educational Gymnastics is gradually replacing our contemporary approach to teaching Self-Testing Activities. This change represents a fundamental shift from the predominate use of the direct to the limitation methods of instruction, allowing each child to progress according to his own level of interest and potential ability.

Normally, self-testing activities are organized and taught on the basis of standardized movements performed with or without equipment or apparatus. For example, "vaulting activities" can be performed on the floor, over small equipment such as hoops or beanbags, or over standard apparatus such as a vaulting box or long horse. Balance activities also illustrate this type of organizational structure with individual stunts such as "turk stand," "one foot balance," or "head stand" performed on or off apparatus. Progression of skill is from the simple to the complex. Lessons and units are developed on the basis of available equipment and apparatus and with selection of stunts based upon the previous ability of each class as well as what was recommended as appropriate skills for each grade level.

New teaching methods, based upon an increased knowledge of "how and why" children learn motor skills, plus the introduction of new and exciting equipment and apparatus, have created a need to reorganize the structural framework of self-testing activities. This is, however, a difficult task since children who have progressed beyond the second or third grade have usually been taught self-testing activities with a standardized format and through a teacher-directed approach. To ask any teacher to completely abandon a well-established way of teaching these activities for the new educational gymnastic approach is an unjust request to both teacher and student.

On the basis of the above, an integration of the contemporary with the educational gymnastic approach is provided in the accompanying chapters. The material provided in Part IV represents a "half-way house" or compromise arrangement to allow for experimentation and a gradual transition toward a new system of organizing and teaching these activities.

Chapter 11 describes the similarities and differences between the contemporary and educational gymnastic approaches to teaching self-testing activities, and explains how one can be integrated into the other. Chapters 12, 13, and 14 include information concerning the content and methods used in the contemporary approach to teaching self-testing activities. Numerous illustrations are provided in each of these chapters to show how small and large apparatus can be used in a variety of interesting and creative ways. Chapter 15 will provide sufficient information for each teacher to experiment with educational gymnastics to determine its value as an approach to teaching self-testing activities.

Teaching Self-Testing Activities

O NE of the most significant changes occurring in the elementary school physical education program is within the self-testing area. Our contemporary approach, which may be simply defined as teaching standardized skills through a predominant use of the direct method, is gradually being replaced by the educational gymnastic* approach. The latter system or approach is fundamentally different in the way skills are organized as well as in the emphasis given to exploratory and creative methods of teaching. Since it is educationally unsound to completely abandon one well-established approach, particularly when teachers and children are accustomed to its format and method, a gradual transition should be followed.

This chapter has, therefore, been organized to show the similarities and differences between the contemporary and educational gymnastic approaches to teaching self-testing activities. It will be recognized that, although there are fundamental differences between these two systems, it is possible to adapt and modify the contemporary approach in order to use the best features of the educational gymnastics. Chapters 12, 13, and 14 are arranged according to the contemporary approach to teaching self-testing activities. Chapter 15 will provide a basic introduction to educational gymnastics allowing each teacher, regardless of grade level, to experiment with this new approach to test its appropriateness and decide upon its possible adoption.

APPROACHES TO TEACHING SELF-TESTING ACTIVITIES

In the "Contemporary Approach" to teaching self-testing activities, all skills are more or less standardized in form. There are, for example, stunts and tumbling skills, beginning from the simple animal walks and progressing to the more difficult stunts such as headsprings and backward extensions. Each skill or movement may be classified as "tumbling," "balancing," or "vaulting" according to the skill and the apparatus used. Progression is generally based upon the premise of simple to complex. This approach has been used in Chapters 12, 13, and 14.

With the "Educational Gymnastic Approach" to teaching self-testing activities, the organization and progression of skills is based upon three ELEMENTS of movement, known as SHAPE, BODY POSITION, and BODY ACTION. All self-testing skills contain one or more of these elements. Each element, in turn, may be subdivided as illustrated in the accompanying chart. Shape, for example, is the "form or arrangement" of the whole body or any one of its parts.

---

*Other names used to describe this approach are "Movement Education" and "Movement Exploration."

A Single or Combination of Movements

May Involve

SHAPE	POSITION	ACTION
The form or arrangement of the whole body or any one of its parts. The body is capable of making shapes which are characteristic of: (1) Curled or stretched, (2) Wide or narrow, (3) Twisted.	The position of the body. Where it is in relationship to the floor, apparatus, or while in flight. The body may be: (1) in a hanging position, (2) balancing on one or more parts on the floor, (3) balancing on one or more parts of apparatus.	The action of the body is how and in what direction it is moving. It may therefore be moving: (1) quickly or slowly, (2) strongly or lightly, (3) in single or continuous movements, (4) in various directions (f o r w a r d, backward, etc.)

It is capable of making shapes which are curled or stretched, wide or narrow, or twisted.

CURLED AND STRETCHED   WIDE AND NARROW   TWISTED

FIG. 11.1   FIG. 11.3   FIG. 11.5

FIG. 11.2   FIG. 11.4   FIG. 11.6

In the preceding examples Figure 11.1 represents a curled shape. In terms of relationship to contemporary stunts and tumbling skills, one could say this is the curled part or position of a forward roll. The wide shape illustrated in Figure 11.3 is performed with part of the body, and could also be described as being similar to the "straddle" position used in vaulting. Finally, Figures 11.5 and 11.6 illustrate twisted positions which are unique in themselves and have no comparable movement in the contemporary approach of classifying skills. Figure 11.6 thus represents one of the fundamental differences between the two approaches. Standardized skills are performed in much the same way by all children. There is very little opportunity on the part of the performer to modify the basic form of the skill. On the other hand, the format of shape, position, and action allows each child maximum freedom to perform a movement which is unique in itself as illustrated by the twisted shapes.

It is important at this point in the discussion to emphasize that this new organizational structure involving the elements of shape, position, and action is used in the *planning, progression,* and *evaluation* of all self-testing skills. These elements become the format for teaching and thus provide the means whereby the limitation and indirect methods of instruction can be utilized to assist each child to learn to understand how his body can be used in an infinite variety of ways (see Chapter 15).

UNIT AND THEME ARRANGEMENT

Most teachers use the "unit" system to organize and teach physical education activities. A unit is defined as the organizing of activities around a central idea or theme. Primary teachers normally organize multiple units of instruction (see Chapter 4). For example, on Monday she may devote a lesson to singing games, on Tuesday to self-testing activities, and on Wednesday to running and tag games. In this case the units are extremely broad in order to cope with the interests and maturity of her particular age group. On the other hand, teachers of Grades Four or Five may plan a three or four week unit on stunts and tumbling, and devote the majority of their time and emphasis to balance type activities. The latter represents a narrow interpretation of a central theme. Nevertheless, both examples are valid and clearly illustrate the flexibility applied to the meaning of a unit or theme.

In the Educational Gymnastic Approach, the terms "unit" or "theme" may be used interchangeably. The majority of teachers who have adopted this approach tend to use "theme" rather than "unit." The reason for this preference is that a theme may be used to describe the central idea of a single lesson or a theme for a series of lessons extending into days or weeks.

CLASSIFICATION OF ACTIVITIES

There are no major differences in the classification of self-testing activities between the contemporary and educational gymnastic approaches. With the exception of "stunts and tumbling" and "individual activities," both approaches classify small pieces of equipment such as beanbags, wands, or hoops as "small apparatus" or "small equipment." Similarly, the common term of "large apparatus" has the same meaning in both approaches, in that it applies to the large equipment such as the vaulting box, wall bars, and to describe all the new fixed and portable agility apparatus.

Small equipment (or apparatus)	Simple Stunts	In the Educational Gymnastic approach, are classified as Individual Activities
	Tumbling Stunts	
	Partner Activities	
	Beanbags, Braids, Indian Clubs	
	Canes, Blocks, Chairs	
	Rope activities	
Large Apparatus	Balance Beam	
	Balance Benches	
	Springboard and Vaulting Box	
	Horizontal Bar	
	Stall Bars	
	Climbing Ropes	
	Jumping Boxes, Planks and Sawhorses	
	Agility Apparatus	

METHODS OF INSTRUCTION

There is at present a great deal of misunderstanding relating to the meaning and application of "direct," "limitation," and "indirect" methods of teaching in all areas of the physical education program. Too often it is inferred that the "traditional" teacher, whatever this means, uses the direct method of instruction, while the "progressive" teacher of Educational Gymnastics uses the limitation and indirect methods. When each teacher analyzes her own approach she will usually discover that she does not fall into either category. In physical education, as in many other subject areas, all three methods are used even within the context of a single lesson. The following definition of each method will provide a basis for understanding the meaning and application of each in both approaches.

Direct Method	Limitation Method	Indirect Method

←———Toward teacher – – – – – – – Toward Student *choice*———→
   control of movement   of movement and use of
   and use of apparatus.   apparatus.

Direct Method

In this method, the teacher structures the physical arrangement of the class (in lines, scatter or some other formation), chooses the type of activity to be performed (a headstand in the contemporary approach or a particular wide shape in the educational gymnastic approach), and prescribes how and where each child is to practice the movement (controls the apparatus selection as well as the method of performing the stunt).

Example: The forward roll will be used to illustrate the direct method. This particular movement is taught in a contemporary gymnastic lesson, hence is a good example of a standardized stunt. The forward roll is also used extensively in Educational Gymnastics. In both approaches the use of the direct method is applied to enable every child to execute this skill with reasonable proficiency. The following would be characteristic of the Direct Method of teaching this skill.

1. Class Organization: The arrangement of the class may be in parallel lines facing a mat, or a scattered formation with each child working within his own area as illustrated in Figure 11.7. The essential aspect is that all children will watch a demonstration and, in turn, will practice the same skill.

FIG. 11.7

2. Choice of Activity: In this example, all children are restricted to practicing a forward roll. The choice is, therefore, that of the teacher.

This method allows the teacher to select skills which all children either need, as in the case of the forward roll, or to stop a class at any time to emphasize a particular point or skill.

Limitation Method

The Limitation Method is a compromise between the Direct and Indirect Methods of teaching.[1] The choice of the activity or how it is to be performed is limited in some way by the teacher.

Example: In teaching a "forward roll," the teacher would limit the choice by indicating she wished the "forward roll" to be practiced on the floor or mats. By posing a challenge, such as "practice the forward roll and see how many variations in leg positions you can make," some freedom is provided. Whenever a teacher allows some freedom of interpretation on the part of the student, she is using the Limitation Method. The latter is a fundamental characteristic of this method.

FIG. 11.8

The Limitation Method is used to a limited degree in teaching standardized skills, since the teacher usually provides some freedom relating to where it is performed as well as some choice in the way it is performed. Its greatest use, however, is in Educational Gymnastics. With the latter, a teacher, through the careful choice of questions, can lead each child to discover many creative interpretations of a movement task. To illustrate, a proposition such as, "See how many twisted shapes you can discover while keeping two parts of your body on the floor" produced the following results:

---

1. A. Bilbrough, and P. Jones, *Physical Education in the Primary Schools* (London: University of London Press Ltd., 1965), Ch. 3.

FIG. 11.9

Indirect Method

The Indirect Method gives each child the opportunity to choose (1) the activity; (2) how he wants to perform it; and (3) where he wants to perform it.[2] This method in context of teaching standardized skills within the contemporary approach has little application. After children have learned a variety of stunts and tumbling skills a teacher could allow them to practice any skill. In this illustration the teacher would have to permit a child to interpret or modify any standardized stunt as he sees fit.

If children have not been taught through the Educational Gymnastics approach the meaning of shape, position, and action, and the proper progression from one movement to another, the application of the Indirect Method will be characterized by chaos and boredom. However, if children understand these terms and sequence development, the use of the Indirect Method has tremendous possibilities in developing individual initiative and creative movement patterns. In the following illustrations, children were initially taught many skills and movement ideas through the Direct and Limitation Methods. When given the opportunity to "practice any sequence" illustrating the Indirect Method, the following types of shapes, positions, and body actions were produced. (See Figures 11.10, 11.11, and 11.12, page 343.)

STRUCTURE OF A LESSON PLAN

Many teachers have been of the opinion that without adequate equipment in variety and numbers, little could be accomplished with thirty to forty children in the instructional time assigned. Obviously, there is some truth in this statement, especially when one is attempting to teach the same skills to all children, regardless of their interest and ability. Recently, teachers have

---

2. G. Kirchner, J. Cunningham, and E. Warrell, *Introduction to Movement Education.* (Dubuque: Wm. C. Brown Company Publishers 1970), Ch. 3.

| FIG. 11.10 | FIG. 11.11 | FIG. 11.12 |

discovered that with a minimum amount of equipment, used in a flexible and creative way, much more can be accomplished in the instructional time assigned for physical education. The accompanying outline of a suggested lesson plan and how it can be modified to meet the various teaching situations will assist most teachers in developing appropriate and interesting self-testing lessons.

A lesson plan for self-testing activities should be considered as a flexible guide to assist teachers in planning and emphasizing one or more skills or movement ideas. It is quite possible to combine previously acquired standardized skills such as forward rolls, headstands, and cartwheels with the elements of shape, position, and action. This is, in fact demonstrated in Chapter 15 showing how to integrate the two approaches, particularly for children beyond the second grade.

LESSON FORMAT FOR SELF-TESTING ACTIVITIES

Length of physical education lessons may vary from 15 minutes to one hour

PART ONE	PART TWO	PART THREE
Introductory or Warm-up Activities	Stunts and Tumbling and Small Apparatus Activities	Large Apparatus Activities

Time: 3 to 5 minutes as a standard allotment regardless of number of minutes for physical education lesson.

Length of time each class will devote to Parts Two and Three will depend upon what is being taught and how much time, space, and apparatus are available.

EXAMPLE OF LESSON PLAN USED IN A CONTEMPORARY APPROACH (30 minutes)

When teaching standardized skills, the direct method is primarily employed. Within the general structure of the suggested lesson plan, each skill is explained and demonstrated followed by a period of practice. A typical lesson plan for teaching standardized skills would contain the following:

Main emphasis:
1. Warm-up.
2. Review of previous stunts.
3. Introduce forward roll and headstand.

Part I: Introductory Activities (5 minutes)
General warm-up activities.

Part II: Stunts and Tumbling and Small Apparatus Activities (10 minutes)
1. Review of previous stunts (may include small apparatus activities)
2. Explanation and demonstration of forward roll.
3. Practice of forward roll.
4. Explanation and demonstration of headstand.
5. Practice of headstand.

Part III: Large Apparatus Activities (10 minutes)
General practice may include practice of previously learned skills on vaulting box, balance beam, or other large apparatus.

Changing time—5 minutes

Underlying the procedure and format of the above lesson is the principle that children learn self-testing activities in a cumulative way beginning from the simple and ending with the complex movements or routines.

EXAMPLE OF LESSON PLAN USED IN THE EDUCATIONAL GYMNASTIC APPROACH (30 minutes)

By comparison, teaching shape, body position, and action through the Educational Gymnastic approach necessitates a major use of the limitation and indirect methods of instruction. Part I of an Educational Gymnastic lesson is similar in purpose and format to a lesson in the Contemporary Approach. Part II, however, differs in that it is used to present movement tasks or challenges with time provided for each child to answer these challenges in a variety of ways with or without small apparatus. It is during this part of the lesson where children learn to work independently according to their own physical and creative ability. Part III is essentially a testing ground for the skills and ideas learned in Part II. The following lesson illustrates the sequential presentation of movement tasks and the relationship of one part of the lesson to another.

Main emphasis:
1. Warm-up.
2. Curl and stretch shapes.
3. Balancing on two and three parts of body.

Part I: Introductory Activity (5 minutes)
General warm-up activities including running, jumping, and making stretch shapes while in flight.

Part II: Floor and Small Apparatus Activities (10 minutes)
1. Individual activities emphasizing single curled and stretched shapes.
2. Individual activities combining single curled and stretched shapes into simple sequences.
3. Using hoops, emphasizing balancing on two then shifting to three different parts of the body.

Part III: Large Apparatus Activities (10 minutes)
Children working in groups on the vaulting box and balance benches. Repeat movement tasks (1), (2) and (3) on each respective large apparatus.

Changing time—(5 minutes)
The above example lesson could represent any primary or intermediate class which had adequate time, (length of lesson should be a minimum of 25-30 minutes), and a minimum amount of small apparatus for Part II, and two or more different types of large apparatus for Part III of the lesson. In the initial lessons, more time is devoted to floor and small apparatus in order to develop sufficient understanding and skill in performing various movements. With primary children the first five or six lessons (or more depending upon age and ability) may be devoted exclusively to floor activities. Boys and girls in Grade Three and above usually need the first two or three lessons devoted exclusively to floor work. As a general rule in the Educational Gymnastic approach, the largest percentage of time in the early lessons is devoted to floor activities with a gradual increase in the amount of time allocated for large apparatus work, as the children demonstrate their readiness to use the larger and more challenging apparatus.

PLANNING PROGRAMS OF INSTRUCTION

According to the previous information, a teacher may elect to plan a program according to a contemporary or an educational gymnastic approach to teaching self-testing activities. Her choice will depend, in part, upon the philosophy of the school, previous programs, and the available time, space, and apparatus. The advantages and disadvantages of each approach are discussed in the following paragraphs.

Planning According to the Contemporary Approach

Within the Contemporary Approach to teaching self-testing activities, a series of units are tentatively outlined for the year. Each unit, such as "tumbling" or "vaulting," would be planned on the basis of the available apparatus, previous experience of the class, and what skills were recommended for that particular grade. All unit development utilizing this format should be tentative since the introduction and progression of stunts is dependent upon the demonstrated ability of the class. The latter will constantly change as children increase their strength, flexibility, and coordination, as well as their general skill. Chapters 12, 13, and 14 contain a wide variety of self-testing skills with suggested grade levels indicated. Teachers, when using this approach, should review each section, such as "stunts and tumbling," "balance bench," and "vaulting box," to select appropriate skills for their grade level. From these activities, tentative lists of skills may be selected to form the nucleus of each unit. As the unit develops, a teacher can add or delete stunts according to the needs and abilities of her class.

Planning According to the Educational Gymnastic Approach

If a teacher decides to use the Educational Gymnastic Approach she must plan for very flexible and certainly tentative units or themes. The underlying principle of allowing children to progress according to their own abilities necessitates a flexible unit structure. In most cases, however, this approach is used in teaching academic subjects, hence teachers should feel more at home with this type of approach than with relatively fixed units of instruction.

During the first year of adopting the Educational Gymnastic approach to teaching self-testing activities, each teacher should boldly experiment with the use of the limitation and indirect methods of instruction to determine how she will use them as well as how much can be learned in future programs. Although Chapter 15 has been organized in such a way that teachers can introduce each of the elements of shape, position, and action in a progressive or sequential order, this need not be followed. The progressive arrangement provided in this chapter should be considered as a guideline or framework to build one's own type of program. It is obvious that primary teachers will have to proceed quite slowly at first since young children have little background or skill in gymnastic type activities. Older children, particularly the eleven and twelve-year-olds, possess a wide background of skills and abilities. Once they have learned the meaning of shape, position, and action, as well as how to work in an informal atmosphere, progress, in the sense of unit or theme development, becomes individualized and increasingly dependent upon the self-direction of each child. In the latter situation, the teacher's role becomes one of a guider rather than the director of a child's total learning experience in self-testing activities.

EVALUATION OF SKILLS

Evaluation of self-testing activities must be considered from the point of view of the teacher as well as that of the students. Each teacher must assess whether she has taught her lesson or unit in such a way that her goals have been effectively achieved. Evaluation from this point of view should be considered as a continuous process of assessing, modifying, and adapting each lesson to meet the changing demands and challenges of her class. Applying this principle to any self-testing lesson or unit, regardless of the structure and methods used, each teacher should evaluate progress on the basis of the following criteria.

Participation: Since time available for physical education is usually quite short, care and effective planning must be taken in the organization of each lesson to permit and encourage maximum participation. Each teacher should, therefore, assess:

FIG. 11.13

1. The time children take to change and enter the gymnasium.
2. The amount of time devoted to explaining and demonstrating skills. Most teachers usually spend too much time explaining, and allow too little time for actual practice.
3. The time available for each child to practice on each type of apparatus. This refers to an effective rotation system within any lesson.

Effective Routine Procedures: Many unnecessary problems and loss of time can be avoided when children know what is expected of them in the gymnasium. Simple routine procedures should, therefore, be established and adhered to from the first lesson. These should include:
1. Arrangement of apparatus—who should be responsible.
2. Rotation procedure—moving from one piece of equipment or apparatus to another.
3. Carrying and putting away equipment and apparatus.

FIG. 11.14

Sufficient Challenge to Children: Whenever teachers are continually confronted with disciplinary problems the reason may be lack of challenge in the tasks given by the teacher. Each teacher should constantly observe the amount of concentration and effort each child is giving to the task in hand. If she notices a general boredom and excessive noise, it may be an indication that the work is either too easy or too hard. In either case, a change is indicated.

FIG. 11.15

Individual Observations and Guidance: In any learning situation, each child needs some guidance and encouragement, regardless of his ability. Too often, we tend to select the outstanding performer for demonstrations and praise. It is the low achiever who really needs attention and encouragement. Hence, in the daily routine of teaching self-testing activities, consideration should be given to:

1. Observing, correcting, and encouraging as many children as possible.
2. Selecting many different children for demonstrations.
3. Recording important and successful techniques that will assist in future lessons.

Evaluation of each student's progress in self-testing activities is a relatively easy task when teaching standardized skills through the contemporary approach, and a difficult task when teaching shape, position, and action through the Educational Gymnastic Approach. In the first case, all skills are performed in the same way thus providing a standard performance. Since these skills are arranged from the simple to the complex, evaluation becomes an assessment of "how many and how well" skills are performed. For example, a primary teacher could list each stunt for her class, then assess each child on how many and how well he performed them.

Evaluation of individual progress using a cumulative number of stunts should be on the basis of individual achievement, with room for individual choice of stunts rather than "the same expectations" for all children. There are simply too many individual variations in skill and maturity to demand the same of all children.

There is a major difference in the way children should be evaluated when using the Educational Gymnastic Approach. The essential purpose of this approach is to assist each child to learn how to use his body in a variety of ways on and off apparatus. Each movement task should produce different shapes and patterns for each child. There is no common standard to judge the progress of each child. Progress is, therefore, an individualized matter and must be evaluated on this basis. Nevertheless, the teacher must still observe and evaluate each child's progress on the basis of some criteria, however subjective and personal it may be.

Since the reader may not be familiar with the meaning of shape, body position, and body action, it will suffice to note at this stage that evaluation

FIG. 11.16

can be made jointly by the teacher and each child. Each child learns to progress at his own rate and according to his potential ability. Evaluation by the teacher becomes the ability to assess whether a child is sufficiently challenged and is continually improving his ability to produce more difficult shapes and movements. Progress, as the teacher will come to observe in this approach to teaching self-testing activities, is as much concerned with the quality of movement as it is with the individuality and variety of the movements each child performs.

General Comments: It must be emphasized that the next three chapters are primarily arranged according to format used in the Contemporary Approach. Teachers can follow this approach and provide a well-rounded and educationally defensible self-testing program for virtually every grade. Nevertheless, the values inherent in the Educational Gymnastic Approach certainly justify a period of experimentation on the part of each classroom teacher. Hence, it is strongly recommended that all teachers read Chapter 15 to determine how this approach could be used in the total self-testing program.

Selected References

Bilbrough, A. and Jones, P. *Physical Education in the Primary Schools*. London: University of London Press Ltd., 1965.

Fait, Hollis F. *Physical Education for the Elementary School Child*. Philadelphia: W. B. Saunders Co., 1964.

Fisher, Hugo; Shawbold, Dean R.; and Wohlford, Paul R. *Individual and Dual Stunts*. Minneapolis: Burgess Publishing Co., 1960.

Halsey, E., and Porter, L. *Physical Education for Children*, Revised Edition. New York: Holt, Rinehart & Winston, Inc., 1967.

Kirchner, G.; Cunningham, J.; and Warrell, E. *Introduction to Movement Education*. Dubuque: Wm. C. Brown Company Publishers, 1970.

Loken, Newton, and Willoughby, Robert. *Complete Book of Gymnastics*. Englewood-Cliffs, New Jersey: Prentice-Hall, Inc., 1959.

Mauldon, E., and Layson, J. *Teaching Gymnastics*. London: MacDonald and Evans, Ltd., 1965.

O'Quinn, G. *Gymnastics for Elementary School Children*. Dubuque: Wm. C. Brown Company Publishers, 1967.

Introductory or Warm-up Activities

N ORMALLY, introductory or warm-up exercises are performed by children during the first part of a physical education lesson. This is particularly true with self-testing activities, as the "warm-up" is considered to be an important conditioner for the more vigorous activities which follow. The recent emphasis on physical fitness also brought renewed interest in this type of activity as a means of developing strength, endurance, and other important factors of general fitness. Both purposes are still valid; however, the manner or style in which this type of activity is handled has changed to be more compatible with our increased understanding of physical growth and development as well as with several important principles of learning.

Although there is a wide variation in the length of physical education periods, the introductory or "warm-up" period should continue to be the first part of any self-testing lesson. Normally, this will last from three to five minutes and involve general and vigorous physical activity. However, prior to discussing the types of activities used in this part of the lesson, several suggestions will be made with respect to gymnasium clothing, changing time, and what children can do prior to the start of each lesson.

GYMNASIUM CLOTHING

It has been the custom in physical education to require all children participating in self-testing activities to change into shorts, T-shirts or blouse, and tennis shoes. This type of clothing still applies with the exception of shoes. Since shoes are a restricting factor, it is strongly suggested that all children participating in this type of activity do not wear shoes or socks. Bare feet assist balance activities, encourage freedom of movement, and encourage children to move safely on or off apparatus with obvious concern for landing. Since most gymnasium floors are either tile or non-splintering wood, this does not present a problem. Children in the intermediate grades who have been used to wearing shoes should not be forced to take them off; they should be permitted the choice. When children experience the freedom of "bare feet," they will soon abandon their shoes.

With primary level children a bolder suggestion is made. When the writer observed primary school children in English schools, he was at first amazed and possibly shocked when he observed five to seven-year-olds enter the gymnasium, take off their clothes, and slip on a pair of shorts. Some girls put on a blouse; however, in the majority of cases they simply wore shorts. If we analyze this situation from a personal, social, and educational point of view, on all counts, there is much to be gained from this procedure. Primary children have little concern for the opposite sex. Even if they are curious of the others' physiological differences, the wholesome atmosphere of a gymnasium with a qualified teacher present is a desirable place to teach respect and understanding of the human body.

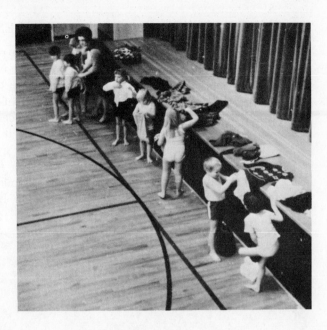

FIG. 12.1

The writer was convinced of this apparent "freedom of clothing" and adopted this procedure in an experimental project. At first, several children were shy; the majority, however, adapted to the changed procedure within one or two lessons. For primary teachers, the time normally allowed for changing was reduced from twelve to four minutes. Children were the first to see this advantage and soon learned not only to change by themselves, but in addition were observed helping each other. Parents were also informed of the new "style" and procedure, and were asked to come and observe their children. When they saw their children changing, but more importantly, the type of activities and learning included in the lessons, not one asked to change the procedure. It is well worthwhile considering, particularly in Grades K-1 where an immense amount of time is lost in tying shoes, undoing buttons, and "herding" children from the dressing room to the gymnasium.

FIG. 12.2

USE OF TIME BEFORE THE LESSON STARTS

The normal procedure in physical education programs is for children to change, enter the gymnasium, and when everyone is present the lesson begins. Teachers will argue that this is necessary because they are required to supervise the dressing room, or that it is impractical to begin while half the class is still out of the gymnasium. The following procedure does not remove any prior responsibilities on the part of the teacher; it does, however, contribute to maximum utilization of every minute in the gymnasium and encourages children to develop self-discipline and respect for the safety of themselves as well as every other member of the class. The following procedure has been adopted in numerous schools and has proven to be extremely effective.

FIG. 12.3

Procedure: As soon as a child has changed and enters the gymnasium he is allowed to practice any of the stunts, tumbling, or small apparatus skills (see next chapter) he has learned in previous lessons. This general rule does not include "free practice" on large apparatus and can be further restricted by the teacher in permitting only those pieces of equipment she feels the children can safely handle by themselves. It must be emphasized that this procedure cannot be initiated until the class as a whole has demonstrated their understanding and ability to work independently without the teacher setting the type of skill to practice. Primary children who have not been taught through a teacher-directed type of program will adapt to this procedure within a few lessons. Older children, particularly those in the upper elementary grades who are accustomed to moving from well-established squad or line formation only when permitted by the teacher, will find difficulty adjusting to this new procedure. Although some classes will adjust very rapidly to this change, others will require more time and patience on the part of the teacher. The latter, however, is worth the effort.

A few suggestions will illustrate how this procedure can be effectively utilized even in the first few lessons. As soon as children have been instructed how and where to change, use one or more of the following ideas while the class is changing.

1. Balls: Indicate to the children that as soon as they have changed they may choose a ball and practice bouncing it (throwing and catching, jumping over it, or playing catch with a partner).
2. Beanbags: Same as suggested above.

FIG. 12.4

FIG. 12.5

3. Hoop: Place on floor and practice jumping over it, jumping in and out of hoop, hopping around hoop, or hold hoop and jumping over it.
4. As skills are taught in future lessons, select one or two to be practiced during this "free practice time" before the lesson begins.

Since children in the intermediate grades have acquired many self-testing skills, a teacher need only to require practice of one or more of these as children enter the gymnasium. Some examples might be:

1. Balance stunts: When children enter the gymnasium after changing, they may practice a "handstand," "cartwheel," "one-foot balance," etc.
2. Balls: Same as above and require bouncing and change of direction (bounce throw into the air and make a full turn of body before bouncing again, etc.)
3. Partners: Do not suggest free practice with a partner until the class has demonstrated their ability to work independently in this type of atmosphere.

TEACHING TECHNIQUES

The atmosphere or tone of any self-testing lesson should be the same as that in any other classroom situation. What the teacher should establish is a setting where all children are actively engaged in learning skills with the teacher assuming the role of a guider or helper. It should be a friendly atmosphere with a minimum amount of noise. Since the teacher does not use a whistle in the classroom, there is no need to use one when teaching self-testing activities. Children should be able to work in the gymnasium and hear your voice at any time. A teacher who consistently raises her voice to be heard will find she is competing with, rather than controlling, the noise of her class.

In the majority of elementary schools the classroom teacher is normally responsible for her own physical education program. Hence, very few teachers will have time to change (other than into tennis shoes) for a gym period and then change back into her street clothes. Since each child is taught to progress according to his own rate and level of ability as well as to be aware of and concerned for the personal safety of himself and others, "spotting" by the teacher is used to a limited degree. Although demonstrations can be given by the teacher, the use of children (who normally possess greater skill than the classroom teacher) for such purposes is preferable. The latter is defensible both from an educational and practical point of view. Hence, on all counts, the necessity for a teacher to change into a gymnasium costume is no longer a vitally important and contentious issue when teaching self-testing activities. This does not, however, rule out the desire on the part of any teacher, particularly those who may be assigned a large percentage of time to physical education, to change if he or she so wishes.

FIG. 12.6

TYPES OF INTRODUCTORY OR WARM-UP ACTIVITIES

Introductory or Warm-up Activities should be vigorous and enjoyable. In the main, both teachers and children dislike performing rigid calisthenics involving exercises of the head, arms and legs, and trunk in a systematic fashion. Traditional calisthenic exercises can be given, however; this writer, as well as many other experts, strongly recommend using other types of vigorous activities. The main reasons underlying this suggestion are:

1. Calisthenics performed in a group situation are uninteresting and are less effective than other types of activities.
2. Three to five minutes of vigorous calisthenics is insufficient time to cause any appreciable increase in the level of physical fitness.
3. Other types of activities have a greater relationship to the second part of the lesson than simple exercises performed to a particular count or cadence.

FIG. 12.7

4. Children vary in physique and level of physical fitness, hence "group-paced" calisthenics may be too demanding for each child. If a teacher prefers calisthenics she should allow children to perform each exercise at their own rate.

In the accompanying pages several methods of presenting introductory or warm-up activities are presented. It is suggested that mimetics who . . . can, and rubber band exercises be preceded by a general activity such as running, skipping, or hopping. Skipping, circuit training, and vigorous tag games need not be preceded by this general and total body activity. Perhaps it is trite to say there is no best way of presenting introductory or warm-up activities. Teachers and children alike enjoy a variation in approach and content. It therefore is desirable for each teacher to become reasonably proficient in each of the following ways of conducting warm-up exercises.

"Mimicking" or "Copying"

In this type of introductory activity, the teacher or a student, without prior instruction to the class, leads them through a series of movements. The leader starts by performing an exercise such as toe touching and the children attempt to copy the movement. As soon as every child is performing the toe touch, the leader shifts to another exercise—again with no warning to the class. Children, in turn, now attempt to copy or mimic this new movement. This pattern is continued through a series of movements.

There are several inherent values in this type of exercise. First, for primary teachers, it is free of the formal or rigid command approach. Furthermore, primary children can more readily learn a movement by mimicking it than by a verbal command or description. Another advantage to the teacher, regardless of grade, is the freedom to vary existing exercises or to create new movements.

"Who Can?"

In this form of exercising children are challenged to perform a movement but are not told exactly how to do it. Each child must develop a creative response to the teacher's "Who can . . . . . ?" question. For example, if a teacher wanted to emphasize a movement involving flexibility she would pose the question "Who can stretch back like a tall swaying tree?" Hence, by direct suggestion, the teacher can stimulate movements that involve all parts of the body. The manner in which each child performs these movements is dependent upon his own creativity. Furthermore, the number of individual or dual movements as well as additional uses of apparatus such as balls, wands, and ropes is limited only by the imagination of the teacher and the class.

The success of this method of exercising is dependent upon the manner in which the teacher selects and presents the questions and how she maintains control throughout the exercise period. Each question should be directed toward enhancing one factor such as strength, endurance, or balance. In order to maintain control, particularly with questions that call for free running or hopping in all directions, a method of stopping children and gaining their attention should also be established. Three basic signals are, therefore, needed to accomplish this task. First, while the teacher is posing a question her hand should be raised above her head. When her hand drops this means START THE MOVEMENT. Second, teach children that one blow on the whistle means STOP—FACE TEACHER AND LISTEN FOR THE NEXT QUESTION. Finally, two blows on the whistle mean RETURN TO YOUR SPOT ON THE HOME BASE LINE. The latter is the original starting position of the class.

To illustrate the simplicity of this method, let us assume a second grade class is in the gymnasium and standing in a line formation. (Home base line.) A few minutes are needed to explain the three signals described in the foregoing paragraph. The procedure shown following should next be performed in chronological order.

First: Line class up on home base line. Tell them to remember their spot.

Second: Raise your hand over your head. Explain what children should do when you drop your hand.

Third: Pose question "Who can . . . . . hop ten times and find a new spot?" Drop your hand. Children now hop to a new spot.

Fourth: One "blow" on your whistle. As the children turn and face you, raise your hand in preparation for the next movement.

Fifth: "Who can . . . run as lightly as he can without moving away from his spot?" Drop your hand.

Sixth: One "blow" on the whistle. Raise your hand.

Seventh: "Who can circle their heads without moving their bodies?"

Eighth: One "blow" on the whistle. Raise hand and continue sequence to cover each part of the body.

Rubber Band Exercises

Exercises performed with rubber bands may be defined as conditioning exercises against a flexible resistance. The unlimited variety of exercises coupled with the negligible cost of old inner tubes should convince most teachers of their apparent worth. Further, they will add spark to the warm-up program and invite added resistance, hence result in potentially greater gains in physical fitness.

How to Cut Old Inner Tube Tires:

Obtain one or two used inner tube tires from your local gas station. The best type is used tractor tire inner tubes; however, regular car size inner tubes are quite satisfactory. Use scissors or an old paper cutter to cut enough bands for every member of your class, plus a few extras. The width of the band should be approximately one and one-half to two inches.*

Safety Rules: The following list of safety rules should be strictly adhered to whenever rubber bands are used.

1. Require each child to inspect his rubber band for rips and worn areas.
2. Provide adequate space for each child.
3. Never permit children to stretch bands toward the face.
4. Match children according to weight and height for all dual exercises.

Suggested exercises: The following list of rubber band exercises are not listed according to their order of difficulty. Initially, each exercise should be per-

---

*See Appendix A for a method of cutting inner tube into the proper size and shape for these exercises.

formed approximately four or five times and at the student's own rate. As strength increases, add to the number of repetitions. Finally, encourage children to design their own exercises involving one, two, and possibly three performers.

No. 1   PULL ACROSS CHEST   No. 2   BEHIND NECK PULL

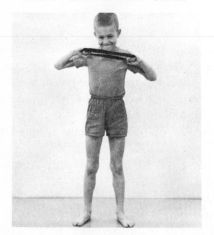

FIG. 12.8   FIG. 12.9

Stand with feet approximately shoulder width apart, back straight, and elbows pointing sideward. Hold rubber band in front of chest. Keeping elbows chest high, pull hands sideward.

Stand with feet approximately shoulder width apart, back straight and elbows pointing sideward. Hold rubber band across back of neck. Keeping elbows elevated and sideward, pull hands sideward.

No. 3: Bow and Arrow

Begin in a standing position with one foot in front of the other, trunk turned slightly to the left and arms extended forward chest high. Grasp rubber band with both hands. Hold right arm straight and pull rubber band toward chest.

No. 4: Straight Arm Pull

Begin with feet approximately shoulder width apart, back straight, and arms extended forward. Hold rubber band in front of chest. Keep arms straight and in line with chest, then pull arms sideward.

No. 5: Arm Flex

Place the right foot slightly in front of the left foot and bend trunk forward. Hold rubber band with right hand and place other end under sole of foot; keeping trunk in a forward leaning position then flex right arm.

No. 6: Upside Down Pull

Place feet approximately shoulder width apart, bend trunk forward and extend arms backward. Hold rubber band above seat. Simultaneously raise arm upward and sideward.

No. 7 Arm Fling	No. 8 Toe Pull

FIG. 12.10	**FIG. 12.11**
Place right foot slightly in front of the left foot, bend trunk forward and extend both arms downward. Hold rubber band in right hand and loop other end under sole of right foot. Simultaneously pull right arm upward and fling left arm upward and backward.	Stand with legs straight and together, bend forward and extend arms downward. Place rubber band under soles of feet and grasp the loop between feet; keeping legs and arms straight then pull rubber band upwards.

No. 9:   SIDE LEG STRETCH

Sit in a long sitting position, hands on floor behind hips and legs straight and together. Loop rubber band just above ankles. Keeping legs straight, pull sideward.

No. 10   SITTING LEG STRETCH

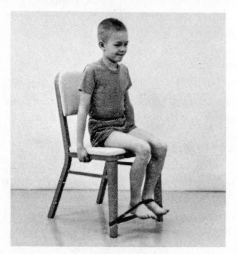

FIG. 12.12

Sit in a chair, back straight, hands grasping seat and knees flexed. Loop rubber band around right front leg of chair and around both ankles. Hold seat of chair with both hands and extend legs forward and upward.

No. 11   ROWING

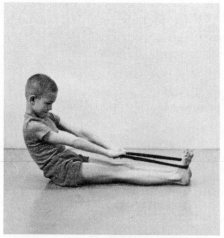

FIG. 12.13

Sit with legs straight and together, trunk slightly forward and arms extended forward. Loop rubber band around soles of feet. Keeping arms and legs straight, extend backward and push toes downward.

No. 12:   LEG PUSH

Sit with left leg extended forward with right leg bent. Grasp rubber band with both hands and place one end under sole of right foot. Raise right leg upward and forward and pull arms toward chest.

No. 13   DOUBLE BACK LEG PUSH   No. 14   WALKING

FIG. 12.14

Begin in front lying position, knees bent, arms backward and upward. Grasp rubber band with both hands and loop other end around ankles of both feet. Keeping arms and trunk straight, push feet backward and downward.

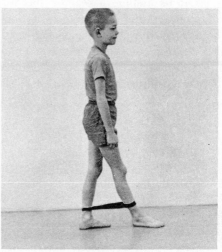

FIG. 12.15

Begin in a walking position with right foot slightly in front of left. Loop rubber band around ankles of both feet. Hold left foot steady and extend right leg forward. Place right foot on floor and shift left foot forward.

Circuit Training

Circuit training is repeating one or more exercises as many times as possible within a set time limit. If a child performs six push-ups, ten curl-ups, and eighteen toe touches within two minutes, this is a simple form of circuit. The number and type of exercises to make a circuit is optional, the variations unlimited.

This type of conditioning exercise program has many advantages, particularly for the self-contained classroom teacher. In the first place, circuit training allows for individual differences. For example, in the illustrations that follow, the number of repetitions for each exercise is determined by each child rather than by the most physically fit child in the class. Also, one of the most important administrative advantages is the set time limit allowed for each circuit. The teacher first determines how much time she wants to devote to circuit training, then proceeds to develop a tailor-made program to meet the needs of her class. An example is provided to show you how to develop a circuit for each member of your class.

Step No. 1: Determine the length of time you want to spend on the circuit. Time may range from 6 - 10 minutes. Example 6 minutes.

Step No. 2: Select appropriate exercises.

Let us assume a teacher has administered the physical fitness test (see Chapter 19) and has noted the majority of students are low in arm and shoulder girdle (bench push-ups), in abdominal (curl-ups), and leg strength and endurance (squat jumps). The circuit training program should contain exercises that will improve these weaknesses. The four exercises shown in the chart following would meet these needs.

Exercises	Max. No.	Training Dose No. 1 (¼ dose)	Jan. 15	Jan. 16	Jan. 17	Etc.
1. Bicycle (legs)	16	4				
2. Push-ups (arms and shoulders)	8	2				
3. Head Raiser (trunk)	6	2				
4. Chest Raiser (trunk)	11	3				

No. 1: Bicycle
No. 2: Push-ups
No. 3: Head Raiser
No. 4: Chest Raiser

No. 1 BICYCLE

No. 2 PUSH-UPS

FIG. 12.16

FIG. 12.17

Rest body weight on head, shoulders and elbows. Raise trunk and legs and place hands on hips. Extend right leg straight up and flex lower leg. Simultaneously lower right leg and extend left leg. Note: Start movement with a slow cadence and gradually increase speed.

Begin in a front lying position, hands approximately shoulder width apart and fingers pointing forward. The head should be a few inches off the floor. Extend arms while keeping the back and legs in a straight line.

No. 3 Head Raiser   No. 4 Chest Raiser

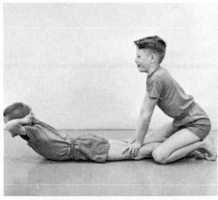

FIG. 12.18   FIG. 12.19

Begin in a back lying position, legs to-   One partner assumes a front lying position
gether and hands laced behind neck. Keep   with his hands laced behind his head. The
seat and legs on the floor and raise head   "anchor" man sits on his partner's feet
upward and forward.   and places his hands just above the knees.
                                              Lower partner raises head and chest off
                                              the floor and keeps elbows sideward
                                              throughout movement.

Step No. 3: Determine maximum number of repetitions for each exercise.

This is the first day involving exercise. Start with exercise number 1, Bicycle. All children attempt to perform as many repetitions of the Bicycle as they can in one minute. Record the number of repetitions under maximum column in the sample chart. Let us assume this is a fifth grade girl and she has performed sixteen bicycle repetitions. Immediately following this test, rest for one minute. Next, perform as many Push-ups as possible in one minute. Rest for one minute and continue procedure to exercises numbers 3 and 4 (Head Raiser and Chest Raiser).

Step No. 4: Set the training dose.

The training dose (see chart) is the actual number of repetitions the child will perform when she starts her circuit program. It may be one-quarter, one-half or three quarters of the maximum number. As a suggestion, start with one-quarter of the maximum number as the child's first training dose. Place these numbers in the first training dose column. Now the child is ready to perform her circuit without any rest between each exercise. In other words, she must try to complete the following three laps of exercises in six minutes:

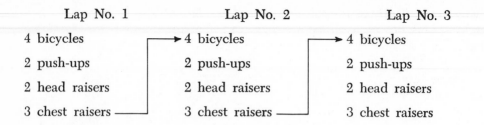

Lap No. 1	Lap No. 2	Lap No. 3
4 bicycles	4 bicycles	4 bicycles
2 push-ups	2 push-ups	2 push-ups
2 head raisers	2 head raisers	2 head raisers
3 chest raisers	3 chest raisers	3 chest raisers

Step No. 5: Attempt to complete the circuit.

Each child has six minutes to complete her circuit. Let us assume this fifth grade girl has completed one lap in two minutes. Now, without rest, she starts her second lap of exercises. This second lap took her two and one-half minutes. This leaves her one and one-half minutes to complete her third lap. Again she immediately starts her third lap and gets to exercise number 2, the Push-ups, and the whistle blows. Record her results under the appropriate date. To illustrate, this child completed two laps and down to exercise number 2 of the third lap. She would record "3-2" under the date and opposite Push-ups.

Step No. 6: After three laps are completed in six minutes.

Continue step number five until a child can perform three laps within six minutes. As soon as a child has completed three laps within the time limit, increase each exercise by one repetition. In our example, the girl would now do five Bicycles, three Push-ups, three Head Raisers, and four Chest Raisers.

The length of time a teacher may wish to devote to a circuit training program will depend upon several factors. The most important consideration is physical fitness needs. If a class scores low on the physical fitness test, it would be wise to require a daily circuit for five to six weeks to increase their level of physical fitness. A teacher may also want to design a ten minute circuit to be performed in the classroom for the days her class may not have access to the gymnasium. In this case, it would be wise to consider student interest and change the exercises in the circuit each month.

There is a wonderful opportunity to help the child who scores extremely low on the physical fitness test. First, attempt to determine the reasons for his or her low fitness. For example, extreme obesity or chronic lack of exercise will cause low scores. Design a circuit for this child to do at home. This may involve drawing stick figures and a short note or interview with the parents. The results may be tremendous if the teacher shows interest in the form of periodical checks with the child and with the parents.

Rope Skipping

The various rope skipping skills illustrated in Chapter 13 can be effectively used as an Introductory Activity. These skills are vigorous and certainly involve coordination of "mind and body." Each, in turn, can be performed while moving in various directions and in varying speeds. Also, for additional challenge and enjoyment, add musical accompaniment such as marches or other "lively" records.

Once children have learned the basic skipping skills, they can be used in the following ways.
1. Skip around the floor using any skipping skill.
2. Add change of speed and direction.
3. Skip to musical accompaniment.
4. Perform three different skipping skills.
5. Adapt the above to a musical accompaniment.

Tag Games

Several Tag Games listed in Chapter 8 involve many of the movements and characteristics suggested for the Introductory Period. The following list may be occasionally used in this part of the lesson for variety and the added "spark of fun."

Name	Page
Beef Steak	154
Snake Catch	156
Crab Tag	158
Broncho Tag	158
Commando	161

SELECTED REFERENCES

DIEM, LISILOTT. *Who Can*, FRANKFORD, A. M. Germany: Wilhelm Limpert Publishers, 1955, Copyright U.S.A., George Williams College, Chicago: 1957.

FAIT, HOLLIS F. *Physical Education for the Elementary School Child.* Philadelphia: W. B. Saunders Co., 1964.

KIRCHNER, G. *Physical Education for Elementary School Children.* Dubuque: Wm. C. Brown Company Publishers, 1966.

KRAUS, HANS, and HIRSCHLAND, RUTH P. *Muscular Fitness and Health,* Journal of the American Association for Health, Physical Education and Recreation, Vol. 24, December, 1953.

MURTHA, JACK. Physical Fitness Program, Sutter County Schools, California: 1962.

President's Council on Physical Fitness, Adult Physical Fitness: A Program for Men and Women, Washington, D.C.: U.S. Government Printing Office, 1963.

President's Council on Youth Fitness, Youth Physical Fitness: Suggested Elements of a School-Centered Program, Parts One and Two, Washington, D.C.: U.S. Government Printing Office, 1961.

Royal Canadian Air Force Exercise Plans for Physical Fitness, Revised U.S. Edition, Pocket Books, Inc., 1962.

SORANI, ROBERT P. *Circuit Training.* Dubuque, Iowa: Wm. C. Brown Company Publishers, 1966.

WALLIS E. L. and LOGAN, G. A. *Exercise for Children.* Englewood-Cliffs, New Jersey: Prentice-Hall Inc., 1966.

WALLIS, E. L. and LOGAN, G. A. *Figure Movement and Body Conditioning Through Exercise.* Englewood-Cliffs, New Jersey: Prentice-Hall, Inc., 1964.
VANNIER, MARYHELEN and FOSTER, MILDRED. *Teaching Physical Education in Elementary Schools*, 4th Edition. Philadelphia: W. B. Saunders Co., 1968.

SUGGESTED FILMS

Title:	"Why Exercise"
Details:	16 mm., color, 14 minutes
Distributor:	Association Films, 3419 Magnolia Boulevard, Burbank, California
Description:	Demonstrates types of activities which develop strength, endurance, and flexibility
Purchase Price:	$152.00 Rental: $54.33

Stunts, Tumbling, and Small Apparatus Activities

P ROBABLY the most familiar self-testing activity to elementary school children is stunts and tumbling. By the fourth grade, children have been exposed to a variety of animal walks, several basic tumbling movements such as forward and backward rolls and perhaps a few dual stunts. The value of these activities is quite obvious; strength, agility, and balance are among the physical fitness elements that can be improved through a balanced program of stunts and tumbling. Because of their truly self-testing nature they also contribute to intangible objectives such as respect for the safety of others and courage through performing a stunt that may appear to be hazardous to the child.

Small apparatus activities are included in this chapter since they are normally taught during the second part of a self-testing lesson. Each of these activities include numerous exciting and challenging skills and also contribute to the development of physical fitness.

It should become evident, when planning a unit of instruction involving these activities, that a general coverage of each area should be the rule rather than the exception. Furthermore, limited equipment should not be the greatest obstacle in providing these activities. The diagrams of Inexpensive Equipment shown in Appendix A can be followed by the least experienced "do it yourself" carpenters.

The general procedure used to teach these self-testing activities is normally a demonstration and explanation of each skill followed by a period of practice and guidance. Within this procedure there are simple techniques that will permit total participation by all children with a minimum of time wasted while waiting in line for a turn. The following suggestions will assist teachers in organizing their lesson to permit maximum activity in an enjoyable and relaxed atmosphere.

1. Teach children to immediately stop their activities when you wish to talk to the whole class. Do not use a whistle; children should consider the gymnasium as another classroom. A simple verbal command such as "stop working and . . . ," or "everybody return to their squads or section places" should be sufficient. The latter should be a "fixed" starting position, usually in "squads" or "groups" spaced around the outside of the gymnasium floor.

2. When there is not enough equipment (which is usually the case), divide the class into working groups to eliminate the problem of "lining up." For example, if you had — mats, benches, stall bars, and Indian clubs, the following arrangement would allow maximum participation.

3. Teach children to remember their section places and to remember what they were practicing from one lesson to the next. Assign certain responsibilities to section leaders, remembering how the apparatus was placed, what they were practicing, and where they rotate to.

FIG. 13.1

STUNTS AND TUMBLING

The accompanying chart contains a list of stunts and tumbling activities that may have been learned in previous grades or may be introduced at the suggested grade levels. Several of these skills will be used in Educational Gymnastics described in Chapter 15 to show how they can be integrated with movements involving shapes, position, or action.

Individual Stunts for Primary and Intermediate Grades (in approximate order of difficulty)

No.	Name of Stunt	Page	K	1	2	3	4	5	6
						Suggested Grade Level			
1.	Camel walk	372	X	X	X				
2.	Tight Rope Walk	372	X	X	X				
3.	Bouncing Ball	372	X	X	X	X			
4.	Log Roll	372	X	X	X				
5.	Wicket Walk	373	X	X	X	X			
6.	Crab Walk	373	X	X	X	X			
7.	Rabbit Jump	373		X	X	X			
8.	Measuring Worm	373		X	X	X			
9.	Seal Walk	374		X	X	X			
10.	Knee Walk	374		X	X	X			
11.	Kangaroo Hop	374	X	X	X	X			
12.	Knee Jump	374		X	X	X			
13.	Side Roll	375	X	X	X				
14.	Turk Stand	375		X	X	X	X		
15.	Bear Dance	375				X	X	X	X
16.	Knee Dip	375				X	X	X	X
17.	Rocker	376	X	X	X	X			
18.	Forward Roll	376		X	X	X			
19.	Backward Roll	376			X	X			
20.	Upswing	376				X	X	X	X
21.	Kip	377						X	X
22.	Seal Slap	377				X	X	X	X
23.	Head Stand	377		X	X	X	X	X	X
24.	Cartwheel	377				X	X	X	X
25.	Handstand	378					X	X	X
26.	Handspring	378					X	X	X

No. 1. Camel Walk (K-2)

FIG. 13.2

Place one foot in front of the other and lock hands behind back to represent a camel's hump. Walk slowly raising head and chest with each step.

No. 2. Tight Rope Walk (K-2)

FIG. 13.3

Draw a line on the floor. Begin in a standing position with arms extended sideward, head up, and both feet on the line. Walk forward placing toe, then heel on the floor.

No. 3. Bouncing Ball (K-3)

FIG. 13.4

Begin this stunt in an erect standing position with arms at side and feet approximately shoulder width apart. Take short jumps and gradually lower the body. Continue jumping and lowering body until the hands touch the floor. This action should simulate a ball coming to rest. Repeat action upward until the standing position is reached.

No. 4. Log Roll (K-2)

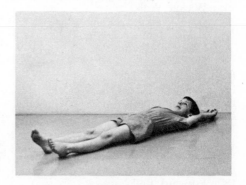

FIG. 13.5

Begin in the back lying position with arms extended overhead and hands locked together. Keep the body in a straight line and roll to side and around to the original position.

No. 5. Wicket Walk (K-3)

FIG. 13.6

Bend forward and grasp the legs just above the ankles. Without releasing the grip, take a short step with the right foot. Continue walking action forward introducing a turn or reverse action and walk backward.

No. 6. Crab Walk (K-3)

FIG. 13.7

Start with hands and feet on the floor. The back should be fairly straight to keep the seat off the floor. Walk forward by lifting the left hand and right leg upward and forward. Walk backward repeating the same action.

No. 7. Rabbit Jump (1-3)

FIG. 13.8

Begin in a squat position with body weight over the toes. Leap forward and land on hands then the feet to simulate a rabbit hop.

No. 8: Measuring Worm (1-3)

FIG. 13.9

Begin in a squat position with arms shoulder width apart and hands on the floor. Without moving the feet, take short steps with the hands until the legs and back are straight. Now, without moving arms, take short steps with the feet until the toes touch the back of the hands.

No. 9: SEAL WALK (1-3)   No. 10: KNEE WALK (1-3)

FIG. 13.10

Begin in prone position, body and legs straight and toes pointed. Keep arms straight and move right hand forward. Shift left hand forward and drag legs simulating the walking action of a seal.

FIG. 13.11

Start with hands and feet on the mat. Reach back and grasp legs just above the ankles. Shift body weight to the left side and take a short step with the right knee. Continue movement with short steps forward.

No. 11: KANGAROO HOP (K-3)

No. 12: KNEE JUMP (1-3)

FIG. 13.12

Begin in a squat position with arms folded across chest and body weight over the toes. Jump up and forward, land on toes and gradually lower body to the starting position.

FIG. 13.13

Stand with feet about shoulder width apart, knees slightly bent and arms raised forward and to the side. Jump up and wrap hands around lower legs, release grip, and land on toes. Landing should be made with knees bent.

No. 13: Side Roll (K-2)

FIG. 13.14

Lie on back with knees tucked in close to stomach and arms wrapped around lower legs. Without releasing grip, roll to the side. Continue rolling until the original position is reached.

No. 14: Turk Stand (1-4)

FIG. 13.15

Begin in a cross-legged position, arms folded across chest and body leaning slightly forward. Without releasing grip, lean forward, extend legs to a standing position. Return to the cross-legged sitting position.

No. 15: Bear Dance (3-6)

FIG. 13.16

Squat down on left foot, extend the right leg forward. Arms may be extended toward the side or folded across the chest. Simultaneously jump forward and draw right leg back and extend left leg forward.

No. 16: Knee Dip (3-6)

FIG. 13.17

Stand on the left foot, bend right leg backward and upward grasping the foot with the right hand. Gradually bend left leg until the right knee touches the floor. Without releasing grip, return to the starting position.

No. 17:   ROCKER (K-3)   No. 18:   FORWARD ROLL (1-3)

FIG. 13.18

FIG. 13.19

Begin in a sitting position with arms wrapped around bent knees. Rock back, raise knees and seat and continue backward roll until the head touches the mat. Return to the starting position.

Begin in a squat position with head up, arm extended slightly forward and fingers pointing straight ahead. Push off from toes, raise seat, and tuck chin to chest. Continue forward movement landing on base of neck and top of shoulders. Push off with hands and continue forward motion to a crouch or standing position.

No. 19:   BACKWARD ROLL (2-3)   No. 20:   UPSWING (3-6)

FIG. 13.20

FIG. 13.21

Begin in a squat position with body weight evenly distributed on fingers and toes. The back should be toward the mat. Push off with hands and roll backward keeping knees to chest and chin down. Continue backward roll until body weight is well over the shoulders. At this point, push off with hands and land on toes.

Begin in a kneeling position, arms extended sideward and backward. Vigorously swing arms forward and upward and at the same time push off from feet and finish in a partially crouched position.

No. 21:   Kip (5-6)

FIG. 13.22

Begin this stunt in a back lying position with arms at side and legs extended. From this position, raise legs, bend knees, and rock back until knees are above head. Note: The fingers should be pointing toward the body. Vigorously thrust legs forward and upward and push off with both hands ending in a partially crouched position.

No. 23:   Head Stand (1-6)

FIG. 13.24

Prior to raising feet off the mat, form a triangle with the hands and forehead. Push off mat with toes of both feet, flex knees, and raise body to a "half-way" position. Once body is in a stable balanced position continue raising legs upward until body forms a straight line.
Note: Too much arch in the back in this position will tend to cause the body to fall forward away from the center of balance.

No. 22:   Seal Slap (3-6)

FIG. 13.23

Begin in a front lying position with toes on mat and hands directly under the shoulders. Simultaneously push off from hands and toes, clap hands in the air and return to starting position.

No. 24:   Cartwheel (3-6)

FIG. 13.25

Begin with back straight, arms extended sideward and legs approximately shoulder width apart. Without bending trunk, bend toward the left placing left hand, then right on the mat and, at the same time, raise right than left leg upward and over toward the opposite side.
Note: In the middle of this stunt, the legs and arms should be fully extended and the body in a straight line.

NO. 25:   HANDSTAND (4-6)

FIG. 13.26

NO. 26:   HANDSPRING (4-6)

FIG. 13.27

Begin this stunt with arms approximately shoulder width apart, hands on mat and fingers slightly bent (aids in maintaining balance). Both feet should also be on the mat in the starting position with the right knee drawn up and close to the chest. With body weight well forward on arms, kick right leg upward and follow with the left. Continue upward movement of legs ending in a near straight line with legs, body, and arms. The head should be well forward to assist in maintaining balance.

This stunt should begin from a standing position. Run forward, skip on left foot, place right foot on mat and, as shown above, place hands on mat with arms extended. Continue upward and forward thrust of right leg followed by left leg. When body is in front of head, push off from hands and land on both feet with knees partially bent.

Combinations of Movements

Stunts and tumbling skills are normally acquired one at a time, however, once learned, they may be performed in a continuous series such as three "forward rolls" or continuous "knee jumps." In addition, children learn to perform routines or sequences involving two or more individual stunts.

Examples of simple and complex sequences are provided for primary and intermediate grades.

Example: Primary level:

MEASURING   RABBIT   SIDE
WORM   JUMP   ROLL

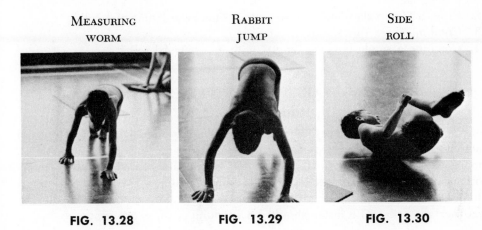

FIG. 13.28   FIG. 13.29   FIG. 13.30

Other combinations:

1. Combine three different animal walk movements into a continuous movement.
2. Combine a "backward diagonal" roll, then a "turk-stand" and finish with a "tight rope walk."
3. Combine two continuous movements and one single movement.
4. Combine two or three movements making the first movement very slow, the next quick, and the last one very slow.

Example: Intermediate level.

JUMP-SLAP HEELS   FORWARD ROLL   HEAD STAND

FIG. 13.31   FIG. 13.32   FIG. 13.33

Other combinations:

1. Combine "measuring worm," "head stand," and a "forward roll" in one smooth and continuous movement. Arrange stunts in your own order of preference.
2. From a "jump-slap-heels" move into a "backward diagonal roll."
3. Combine three quick movements.
4. Combine a single balance "stunt" with a "sideward roll."

PARTNER ACTIVITIES

The use of a partner in self-testing activities can be considered as one of the most versatile "pieces" of equipment. The accompanying list of partner activities illustrate how a partner can be used as an object or resistance, a place of balance, or an obstacle to vault over. There are, of course, many other stunts that could be listed. In addition, if children are given the opportunity, they are capable of inventing many challenging and creative dual or partner activities. The latter should be encouraged in every grade.

Partner Stunts and Activities for Primary and Intermediate
Grades (in approximate order of difficulty)

No.	Name of Stunt	Page	Suggested Grade Level						
			K	1	2	3	4	5	6
1.	Leap Frog	381	X	X	X	X			
2.	Rocking Chair	381		X	X	X	X		
3.	Wheelbarrow	381		X	X	X	X	X	X
4.	Chinese Get-up	381			X	X	X	X	X
5.	Knee Stand	382				X	X	X	X
6.	Leg Wrestling	382					X	X	X
7.	Elephant Walk	382					X	X	X
8.	Pig Walk	382					X	X	X
9.	Rooster Fight	383					X	X	X
10.	Crab Fight	383				X	X	X	X
11.	Shoulder Wrestling	383				X	X	X	X
12.	Elbow Wrestling	383					X	X	X
13.	Handspring Over Partner	384					X	X	X
14.	Knee Handspring	384					X	X	X

No. 1: Leap Frog (K-3)

FIG. 13.34

One partner assumes a squat position keeping his head tilted downward. The other partner assumes a semi-crouched position about two feet behind, with his hands resting on partner's shoulders. Back partner spreads legs and leaps over his partner. Continue sequence for several jumps.

No. 2: Rocking Chair (1-4)

FIG. 13.35

One partner lies on floor with his knees bent and arms extended upward. The other stands at the foot of his partner, bends forward and grasps his partner's hands. One partner rocks back pulling the other upward and forward until both have changed position.

No. 3: Wheelbarrow (1-6)

FIG. 13.36

One partner lies on floor, spreads legs and extends his arms. The other partner stands between the extended legs and grasps his partner's lower legs. Lead partner takes short steps with his hands while the other player follows with short walking steps.

No. 4: Chinese Get-up (2-6)

FIG. 13.37

Partners begin in a back to back position with elbows locked, knees together and feet flat on the floor. Both rise off the floor by pushing against each other and, if necessary, by taking short backward steps.

No. 5:   KNEE STAND (3-6)   No. 6:   LEG WRESTLING (4-6)

FIG. 13.38   **FIG. 13.39**

Base partner places legs about shoulder width apart, bend forward and places his head between partner's legs. Top partner places his hands on base's shoulders and base partner grasps thighs of upper partner. Base begins to stand up while top partner places his feet on base's thighs, releases hands from partner's shoulders and begins to arch forward.

Partners begin in a back lying position with each facing in opposite directions. On signal "go," both raise inside leg to a crossed-knee position. From the crossed-knee position, each partner's leg downward until his leg touches the mat.

No. 7:   ELEPHANT WALK (4-6)

No. 8:   PIG WALK (4-6)

FIG. 13.40   **FIG. 13.41**

One partner sits on floor with legs extended sideward while upper partner bends down, places hands between legs and his feet opposite sitting partner's shoulders. Lower partner wraps his legs around trunk and places hands over seat of upper partner. Lower partner rises off floor and takes short "elephant-like" steps while upper partner holds on.

One partner lies on the floor with arms sideways and hands pointing forward. Upper partner kneels down, places his knees on each side of his partner's waist and extends lower legs until his feet are under his partner's face. Upper partner's hands should be opposite the thighs of his lower partner. Lower partner wraps his legs around his partner's trunk then grasps the lower legs just above the ankles. Take short "pig-like" steps in this position.

No. 9: ROOSTER FIGHT (4-6)

FIG. 13.42

Stand on one leg and arms folded across chest. At command "go," attempt to push (not hit) opponent off balance. As soon as one player touches the floor with his "free" foot, the other partner is declared the winner.

No. 10: CRAB FIGHT (3-6)

FIG. 13.43

Partners assume a "crab walk" position with hands and feet on the mat and seat off the mat. On signal "go," each attempts to push the other off balance. As soon as one player touches the mat with his seat or falls over, the other is declared the winner.

No. 11: SHOULDER WRESTLING (3-6)

FIG. 13.44

Partners assume a kneeling position with hands locked behind back and shoulders touching. On signal and without losing contact with shoulders, one partner attempts to push the other off balance.

No. 12: ELBOW WRESTLING (4-6)

FIG. 13.45

Partners assume a full kneeling position with right elbows on the mat and holding hands in front. The left forearm should be in contact with the mat. On signal, and without taking elbows off mat, one partner attempts to push the other's hand to the mat.

No. 13: Handspring over Partner (4-6)   No. 14: Knee Handspring (4-6)

FIG. 13.46

FIG. 13.47

One partner kneels on mat, places hands well apart, and tucks head toward chest. The standing partner places his hand opposite the trunk of the kneeling partner, keeps arm straight, and raises one leg off the mat. Keeping the arms straight, kick upward with free leg, push off with back leg and "roll" over partner.

One partner lies on his back with knees bent and together and arms extended forward. Standing partner places hands on partner's knees, lowers body forward, and raises one leg slightly off the mat. Top partner swings top leg upward and pushes off lower leg and continues forward movement placing his shoulders against lower partner's hands. Lower partner keeps his arms extended to assist top partner's forward motion.

HOOPS

The introduction of hoop activities to any self-testing program will add challenge and variety. Hoops are inexpensive, easily stored, and, more important, a most versatile piece of equipment. A few of the more common and popular hoop activities are listed and illustrated in the accompanying pages. Additional stunts can be developed by application of the limitation method. For example, ask children to develop a stunt involving "vaulting," "balancing," or "twirling."

	Hoop Activities for Primary and Intermediate Grades								
				Suggested Grade Level					
No.	Name of Stunt	Page	K	1	2	3	4	5	6
1.	Hula Hooping	385	X	X	X	X	X	X	X
2.	Run Bowl and Jump Through	385				X	X	X	X
3.	Twirl Hoop on Parts of Body	386	X	X	X	X	X	X	X
4.	Balancing Hoop on Parts of Body	386	X	X	X	X	X	X	X
5.	Individual Positions	386	X	X	X	X	X	X	X
6.	Partner Activities	387		X	X	X	X	X	X
7.	Partner Activities	387		X	X	X	X	X	X

No. 1: Hula Hooping

FIG. 13.48

No. 2: Run Bowl and Jump Through

FIG. 13.49

No. 3: Twirl Hoop on Parts of Body

FIG. 13.50

No. 4: Balancing Hoop on Parts of Body

FIG. 13.51

No. 5: Individual Positions

FIG. 13.52

No. 6: Partner Activities

FIG. 13.53

No. 7: Partner Activities

FIG. 13.54

BEANBAGS, BRAIDS, AND INDIAN CLUBS

Too often beanbags, braids, or Indian clubs are not used to their greatest advantage in the self-testing program. The beanbag is used extensively by primary teachers in numerous throwing and catching activities. Rarely is it used as an obstacle to manipulate the body around or over, in combination with other inexpensive pieces of equipment. Similarly, braids and Indian clubs can be used in much the same way as the beanbag. When suitable challenges involving this type of equipment are presented to any age group in the elementary school, they will react with enthusiasm.

Considering the existing shortage of equipment in the majority of elementary schools, these "bits and pieces" of equipment can serve a very useful purpose. Most teachers can usually find enough scraps and make sufficient sets for each child in the class. Discarded bowling pins can usually be obtained from the local bowling alley and make excellent Indian clubs. Braids can be made from spare pieces of cloth as can beanbags.

A few examples are provided for each type of apparatus to show the versatility of this equipment. These examples should be considered as a starting point for using this type of equipment. Re-emphasizing a previous point, the use of the Limitation Method can produce many creative and challenging stunts performed with a beanbag, braid, or Indian club.

Stunts and Activities Using Beanbags, Braids, and Indian Clubs

No.	Name of Stunt	Page	K	1	2	3	4	5	6
1.	Balancing on the Beanbag	388	X	X	X	X	X	X	X
2.	Braids—backward arch	389	X	X	X	X	X	X	X
3.	Jump Through	389				X	X	X	X

No. 1:   Balancing on the Beanbag

FIG. 13.55

No. 2:   Braids-Backward Arch   No. 3:   Jump Through

FIG. 13.56

FIG. 13.57

BLOCKS, CHAIRS, AND WANDS

The use of this type of equipment has become increasingly popular in elementary school physical education programs. Initially, lack of commercial equipment forced teachers to improvise what was available or make equipment from scraps of wood. Although the situation has improved in many schools, the value and popularity of blocks, wands, and chairs have earned them a permanent place in the program.

Prior to using this equipment in the gymnasium or classroom a simple set of safety rules should be established and understood by all children. The list should not be extensive; it should, however, include the following points.

1. Check all equipment before using (look for splinters in wands, loose or unstable chairs, etc.).
2. Establish a safe procedure for obtaining and returning equipment.
3. When equipment is being used, make sure there is sufficient space around each child to prevent interference of one child with another.

The following stunts were developed by children and represent only a few of the many that can be designed for each piece of equipment. An additional suggestion is to ask the children to give names to their stunts and record them for future use. Simple stick figures will help teachers to remember unique stunts from year to year.

Stunts and Activities Using Blocks, Chairs, and Wands

No.	Name of Stunt	Page	K	1	2	3	4	5	6
1.	Floor Touch	390	X	X	X	X			
2.	Side Balance	390	X	X	X	X			
3.	Over the Hill	391		X	X	X	X		
4.	Jump to Seat	391				X	X	X	X
5.	Leg dips	391				X	X	X	X
6.	Squat and Stretch	391	X	X	X	X	X	X	X
7.	Human Bridge	392		X	X	X	X	X	X
8.	Hand Balance	392		X	X	X	X	X	X
9.	Foot Balance	392		X	X	X	X	X	X
10.	Twist-away	392			X	X	X	X	X
11.	Back Touch	393				X	X	X	X
12.	Floor Touch	393			X	X	X	X	X
13.	Foot Balance	393	X	X	X	X	X		
14.	Jump Through Stick	393				X	X		X
15.	One Foot Balance	394		X	X	X	X	X	X
16.	Forward Roll Off Blocks	394			X	X	X	X	X
17.	Individual Balance	394			X	X	X	X	X

NO. 1: FLOOR TOUCH (K-3)

NO. 2: SIDE BALANCE (K-3)

FIG. 13.58

FIG. 13.59

Stand on left leg, right foot resting on chair, back straight and arm extended sideward. Keep both legs straight, bend forward and downward, and place hands on floor.

Lie across chair, right arms extended downward and left arm resting on left side. Simultaneously raise left arm and leg.

No. 3: Over the Hill (1-4)

FIG. 13.60

Begin in backward sitting position, back straight, knees bent, and left hand on top of chair. Raise left leg upward to top of chair, raise left hand to allow leg to continue forward, then downward.

No. 4: Jump to Seat (3-6)

FIG. 13.61

Stand approximately one foot away from chair, and extend arms backward and upward. Simultaneously swing arms forward and upward and push off toes. Land on seat of chair with knees bent and arms sideward for balance.

No. 5: Leg Dips (3-6)

FIG. 13.62

Stand on chair, bend forward, reach back and grasp top of chair. Simultaneously bend left knee and extend right leg forward.

No. 6: Squat and Stretch (K-6)

FIG. 13.63

Begin in squat position, arms extended forward and grasp lower back legs of chair. Keep hands on chair, shift forward and upward until upper trunk touches back of chair and legs are extended.

No. 7:   HUMAN BRIDGE (2-6)   No. 8:   HAND BALANCE (1-6)

FIG. 13.64

FIG. 13.65

Sit on floor, arms extended backward with fingers pointing toward the chair. The heels rest on the nearer edge of the chair. Raise seat up until trunk and legs form a straight line. At the top of this movement, the shoulders should be over the hands.

Stand with legs extended and feet approximately shoulder width apart. Place index finger of right hand under end of wand and grasp middle of wand with the left hand. Release left hand and balance wand on index finger.

No. 9:   FOOT BALANCE (1-6)   No. 10:   TWIST-AWAY (3-6)

FIG. 13.66

FIG. 13.67

Stand with right foot slightly in front of the left. Place end of wand near big toe and hold opposite end with the left hand. Raise right foot off floor, release right hand, and balance wand on foot.

Partners stand with feet about shoulder width apart, knees slightly flexed, and grasping wand with palms facing downward. Each partner attempts to twist to his right. As soon as one partner releases his grip, the other is declared the winner.

No. 11: Back Touch (4-6)

FIG. 13.68

Begin with legs straight, feet approximately shoulder width apart, and grasp wand close to one end. Arch backward, place end of wand on mat, and continue arching backward and downward.

No. 12: Floor Touch (2-6)

FIG. 13.69

Partners sit on floor with knees bent and toes touching. Grasp wand with palms facing down and arms completely extended. The wand must be parallel to the floor. On signal from the teacher, each child tries to touch the wand to the floor on his right side. Change sides after each contest.

No. 13: Foot Balance (K-4)

FIG. 13.70

Begin in a back lying position, hold wand above head and place feet under wand. Release hands and extend legs upward keeping wand balanced across feet.

No. 14: Jump Through Stick (4-6)

FIG. 13.71

Stand with knees partially bent and feet about twelve inches apart. Hold wand with arms spread apart and fingers grasping with palms facing downward. Keeping arms straight, jump upward and over wand landing in front with knees slightly bent.

No. 15:   One Foot Balance (1-6)

FIG. 13.72

No. 16:   Forward Roll Off Blocks   No. 17:   Individual Balance
              (3-6)   (2-6)

FIG. 13.73

FIG. 13.74

ROPE SKIPPING

There are two basic types of rope skipping activities that children perform in the primary and intermediate grades. One kind is "rope jumping" which means to leap or spring free from the ground, to bounce or to jolt. This type of activity is performed with the long rope turned by two students. The second type is "rope skipping" which includes light and graceful leaps over a rope turned by an individual. In the following paragraphs information pertaining to the correct length and thickness of ropes and a list of skills will be provided.*

Long Rope Jumping

Rope jumping may be performed with one or more pupils jumping over a rope turned by two pupils. To teach this activity, begin with the progression of skills listed under the Single Performer. After the basic entry and jumping skills are mastered, introduce the dual activities listed under Two Performers. To assist in teaching both types of jumping activities, use the suggested list of Rope Jumping Rhymes on page 397.

Single Performer with Two Pupils Turning Rope:

There are two ways a rope may be turned for jumping activities. When the rope is turning forward and toward the incoming jumper it is called the "front door" (see Figure 13.75). If the rope is turning backward and away from the jumper it is called the "back door."

FRONT DOOR

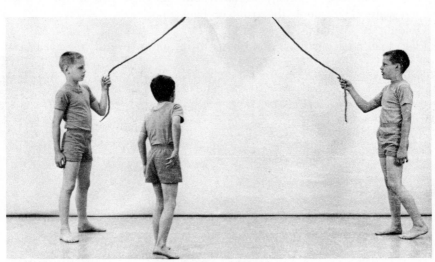

FIG. 13.75

Front Door: Children turn the rope toward the jumper (clockwise). The jumper waits until the rope is moving away from him before he runs in the "front door."

*See Appendix A for suggestions relating to measuring, cutting, marking, and storing ropes.

Back Door: Children turn the rope away from the jumper (counterclockwise). The jumper waits until the rope has passed the highest peak and is moving downward before he runs in the "back door."

The following progression of rope jumping activities may be performed by entering through the front or back door.

1. Run under rope.
2. Run in, jump once, run out.
3. Run in, jump several times, run out.
4. Run in, jump on one foot, run out.
5. Run in, jump several times on one foot, run out.
6. Run in, jump making ¼, ½, ¾ or full turns with each jump, run out.
7. Run in, jump on alternate feet, run out.
8. Run in, touch the floor with hands on every other jump, run out.
9. Run in, take a squat position (on all fours) and jump in this position, run out.
10. Run in, jump up and touch toes, land and run out.

Two Performers With Two Pupils Turning Rope

All of the rope jumping stunts listed following can be performed by partners entering through the front or back door.

1. Holding inside hands, repeat (1) to (6) as listed.
2. Place arm over partner's shoulder, run in, jump several times, run out.

SHOULDER HOLD

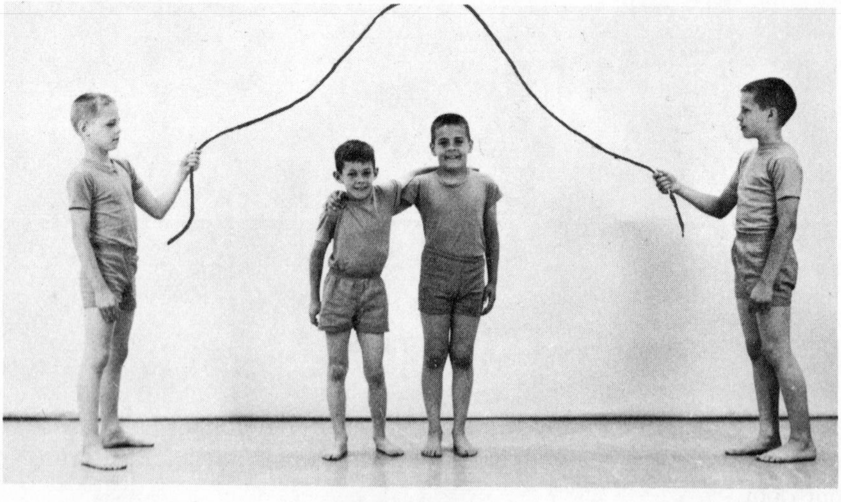

FIG. 13.76

Partners place one hand on each other's shoulder and jump over rope as it turns forward or backward.

3. Run in, stand back to back, jump several times, run out.
4. Run in, stand facing partner, hold partner's right leg, jump several times, release grip and run out (see Figure 13.77).

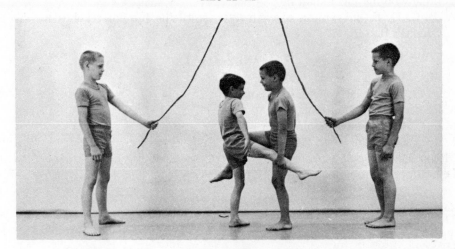

FIG. 13.77

Partners stand facing each other and grasp just below the knee of the right leg. Partners jump over the rope as it turns forward or backward.

5. Run in, face partner, jump several times, change places, jump several times, change places, jump a few more times, run out.
6. Run in, face partner, place hands on each other's shoulders, jump several times, run out.

Rope Jumping Rhymes

Rope jumping rhymes, like singing games, have been handed down for many generations. These rhymes may be repeated as children perform the various rope jumping activities. Encourage children to use their own versions of the following favorites.

MABEL, MABEL

Mabel, Mabel, set the table,
Don't forget the salt, vinegar, pepper . . .
(Turners turn "pepper" on the last word.)

FUDGE, FUDGE

Fudge, Fudge, tell the judge,
Mama's got a new born baby.
Wrap it up in tissue paper,
Send it down the elevator,

Elevator one, splits . . . Elevators two . . . splits, etc., until the jumper misses.
(Jumper performs splits on the word "splits.")

APPLE, APPLE

Apple, Apple, up in the tree,
Tell me who my lover shall be,
A, B, C, D, E. etc. (jump to each letter until the jumper reaches his sweetheart's first initial)

MAMA, MAMA

Mama, Mama, I am sick,
Send for the doctor, quick, quick, quick,
Mama, Mama, turn around,
Mama, Mama, touch the ground,
Mama, Mama, are you through?
Mama, Mama, spell your name.
(Child performs actions indicated in the verse)

DOWN BY THE MEADOW

Down by the meadow where the green grass grows,
There sits (call name of jumper) sweet as a rose.
She sang, she sang, she sang, she sang so sweet,
And along came (jumper's sweetheart's name), and
Kissed her on the cheek.
How many kisses did she get?
1, 2, 3, 4, etc.
(Child keeps jumping until she misses)

ALL IN TOGETHER

All in together, this fine weather,
January, February, March, etc.
(Jumper run in on the month of his birthday)
All out together, this fine weather,
January, February, March, etc.
(Jumpers run out on the month of his birthday).

HOKEY POKEY

Hokey Pokey went to France,
To teach the ladies how to dance,
First on the heels, then on the toes,
Give a high kick and around you go.
A bow to the captain, a salute to the queen,
And turn your back on the submarine.
(Child performs action indicated in the rhyme.)

I LOVE COFFEE

I love coffee, I love tea, I love . . . (name)
I dislike coffee, I dislike tea, I dislike . . . (name)
So go away from me.
(Child who is jumping calls the name of another child who comes in, then
    goes out.)

Single Rope Skipping

LENGTH OF ROPE: There are several kinds and thicknesses of rope
that can be used for individual rope skipping. Probably three-eighths inch
sash cord is the best; however, any rope, either sash or plastic, up to one-half
inch in thickness, is quite acceptable. Of equal importance is the proper
length of rope for each child. To determine the correct length have each
child stand in the center of the rope; if long enough, it should extend from
armpit to armpit (Figure 13.78). An incorrect length will adversely affect
rope skipping performance.

ROPE LENGTH

ARM POSITION

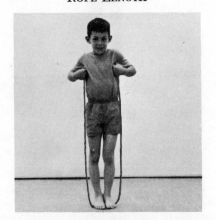

FIG. 13.78

FIG. 13.79

CORRECT ROPE SKIPPING FORM: The ends of the rope should be held
loosely in the fingers with the thumb placed on top of the rope and pointing
to the side (Figure 13.79). The elbows are held close to the side with the
forearms and hands pointing slightly forward and away from the body. To
start the rope turning, swing the arms and shoulders in a circular motion;
once the rope begins to follow a circular motion, all further action should
be initiated from the wrists and fingers.

PROGRESSION OF ROPE SKIPPING SKILLS: Rope skipping skills should
progress from the simple "two foot basic" with a rebound step between each

jump to the more complex rhythmic skills. In the majority of cases, girls will initially appear to be superior to boys not only in ability but in grace and form. With practice, however, boys will catch up to their counterparts, and, in some cases, demonstrate equal grace and form even in the more advanced skills. Several of the following skills are illustrated in the latter part of this section.

1. Rope turning forward—two foot basic (see Figures 13.80 and 13.81).
2. Rope turning backward—two foot basic.
3. Rope turning forward—hop on one foot (see Figures 13.82 and 13.83).

Two Foot Basic Step

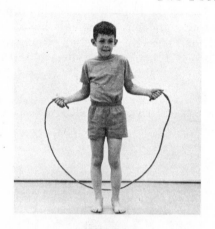

FIG. 13.80   **FIG. 13.81**

There are two jumps in place for each complete turn of the rope. Pull rope around and jump over it and . . .

. . . take a second rebound jump as rope is passing backward and upward.

4. Rope turning backward—hop on one foot.
5. Rope turning forward—hop on right then hop on left foot without a rebound step.
6. Rope turning backward—hop on right then hop on left foot without a rebound step.
7. Rope turning forward—alternate step (see Figure 13.84).
8. Rope turning backward—alternate step.
9. Rope turning forward—alternate swing step (see Figure 13.85).
10. Rope turning backward—alternate swing step.
11. Rope turning forward—progress forward jumping over rope with right foot then left foot and no rebound steps.
12. Rope turning backward—progress backward jumping over rope with right foot then left foot and no rebound step.

ONE FOOT HOP

FIG. 13.82

The one foot hop may be performed with each turn of the rope or with a rebound step after each jump over the rope. In the above illustration the child is preparing to jump over the rope.

FIG. 13.83

The child has jumped over the rope and is taking a rebound hop while the rope is passing over the head.

ALTERNATE STEP

FIG. 13.84

The alternate step involves a jump over rope with right foot, (jump), a second hop on same foot (rebound), then a jump over rope with left foot (jump) and another hop on same foot (rebound). The rhythm should be . . . jump right, rebound right, jump left, rebound left, etc. During the rebound step the rope is passing overhead.

ALTERNATE STEP-LEG SWING

FIG. 13.85

This variation is basically the same as the Alternate Step with the "free leg" during the rebound hop swinging to the side.

13. Rope turning forward—move sideways jumping over rope with right foot then left foot and no rebound step.
14. Rope turning forward—rocker step (see Figures 13.86 and 13.87).

ROCKER STEP

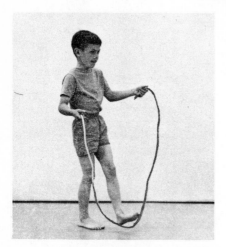

FIG. 13.86

FIG. 13.87

In executing this step, one leg is always forward with a shift of weight from the back to the front or lead foot. As the rope passes under the front foot the weight should be transferring forward thus allowing back foot to raise and permit rope to pass under.

After rope passes under back foot and begins its upward and forward arch the performer should again "rock" back transferring weight to back foot. In the above illustration the child is beginning to transfer weight to the forward foot.

15. Rope turning forward—two foot basic step and cross feet on each alternate jump.
16. Rope turning forward—two foot basic with no rebound step, cross feet on each jump alternating right over left, then left over right.
17. Rope turning forward—two foot basic and click heels on each alternate jump.
18. Rope turning forward—two foot basic with no rebound step, click heels on each step.
19. Rope turning forward—"Pepper"—rope must make two full turns while performer's feet are off the ground.
20. Rope turning forward—Doubles—enter front (see Figures 13.88 and 13.89).
21. Rope turning forward—Doubles—enter back
22. Rope turning forward—Doubles—one in (see Figures 13.90 and 13.91).

ENTER FRONT

FIG. 13.88

Partner with rope performs a two foot basic step (jump, rebound, jump, rebound). As the rope comes forward and downward, outside partner enters and places his hands on partner's waist.

FIG. 13.89

Both jump rope and continue alternate rebounding and jumping rhythm.

ONE IN

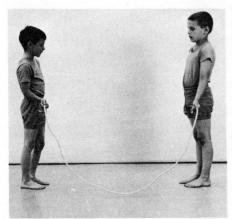

FIG. 13.90

Partners swing rope to half time rhythm (jump-rebound-jump). As rope swings back, one partner turns inward.

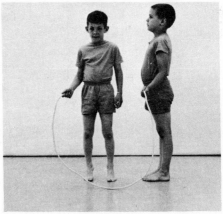

FIG. 13.91

As the rope travels downward and passes inside partner he executes a jump over rope then a rebound hop in preparation of the next jump.

PYRAMID BUILDING

A human pyramid is usually considered to be a group of students forming a "pyramid-like" human structure with one child at the top and all other participants gradually tapering to the sides. This is known as a "True Pyramid"; however, there are other kinds of pyramids which may have high points somewhere within the pyramid or even at the ends. The following block illustrations may be used as basic guides in constructing pyramids with two, three, or more students.

True Pyramid (Joined)

Modified Pyramid (Joined)

Modified Pyramid (Unjoined Groups)

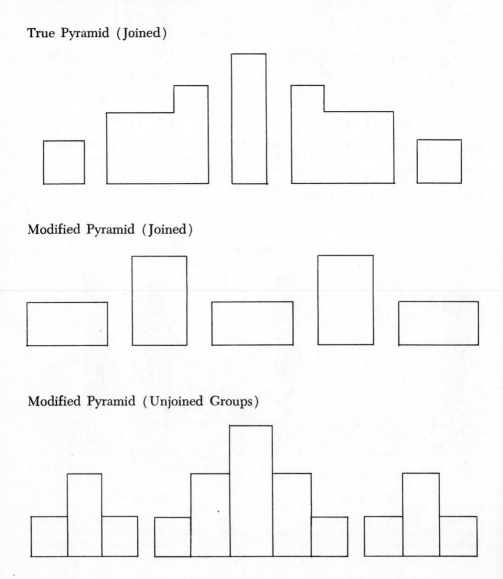

How to Teach Pyramid Building

In the accompanying chart there is a suggested list of skill beginning with individual poses for center, side, and end positions. These should be learned first and then individuals should progress to the double activities. At this point a policy should be established to require the heaviest and strongest students to act as the base and the lighter student as the top.

				Grade Level		
No.	Name of Stunt	Position	Page	4	5	6
1.	Stride Stand	center (single)	406	X	X	X
2.	Inclined Stand	center (single)	406	X	X	X
3.	Cross Legged Stand	center (single)	407	X	X	X
4.	Head Stand	center (single)	407		X	X
5.	Attention Stand	center (single)	407	X	X	X
6.	Dog Stand	end (single)	407	X	X	X
7.	Bridge Stand	end (single)	408	X	X	X
8.	Forward Incline Stand	end (single)	408	X	X	X
9.	Balance Stand	end (single)	408	X	X	X
10.	Forward Bend	side (single)	408	X	X	X
11.	Knee Stand	side (single)	409	X	X	X
12.	Knee Scale	side (single)	409	X	X	X
13.	Kneeling Arch	center (2-man)	409	X	X	X
14.	Handstand Arch	end (2-man)	409	X	X	X
15.	Base Stand	end (2-man)	410	X	X	X
16.	Headstand Arch	end (2-man)	410		X	X
17.	Inclined Handstand	end (2-man)	410		X	X
18.	Double Incline	side (2-man)	410	X	X	X
19.	Double Headstand	center (3-man)	411	X	X	X
20.	Stride Stand	center (3-man)	411	X	X	X
21.	Shoulder Stand	end (3-man)	412		X	X
22.	High Center Pyramid	center (4-man)	412		X	X
23.	Center Arch	center (4-man)	413		X	X
24.	Long Stand	center (4-man)	413		X	X

Pyramids

Once the dual stunts are learned it is possible to combine these positions such as two "base stands" (Illustration No. 15) facing each other and one individual pose such as "dog stand" (Illustration No. 6) on each end facing towards the center, forming a symmetrical six man pyramid. The remaining three and four man pyramids listed in the accompanying chart are provided to give additional illustrations. Beyond this point, it is the imagination of the teacher and her students that should be used to design and construct an unlimited variety of pyramids.

Since pyramid building involves teamwork and timing a standard procedure or set of whistle "cues" should be developed by each teacher. To illustrate, the first blow of the whistle would mean all stand at attention and face one direction. The second blow would signal all participants to move into the ready or primary position. A third blow may be necessary for two and three man high pyramids to shift into the final position of the upper participants. A similar procedure should be followed to dismount the pyramid back to the starting formation.

No. 1: STRIDE STAND (4-6)   No. 2: INCLINED STAND (4-6)

FIG. 13.92

Stand with legs partially flexed or fully extended. The arm position may be over head, sideward, or at side of body.

FIG. 13.93

Stand with left leg partially bent, right leg extending back, trunk leaning forward and arms extended forward and upward.

No. 3:   CROSS LEGGED STAND (4-6)

FIG. 13.94

Sit with legs crossed, back straight and arms extended sideward and upward. Optional position of the arms will depend upon the type of pyramid.

No. 4:   HEAD STAND (5-6)

FIG. 13.95

Form a triangle with forearms and head and raise body into an arched position. Leg positions may be changed to stride, scissors, or one leg upward and one leg parallel to mat.

No. 5:   ATTENTION STAND (4-6)

FIG. 13.96

Stand with legs together, body erect, and arms forming an arch above the head. Arm position may also be forward, sideward or extending backward.

No. 6:   DOG STAND (4-6)

FIG. 13.97

Assume a kneeling position with arms straight, head up, and a slight incline to trunk.

No. 7:　BRIDGE STAND (4-6)　　No. 8:　FORWARD INCLINE STAND (4-6)

FIG. 13.98

FIG. 13.99

Sit on mat with knees bent and place hands immediately below shoulders. Raise trunk upward until trunk and thighs form a straight line.

Balance on knees and lower legs and arch body backward with arms straight and together. Vary arm position to fit the desired theme of the pyramid.

No. 9:　BALANCE STAND (4-6)　　No. 10:　FORWARD BEND (4-6)

FIG. 13.100

FIG. 13.101

Stand on left foot, bend left leg slightly, extend right leg back and lower trunk forward. The arms may be pointed forward, sideward, or backward.

Stand with legs together and arch body and arms forward.

No. 11: Knee Stand (4-6)

FIG. 13.102

Balance on both knees with lower legs together and pointing back. The upper legs and trunk should form a straight line. Arms may be forward, overhead, or sideward.

No. 12: Knee Scale (4-6)

FIG. 13.103

Kneel on right leg and extend left leg forward. Hold trunk and head erect and extend arms upward and together.

No. 13: Kneeling Arch (4-6)

FIG. 13.104

Partners kneel on opposite legs with opposite legs forming a right angle and facing each other. Extend both arms forward and upward forming an arch.

No. 14: Handstand Arch (4-6)

FIG. 13.105

Support stands in a stride position while other partner executes a handstand. Support grasps partner's legs just below the ankles.

No. 15:   BASE STAND (4-6)   No. 16:   HEADSTAND ARCH (5-6)

FIG. 13.106

One partner assumes a kneeling position with trunk slightly inclined toward center of pyramid. Top partner assumes a stride position on base's back and extends arms in opposite directions.

FIG. 13.107

One partner assumes a kneeling position with trunk slightly inclined forward toward center of pyramid. Other partner performs a headstand and arches his body toward his partner's extended arms.

No. 17:   INCLINED HANDSTAND (5-6)   No. 18:   DOUBLE INCLINE (4-6)

FIG. 13.108

Base partner assumes an erect sitting position with hands grasping partner's legs. Handstander places his hands opposite base's ankles and, with partner's assistance, shifts to an inclined handstand position.

FIG. 13.109

Partners assume a front lying position with heads touching. Extend arms forming a straight line with legs and trunk.

No. 19: Double Headstand (4-6)

FIG. 13.110

FIG. 13.111

Center man stands erect with arms at side while end partners take a kneeling position on each side of center.

Center extends arms sideward while end partners execute a headstand. Center partner holds feet of end partners.

No. 20: Stride Stand (4-6)

FIG. 13.112

FIG. 13.113

Base partners take a kneeling position with backs slightly inclined forward. Top man stands behind ground men with one hand on the shoulders of each base.

Top man stands on lower backs of ground men and extends arms sideward.

No. 21: Shoulder Stand (5-6)

FIG. 13.114

FIG. 13.115

End partners kneel on opposite legs and face each other. Top man places hands on forward base and rear base grasps his ankles.

Top man leans forward and maintains extended arms and an erect body as rear base lifts his legs and places them on his shoulders.

No. 22: High Center Pyramid (5-6)

FIG. 13.116

FIG. 13.117

One partner sits on base's shoulders with arms extended sideward and downward. End partners take the first position of the headstand.

End partners execute a headstand while base grasps ankles of end partners. Top man raises arms upward to an extended sideward position or continues upward to an overhead position.

No. 23:   Center Arch (5-6)

FIG. 13.118

FIG. 13.119

End partners kneel on opposite legs, place one hand on knee and opposite hand at side. Center partners stand back to back with arms extended forward and upward.

Simultaneously end partners grasp waists of center partners as center partners arch backward and raise arms upward and backward until hands touch.

No. 24:   Long Stand (5-6)

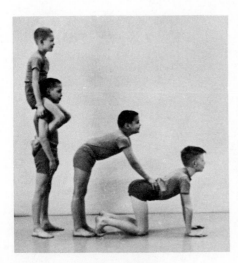

FIG. 13.120

FIG. 13.121

One partner sits on base's shoulder while partner of other pair rests his hand on base's lower back.

Rear couple assist in the upward extension of center man's legs until his feet are resting on the upper man's shoulders.

Selected References

FAIT, HOLLIS F. *Physical Education for the Elementary School Child.* Philadelphia: W. B. Saunders Co., 1964.

FISHER, HUGO; SHAWBOLD, DEAN R.; and WOHLFORD, PAUL R. *Individual and Dual Stunts.* Minneapolis: Burgess Publishing Co., 1960.

HORNE, VIRGINIA LEE, *Stunts and Tumbling for Girls.* New York: The Ronald Press Co., 1943.

KIRCHNER, G. *Physical Education for Elementary School Children.* Dubuque: Wm. C. Brown Company Publishers, 1966.

LOKEN, NEWTON, and WILLOUGHBY, ROBERT. *Complete Book of Gymnastics.* Englewood Cliffs, New Jersey: Prentice-Hall, Inc., 1959.

O'QUINN, G., *Gymnastics for Elementary School Children.* Dubuque: Wm. C. Brown Company Publishers, 1967.

RUFF, W. K., *Gymnastics Beginner to Competitor.* Dubuque: Wm. C. Brown Company Publishers, 1968.

SCHURR, E. L. *Movement Experiences for Children; Curriculum and Methods for Elementary School Physical Education.* New York: Appleton-Century-Crofts, 1967.

Stunts and Tumbling for Elementary Schools, Office of Superintendent of Schools, Sacramento County, Sacramento, California, 1959.

VANNIER, MARYHELEN, and FOSTER, MILDRED. *Teaching Physical Education in Elementary Schools,* Fourth Edition. Philadelphia: W. B. Saunders Co. 1968.

Large Apparatus Activities

C
H
A
P
T
E
R

14

T HE fundamental purpose of large apparatus in any self-testing program is to provide an opportunity for each child to test his ability on more challenging apparatus. This statement assumes that there is sufficient apparatus available and that children are ready to test their abilities. Each program will obviously vary with reference to the readiness of children to use large apparatus, hence must be planned to cope with a wide range of ability.

An important consideration has been given to the cost of this apparatus. Hence, wherever possible, the writer has provided diagrams and instructions for constructing "homemade" apparatus. A large percentage of this apparatus can be made by interested teachers or parents with a very small capital outlay.

BALANCE BEAM AND BENCHES*

The balance beam or bench has been used in self-testing programs for a number of years. It has, however, been used in a very limited way, which is usually flat on the ground with children performing stunts on or across the long axis (Figure 14.1). When the balance beam or bench (now fitted with a hook on one end as illustrated) is placed at different angles or used in combination with other apparatus, the variety of movements and challenges becomes infinitely greater. This applies to teaching standardized skills as well as when teaching shapes, position, or action through the Educational Gymnastic Approach.

Activities performed on the balance beam or bench require two types of balance skill. The first is static balance which is the ability to maintain a fixed stationary position. An example of this type of balance skill is the foot and knee balance. The second type, known as dynamic balance, is maintaining correct body position while moving. Examples of this type of balance

FIG. 14.1

*See Appendix A for a diagram of a homemade balance beam or bench.

FIG. 14.2

are walking forward and backward or one foot hop. Each of the latter skills are illustrated in the accompanying pages. The majority of primary level balance skills are basically dynamic in nature. As strength and skill increase, the more advanced static balance activities may be introduced.

The following skills are arranged in their approximate order of difficulty. To assist in learning these skills, have the children practice all stunts on the floor before attempting them on the balance beam or bench. Any fixed line on the floor will serve as an imaginary balance beam or bench.

No.	Name of Stunt	Page	Suggested Grade Level						
			K	1	2	3	4	5	6
1.	Forward Walk	418	X	X	X	X			
2.	Backward Walk	418	X	X	X	X			
3.	Run Forward	418	X	X	X	X	X		
4.	Sliding	418	X	X	X	X	X		
5.	Galloping	419	X	X	X	X	X		
6.	One Foot Hop	419		X	X	X	X	X	X
7.	Side Stepping	419		X	X	X	X	X	X
8.	Leg Swing	419		X	X	X	X	X	X
9.	Pick Up Eraser	419		X	X	X	X	X	X
10.	Step Under Wand	420			X	X	X	X	X
11.	Foot and Knee Balance	420			X	X	X	X	X
12.	Front Support	420				X	X	X	X
13.	Knee Balance	420				X	X	X	X
14.	Rear Support	420				X	X	X	X
15.	Side Balance	421				X	X	X	X
16.	Side Leg Extension	421					X	X	X
17.	Cat Walk	421					X	X	X
18.	Squat on One Leg	421					X	X	X
19.	Leg Raiser	422					X	X	X
20.	Jack Knife	422					X	X	X
21.	Front Balance	422					X	X	X
22.	Swing Turn	422					X	X	X
23.	Squat Mount	422					X	X	X
24.	Rear Dismount	423					X	X	X
25.	Front Dismount	423					X	X	X

No. 1:   FORWARD WALK (K-3)   No. 2:   BACKWARD WALK (K-3)

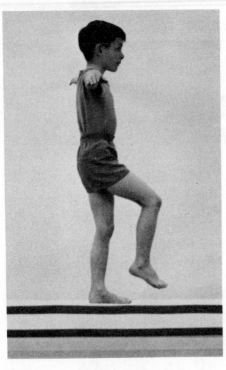

FIG. 14.3   FIG. 14.4

Stand on the balance beam with arms ex-   Stand on the balance beam with arms extended sideward, head up, back straight   tended sideward, head up, back straight
and body weight on the left foot. Raise   and body weight on the right foot. Shift
Right foot upward and forward. Place the   left leg backward placing toe then heel
toe then the heel of the left foot on the   on the balance beam.
balance beam.

No. 3:   RUN FORWARD (K-4)

Begin with head up, back straight, and arms extended sideward. Shift body weight to left foot and raise right foot off balance beam in preparation for the next running step. Swing right leg forward and push off from left toe. At this point both feet should be off the beam. Land on toe then heel of the right foot.

No. 4:   SLIDING (K-4)

Stand sideways on the beam with arms extended sideward and body weight over right foot. Slide left foot to the left. Shift body weight to left foot and slide right foot close to the left foot.

No. 5: GALLOPING (K-4)   No. 6: ONE FOOT HOP (1-6)

FIG. 14.5   **FIG. 14.6**

Stand on beam with head up, back
straight and arms extended sideward.
Shift body weight to the right foot and
raise left foot upward and forward. Simultaneously place left foot on beam and shift
right toe close to the heel of the left
foot. Note: In galloping, one foot always
remains the lead foot.

Stand on the right foot, raise left foot
backward and upward and extend arms
sideward. Take off from toe of right foot,
hop forward and land on toe then heel
of the same foot.

No. 7: SIDE STEPPING (1-6)

Stand on beam with feet shoulder width apart and arms extended sideways. Shift weight to left foot, cross right foot in front of left then place on
beam.

No. 8: LEG SWING (1-6)

Stand on the right foot with head up, trunk bent forward, arms sideways,
left leg backwards and off the beam. Swing left leg downward, forward and
upward, and raise trunk upward.

No. 9: PICK UP ERASER (1-6)

Place a small object such as an eraser in the middle of the balance beam.
Walk to the object, bend knees, extend right arm downward and left arm
backward and upward. Pick up object, stand up and walk to the end of the
balance beam.

No. 10: STEP UNDER WAND
(2-6)

No. 11: FOOT AND KNEE
BALANCE (2-6)

FIG. 14.7

One partner stands near center of beam and holds wand about three feet above and across the beam. The other partner walks to the center, bends down and passes under the wand with short steps.

FIG. 14.8

Begin with left foot well in front of the right, knees bent and arms extended sideward. Bend knees until the knee of the right leg rests on the beam. Hold position for a few seconds then extend and return to starting position.

No. 12: FRONT SUPPORT (3-6)

Begin in a standing position then kneel down placing hands and knees on beam. Gradually walk backward on toes until the legs and trunk form a straight line.

No. 13: KNEE BALANCE (3-6)

Begin in a standing position then kneel down placing hands and knees on the beam. Raise right leg upward. Keeping right leg extended upward, lower head and place forehead on the beam.

No. 14: REAR SUPPORT (3-6)

Sit on beam with legs straight, arms extended backward and hands grasping sides of beam. Lift seat off beam until trunk and legs form a straight line.

No. 15: SIDE BALANCE (3-6)

FIG. 14.9

Walk to the center of the balance beam
and stop with right foot in front of the
left. Turn right foot sideways, shift weight
to ball of foot, and lift left foot off beam.
Continue shifting sideward, arch back,
and raise left leg.

No. 16: SIDE LEG EXTENSION (4-6)

Walk to the center of the beam and stop with feet together. Shift weight
to left foot, raise extended right leg sideward and trunk slightly to the left.

No. 17: CAT WALK (4-6)

Begin in a partially crouched position with hands and feet on the beam.
Walk forward lifting right hand and foot at the same time. Shift weight to
right side and move left hand and foot.

No. 18: SQUAT ON ONE LEG (4-6)

FIG. 14.10

Stand on right foot, arms extended sideward and left foot off beam. Bend right
knee and raise extended left leg forward
and upward. Lower body until right knee
is fully flexed and heel of left foot is resting on the balance beam.

No. 19:   Leg Raiser (4-6)

Lie on back with hands grasping lower edge of balance beam. Keeping legs straight, raise upward until feet are above head and seat is off balance beam.

No. 20:   Jack Knife (4-6)

No. 21:   Front Balance (4-6)

FIG. 14.11

FIG. 14.12

Sit on the beam with legs extended, heels of both feet resting on the beam and hands holding top edge of beam. Bend knees and raise feet off beam. Continue upward movement of feet, lower trunk backward and straighten legs. After practice, raise legs upward without bending knees.

Begin with right foot in front of left and arms extended sideward. Lean forward, shift weight to front foot and extend left leg backward. Continue raising back leg and arch back.

No. 22:   Swing Turn (4-6)

Walk to the center of the beam, shift weight to right foot and swing left leg forward. Continue swinging left leg forward, lift up on ball of foot, and make a half turn thus facing opposite direction.

No. 23:   Squat Mount (4-6)

FIG. 14.13

Stand with feet about shoulder width apart, body erect and hands resting on balance beam. (Beam should be three to four feet high.) Keeping hand on beam, jump upward and slightly forward and place feet on beam.

No. 24: REAR DISMOUNT (4-6)

Sit on balance beam with legs straight and hands grasping edge of beam. Raise trunk upward until trunk and legs form a straight line. Shift legs upward then sideward, push from hands and land on both feet on the side of the balance beam.

No. 25: FRONT DISMOUNT (4-6)

FIG. 14.14

Begin in a crouched position with arms straight and hands grasping outside edge of balance beam. Extend legs backward until the head, trunk, and legs are in a straight line. Lift legs upward and sideward, push off with hands, and land on both feet on the side of the balance beam.

SPRINGBOARD, BEATBOARD, MINI-TRAMP, AND VAULTING BOX*

The springboard and vaulting box are two of the oldest and most popular apparatus used in the self-testing program. In this chapter the term "vaulting box" will include other similar apparatus such as the "vaulting bench" and "long horse" since they are used in much the same way. Teachers who do not have a vaulting box should refer to the diagrams of inexpensive equipment contained in Appendix A. The latter can be constructed with a minimum capital outlay and by the custodian or an interested parent.

The majority of vaulting stunts are normally performed from the springboard or mini-tramp on to a mat. Once children have developed sufficient skill in using the springboard and controlling their bodies in flight, the vaulting box can be added to provide greater challenge and versatility of movements. The approach, take-off, and landing are essentially the same for all vaulting activities, hence children should practice these movements until they become almost automatic. A well executed and consistent take-off allows a child to concentrate on height and execution of a specific vault.

---

*See Appendix A for a diagram of a homemade vaulting box.

Approach and Take-off

FIG. 14.15

FIG. 14.16

Begin several yards back from take-off point. Run toward springboard and take off on left foot.

Continue forward bring both feet together and land on balls of feet approximately six to twelve inches away from end of board. Note slight knee bend at moment of contact.

FIG. 14.17

Push off board in an upward and slightly forward direction. Note: Most children will lean too far forward, thus lose height and control on landing.

Stunts Performed with Springboard, Beatboard, and Vaulting Box

No. Name of Stunt	Page	Suggested Grade Level K	1	2	3	4	5	6
Springboard, Beatboard, or Trampet								
1. Clap hand overhead	425				X	X	X	X
2. Clap hands behind back	425				X	X	X	X
3. Jump and tuck	425				X	X	X	X
4. Jump and turn	425				X	X	X	X
5. Jump and arch	426				X	X	X	X
6. Jump and straddle legs	426					X	X	X
7. Jump and pike	426					X	X	X
Vaulting Box (adjust height of box to level of skill)								
8. Squat vault	426					X	X	X
9. Straddle vault	427					X	X	X
10. Flank vault	427						X	X
11. Head vault	427						X	X

No. 1: CLAP HANDS OVERHEAD (3-6)

FIG. 14.18

Clap hands overhead. Emphasize the knee bend on landing to absorb shock and to maintain control.

No. 2: CLAP HANDS BEHIND BACK (3-6)

FIG. 14.19

Clap hands behind back (or under legs).

No. 3: JUMP AND TUCK (3-6)

FIG. 14.20

No. 4: JUMP AND TURN (3-6)

FIG. 14.21

No. 5:   JUMP AND ARCH (3-6)   No. 6:   JUMP AND STRADDLE LEGS
                                                      (4-6)

FIG. 14.22

FIG. 14.23

No. 7:   JUMP AND PIKE (4-6)   No. 8:   SQUAT VAULT (4-6)

FIG. 14.24

FIG. 14.25

Squat Vault: From a two foot take-off
reach upward and slightly forward, touching hands on the top of the vaulting box.
Simultaneously tuck knees close to chest
and continue forward and upward. Land
with a gradual bending of the knees.

No. 9: STRADDLE VAULT
     (4-6)

FIG. 14.26

Straddle Vault: From a two
foot take-off simultaneously
reach forward with extended
arms and extend legs sideward.
It is extremely important in
this vault to gain maximum
height to insure foot clearance.
Continue forward, bring legs
together, and land with a gradual bending of the knees.

No. 10: FLANK VAULT
     (5-6)

FIG. 14.27

Flank Vault: From a two foot
take-off simultaneously reach
forward with both arms and
extend legs toward the right
side. As the legs move forward
and sideways release right hand
and continue forward movement, landing with a gradual
bending of the knees.

No. 11: HEAD VAULT (5-6)

FIG. 14.28

Head Vault: From a two foot
take-off place hands then head
on top of box as the body extends upward and over. When
the body is in a forward "overbalanced" position push off
from tips of fingers and land
with a gradual bending of the
knees. Note: Most children will
tend to push off before they
reach the "overbalanced" position. The latter will cause a
"dropping" on to the box rather
than a gradual arching and
landing as shown above.

HORIZONTAL BAR, HORIZONTAL LADDER, AND STALL BARS*

Many of the skills listed under each of the following apparatus may also be performed on other types of apparatus. The latter applies to many of the new Agility Apparatus as well as to existing outdoor play equipment such as the Climbing Cube and Swedish Gym.

Horizontal Bar (Chinning Bar)

Inasmuch as stunts performed on the horizontal bar require a great deal of arm and shoulder strength and endurance, teachers should keep this factor in mind by beginning with one or two repetitions of each skill. When a child is able to perform five or six repetitions of the first stunt, allow him to progress to the next one listed in the chart which follows.

TEACHING SUGGESTIONS:

Stunts performed on the horizontal bar are, by comparison to those on other indoor apparatus, extremely difficult for elementary school-age children. Hence, a great deal of encouragement must be shown by the teacher. In most cases, it is lack of sufficient arm and shoulder strength rather than an inherent absence of skill that will create an initial disinterest in this apparatus. The following suggestions will not make the teacher's task any easier but will assist in preventing unnecessary accidents.
1. Check equipment before allowing children to perform any stunt.
2. Make sure you are in the proper position to "spot" for safety.
3. Begin with simple stunts and progress to the more difficult.

HORIZONTAL BAR

No. Name of Stunt	Page	K	1	2	3	4	5	6
			Suggested Grade Level					
1. Hang Like a Monkey	429		X	X	X	X	X	
2. Roll Over Barrow	429		X	X	X	X	X	X
3. Pull-Ups	429		X	X	X	X	X	X
4. Skin the Cat	429			X	X	X	X	X
5. Scramble Over Fence	430			X	X	X	X	X
6. Pull Over	430			X	X	X	X	X
7. Bird's Nest	430			X	X	X	X	X
8. Rocking Chair Swing	430				X	X	X	X

*See Appendix A for a diagram of an inexpensive horizontal bar.

No. 1:   Hang like a Monkey (1-5)

FIG. 14.29

Jump up, grasp bar with palms forward and hands about twelve inches apart. Swing right leg up and over the bar. Rest heel of right leg on top of bar. Bring left leg up and over right leg and rest back of left leg on the top of the right foot.

No. 2:   Roll Over Barrow (1-6)

FIG. 14.30

Jump up and take a front support position with arms straight and hands on top of bar (front grip). Bend at the waist, drop head forward, roll over the bar and bring legs down and release grip.

No. 3:   Pull-ups (1-6)

FIG. 14.31

Jump up and grasp bar with a front (palms facing forward) or reverse (palms facing backward) grip. Pull upward with arms until the chin is even with the bar. Do not allow children to kick with legs as they swing forward and upward.

No. 4:   Skin the Cat (2-6)

FIG. 14.32

Jump up, grasp bar wth a front grip (palms facing forward) and swing legs forward and upward and flex knees. Move both feet under bar between hands then gradually lower legs to an extended position. Release and drop or return to original position.

No. 5:   SCRAMBLE OVER FENCE (2-6)   No. 6:   PULL OVER (2-6)

FIG. 14.34

FIG. 14.33

Begin in a front support position (arms
straight and palms downward) and swing
left leg upward and over the bar to a rest
position next to the left hand. Release left
hand, shift body weight to left thigh, and
grasp bar on outside of left leg. Repeat
action with right side, holding resting
position for a few seconds and jump to
ground.

Stand facing the bar, arms extended overhead and knees slightly bent. Jump up,
grasp bar with palms facing forward and
raise legs upward and close to the bar.
Continue upward by flexing the arms then
bend at waist and roll over bar to a front
support position.

No. 8:   ROCKING CHAIR SWING (3-6)

No. 7:   BIRD'S NEST (2-6)

FIG. 14.35

FIG. 14.36

Jump up and grasp bar with palms facing
forward. Draw both legs up and through
arms, drop legs over bar and rest back of
knees firmly against bar.
Simultaneously shift lower legs backward
and arch back ending with back of heels
resting against bar, back fully arched and
arms extended.

Jump up and grasp bar with palms facing
forward and hands about shoulder width
apart. Draw both legs up and through
bar, drop knees over and rest back of
knees firmly against bar. Keep knees bent,
release grip and swing back and forth.
Reach upward, grasp bar and return to
starting position.

Horizontal Ladder

Activities performed on the horizontal or overhead ladder are similar to chinning bar activities. Both require a great deal of strength and endurance of the arm and shoulder girdle muscles. Therefore, follow the progression of skills outlined in the chart following and do not require full travels, that is, all the way across, until sufficient strength and endurance are developed. As a starting point, require one-quarter distance across for all traveling movements. Each day increase the number of rungs until the full distance can be accomplished without undue stress.

TEACHING SUGGESTIONS:

The following safety hints require continuous reinforcement. Take a few minutes before the children begin to play or practice stunts on the apparatus and stress the following:
1. Check the apparatus before allowing pupils to perform stunts.
2. Stand close to performer while he is attempting to do a difficult stunt in order to assist the child and to prevent accidents.
3. Require each pupil to wait his turn at least five feet away from the apparatus.
4. Allow only two pupils on the ladder at the same time.
5. The second pupil should not begin his stunt until the first pupil is at least halfway across the ladder.
6. Require pupils to travel in the same direction.
7. All movements require that one hand be in contact with the apparatus. Emphasize this safety precaution.
8. Do not permit children to touch or hinder a child who is performing a stunt on the horizontal ladder.

HORIZONTAL LADDER

No. Name of Stunt	Page	\multicolumn{7}{c}{Suggested Grade Level}						
		K	1	2	3	4	5	6
1. Swing and Drop	432		X	X	X	X	X	
2. Chinning	432		X	X	X	X	X	X
3. Side Rail Traveling	432			X	X	X	X	X
4. Double Rail Traveling	433			X	X	X	X	X
5. Single Rung Traveling	433			X	X	X	X	X
6. Rung Travel Sideways	433			X	X	X	X	X

FIG. 14.37

No. 1: Swing and Drop (1-5)

Climb up the end of the ladder, rest feet on top step, and one hand grasping each side pole. Reach forward and grasp the second or third rung with one hand, followed by the other, grip with palms forward. Swing forward by raising legs upward and forward. Swing backward by "pulling" legs downward and backward. Stop swinging, look downward at landing place, then release both hands and land on ball of feet with knees bending to absorb the fall.

FIG. 14.38

No. 2: Chinning (1-6)

Climb up the end of the ladder, rest feet on top step, and one hand grasping each pole. Reach forward and grasp the second or third rung with one hand, followed by the other. Grip the palms forward or backward. (Allow children to choose their own grip.) Keeping trunk and legs straight, pull upward until the chin is above the bar. Return to starting position before releasing grip and landing on ground below.

FIG. 14.39

No. 3: Side Rail Traveling (2-6)

Climb up the end of the ladder, rest feet on top step, and one hand grasping each side pole. Turn body toward the right, release left hand and regrasp right pole with left hand. Place right hand on outside of rail, palms facing inside, and left hand forward and right hand and palms facing outside. Shift forward by releasing right hand, swinging body forward and regrasping rail with right hand. Repeat with left hand, etc., to the far end of the rail. Climb down far end of ladder.

No. 4: DOUBLE RAIL TRAVELING
(2-6)

Climb up one end of the ladder, rest feet on top step, and one hand grasping each side pole. Grasp both side rails with palms of both hands facing in and swing to a hanging position. Travel forward by sliding one hand forward, then the other. Do not release grip, slide hands the full length of the ladder.

FIG. 14.40

No. 5: SINGLE RUNG TRAVELING
(2-6)

Climb up one end of the ladder, rest feet on top step, and one hand grasping each side pole. Reach forward and grasp the second rung with one hand, palm facing forward, and the third rung with the other hand. Simultaneously shift body forward toward the forward hand and release back hand. Continue forward grasping the next rung. Repeat movement with opposite hand and continue traveling forward to opposite end. Dismount by dropping or by climbing down opposite end of ladder.

FIG. 14.41

No. 6: RUNG TRAVEL SIDEWAYS
(2-6)

Climb up one end of ladder, rest feet on top step and one hand grasping each side pole. Reach forward and grasp the second rung with the left hand with palms facing the head. Grasp the first rung with the right hand with palms facing the head. Swing to a hanging position. Shift the right hand to the same rung as the left hand, again, with palms facing the same direction. Shift the left hand to the next rung grasping it with palms facing head. Continue traveling with body swinging from side to side and the left hand always leading the right.

FIG. 14.42

Stall (Wall) Bars

Stall bars have been used in elementary school physical education programs for many years. They are still a very valuable apparatus for developing strength, flexibility, as well as many gymnastic skills. The following stunts will provide the classroom teacher with some basic ideas. Allow children to develop their own stunts and record (use stick figures) for future programs.

STALL BARS

No.	Name of Stunt	Page	K	1	2	3	4	5	6
			Suggested Grade Level						
1.	Pendulum Swing	434		X	X	X	X	X	X
2.	Side Lean	434		X	X	X	X	X	X
3.	Hand Walking	435	X	X	X	X	X	X	X
4.	Handstand	435				X	X	X	X
5.	Foot Hang	435				X	X	X	X

No. 1: PENDULUM SWING (1-6)   No. 2: SIDE LEAN (1-6)

FIG. 14.43

FIG. 14.44

Grasp the bar with the palm of hands pointing forward. Keep the legs together and swing body toward the left then right side.

Climb up a few rungs, hold bar with right hand and rest right foot on a lower bar. Swing body outward. Return to starting position.

No. 3: Hand Walking (K-6)

No.4: Handstand (3-6)

FIG. 14.45

FIG. 14.46

Climb up a few rungs. Keep one hand and foot on the bars and reach sideways with free hand and foot. Slide hands and legs together and repeat.

Begin with hands on the floor and approximately one foot away from the stall bars. Push off from the right foot and follow with the left. Lock toes under bar and hold position.

No. 5: Foot Hang (3-6)

FIG. 14.47

Climb up bars and place toes over bar while holding a grip with both hands. (Grip any bar/bars.) Gradually "hand walk" down until the reverse vertical position is reached. Remove one hand at a time to test the strength of the toe grip. (Spotters should be present for this stunt.)

CLIMBING ROPES

Various climbing and swinging skills may be performed with a hanging rope even with primary level children. With proper instruction, including a progression from the simple to more complex skills, six and seven-year-olds can develop sufficient skill and strength to climb to the top of a twenty foot rope. Older children, particularly girls who have started their preadolescent growth spurt, may not have developed sufficient strength to raise their bodies up the vertical rope. The latter requires additional patience and understanding on the part of the teacher.

The following skills should be introduced as listed in the accompanying chart. If two or more ropes are hung in a parallel row additional skills requiring vertical climb, transfer to other ropes, and upside-down descents can be performed by the advanced performer.

STUNTS PERFORMED WITH CLIMBING ROPE

No. Name of Stunt	Page	Suggested Grade Level K	1	2	3	4	5	6
1. Chinning–no leg support	436	X	X	X	X	X	X	X
2. Chin and Tuck	436	X	X	X	X	X	X	X
3. Double Rope Hang	437	X	X	X	X	X	X	X
4. Reverse Hang	437					X	X	X
5. Swinging	437	X	X	X	X	X	X	X
6. Climbing	437	X	X	X	X	X	X	X

No. 1: Chinning–No Leg Support (K-6)

FIG. 14.48

From a standing position reach up and grasp the rope with both hands. Without using the legs pull body upward until the chin is opposite the highest hand.

No. 2: Chin and Tuck (K-6)

FIG. 14.49

From a standing position reach up and grasp rope with both hands. Hold position and draw knees upward toward chest.

No. 3: Double   No. 4:   No. 5: Swinging
Rope Hang (K-6) Reverse Hang (4-6)   (K-6)

FIG. 14.50   **FIG. 14.51**   **FIG. 14.52**

Grasp two ropes and pull body upward and over. Continue over to a standing position or return to starting position.

Grasp the rope and pull body upward and over to a straddle position. Gradually extend legs upward until the body is in a vertical position.

Allow the children to grasp the rope at their own desired height. Gradually introduce additional body movements and positions while swinging. (Add twist, chin, legs straddle, etc.)

No. 6: Climbing (K-6)

FIG. 14.53   **FIG. 14.54**   **FIG. 14.55**

(Follow second boy from window)
Grasp rope with one hand slightly above the other.

Pull body upward and loop the rope over the top of right foot. Left foot is then placed on top of the rope thus "locking" foot position. Note: The other three climbers have failed to secure this position, hence will find climbing extremely difficult.

Hold the locked foot position and extend arms upward, one at a time. As soon as a firm grip is secured, pull body upward to new position. Note: Never allow children to slide down (this will cause severe burning). They must descend by a "hand-over-hand" action.

JUMPING BOXES, PLANKS, AND SAWHORSES*

The criteria for purchasing or making any apparatus should include such factors as usefulness, safety, and durability. This apparatus not only meets this criteria but, in addition, is within the budget of virtually any school. Another advantage, even for schools which can afford more expensive apparatus, is the possibility of obtaining this apparatus within days providing there is an interested "do-it-yourself" teacher or parent willing to help. The diagrams and instructions for this equipment included in Appendix A provide sufficient information for constructing a set of jumping boxes, a sawhorse, and a few suggestions for cutting and preparing planks.

It is quite obvious this apparatus may be used as a substitute for the balance beam, benches, or vaulting box. The sawhorse can be covered with a large tumbling mat and used quite effectively as a vaulting box. Hence, rather than attempting to provide additional stunts, the space will be used to show how this apparatus can be used as a substitute for other apparatus as well as an additional challenge not provided by the latter.

FIG. 14.56

FIG. 14.57

*See Appendix A for instructions and diagram to construct boxes and sawhorse.

AGILITY ROPES*

Agility Ropes are essentially two ropes that can be arranged in a variety of ways across the gymnasium. These ropes are specifically constructed to prevent sagging even with the combined weight of twenty or more children. This apparatus is also sufficiently light enough for primary children to carry and mount with a minimum of assistance by the classroom teacher.

FIG. 14.58

The following illustrations will indicate the versatility of these ropes for climbing, hanging, and other agility movements.

FIG. 14.59   **FIG. 14.60**

---

*Agility Ropes may be purchased from Educational Consultants Ltd., P.O. Box 404, North Vancouver, British Columbia, Canada.

FIG. 14.61

FIG. 14.62

SELECTED REFERENCES

LOKEN, NEWTON C., and WILLOUGHBY, ROBERT J. *Complete Book of Gymnastics.*
    Englewood Cliffs, New Jersey: Prentice-Hall, Inc., 1959.
O'QUINN, GARLAND, JR. *Gymnastics for Elementary School Children.* Dubuque:
    Wm. C. Brown Company Publishers, 1967.
Physical Education Activities for Grades K-6, Kansas State Department of Public
    Instruction, 1962.
Physical Education: Grade Two, San Diego City Schools, California, 1962.
Playground Equipment Safety, Unpublished Material, Department of Education,
    Baltimore, Maryland, 1961.
RUFF, W. K. *Gymnastics Beginner to Competitor.* Dubuque: Wm. C. Brown Com-
    pany Publishers, 1968.
Swedish Gym. The Delmer F. Harris Co., Concordia, Kansas, 1962.
VANNIER, M. and FOSTER, M. *Teaching Physical Education in Elementary Schools,*
    Fourth Edition. Philadelphia: W. B. Saunders Co., 1968.

Educational
Gymnastics

15

Definition and Purpose
Values of Educational Gymnastics
Teaching Patterns
Suggested Procedure to Introduce Educational
    Gymnastics
Individual and Small Apparatus Activities
Large Apparatus Activities
Visual Aids

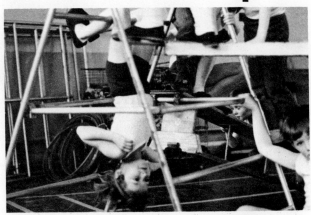

T HE purpose of this chapter is to provide a basic understanding of the nature, purpose, and methods used within Educational Gymnastics. Care has been taken to present this approach in a simplified and sequential manner. Each piece of equipment and apparatus used within the Contemporary Approach to teaching self-testing activities is also used within this new approach. Immediate comparisons can be made to previous chapters in order to understand the similarities and unique differences between the two approaches. An attempt has also been made to show how many of the ideas and skills from each approach may be integrated into any self-testing program.

DEFINITION AND PURPOSE

In contemporary literature, Educational Gymnastics* is defined as an approach or system of teaching children to become aware of their physical abilities and to use them effectively in the daily activities involving play, work, and creative expression.[1] This definition, however, could be used to interpret the general meaning of contemporary physical education as defined in Chapter 1. As such, it is inadequate in clarifying the essential meaning of Educational Gymnastics. Upon analysis of the latter approach, there is a unique organization of all skills (shape, position, and action). This method of organizing and progression of all movement skills is fundamentally different from our contemporary way of classifying skills within the Games,

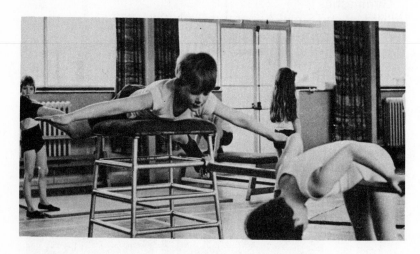

FIG. 15.1

---

*Other terms are "Movement Education," "Movement Exploration," "Basic Movement," and "Indirect Method."

1. M. North, *A Simple Guide to Movement Teaching.* (Exeter: Wheaton & Co., 1964), Chapter 1.

Dance, and Self-Testing areas. Secondly, this new approach predominately utilizes methods and techniques which stimulate and encourage exploratory and creative movements on the part of each child. Although this approach can be applied to virtually every area of the physical education program, it is normally restricted to the medium of self-testing or gymnastic type activities.

On the basis of the above criteria, Educational Gymnastics may be defined as an individualized and exploratory approach to teaching children to use their creative and physical abilities through the medium of self-testing activities.

FIG. 15.2

Since Educational Gymnastics encourages children to use their natural tendencies and to progress according to their own level of interest and creative ability, its purposes become self-evident. Providing an informal teaching atmosphere is created, coupled with adequate facilities and equipment, the following general purposes can be realized through Educational Gymnastics.[1]

1. To assist children to become physically fit and skillful in a variety of situations. This infers we should help children increase their coordination and flexibility of mind as well as body.

2. To teach children to understand movement so they can build movement sequences from an ever-increasing understanding of what, where, and how the body can move.

---

1. G. Kirchner, J. Cunningham, and E. Warrell, *Introduction to Movement Education*, Dubuque: Wm. C. Brown Company Publishers, 1970, Chapter 1.

3. To encourage self-discipline and self-reliance so children can work on their own ideas individually, in pairs, or in groups.
4. To provide maximum enjoyment and opportunities for creative expression.

VALUES OF EDUCATIONAL GYMNASTICS

When the underlying principles and methods of Educational Gymnastics are effectively applied through the medium of self-testing activities, the following values are inherent in such an approach.

Values to the Student

Through the Educational Gymnastic approach a child's physical attributes, such as his strength, endurance, and coordination are developed in a natural and functional manner. His level of motor skill will increase according to his own level of ability, readiness, and personal motivation. It is axiomatic that this approach permits the outstanding performer to progress as rapidly as he is capable of developing. Similarly, the less able are not measured against an arbitrary standard, hence can achieve success and personal satisfaction according to realistic tasks and challenges.

FIG. 15.3   FIG. 15.4

A child must also learn through this approach to work as a member of a group as well as to work independently within the structure of a group setting. Through this medium he must learn to be tolerant, self-confident, and self-reliant. Finally, since a child is taught to progress according to his own level of ability, the potential for accidents and injury is greatly reduced. When children are not forced to attempt skills that they are incapable of performing, accidents are greatly reduced. The inherent value to each child is that he learns to be responsible for his own safety as well as being cognizant of the safety of others. The latter value has immeasurable benefits in later life.

FIG. 15.5   **FIG. 15.6**   **FIG. 15.7**

Value to the Teacher

From the teacher's point of view, Educational Gymnastics has numerous advantages. Since this approach allows children to learn in an informal and creative atmosphere, the teacher has an opportunity to observe the child in a noncompetitive and self-expressive situation. Observation of children in this type of setting provides important insights to understanding the personality of each child.

Since the teacher uses a normal conversational speaking voice instead of formal commands there is no longer a need to use a whistle or use methods of instruction which are different than those applied in the classroom. Also, the methods and techniques used in this approach emphasize a creative movement interpretation on the part of each child. Demonstrations by the teachers are, therefore, clearly "out-of-place," and it is no longer necessary for a classroom teacher to change into a gymnasium costume when teaching educational gymnastics. It should be emphasized at this point that Educational Gymnastics is not a "replacement" of all parts of the physical education program. There is and will continue to be a need for classroom teachers to be proficient in the skills of other areas of the program such as individual and team sports. When teaching the latter activities, it is desirable to change into a suitable costume and, if necessary, demonstrate skills of the various activities.

Perhaps the most significant change inherent in Educational Gymnastics is the change in the role of the teacher. With the shift in the responsibility for choosing appropriate equipment and movement ideas to the child, the teacher, in turn, assumes the role of a "guider" rather than a "director" of the learning experience. The importance of the teacher, however, is in no

FIG. 15.8   FIG. 15.9

way reduced; it is enhanced and enriched by the individualized and creative
nature of this approach. As teachers will come to realize, such an approach
provides more time for individual observation and time to assist each child
to develop his movement skills and ideas.

TEACHING PATTERNS

One of the most difficult tasks in the field of education is to attempt to
explain a new approach to teaching. Teachers, like all other professions, judge
new ideas, methods, and approaches on the basis of their own prior experience. In addition, most teachers normally have an opportunity to observe
other teachers using new methods and techniques or view sample lessons on
film or video tape. This may not be the case with Educational Gymnastics.
Recognizing the limitations, the following material has been organized and
extensively illustrated to provide each teacher with a basic guideline to follow
when attempting to introduce this new and exciting way of teaching children
self-testing activities.

An Overview

Within the accompanying chart, there are three essential aspects of this
approach to teaching. In Chapter 11, the main elements of movement were
described and compared to the contemporary approach used to teach self-
testing activities. In this chapter, each element of Shape, Body Position, and
Body Action will be progressively introduced through INDIVIDUAL and
SMALL APPARATUS ACTIVITIES. Illustrations will be provided to show
how these elements may be taught using individual activities, partner's hoops,

beanbags, and other small apparatus. A similar procedure will be followed with the large apparatus. Teachers need only to refer to the small or large apparatus which they have available at their school.

STRUCTURE OF EDUCATIONAL GYMNASTICS		
ELEMENTS OF MOVEMENT TO BE TAUGHT	METHODS OF TEACHING TO BE USED	LESSON CONTENT
Shape: The form or arrangement of the whole body or any of its parts. The body is capable of making such shapes as curled, stretched, wide, narrow, and twisted. *Position:* The position or balance of the body in relation to the floor, apparatus, or while in flight. The body may balance on one or more of its parts on the floor, apparatus, or demonstrate balance while in flight. *Action:* The action of the body is how and where it is moving. The body may move with a quick, slow, light, or gentle movement in various directions.	*Direct:* Choice of activity and how it is to be performed determined by the teacher. *Limitation:* Choice of activity and how it is to be performed limited in some way by the teacher. *Indirect:* Choice of activity and how it is to be performed determined by the student.	*Part One:* Introductory Activities. General activities emphasizing vigorous and total body movements. *Part Two:* Floor Activities Individual Activities Partner Activities Beanbags, braids, and Indian clubs. Blocks, Chairs, and Wands Individual ropes *Part Three:* Large Apparatus Activities Balance beam or bench Springboard and Vaulting Box Horizontal Stall Bars and Ladder Climbing Ropes Jumping Boxes, Sawhorse, and Planks Agility Ropes

The general format and procedure for introducing Educational Gymnastics described in this chapter may be followed within any grade in the elementary school. It is recognized, however, that older children, particularly those beyond the second grade, have already learned numerous self-testing skills. The latter can be incorporated in this new approach. In addition, the interest span and general maturity of these children must also be taken into consideration when choosing the type of movement tasks as well as the arrangement of apparatus. These variations will become quite clear through the various illustrations provided in this chapter.

As previously explained, the structure of an Educational Gymnastic lesson normally includes three closely related parts. Part One is the Introductory or Warm-up period and lasts approximately three to five minutes. The various types of activities used in this part of the lesson have been described in Chapter 12. The latter may be used in Educational Gymnastics for the same purpose. However, in the initial stages of this approach this Introductory Period is EXTREMELY VALUABLE in establishing the proper atmosphere for learning. Therefore, several lessons will be described in detail to show how this important part of the lesson can be used to develop the proper classroom atmosphere, normal routine procedure, as well as several important movement skills.

Part Two is normally defined as "Floor Work" and is used to introduce one or more elements of movement using individual activities or a variety of small apparatus. This part of the lesson is designed to give every child an opportunity to develop skill and movement understanding on the floor or with small apparatus. Part Three, known as Large Apparatus Activities, is used to further expand a child's skill and movement ideas by providing large and more challenging equipment to test out and expand the movement ideas learned in the previous part of the lesson.

Obviously, when first introducing Educational Gymnastics, children do not have sufficient skill or understanding of movement to apply to large apparatus. The allocation of time to each part of a lesson during the first exploratory year will look something like the accompanying chart. Regardless of the available time for each lesson during the first part of the year, more time must be devoted to Individual and Small Apparatus activities until sufficient skill and movement understanding is acquired. Gradually, more time

LESSON PLAN FOR EDUCATIONAL GYMNASTICS

← ———————————— Length of physical education period ———————————— →

First Part of year ↓ Latter Part of year	PART ONE: INTRODUCTORY ACTIVITIES	PART TWO: INDIVIDUAL AND SMALL APPARATUS ACTIVITIES	PART THREE: LARGE APPARATUS ACTIVITIES
	Devote approximately three to five minutes to this activity throughout the school year.	Devote more time to this part during first half of year and gradually decrease as movement ideas are developed.	Devote less time to this section during early part of year and gradually increase time as skill and movement ideas develop through use of individual and small apparatus activities.

can be devoted to Large Apparatus activities. There is, of course, no rigid line of demarcation between these two closely related parts of the lesson, hence the use of small and large apparatus during any part of the lesson is, at times, useful and appropriate.

SUGGESTED PROCEDURE TO INTRODUCE EDUCATIONAL GYMNASTICS

Teaching self-testing activities through the Educational Gymnastic approach is as much dependent upon the creation of an atmosphere in which a child or group of children can work safely and independently as it is with the teacher's knowledge of how to introduce skills and movement ideas in a systematic and progressive way. To emphasize the importance of this statement, one must remember that the Contemporary Approach to teaching self-testing activities stressed the importance of the direct method which required the teacher to "plan" what and how each skill was to be performed. In the latter method of teaching, emphasis is given to following orders rather than encouraging children to "think" for themselves or produce creative movements. Hence, the shift from a predominately formal "teacher-directed" to a learning atmosphere, which is characterized by informality and with the main responsibility for learning shifted to the learner, is a tremendous challenge for both teacher and class. The rewards inherent in this transition are worth the patience and effort required of the teacher and, of course, the children under her charge.

It is vitally important, therefore, that the initial lessons, particularly for children beyond the second grade, be more concerned with establishing the "atmosphere for learning" than with the teaching of the introductory movement skills and ideas. The latter will come much more rapidly and effectively only when children learn to work independently at their own rate and according to their own ability. Hence, to assist teachers in this important "initial step," the first few lessons will be described in detail. The progressive introduction of movement skills begins under INDIVIDUAL ACTIVITIES (see page 461). This latter section has also been described in detail to show how movement ideas can be progressively added to each child's movement vocabulary. Once a teacher acquires the basic movement vocabulary, she will, in turn, develop variations in this suggested procedure. The latter is extremely important since successful teaching is dependent upon the freedom each teacher has to draw upon her own unique talents and creative ideas*

---

* There are a number of educational gymnastic films now available for purchase or rental. A brief description of several useful films will be provided in the Selected Reference.

During the first few lessons it is imperative that the following procedures, skills, and understanding be learned by all children. These hold the key to the success and enjoyment of using the Educational Gymnastic Approach.

1. Teach children to change, enter the gymnasium, and begin independent practice while waiting for the lesson to begin. The changing procedure described below was developed through this approach.
2. Teach children to work independently with concern for the safety of self and every other member of the class.
3. Teach children to work in an atmosphere where your normal speaking voice can be heard. Raising one's normal speaking voice or relying upon a whistle is not compatible with this method of teaching.
4. Teach children the basic meaning and purpose of educational gymnastics. Each child must learn that he will be responsible for developing his own movement ideas and that he must only attempt skills that are within reach of his own level of ability.
5. Teach children routine procedures relating to "Section places" (squads), carrying and arranging apparatus.

Introductory Lessons

Emphasis:
1. Establish changing and "free practice" procedures.
2. Teach meaning and use of "squad" or "section places."
3. Teach children to move, stop, and listen to your "verbal" commands.
4. Begin to teach movement skills in a systematic and progressive way (see "Individual Movements," page 461).

Since many of the methods and procedures outlined above may be new to both the teacher and class a gradual introduction is suggested. Primary children, particularly those in Kindergarten and Grade One, will require a lot of assistance and "patience" during these initial lessons. Once they learn the basic procedure relating to changing, free practice, and section places, they will adapt very well to the informal atmosphere of Educational Gymnastics. Prior experience of older children is both a help and a hindrance, hence they will need more time to adjust to the informal atmosphere and to working on their own. A few suggestions will be made for each level.

Suggestions for Primary Teachers

If the classroom is near the gymnasium, primary teachers can either have the children change in the classroom or, if she prefers, in the gymnasium. Primary children need wear only shorts and a T-shirt or blouse. No shoes are necessary, in fact, they are a hindrance to Educational Gymnastics. With respect to shy children, do not force them to change in front of others; they will gradually lose their inhibitions as they observe other children "casually" change. Also encourage children to help each other change, particularly with those "difficult back buttons."

FIG. 15.10

FIRST LESSON: ESTABLISH SECTION PLACES

During the first lesson divide the class into four groups. For Primary level use the term "section places." Once in their section places emphasize they must remember their places and return quietly whenever you ask them to "return to your section places." At this point, try the following: (In question form)

FIG. 15.11

"Now, stand up and see if you can walk around the gymnasium, without touching anyone, and when I say 'section places,' walk back and sit down." Repeat and stress walking in different directions.
Repeat with a run.
Repeat with a hop, skip, or gallop.

For remainder of lesson (if any time remains), allow children to practice animal walks or some other self-testing skills.

SECOND LESSON: INTRODUCE FREE PRACTICE
AND WORKING IN THEIR OWN SPACE

Indicate to the class that you have placed beanbags, hoops, and balls (or whatever equipment you select) on the floor. As soon as they have changed they may choose one piece of equipment and begin to practice while the rest of the children are changing. If desired, impose restrictions such as only practice jumping over beanbags or hoops.

From this point it is possible to begin to follow the general format of a lesson.

FIG. 15.12

Part One: Introductory Activity

Repeat "Section Places"

Next, introduce "FINDING YOUR OWN SPACE IN THE GYMNA-SIUM." Children must learn to find a place on the gymnasium floor where they can practice a skill or movement without interfering with the movements of other children. Young children will also tend to "bunch up" near the teacher. Keeping these points in mind, direct the class to run and find their "own place" on the floor. Check the spacing and stress the use of "all the gymnasium." Repeat running, hopping, or galloping, then find a new "space" when you say "stop and find a new space." This spacing will require constant attention throughout the first year.

For remainder of lesson choose any self-testing activity for practice. This time, however, emphasize practicing "in your own space."

THIRD LESSON: RUN, JUMP, AND LAND

Part One: Introductory Activities

Repeat running in different directions.

Introduce run and stop in different positions. For example:

1. Run and stop with hands and feet on the floor.
2. Run and stop with "just one foot on the floor."
3. Run and stop in any position you like.

FIG. 15.13

Introduce run, jump into the air and land "softly and safely" on two feet. Emphasize knees must be bent when they land. Repeat and reemphasize running in different directions.

If the class is progressing faster than you anticipated, add "making a shape or a turn in the air before landing."

For remainder of lesson, choose any self-testing activity or continue to explore other possibilities with the above. Do not be in a hurry during these first few lessons.

LESSONS FOUR TO . . . . WHATEVER NUMBER IS NECESSARY

During the first few lessons the Introductory Activities will take more time until the general idea and procedure is established. As children learn to move in this "informal" atmosphere, many additional movements can be included and with almost continuous activity on the part of EVERY CHILD.

From Lesson Four on progression will depend upon the general level of ability and interest of each class. Eventually, however, each child must be able to run, jump, land, and roll on the floor (with or without a mat) from various heights and directions without hurting himself or colliding with others in the class. This ability to move on or off apparatus within the limits of one's physical ability coupled with an awareness of the presence and safety of others in the class is A FUNDAMENTAL PREREQUISITE to all future lessons. Children must be able to perform the (1) sideways log roll; (2) side curled roll; (3) backward diagonal roll; (4) forward roll; and (5) backward roll with a high level of proficiency.

Therefore the number of lessons required to teach these skills will be dependent upon previous background and ability of the children. Each skill is described in the accompanying paragraphs. The direct method is also strongly suggested when teaching these skills to insure they are learned correctly by every child.

1. The sideways log roll should be taught with children rolling, and before they collide, jumping up, running to a new place before rolling again.

FIG. 15.14

FIG. 15.15

FIG. 15.16

2. The sideways safety or curled roll should be performed with elbows, knees, and nose "hidden" or tucked in. When in this position, no injury will result. Start this on the floor or mat, then introduce a walk, land, and roll.

FIG. 15.17   **FIG. 15.18**

3. The backward diagonal roll is one of the most important safety rolls. It is used as a means of rolling backward with a gradual dissipation of speed, thus preventing injury as well as providing an effective and graceful means of shifting from one movement to another. The use of this movement in sports and other play activities cannot be overemphasized. It is one of the most useful safety skills to be taught in the self-testing program.

FIG. 15.19   **FIG. 15.20**

4. One of the most important safety skills is the forward roll. Most children have already learned this skill before they come to school and can usually demonstrate many variations involving different leg and arm positions. The essential part of this skill is to tuck the chin in and roll from the top of the shoulders (head should not touch the floor or mat).

FIG. 15.21   FIG. 15.22   FIG. 15.23

5. In all self-testing activities, no child should be forced to attempt a skill that he is potentially incapable of performing. This is particularly true with the backward roll. As the child rolls backward the weight of the body must be taken on the arms, not on the head and neck. Children who do not possess sufficient arm strength or who are excessively overweight cannot and should not attempt this skill. They can, however, successfully perform the backward diagonal roll.

FIG. 15.24   FIG. 15.25   FIG. 15.26

Once children have learned to run at various speeds and in different directions as well as to perform the basic safety rolls, the scope of Introductory Activities becomes unlimited. As children learn various shapes, positions, and actions during the second part of the lesson (Individual and Small Apparatus Activities), they may be incorporated into numerous movement sequences in future lessons. To illustrate, in the second part of the lesson, children will be taught to balance on different parts of their bodies. They will apply this to a beanbag in the form of "making a balance position with one part of the body on the beanbag." Hence in a future lesson the Introductory Activity may see beanbags scattered over the floor and the teacher posing the following task. "Run in various directions and when I say 'stop,' find a beanbag and make a balance shape on or over it." The next question could be "Do a sideways safety roll and continue running emphasizing 'quick then slow' speed. The essential characteristic of the Introductory Activity Period should be *continuous* and vigorous activities with a relationship to the skills and movement ideas of the second part of the lesson.

If the above procedures and skills have been learned it is time to begin to teach movement skills and understandings during the second part of the lesson. From this point, for each future lesson, repeat one or more of the skills learned during the previous Introductory periods, then begin with the second part of the lesson and introduce the first shape as described on page 462. As the reader will note, numerous suggestions are provided within this "Individual Activities" section to show how curled and stretched shapes may be introduced into Part Two of the lesson. Do not include Part Three of the lesson until the children have developed sufficient understanding and skill, using individual, partner, and other small apparatus. However, after ten or more lessons, and providing large apparatus is available, allow children, during the third part of the lesson to simply explore the use of this equipment. Later, the movement ideas and skills learned during the second part of the lesson can be applied to larger apparatus.

Suggestions for Intermediate Teachers

The four points of emphasis that must be stressed during the first few lessons are equally applicable to intermediate level children. However, the methods and techniques used to create this informal teaching atmosphere with upper elementary school-age children should take into consideration the methods of teaching used by previous teachers, what skills they have learned in previous grades, and their receptiveness to new ideas.

Generally speaking, most elementary school children have been taught by a formal "teacher-direct approach." They have learned to perform warm-up exercises according to a count or cadence and have also been taught a wide variety of stunts, tumbling, and other gymnastic skills. Also it has normally been the practice to require every child to change, and when all are in the gymnasium, the lesson begins.

It is, therefore, suggested that the forepart of the first few lessons be used to develop this new procedure of changing, entering the gymnasium, and participating in a form of free practice while waiting for the remainder of the class to change. Carry on with your regular lesson plans but emphasize to the class you are no longer going to use a whistle and they must work quietly in order to hear your instructions. Indicate that they may participate without wearing shoes and encourage them to try their stunts without shoes, asking for their reactions.

The first part of a Contemporary Self-Testing lesson normally begins from squad lines and includes all running around the gymnasium (usually in a counterclockwise direction around the outside of the gymnasium floor). After a few minutes they are normally given a set of conditioning exercises. To assist these older children to move to a more independent approach required in the Introductory Activity period of an Educational Gymnastic lesson, introduce the following ideas:

1. Instead of beginning with a run around the outside of the gymnasium, (see Figure 15.27), tell them to run in different directions (see Figure 15.28), and WITHOUT TOUCHING any other student. Stress they must move quietly in order to hear your next command. Once they can move in various directions, add one or more of the following:

FIG. 15.27

FIG. 15.28

2. Stop and find a spot (or called "space") on the floor without interfering with any other student.
3. Run and when you say 'stop,' they must stop on one foot, with a foot and a hand on the floor, or whatever you suggest.
4. Run, jump, and land with a full knees' bend.
5. Run, jump, land, and immediately perform a sideways roll, forward roll, backward diagonal roll, or backward roll. If children cannot perform any of these stunts, use the next few lessons to teach these skills.

FIG. 15.29   **FIG. 15.30**   **FIG. 15.31**

As with the primary level children the above informal atmosphere plus the few important safety skills of landing and rolling are vitally important to the success of all future lessons. Hence, before intermediate level school children are permitted to move into the second part of a regular Educational Gymnastic lesson, take the time to insure these skills are correctly learned.

As soon as each teacher feels she is ready to teach the first shapes described under Individual Activities, turn to page 462. Use the next five or six lessons, (or more if desired) and teach only Part One: Introductory Activities, and Part Two: Individual and Small Apparatus Activities. The first few lessons should look like the following:

First Lesson

Part One: Introductory Activities

1. Run in different directions.
2. Run in different directions with varying speed (first fast, then slow, as determined by each child).
3. Run, jump, and land on the floor.
4. Run, jump, make a shape in the air, and land.
5. Repeat No. 4, land, and perform a sideways roll.

FIG. 15.32

Part Two: Individual and Small Apparatus Activities

1. Have children find a "space" on the floor (make sure all space is effectively used).
2. Introduce curled and stretched shapes. (See page 462).

Since older children can perform numerous stunts and tumbling skills, ask them to perform one of these familiar stunts, then see if they can make a curled or stretch shape from the first movement. It is helpful, during these early lessons, to allow children to move from what is familiar to this new form of movement.

Second Lesson

Part One: Introductory Activities

Repeat Lesson One.
Add run, jump, and make a curled shape in flight. Same with stretch shape.

Part Two: Individual and Small Apparatus Activities

Repeat Lesson One.
Add making different curled and stretched shapes from standing, sitting, or other positions.

FIG. 15.33

Note: If you "run out of ideas," allow children to practice other contemporary skills such as headstands, cartwheels, or large apparatus skills such as vaulting. This is not considered reverting to the Contemporary Approach. When given this opportunity stress they must work independently or in groups. Also, if you note the class as a whole cannot work independently establish fixed squads (one for vaulting, one for large mat work, and one for horizontal bar) and set skills to be practiced on each piece of equipment.

THIRD LESSON

Part One: Introductory Activities

Repeat previous lesson or refer to Chapter 12 for new ideas.

Part Two: Individual or Small Apparatus Activities

Repeat part of previous lesson.

Add BODY POSITION (see page 466).

At this stage children should have developed the ability to work independently and possess the beginning ideas or curl and stretch shapes plus body position. From this point on, progress is as much dependent upon the ability of the class as it is with the creative ability of each teacher. There will always be lessons where nothing seems to go right as when the class may need more time to develop the capacity to work independently. If a teacher can stay with this "teething" stage the results will be enormously gratifying to both teacher and each member of her class. It is a most exciting approach to teaching self-testing activities and, as teachers will come to recognize, an approach which has unlimited movement possibilities.

INDIVIDUAL AND SMALL APPARATUS ACTIVITIES

The activities included in this section should primarily be used during PART TWO of an EDUCATIONAL GYMNASTIC LESSON. Each movement idea and skill is first introduced within INDIVIDUAL ACTIVITIES then may be repeated with each additional small apparatus. As soon as a teacher develops a basic approach within the INDIVIDUAL ACTIVITIES, she should refer to other suggested small apparatus and incorporate these activities in the lesson. The latter will provide numerous challenging ideas that are not available with individual movements.

Individual Activities

Individual activities include all shapes, positions, and actions a child can perform without any apparatus. The mat may be used, however, in this instance as it is not classified as a piece of equipment.

The introduction of Individual Activities or Movements begins with shape and adds action or position as skill and understanding dictate. Initially, this format and method may appear to be too unstructured and complicated. After a few lessons, however, most teachers are able to construct lessons and themes with relative ease. Children, too, find this method enjoyable and challenging and accordingly adapt to the new format and methods in a very short period of time.

STRETCH AND CURLED SHAPES

The human body is capable of making an infinite variety of curled and stretch shapes involving the whole or any part of the body. Assisting children to find or discover what stretch and curl shapes their bodies are capable of doing should start from the familiar and simple, then gradually shift to the more complex. Once a child has developed a "movement vocabulary" which is simply knowing what shapes his body is capable of making, greater freedom should be permitted. Variety of shapes, however, without concern for form hinders both physical and intellectual development. Progression of each shape or combinations of shapes involves thought, repetition, and constant attention on the part of the teacher and child.

FIG. 15.34   FIG. 15.35   FIG. 15.36

One of the first problems facing a teacher who has not used the format and methods of Educational Gymnastics is where and how to begin. There are several approaches that can be used; however, since any child beyond the first grade will have had some prior experience in "stunts and tumbling," this factor should be taken into consideration. Although intermediate level children may follow the suggested outline below, care should be taken to present sufficiently challenging tasks for this age group. The accompanying suggested format will provide sufficient information to assist each teacher in coping with the interests and abilities of each respective age level. Teachers should modify and adjust their programs to meet the specific abilities of their class.

Teaching Progression for Curl and Stretch Shapes
from
Single or Combined Curled and Stretch Shapes
to
Combining Shape, Body Position, and Body Action

The above suggested teaching progression begins with single shapes, then adds BODY POSITION and Body Action. The LIMITATION METHOD is primarily used and requires the teacher to ask a question(s) which will challenge each child to move in a particular way. Although each teacher will develop her own style of asking questions, the following phrases and words have proven to be successful.

Can you *make* a ("curled") shape?	Could you change . . . . . ?
Can you *discover* a new . . . . . ?	Try to add on to . . . . . ?
Can you *add* to this by . . . ?	Try to vary . . . . . ?
Can you *find* another way of . . . ?	How many different . . . . . ?
Can you *add* a different way to . . . . ?	Are you able to . . . . . ?
Can you *vary* your shape to . . . . . ?	See if you can . . . . . ?
Can you *improve* on the . . . . . ?	Attempt to do . . . . . ?
Could you move from . . . . . . ?	Is it possible to . . . . . ?
Could you shift . . . . . . ?	

In the above type of questioning avoid the expression "I" want you to do . . . . , since it gives the impression that *you* and not the child want something very particular. The key words should be to stimulate a creative interpretation of a task or challenge posed by your question.

Once you have posed a question it is usually necessary to give some command to start. Probably the most common and informal beginning is "off" or "away you go." Children will react extremely well to this type of comment. Other expressions could be—"and begin" or "start."

DEVELOPING SINGLE OR COMBINED CURLED OR STRETCH SHAPES

The initial phase of teaching curl and stretch shapes is to assist each child to understand the meaning of the words as well as to learn what variety of stretch and curl shapes he is capable of making. Hence, the first shapes should involve the whole body, then progress to individual parts.

Questions should encourage making shapes from the following starting positions:

. . . . for curled shapes
1. from a sitting position
2. from a standing position
3. while in flight
4. from a front, back, or side lying position
5. from a curled position to another curled position

. . . . . . for stretch shapes
1. from a standing position
2. while in flight
3. from a sitting position
4. from a front, back, or side lying position
5. from a stretched position to another stretched position

Progression should be from a stationary position into a curled or stretch shape. A teacher may begin with questions directed at curled shapes (from 1-5) then try the same with stretch shapes (1-5) or alternately from one to the other. The following example will illustrate the shapes children produced by attempting to answer the following questions.

SITUATION: If mats (large or small) are available, ask the children to place them in a scattered fashion on the floor. Next, ask children to "find a space in the gymnasium and sit down." When there are only a few mats available, stress that "some boys and girls NEED NOT SIT on a mat."

QUESTION: "Can you curl up and make a very small ball-like shape?"

FIG. 15.37

Allow sufficient time for experimentation. Also, during this time the teacher should look for unusual curled shapes and provide encouragement and praise wherever necessary. Choose one or two good shapes (not always the same children) and let them show the rest of the class. Move right into another question.

QUESTION: "Can you make a stretch shape from a standing position?" Time for practice and observation.

FIG. 15.38   FIG. 15.39

You will observe some children will stretch with legs together, others will stretch upward, and still others will simply stretch one hand or arm in their movement answer to your question. The essential point in these initial attempts is that the children are beginning to "think" out their own answers. QUESTION: (To combine both shapes): See if you can repeat your stretch shape or find a new one then change into a curled shape.

FIG. 15.40   FIG. 15.41   FIG. 15.42

It is virtually impossible to suggest how many questions to pose or how long to allow for practice. Also, during the early phase of introducing this approach the children usually lack sufficient background and movement vocabulary to continue with stretch and curl as a single theme. Other shapes such as "wide and narrow" and "twisting" (see later sections) may be used during these initial lessons to provide challenging variations of these basic movement tasks. As the class increases their understanding and ability to perform numerous stretch and curl shapes, single lessons can be devoted to perfecting individual shapes or whole sequences. Also, the addition of partners and small apparatus provides tremendous scope and challenge for lesson themes which concentrate on stretch and curl shapes. This will be illustrated in the later sections.

COMBINING STRETCH AND CURL SHAPES WITH BODY POSITION OR BODY ACTION

At this stage, children should be able to perform a variety of individual curl or stretch shapes into a simple SEQUENCE (a continuous series of movements). No concern has been given to the action that was involved in each shape nor *where* the body was balancing as the shape was performed. It is now possible to add these latter elements to a child's movement vocabulary.

Adding Body Position:

Body Position is where the body is in relationship to the floor, apparatus, or while in flight. At this stage we are, however, only concerned with Individual Movements involving stretch and curl in relationship to the floor. Once the meaning of the following positions are learned they can be applied to any shape on or off apparatus.

Prior to combining stretch and curl shapes with Body Position pose a series of questions that will make the children conscious of where they are balancing or what is commonly called "TAKING YOUR WEIGHT ON. . . . ." The following balance positions should be attempted before combining shapes with these positions.

1. Balance (or taking the weight on) four parts of the body. (See Figure 15.43)

2. Balance (or taking the weight on) three parts of the body. (See Figure 15.44)

3. Balance (or taking the weight on) two parts of the body. (See Figure 15.45)

4. Balance (or taking the weight on) one part of the body.

5. Balance on specific parts of the body, such as two hands, or knees, on your back, side, upside down.

FIG. 15.43

FIG. 15.44

FIG. 15.45

6. Change balance positions from four to three; from three to two, or back to four.
7. Change balance positions from side to back; from back to stomach; from stomach to standing on one foot.

Example questions and movement answers:

QUESTION: How many remember the "measuring worm" (or push-up)? Start from the crouched position and walk forward on your hands and stop whenever you like and change from a four-point balance (two hands and two feet) to a position where you can put the weight of your body on three parts. Show one or two good examples.

QUESTION: See if you can find (or discover) a new position where you can take the weight on four (or three, two, or one) parts.

FIG. 15.46

QUESTIONS (For Primary):
1. Can you "take the weight on two hands and two knees" (four parts)
2. What other position can you discover where four parts of your body can take the weight?
3. See if you can balance on your back without using your hands.
4. Try to balance on your side using just one hand and any other part of your body.

Some results:

FIG. 15.47

FIG. 15.48

QUESTIONS (For Intermediate):
1. Find a balance position where you are "taking the weight" of the body on four different parts.
2. Shift to a new position on four parts but do not use one hand (or foot, or seat, etc.)
3. Make four different positions which start with a two-point balance, shift to three parts, then four, and finally back to two parts.
Some results:

FIG. 15.49   FIG. 15.50

As soon as the class understands the meaning of Body Position or "taking the weight on" one or more parts of the body, they can combine stretch and curl shapes with this element. This combination may involve the following: Combining a curled or stretch shape with a body position, for example, (Primary)   "Can you make a curled shape then move to a new position where you take the weight on four parts of your body."

FIG. 15.51

FIG. 15.52

Intermediate: See if you can move from a curled shape to a position where
   you take the weight on four parts.

FIG. 15.53   FIG. 15.54

Other combinations could be: (1) Weight on hands and a stretch shape; (2)
   Weight on two parts and a curled shape; (3) Weight on side or back
   and make a stretch shape.
Intermediate: "Can you move from a headstand (weight on three parts) to
   another stretch shape on your back (or side)?" (See Figs. 15.55, 15.56,
   and 15.57.)

Adding Body Action:

   The action of the body includes *how* it is moving such as quick or slow
and in *what* direction the body is moving. Action may, therefore, be combined with shapes, moving, for example, quickly from a curled or stretch
shape. This element may also be involved in the execution of any shape as
performing three slow and continuous curled shapes.

FIG. 15.55	**FIG. 15.56**	**FIG. 15.57**

Direction, as the second aspect of Action, includes all the possible directions or pathways the body can take. This is where children learn to perform shape and position with a conscious awareness of direction. When this occurs the variety or combinations of movements becomes infinite. To illustrate, the following question was posed to primary and intermediate level children: "See if you can make a sequence of stretch and curl shapes, and move in a sideways direction." Allow practice, then add a "quick" curl and a "slow" stretch as part of the sequence.

An Intermediate level answer:

FIG. 15.58	**FIG. 15.59**	**FIG. 15.60**

If we review at this stage that of using the LIMITATION method in relationship to the format and progression of skill development, it becomes quite
obvious the children are developing an ever-increasing range of movement
possibilities.

A Single Skill or

Combination of Movements

May Involve

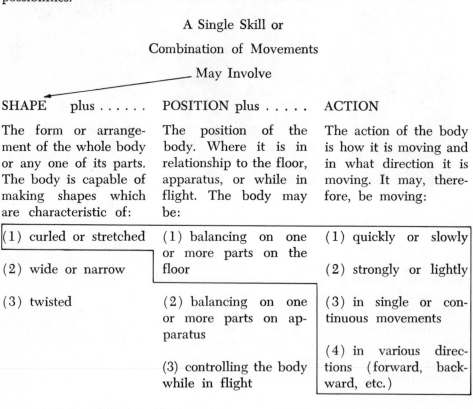

SHAPE plus	POSITION plus	ACTION
The form or arrange-ment of the whole body or any one of its parts. The body is capable of making shapes which are characteristic of:	The position of the body. Where it is in relationship to the floor, apparatus, or while in flight. The body may be:	The action of the body is how it is moving and in what direction it is moving. It may, there-fore, be moving:
(1) curled or stretched	(1) balancing on one or more parts on the floor	(1) quickly or slowly
(2) wide or narrow		(2) strongly or lightly
(3) twisted	(2) balancing on one or more parts on ap-paratus	(3) in single or con-tinuous movements
	(3) controlling the body while in flight	(4) in various direc-tions (forward, back-ward, etc.)

In the heavy "outlined" area of the chart it can be seen that movement
skills have progressed from single curl or stretch shapes to combining shape
and position, then finally the addition of body action expressed in terms of
"how" and in "what" direction the movement takes place. If children have
developed sufficient skill and understanding through the limitation method
of instruction, they are ready to develop a wide variety of interesting sequences involving one or more elements of SHAPE, POSITION, and AC-
TION.

Variety for its own sake should be avoided. At this stage, both at the
primary and intermediate levels, children should concentrate on developing
rather simple movements or sequences and show more concern for quality
and understanding the relationships of one movement skill to another. This
should be a time for practice and refinement of skill; a time for both teacher
and child to explore, observe, and refine the movement sequence.

FIG. 15.61

The following examples illustrate what primary and intermediate children are capable of producing:

A Primary sequence: An Intermediate sequence:

FIG. 15.62   FIG. 15.65

FIG. 15.63   FIG. 15.66

FIG. 15.64   FIG. 15.67

WIDE AND NARROW SHAPES

Wide and narrow, like curl and stretch, are contrasting shapes. A wide shape requires the legs or arms, or both, to be, in some way, away from the trunk. By contrast, a narrow shape is characterized by its thinness which means the arms or legs must be close together or in line with the trunk. The following illustrations show contrasting wide and narrow shapes.

FIG. 15.68

FIG. 15.69

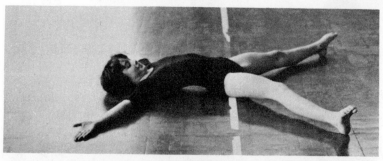

FIG. 15.70

FIG. 15.71

FIG. 15.72   FIG. 15.73

TEACHING PROGRESSION OF WIDE AND NARROW SHAPES

The same procedure for stretch and curl shapes is used to teach wide and narrow shapes. However, if a teacher has covered the previous section it is possible to integrate some stretch and curl shapes as these new shapes are introduced.

TEACHING PROGRESSION
   from:
Single or combined wide and narrow
   shapes to:
Combining Shape, Position, and Action

Note: If curl and stretch shapes have been previously introduced, they can be integrated at any stage of teaching wide and narrow shape.

DEVELOPING SINGLE OR COMBINED WIDE AND NARROW SHAPES

If a teacher has begun with stretch and curl shapes the children will have learned there are numerous starting positions from which a shape may be performed. The same starting points can be used with wide and narrow shapes. Questions should encourage making various wide and narrow shapes from the following starting position. In addition, add stretch and curl shapes at any stage in the suggested progression.

For wide and narrow shapes
1. from a standing position
2. while in flight
3. from a sitting position
4. from a front, back, or side lying position
5. from a wide to a narrow position
6. from a narrow to a wide position
7. from a curled or stretched to a wide or narrow position.

The following illustrations will indicate the typical answers produced by primary and intermediate level children to the questions posed.

Question: "How many different wide shapes can you make while keeping two feet on the floor?"

primary   intermediate

FIG. 15.74   FIG. 15.75

Other questions:

Is it possible to make a wide shape with just your legs (or just arms, or one arm and one leg)?

Is it possible to repeat any wide or narrow shape while in flight?

FIG. 15.76   FIG. 15.77

Although the same question is posed to both levels, the quality of movement of older boys and girls should be observable. Even though the main element is a wide or narrow shape, teachers should now begin to observe and comment on take-off, height of the jump, quality of shape performed, control on landing, and the general awareness on the part of the child with respect to what he is attempting to accomplish. Repetition of the same movement should be required by the teacher to encourage improvement and retention of any skill. Retention of any skill requires continuous practice.

The addition of stretch and curl could be introduced at this stage. For example, from the wide shape. . . . . "Change your shape to curled and then to the first wide shape."

| FIG. 15.78 | FIG. 15.79 | FIG. 15.80 |

COMBINING WIDE AND NARROW SHAPES WITH BODY POSITION OR BODY ACTION

If the previous individual and combined shapes have been introduced as well as the progression suggested under "curl and stretch," the following individual and combination of movements are possible. As each teacher and

SHAPE		POSITION		ACTION
curl	*Plus*	on the	*Plus*	—quick or slow
stretch	"with or from" a	floor or	moving a	—strong or light
wide	position which	in flight	particular way	—single or contin-
narrow	takes the weight		or in a particular	uous
	on one or more		direction.	—in various direc-
	parts of the body.			tions

her class learn the various shapes, positions, and actions, lessons can be developed to emphasize one or more elements. For example, a teacher may notice all children have difficulty in moving from one shape to another with

any form of "controlled" action. On this basis she may arrange a series of challenges stressing the following:
1. Moving from one shape to another with slow, controlled, and continuous movements.
2. Making strong forceful movements alternating with light or gentle movements.
3. Movements emphasizing position only; taking the weight on various parts of the body.
4. Movements emphasizing wide and narrow and taking the weight on different parts.
5. Sequence combining wide and narrow with stretch and curl shapes.

The addition of wide and narrow shapes to a child's "movement vocabulary" adds possibilities to the type and quality of his sequence involving one or more elements. Parts of a sequence are provided to illustrate the possible variety and quality that should be expected at this stage of development. Children in the intermediate grades should draw upon their previous gymnastic skills such as headstands, forward rolls, or handsprings, and incorporate these skills into their sequences.

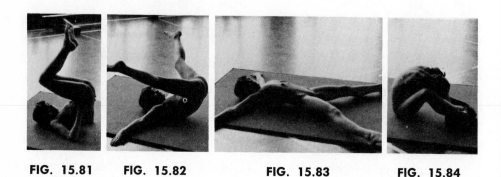

FIG. 15.81   **FIG. 15.82**   **FIG. 15.83**   **FIG. 15.84**

TWISTED SHAPES

A twisted shape can be performed in two ways. First, by holding one part of the body in a fixed or stabilized position such as on the floor or apparatus, then turning the body or any part of it away from the fixed base. In Figure 15.85 the body is fixed or stabilized by two feet restricting the degree of twisting away from this stationary base. A twisted shape may also be made when the body is in flight. In this case, as illustrated in Figure 15.86, one part of the body is held in a fixed position while the other part turns away from the "fixed" part producing a twisted shape. Although it could be argued that the latter was a "turn" (usually defined as rotation of the body and loss of a fixed contact), with younger children the synonymous use of "twist" and "turn" is quite acceptable at this stage of their development. Later the refinement in meaning can be made.

FIG. 15.85   **FIG. 15.86**

TEACHING PROGRESSION FOR TWISTED SHAPES

As with the previous two shapes, the important task for the teacher is to teach the meaning of "twisting" through simple tasks, later variety and complexity of twisting shapes can be introduced. The accompanying chart illustrates how twisted shapes can be independently introduced, or, at various stages, integrated with "stretch and curl" and "wide and narrow" shapes.

TEACHING PROGRESSION   ADDING OTHER SHAPES

Single or combined twisted
   shapes ← — — — — — — — — — — — — — adding single or combined
         ↓   "stretch and curl" and "wide
                                     and narrow" shapes
Combining twisted shapes with
Body Position or Body Action ← — — — — adding above to twisted
         ↓

Sequence Building—combining
Shape, Position, and Action ← — — — — — — adding above to twisted

DEVELOPING SINGLE OR COMBINED TWISTED SHAPES

The same procedure used with the previous shapes is followed with twisted shapes. Since twisting is an extremely important element not only to the quality of any future sequence, but also to the inherent contribution to the maintenance and improvement of flexibility, time should be taken to practice numerous individual twisted shapes before integrating them with wide, narrow, curled, or stretch shapes. The individual illustrations shown in Figures 15.87, 15.88 and 15.89 will indicate the wide range of twisted movement that can be performed from the basic standing, sitting, and lying positions.

FIG. 15.87   **FIG. 15.88**   **FIG. 15.89**

When individual twisting positions have been extensively explored, add twisting to the previous stretch, curl, wide or narrow shape. The following questions illustrate this possible combination.

QUESTION: Make a wide shape. "Now, can you keep one or more parts of your body glued to the floor and twist any part of your body?—what other ways can you twist?"

Other questions should be directed at combining twisting with one or more of the other shapes. Some combinations could be:

    Wide—Narrow—Twisted
    Stretched—Twisted—Curled
    Twisted—Curled—Wide—Twisted
    Wide and Twisted—Narrow—Stretched and Twisted

The latter sequence adds a new dimension to a child's "movement vocabulary." He should see the additional possibility of producing shapes which are combinations of individual shapes. When the latter sequence was presented to a group of fourth grade children they produced the following:

wide and twisted   narrow and twisted   stretched and twisted.

FIG. 15.90   FIG. 15.91   FIG. 15.92

COMBINING TWISTED SHAPES WITH BODY POSITION OR BODY ACTION

Elements of Body Position or Body Action may be integrated into any individual twisted shape or stressed as a "linking" from one twisted shape to another shape or action.

Examples of Integrating Position or Action with Twisted Shapes.

1. Make a twisted shape in a slow and continuous movement, then recoil back to the starting position as quickly as possible.
2. Get into a headstand position (balancing on three parts) and make a twisted shape.
3. Show a strong movement as you make a twisted shape and a contrasting light or gentle recoiling action as you shift into a new twisted shape.
4. Execute any "sports skill" (examples: baseball swing, throwing a ball, or catching a forward pass on the run) which involves a twisting action. This type of challenge is enjoyed by the boys and girls in the intermediate grades. It is also useful to show relationships in the movements learned in gymnastics to other sports, (see Figures 15.93, 15.94 and 15.95).

If a teacher has followed the suggested procedure for introducing each of the various shapes and accompanying body positions and actions, the possible variety of movements are almost unlimited. Variety during the initial stages of introducing this format of teaching was necessary since the children did not have sufficient "movement vocabularies" to occupy themselves for a full class period. It should now be possible to emphasize a particular theme which would stress one or two basic factors. For example, a theme (which is defined as a basic movement idea) for a sequence could be "twisting and continuity of movement." In this case, other shapes, such as stretch, curl, or wide, could be present in a sequence, but the *essential* aspects of concern both to the teacher and child would be the quality of each twisting movement and how well the continuity is expressed from one movement to another.

FIG. 15.93   FIG. 15.94   FIG. 15.95

Indirect Method of Teaching Skills

We have previously defined the DIRECT method as being "teacher-directed" with little or no choice allowed to the children. This was followed by the LIMITATION method where some choice is allowed both in the type of activity as well as where it is performed. As additional apparatus is introduced, more choice is possible.

The Indirect Method simply means children may practice any movement they desire on any or all available apparatus. The application of this method without any background in shape, position, and action, as well as the demonstrated ability to move with care and concern for the safety of oneself and others present in the gymnasium, is utter folly. This method has value and application in teaching self-testing activities only when children have demonstrated the ability to learn in this type of atmosphere.

At this stage in the gradual adoption of the new format for teaching gymnastic skills a teacher would say, at any point during the FLOOR WORK part of the lesson, "practice your sequences or individual movements." This is the extreme end of the LIMITATION METHOD; it is not simply a permissive atmosphere where children move without any conscious awareness of how or why they are moving.

Partner Activities

When Partner Activities are first introduced into the second part of the lesson, the same progression used to introduce individual shapes, position, and action can be used. Variations in this basic approach should be made by each teacher to cope with the interests and abilities of her class. Also, each teacher will have found certain techniques more suitable to her own style of teaching, hence, will modify and adjust her form of questioning and the way she observes and evaluates until she feels competent and satisfied with the results she is getting from each child.

In order to provide some guidance, the basic progression for introducing partners will be outlined for single and combined shapes, followed by the introduction of position and action and finally sequence building involving all three elements.

DEVELOPING SINGLE OR COMBINED SHAPES

In the following outline it is possible to use partners with each of the three basic shapes in three very different and challenging ways. Using "wide and narrow" as an example, the following movement tasks could be developed into a series of questions.

SHAPE		WAY A PARTNER IS USED	
	(1)	or (2) or	(3)
curl or stretch	single or	matching shapes	contrasting shapes
wide or narrow	unified	with a partner	with a partner
twisted	shape with		
	a partner		

FIG. 15.96

FIG. 15.97

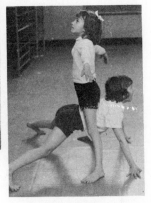

FIG. 15.98

Single Shapes (partners are considered as a single unit)
1. Make a wide (or narrow) shape with your partner.

FIG. 15.99   FIG. 15.100

2. One partner making a wide shape while the other makes a narrow shape. Both must be joined.
3. Make a wide shape, change to narrow shape without losing contact with your partner.

MATCHING AND CONTRASTING SHAPES

It is now possible to return to all the questions and examples listed under Individual Shapes for "wide and narrow" and repeat them in the form of "matching" or "contrasting" shapes with a partner. For example, the previous question "How many different wide or narrow shapes can you make while standing on two feet?" can now be performed by one child attempting to match his partner.

FIG. 15.101

FIG. 15.102

Combining Shape with Body Position or Action

Virtually all of the movement tasks suggested and illustrated under curl and stretch, wide and narrow, and twisted, may be applied to partner activities. Emphasis in this case may be on matching or contrasting movements. Other tasks or movement challenges may be posed to emphasize position or action while partners work as a single unit or as individuals attempting to match or contrast each other's shapes and movement patterns. Several examples for both levels are provided to give additional ideas with respect to how partner activities may be exploited.

Primary Level: Emphasis Position

1. See how many "bridge shapes" you can make with your partner.

FIG. 15.105

FIG. 15.103   FIG. 15.104

2. Make another bridge shape with one partner "taking the weight" (balancing) on four parts of his body.
3. Repeat above with both taking the weight on (a) two parts, (b) knees, (c) one foot and one hand, etc.

Emphasis: Action

1. Show a matching stretch and curl sequence which moves forward and sideways.
2. Show a contrasting "twisted" sequence where one moves slowly and the other moves quickly from one shape to another.
3. Produce a matching sequence which has one stretch and curl shape, one twisted shape and two different directions.

Intermediate Level: Emphasis Position
1. Make a bridge shape with your partner with feet (or hands or head or side) in opposite positions (one up, the other down).
2. Make a single shape where each partner is taking the weight on one (or two, three, or four) parts of his body.

FIG. 15.106   FIG. 15.107

Emphasis: Action
1. Develop a matching stretch and curl sequence which shows change of direction.
2. Produce a contrasting wide and narrow sequence with wide shapes emphasizing strong movement and narrow shapes light and gentle movements.
3. Make a matching sequence which emphasizes twisting and flight.

This stage in the addition of various elements of shape, position, and action should be considered as a simple extension of the above. Combining these elements into sequences adds to the challenge as well as tests the creative ability of the children. One must not forget the prior experience of intermediate level children who have learned to perform such stunts as the cartwheel, forward roll, or handspring. These skills should be integrated into sequence work. The following examples show again the quality of sequence work.

"Can you make a sequence with your partner to show a matching narrow, curl, and stretch shape?" (See Figures 15.108, 15.109, and 15.110.)

"Work out a sequence which includes a matching shape in flight." (See Figures 15.111, 15.112, and 15.113.)

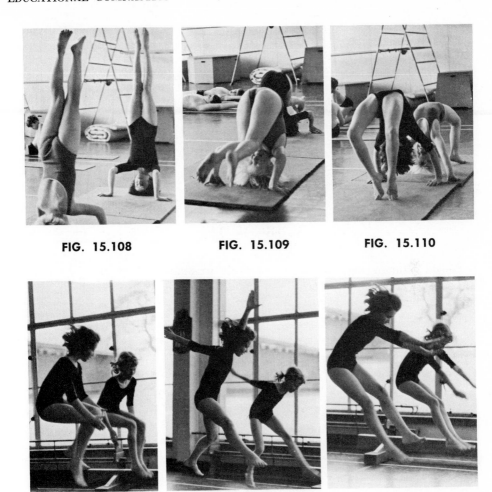

FIG. 15.108   FIG. 15.109   FIG. 15.110

FIG. 15.111   FIG. 15.112   FIG. 15.113

Hoop Activities

The previous section on Partner Activities has given the reader an indication of the extent an additional "piece" of apparatus can improve or challenge the physical and intellectual abilities of children. Hoop activities can accomplish the same. Within this Educational Gymnastic approach, the hoop can be used in two complementary ways. In the first instance the hoop is in contact with the body (held or balanced) as illustrated in Figure 15.114. This provides an extension for any individual shape or sequence or movement. The shape of the body is in some relationship to the hoop. In the second case, the body is not in direct contact with the hoop (not held or

FIG. 15.114

balanced), hence may act as an obstacle to maneuver around or through. Shape and action in the latter situation must have some relationship to the hoop as illustrated in Figures 15.115 and 15.116.

FIG. 15.115

FIG. 15.116

The identical procedure used with Individual Activities may be followed with Hoop Activities. Teachers should review the questions listed under single or combined shapes, combining shapes with body position or action in the Individual and Partner Activities sections to see how hoops could be incorporated into the progressive introduction of shapes, position, and action. In addition, the following illustrations and suggestions should provide adequate guidance in the use of hoop activities.

SINGLE OR COMBINED SHAPES

As suggested, there are two basic ways hoops can be used in this approach. A few suggested ideas and questions for each grade level will indicate the possible application of hoops.

SHAPE	WAYS A HOOP CAN BE USED	
curl and stretch wide and narrow twisted	(1) in contact with the body	(2) not in contact with the body

Primary (in contact with body)
1. Stretch shapes with hoop held high, to the side or low.
2. Wide or narrow shapes while holding hoop with one hand.
3. Placing one or more parts on hoop and make a wide or stretched shape.

FIG. 15.117

FIG. 15.118

Intermediate (not in contact with the body)
1. Make a bridge shape over the hoop.
2. Rest hoop against wall or obstacle and show and stretch, wide or twisted shape to the hoop.
3. Place one part of body inside the hoop and show a balance shape.

FIG. 15.119   **FIG. 15.120**   **FIG. 15.121**

COMBINING SHAPE WITH BODY POSITION OR ACTION

Since the same procedure is continued with the addition of body position and body action, a few additional ideas are provided to illustrate how hoops can be incorporated into combined movements.

Primary Level:

1. Lie on your back and see if you can make a shape with the hoop.

FIG. 15.122

2. Make a bridge shape touching four parts on the hoop.
3. Travel around the gymnasium holding the hoop in a high then a low position to the body.

Intermediate Level:

1. Lie on your back and place hands and feet on the hoop. Roll sideways without losing contact with the hoop.
2. Place the hoop on the floor. Begin a few yards away from your hoop, run and jump and land with three parts resting in the middle of the hoop.

3. Place hoop on the floor. See how many different balance positions you can make while remaining in the middle of the hoop.

FIG. 15.123

The following sequence illustrates how a hoop may be used to show a relationship of shape, position or action to the hoop.

Sequences emphasizing different body positions.

FIG. 15.124

FIG. 15.125

FIG. 15.126

Beanbags, Braids, and Indian Clubs

If the teacher has followed the suggested progression, beginning with Individual Activities, Partners, then Hoops, it should be reasonably clear how one should use beanbags, braids, or Indian clubs within this approach. There are many possible uses of this type of equipment. For example, a beanbag can be used individually with a particular shape or combined sequence. Indian clubs and hoops can be used to develop variations in particular shapes or used simply as an obstacle when one wishes to emphasize change of direction. A list of simple and rather complex examples are listed under the following headings to provide ideas and suggestions for each classroom teacher.

SINGLE AND COMBINED SHAPES

1. Beanbag on floor. Make wide and narrow (and other) shapes keeping one part of the body on the beanbag.
2. From a standing (sitting or lying) position make a shape while balancing the beanbag on your head (or on any other part of the body).

FIG. 15.127

3. Hold the beanbag between knees (or ankles, hand, etc.) and shift from a curled to a stretch shape without dropping the beanbag.
4. Combine the use of a beanbag and braid in making shapes.

FIG. 15.128   FIG. 15.129

COMBINING SHAPE WITH BODY POSITION OR BODY ACTION

1. Place three or four Indian clubs on the floor in a scattered arrangement and travel around each Indian club. Repeat and jump over each Indian club.
   Repeat and change directions as you jump over.
2. Place the braid around one wrist and one ankle and find a balance position where the weight is taken on three parts.
3. Use a braid in making three shapes involving a stretch, curl, and twist. Shift from each shape into another with a change of direction and speed.
4. In partners, using two braids, make a sequence which stresses changing direction.

Sequence building should now include a wide variation of shapes and movement patterns. The possible use of partners and hoops can also be added to any sequence as well as the wide variety of standardized stunts learned in previous grades.

The following question was posed to intermediate level children.
Question: Develop a sequence with a beanbag, blocks, or braid. With no additional comments, the following shapes and movement ideas were produced.

FIG. 15.130   FIG. 15.131   FIG. 15.132

Blocks, Wands, and Chairs

The addition of this type of equipment to the second part of a lesson further increases the scope of individual and combined sequence work. Since the general format and progression have been established in previous sections, only sample uses will be illustrated in the accompanying pages. Other small equipment such as beanbags and hoops may also be combined with wands, chairs, and blocks.

SINGLE AND COMBINED SHAPES

Wands: Emphasis Stretch and Curl

1. Use the wand to produce a stretch shape.
2. Make a curled shape with a wand.

FIG. 15.133

3. Place the wand on the floor and make a bridge shape over it.
4. With partner, show a wide and a narrow shape.

FIG. 15.134

FIG. 15.135

Blocks: Emphasis Balance

1. Place one part of the body on the block and show a wide (or narrow) shape.

FIG. 15.136

2. Place one hand on the block and show a twisted shape.
3. Use a block and wand and show a balance position which emphasizes twisting as a theme.
4. Combine blocks and hoop into a new balance position where the weight is taken on two or more parts of the body.

FIG. 15.137

FIG. 15.138

Chairs and Canes: Emphasis Twisting
1. Make three twisted shapes with a chair.
2. Place a cane across the seats of two chairs and show a twisted shape below and above the cane.

FIG. 15.139

FIG. 15.140

FIG. 15.141

COMBINE SHAPE WITH BODY POSITION OR BODY ACTION

Wands: Emphasis Shape and Action
1. Hold the wand with both hands and shift from a wide to a narrow shape in a slow and continuous movement.
2. Repeat above moving slowly into the wide shape and quickly into the narrow.
3. Place the wand on the floor. Start three or four yards away, run toward the wand, jump and show a wide or a twisted shape over the wand.
4. Repeat above and after landing roll into another twisted shape.

Chairs and Canes: Emphasis Flight and Change of Direction
1. Combine chair and canes to show a theme which emphasizes flight and changing directions.
2. Use a chair to show change of direction.

Combining Small Equipment: To see how well the class is progressing with sequence development, allow them to choose one or more pieces of equipment and develop a theme of their own choice. Allow them to choose from a "pool" of equipment, including beanbags, hoops, partners, braids, chairs, wands, and canes.

Individual Ropes

Individual ropes may be used to enhance or complement a single shape, act as a point of contact in partner work, or be used as an obstacle to maneuver around or through. Several examples of this very versatile piece of equipment are shown under Single and Combined Shapes.

SINGLE AND COMBINED SHAPES
1. Use the rope to show a series of holes which represent wide and narrow shapes.
2. Tie the ends of the rope together and make a curled or a stretch shape.
3. With a partner and two ropes make a twisted shape.
4. Use a rope and a hoop and develop a contrasting wide and narrow shape.

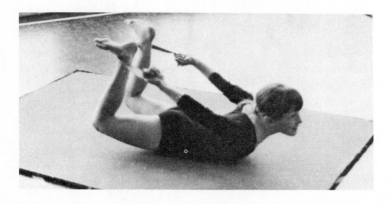

FIG. 15.142

Combining Shape with Body Position or Body Action

1. Use a rope to show a twisted shape and a change of direction.
2. With a partner produce a strong and contrasting light movement.
3. With a partner develop a sequence using two ropes and emphasizing stretch and curl.
4. Find how many balance positions can be made using a block and rope.

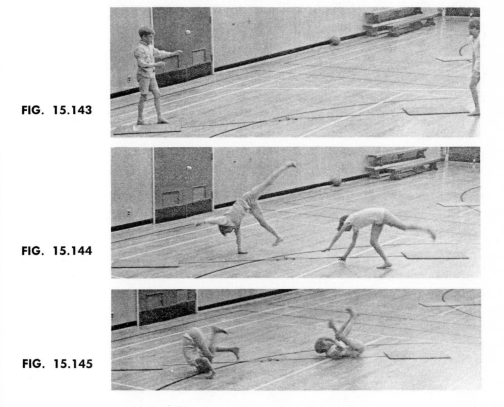

FIG. 15.143

FIG. 15.144

FIG. 15.145

LARGE APPARATUS ACTIVITIES

The balance beam or bench, when arranged in creative and challenging positions, can be used to test and further extend the skills and movement ideas learned during the second part of the lesson. The balance bench with hooks attached to one end is the more versatile apparatus since it can be "attached" to other apparatus, such as stall bar, box, sawhorse, and even climbing ropes.

Since most children have used the balance bench while in a horizontal position, it is wise to begin with this arrangement and then gradually introduce

FIG. 15.146

other individual or combined arrangements. Once children have acquired an understanding of the meaning of Shape, Position, and Action, as well as a working knowledge of sequence building, they will begin to develop their own arrangements of apparatus to complement their movement ideas.

During the first few lessons, allow children to explore the possible uses of the balance beam or bench without asking them to apply a specific shape, position, or action with this apparatus. Children must be familiar and feel safe on apparatus before a challenge is presented. Normally, one or two exploratory lessons, even with primary children, is sufficient to develop this "feeling of security."

FIG. 15.147

Many of the movement tasks presented earlier in this chapter can be applied to the balance beam or bench. Teachers should begin with these ideas and gradually introduce more creative arrangements of this apparatus as the skill, competence, and understanding of the children develop.

FIG. 15.148

FIG. 15.149

In addition, several examples of applying single and combined movements to the balance beam or bench are described and illustrated in the next section. The latter should provide a starting point for each teacher with respect to the potential use and possible arrangement of this apparatus.

Applying Single or Combined Shapes to the Balance Beam or Bench

One of the first tasks of the teacher is to assist children to use the balance beam or bench in a variety of ways when performing single or combined shapes. A movement task such as "See if you can make a twisted shape on the balance bench (or beam)," will usually produce something like the shapes illustrated in Figure 15.150. In the first instance the parallel arrangement of

FIG. 15.150

the benches lacks imagination. Also, the use of the word "ON" encourages all children to begin their movements from the same starting position. Questions should be presented in such a way that children begin to see the apparatus in a much wider perspective. Rephrasing the question to "Can you make a series of twisted shapes using various parts of the balance bench?" allows for greater scope as illustrated in Figures 15.151 and 15.152.

FIG. 15.151

FIG. 15.152

The following questions involving the three basic shapes illustrate the potential use of the balance bench in extending movement ideas developed during the Floor Activities part of a lesson.

Curl and Stretch: "Can you make a stretch shape with part of your body on the bench and part on the floor?" . . . . . "Change to a new stretch position with another part on the bench."

FIG. 15.153

FIG. 15.154

Wide and Narrow: "With your partner, make a wide shape with only one partner in contact with the bench."
Twisted: "Make a series of twisted shapes as you move from one end of the beam to the other."

FIG. 15.155

FIG. 15.156

FIG. 15.157

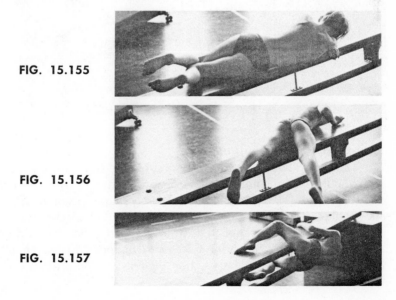

APPLYING COMBINED MOVEMENTS TO
THE BALANCE BEAM OR BENCH

When applying movement ideas to the balance beam or bench the latter should be considered as either a point of contact or an obstacle to move around, across, or over (in flight). The following movements illustrate this application.

1. Move around the benches showing a quick change of direction.
2. Travel across the benches by changing from three to two points of balance.
3. Develop a sequence traveling across the bench and include a twisted shape, balancing on side and a change of direction.
4. Begin anywhere on the floor, run and jump on to a bench, then leap off, land, and make a safety roll (may be a sideway, diagonal, or forward roll).

Repeat and perform a stretch, twisted, or curled shape before landing.

FIG. 15.158

Springboard and Vaulting Box

The springboard, beatboard, mini-tramp and vaulting box can be used individually or in combination with other apparatus to provide interesting and challenging movement tasks involving shape, position, and action. Teachers should review the movement tasks provided in the previous chapter to see how they can be applied to this apparatus. Several additional examples are provided under Single or Combined Shapes and movements to illustrate how the apparatus can be used as well as to show a variety of movement ideas.

APPLYING SINGLE OR COMBINED SHAPES TO THE SPRINGBOARD,
BEATBOARD, MINI-TRAMP, OR VAULTING BOX

All individual shapes performed in flight from the floor can now be applied to the springboard, beatboard, or mini-tramp. The latter provides additional height and time to execute curled or stretched, wide or narrow, or twisted shapes. In addition, children have learned safety rolls (sideward, backward, and forward roll); therefore, should be able to land and roll with grace and ease. The following movement tasks illustrate the additional challenge and increased quality of movements performed from the springboard, beatboard, or mini-tramp. Similar movements may also be performed from the vaulting box as illustrated in Figure 15.159.

FIG. 15.159

FIG. 15.160

FIG. 15.161

The vaulting box should also be used as an additional challenge for shapes. Teachers should encourage the use of all parts of the box (top, side, and end) when performing shapes as well as to provide movement tasks which require children to approach and dismount in various directions. Movement tasks listed below will provide a starting point for teachers who are in the beginning stages of using this apparatus in this new and challenging approach.

FIG. 15.162

FIG. 15.163

FIG. 15.164

1. Make a stretch (wide or twisted) shape on the side, end, and top of the box.

FIG. 15.165

2. Combine a wide and twisted shape along the top of the box.
3. With a partner or group make a long shape on the side or top of the box.

FIG. 15.166

FIG. 15.167

APPLYING COMBINED MOVEMENTS TO THE
SPRINGBOARD AND VAULTING BOX

Sequence involving shapes, position, and action can now be designed to include the springboard and vaulting box individually or in combination with other small and large apparatus. The selection and arrangement of this apparatus should complement the shapes and movements contained in the sequence. Excessive rearrangement of apparatus serves little purpose in the development of movement skills, hence teachers should caution children if they tend to waste time in arranging apparatus. One arrangement of apparatus should last for several lessons.

USING THE STAGE AS A PIECE OF APPARATUS

FIG. 15.168

Horizontal Bar, Stall Bars and Ladder

The use of horizontal bar and overhead ladder in teaching shape, position, and action has limited possibilities. The horizontal bar, for example, may be used for movement tasks involving shape and some sequences which stress body position. In the main, however, neither of these first two pieces of equipment are as versatile as the stall bars. On the basis of the latter, several examples of movement tasks stressing single and combined shapes will be illustrated along with additional suggested ideas. When the stall bars are combined with other apparatus there are greater challenges for sequence work involving combined shapes and movements.

APPLYING SINGLE AND COMBINED SHAPES TO THE STALL BARS

One of the most important features of the stall bars is the variable height a student may select to perform a shape. The following movements tasks show how the stall bars may be effectively exploited.

1. Make a wide or narrow shape while on the stall bars.
2. See how many "letters of the alphabet" you can make on the stall bars.
3. Make a twisted shape.

FIG. 15.169

FIG. 15.170

FIG. 15.171

APPLYING COMBINED MOVEMENTS TO THE STALL BARS

Movement tasks which require children to balance or hang on different parts may be applied to the stall bars. Since many children lack sufficient arm and shoulder girdle strength the lower rungs of the stall bars are extremely useful during the early stages of sequence development. Children will attempt such tasks as hanging upside down with their hands touching the floor. Later, with practice and increased skill and strength, more daring movements can be attempted. In addition to the movement tasks provided under Individual and Small Apparatus Activities, the following tasks will show how other apparatus can be used in conjunction with the stall bars.

1. Make a shape which uses the floor and stall bars as a point of balance.
2. Make a series of shapes which require three points of contact with the stall bars.
3. Find three different shapes while the body is sideways or upside down on the stall bars.

FIG. 15.172　　　　　　　　　　　　　　　　　FIG. 15.174

FIG. 15.173

4. Develop a sequence showing change of direction and wide and narrow shapes.
5. Travel up the bench, across stall bars and down, showing twisted and curled shapes.

Climbing Rope

There are numerous and extremely enjoyable and challenging individual and combined shapes, positions, and body actions that can be applied to the vertical or swing rope. When children are given the opportunity to combine the rope with other apparatus, they will create the most unusual and challenging arrangements to complement their sequences. Several combined apparatus arrangements are illustrated in this section.

FIG. 15.175

Applying Single and Combined Shapes to the Climbing Rope

All single and combined shapes should be performed with the rope in a stationary and vertical position before they are attempted while the rope is swinging. The following movement tasks will provide an additional supplement to the tasks and challenges presented earlier in this chapter.

Stationary:

1. From a supporting position using two hands see how many different body shapes you can produce.

FIG. 15.176

FIG. 15.177

2. Use the floor and rope and repeat above.
3. If two ropes are hanging parallel, repeat 1. and 2. above.
4. Make a wide shape from an upside-down position (or make a stretch, then a curled shape).

While swinging:
1. Repeat above.
2. Repeat above, then land and roll on to mat (safety rolls).
3. Repeat above landing backward and performing a backward diagonal roll.

APPLYING COMBINED MOVEMENTS TO THE
CLIMBING ROPE AND OTHER APPARATUS

Sequence work should include movements from one type of apparatus to another illustrating continuity of movement. The rope, when combined with benches, boxes, and planks can provide this linking of movements as well as an exciting challenge for children.

Jumping Boxes, Sawhorse, and Planks

There are situations where apparatus is difficult to define as being small or large. The vaulting boxes and sawhorse may be used more effectively during the Floor Activity part of the lesson rather than as Large Apparatus. This distinction, however, is unimportant as teachers will develop lessons where there is a constant overlap between Floor Activities and Large Apparatus Activities. Classification of apparatus depends more upon the purpose it is serving than upon its relative size. This is illustrated in several of the accompanying examples.

FIG. 15.178

APPLYING SINGLE AND COMBINED SHAPES TO
VAULTING BOXES, SAWHORSES AND PLANKS

The boxes and sawhorses provide excellent opportunities for movement
tasks involving shape. In Figure 15.179, for example, children were asked to
make a series of wide or narrow shapes using the box or sawhorse. The chal-

FIG. 15.179

FIG. 15.180

FIG. 15.181

FIG. 15.182

FIG. 15.183

lenge presented in Figure 15.180 was to make a shape on top or side of a box. Jump and make another shape in flight produced a variety of interesting shapes as illustrated in Figures 15.181, 15.182, and 15.183. The sawhorse also provides additional challenges when a movement task requires children to make a wide or twisted shape on the horse.

APPLYING COMBINED MOVEMENTS TO VAULTING
BOXES, SAWHORSES OR PLANKS

Many of the movement tasks presented under Balance Beam and Bench, Vaulting Box, as well as with individual and small apparatus activities, may be applied to this apparatus. Teachers should review these sections for the initial ideas of using this equipment. Also, the combination of other small apparatus such as hoops, partners, and canes with one or more pieces of this apparatus will provide extremely interesting challenges.

Agility Apparatus

One of the most significant contributions in the self-testing area has been the development of new and challenging Agility Apparatus. Most of this apparatus has been developed in England for use in the Education Gymnastic or Movement Education Programs. It has been specifically designed to provide more challenging tasks which traditional gymnastic apparatus cannot provide. Generally speaking, this new apparatus is higher, wider, and flexible in its arrangement. Some apparatus is also portable thus allowing it to be used in the gymnasium or out-of-doors.

Since this apparatus is relatively new to the majority of readers, several of the more popular designs are illustrated in the accompanying pages.

Teachers who are hesitant to use the following apparatus are reminded that a child will not attempt a movement task on any piece of equipment until he is physically and mentally ready. This is emphasized in this approach to teaching Shape, Position, and Action. If the latter is adhered to in principle and practice, accidents should be a rare occurrence. This is not just an opinion held by the writer, it is a proven fact. There are fewer accidents in Educational Gymnastic programs than in contemporary programs emphasizing the teacher-directed approach to teaching standardized skills.

Types of Agility Apparatus

The following examples of commercial agility apparatus are far from complete. They do, however, represent the kinds of apparatus that are suitable for various age levels.

J. E. G. Apparatus

FIG. 15.184

Agility Ropes

FIG. 15.185

Whittle Primary P. E. Equipment

FIG. 15.186

South Hampton (Cave)

FIG. 15.187

Nissen No. 223 Wall Gym

FIG. 15.188

SELECTED REFERENCES

BILBROUGH A., and JONES, P. *Physical Education in the Primary Schools.*° London: University of London Press, 1967.

CAMERON, W. McD., and PLEASANCE, PEGGY. *Education in Movement.* Oxford: Basil Blackwell & Mott, Ltd., 1965.

HALSEY, ELIZABETH. *Inquiry and Invention on Physical Education.* Philadelphia: Lea and Febiger, 1964.

HALSEY, ELIZABETH and PORTER, L. *Physical Education for Children,* 2nd Edition. New York: Holt, Rinehart & Winston, Inc., 1967.

HOWARD, S. "The Movement Education Approach to Teaching in English Elementary Schools," *American Journal for Health Physical Education and Recreation.* January, 1967, page 31.

Inner London Education Authority, Educational Gymnastics.° London: 1966.

KIRCHNER, G.; CUNNINGHAM, J.; and WARRELL, E. *Introduction to Movement Education.* Dubuque: Wm. C. Brown Company Publishers, 1970.

LABAN, R. *Modern Educational Dance.*° London: Macdonald and Evans, 1948.

LABAN, R. and ULLMANN, L. *The Mastery of Movement.*° London: Macdonald & Evans, 1960.

*All books listed with an asterisk may be purchased from the Ling Book Shop, Ling House, 10, Nottingham Place, London W C 1.

LOCKS, L. F. "The Movement Movement," *American Journal for Health, Physical Education and Recreation.* January, 1966, page 26.

LUDWIG, E. A. "Towards an Understanding of Basic Movement Education in the Elementary Schools." *American Journal for Health, Physical Education and Recreation.* March, 1968, page 27.

MAULDIN, E., and LAYSON, J. *Teaching Gymnastics.*° London: Macdonald & Evans, Ltd., 1965.

Ministry of Education, Moving and Growing. London: Her Majesty's Stationery Office,° 1952.

Ministry of Education, Planning the Program.° London: Her Majesty's Stationery Office, 1965.

NORTH, MARION. *A Simple Guide to Movement Teaching.*° Exeter: Wheaton & Co., 1964.

Ontario Department of Education, Physical Education Health, Interim Revision. Toronto: 1967.

SIMONS, W. M. M. Educational Gymnastics—Its Meaning, Uses and Abuses, Canadian Journal of Health, Physical Education and Recreation, page 6.

WISEMAN, E. D. "Movement Education—What It Is and What It Is Not," Canadian Journal of Health, Physical Education and Recreation, page 6.

VISUAL AIDS

The accompanying list of Movement Education films have been previewed by the writer or recommended by leading experts in the field. Wherever possible the prices and any other salient aspect relating to preview fees are provided.

Simon Fraser University's Film Series

Simon Fraser University's Film Series contains five instructional films on Educational Gymnastics (Movement Education) specifically designed to be used by classroom teachers and for teacher training programs. The films in this series were taken under normal teaching conditions in a typical elementary school in British Columbia, Canada. Children ranging in age from five to thirteen were filmed at sequential periods over a period of one school year. Film sequences were selected from over twenty thousand feet of film, illustrating the basic elements of Movement Education, creative uses of equipment and apparatus, and numerous examples of various methods and techniques used in this approach. This series may, therefore, be considered a complementary visual supplement to Chapter 15 in this book or to any available text on the subject of Movement Education.

The following five films may be purchased from Universal Education and Visual Arts, 2450 Victoria Park Avenue, Willowdale 425, Toronto, Canada. Delivery time is normally ten days.

FILM NO. 1: INTRODUCTION TO MOVEMENT EDUCATION
(36 minutes, sound, color)

Film No. 1 is designed to give classroom teachers, with no prior knowledge of Educational Gymnastics, a general overview of the content and methods that are used in this approach to teaching physical activities. In the initial sequences, the philosophy underlying this approach is presented to show the compatibility of Movement Education to the modern concept of education. This is followed by a description of the three basic elements of Movement Education and how they are taught. Strong emphasis is given to the limitation and indirect methods of instruction in this and all remaining films of this series. Special attention is also given to "safety training," a procedure which must be understood and emphasized in every lesson utilizing this approach. Since this is an introductory film we have attempted to show a wide variety of small and large apparatus used in typical lessons throughout this project. Continuous reference is made in this film to more elaborate coverages of key aspects of Movement Education in the remaining four films.

FILM NO. 2: DEVELOPING RANGE AND UNDERSTANDING
OF MOVEMENT (29 minutes, sound, color)

This film describes one of the primary elements of Movement Education most commonly defined as "Body Awareness." It illustrates how children learn to control and manipulate the weight of the body on the floor, with small equipment and with large apparatus. Several sequences show children of various ages using Agility or Climbing Apparatus.

A major emphasis of this film has been to illustrate movement tasks requiring children to move and balance on different parts of the body, to work with a partner and within a group, and to develop specific themes of stretch, curl, and twist. Excerpts of a lesson plan titled "feet high" is also included to show how two parts of a lesson complement each other.

FILM NO. 3: UNDERSTANDING SPACE AND DIRECTIONAL
MOVEMENTS (26 minutes, sound, color)

This film illustrates how teachers can assist children to develop a conceptual understanding and an effective use of general and limited space. It shows how to gradually expand a child's movement vocabulary to include such directional movements as forward, sideways, across, around, and through.

The first part of the film attempts to lay the groundwork for this important aspect of Educational Gymnastics. Children are shown in their initial lessons developing the full use of all available space on or off apparatus. Several scenes clearly illustrate how children develop spatial awareness as well as an awareness of the safety of themselves and other members of the class. A lesson plan emphasizing the use of general and limited space is also provided as a guideline for beginning teachers. Numerous illustrations of constructive and creative use of equipment and apparatus have been included to show how children, when given the opportunity, can become the initiators of their own learning experiences.

FILM No. 4: HOW TO DEVELOP A THEME
(31 minutes, sound, color)

The primary purpose of this film is to show, in a sequential pattern, how Movement Education is taught through a series of themes. Although a theme is similar to the contemporary "instructional unit," it has a uniqueness of its own and needs general clarification. Hence, the film illustrates how a theme is first introduced to a variety of age levels and how it is developed in progressive stages.

One of the most interesting aspects of this film is the "before and after" visual demonstration showing a general improvement in a child's ability to draw upon an increased movement vocabulary. The themes of "stretch and curl" and "twisting" are illustrated both at primary and intermediate levels to show contrast in abilities, particularly in the use of small equipment and large apparatus.

FILM No. 5: QUALITIES OF MOVEMENT (27 minutes, sound, color)

This film describes what Rudolf Laban defined as the qualities of movement. A distinction is first drawn between the term "quality" as it is generally understood in gymnastics and other sports and the "qualities" of movement as defined by the originator of Movement Education.

In the remaining portion of the film, the qualities of "force," "time," and "flow" are illustrated by a variety of age levels. A theme combining all three qualities is included to show how each quality can be integrated into one theme. For interest and comparison, a sequence performed by a group of university students has been included in the latter part of the film.

Individual Films

TITLE: CHILDREN IN ACTION

Details: 16 mm., color, sound, 24 minutes
Distributor: Divisional Education Offices, Education Offices, Market Street, Nelson, Lancashire, England
Description:

This film was directed by Percy Jones (co-author of Physical Education in the Primary Schools) and shows upper elementary school-age children participating in various aspects of a movement education lesson. There are excellent illustrations of individual and partner sequences. Apparatus arrangement is also worth special notation. The presentation of movement tasks as well as methods of increasing the challenges on the floor and apparatus has been exceptionally well illustrated.

TITLE: MOVEMENT EDUCATION IN THE PRIMARY SCHOOL
Details: 16 mm., color, sound, 26 minutes
Distributor: Somerset County Council Film Library, Mount Street, Bridgwater, Somerset, England
Description:
   The basic elements of Space, Weight, and Time are illustrated in this film. Children ranging in age from seven to eleven are shown developing movement skills during the movement training and apparatus part of the lesson. The concepts of space, weight, and time are clearly described and illustrated. Teachers will find many ideas relating to technique and the creative use of apparatus throughout this film.

TITLE: JUNIOR SCHOOL PHYSICAL EDUCATION LESSON
Details: 16 mm., color, sound, 25 minutes
Distributor: County Film Library, 2 Walton's Parade, Preston, Lancashire, England
Description:
   This film shows a typical English junior-level group of students in a physical education lesson. The children have been given instruction prior to going into the recreation area. They demonstrate the use of various apparatus, how to work alone, in pairs, and in groups. The teacher's role is shown as a guider of the activities.

TITLE: AND SO THEY MOVE
Details: 16 mm., black and white, sound, 20 minutes
Distributor: Audio-Visual Center, Michigan State University, East Lansing, Michigan
Description:
   This is a film showing the application of movement education to physically handicapped elementary school children. Numerous practical and meaningful activities in fundamental movement experiences are presented with accompanying theoretical narration on the value of the activities. Suggestions are included for sequence in programming based on a problem-solving approach.

TITLE: BASIC MOVEMENT EDUCATION IN ENGLAND

Details: 16 mm, black and white, sound, 19 minutes

Distributor: Audio-Visual Education Center, University of Michigan, 720
             East Huron Street, Ann Arbor, Michigan
             Purchase Price $85.00;   Rental $4.25

Description:
    This film describes movement education from primary grades through
teacher training in England. The use of small and large apparatus is shown
in a variety of interesting situations. The film demonstrates how to bring a
child to an awareness of his relationship to space, time, and force.

TITLE: MOVEMENT EXPERIENCES FOR CHILDREN

Details: 16 mm., black and white, sound, 7 minutes

Distributor: Department of Instructional Media Distribution, Altgeld 114,
             Northern Illinois University, DeKalb, Illinois

Description:
    A short documentary film on the need for children to move and to
learn to move well which includes delightful pictures of children in natural
outdoor activities followed by a view of an experimental indoor program
using a problem-solving approach.

TITLE: MOVEMENT EXPERIENCES FOR PRIMARY CHILDREN

Details: 16 mm., color, sound, 17 minutes

Distributor: Department of Instructional Media Distribution, Altgeld 114,
             Northern Illinois University, DeKalb, Illinois

Description:
    This film includes a comprehensive coverage of how movement ideas of
movement education is taught to elementary school children. Children are
shown developing movement ideas on the floor and later on a wide variety
of apparatus and new agility equipment. Emphasis is given to appropriate
teaching methods used in movement education.

TITLE: MOVEMENT EDUCATION IN PHYSICAL EDUCATION

Details: 16 mm., black and white, sound, 20 minutes
             Purchase Price $145.00;   Rental $25.00

Distributor: Hayes Kruger, Louise Duffy School, 95 Westminster Drive, West
             Hartford, Connecticut

Description:
    This film interprets movement education through narration in question-
answer form. Two teachers from the program provide much information
on a variety of activities from K-6. The film demonstrates the methodology
of the problem-solving approach, emphasizes the importance of a well-

structured environment, and discusses the relationship to good traditional programming.

TITLE: MOVEMENT EDUCATION IN PHYSICAL EDUCATION
Details: 16 mm., black and white, sound, 17 minutes
            Purchase Price $50.00;   Rental $3.00
Distributor: The Audio-Visual Center, Division and Extension and University
            Services, University of Iowa, Iowa City, Iowa. (Films not avail-
            able for rental or preview outside U.S.A.)
Description:
    In this film, emphasis is placed on present movement patterns based on skills for daily work and play activities to children in the first grade and the relationship of these patterns in their activities throughout the elementary grades.

TITLE: TIME AND SPACE AWARENESS
Details: 16 mm., black and white, sound, 8 minutes
            Purchase Price $25.00;   Rental $1.65
Distributor: The Audio-Visual Center, Division and Extension and University
            Services, University of Iowa, Iowa City, Iowa. (Films not avail-
            able for rental or preview outside U.S.A.)
Description:
    This film illustrates a sample lesson emphasizing time and space, two of the components of movement which are then transferred to a game situation.

TITLE: MOVEMENT EDUCATION—GUIDED EXPLORATION
Details: 16 mm., black and white, sound, 8 minutes
            Purchase Price $25.00;   Rental $1.65
Distributor: The Audio-Visual Center, Division and Extension and University
            Services, University of Iowa, Iowa City, Iowa. (Films not avail-
            able for rental or preview outside U.S.A.)
Description:
    The teaching techniques used as children explore with hoops, jump ropes, and balls are highlighted in this demonstration film.

TITLE: MOVEMENT EDUCATION—THE PROBLEM-SOLVING TECHNIQUE
Details: 16 mm., black and white, sound, 12 minutes
            Purchase Price $30.00;   Rental $1.65
Distributor: The Audio-Visual Center, Division and Extension and University
            Services, University of Iowa, Iowa City, Iowa. (Films not avail-
            able for rental or preview outside U.S.A.)

Description:

This film demonstrates keen fifth graders developing a dance using simple folk steps and music. The emphasis is on the teaching techniques of problem-solving rather than on the finished dance product.

TITLE: EDUCATIONAL GYMNASTICS IN ENGLAND—FROM PRIMARY TO COLLEGE LEVEL PROGRAMS

Details: 16 mm., color, sound, 30 minutes.

Distributor: Audio-Visual Centre, Simon Fraser University, Burnaby 2, B.C., Canada.

Description:

This film is a visual documentation of Dr. Kirchner's observations of educational gymnastic programs in England (1969). The film illustrates the role and emphasis of educational gymnastics in elementary, high school, and college programs. In the majority of scenes, typical programs are shown to illustrate the methods used, levels of performance and differences in facilities and equipment. The film also shows a few advanced educational gymnastic programs to illustrate the quality of performance that can be reached through this type of program.

Dance Activities

Dance activities for elementary school children include fundamental rhythmical skills, folk dances, singing games, and creative rhythms. Chapter 16 provides a description and illustration of the basic or fundamental locomotor and non-locomotor skills. These skills are the foundation or underlying movements of all dance activities. Chapter 17 contains traditional folk dances and singing games with each placed in appropriate grade levels. Chapter 18 of this section, Creative Rhythms, presents a suggested approach to teaching pantomime and interpretative movements.

Fundamental Rhythm Skills

Teaching Suggestions
Locomotor Movements
Non-Locomotor Movements

T HE basic or fundamental skills of rhythm and dance activities include eight locomotor steps and six non-locomotor or axial movements. Locomotor skills such as walking, hopping, and leaping are the foundations upon which all dance steps are based. For example, a combination of three running steps and one hop in proper rhythmic relationship produces a schottische step, or a step, slide, step to three-quarter time produces a waltz. Non-locomotor or axial movements such as swinging and swaying and bending and stretching are not only used in combination with the traditional dance steps to enhance grace of movement but in addition become the basic framework for all pantomime and creative dance activities. The ability of a child to sway "like a tall fir tree" or swing "like the old rusty gate" requires an individual perception of this movement coupled with an ability to move the body through its maximum range wth grace and ease.

Although primary level singing games and pantomime activities involve many dance steps and axial movements, special attention should be devoted to each of these movements within each grade level. It is impossible, however, to indicate proficiency levels by grade or by sex for each of the fundamental rhythmical skills. A more feasible approach is to list the recurring common faults of each locomotor and non-locomotor movement and to indicate methods of correcting these errors. This chapter presents the latter approach with each skill illustrated, then accompanied by a list of common faults and instructional activities. The use of the list of records provided for each skill will depend upon the age of the children as well as the specific part of the skill that is being emphasized.

TEACHING SUGGESTIONS

Teachers are well aware of the fact that there is no best or correct way to teach fundamental rhythm skills. Obviously, the method used will depend upon such factors as age of the student, observed deficiencies, available space, and probably more important, the special talents of the teacher. Certain problems, however, are faced by most teachers when introducing these dance activities. The following suggestions will assist in overcoming these problems or may provide new ideas which can be incorporated into an established method of presentation.

1. Provide sufficient space for each child to move without fear of physical hazards or a need to restrict movements.
2. Encourage children to recognize skillful and creative performances. When a child demonstrates a graceful movement, allow the remainder of the class to watch this child and attempt to analyze and explain why the movement was graceful or well executed.
3. Recognize that a certain amount of noise, particularly that resulting from natural or spontaneous enjoyment, is desirable.

4. Provide experiences that involve locomotor and non-locomotor movements, as well as a combination of both.
5. Provide praise and encouragement rather than scolding or ridicule for incorrect movements.
6. Do not expect or encourage uniformity of response.

LOCOMOTOR MOVEMENTS

Each of the eight locomotor movements described in the accompanying pages is performed with an even or uneven rhythm. The walk, run, jump, hop, and leap involve an even rhythm while the skip, gallop, and slide require an uneven rhythmic pattern.

Walking

Walking is a transfer of weight from one foot to the other while moving in a forward or backward direction. One foot must always be in contact with the floor. The right arm swings forward paralleling and accompanying

FIG. 16.1

FIG. 16.2

The child's left arm and right leg are in the forward position. In walking, the heel of the front foot should contact the ground first then the ball of the foot and finally the weight should be over the toes in preparation for the next step.

The right foot maintains contact with the floor while the left leg and right arm are brought forward and the left arm shifts downward and backward. A normal walking movement should be a relaxed, free flowing movement of the arms and legs with back straight and head erect to permit child to look straight ahead rather than at his feet.

the forward movement of the left leg; this is followed by the same action with the left arm and right leg.

COMMON FAULTS IN WALKING

1. Walking with toes turning inward (usually classified as pigeon-toed).
2. Walking with toes turning outward.
3. Dragging the heel rather than distinctly pushing upward and forward from the toe. This is well illustrated by scuffing of the heels.
4. Walking with poor posture. A typical example is the child who walks with an exaggerated forward, backward, or sideward lean.
5. Walking with an incorrect arm action. In this case the right arm comes forward with the right foot rather than the left arm. No arm action or simple arm hanging may also be noted.
6. Walking with a stiff knee giving the appearance of a goose step. This is usually accompanied with a complementary stiff arm swing.

WALKING ACTIVITIES

1. Walk informally about the room. This should be an easy relaxed walk that is most natural to the child.
2. Same as (1) but in a circle.
3. Same as (2) with a change in direction.
4. Walk in different ways. For example, short or long steps, fast or slow, hard or soft, high or low.

RECORD ACCOMPANIMENT FOR WALKING ACTIVITIES

Title of Record	No. of Record	Movements	Grade Level
1. "Childhood Rhythms"	Series I, No. 101	walk, run, skip	K-1
2. "Childhood Rhythms"	Series I, No. 102	duck, camel horse, elephant	K-1
3. R.C.A. Rhythmic Activities E-72	45-5004-A (Hollaendre)	walk	K-3
4. "Childhood Rhythms"	Series II, No. 202	walk, hop	3
5. Elementary Rhythms	AED 2, PJ-8	walk	2-3
6. Linden, Rhythmic Activities	1000-A	walk	2-3
7. "Basic Rhythms" Kay Ortmans Productions, Ltd.	Album I, No. 1	walk, run	K-1
8. "Rhythm Time," Bowmar Records	No. 1550	walk, run, skip	K-2
9. "Fundamental Steps and Rhythms," Folkraft	Album 20, No. 1440	walk	K-2

5. Walk to a change of tempo, single or double time.
6. Walk on heels with exaggerated arm movements.
7. Walk on tiptoes.
8. Walk slowly for balance. using two, three, or four beats per measure.
9. Walk sidewards by crossing one foot in front of the other.
10. Pantomime walking, a "happy" or "sad" walk, carry a heavy or light load, a young or old man, etc.

Running

This movement consists of a transfer of weight from one foot to another with a momentary loss of contact with the floor by both feet.

COMMON FAULTS IN RUNNING

1. Running with heel touching the floor first, followed with a "rocking motion" forward to ball of foot. In dance activities the running step should be performed on the ball of the foot or on the toes.
2. Throwing legs out to side on the forward motion.
3. Running with toe turning inward on what is classified as pigeon-toed.
4. Running with toes turning outward.

FIG. 16.3

FIG. 16.4

In the above illustration the child has landed on his left foot and is beginning to shift his right leg and left arm forward. The right arm continues backward in opposition to the left leg action. Note the slight forward lean in the running position.

In the middle of the running position, both feet should be off the ground. Rhythmic activities, involving a running step, usually require the landing to be on the balls of the feet or possibly on the toes.

5. Running with incorrect arm action. In this case, the right arm comes forward with the right foot rather than the left arm forward with the right.
6. Running "out-of-time" to music.

RUNNING ACTIVITIES

1. Running informally about the room.
2. Running around room in small groups.
3. Running with short or long steps.
4. Running with high knee lift.
5. Running backwards.
6. Running to a change in tempo—single or double time.
7. Running on heels or tiptoes.
8. Pantomime running, like tall man, dog, elephant, etc.

RECORD ACCOMPANIMENT FOR RUNNING ACTIVITIES

Title of Record	No. of Record	Movements	Grade Level
1. Childhood Rhythm	Series I, No. 101	run	K-3
2. Childhood Rhythm	Series III, No. 303	run	K-3
3. Elementary Rhythm	AED 2, PJ 8	walk, run	2-3
4. Rainbow Rhythms	Series 1	run, hop, skip	K-3
5. Rhythm Times, Bowmar	1550-A	run	K-3
6. Rhythm Times, Bowmar	1552-A	run	2-3
7. "Basic Rhythms," Kay Ortmans Productions, Ltd.	Album I, No. 1, 3 and 4	run	K-1
8. "Fundamental Steps and Rhythms," Folkraft	No. 1441	run	K-2

Jumping

Jumping is a transfer of weight from one foot or from both feet to both feet.

COMMON FAULTS IN JUMPING

1. Landing on heels or landing "flat-footed."
2. Landing on one foot (hop) rather than on both feet.
3. Jumping (take-off) and landing with stiff knees and ankles.
4. Trunk bent too far forward producing an exaggerated forward movement as the child lands.

JUMPING ACTIVITIES

1. Jump in place. The first jumps should just clear the floor, then gradually increase the height of each jump.

FIG. 16.5

Begin this movement with feet about shoulder width apart, trunk tilted slightly forward and weight well forward on toes. Bend the knees and raise arms sideward and backward.

FIG. 16.6

Extend the legs and swing arms forward and upward or toward the body as illustrated in the above picture. After the momentary loss of contact with the floor, land on the toes and gradually flex the knees and shift arms sideways ready for the next jump.

2. Jump with feet together and gradually spread legs on each jump.
3. Jump forward, sideward, and backward.
4. Jump in place with a higher jump on an accent. Use 4/4, 3/4 or 2/4 rhythm.
5. Jump in place to a 4/4 rhythm and perform a 1/4 turn on each accent.
6. Jump in place to a 4/4 rhythm and require different positions in the air on each accent. Such positions could be feet apart with right leg forward and left leg back.

RECORD ACCOMPANIMENT FOR JUMPING ACTIVITIES

Title of Record	No. of Record	Movements	Grade Level
1. "Childhood Rhythms"	Series I, No. 102	jump	K-3
2. Linden Rhythmic Activities	1001B	jump	K-3
3. Elementary Rhythms	AED 2, PJ-8	walk, jump, run	K-3
4. Elementary Rhythms	AED 3	jump	K-2
5. Rainbow Rhythms	Series 2	jump	K-3
6. Childhood Rhythms	Series II, No. 204	jump	2-3
7. Fundamental Steps and Rhythms, Folkraft	No. 1442	jump	K-2

Hopping

Hopping is a transfer of weight from one foot to the same foot. In the upward phase of this movement, the toe is the last to leave the floor; in the downward movement the toe is the first to contact the floor.

COMMON FAULTS IN HOPPING

1. Landing on heel or landing "flat-footed."
2. Hopping (take-off) and landing with stiff knees and ankles.
3. Trunk bent too far forward, producing an exaggerated forward movement as the child lands.

HOPPING ACTIVITIES

1. Hop in place. The first hop should just clear the floor with each succeeding hop gradually increasing in height.

FIG. 16.7	**FIG. 16.8**
Stand on one foot, trunk leaning slightly forward, knees partially bent, and arms extended sideways.	Extend knee of left leg and push off floor with toe. On the upward lift, flex right knee and keep arms extended sideward for balance. Land on toe of left foot and repeat movement.

2. Hop forward, sideward, and backward.
3. Hop in place with a higher hop on accent. Use 4/4, 3/4 or 2/4 rhythm.
4. Hop in place and make a 1/4 turn on each accent.
5. Hop in place to a 4/4 rhythm. Require different positions in the air on accent. Such positions could be right leg forward, arms sidewards or overhead.

6. Hop several times on one foot then, without losing rhythm, switch to the other foot.

RECORD ACCOMPANIMENT FOR HOPPING ACTIVITIES

Title of Record	No. of Record	Movements	Grade Level
1. Rainbow Rhythms	Series 2	hop	2-3
2. Rainbow Rhythms	Series 1	hop, run, skip	K-3
3. Childhood Rhythms	Series II, No. 204	hop	K-3
4. Childhood Rhythms	Series V, No. 503	hop	2-3
5. Childhood Rhythms	Series III, No. 302	hop	K-1
6. Rhythm Band	Vol. 2, 13141A	hop	2-3

Leaping

A leap is a transfer of weight from one foot to the other foot. The toe of the take-off foot is the last to leave the floor while the toe of the landing foot is the first to contact the floor. It should be noted the main difference between a leap and a run is that the former has a more sustained loss of contact with the floor as well as a greater height and distance covered.

FIG. 16.9

FIG. 16.10

In the illustration shown above, the child has just extended his left leg and is momentarily off the ground. The right knee is flexed and ready to extend forward and downward. Both arms are in an exaggerated position to assist in the upward and forward movement.

As the child lands on his right toe, the left knee is flexed and both arms lowered to assist in balance as well as to prepare for the next leap.

COMMON FAULTS IN LEAPING

1. Landing on the heel or landing "flat-footed."
2. Landing on both feet.
3. Trunk bent too far forward, producing an exaggerated forward movement as the child lands.
4. Leaping (take-off) and landing with stiff knees and ankles.
5. Failing to swing arms forward to assist in forward movement.

LEAPING ACTIVITIES

1. Run forward a few steps, then leap. Alternate the take-off foot.
2. Leaping for height and distance.
3. Hop in place a few times then leap forward or sideward.
4. Leap on accent — use 4/4, 3/4, or 2/4 time..

RECORD ACCOMPANIMENT FOR LEAPING ACTIVITIES

Title of Record	No. of Record	Movements	Grade Level
1. Childhood Rhythms	Series II, No. 205	leap	K-3
2. Childhood Rhythms	Series III, No. 302	leap	2-3
3. R.C.A. Rhythmic Activities	Vol. 2 45-5007 B	leap	K-3
4. Rhythm Band	Vol. 2 13140-A	leap	2-3
5. Rhythm Band	Vol. 2 13142-A	leap	2-3
6. R.C.A. Rhythmic Activities	E72, 45-5006-A	leap	2-3
7. "Music for Movement," Kay Ortmans Productions, Ltd.	Album I, No. 2	leap, skip, run	K-2
8. "Children Rhymes"	Series IX, No. 902	leap	K-2

Sliding

A slide is actually a gallop performed in a sideward direction.

COMMON FAULTS IN SLIDING

1. Sliding on heels rather than on balls of feet and toes.
2. Sliding foot too far to side.
3. Leaning too far over toward the lead foot.

SLIDING ACTIVITIES

1. In circle or line formation—slide to right then to left.
2. Slide four steps to right, make 1/2 turn, then four steps to the left.
3. With partners slide four steps right then four steps left.

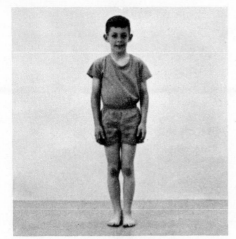

FIG. 16.11

Begin with feet together, arms extended
and resting on side of legs and weight
evenly distributed on both feet.

FIG. 16.12

Step right foot to right side, then bring
left foot to right in a closing movement.

RECORD ACCOMPANIMENT FOR SLIDING ACTIVITIES

Title of Record	No. of Record	Movements	Grade Level
1. Childhood Rhythms	Series V, No. 505	slide	K-3
2. Linden, Rhythmic Activities	1000 B	slide	K-3
3. Childhood Rhythms	Series 5, No. 501	slide	2-3
4. Childhood Rhythms	Series 5, No. 502	slide	K-3
5. Rhythm Band	Vol. 2 3140-B	slide	2-3
6. Rhythm Band	Vol. 2 13140-A	slide	2-3
7. Toy Shop	No. 106	slide	K-3
8. "Fundamental Steps and Rhythms," Folkraft	No. 1442	slide	K-3

Skipping

A skip is a combination of a long step and a short hop alternating the
lead foot after each hop.

COMMON FAULTS IN SKIPPING

1. Skipping on the same foot.
2. Inability to hop on both feet.
3. Landing flat-footed rather than on toes.

4. Failing to swing arms in opposition to leg movements.
5. Leaning too far forward or backward.
6. Failing to skip in time with music.

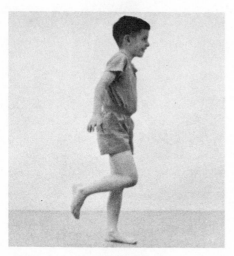

FIG. 16.13

The child has just landed on his left foot and immediately takes a short hop on the same foot and begins to swing the right foot forward for the next step.

FIG. 16.14

Continue swinging right leg forward and land on right foot. The weight should be over the toes of this foot. Hop on right foot and swing left foot forward in preparation for the next step.

RECORD ACCOMPANIMENT FOR SKIPPING ACTIVITIES

Title of Record	No. of Record	Movements	Grade Level
1. Childhood Rhythms	Series 1, No. 101-102	skip	K-1
2. Childhood Rhythms	Series 3, No. 303	skip	K-3
3. Rainbow Rhythms (voice)	Series 1	skip, run, hop	K-3
4. Linden Rhythmic Activities	1002B	skip	2-3
5. Linden Rhythmic Activities	1000A	skip	K-3
6. Elementary Rhythms	AED 2 PJ-8	skip	2-3
7. "Rhythm Time," Bowmar Records	1550	skip, walk, run	K-2
8. Rhythm Activities, Bassett-Chestnut Productions	1000	walk, skip	K-2
9. Fundamental Steps and Rhythms, Folkraft	1441	skip	K-2

SKIPPING ACTIVITIES

1. Skipping forward or backward in circle formation.
2. Skip with partner — hand crossed in skating position.
3. Skip four long steps forward then for short steps backward.
4. Skip four steps beginning with right foot then four steps beginning with left foot.
5. Skip diagonally right for three steps (R-L-R) and bring feet together on fourth count. Repeat to left.

Galloping

A gallop is moving in a forward direction with the same foot always in front. The weight is transferred from the leading foot to the closing or back foot. It is a combination of a walk and a run.

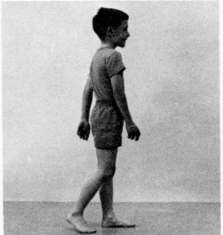

FIG. 16.15	FIG. 16.16
In the illustration above, the child has just finished the run and has walked forward on his left foot.	With the weight now over the left foot, shift the right toe close to the heel of the left foot then shift weight back to right foot in preparation for the next run and step.

COMMON FAULTS IN GALLOPING

1. Landing on heels rather than on toes.
2. Stiff legs — both knees should be bent.
3. Failure to shift weight to forward foot then to back foot.
4. Arms may be too rigid or not moving in opposition to foot action.
5. Failing to keep time with music.

GALLOPING ACTIVITIES

1. Gallop with left foot forward, stop, then right foot forward.
2. Gallop around circle.
3. Gallop in different directions.
4. Gallop and pantomime horses—slow, fast, young, old, etc.

RECORD ACCOMPANIMENT FOR GALLOPING ACTIVITIES

Title of Record	No. of Record	Movements	Grade Level
1. Childhood Rhythms	Series 1, No. 101	gallop	K-1
2. Linden Rhythmic Activities	1002 B	gallop	K-3
3. Linden Rhythmic Activities	1000 B	gallop	2-3
4. Childhood Rhythms	Series 1, No. 102	gallop	K-1
5. Toy Shop	No. 105	gallop	K-1
6. Childhood Rhythms	Series 5, No. 505	gallop	2-3
7. Childhood Rhythms	Series 5, No. 502	gallop	2-3
8. Elementary Rhythm	AED 2 PJ-8	gallop	K-3
9. Elementary Rhythm	AED 1	gallop	K-3

NON-LOCOMOTOR MOVEMENTS

There are five non-locomotor or axial movements that are performed from a relatively stable base of support. Each of these movements is usually performed while standing, kneeling, sitting, lying; however, they may be combined with a locomotor skill. Each axial movement may be performed to an even or uneven rhythm, depending on the type of interpretation desired.

Swinging and Swaying

Swinging is a pendular movement with the axis of support above the moving parts. To illustrate, an arm may swing from the shoulder in a downward and backward movement or a leg may swing from side to side. Swaying is the same type of movement with the support below the moving parts.

COMMON FAULTS IN SWINGING AND SWAYING

1. Lack of flexibility — unable to swing or sway through the full range of movement.
2. Inability to distinguish between a swing (support is above moving part —shoulders to arms) and sway (support is below moving part—waist to shoulders).
3. Rigid movements rather than graceful and continuous movements.

SWINGING AND SWAYING ACTIVITIES

1. Swing arms forward and backward and side to side.
2. Sway arms overhead in a frontward and backward and sideward direction.
3. Repeat (1) with legs.

FIG. 16.17

Swinging: The arm swinging movement shown above should be performed with feet well apart. As the arms swing from the right to left side, the body weight should shift to the left foot to permit a free unchecked pendular movement.

FIG. 16.18

Swaying: Begin the arm swaying motion with legs well apart, weight on left foot, and trunk bent to the left side. Shift arms toward the opposite side and transfer weight to opposite foot.

RECORD ACCOMPANIMENT FOR SWINGING AND SWAYING MOVEMENTS

Title of Record	No. of Record	Movements	Grade Level
1 Childhood Rhythms	Series 3, No. 305	swing	K-3
2. Linden Rhythmic Activities	1001 A	swing	2-3
3. Rainbow Rhythms	Series 2, No. 2-A	swing	2-3
4. Elementary Rhythms	AED 4 A	swing	2-3
5. Elementary Rhythms	AED 4 B	swing	2-3
6. Rainbow Rhythms	Series 2	swing	2-3
7. Rhythm Time, Bowmar Records	1551	swing, sway	K-2
8. "Music for Movement," Wayne State University, Audio-Visual Materials, Consultation Bureau	Vol. I, side 3	swing, sway	K-2
9. "Music for Physical Fitness," L. P. Record	side 2	swing, sway	K-2

4. Allow children to experiment with this movement. "How many parts of the body can swing, can sway?"
5. Swing or sway various parts of body in pantomime. Example: Sway like a tree, windshield wiper, etc. Change tempo with each pantomime movement.

Bending and Stretching

Bending is flexing any or all parts of the body, while stretching is extending the same. Both movements may be done in a relaxed or vigorous fashion and with even or uneven rhythm.

FIG. 16.19	FIG. 16.20

Bending: Begin this axial movement by relaxing neck, shoulder, and trunk muscles, and gradually lower trunk toward the floor. By keeping the legs straight the child will stretch the leg and back muscles thus increasing his range of motion.

Stretching: After bending forward as far as possible, begin a slow upward movement, raising arms upward and backward. Hold the stretch position for a few seconds then repeat the bending movement.

COMMON FAULTS IN BENDING AND STRETCHING

1. The inability to bend or stretch to full range of movement.
2. The inability to bend from waist or to the side without grotesque movement

BENDING AND STRETCHING ACTIVITIES

1. Bend and stretch different parts of body—arms, legs, trunk.
2. Imitate things that bend or stretch—tree, snake, dog, etc.

3. Assume different sitting or lying positions and explore different bending and stretching movements.
4. Bend and stretch to musical accompaniment.
5. Stretch one arm slowly and bend it back rapidly. Reverse movement.
6. Bend one part of body (arms) while stretching the other (legs).

RECORD ACCOMPANIMENT FOR BENDING AND STRETCHING MOVEMENTS

Title of Record	No. of Record	Movements	Grade Level
1. Childhood Rhythm	Series 2, No. 201	stretch, bend	2-3
2. Linden Rhythmic Activities	1001 A	stretch, bend	2-3
3. Rainbow Rhythms	Series 2	stretch, bend	K-3
4. Childhood Rhythms	Series 5, No. 506	stretch, bend	2-3
5. Rhythm Band	Vol. 2, 3140 B	stretch, bend	K-1
6. Rhythm Time	1552 B	stretch, bend	2-3
7. "Happy Times," Educational Dance Recordings	S 6.1	stretch, bend	2-3

Rising and Falling

Rising is a slow contractual movement of any or all parts of the body while moving from a lower to a higher level. Falling, on the other hand, is a controlled gradual relaxation by any or all parts of the body while moving from a higher to a lower level.

COMMON FAULTS OF RISING AND FALLING

1. Dropping to floor rather than a gradual descent through a slow relaxation of muscles.
2. Rapidly rising off floor rather than a gradual and graceful movement.
3. Using arms to stop the fall — the hands should touch floor; however, they, together with arms and shoulder muscles, should relax.

RISING AND FALLING ACTIVITIES

1. From an exact standing position, have children gradually relax muscles and "drop" to a front lying, back lying, or side lying position.
2. From an exact standing position, have children relax muscles and lower body one half or three quarters toward floor then rise back to the standing position.
3. Assume various positions on the floor, (crouched, sitting on feet, etc.) and rise back to the standing position.
4. Have partners hold hands and rise and fall to floor.

FIG. 16.21

FIG. 16.22

Rising: In the above illustration the child has begun to raise his body upward from a partially crouched position. This should be a lifting action rather than a swinging or stretching movement.

Falling: At the height of this movement, the body should be in an erect position with weight on toes and arms extended overhead. Begin the falling action by a slow relaxation of all muscles rather than the arms, then the neck and so on until a full crouched position is attained.

MUSICAL ACCOMPANIMENT FOR RISING AND FALLING MOVEMENTS

	Title of Record	No. of Record	Movements	Grade Level
1.	Childhood Rhythms	Series 2, No. 201	fall, recover	K-2
2.	Linden Rhythmic Activities	1001 B	fall, recover	2-3
3.	Elementary Rhythm	AED 2	fall, recover	K-1
4.	Childhood Rhythms	Series 5, No. 504	fall, recover	2-3
5.	Childhood Rhythms	Series 2, No. 205	fall, recover	K-1
6.	Rhythm Time	1552 B	run, fall	2-3
7.	Rhythm Time	1551 A	fall, recover	2-3
8.	Childhood Rhythms	Series 2, No. 206	fall, recover	K-3

Twisting and Turning

Twisting is a rotation of the body or any part of the body while maintaining a stable base of support. Turning is a partial or total rotation of the body and a shifting of the base of support.

COMMON FAULTS IN TWISTING AND TURNING

1. Losing balance while twisting parts of body.
2. Inability to judge and perform a full turn.

FIG. 16.23

FIG. 16.24

Twisting: Stand with legs extended, feet apart, and arms spread sideward. Twist body toward the left side and continue backward without moving feet off the floor. Return to the starting position then twist to the right side.

Turning: Begin with legs extended, feet apart and arms spread sideward. Start to twist body toward the left side and, as body weight shifts to left foot, lift the right foot and take a short step around the toe of the left foot. Continue this turning movement to the starting position.

MUSICAL ACCOMPANIMENT FOR TWISTING AND TURNING MOVEMENTS			
Title of Record	No. of Record	Movements	Grade Level
1. Childhood Rhythms	Series 2, No. 201	twist, turn	2-3
2. Rainbow Rhythms	Series 1	twist, turn	K-3
3. Elementary Rhythms	AED 1	twist, turn	2-3
4. Rainbow Rhythms	Series 2	twist, turn	K-3
5. Rhythm Band	Vol. 2, 13142 A	twist, turn	2-3
6. "Music for Physical Fitness," L.P. Record	Side 2	twist, turn	K-3

TWISTING AND TURNING ACTIVITIES

1. Turning body a quarter, half, or full turn to right then to the left.
2. Turning body to music.

3. Turning to pantomime movements — tops, doors, washing machine, etc..
4. Let children experiment with all parts of the body to see how many different parts of the body as well as the number of combinations they can twist.
5. Twist to pantomime movements — trees and wind.

Striking and Dodging

Striking is a percussion-type movement directed toward an object or
person. The latter may be real or imaginary. Dodging is a quick shifting
of one or all parts of the body directed away from a stationary or moving
object.

FIG. 16.25	FIG. 16.26

Striking: The child, in the above illustration, is pretending to chop wood. Begin with feet apart, arms over head with
hands held close together. Forceably
lower hands, flex and twist trunk downward simulating a pounding or striking
action.

Dodging: The child, in the above illustration, is pretending to move away from
a ball thrown toward his right side. Start
in a standing position with legs slightly
apart and weight evenly distributed on
both feet. Shift weight to right foot, raise
left leg and shift body sidewards away
from base of support. Repeat action to
opposite side.

COMMON FAULTS IN STRIKING AND DODGING

1. Inability to forceably repeat a movement two or more times.
2. Rigid or inflexible movements rather than smooth total body movement.

STRIKING AND DODGING ACTIVITIES

1. Beating movements to pantomime — beat drum, chest, tree (woodpecker).
2. Beating movements using other parts of the body — feet, knee, elbow, etc.
3. Striking movements to pantomime — tennis, volleyball, etc.

MUSICAL ACCOMPANIMENT FOR STRIKING AND DODGING MOVEMENTS			
Title of Record	No. of Record	Movements	Grade Level
1. Rhythm Band	Vol. 2 3140 B	striking, dodging	2-3
2. Rhythm Time	1552 B	striking, dodging	2-3
3. "Music for Movement," Wayne State University, Detroit, Audio-Visual Materials, Consultation Bureau	Vol. 1 Side 2	strike, dodge	K-3

Pushing and Pulling

Pushing is directing a force or object away from the base of support such as pushing a door open or pushing with one foot against an imaginary object. Pulling is directing a force of object toward oneself such as pulling a wagon.

FIG. 16.27

Pushing: Begin with arms chest high, back straight, one foot in front of the other and weight on back foot. Shift body forward in a forceful movement until weight is well over the front foot. Repeat similar actions with one arm, head or one foot.

FIG. 16.28

Pulling: Begin with trunk flexed, arms extended forward, and weight on front foot. Draw arms backward and upward to simulate pulling of a heavy object.

COMMON FAULTS IN PUSHING AND PULLING

1. Inability to maintain balance throughout the pushing or pulling action.
2. Rigid or inflexible movements rather than smooth extended thrusts.
3. Lack of balance when performing a push with one leg while standing on the other.

PUSHING AND PULLING ACTIVITIES

1. Pushing and pulling movements to pantomime — chop wood, boxing, rowing, etc.
2. Partner pulling and pushing movements in pantomime.
3. Using small objects such as wands, balls, books, etc., and pantomime movements of a story, song, or verse.
4. Tell a story and substitute movements for pushing and pulling as well as other non-locomotor movements.

MUSICAL ACCOMPANIMENT FOR PUSHING AND PULLING MOVEMENTS

Title of Record	No. of Record	Movements	Grade Level
1. Elementary Rhythms	AED 2 PJ-9	push, pull	2-3
2. Childhood Rhythms	Series 1, No. 105	push, pull	K-3
3. RCA Rhythmic Activities	E 72 15-5004 A	push, pull	3
4. Rainbow Rhythms	Series 2, No. 213	push, pull	K-3
5. "Music for Movement," Kay Ortman's Productions, Ltd.	Album 1 No. 4	push, pull	K-2

SELECTED REFERENCES

AINSWORTH, DOROTHY S., and EVANS, RUTH. *Basic Rhythms.* New York: Chartwell House, Inc., 1954.

ANDERSON, M. H.; ELLIOT, M. E.; and LABERGE, J. *Play with a Purpose.* New York: Harper & Row. Publishers, 1966.

ANDREWS, GLADYS; SAURBORN, JEANNETTE; and SCHNEIDER, ELSA. *Physical Education for Today's Boys and Girls.* Boston: Allyn and Bacon, Inc., 1960.

EVANS, RUTH; BACON, THELMA; BACON, MARY E.; and STAPELTON, JOIE L. *Physical Education for Elementary Schools.* New York: McGraw-Hill Book Company 1958.

EVANS, RUTH, and BATTIS, EMMA. *Childhood Rhythms.* New York: Chartwell House, Inc., 1954.

GILBERT, PIA, and LOCKHART, AILEENE. *Music for the Modern Dance.* Wm. C. Brown Company Publishers, Dubuque, Iowa, 1961.

KULLWITSKY, OLGA, and KALTMAN, FRANK L. *Teacher's Dance Handbook Number One: Kindergarten to Sixth Year.* Newark: Bluebird Publishing Co., 1959.

LOCKHART, AILEENE, and PEASE, ESTHER. *Modern Dance: Building and Teaching Lessons,* 3rd Edition. Wm. C. Brown Company Publishers, Dubuque, Iowa, 1965.

Moving and Growing. London: Ministry of Education and Central Office of Information, His Majesty's Stationery Office, 1952.

MURRAY, R. L. *Dance in Elementary Education,* Second Edition. New York: Harper & Row, Publishers, 1963.

SAFFRAN, R. *First Book of Creative Rhythms.* New York: Holt, Rinehart & Winston, Inc., 1963.

THACKERY, R. M. *Music and Physical Education,* Revised Edition. London: G. Bell and Sons, Ltd., 1965.

SUGGESTED FILMS

Title:	"Discovering Rhythm"
Details:	16 mm., color, sound
Distributor:	Universal Education and Visual Arts, 221 Park Avenue South, New York
Description:	Demonstrates to children that rhythm is an outgrowth of activities they actually do. Illustrates fundamental movements
Purchase Price:	$120.00

Traditional and Contemporary Dances

Singing Games
Folk Dances
Square Dances

ALL dances that are performed in the elementary school may be broadly classified under the general heading of Traditional and Contemporary Dances. This classification includes singing games and traditional dances of past cultures as well as the contemporary dances of the generation.

In this chapter, three general sections have been organized on the basis of "ease of use" rather than on established dance criteria. The first major section titled "Singing Games" includes a wide selection of the more popular singing games enjoyed by children in the first two or three grades. The next section on "Folk Dances" includes appropriate traditional and contemporary dances for primary and intermediate grades. Although suggested grade levels are provided for each dance, teachers should select each dance on the basis of the children's dance background and their demonstrated interests. "Square Dances" are included in the latter section in order to provide additional teaching suggestions, also a Glossary of Terms.

SINGING GAMES

Singing games are part of the dance heritage of every country. They are, in essence, the forerunners of the more complicated traditional and contemporary dances. As such, they provide a foundation upon which the more advanced dances can be built. Because of the cultural and historical significance of folk singing games, primary teachers should take time to provide interesting and appropriate materials relating to their origin, the customs of the people, and the meaning of the various dance movements. There are many ways of presenting this information, such as reading stories and poems about the people, displaying pictures, dolls, and articles, or by showing a film about the country.

Most primary singing games are individual or partner activities; however, both types are performed within a total group situation. Since five, six, and seven-year-olds are basically individualistic, the singing games listed in the accompanying chart may be performed individually while in a line, circle, or scattered pattern. With practice and maturity, children in the second and third grades progress to more advanced folk dances involving intricate patterns and total group participation.

How to Teach Singing Games

Teaching singing games to children in the primary grades, particularly to five and six-year-olds, should be an enjoyable experience for teachers and a creative experience for children. From the point of view of children, their uninhibited behaviour and joy of movement makes singing games an appropriate activity. Once they learn the words they will provide their own accompaniment and an infinite variety of interesting and creative versions of each singing game.

Since there are wide variances in maturity, motor ability, and interests among early primary children, no single method of teaching this type of activity will prove successful. Each teacher should, therefore, experiment with several approaches until she finds a method most suitable to her own style of teaching. Usually this is a combination of methods and technique rather than one "special" approach. The following suggestions may be helpful to teachers who are in the process of developing a suitable approach to teaching these activities.

1. Use a musical accompaniment that permits you to work freely with the children. This implies the use of commercial records or a tape recording of your own piano accompaniment.
2. Give the name of the folk dance or singing game, its origin, and mention something about the customs of the people. To illustrate, show motion pictures, slides, or photographs of and about the people.
3. Teach the words of the singing game first; teach the movement later. Children should practice singing the song until it is nearly memorized.
4. Teach the basic steps of the singing game after the children have learned the verses of the song.
5. Combine the basic steps with the words and music.
6. Attempt to create a permissive atmosphere whereby children feel free to express their own ideas and movements.

How to Create Singing Games

Through singing games, children learn to walk, run, skip, or perform a combination of these basic dance steps to a musical accompaniment. As soon as children have developed this ability to move rhythmically to music, they can create their own singing games. This may be accomplished by allowing them to develop their own dance to favorite nursery rhymes or songs. For example, "Sing a Song of Sixpence" or "I Saw a Ship a Sailing" have simple phrases and a rhythmical melody which provide the necessary ingredients for a new singing game. In addition, children may wish to write their own verses about animals, space ships, or special events, and then try to apply them to musical accompaniment. The latter task of finding the appropriate music usually becomes a joint venture for the teacher and her class. The supplementary list of singing games and available records on the accompanying page will be of general assistance. Children should also be encouraged to create their own music. Perhaps too, some children may be fortunate enough to have a teacher with a musical background and the talent to write musical accompaniments to fit the various verses written by them.

SINGING GAMES FOR PRIMARY GRADES*

Name of Dance (Arranged in approximate order of difficulty)	Formation	Origin	Page	Grade level K	1	2	3
1. Baa, Baa, Black Sheep	Circle	English	553	X			
2. Hickory, Dickory, Dock	Circle	English	553	X			
3. Ring Around The Rosy	Circle	English	553	X	X		
4. Farmer In The Dell	Circle	English	554	X	X		
5. Sally Go Round The Moon	Circle	American	554	X	X		
6. The Muffin Man	Circle	English	555	X	X		
7. Loobie Loo	Circle	English	555	X	X		
8. Did You Ever See a Lassie?	Circle	Scottish	556	X	X		
9. How D'Ye Do My Partner	Circle	Swedish	557		X	X	
10. Oats, Peas, Beans, and Barley	Circle	English	557		X	X	
11. A Hunting We Will Go	Line	English	558		X	X	
12. Round and Round the Village			559		X	X	
13. Jolly Is the Miller	Circle	English	559			X	X
14. Shoo Fly	Circle	American	560			X	X
15. Paw Paw Patch		American	560				X
16. Skip To My Lou	Circle	American	561				X

Supplementary List of Singing Games**

Name	Origin	Formation	Grade Level K	1	2	3	Record Source
Bluebird	American	Circle	X	X			Folkraft 1180: Bowmar A 1 No. 3
Rig-a-Jig-Jig	American	Circle			X	X	Folkraft 1199, Pioneer 1199
Mulberry Bush	English	Circle	X	X			Bowmar A1 Folkraft 1183
Thread Follows The Needle					X	X	Bowmar A C III
London Bridge	English	lines	X	X			RCA 45-5065 A, Bowmar 36 A1 (2)
Little Miss Muffet	English			X	X		Childhood Rhythms. Series 7 No. 703
I Should Like to Go to Shetland	English	Circle	X	X			Folkraft 1190
Sing a Song of Sixpence	English	Circle			X	X	Folkraft 1180
Carrousel (Merry-go-Round)	Swedish	Circle			X	X	Folkraft 1183, RCA Victor 41-6179; Pioneer 3004-A
Hansel and Gretel	German	Circle			X	X	Folkraft 1193

*See supplementary list of singing games.
**See Selected References for addresses of Record Companies.

No. 1: Baa, Baa, Black Sheep (K)

Musical Accompaniment
Childhood Rhythms, Series 7,
No. 701

Measure Song

1-8 Baa, baa, black sheep,
  Have you any wool?
  Yes sir, yes sir,
  Three bags full.

1-8 One for my master,
  One for my dame,
  And one for the little boy
  Who lives in the lane.

Formation
Single circle, facing center and hands
joined. One child in center of circle.

Pattern

Eight walking steps right. Place hands
on hips and nod on word "yes," hold
three fingers up on word "three" and
arms out to show a large bag.

Turn right and bow or curtsy
Turn left and bow or curtsy
Face center and bow or curtsy.

No. 2: Hickory, Dickory, Dock (K)

Musical Accompaniment
Childhood Rhythms, Series 7,
No. 702
Square Dance Associates
Album 12, No. 8

Measure Song
1-4 Hickory, dickory, dock!
5-8 The mouse ran up the clock

1-4 The clock struck one,
  The mouse ran down,
5-8 Hickory, Dickory, Dock.

Formation
Double circle with inside hands on
partner's shoulder and both facing
counterclockwise. One child is the
"mouse," the other the "clock."

Pattern
Sway toward center of circle.
Sway toward outside. Stamp one foot,
then the other.
Mouse runs clockwise around his partner then stamps feet as above. Clock
claps hands on word "one." Mouse
runs counterclockwise. Repeat swaying and stamping movements.

No. 3: Ring Around The Rosy (K-1)

Musical Accompaniment
Folkraft 1199
Measure Song
1-6 Ring-a-Round a Rosy
  A pocket full of posies,
  Ashes, ashes*
  All fall down.
7-8

Formation
Single circle, players join hands
and face center.
Pattern
With joined hands, walk or skip
around the circle.

Drop to a squatting position.

---

*Other words are "hush-a, hush-a", "at-choo, at-choo" or "one, two, three".

Teaching suggestions:
Use the following verse as a substitute for the one described.
Ring around the rosy,
A pocket full of posies,
One, two, three,
And squat where you be.

No. 4: Farmer In The Dell (K-1)

Musical Accompaniment	Formation
Folkraft 1182	Single circle facing center with hands
RCA Victor 45-5066 A	joined. One child, (the "farmer") is
Bowmar Singing Games, Album II	in the center of the circle.

Measure	Song	Pattern
1-2	The farmer in the dell,	All walking left around circle, singing
3-4	The farmer in the dell,	verse while the "farmer" looks about
5-6	Heigh-ho! the cherry-o,	for a wife.
7-8	The farmer in the dell	Continue to walk around circle as
1-2	The farmer takes a wife,	"farmer" chooses a wife who joins him
3-4	The farmer takes a wife,	at center of circle.
5-6	Heigh-ho! the cherry-o,	Repeat procedure as directed.
7-8	The farmer takes a wife.	Repeat procedure as directed.
1-8	The wife takes the child, etc.	Repeat procedure as directed.
1-8	The child takes the nurse, etc.	Repeat procedure as directed.
1-8	The nurse takes the dog, etc.	Repeat procedure as directed.
1-8	The dog takes the cat, etc.	Repeat procedure as directed.
1-8	The cat takes the rat, etc.	Children in center crowd around
1-8	The rat takes the cheese, etc.	"cheese" and clap their hands over
1-8	The cheese stands alone	the "cheese's" head, while circle play-
1-8	The farmer runs away, etc.	ers stand still, clap hands, and sing
1-8	Repeat for each player as he leaves center of circle.	verse.

Continue walking as the "farmer," then wife, etc. leave the center of circle.
Note: "Cheese" remains and becomes the new "farmer."

Teaching suggestions:
This song may be sung "derry-o," "dairy-o," or "the dearie-o."

No. 5: "Sally Go Round The Moon" (K-1)

Musical Accompaniment	Formation
Folkraft 1198	Single circle facing center with hands
RCA Victor 45-5064	joined.

Measure	Song	Pattern
1-8	Sally, go round the stars, Sally, go round the moon, Sally, go round the chimney pots, On a Sunday afternoon Whoops! (or Who-ee)	Walk, run, skip, or slide around the circle. On the word "whoops," all jump into air and clap hands or perform any movement they wish.
1-8	Repeat above	Repeat action in opposite direction.

No. 6: The Muffin Man (K-1)

Musical Accompaniment

Folkraft 1188

RCA Victor 45-5065

Formation

Single circle facing center with one child (the "muffin man") in the center of the circle.

Measure	Song	Pattern
1-2	Oh, have you seen the muffin man,	Children join hands and circle to the left using a walk or a slow skip step.
3-4	The muffin, the muffin man,	
5-6	Oh, have you seen the muffin man,	
7-8	Who lives in Drury Lane?*	
1-2	Oh yes, we've seen the muffin man,	Children in circle stand facing center and clap hands while singing "The Muffin Man." The child in center chooses a partner from circle and brings him or her back to center. (Skaters position.) This child becomes the new "muffin man" while the "old" partner returns to circle.
3-4	The muffin man, the muffin man	
5-6	Oh yes, we've seen the muffin man,	
7-8	Who lives in Drury Lane.	

Teaching suggestions:

With large numbers of children start with two muffin men in center of circle.

No. 7: Loobie Loo (K-1)

Musical Accompaniment

Folkraft 1184

RCA Victor 45-5067

Childhood Rhythms

Series 7, No. 706

Bowmar Singing Games

Album 1, No. 1514

Formation

Single circle facing center with hands joined.

Measure	Song	Pattern
1-3	Here we go Loobie Loo,	Circle left using a walk, skip, or slide step. Sing chorus at start, between
3-4	Here we go Loobie Light,	

---

*Substitute "across the way" as an American adaption.

5-6 Here we go Loobie Loo,

7-8 All on a Saturday night. Song (Verse No. 1):

stanzas, and at end of game.

Everyone drops hands and faces center.

1-2 I put my right hand in,

Place right hand toward center of circle.

3-4 I put my right hand out,

5-6 I give my hand a shake, shake, shake

Turn, place right hand away from circle.

Shake hand.

7-8 And turn myself about.

Turn in place.

Verse:

No: Repeat chorus after each verse.

2. I put my left hand in, etc.

3. I put my both hands in, etc.

4. I put my right foot in, etc.

5. I put my left foot in, etc.

6. I put my elbows in, etc.

7. I put my shoulders in, etc.

8. I put my big head in, etc.

9. I put my whole self in, etc.

Repeat each verse according to the movement suggested.

No. 8: Did you Ever See a Lassie (K-1)

Musical Accompaniment
Folkraft 1183
RCA Victor 45-5066
Pioneer 3012-B
Bowmar Album 1.

Formation
Single circle facing center with hands joined. One child is in the center of the circle.

Measure Song

1-8 Did you ever see a lassie, ("laddie" when boy is in center)
A lassie, a lassie,
Did you ever see a lassie,
Go this way and that?
Chorus

Pattern
All join hands and skip to left swinging joined hands.

9-16 Go this way and that way.
Go this way and that way.
Did you ever see a lassie
Go this way and that?

All stop, release hands, face child in center and imitate his movements. Repeat singing game with a new leader in the center.

Teaching suggestions:

Once the children have learned the basic movements, have them create impressions such as birds, animals, mechanical toys, etc. Also instead of skipping, walk using swing and sway, stamping, and clapping.

No. 9: How D'Ye Do My Partner (1-2)

Musical Accompaniment	Formation
Folkraft 1190	Double circle with partners facing.
Pioneer 3012	Girls are on the outside circle.
RCA Victor 21 685	
Bowmar, Album 1, No. 1513 A	

Measure	Song	Pattern
1-2	How d'ye do my partner	Boys bow to partners.
3-4	How d'ye do today?	Girls curtsy to partners.
5-6	Will you skip in a circle?	Boy offers hand to partner.
7-8	I will show you the way.	Join inside hands and turn counter-clockwise.

Chorus:

1-8	Tra, la, la, la, la, la, Tra, la, la, la, la, la, Tra, la, la, la, la, la, Tra, la, la, la, la, la,	With joined hands, skip around the circle.
1-6	Repeat song	Repeat directions 1-6
7-8	And I thank you, Good day.	Stop, release hands, face partner; boys bow and girls curtsy. Change partners by players in both circles moving one step to their own right and repeat singing game.

No. 10: Oats, Peas, Beans, and Barley (1-2)

Musical Accompaniment	Formation
Folkraft 1182	Single circle facing center with hands joined. One child in the center of the circle is the "farmer."
RCA Victor 45-5067	
Folk Dancer MH 1110-A	
Pioneer 3012	

Measure	Song	Pattern
1-2	Oats, peas, beans, and barley grow,	"Farmer" in center of circle stands while children in circle circle left with small walking steps.
3-4	Oats, peas, beans, and barley grow,	
5-6	Do you or I or anyone know	
7-8	How oats, peas, beans, and barley grow?	
1-2	First the farmer sows his seed,	Children in circle stop, face center, and all dramatize words of song.
3-4	Then he stands and takes his ease,	

5-6 Stamps his foot and claps his
hand,
7-8 And turns around to view the
land.
1-2 Waiting for a partner,   Children in circle skip left as "farmer"
3-4 Waiting for a partner,   skips around inside circle and picks
5-6 Open the ring and choose one   a new partner. "Farmer" and new
in.   partner skip around inside circle.
7-8 While we all gaily dance and
sing.
Song
Tra, la, la, la, la, la   The two "farmers" continue to skip
Tra, la, la, la, la, la   inside the circle while others join
Tra, la, la, la, la, la, la, la   hands and circle left. "Old farmer"
Tra, la, la, la, la, la   joins the ring and "new farmer" repeats pattern.

No. 11: A Hunting We Will Go (1-2)

Musical Accompaniment   Formation
Folkraft F1191   Two parallel lines facing each other
RCA Victor 45-5064   with girls on one side and boys on the
Childhood Rhythms,   other.
Series 7, No. 705.
Measure   Song   Pattern
1-4 Oh, a-hunting we will go, A-   Head couples join inside hands and
hunting we will go,   skip down between lines to the foot
      of the set.
5-8 We'll catch a fox and put him   Head couple turn around, change
in a box.   hands and skip back to head of set.
And then we'll let him go.   All other players clap hands while
Chorus: head couple is skipping down and
      back.
1-8 Tra, la, la, la, la, la, la,   Head couple skips around the left side
Tra, la, la, la, la, la,   of set followed by other couples. When
Tra, la, la, la, la, la,   the head couple reach the foot of the
la, la, la, la,   line they form an arch under which
Tra, la, la, la, la, la,   all other couples pass through. Head
      couple remains while the second cou-
      ple becomes the head couple.

No. 12: Round and Round the Village (1-2)

(Go In and Out the Windows)

Musical Accompaniment

Folkraft 1191

Pioneer 3001-B

Formation

Single circle with all facing center and hands joined. One or more players are on the outside of the circle.

Measure	Song	Pattern
1-2	Go round and round the village,	Children join hands and hold them high as "it" (s) skip to the right around the outside.
3-4	Go round and round the village,	
5-6	Go round and round the village,	
7-8	As we have done before.	
1-2	Go in and out the windows,	"It" skips in and out under the raised arms (windows)
3-4	Go in and out the windows,	
5-6	Go in and out the windows,	
7-8	As we have done before.	
1-2	Now go and choose a partner,	"It" skips around the inside of circle, stops and bows or curtsies in front of a partner he or she has chosen.
3-4	Now go and choose a partner,	
5-6	Now go and choose a partner,	
7-8	As we have done before.	
1-2	Now follow me to London	"It" skips around inside the circle followed by his new partner. Circle players skip in the opposite direction.
3-4	Now follow me to London	
5-6	Now follow me to London,	
7-8	As we have done before.	
1-2	Shake hands before you leave me,	The circle players remain in place, clap their hands and sing while inside players shake hands and bow or curtsy. The chosen player(s) then go to the outside of the circle while other players return to the circle.
3-4	Shake hands before you leave me,	
5-6	Shake hands before you leave me,	
7-8	As we have done before.	

No. 13: Jolly is the Miller (2-3)

Musical Accompaniment

Folkraft 1192

Childhood Rhythms, Series 6

No. 602

Formation

Partners form a double circle with girls on outside. One player (the "miller") stands in the center.

RCA Victor 45-5067

Measure	Song	Pattern
1-2	Jolly is the miller who lives by the mill.	Couples join inside hands and walk counterclockwise singing the song. During the second line children in inner circle extend left arms sideward to form a mill wheel. On the last word of the song, ("back"), partners drop hands and children in inner circle step forward while those in outer circle step backward. The extra player tries to secure a partner during this exchange. The child without a partner goes to the center. Repeat entire dance with new partner.
3-4	The wheel turns around of its own free will,	
5-6	One hand in the hopper and the other in the sack,	
7-8	The hub goes forward and the rim turns back.	

No. 14: Shoo Fly (2-3)

Musical Accompaniment
Folkraft 1185

Measure Song

Formation
Double circle with girls on the outside.
Pattern

1-2 Shoo, fly, don't bother me;
Shoe, fly, don't bother me.

Players join hands and walk four steps toward center, then four steps backward.
Repeat 1-2.

3-4 Shoo, fly, don't bother me,
For I belong to somebody.
5-8 Repeat 1-4
Chorus

Repeat 1-4.

9-16 I feel, I feel,
I feel like a morning star;
I feel, I feel,
I feel like a morning star.

Partners join hands and walk around each other in clockwise direction. Repeat. On last "morning star," boy raises his left hand and turns his partner under his arm. Girl is now on boy's left. The girl on the boy's right becomes his new partner.
Join hands and repeat dance.

No. 15: Paw Paw Patch (3)

Musical Accompaniment
Folkraft 1181
Burns Wheeler, Album 6, No. 516

Formation
Columns of four to six couples with partners facing.

Measure	Song	Pattern
1-2	Where, O where is sweet little Sally?	First girl turns right and circles clockwise and goes once around the set, with sixteen skipping steps.
3-4	Where, O where is sweet little Sally?	
5-6	Where, O where is sweet little Sally?	
7-8	Way down yonder in the paw paw patch.	
1-2	Come on, boys, let's go find her,	First girl takes the first boy's left hand in her right hand and leads line of boys around the set. Boys may join hands.
3-4	Come on, boys, let's go find her,	
5-6	Come on, boys, let's go find her,	Girls in line clap hands. All finish in place facing the front.
7-8	Way down yonder in paw paw patch.	
1-2	Pickin' up paw paws, putting 'em in her pocket,	Partners join hands and follow first couple once around to the right. First couple turns away from each other with boy going left and girl going right, and skip to the foot of line. The rest of the line moves one place forward.
3-4	Pickin' up paw paws, putting 'em in her pocket.	
5-6	Pickin' up paw paws, putting 'em in her pocket,	
7-8	Way down yonder in paw paw patch.	Repeat entire dance with each new "first" girl leading.

No. 16: Skip to My Lou (3)

Musical Accompaniment	Formation
Bowmar Singing Games Album 3, No. 1522-A	Single circle with partners side by side. Girl is on boy's right.
Folkraft 1192	
Folk Dancers MH 111-A	
Pioneer 3003-A	

Measure	Song	Pattern
	Verse No. 1	
1-2	Boys to the center, Skip to my Lou,	Boys walk four steps forward and four steps backward.
3-4	Boys to the outside, Skip to my Lou,	Repeat 1-4.
5-6	Boys to the center, Skip to my Lou,	

7-8 Skip to my Lou, my darling.
   Verse No. 2

1-2 Girls to the center, Skip to Repeat pattern as described above.
   my Lou,

3-4 Girls to outside, Skip to my
   Lou,

5-6 Girls to the center, Skip to
   my Lou,

7-8 Skip to my Lou, my darling.
   Verse No. 3

1-6 Swing your partner, Skip to Partners join both hands and swing
   my Lou, (3 times)   or skip around in place.

7-8 Skip to my Lou, my darling.
   Verse No. 4

1-6 I've lost my partner now   Release hands and girls walk forward,
   what'll I do (3 times)   boys turn and walk in the opposite
                  direction.

7-8 Skip to my Lou, my darling.
   Verse No. 5

1-6 I've got another one, prettier New partners promenade counter-
   too, (3 times)   clockwise to original position with

7-8 Skip to my Lou, my darling. girl on boy's right.
                  Repeat dance with new partner.

FOLK DANCES

Traditional and Contemporary dances are dance patterns of past and present cultures. Generally speaking, when a dance such as Gustaf's Skoal has been handed down from many generations, it is designated as a traditional folk dance. On the other hand, a dance which originates within our own generation and is performed to recent or popular music is usually designated as a contemporary dance. Examples of the latter would be the "Patty Cake Dance," "Hitch Hiker," and the "Twist." Both types of dances, however, express some aspect of the culture from which they originated. The "Danish Dance of Greeting" and "Sicilian Circle" are examples of how dances can be used as a method of greeting or meeting others. Other dances, such as the "Sailor's Hornpipe" and our American "Indian Dance," are part of a ceremonial or religious custom.

How to Teach Traditional and Contemporary Dances

Obviously there is no "best way" of teaching children traditional and contemporary dances. The method a teacher uses will depend upon such factors as the age of the children, their previous dance experience, and the difficulty of the dance that is being introduced. The following suggestions should be given consideration when developing a basic approach to teaching these dances.

1. Acquire a general background of the people and customs of each dance selected for presentation to the class.
2. Present the background information about the dance in relationship to class interest and maturity. Make it meaningful to the children.
3. Use audiovisual aids such as costumes, scenery, and folk songs to stimulate interest and a deeper understanding of the people and customs represented in the dance.
4. Allow the children to hear the music prior to learning the dance patterns.
5. Teach the dance by phases rather than by counts.
6. When teaching the steps of the dance, use a slower tempo; after it is learned, increase the tempo to the appropriate speed of the dance.
7. Look for general problems such as starting off with the wrong foot, and correct these difficulties; later, provide individual assistance.
8. When teaching a dance, indicate any change in dance formation just before the beginning of the new phase.
9. Encourage creative expression within the pattern of the dance. Many of the older traditional dances may require movements that are uncomfortable or too rigid for children to perform. Where creative variations do not change the basic theme of the dance, they should be encouraged.
10. Avoid spending too much time on one dance.

TRADITIONAL AND CONTEMPORARY DANCES

No.		Type of Dance	Origin	Page	Grade Level						
					K	1	2	3	4	5	6
1.	Children's Polka	Circle	German	564	X	X	X				
2.	Danish Dance of Greeting	Circle	Danish	565		X	X				
3.	Circassian Circle	Circle	English	565		X	X	X			
4.	Pop Goes the Weasel	Circle	American	566			X	X			
5.	Bleking	Circle	Swedish	566			X				
6.	Cshebogar	Circle	Hungarian	567				X	X		
7.	Glow Worm Mixer	Circle	American	567				X			
8.	Little Brown Jug	Circle	American	568				X			
9.	Grand March	Line	American	568				X	X	X	
10.	Oh Susanna	Circle	American	569				X	X		
11.	Schottische	Circle	Scottish	569				X	X		
12.	Badger Gavotte	Circle	American	570				X	X		
13.	Norwegian Mountain March	Circle	Norwegian	570				X	X		
14.	Heel and Toe Polka	Circle	German	571					X	X	
15.	Oklahoma Mixer	Circle	American	571					X	X	
16.	Rye Waltz	Circle	American	572					X	X	

Supplementary List of Traditional and Contemporary Dances

Name	Origin	Formation	K	1	2	3	4	5	6	Record Source
Shoemaker's Dance	Danish	circle		X	X					Folkraft 1187; RCA EPA 4141, Bowmar Album 4 RCA 6176
Chimes of Dunkirk	French	circle		X	X					
Jingle Bells	American				X	X				
Jump Jim Joe	American				X	X				Folkraft 1180; Bowmar, Album 3
Gustaf's Skoal	Swedish	quadrille				X	X	X		Bowmar, Album 4, Folkraft 1175
Greensleeves	English	circle				X	X			
Seven Steps	German	circle				X	X			World of Fun, M-101; Folkraft 1163
Troika	Russian	threes					X	X	X	World of Fun 105;
Mayim	Israeli	circle					X	X	X	Folkraft 1108
Hop Morr Anika	Swedish	circle					X	X	X	RCA 4142
Crested Hen	Danish	threes						X	X	RCA 6176
Road to The Isles	Scottish	couples					X	X	X	IMP 1005A
Horah	Israeli	circle					X	X	X	Folkraft 1110
Jessie Polka	American	couples						X	X	Folkraft 1071
Put Your Little Foot	American	couple						X	X	Folkraft 1165
Highland Schottische	Scottish	circle						X	X	RCA 45-6179
Varsovienne	American	circle							X	Windsor 7516
Manitow	Canadian	circle						X	X	Lloyd Shaw 6-141

No. 1: Children's Polka (Kinderpolka) (1-3)

Musical Accompaniment
RCA Victor 45-6179
Burns, Evans and Wheeler
   Album 1, No. 124
Pioneer 3004-B

Formation
Single circle with partners facing, both arms extended sideward with hands joined.

Measure	Action
1-2	Take two slides toward center; step lightly three times.
3-4	Take two slides away from center; step lightly three times.
5-8	Repeat action of measure 1-4.
9-10	Slap own knees once, clap own hands once, and clap partner's hands three times.

11-12 Repeat action of measures 9-10.
13   Hop, placing right heel forward, place right elbow in left hand and shake finger three times.
14   Repeat action of Measure 13 with left foot.
15-16 Turn in place with four running steps and step lightly three times.

Teaching suggestions:
To help children learn dance pattern, count in this manner:
Step, step, tap, tap, tap. Repeat.
Slap, clap, clap, clap, clap. Repeat.
Hop, one, two, three. Repeat.
Turn around now, tap, tap, tap.

No. 2: Danish Dance of Greeting (2-3)

Musical Accompaniment	Formation
Folkraft 1187	Single circle of couples with all facing
RCA Victor 41-6183	center. The girl is on the right side of
Pioneer 3014-B	the boy.
Burns, Evans and Wheeler,	
Album 1, No. 126 (with words)	

Measure	Song	Pattern
1.	Clap, clap, bow.	Clap hands twice, turn and bow to partner (girls should curtsy).
2.	Clap, clap, bow.	Clap hands twice and bow to child on the other side (neighbor).
3.	Stamp, stamp.	Stamp on the right then on the left foot.
4.	Turn yourself around.	Turn around in place with four running steps.
5-8	Repeat words.	Repeat all.
9-12	Tra, la, la, la, la, etc.	All join hands and circle to the right with sixteen short running steps.
13-16	Tra, la, la, la, la, etc.	Repeat action to the left.

No. 3: Circassian Circle (Mixer) (2-4)

Musical Accompaniment	Formation
Folkraft 1247	Single circle of couples with all facing center. Girl is on the boy's right side.

Measure	Action
1-4	All join hands and walk four steps toward center of circle, then four steps backward.
5-8	Girls walk four steps toward the center, clapping on the fourth step, and four steps backward to place.
9-12	Boys walk four steps to center, then turn left and walk forward three steps to girl who was originally on his left.

13-16 Boys take four skips with new partner, and four walking steps (promenade) around circle, with girls on the outside.

Repeat dance with new partners.

No. 4: Pop Goes the Weasel (3-4)

Musical Accompaniment	Formation
Childhood Rhythms, Series 4, No. 403 (words)	Double circle in sets of four children. Girl is on partner's right. Couples facing clockwise are couples No. 1, while
World of Fun, M-104-B	couples facing counterclockwise are
Folkraft 1329	couples No. 2.

Measure   Action

1-4   Join hands in a circle of four and circle left with eight skipping or sliding steps.

5-6   Walk two steps forward raising joined hands then two steps backward lowering hands.

7-8   Couples No. 1 raise their joined hands to form an arch as No. 2 couples pass under. No. 2 couples continue forward to meet new couples.

Variation of Pop Goes the Weasel

Formation

Three children form a set with two children joining inside hands. The third child stands in front with his back to the other two and extends his hands back and holds the outside hands of the other two. All three face counterclockwise in a large circle.

Measure   Action

1-6   All sets skip around in a large circle.

7-8   On "pop" the child in front skips backward under the raised inside hands of the back couple and continues backward meeting the couple behind him.

9-14   Repeat measures 1-6.

15-16   Repeat measures 7-8.

No. 5: Bleking (3)

Musical Accompaniment	Formation
Pioneer 3016	Single circle with partners facing. Part-
Folkraft 1188	ners extend arms forward at shoulder
Childhood Rhythms, Series 8, No. 804	height and join hands.
RCA Victor 41-6169	

Measure	Action
1-8	Hop on left foot, right heel forward, right arms forward and pull left arm back. (Count 1.) Continue for seven more counts.
9-12	Partners facing, arms extended sidewards and hands joined. Take seven step-hops clockwise and end with a stamp on last count. Child with back to center starts with left foot; other partner starts with right. Dance two step hops per measure moving arms down and up with each step hop.
13-16	Turn counterclockwise and repeat seven step hops, ending with a stamp.

Teaching suggestions:

Teach the Bleking step in a single circle formation and without partners.

No. 6: Cshebogar (4-5)

Musical Accompaniment	Formation
Folkraft 1196	Single circle of couples with hands joined. Couples facing center with girl on boy's right side.

Measure	Action
1-4	Take eight slide steps to the left.
5-8	Take eight slide steps to the right.
1-4	Four walking steps to the center, raising the hands high as you go. Four walking steps backward to place lowering hands as you return.
5-8	Face partner and place right hand on his or her waist. Raise left arm and pull away from partner and skip around him. (This is a Hungarian turn.)
1-4	Face partner, join hands with arms held at shoulder height. Slide four steps slowly toward the center of the circle bending toward the center as you slide. Boys start with left foot and girls with right foot.
5-8	Four step-draw steps outward.
1-4	Two draw steps in and two draw steps out.
5-8	Then do the Hungarian turn again.

No. 7: Glow Worm Mixer (4)

Musical Accompaniment	Formation
MacGregor 310-B	Players form a double circle and all
Windsor 4613-B	face counterclockwise. Boy stands on inside circle and holds the girl's left hand in his right.

Measure	Action
1-2	Walk forward four steps.
3-4	Partners face each other, then boys, beginning with left foot, take four short steps backward and away, while girls do same.

5-6   All face diagonally to the right. Start on left foot and walk four steps and meet new partner.

7-8   New partner joins hands and walks four steps clockwise in a small circle. Repeat dance with new partner.

No. 8: Little Brown Jug (4)

Musical Accompaniment
Columbia 36021
Folkraft 1204

Formation
Double circle with partners facing each other. Hands are joined and raised to shoulder height. Girls are on the outside circle.

Measure

Action

1-8   Boy touches his left heel to side then left toe next to right foot. Repeat movement. Take four slide steps to the left. Girls start with outside foot and do the same.

9-16   Repeat measures one through eight with four slides to the right.

17-24 Clap own thighs four times then own hands together four times.

25-32 Partners clap right hands together four times then left hands together four times.

33-40 Hook right elbows with partner and skip around in a circle with eight skipping steps.

41-56 Repeat clapping sequence of measures seventeen to twenty-four and twenty-five to thirty-two.

57-64 Hook left elbows and repeat turns.

No. 9: Grand March (4-6)

Musical Accompaniment
Any marching record

Formation
Boys line up on one side of the room and girls on the other side. All face the foot of the room. The teacher stands in the center of the end line at the head of the room.

Call

Action

Come down the center in twos.

March to meet partners at the foot of the room. As the couples meet they turn, join hands, and march to the head of the room where the teacher is standing to give directions.

Twos right and twos left.

The first couple turns to the right, the second to the left, etc.

Come down the center in fours.

When the two head couples meet at the foot of the room, they hold hands and walk four abreast down the center.

Fours right and fours left.

Come down the center in eights.

When children reach the front of the room, they divide again with four going to the right and four going to the left, etc.

When the lines of fours meet at the front of the room, join hands to form a line of eight abreast. The lines of eight march to the head of the room and halt.

Note: This process may be reversed with lines of eight dividing into columns of four. The column of fours march back to the other end of the room where the two columns merge into one column of fours. The fours divide at the head of the room, etc. until all are back to original position of one couple.

No. 10: Oh Susanna (4-5)

Musical Accompaniment
RCA Victor 45-6178
Folkraft 1186

Formation
Partners stand in a single circle, face center with hands joined. The girl is on the boy's right side.

Measure

Action

1-16 All take eight sliding steps to the right and eight sliding steps to the left.

1-4   All take four steps to the center and four steps back.

5-8   Repeat measures one through four.

1-4   Release hands and girls walk four steps toward center of circle and four steps back. Boys stand in place and clap hands.

5-8   Boys to center while girls clap hands.

1-2   Do-si-do with partner.

3-4   Do-si-do with corner girl.

5-8   Everyone promenade around the circle.

No. 11: Schottische (4-5)

Musical Accompaniment
MacGregor 400A
Folkraft 1101

Formation
Double circle with partners facing counterclockwise. Boys are on the inside circle and hold partners in an open dance position.

Measure   Action
1-2   Partners start with outside foot, run forward three steps and hop on outside foot and extend inside foot forward.
3-4   Begin with inside foot and repeat action.
5-6   All perform four step-hops in place.

Repeat the first six measures as often as desired or substitute the following variations for measures five and six.

Variation One: Partners drop hands and dance four skip-hops in place, turning away from each other on the first step and ending in the starting position on the fourth step-hop.

Variation Two: Gents take four step-hops in place and girls turn under their arms. On the next turn, reverse movements with the gents turning under the girls' raised arms.

Variation Three: Partners join hands about waist high and both turn under raised arms, continue around and back to the starting position.

No. 12: Badger Gavotte (4-5)

Musical Accompaniment	Formation
MacGregor 610B	Double circle with couples facing counterclockwise. Partners join hands. Girl is on the boy's right side.
Folkraft 1094	

Measure   Action
1-2   Begin with the outside foot (boy's left; girl's right), walk forward four steps, face partner, join both hands, take three slide steps to the boy's left, and touch right toe behind left foot.
3-4   Repeat measures one and two in the opposite direction.
5-8   Change to a closed dance position and all take eight two-steps progressing counterclockwise with boys starting with left foot and girls with right foot. Repeat dance until music ends.

No. 13: Norwegian Mountain March (4-5)

Musical Accompaniment	Formation
Folkraft 1177	Circle in sets of three children and all facing counterclockwise. The "set" is composed of one boy in the center and slightly in front of the two side girls. The boy holds inside hands of two side girls and the two girls join outside hands forming a triangle.
RCA Victor 45-6173	

Measure   Action
1-8   Starting with right foot, all take eight step-hops forward. All should accent the first step of each measure and the leader should occasionally glance over his right and left shoulders at his partners.

9-10 Boys move backward with step-hops under the raised arms of the two girls.

11-12 Girl of right side of set turns under the boy's left arm with four step-hops.

13-14 Girl on the left side of the set turns under the boy's right arm with four step-hops.

15-16 Boys now turn under their own left hand with four step-hops.
Repeat entire dance as often as desired.

No. 14: Heel and Toe Polka (5-6)

Musical Accompaniment
Burns, Evans and Wheeler
Album 2, No. 225
Folkraft 1166
MacGregor 400B

Formation
Double circle with partners facing counterclockwise. Open dance position with girl on boy's right side.

Measure   Action

1-2 Partners touch outside heel forward and bend slightly backward. Touch toes of outside foot backward and bend slightly forward and take three running steps forward. (Heel and toe, and step, step, step.)

3-4 Repeat 1-2 with inside foot.

5-8 Repeat measures one to four.

9-16 Partners face each other, boy places hands at girl's waist and girl places hands on boy's shoulders. All polka around circle in counterclockwise direction.

No. 15: Oklahoma Mixer (5-6)

Musical Accompaniment
Folkraft 1035
Methodist World of Fun 102
MacGregor 400

Formation
Double circle of couples with girl on boy's right side. Take the Varsovienne position with left foot free.

Measure   Action

1-2 Begin with left foot, take two two-steps.

3-4 Begin with left foot, take four walking steps forward.

5-8 Repeat measures one through four.

9-12 Place left heel forward and to the left, then left toe opposite right foot. Hold left hand, release right, girls walk to center of circle in front of boys as boys move to the outside of circle. The girls finish facing clockwise and boys facing counterclockwise.

13-16 Boy does a right heel and toe and takes three steps in place. Girl does a right heel and toe and walks to boy behind.
Repeat dance with new partner.

No. 16: Rye Waltz (5-6)

Musical Accompaniment

Folkraft 1103

Formation

Double circle with boys in the center facing girls. Partners take an open dance position.

Measure

Action

1-4   Boys extend toe of left foot to the side and return to inside of right foot. Repeat point and close. (Girl performs same movement with right foot.) Girl takes three slide steps to the boy's left and touches right toe behind left foot.

5-8   Repeat in opposite direction.

9-16   Waltz around the room with boys using their right shoulders to lead.

SQUARE DANCES

American folk dances include mixers, couples, longways, circles, and square dances that have been developed in this country during the past few hundred years. Of all these American folk dances, square dances have become the most popular with upper elementary school children. There is no single reason, however, for this growth in popularity. Probably the simplicity of the steps involved and the enjoyment of participation could well be two important reasons for their general appeal.

Additional teaching suggestions are listed following to assist teachers in presenting the various types of square dance patterns. A list of basic terms that are used in square dances is also provided in the accompanying pages.

1. Emphasize fun and enjoyment rather than the perfection of each and every skill.
2. Teach all square dance movements from a circle formation with girls standing on the right side of the boys.
3. Select square dances that involve simple patterns and introduce them at a slower speed.
4. When the dance is learned the teacher should call the dance patterns without music, then with a musical accompaniment. Once the dance is learned, the teacher may continue to call her own dance or use a record with the calls included.
5. The majority of square dancing is done with a shuffle step rather than a run or a hop. Hence, emphasize a smooth and graceful slipping action with the landing phase on the ball of the foot rather than on the heel.
6. The success of square dancing depends, in part, upon keeping the square of four couples symmetrical and partners parallel. Constantly check to see that children maintain the square and partners do not wander away from each other.
7. Encourage children not only to call their own dances, but, in addition, to create their own sequences of square dance figures.

SQUARE DANCES

No.	Name	Type	Page	Suggested Grade Level						
				K	1	2	3	4	5	6
1	Sicilian Circle	circle	573					X	X	X
2	Virginia Reel	longways	574				X	X	X	X
3	Solomon Levi	square	575					X	X	X
4	Oh Johnny	circle	576					X	X	X
5	Red River Valley	square	576						X	X

Supplementary List of American Square Dances

Name	Origin	Formation	Grade Level				Record Source
			3	4	5	6	
Texas Star (with call)	American	Square			X	X	Folkraft 1256
Hinky Dinky Parley Vous (with call)	French	Square		X	X	X	Folkraft 1023
Let's Square Dance (Caller Dick Crews)	American	Square		X	X	X	RCA 3001 (Album 1 and 2)
Jonsey Square Dances (Caller Fenton Jones)	American	Square		X	X	X	MacGregor (Album 4, 7, 8)

No. 1: Sicilian Circle (4-6)

Musical Accompaniment
Windsor A7S4A

Formation
Circle of "sets of four" with couple facing couple. The girl should be on partner's right side.

Measures	Call	Action
1-2	Now everybody forward and back.	Join inside hands with partner. Four steps forward toward opposite couple and four steps backward to place.
5-8	Circle four hands around.	Join hands and circle left with eight walking steps and finish in original places.
1-4	Ladies chain.	Ladies chain across and back with the two ladies changing places. The gentleman takes the approaching lady's left hand in his left, places his right arm around her waist and pivots backward to reface the opposite couple.

5-8	Chain the ladies back again.	The ladies return to their original positions with the same movement.
1-4	Right and left through.	Right and left with opposite couple, over and back. Walk forward to opposite's place, passing right shoulders with opposite, then keeping side by side as though inside hands were joined, turn half around as a couple (man turns backward while lady turns forward) and reface opposite.
5-8	Right and left back.	Repeat the same movement returning to original place.
1-4	Forward and back.	Forward and back.
5-8	Forward again, pass through.	All walk forward eight steps, passing opposite by right shoulder, to meet new couple.
Repeat dance with new couple.

No. 2: Virginia Reel (3-6)

Musical Accompaniment
Burns, Album J. No. 558
RCA Victor 45-6180
Folkraft 1249

Formation
Six couples in file formation with partners facing each other. Boys are on the caller's right.

Measure	Call	Action
1-8	Bow to your partner. Go forward and back. Go forward and back again.	Players take three skips forward and curtsy or bow, then skip back. Repeat.
9-12	Now forward again with right elbow swing, and all the way back.	Partners hook right elbows, turn once around, then back.
13-16	Now forward again with left elbow swing and all the way back.	Partners join left hands, turn once around, then back.
1-4	Now forward again with a two hand swing and all the way back.	Partners join both hands and turn clockwise and back.
5-8	Forward again with a do-si-do.	All partners do a do-si-do.
9-16	The head two sasshay down the middle and all the way back to the head of the set.	Head couple joins hands and slide down center of set and back.

2-8 Cast off, with boys going left and girls going right.	All face the caller with the boys' line skipping left and girls' line skipping right, ending at the foot of the set.
9-16 Form an arch and all pass through.	The head couple meets at the foot of the set, joins hands and raises them to form an arch. The second couple leads the other couples through the arch and moves to the head of the line to become the new head couple. Repeat dance with each new head couple.

No. 3: Solomon Levi (4-6)

Musical Accompaniment	Formation
MacGregor 007-4A (with call)	Square of four couples who are numbered counterclockwise. Girl is boy's right side.

Measure Call	Action
1-4 Everyone swing your honey; swing her high and low.	Swing partner.
5-16 Allemande left with left hand, and around the ring you go. A grand old right and left.	Left hand to corner, walk around corner back to partner. Extend right hand to partner, left to next lady, alternating right and left hands until partners meet.
Walk on your heel and toe and meet your honey, give her a twirl, and around the ring you go. Chorus:	Give partner a swing and promenade.
1-8 Oh Solomon Levi, tra la la la la la Oh Solomon Levi, tra la la la la la	All sing and promenade around set and back to home position.
1-4 First couple separate, go round the outside track,	Boy of couple one goes left and girl goes right around outside of set.
5-8 Keep going around the set, you pass coming back,	Continue around set to home position.
1-4 Pass right by your partner, salute your corners all,	Pass partner and bow to corner dancers.
5-8 Turn around and swing your own, and promenade the hall.	Turn and swing partners and promenade the hall.

1-8	Sing chorus.

Promenade around set.
Repeat dance with number two, three, and four couples leading. After couple four completes their turn, have all four couples separate and repeat dance.

No. 4: Oh Johnny (4-6)

Musical Accompaniment
MacGregor 652-A
  (with call)

Formation
Single circle with girls on boys' right. All join hands.

Measure Call

Action
All couples move to the right in walking steps.

1-4	All join hands and circle the ring.
5-8	Stop where you are and give your honey a swing.
9-12	Swing that litle gal behind you.
13-16	You swing your own.
1-4	Allemande left with the corner gal.
5-8	Do-si-do your own.

In closed dance position, swing partners.
Boy swings girl on his left.

Boy swings girl on his right.
Turn to corners, give left hand to corner girl, walk around her and return to partner. Fold arms and pass right shoulder to right shoulder around partner and back to the corner girl who becomes new partner.

9-12	Now you all promenade with your sweet corner maid,
13-16	Singing, "Oh, Johnny, Oh, Johnny, Oh."

Everyone promenade.

Repeat dance.

No. 5: Red River Valley (5-6)

Musical Accompaniment
Imperial 1096
MacGregor Album 8
  (with call)

Formation
Square of four couples who are numbered counterclockwise. Girl is on boy's right.

Measure Call

Action
Everyone joins hands.

1-4	All join hands in the valley.
5-8	And circle to the left and to the right.
1-4	And you swing the girl in the valley.

With joined hands, walk four steps left and back four steps to the right.
Boys swing corner girls (girl on boy's left).

5-8	Now swing that Red River Gal.	Boys return to their own partners and swing.
1-4	Now you lead right down the valley.	Number one and three couples walk to the couple on their right and join hands in a circle.
5-8	And you circle to the left then to the right.	Walk four steps to the left and back four steps to the right.
9-12	Two ladies star in the valley.	Girls star with right hands in the center of the set and walk once around clockwise.
13-16	Now swing with the Red River Gal.	Boys swing partners.
1-4	Same couples to the left down the valley.	Numbers one and three couples walk to their left and join hands with new couples.
5-8	And you circle to the left and to the right.	Walk four steps to the left and back four steps to the right.
9-12	Now two gents star in the valley.	Boys star with their right hands and turn once around clockwise.
13-16	And you swing that Red River Gal.	Everyone swings with their partner. Repeat entire dance with two side couples taking the active part. Instead of a star, do-si-do the second time and elbow swing the third, etc.

Glossary of Terms

The following words and phrases occur frequently in the folk and square dances for the intermediate grades.

Active couple(s): The couple(s) who are designated to start the dance or to whom a part of the dance is addressed.

Advance: To move in a forward direction usually with walking steps.

Allemande Left: From a circle or square formation with all dancers facing the center, the boy joins his left hand with the girl on his left and walks once around counterclockwise and back to starting position.

Allemande Right: Same as Allemande Left only toward opposite direction.

Arch: Two dancers join inside hands and raise arms upward to form an arch.

Balance: In square dancing the usual following a "swing your partner," partners face each other, join right hands, step back, with weight on the left foot, and with right heel touching in front. Both partners may also bow slightly.

Bow and Curtsy: The bow, performed by the boys, may be a simple nod of the head or an elaborate and pronounced deep bend of the trunk.

The curtsy, performed by the girls, may be a simple nod of the head or an elaborate and pronounced deep bend of the knees and a graceful sideward extension of dancing costume.

Break: Release hands.

Chain: (Ladies chain). In square dancing, the ladies move across to the opposite couple extending right hands to each other as they pass then left hands to opposite gent. The gent places his right hand behind lady's back grasping her right hand and turns her one full turn counterclockwise.

Clockwise: Move in the same direction as the hands of a clock.

Corner: When facing the center, the boy's corner is the girl on his left and the girl's corner is the boy on her right.

Counterclockwise: Move in the opposite direction as the hands of a clock.

Divide or Split the Ring: Active couples pass through the opposite couple.

Do-si-do: These words mean "back to back" and usually involve two persons facing each other. Two dancers walk forward, pass right shoulders and, without turning, move to the right passing back to back, then walk backward to starting position.

Forward and Back: This figure may involve one or more dancers facing each other. Both sides advance four steps forward (or three steps and a bow) and four steps backward.

Grand Right and Left: This is a weaving pattern and usually follows an Allemande Left. Face partner and join right hands, pass and give left hand to the next dancer, and continue weaving around set.

Head Couple: In square dancing, the head couple is the couple nearest to the music or caller.

Home: The original starting place at beginning of dance.

Honor: Salute or bow to partner or other dancers.

Opposite: The person or couple directly across the square.

Promenade: Partners join their inside hands in a skater's position and walk counterclockwise around set.

Sashay: This is the American term for the French term "chasse." These are sliding steps sideward.

Separate: Partners leave each other and move in opposite directions.

Square: Four couples with each forming one side of a square.

Star or Wheel: Two or more dancers join right hands in center of the set and walk forward or backward as directed.

Swing: This is a rhythmic rotation of a couple with a walking step, buzz step, two-step, or skip. The swing may be a one hand, two hand, elbow, or waist swing.

Varsovienne Position: The boy stands slightly behind and to the left of his partner. While both are facing the same direction, the girl raises both hands to about shoulder height and the boy joins his right hand with the girl's right hand; his left hand with the girl's left hand.

SELECTED REFERENCES

"A Guidebook for Rhythms in the Elementary School District No. 4," Lane County, Oregon: 1960.

ANDREWS, GLADYS; SAURHORN, JEANETTE; and SCHNEIDER, ELSA. *Physical Education for Today's Boys and Girls*. Boston: Allyn & Bacon, Inc., 1960.

ELLFELDT, LOIS. *Folk Dance*. Dubuque: Wm. C. Brown Company Publishers, 1969.

KADMAN, G., and HODES, T. *Israeli Folk Dances*. Tel Aviv: Education and Culture Centre, 1959.

KRAUS, R. *A Pocket Guide of Folk and Square Dances and Singing Games*, Prentice-Hall, Inc., 1966.

KULBITSKY, OLGA, and KALTMAN, FRANK L. *Teacher's Dance Handbook, Number One, Kindergarten to Sixth Year*. Newark: Bluebird Publishing Co., 1960.

LATCHAW, MARJORIE, and PYATT, JEAN. *Folk and Square Dances and Singing Games for Elementary Schools*. Englewood-Cliffs, New Jersey: Prentice-Hall, Inc., 1966.

MONSOUR, S., COHEN, M. C., and LINDELL, P. E. *Rhythm in Music and Dance for Children*. Belmont, California: 1966.

MURRAY, RUTH L. *Dance in Elementary Education*, Second Edition. New York: Harper & Row, Publishers, 1963.

MYNATT, C. V., and KAIMAN, B. D. *Folk Dancing: for Students and Teachers*. Dubuque: Wm. C. Brown Company Publishers, 1969.

O'RAFFERTY, P. *The Irish Folk Dance Book*. London: Peterson Publications Ltd., (with music).

"Physical Education for Boys and Girls: Course of Study, Elementary School, Grades 3-4," Curriculum Department, Elementary School Division, Modesto City Schools, Modesto, California, 1961.

"Physical Education Rhythmic Activities: Teaching Guide Grades 3, 4, 5, 6," Publication No. EC-198 Division of Instructional Services, Los Angeles City Schools, Los Angeles, 1958.

Society for International Folk Dancing. *A Selection of European Folk Dances, Vols. 1 and 2*. New York: Pergamon Press, Inc., 1964 (with music).

STUART, FRANCES R., and GIBSON, VIRGINIA L. *Rhythmic Activities: Series III*, Minneapolis: Burgess Publishing Co., 1961.

The Royal Scottish Country Dance Society. *Twenty-four Favourite Scottish Country Dances*. London: Paterson's Publications Ltd., (with music).

WAKEFIELD, E. E. *Folk Dancing in America*. New York: J. Lowell Pratt & Co., 1966.

SOURCES OF RECORDS

Bowmar Company, 12 Cleveland Street, Valhalla, New York.

Bowman Records, 4921 Santa Monica Blvd., Los Angeles 29, California.

Burns Record Company, 755 Chickadee Lane, Stratford, Conn.

Canadian Folk Dance Record Service, 605 King Street West, Toronto 2B, Ontario, Canada.

Childhood Rhythms, 326 Forest Park Avenue, Springfield, Massachusetts.

Columbia Records, 1473 Barnum Avenue, Bridgeport, Conn.

Folk Dancer, Box 201, Flushing, Long Island, New York.

Folkraft Record Company, 7 Oliver Street, Newark, New York.

Israeli Music Foundation, 731 Broadway, New York.

Lloyd Shaw Recording Co., Box 203, Colorado Springs, Colorado.

MacGregor Records, 2005 Labrance, Houston, Texas.

Methodist Publishing House, 150 Fifth Avenue, New York.
RCA Victor Record Division, 155 East 24th Street, New York.
Square Dance Associates, 102 N Columbus Avenue, Freeport, New York.
Windsor Records, 5528 North Rosemead Blvd., Temple City, California.

SUGGESTED FILMS

Title:	"Tinkling"
Details:	16 mm., 11 minutes, color, sound
Distributor:	General Learning Cooperation, 3 East 54th Street, New York
Description:	Instructions and teaching techniques for Philippine stick dances

Creative Rhythms

Pantomime Movements
Interpretative Movements
Resource Materials

C REATIVE rhythms are movements children use to communicate their understandings and to express their feelings about things and ideas. Through rhythmic pantomime or imitation children reveal their understanding of moving things. Initially the child must learn to move like "something" which may be an animal, a mechanical object, or a movement of nature. These pantomime movements may require an initial demonstration or general verbal guidance by the teacher. The second type of creative rhythms is interpretative movements used to express feelings rather than to imitate a particular thing or idea. The quality and direction of these movements are not dependent upon the direct guidance of the teacher. They must, to be truly interpretative, rely upon the mood, intelligence, and personal feelings of the child. With the latter movements, the teacher can set the stage and provide musical accompaniment for each child to express his own feelings and ideas.

The way a teacher structures the classroom setting to foster pantomime or interpretative movements will depend, to some extent, upon the age of the children. More specifically, however, it is their immediate interests, feelings, and ideas, and the type of musical accompaniment that will initiate creative movements. Since there is no set format or pattern for introducing pantomime or interpretative movements, each teacher will gradually work out her own way of developing them. For teachers who have had little or no experience with creative rhythms, some guidance is indicated. Therefore, to assist primary teachers in developing a pattern, two sample lessons are provided to show how pantomime and interpretative movements are fostered through direct and indirect guidance of the teacher. Three charts are also provided to indicate the various types of animal, mechanical, and nature movements that can be expressed through rhythmic pantomime and interpretative movements. Several pantomime movements, such as Lumber Loader and Raggedy Andy, are illustrated in the last section of this chapter to provide additional examples of how various objects can be interpreted.

PANTOMINE MOVEMENTS

Rhythmic pantomime provides each child with an opportunity to learn a movement by copying the teacher, another child, or the actual movement of an animal or mechanical object. Once the movement is understood the child may pantomime it, adding whatever creativity he so desires.

Lesson in Mechanical Pantomime (Grade K-1)

The following lesson could be used for five- and six-year-olds who are familiar with various mechanical objects. The primary purpose is to encourage or stimulate each child to pantomime these movements. An attempt has been made to provide ideas and movements that are familiar to this age group. Once the basic movement patterns are understood and the children appear to be at ease, guide rather than direct them into other mechanical movements.

Lesson No. One: Mechanical Objects

Basic theme: Pantomime
Musical Accompaniment: Records
Grade: K-1
Formation: Circle

Suggested Teaching Procedure

A. Movement Introduction:
   Arrange children in a circle formation and seated on the floor. Use the following questions to familiarize the children with various body movements.
   1. What parts of your body can you move while you are sitting?
   2. If no circular movements: Can your arms go round and round?
   3. What else can you make go round and round?
   4. To combine movements: Can you move part of your body round and round and up and down?

Possible Responses from Children

A. Movement Introduction:
   The responses listed following will probably result from your questions. Unique variations should be encouraged through praise and example.
   1. Arms, legs, and head may move from side to side or in a circular fashion.
   2. Arms may circle above head, at side, or in front of body.

   3. Trunk or smaller segments such as wrists and feet.
   4. Bending forward while circling arms and raising them up and down.

General comment. Through the use of simple questions it is possible to initiate bending, turning, and swinging movements of the body. When there is a definite absence of a particular type of movement such as circling, the head, arms, or legs pose a question that will guide them into this type of response.

B. Movement of Mechanical Objects
   1. Can you show me something that is mechanical that goes round and round? (Do not say "such as a top or washing machine," or they will simply duplicate your request.)

B. Movement of Mechanical Objects
   1. Allow all children to stand and pantomime any mechanical object. Responses may be top, merry-go-round, or airplane propeller.

2. If no response, suggest a top or merry-go-round.

2. Select one or two of the best responses and have class watch them.

Introduce Musical Accompaniment: Childhood Rhythms, Series 1, No. 104, Top.

3. I have some music that goes round and round. Let's see if we can all be tops. When the music starts, all the "tops" can spin but when the music stops, the "tops" must stop.

3. Response may vary from total body turning to turning and shifting from high to a low position. Stop and start music, pointing to various children for praise and encouragement.

4. In the summertime when the sun is hot, what goes round and round and helps the grass grow?

4. Arms may be extended at sides and body makes a full turn.

Introduce Second Musical Accompaniment: Childhood Rhythms, Series 1, No. 104, Round and Round.

5. When I play this new music you can all be lawn sprinklers. When the music stops let's all move to a new place to help some new grass grow.

5. Stop and start record and encourage creative responses by suggesting a high, low, fast, lazy sprinkler.

Additional Suggestions:
Join hands in circle formation.

1. Can our circle go up and down together. (Give commands.)

1. Stand, jump up, bend down, and sit on floor.

2. Can we pop up and down like a toaster? (Childhood Rhythms, Series 2, No. 205, Jumping Jacks.)

2. Stop and start music.

Break hand grasp but keep in circle.

1. Can we all be teeter-totters that go up and down. (Childhood Rhythms, Series 2, No. 201, Up and Down.)

1. Individual movements simulating the movements of the teeter-totter.

Continue pattern suggesting additional mechanical objects. Complete the lesson with a story or poem that relates to the general theme.

INTERPRETATIVE MOVEMENTS

Interpretative movements are the highest level or form of creative expression for children. Because of the creativity involved, teachers can only structure the setting, encourage, and possibly hope for responses that are expressions of feeling and imagination. Left to their own imaginations, children once stimulated by a question or musical accompaniment will develop and endlessly improvise their own movements.

Lesson in Interpretative Movements (Grades 2-3)

This lesson is written for Grades Two or Three. Its purpose is to stimulate light and heavy movements with emphasis on the quality rather than the direction of the response. A short discussion should precede this lesson to familiarize children about new words and concepts of clouds as part of nature. This can be done through class discussion or reading stories and poems about clouds.

Lesson No. Two: Clouds and Nature*

Basic Theme: Interpretative Movements
Grade: 2-3
Formation: Multiple (scattered, line and circle)

Suggested Teaching Procedure

A. Movement Introduction:
Arrange children in scattered formation and seated on the floor. The following questions and discussion period will provide the initial stimulus for later interpretative movements.

1. Think of coming to school on a nice warm day when the sky is filled with pretty white clouds. What do the clouds look like?

2. If you could touch a cloud, what do you think it would feel like?

3. If you were a big cloud, what would you do on a nice warm day?

Possible Responses from Children

A. Movement Introduction:
The type of response to your questions will be to tangible objects that are familiar to this age group.

1. Mashed potatoes, cotton candy, or cotton balls.

2. Soft and fluffy like whipped cream, daddy's shaving cream.

3. Sleep, fly around and look at everyone, ride with the wind.

---

*The initial format for this lesson was developed by Mrs. Louise Stratton, Eastern Washington State College.

B. *Interpretative Movements*:
1. Let's all move about the room as if we were clouds in the sky.
2. To indicate light movements: Can you run very lightly on the tips of your toes?
3. What else is soft and light and makes you feel like moving as you did?

B. *Interpretative Movements*:
1. Running, romping, moving on tiptoes or heavy pronounced steps.
2. Running lightly, swinging or swaying, etc.

3. Kitten, bunny, feathers.

Introduce Musical Accompaniment: tambourine, triangle, or song bells.

4. Can you move your arms and your whole body very softly and lightly while I play the triangle? (Vary speed, but always keep intensity very soft.)
5. Seated in scattered formation: We have talked about light and soft things and moved so we felt that way. What is very different from softness?
6. What can you think of that is just the opposite of soft fluffy clouds?
7. Can you move around the room again, but this time we will be heavy and hard. (Use drum or blocks for accompaniment.)

4. Children may remain in same spot or may shift about the room with light expressive movements.

5. Stones, big and fat, heavy, rough.

6. Giants, elephants, sledge hammer.

7. Heavy pounding with feet, clenched fists, dragging arms to imitate elephant walk.

Additional Suggestions:

Reorganize class into partners or small groups and pose questions that require a group effort to express the movement. For example, with children in partners, ask them to interpret two thunder clouds moving toward each other. Continue lesson emphasizing soft and heavy movements. The conclusion may be a discussion of the movements or play a record and allow each child to interpret the music.

RESOURCE MATERIALS

The two sample lessons in this chapter will assist in developing a basic approach to teaching pantomime and interpretative movements. Numerous other methods and techniques may be used with equal success. However, as an additional source of creative movements, three charts containing possible animal, mechanical, and nature movements are provided in the accompanying pages.

Animal Movements

Animal	Page*	Suggested Type of Movement	Musical Accompaniment	
			Record	Instrument
Bear		Heavy slow walk, running, climbing	Childhood Rhy. Series 5, Re. 501, Bears	Drum (slow)
Camel	372	Slow bouncy walk, carrying object	Childhood Rhy. Series 1, Re. 103, Camels	Drum (uneven)
Elephant	382	Heavy slow rocking walk, lifting object	Childhood Rhy. Series 1, Re. 103, Elephants	Drum (slow, heavy)
Frog		Hopping, jumping, bouncing, bending	Childhood Rhy. Series 5, Re. 501, Frogs	Drum (short, quick)
Worm	373	Curling, bending, stretching		Scraper
Monkey		Fast crawl, bent knee jumps, runs		Woodblock
Rabbit	373	Jumping, bending, running, sniffing	RCA Rhy. Ser. Vol. 2, 45-5007 Happy and Light of Heart	Woodblock
Soldier	590	Crawling, running, marching	RCA Rhy. Ser. Vol. 2, 45-5007 Soldiers March	Drum or drum rolls
Tall Man— Short Man	592	Bending and stretching, bent knee walk, tiptoe walk	Childhood Rhy. Series 2, Re. 201 Fast & Slow	Drum (fast and light, heavy and slow)
Cat		Cautious walking, running, playing, stretching	Cap. 2 Pussy Cat Parade	Woodblock sticks
Chicken		Choppy, quick walk, scratching, pecking, flapping arms	Rhythm Time ES — 102	Woodblock (short, quick)
Raggedy Andy	591	Loose, floppy walk, swinging, bending		drum tambourine
Giant	591	Slow, heavy walk and run, exaggerated movements	Childhood Rhy. Series 1 Re. 106 Giants	Drum (heavy, slow), cymbal
Horse		Galloping, prancing (knees high), walking, carrying rider	Childhood Rhy. Series 1 Re. 102 Horse	Woodblock
Butterflies		Light sustained movements, use of arms, soft runs and skips	RCA Rhy. Ser. Vol. 2, 45-5005 Waltz	Gong Cymbal

*Several animal movements are illustrated at the end of this chapter or in an earlier chapter. Turn to the appropriate page for a description of the movement.

The suggested movements described in each chart may be performed with the musical accompaniment listed on the right side of each chart. The suggested list of records and instrumental accompaniments should be considered as illustrative samples. Each teacher should, therefore, develop a similar resource chart and list those records that have been successful in creating various types of creative responses.

Mechanical Movements

Mechanical Objects	Page	Suggested Type of Movement	Musical Accompaniment	
			Record	Instrument
Bull dozer	592	Pushing, bending, walking show effort		Drum Scrapers
Dump Truck	593	Bending and stretching, lifting, locomotion, show effort	Childhood Rhy. Series 2, Re. 201 Up & Down	Drum
Lumber Loader	593	Bending and stretching, lifting, slow, sustained, show effort	Childhood Rhy. Series 1, Re. 104 Elevators	Drum
Washing Machine	594	Twisting, rolling, bouncing	RCA Rhy. Ser. Vol. 2, 45-5004 March from Nut.	Scraper Drum
Ditch-digger	594	Bend and stretch, push and lift, show effort		Drum
Lawn Sprinkler	595	Twisting, turning, bending, stretching	Childhood Rhy. Series 2, Re. 201 Round & Round	Shakers Maracas
Top		Twisting, turning, running, skipping, walking, falling	Childhood Rhy. Series 1, Re. 104 Top	Scraper Cymbal, Gong
Clocks		Locomotion, (percussive), swing and sway (stiff)	RCA Rhy. Ser. Vol. 3 Clock	Woodblock
Percolate		Rising and falling, jiggling and bobbing (loose and floppy)		Woodblock (accelerating beat)
Pop-up Toaster		Rising and falling, bending and stretching, hopping, jumping	Childhood Rhy. Series 2, Re. 205 Jumping Jacks	Woodblock Drum
Airplanes		Rising and falling, sustained arm movements with running	Childhood Rhy. Series 1, Re. 104 Airplanes	Drum (vibratory beats)
Typewriter		Walking, hopping, jumping (short, quick) bending, stretching		Woodblock Triangle Bell

Nature Movements

Object of Nature	Page	Suggested Type of Movement	Musical Accompaniment	
			Record	Instrument
Wind		Use of arms, turning, smooth run, bending and stretching while running	Let's Play Kagortman Ser. 2 P. J.	Drum Tambourine
Rain		Rising and falling, bending and stretching, shaking	Garden Varieties AED 4	Shakers Maracas
Flowers		Bending and stretching, swinging and swaying	Garden Varieties AED 4	Drum Tambourine
Bees		Swinging and swaying, whipping and slashing with arms and trunk	Garden Varieties AED 4	Drum Tambourine
Sun		Rising and falling, bending and stretching, big and small movements	Garden Varieties AED 4	Gong Cymbal
Clouds		Sustained, smooth movements, tiptoe walks and runs, swinging and swaying	Rhythm Time 104	Cymbal Drum
Shadows		Darting walks and runs, bending and stretching, strike dodging	Rhythm Time 104	Drum Woodblock
Moon		Rising and falling, bending and stretching, sustained locomotion	Rhythm Time 104	Drum
Waves		Rising and falling, skipping, swinging and swaying, dynamic falls	RCA Rhy. Ser. Vol. 2, 45-5006	Drum (loud and soft) Cymbal
Fire		Striking and dodging, jumping, turning, hopping, stretching		Drum (first slow, loud and soft)
Smoke		Rising, turning, swinging, swaying, running, skipping, stretching		Cymbal Tambourine

PANTOMIME MOVEMENTS

SOLDIER

FIG. 18.1

The soldier march is basically the same as a walk with a general exaggeration of all movements. Stress head up, shoulders back, and a high arm swing.

FIG. 18.2

Check the position of arms and feet. The left arm and right foot always come forward together. Also, the toes should point straight ahead rather than inward (pigeon-toed) or toward the side.

MARCHING ON HEELS AND TOES

FIG. 18.3

In order to maintain balance while marching on the heels, it is necessary to spread the feet a little more than a normal march position. The arm swing should start almost from behind the back to assist the child in staying on his heels.

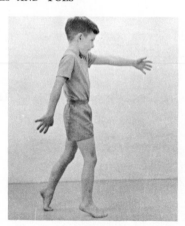

FIG. 18.4

This is the same movement as normal marching except the child stays on his toes.

GIANT

FIG. 18.5

FIG. 18.6

This movement must emphasize a slow heavy stomping action. Raise the left arm and leg then. . .

. . . lower leg and arm, and drop head and shoulders toward the ground.

RAGGEDY ANDY

FIG. 18.7

FIG. 18.8

The Raggedy Andy movement is a shifting of the limp, or relaxed body in virtually any direction. Stress a slight bend of knees, trunk bent forward, and arms dangling down.

To move like Raggedy Andy, the body should swing from side to side without raising trunk or bending elbows. The arms should swing from shoulders as if they were tied on just below the head.

TALL MAN — SHORT MAN

FIG. 18.9

FIG. 18.10

To pantomime a tall man, stress "on toes," body erect, and arms extended over head.

A short man can be mimicked by lowering body to a partial crouched position. Exaggerate the arm swing to maintain balance while walking in this position.

BULL DOZER

FIG. 18.11

FIG. 18.12

In pretending to be a bull dozer, join fingers and bend elbows sideways to represent the blade.

Lower body forward and downward bringing "blade" into position to move a pile of earth.

Dump Truck

FIG. 18.13

FIG. 18.14

A child's head and trunk can represent the cab of a large dump truck. The extended arms represent the back of the truck. To illustrate, the child in the picture above is backing up to dump a load of gravel.

The dumping action can be performed by a slow "jerking" upward and backward, each time with a slight lowering of the "bed" of the truck.

Lumber Loader

FIG. 18.15

FIG. 18.16

A lumber loader is a small truck with a platform in front that can be raised or lowered. To pantomime this machine, the child above is lowering his platform to "pick up" a load of lumber.

After placing his platform under the stack of lumber, he rises upward very gradually and, from here may back up, move forward, or move like a truck to any position desired.

Ditch Digger

FIG. 18.17

FIG. 18.18

A ditch digger is a cab movement on four wheels. The long arm extending in front of the cab has a "scoop" shovel on the end. To pantomime this activity, the child's body represents the cab, his arms represent the long arm of the shovel, while his hands act as the scoop. Bend arms downward to "scoop" up earth then . . .

. . . lift arms upward and sideward dumping earth at side of ditch.

Washing Machine

FIG. 18.19

FIG. 18.20

To imitate the inside action of a washing machine, spread stiff legs sideward and arms sideward and downward. The trunk and arms represent the rotating blade. Keep feet on floor and twist to the left.

Twist back to the right. This movement should simulate the swift backward and forward action of the blade action.

LAWN SPRINKLER

FIG. 18.21

FIG. 18.22

This particular lawn sprinkler is the kind that swings one half the way around in "jerky" movements, then swings back to the starting position. Keep feet on floor, arms extended and swing arms toward left in "jerky" movements. . .

. . . simulating the rotary action of the sprinkler.

ARCHERY

FIG. 18.23

FIG. 18.24

Archery can be pantomimed from drawing out the arrow from the quiver to shooting a deer. In the above illustration, the child is pretending to hold the bow in his left hand and the arrow in his right hand.

Draw the arrow back, aim and shoot.

BASEBALL SWING

FIG. 18.25

In the above illustration the child is holding a bat in the "ready" position.

FIG. 18.26

Swing downward and forward simulating hitting a ball and follow through around the left side of the body.

VOLLEYBALL

FIG. 18.27

The child is pretending he is getting ready to hit a volleyball. Note the position of the hands with fingers spread and thumbs close to each other. The knees are partially bent.

FIG. 18.28

Hit the ball upward and forward and follow through with hands and arms.

BOWLING

FIG. 18.29

FIG. 18.30

Pretend to hold a bowling ball in the right hand. Keep eyes on target, swing right arm backward and upward and left arm forward.

Swing right arm downward and forward, shift weight to left foot and swing left arm backward.

FOOTBALL THROW

FIG. 18.31

FIG. 18.32

Pretend to hold a football in the right hand. Bring ball back close to ear and behind the head and shift weight to back foot.

Bring arm forward, release ball and follow through with right hand in the direction of the ball.

SELECTED REFERENCES

AINSWORTH, DOROTHY S., and EVANS, RUTH. *Basic Rhythms*. New York: Chartwell House, Inc., 1954.

ANDREWS, GLADYS. *Creative Rhythmic Movement for Children*. New York: Prentice-Hall, Inc., 1954.

ANDREWS, GLADYS; SAURBORN, JEANETTE; and SCHNEIDER, ELSA. *Physical Education for Today's Boys and Girls*. Boston: Allyn & Bacon, Inc., 1960.

DIEM, LISILOTT, *Who Can*. Frankfort A.M. Germany: Wilhelm Limpert, Publishers, 1955, Copyright U.S.A., George Williams College, Chicago, 1957.

HALSEY, E., and PORTER, L. *Physical Education for Children*, Revised Edition, New York: Holt, Rinehart & Winston, Inc., 1967.

KULBITSKY, OLGA and KALTMAN, FRANK L. *Teacher's Dance Handbook Number One: Kindergarten to Sixth Year*. Newark: Bluebird Publishing Co., 1959.

LATCHAW, MARJORIE and PYATT, JEAN. *Dance for Children*. Englewood-Cliffs, New Jersey: Prentice-Hall, Inc., 1958.

MONSOUR, S.; COHEN, M. C.; and LINDELL, P. E. *Rhythm in Music and Dance for Children*. Belmont: California, 1966.

Moving and Growing. London: Ministry of Education and Central Office of Information, Her Majesty's Stationery Office, 1952.

MURRAY, RUTH, L. *Dance in Elementary Education*, 2nd Edition. New York: Harper & Row, Publishers, 1963.

SAFFRAN, R. *First Book of Creative Rhythms*. New York: Holt, Rinehart & Winston, Inc., 1963.

THACKERY, R. M. *Music and Physical Education*, Revised Edition. London: G. Bell and Sons, Ltd., 1965.

VANNIER, M., and FOSTER, M. *Teaching Physical Education in Elementary Schools*, Fourth Edition. Philadelphia: W. B. Saunders Company, 1968.

SUGGESTED FILMS

Title:	"Building Children's Personalities With Creative Dancing"
Details:	16 mm., 30 minutes, color
Distributor:	Bailey Films, 6509 Lonpre Avenue, Hollywood, California
Description:	Shows how a skillful teacher can lead children through the phases of creative dance expression
Purchase Price:	$275.00; Rental $15.00
Title:	"Learning Through Movement"
Details:	16 mm., 32 minutes, black and white, sound
Distributor:	S. L. Film Productions, 5126 Nartwick Street, Los Angeles, California
Description:	Explores the multiplicity of learning concepts that a child can experience in a creative dance class
Purchase Price:	$165.00; Rental $20.00
Title:	"Creative Dance in the Junior School"
Details:	16 mm., 40 minutes, color, sound
Distributor:	County Film Library, 2 Walton's Parade, Preston, Lancashire

Description: Illustrates progression of dance through the junior
                        school (intermediate level); shows dances composed
                        by children

Title: "Music and Movement"
Details: 16 mm., color, sound, 13 minutes
Distributor: Rank Audio-Visual, Ltd., Woodger Road, Shepherds
                        Bush, London, Wisconsin
Description: A high standard of work from six-year-olds showing
                        response to music and how the use of percussion
                        and visual stimuli develop quality of movement

Physical Fitness Evaluation

Chapter 19:   TESTING AND FOLLOW-UP
PROCEDURES

In 1953 Dr. Hans Kraus and Ruth Hirschland released the results of a study which compared the muscular fitness of American and European children. A test designed to measure minimum muscular fitness revealed American children of ages six to thirteen produced a discouraging fifty-seven percent failure while a comparable European sample produced a surprisingly low eight percent failure. Numerous follow-up studies were conducted to evaluate Kraus's original findings; all, however, revealed similar results.

There has been an unprecedented interest in the elementary school physical education program during the past ten years. The contributions of the President's Council on Youth Fitness has done much to make the public aware of the physical fitness needs of children, youth, and adults. National and State physical education organizations have also given top priority to providing consulting services, testing manuals, program guides, as well as sponsoring numerous conferences for elementary school teachers. The result of this general interest has been improved programs and a general increase in the level of physical fitness of elementary school-age children.

As a related point of interest, the author recently completed a study which compared the physical fitness of children in several countries.[1] In the accompanying chart, Scotland produced the most significant figures with respect to the general level of fitness. The latter sample, however, was obtained from Inverness, which is located in the north of Scotland, hence represents a typical rural area. On the other hand, England's sample population represents a typical urban community. The Canadian and American samples are cross sections of urban and rural populations. On this basis and recognizing the limitations of this study, the United States results are most impressive. The picture is certainly much brighter than the 1953 Kraus-Hirschland report. Other studies have also confirmed this general increase in the physical fitness of elementary school-age children.

Contemporary physical education programs by interest and nature stress the importance of physical fitness as a means rather than an end in itself. Further, the trend toward individualized instructional programs enhance rather than deter the potential of raising every child's level of physical fitness. Hence, continuous assessment of every child's physical fitness should be made on an individual basis and only if the results are used in a positive way.

The test battery described in the next chapter was developed for general classroom use rather than to be administered by specially trained personnel. The norms for the test include thirty thousand children representing rural and urban populations from six states. In addition, cumulative record cards and general information relating to follow-up programs are provided

---

1. G. Kirchner, *"Comparative International Survey of the Physical Fitness of Elementary School Age Children,"* Department of Physical Development Studies, Simon Fraser University, 1967.

to illustrate what positive steps can be followed to raise and maintain adequate levels of physical fitness.

Percentage of Children from each Country Achieving Superior, Good, Average, Below Average, and Poor Ratings on the Elementary School Physical Fitness Test.

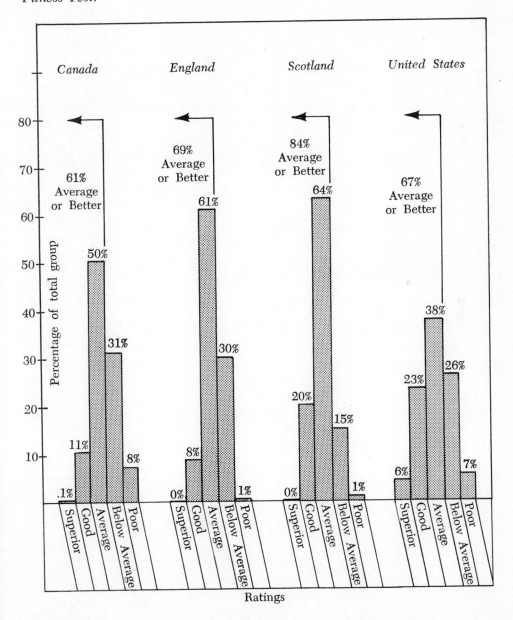

Testing and Follow-up Procedures

C
H
A
P
T
E
R

19

T HIS chapter contains an inexpensive and easy to administer physical fitness test for boys and girls of ages six to twelve. The five item test battery was designed to be administered by classroom teachers with a minimum of facilities and equipment. Scores from each test item are added to produce one cumulative score which represents a child's current level of physical fitness. Also included are sample score sheets, methods of interpreting individual and group scores, separate norms for boys and girls, and follow-up materials for teachers and parents.

WHAT THE TEST MEASURES

This test battery is designed to measure strength, endurance, power, and speed which are considered to be basic elements of physical fitness. If a child performs well on each of these test items, he is believed to be physically fit. In other words, we assume that a high score in the key of fundamental elements of physical fitness is an indication that the child possesses adequate strength and vitality to carry out the duties of his daily life as well as the energy to meet unforeseen emergencies. On the other hand, if his level of performance is low we assume the child does not have sufficient strength and vitality to meet his daily life activities nor any reserve energy to meet unexpected emergencies.

Any physical fitness test item that is designed for use by classroom teachers must possess certain distinguishing characteristics. First, it must be a reliable and valid measure of a specific element of physical fitness. Each test item must be readily adaptable to the varying and unique conditions which exist in many elementary schools. Such factors as available facilities, age of children, and size of class must be considered important elements in the selection of any test item. Finally, each test item should be highly motivating and, as far as possible, free of elements that may cause accidents or physical harm. These criteria were used as fundamental guides throughout the development of this test battery.

HOW TO ADMINISTER THE TEST

This section deals with the administration and scoring of the test battery. The suggested procedures should help the teacher administer the battery in a relatively short period of time and with a maximum of ease.

Health Status

Test those children in your class who are physically able to participate in the regular physical education program. If available, the health records of each student should be checked to detect any child who may be permanently disabled as a result of a chronic disease such as rheumatic fever or diabetes. In addition, it is advisable to exempt those children who have recently returned to school after a temporary illness.

Pupil Orientation

Each test item should be thoroughly explained and demonstrated to the group before being administered. Since practice does not reduce the validity of these test items, they may be given as regular exercises prior to the actual testing day.

Equipment

The following equipment should be secured before the tests are administered: stop watch, measuring tape, several mats and chairs, adhesive tape, yardstick, and a class score sheet.

Student Helpers

The time required to administer this test battery can be greatly reduced by student helpers. It is recommended that children in the third grade and above be used as helpers. Teachers in Grades One and Two should do all the testing or obtain help from other teachers or from more mature students. Therefore, the amount of time necessary to administer this test battery will depend upon the age of the children and the number of assistants.

Space Requirement

Since each teacher will have to administer this battery with the facilities available in her school, it is difficult to recommend a standard space for each test item. If a gymnasium is not available, the standing broad jump, bench push-ups, curl-ups, and squat jump tests can be administered in a classroom. The 30-yard dash test may be run indoors on the gymnasium floor, in a corridor, or out-of-doors on any suitable surface area.

The layout of equipment shown in the diagram below is suggested as a desirable plan for an average size gymnasium. Upon entering the gymnasium students should be seated according to their order on the class score sheet. The mats are placed close to the wall and approximately five feet apart. The measuring tape(s) for the standing broad jump test is placed between the mats. The run for the 30-yard dash test is placed on a diagonal to the gymnasium floor with at least ten feet clearance beyond the finish line. The recording table is placed approximately in the middle of the floor to facilitate recording and to permit the teacher to check the procedures of student helpers.

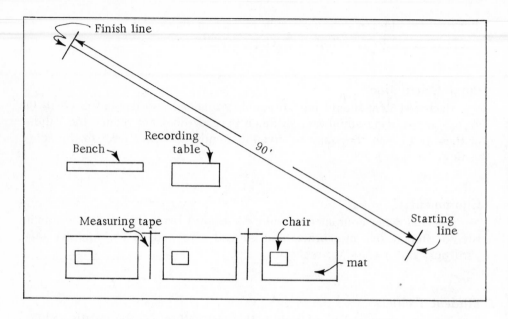

Class Score Sheet

The class score sheet on page 609 should be used for all tabulations. Two sample cases shown on this sheet will illustrate how to record individual scores as well as how to estimate the total physical fitness of each child.

Test Item	*Case No. 1* John Smith — Age 6	*Case No. 2* Mary White — Age 7
Standing broad jumps	40 inches	44 inches
Bench push-ups	24	30
Curl-ups	10	28
Squat jump	14	40
30-yard dash	6.4 seconds	5.6 seconds

Read the directions from 1-7 and note how each score is recorded on the example score sheet following.

1. Arrange children according to sex and age. (John Smith is six; Mary White is seven.)
2. Record the score for each test item under the *Score* column.
3. Record the points for each test under the *Point* column which corresponds to the child's sex and age. To find the points for each test item, turn to the norms on pages 618 through 645.
4. Record the rating for each test item under the *Rating* column. The Superior, Good, Average, Below Average and Poor ratings are found on the

CLASS SCORE SHEET (EXAMPLE)

Key
S = Score
P = Points
R = Rating

Ratings
1 – Superior
2 – Good
3 – Average
4 – Below Average
5 – Poor

Class _____
Date _____

Name	Age	Power No. 1 Standing Broad Jump			Strength and Endurance No. 2 Bench Push-ups			No. 3 Curl-ups			No. 4 Squat Jump			Speed No. 5 30-yard Dash			Physical Fitness Total	Rating
		S	P	R	S	P	R	S	P	R	S	P	R	S	P	R		
Boys																		
1. John Smith	6	40	52	3	24	59	2	10	51	3	14	47	3	6.4	52	3	261	3
2.																		
3.																		
Girls																		
1. Mary White	7	44	61	2	30	67	1	28	65	1	40	71	1	5.6	65	1	329	1
2.																		
3.																		

right side of each scoring table. (John's 52 points for the standing broad jump test place him in the Average bracket, while Mary's 61 points for the same test place her in the Good bracket.)

5. Add the points for the five tests and place this sum in the *Total* column under points. (John's total is 261 points; Mary's total is 329 points.)

6. Record the rating for the points under the *Total* column. John's 261 points give him an average rating for total physical fitness; Mary's 329 points give her a superior rating for total physical fitness.

7. In the majority of cases, a child will have a birthday between September and June of the next year. However, use the same age norm for each child that was used in September for all succeeding test administrations throughout each respective school year. To illustrate, John Smith's birthday was January 13, 1964. Since he started with the six year norm, any further tests John takes would use the same norm rather than shifting to the seven year norm.

Order of Tests

The order in which the tests of this battery are given is determined by the fatigue factor, by the number of testing periods allocated, and by the facilities available. The following order is therefore recommended for one or more testing periods: (1) standing broad jump, (2) bench push-ups, (3) curl-ups, (4) squat jump, and (5) 30-yard dash.

DESCRIPTION OF TEST ITEMS

The standard administrative procedures for the five tests of this battery are shown on pages 610 through 614. Care should be taken to assure that each test is performed as close as possible to the procedures described under Starting Position and Movement.

TEST NO. 1: STANDING BROAD JUMP

FIG. 19.1   **FIG. 19.2**   **FIG. 19.3**

Purpose: To measure power.

Equipment: A measuring tape and a yardstick. Arrange equipment as shown in the diagram below.

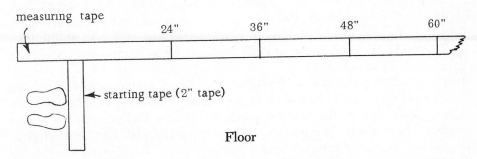

Floor

Starting Position: The pupil assumes a squat position with his arms extended backward and with the toes of both feet parallel to and back of the starting tape. (Figure 19.1)

Movement: The pupil starts the jump by shifting his arms forward and upward. As soon as his feet leave the floor (Figure 19.2) he flexes his legs and continues to swing his arms forward. The pupil lands with feet parallel, trunk flexed, and his arms extended in a forward direction (Figure 19.3)

Scoring: Allow one practice jump. The second jump is recorded. A tape measure is used to measure the distance to the nearest inch from the take-off line to the nearest heel position. An accurate reading can be taken if the recorder places a yardstick behind the heels of the jumper (Figure 19.3) and at right angles to the measuring tape. If the pupil steps with one foot and then jumps, touches the floor with his hands before landing, or falls backward after landing, the jump is repeated.

Precautions: Encourage the subject to flex his knees in the starting position to assure maximum thrust from the knee muscles.

TEST NO. 2: BENCH PUSH-UPS

FIG. 19.4

FIG. 19.5

Purpose: To measure the strength and endurance of the forearm, the arm, and the shoulder girdle muscles.

Equipment: A chair (the seat of the chair should be approximately 14 to 17 inches above the mat) and a mat. Place chair on the mat.

Starting Position: The pupil grasps the nearer corners of the chair and assumes a front leaning rest position with legs together and both feet on the mat. The body should form a straight line and be at right angles with the arms. (Figure 19.4)

Movement: The pupil lowers his body and flexes at the elbows until his chest touches the nearer edge of the chair. (Figure 19.5) The arms are then extended to the starting position. (Figure 19.4)

Scoring: The score is the number of push-ups performed. Stop the pupil at the end of the fiftieth push-up.

Precautions: Place one hand on the nearer edge of the chair to make certain the chest touches on every downward movement.

TEST NO. 3: CURL-UPS

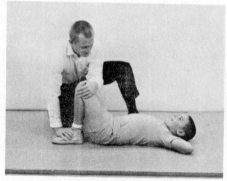 

FIG. 19.6   FIG. 19.7

Purpose: To measure the strength and endurance of the trunk flexor muscles.

Equipment: A mat.

Starting Position: The pupil assumes a back lying position with knees bent, soles of the feet flat on the floor, and the fingers laced behind the head. The tester places his right hand on the pupil's feet, holding them down and close to the buttocks, while the left hand is placed across the top of the pupil's knees. (Figure 19.6)

Movement: The pupil sits up, touches the tester's hand (Figure 19.7) and returns to the starting position. (Figure 19.6) It should be noted that a child's physique will determine whether he is able to touch the tester's hand with his head, chin, or chest. Touching with the head should be considered as an acceptable performance for all children.

Scoring: The score is the number of times the pupil sits up and touches the tester's hand. Stop the pupil at the fiftieth curl-up.

Precautions: Prevent the pupil from using his elbows in bracing or pushing against the floor as he rises up. Keep the pupil's heels close to his buttocks throughout the exercise.

TEST NO. 4: SQUAT JUMP

| FIG. 19.8 | FIG. 19.9 | FIG. 19.10 |

Purpose: To measure the strength and endurance of the trunk and leg extensor muscles.

Equipment: A mat.

Starting Position: The pupil assumes a crouched position with the arms at the sides of the legs and the fingers resting on the mat. (Figure 19.8)

Movement: The pupil jumps to a height at which his feet are approximately four inches above the mat. The arms remain at the pupil's sides to maintain balance. (Figure 19.9) The pupil returns to the starting position and continues the exercise. (Figure 19.10)

Note: When returning from the position shown in Figure 19.9 to the position shown in Figure 19.10, it is important that the force generated from this movement be absorbed with the arms and hands (fingers) instead of the knees and the legs. Each pupil should be completely instructed as to the correct procedure.

TEST No. 5: THIRTY-YARD DASH

FIG: 19.11

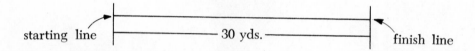

starting line ┣━━━━━━ 30 yds. ━━━━━━┫ finish line

Purpose: To measure speed.

Equipment: A stop watch, measuring tape, and a finish tape. An indoor area such as the gymnasium floor, or an outdoor area such as the playing field may be used for the thirty-yard dash.

Starting Position: The pupil assumes a standing starting position immediately behind the starting mark.

Movement: At the command "go" the pupil runs as fast as possible through the thirty-yard distance (Figure 19.11) passing through the finish tape at the thirty-yard mark.

Scoring: The score is the number of seconds required to run thirty yards. Record to the nearest tenth of a second.

Precautions: Explain the purpose of the test. In order to maintain maximum speed, encourage the pupil to run at top speed for a short distance beyond the finish line.

HOW TO INTERPRET THE TEST

There are separate norms for boys and girls from six to twelve years of age. Pupils are classified as being superior, good, average, below average, or poor in each test item as well as in total physical fitness as measured by the sum of the five tests.

The T-scale was used to transfer a child's raw score on each test item into equivalent points.[1] This common scale permits the performance on any test item to be compared with the performance on any of the other four tests of the battery. The points can also be added to give a total physical fitness score. A teacher simply has to look at the rating corresponding to the points a child receives to estimate his level of physical fitness. By comparing a pupil's performance from one trial to another, we can also estimate whether he is decreasing, maintaining, or increasing his level of physical fitness.

Interpreting Individual Scores

A child's score on the five test items indicates his present level of power, strength, endurance, and speed. The points under Physical Fitness (see the example Class Score Sheet on page 617) give an overall estimate of a child's present level of physical fitness. A further indication of a boy or girl's physical status can be obtained by comparing his or her score with the average performance shown in the chart following.

AVERAGE PERFORMANCE CHART

Test Item	6 yrs		7 yrs		8 yrs		9 yrs		10 yrs		11 yrs		12 yrs	
	Boys	Girls	Boys	Girls	Boys	Girls	Boys	Girls	Boys	Girls	Boys	Girls	Boys	Girls
1. Standing Broad Jump	39	36	44	41	47	44	50	47	54	50	57	53	59	53
2. Bench Push-ups	14	12	16	12	17	13	17	11	18	11	19	10	18	9
3. Curl-ups	9	9	13	12	16	15	19	17	22	20	26	22	28	20
4. Squat Jump	16	16	20	20	22	22	24	24	29	25	31	28	28	23
5. Thirty Yard Dash	6.4	6.8	5.9	6.3	5.8	5.9	5.4	5.5	5.4	5.5	5.0	5.2	4.9	5.3

The sample case which follows will further explain the use of the scoring tables as well as illustrate how a child's level of fitness can be interpreted.

Name	Age	Test Items	Testing Dates	
			Sept. 1969	June 1970
Alan Jones	8	Standing Broad Jump	62 inches	63 inches
		Bench Push-ups	9	24
		Curl-ups	3	25
		Squat Jump	16	27
		30-yd. dash	6.4 seconds	5.2 seconds

---

1. H. E. Garrett, *Statistics in Psychology and Education,* Fourth edition, (New York: Longmans, Green and Company, 1952), p. 308.

Using the score table for eight-year-old boys on page 622 we have transferred Alan Jones' raw scores into equivalent points. (See score sheet following.) In terms of the individual components of physical fitness measured in September, 1969, Alan was superior in power (standing broad jump), below average in arm and shoulder girdle strength and endurance (bench push-ups), poor in abdominal strength and endurance (curl-ups), below average in leg strength and endurance (squat jump), and below average in speed (30-yd. dash). His total of 222 points, therefore, placed him in the below average bracket of physical fitness.

By comparing Alan's raw score for the standing broad jump test with the average performance for eight-year-old boys (see Average Performance Chart on page 615), we see his 62 inches is well above the mean jump of 47 inches. In the area of strength and endurance, the scores for the bench push-ups (9), curl-ups (3), and squat jumps (16) tests are appreciably below the average performance of fitness. These scores are relatively poor, indicating the inability to continue an exercise for too long without showing signs of weakness or fatigue. Alan's score of 6.4 seconds for the 30-yd. dash test also reveals a low level of performance in the area of speed.

If we compare the scores made in September, 1969, and in June, 1970, we note a slight improvement in power, a general increase in strength and endurance, and a marked increase in speed. In a period of nine months his rating has changed from Below Average to Good, thus showing a significant improvement in his general level of physical fitness.

An adequate understanding of each child's level of physical fitness can provide an effective method for the teacher to plan physical education programs. For example, if the majority of boys and girls in a third grade class were below the average performance in the strength and endurance items, this would indicate a need for activities involving general body strength as well as an emphasis on movements requiring numerous repetitions. Other teachers may find their classes to be in the average or better grouping, which would indicate that their present physical education programs were adequate with no major modifications necessary.

CLASS SCORE SHEET (EXAMPLE)

Class ——————

Date ——————

Key
S = Score
P = Points
R = Rating

Ratings
1 – Superior
2 – Good
3 – Average
4 – Below Average
5 – Poor

Boys	Age	Power			Strength and Endurance									Speed			Physical Fitness	
		No. 1 Standing Broad Jump			No. 2 Bench Push-ups			No. 3 Curl-ups			No. 4 Squat Jump			No. 5 30-yd. Dash			Total	Rating
		S	P	R	S	P	R	S	P	R	S	P	R	S	P	R		
Sept. 1969 Alan Jones	8	62	66	1	9	40	4	3	34	5	16	44	4	6.4	38	4	222	4
June 1970 Alan Jones	8	63	67	1	24	56	2	25	56	2	27	54	3	5.2	59	2	292	2

NORMS FOR BOYS AND GIRLS
(SIX THROUGH TWELVE YEARS)

BOYS — SIX YEARS

PHYSICAL FITNESS ELEMENTS											
POWER		STRENGTH AND ENDURANCE						SPEED		TOTAL PHYSICAL FITNESS	
Standing Broad Jump		Bench Push-ups		Curl-ups		Squat Jump		30-yd. Dash			
Score (In.)	Points	Score (No.)	Points	Score (No.)	Points	Score (No.)	Points	Score (Sec.)	Points	Points	Rating
63	81	50	74	50	75	50	76	4.4	80		
62	80	49	72	49	74	49	75	4.5	77		
61	79	48	72	48	74	48	75	4.6	76		S
60	79	47	72	47	74	47	74	4.7	75		
59	77	46	72	46	74	46	74	4.8	74		U
58	75	45	71	45	74	45	73	4.9	73		
57	74	44	71	44	73	44	73	5.0	70		P
56	72	43	71	43	73	43	73	5.1	69		
55	71	42	71	42	72	42	72	5.2	68		E
54	70	41	70	41	72	41	72	5.3	67	326-up	
53	69	40	70	40	72	40	71	5.4	65		R
52	68	39	69	39	71	39	69				
51	67	38	68	38	70	38	69				I
50	66	37	68	37	69	37	68				
		36	67	36	69	36	68				O
		35	67	35	69	35	67				
		34	66	34	68	34	67				R
		33	66	33	68	33	66				
		32	65	32	67	32	66				
		31	65	31	67	31	66				
				30	66	30	65				
				29	66						
				28	65						
49	64	30	64	27	64	29	63	5.5	64		
48	63	29	63	26	64	28	62	5.6	63		
47	61	28	62	25	63	27	62	5.7	63		
46	60	27	62	24	63	26	61	5.8	62		G
45	59	26	61	23	62	25	60	5.9	61		
44	57	25	60	22	62	24	59			281-	O
43	56	24	59	21	61	23	58			325	

BOYS — SIX YEARS (*Continued*)

PHYSICAL FITNESS ELEMENTS

| POWER | STRENGTH AND ENDURANCE | | | | | | SPEED | | TOTAL PHYSICAL FITNESS | |
| Standing Broad Jump | | Bench Push-ups | | Curl-ups | | Squat Jump | | 30-yd. Dash | | | |
Score (In.)	Points	Score (No.)	Points	Score (No.)	Points	Score (No.)	Points	Score (Sec.)	Points	Points	Rating
42	55	23	59	20	60	22	57				O
		22	58	19	58	21	56				
		21	57	18	58	20	55				D
		20	56	17	57						
		19	55	16	57						
				15	56						
				14	55						
41	53	18	54	13	54	19	53	6.0	54		
40	52	17	53	12	53	18	52	6.1	54		
39	50	16	52	11	52	17	51	6.2	53		A
38	49	15	51	10	51	16	50	6.3	53		V
37	47	14	50	9	50	15	49	6.4	52		E
36	46	13	48	8	48	14	47	6.5	48	228-	R
		12	47	7	47	13	46	6.6	48	280	A
		11	46	6	46			6.7	47		G
		10	45					6.8	46		E
								6.9	45		
35	44	9	43	5	44	12	44	7.0	41		B A
34	43	8	41	4	42	11	43	7.1	40		E V
33	41	7	40	3	40	10	41	7.2	39	180-	L E
32	40	6	38	2	38	9	39	7.3	38	227	O R
31	39	5	36			8	37	7.4	38		W A
30	38					7	36	7.5	37		G
29	36							7.6	36		E
28	35							7.7	35		
27	33	4	34	1	34	6	34	7.8	34		
26	32	3	32			5	32	7.9	33		
25	30	2	28			4	30	8.0	30		
24	29	1	25			3	28	8.1	29		P
23	28					2	25	8.2	28		
22	27					1	19	8.3	27		O
21	26							8.4	26	179-	
20	26							8.5	26	below	O
19	25							8.6	25		
18	24							8.7	25		R
								8.8	24		
								8.9	24		
								9.0	23		
								9.1	22		

BOYS — SEVEN YEARS

PHYSICAL FITNESS ELEMENTS											
POWER		STRENGTH AND ENDURANCE						SPEED		TOTAL PHYSICAL FITNESS	
Standing Broad Jump		Bench Push-ups		Curl-ups		Squat Jump		30-yd. Dash			
Score (In.)	Points	Score (No.)	Points	Score (No.)	Points	Score (No.)	Points	Score (Sec.)	Points	Points	Rating
68	79	50	72	50	72	50	72	4.0	80		
67	78	49	70	49	70	49	70	4.1	79		
66	77	48	69	48	69	48	70	4.2	79		
65	76	47	68	47	68	47	69	4.3	78		S
64	76	46	68	46	67	46	69	4.4	77		U
63	74	45	68	45	67	45	68	4.5	76		P
62	73	44	67	44	67	44	67	4.6	75	325-up	E
61	72	43	67	43	66	43	67	4.7	73		R
60	71	42	67	42	66	42	66	4.8	70		I
59	70	41	66	41	66	41	66	4.9	68		O
58	69	40	66	40	66	40	66	5.0	67		R
57	68	39	65	39	65	39	65	5.1	65		
56	67	38	65	38	65			5.2	65		
55	66	37	65								
54	65	36	65								
53	63	35	64	37	64	38	64	5.3	64		
52	62	34	64	36	64	37	63	5.4	64		
51	60	33	63	35	64	36	63	5.5	58		
50	59	32	63	34	64	35	62	5.6	57		
49	57	31	62	33	63	34	61	5.7	57		
48	56	30	62	32	63	33	61				
47	55	29	61	31	63	32	60				
		28	60	30	62	31	60				G
		27	60	29	61	30	59			277-	O
		26	59	28	60	29	58			324	O
		25	58	27	60	28	57				D
		24	57	26	60	27	56				
		23	57	25	59	26	56				
		22	56	24	58	25	55				
		21	55	23	58						
				22	57						
				21	57						
				20	56						
				19	55						
46	53	20	54	18	54	24	54	5.8	54		
45	52	19	53	17	53	23	53	5.9	50		A
44	51	18	52	16	52	22	52	6.0	48		V
43	49	17	51	15	52	21	51	6.1	48	227-	E
42	48	16	50	14	51	20	50	6.2	47	276	R
41	47	15	49	13	50	19	49	6.3	47		A
40	46	14	48	12	49	18	48	6.4	46		G
		13	47	11	48	17	47	6.5	45		E
		12	46	10	47	16	46				
				9	45	15	45				

BOYS — SEVEN YEARS *(Continued)*

PHYSICAL FITNESS ELEMENTS

POWER		STRENGTH AND ENDURANCE						SPEED		TOTAL PHYSICAL FITNESS	
Standing Broad Jump		Bench Push-ups		Curl-ups		Squat Jump		30-yd. Dash			
Score (In.)	Points	Score (No.)	Points	Score (No.)	Points	Score (No.)	Points	Score (Sec.)	Points	Points	Rating
39	44	11	44	8	44	14	44	6.6	43		B A
38	43	10	43	7	43	13	42	6.7	42		E V
37	42	9	41	6	41	12	41	6.8	41	178-	L E
36	40	8	40	5	40	11	40	6.9	39	226	O R
35	38	7	38	4	38	10	38	7.0	35		W A
34	37	6	37	3	36	9	36				G
33	35					8	35				E
32	34	5	34	2	34	7	33	7.1	34		
31	33	4	33	1	31	6	32	7.2	33		
30	32	3	30			5	30	7.3	33		
29	30	2	29			4	28	7.4	32		
28	29	1	25			3	25	7.5	31		
27	28					2	21	7.6	29		
26	27					1	19	7.7	28		
25	25							7.8	27		P
24	23							7.9	27		O
23	22							8.0	26	177-	O
22	21							8.1	26	down	R
21	19							8.2	25		
								8.3	25		
								8.4	24		
								8.5	24		
								8.6	23		
								8.7	23		
								8.8	22		
								8.9	21		
								9.0	21		
								9.1	20		
								9.2	19		
								9.3	19		

BOYS – EIGHT YEARS

PHYSICAL FITNESS ELEMENTS											
POWER		STRENGTH AND ENDURANCE						SPEED		TOTAL PHYSICAL FITNESS	
Standing Broad Jump		Bench Push-ups		Curl-ups		Squat Jump		30-yd. Dash			
Score (In.)	Points	Score (No.)	Points	Score (No.)	Points	Score (No.)	Points	Score (Sec.)	Points	Points	Rating
74	78	50	72	50	72	50	70	3.9	78		
73	77	49	70	49	70	49	67	4.0	76		
72	77	48	68	48	68	48	65	4.1	75		
71	75	47	67	47	68	47	65	4.2	74		
70	74	46	67	46	66			4.3	73		S
69	73	45	67	45	65			4.4	72		U
68	72	44	66	44	65			4.5	72		P
67	71	43	66					4.6	71	326-up	E
66	70	42	65					4.7	71		R
65	69	41	65					4.8	70		I
64	68	40	65					4.9	66		O
63	67										R
62	66										
61	66										
60	65										
59	64	39	64	43	64	46	64	5.0	64		
58	63	38	64	42	63	45	64	5.1	60		
57	62	37	63	41	63	44	63	5.2	59		
56	61	36	63	40	63	43	63	5.3	56		
55	60	35	62	39	63	42	63				
54	59	34	62	38	62	41	62				
53	57	33	61	37	62	40	62				
52	56	32	61	36	61	39	61				
51	55	31	60	35	61	38	61				G
		30	60	34	60	37	60			276-	O
		29	59	33	60	36	60			325	O
		28	58	32	59	35	59				D
		27	58	31	59	34	58				
		26	57	30	59	33	58				
		25	57	29	58	32	57				
		24	56	28	57	31	57				
		23	55	27	57	30	56				
				26	56	29	55				
				25	56	28	55				
				24	55						
				23	55						

BOYS – EIGHT YEARS *(Continued)*

PHYSICAL FITNESS ELEMENTS									
POWER	STRENGTH AND ENDURANCE						SPEED	TOTAL PHYSICAL FITNESS	
Standing Broad Jump	Bench Push-ups		Curl-ups		Squat Jump		30-yd. Dash		
Score Points (In.)	Score Points (No.)		Score Points (No.)		Score Points (No.)		Score Points (Sec.)		Points	Rating
50 54	22 54		22 54		27 54		5.4 54			
49 52	21 54		21 54		26 53		5.5 52			
48 51	20 53		20 53		25 53		5.6 52			A
47 50	19 51		19 52		24 52		5,7 51			V
46 48	18 50		18 51		23 51		5.8 50		227-	E
45 47	17 50		17 51		22 50		5.9 46		275	R
44 46	16 49		16 50		21 49					A
	15 48		15 49		20 48					G
	14 47		14 48		19 47					E
	13 46		13 47		18 46					
	12 45		12 46		17 45					
			11 45							
43 44	11 43		10 44		16 44		6.0 43			B A
42 43	10 42		9 42		15 43		6.1 42			E V
41 41	9 40		8 41		14 42		6.2 40		177-	L E
40 40	8 39		7 40		13 41		6.3 39		226	O R
39 39	7 37		6 39		12 40		6.4 38			W A
38 38	6 36		5 38		11 39		6.5 37			G
37 37			4 36		10 37		6.6 36			E
36 35					9 35		6.7 35			
35 33	5 34		3 34		8 34		6.8 34			
34 32	4 30		2 32		7 33		6.9 32			
33 31	3 29		1 29		6 31		7.0 31			
32 31	2 27				5 29		7.1 30			
31 30	1 25				4 28		7.2 29			
30 29					3 25		7.3 28			
29 27					2 23		7.4 28			
28 26					1 19		7.5 27			
27 25							7.6 26			P
26 24							7.7 25			O
25 22							7.8 24		176-	O
24 21							7.9 24		down	R
23 19							8.0 23			
22 19							8.1 23			
							8.2 22			
							8.3 22			
							8.4 21			
							8.5 21			
							8.6 20			
							8.7 20			
							8.8 19			
							8.9 18			

BOYS – NINE YEARS

PHYSICAL FITNESS ELEMENTS

POWER	STRENGTH AND ENDURANCE			SPEED	TOTAL PHYSICAL FITNESS	
Standing Broad Jump	Bench Push-ups	Curl-ups	Squat Jump	30-yd. Dash		
Score (In.) / Points	Score (No.) / Points	Score (No.) / Points	Score (No.) / Points	Score (Sec.) / Points	Points	Rating
77 81	50 76	50 72	50 70	3.7 77		S
76 79	49 72	49 70	49 68	3.8 77		U
75 77	48 72	48 70	48 67	3.9 76		P
74 76	47 70	47 68	47 66	4.0 76		E
73 76	46 69	46 66		4.1 75		R
72 75	45 68	45 66		4.2 75		I
71 74	44 68	44 65		4.3 73	329-up	O
70 73	43 68	43 65		4.4 70		R
69 72	42 67			4.5 69		
68 72	41 67			4.6 69		
67 70	40 67			4.7 68		
66 69	39 66					
65 68	38 66					
64 67	37 65					
63 66	36 65					
62 65	35 64	42 64	46 64	4.8 64		
61 64	34 64	41 64	45 62	4.9 60		
60 63	33 63	40 63	44 62	5.0 56		
59 62	32 63	39 63	43 61	5.1 55		
58 60	31 62	38 62	42 61	5.2 55		G
57 59	30 61	37 62	41 60			O
56 58	29 60	36 61	40 60			O
55 57	28 59	35 61	39 59		276-	D
54 56	27 58	34 60	38 59		328	
	26 58	33 60	37 58			
	25 57	32 59	36 58			
	24 56	31 59	35 57			
	23 56	30 58	34 57			
	22 55	29 57	33 56			
		28 56	32 55			
		27 56	31 55			
		26 55				
		25 55				
53 54	21 54	24 54	30 54	5.3 53		
52 53	20 53	23 53	29 53	5.4 50		A
51 51	19 51	22 52	28 53	5.5 47		V
50 50	18 51	21 52	27 52	5.6 45		E
49 48	17 50	20 51	26 52		225-	R
48 47	16 49	19 50	25 51		275	A
47 45	15 48	18 49	24 50			G
	14 47	17 48	23 49			E
	13 46	16 48	22 48			
	12 45	15 47	21 47			
		14 46	20 46			
		13 45	19 45			

BOYS – NINE YEARS (Continued)

PHYSICAL FITNESS ELEMENTS											
POWER		STRENGTH AND ENDURANCE						SPEED		TOTAL PHYSICAL FITNESS	
Standing Broad Jump		Bench Push-ups		Curl-ups		Squat Jump		30-yd. Dash			
Score (In.)	Points	Score (No.)	Points	Score (No.)	Points	Score (No.)	Points	Score (Sec.)	Points	Points	Rating
46	44	11	43	12	44	18	44	5.7	44		
45	43	10	42	11	43	17	43	5.8	40		B A
44	42	9	40	10	42	16	42	5.9	40		E V
43	41	8	40	9	41	15	41	6.0	37	176-	L E
42	39	7	38	8	40	14	40	6.1	36	224	O R
41	38	6	37	7	39	13	39	6.2	36		W A
40	37	5	35	6	37	12	38	6.3	35		G
39	36			5	36	11	37				E
38	35					10	35				
37	33	4	34	4	34	9	34	6.4	34		
36	32	3	32	3	33	8	33	6.5	32		
35	30	2	29	2	31	7	31	6.6	31		
34	29	1	25	1	28	6	30	6.7	30		
33	28					5	28	6.8	28		
32	27					4	26	6.9	26		
31	26					3	25	7.0	25		
30	25					2	20	7.1	25		
29	24					1	19	7.2	24		P
28	23							7.3	24	175-	O
27	22							7.4	23	down	O
26	21							7.5	22		R
25	20							7.6	22		
24	19							7.7	20		
								7.8	20		
								7.9	19		
								8.0	19		
								8.1	18		
								8.2	18		
								8.3	17		
								8.4	17		

BOYS — TEN YEARS

PHYSICAL FITNESS ELEMENTS											
POWER	STRENGTH AND ENDURANCE						SPEED		TOTAL PHYSICAL FITNESS		
Standing Broad Jump	Bench Push-ups		Curl-ups		Squat Jump		30-yd. Dash				
Score (In.)	Points	Score (No.)	Points	Score (No.)	Points	Score (No.)	Points	Score (Sec.)	Points	Points	Rating
83	80	50	74	50	70	50	70	3.5	80		
82	80	49	72	49	68	49	69	3.6	80		
81	78	48	70	48	67	48	68	3.7	77		
80	78	47	70	47	66	47	67	3.8	75		
79	77	46	69	46	65			3.9	74		
78	77	45	69					4.0	73		S
77	76	44	68					4.1	73		U
76	76	43	68					4.2	72		P
75	75	42	67					4.3	70	328-up	E
74	74	41	66					4.4	68		R
73	73	40	66					4,5	65		I
72	72	39	65								O
71	71	38	65								R
70	70										
69	69										
68	68										
67	67										
66	66										
65	64	37	64	45	63	46	64	4.6	63		
64	63	36	64	44	62	45	64	4.7	61		
63	62	35	63	43	62	44	62	4.8	58		
62	60	34	63	42	61	43	60	4.9	55		
61	59	33	62	41	61	42	60				
60	58	32	62	40	60	41	59				G
59	56	31	61	39	60	40	58			275-	O
58	55	30	60	38	59	39	57			327	O
		29	58	37	59	38	56				D
		28	58	36	58	37	56				
		27	57	35	58	36	55				
		26	57	34	57	35	55				
		25	56	33	57						
		24	55	32	56						
		23	55	31	55						
				30	55						

BOYS – TEN YEARS *(Continued)*

PHYSICAL FITNESS ELEMENTS						
POWER	STRENGTH AND ENDURANCE				SPEED	TOTAL PHYSICAL FITNESS
Standing Broad Jump	Bench Push-ups	Curl-ups		Squat Jump	30-yd. Dash	
Score Points (In.)	Score Points (No.)	Score Points (No.)		Score Points (No.)	Score Points (Sec.)	Points Rating
57 54	22 54	29 54		34 54	5.0 52	
56 53	21 54	28 53		33 53	5.1 52	
55 52	20 53	27 53		32 53	5.2 51	
54 50	19 51	26 52		31 52	5.3 51	A
53 49	18 50	25 52		30 51	5.4 50	V
52 48	17 49	24 51		29 50	5.5 46	226- E
51 46	16 48	23 51		28 49		274 R
50 45	15 47	22 50		27 49		A
	14 46	21 49		26 48		G
	13 45	20 48		25 48		E
		19 46		24 47		
		18 45		23 46		
		17 45		22 45		
				21 45		
49 44	12 44	16 44		20 44	5.6 43	
48 43	11 43	15 44		19 42	5.7 42	B A
47 41	10 42	14 43		18 41	5.8 40	E V
46 40	9 40	13 42		17 40	5.9 38	175- L E
45 39	8 39	12 41		16 40	6.0 35	225 O R
44 38	7 38	11 40		15 39		W A
43 37	6 37	10 39		14 37		G
42 36	5 35	9 38		13 37		E
41 35		8 37		12 36		
		7 35		11 35		
40 34	4 33	6 34		10 34	6.1 34	
39 32	3 32	5 33		9 32	6.2 32	
38 31	2 30	4 32		8 31	6.3 30	
37 30	1 26	3 31		7 30	6.4 30	
36 29		2 29		6 29	6.5 29	
35 28		1 26		5 28	6.6 29	
34 27				4 25	6.7 27	
33 26				3 22	6.8 26	P
32 25				2 19	6.9 25	O
31 24				1 18	7.0 25	174- O
30 23					7.1 24	down R
29 21					7.2 24	
28 20					7.3 23	
27 19					7.4 23	
					7.5 23	
					7.6 22	
					7.7 22	
					7.8 20	
					7.9 20	
					8.0 19	
					8.1 18	

BOYS – ELEVEN YEARS

PHYSICAL FITNESS ELEMENTS											
POWER		STRENGTH AND ENDURANCE						SPEED		TOTAL PHYSICAL FITNESS	
Standing Broad Jump		Bench Push-ups		Curl-ups		Squat Jump		30-yd. Dash			
Score (In.)	Points	Score (No.)	Points	Score (No.)	Points	Score (No.)	Points	Score (Sec.)	Points	Points	Rating
85	81	50	74	50	70	50	72	3.5	80		
84	80	49	72	49	67	49	70	3.6	79		
83	79	48	70			48	68	3.7	77		
82	78	47	69			47	66	3.8	75		
81	77	46	68					3.9	73		S
80	76	45	67					4.0	71		U
79	76	44	67					4.1	70		P
78	75	43	66					4.2	70	331-up	E
77	73	42	66					4.3	67		R
76	72	41	65								I
75	70	40	65								O
74	69										R
73	68										
72	67										
71	66										
70	66										
69	64	39	64	48	64	46	64	4.4	64		
68	63	38	64	47	62	45	62	4.5	60		
67	62	37	63	46	61	44	60	4.6	58		
66	60	36	63	45	60	43	60	4.7	56		
65	59	35	62	44	60	42	58				
64	58	34	61	43	59	41	56				
63	57	33	61	42	58	40	56				G
62	56	32	60	41	58					277-330	O
61	55	31	59	40	57						O
		30	59	39	57						D
		29	58	38	56						
		28	57	37	56						
		27	57	36	55						
		26	56	35	55						
		25	56								
		24	55								

BOYS — ELEVEN YEARS *(Continued)*

PHYSICAL FITNESS ELEMENTS							
POWER	STRENGTH AND ENDURANCE				SPEED	TOTAL PHYSICAL FITNESS	
Standing Broad Jump	Bench Push-ups	Curl-ups		Squat Jump	30-yd. Dash		
Score Points (In.)	Score Points (No.)	Score Points (No.)		Score Points (No.)	Score Points (Sec.)	Points	Rating
60 54	23 54	34 54		39 54	4.8 54		
59 52	22 54	33 54		38 54	4.9 52		
58 51	21 53	32 53		37 53	5.0 50		
57 50	20 52	31 53		36 53	5.1 47		
56 48	19 50	30 52		35 52	5.2 45		A
55 47	18 49	29 52		34 52			V
54 46	17 49	28 51		33 51		226-	E
53 45	16 48	27 51		32 51		276	R
	15 47	26 50		31 50			A
	14 46	25 49		30 49			G
	13 45	24 48		29 48			E
		23 48		28 48			
		22 47		27 47			
		21 46		26 46			
		20 46		25 46			
				24 45			
52 44	12 44	19 44		23 44	5.3 42		
51 43	11 43	18 44		22 44	5.4 40		
50 41	10 42	17 43		21 43	5.5 39		
49 40	9 40	16 42		20 42	5.6 39		B A
48 39	8 39	15 41		19 41	5.7 37		E V
47 38	7 38	14 40		18 40	5.8 35	177-	L E
46 37	6 37	13 40		17 39		225	O R
45 35	5 36	12 39		16 38			W A
		11 38		15 38			G
		10 37		14 37			E
		9 36		13 36			
		8 36		12 35			
				11 35			
44 34	4 34	7 34		10 34	5.9 33		
43 33	3 32	6 33		9 33	6.0 31		
42 32	2 29	5 32		8 32	6.1 30		
41 31	1 26	4 31		7 30	6.2 29		
40 30		3 29		6 29	6.3 28		
39 29		2 27		5 27	6.4 27		
38 28		1 25		4 25	6.5 26		P
37 27				3 23	6.6 26	176-	O
36 26				2 22	6.7 25	down	O
35 25				1 19	6.8 24		R
34 24					6.9 24		
33 23					7.0 23		
32 21					7.1 22		
31 19					7.2 21		
					7.3 21		
					7.4 20		
					7.5 19		

BOYS — TWELVE YEARS

PHYSICAL FITNESS ELEMENTS										
POWER	STRENGTH AND ENDURANCE						SPEED		TOTAL PHYSICAL FITNESS	
Standing Broad Jump	Bench Push-ups		Curl-ups		Squat Jump		30-yd. Dash			
Score Points (In.)	Score Points (No.)		Score Points (No.)		Score Points (No.)		Score Points (Sec.)		Points	Rating
88 80	50 74		50 70		50 70		3.5 79			
87 79	49 72		49 70		49 68		3.6 77			
86 77	48 72		48 68				3.7 76			
85 76	47 70		47 68				3.8 75			
84 75	46 70		46 66				3.9 72			S
83 74	45 68		45 66				4.0 69			U
82 73	44 68						4.1 68			P
81 72	43 67						4.2 66		330-up	E
80 71	42 66									R
79 71	41 66									I
78 70	40 65									O
77 69										R
76 68										
75 67										
74 66										
73 65										
72 64	39 64		44 64		48 64		4.3 64			
71 63	38 64		43 62		47 62		4.4 62			
70 62	37 63		42 60		46 60		4.5 60			
69 61	36 63		41 59		45 60		4,6 58			
68 60	35 62		40 57		44 59		4.7 56			
67 59	34 62		39 57		43 59					
66 58	33 61		38 56		42 58					G
65 57	32 61		37 56		41 58					O
64 56	31 60		36 55		40 57				276-329	O
63 55	30 59		35 55		39 57					D
	29 59				38 56					
	28 58				37 56					
	27 58				36 55					
	26 57									
	25 57									
	24 56									
	23 55									

BOYS – TWELVE YEARS *(Continued)*

PHYSICAL FITNESS ELEMENTS						
POWER	STRENGTH AND ENDURANCE				SPEED	TOTAL PHYSICAL FITNESS
Standing Broad Jump	Bench Push-ups	Curl-ups		Squat Jump	30-yd. Dash	
Score Points (In.)	Score Points (No.)	Score Points (No.)		Score Points (No.)	Score Points (Sec.)	Points · Rating
62 54	22 54	34 54		35 54	4.8 54	
61 52	21 54	33 54		34 54	4.9 52	
60 51	20 53	32 53		33 53	5.0 49	
59 50	19 51	31 53		32 53	5.1 47	
58 49	18 50	30 52		31 52	5.2 46	A
57 47	17 49	29 51		30 52		V
56 46	16 49	28 51		29 51		E
55 46	15 48	27 50		28 50	226-	R
54 45	14 47	26 49		27 49	275	A
	13 46	25 49		26 48		G
	12 45	24 47		25 47		E
		23 47		24 47		
		22 46		23 46		
		21 45		22 45		
		20 45		21 45		
53 43	11 44	19 44		20 44	5.3 44	
52 42	10 43	18 44		19 43	5.4 42	
51 41	9 41	17 43		18 42	5.5 40	
50 40	8 40	16 42		17 42	5.6 39	B A
49 39	7 40	15 42		16 41	5.7 38	E V
48 38	6 39	14 41		15 40	5.8 35	L E
47 36	5 37	13 40		14 39		O R
46 35	4 35	12 40		13 38	175-	W A
		11 38		12 38	225	G
		10 37		11 37		E
		9 36		10 36		
		8 35		9 35		
		7 35				
45 34	3 33	6 34		8 34	5.9 33	
44 33	2 31	5 33		7 33	6.0 31	
43 32	1 28	4 32		6 32	6.1 31	
42 32		3 30		5 30	6.2 30	
41 31		2 28		4 29	6.3 30	
40 30		1 26		3 26	6.4 29	
39 29				2 28	6.5 28	P
38 28				1 19	6.6 28	O
37 27					6.7 27	O
36 26					6.8 26	R
35 25					6.9 25	
34 22					7.0 24	174-
33 20					7.1 24	down
32 19					7.2 23	
					7.3 23	
					7.4 22	
					7.5 20	

GIRLS – SIX YEARS

PHYSICAL FITNESS ELEMENTS											
POWER		STRENGTH AND ENDURANCE						SPEED		TOTAL PHYSICAL FITNESS	
Standing Broad Jump		Bench Push-ups		Curl-ups		Squat Jump		30-yd. Dash			
Score (In.)	Points	Score (No.)	Points	Score (No.)	Points	Score (No.)	Points	Score (Sec.)	Points	Points	Rating
60	84	50	82	50	82	50	78	4.5	80		
59	83	49	82	49	80	49	76	4.6	78		
58	81	48	80	48	76	48	75	4.7	76		
57	79	47	78	47	76	47	75	4.8	74		
56	78	46	77	46	75	46	74	4.9	73		
55	77	45	77	45	75	45	74	5.0	72		
54	76	44	76	44	73	44	73	5.1	71		
53	75	43	76	43	73	43	72	5.2	70		
52	74	42	75	42	72	42	72	5.3	69		
51	72	41	75	41	72	41	71	5.4	67		S
50	70	40	73	40	71	40	71	5.5	66		U
49	68	39	73	39	71	39	70	5.6	65	326-up	P
48	68	38	72	38	70	38	70				E
47	66	37	72	37	70	37	69				R
		36	71	36	69	36	68				I
		35	71	35	69	35	68				O
		34	70	34	68	34	67				R
		33	70	33	68	33	66				
		32	69	32	67	32	65				
		31	68	31	67						
		30	67	30	66						
		29	66	29	66						
		28	66	28	65						
		27	65	27	65						
46	64	26	64	26	64	31	64	5.7	64		
45	63	25	63	25	63	30	63	5.8	60		
44	61	24	63	24	63	29	62	5.9	59		
43	59	23	62	23	62	28	62	6.0	57		
42	58	22	61	22	62	27	61	6.1	56		
41	56	21	60	21	61	26	60	6.2	56	275-	G
40	55	20	60	20	60	25	59	6.3	55	325	O
		19	58	19	59	24	58				O
		18	57	18	59	23	57				D
		17	56	17	58	22	56				
		16	55	16	57	21	55				
				15	56						
				14	55						
39	54	15	54	13	54	20	54	6.4	54		A
38	53	14	53	12	53	19	53	6.5	52		V
37	51	13	52	11	52	18	52	6.6	51	228-	E
36	50	12	50	10	51	17	51	6.7	51	274	R
35	48	11	49	9	49	16	50	6.8	50		A
34	47	10	47	8	48	15	48	6.9	49		G
33	45	9	46	7	46	14	47	7.0	45		E
				6	45	13	45				

GIRLS — SIX YEARS *(Continued)*

PHYSICAL FITNESS ELEMENTS											
POWER		STRENGTH AND ENDURANCE						SPEED		TOTAL PHYSICAL FITNESS	
Standing Broad Jump		Bench Push-ups		Curl-ups		Squat Jump		30-yd. Dash			
Score (In.)	Points	Score (No.)	Points	Score (No.)	Points	Score (No.)	Points	Score (Sec.)	Points	Points	Rating
32	43	8	44	5	43	12	44	7.1	44		
31	42	7	42	4	41	11	43	7.2	43		BELOW
30	40	6	41	3	39	10	41	7.3	42		AVERAGE
29	39	5	39	2	37	9	40	7.4	40	180-227	
28	38	4	37			8	38	7.5	39		
27	37	3	35			7	36	7.6	38		
								7.7	37		
								7.8	36		
								7.9	35		
26	34	2	33	1	33	6	34	8.0	33		
25	32	1	28			5	32	8.1	33		
24	31					4	29	8.2	32		
23	30					3	26	8.3	31		
22	29					2	23	8.4	30		
21	28					1	19	8.5	29		POOR
20	27							8.6	28		
19	26							8.7	27	179-down	
18	25							8.8	26		
17	25							8.9	26		
16	24							9.0	25		
								9.1	24		
								9.2	23		
								9.3	20		
								9.4	19		
								9.5	18		

GIRLS — SEVEN YEARS

PHYSICAL FITNESS ELEMENTS											
POWER		STRENGTH AND ENDURANCE						SPEED		TOTAL PHYSICAL FITNESS	
Standing Broad Jump		Bench Push-ups		Curl-ups		Squat Jump		30-yd. Dash			
Score (In.)	Points	Score (No.)	Points	Score (No.)	Points	Score (No.)	Points	Score (Sec.)	Points	Points	Rating
66	80	50	82	50	74	50	74	4.0	80		
65	79	49	80	49	74	49	73	4.1	80		
64	78	48	78	48	72	48	72	4.2	79		
63	77	47	76	47	72	47	72	4.3	78		
62	76	46	76	46	71	46	71	4.4	76		
61	76	45	74	45	71	45	70	4.5	75		
60	75	44	74	44	70	44	69	4.6	74		S
59	74	43	72	43	70	43	68	4.7	73		U
58	74	42	72	42	69	42	68	4.8	72		P
57	73	41	70	41	69	41	67	4.9	70	326-up	E R
56	72	40	70	40	68	40	66	5.0	68		I
55	71	39	69	39	68	39	65	5.1	67		O
54	69	38	69	38	67			5.2	65		R
53	68	37	68	37	67						
52	66	36	68	36	66						
		35	67	35	66						
		34	67	34	65						
		33	66	33	65						
		32	66								
		31	65								
		30	65								
51	64	29	64	32	64	38	64	5.3	63		
50	63	28	63	31	63	37	64	5.4	62		
49	61	27	63	30	63	36	63	5.5	61		
48	60	26	62	29	62	35	63	5.6	60		
47	58	25	62	28	62	34	62	5.7	59		
46	57	24	61	27	61	33	62	5.8	58		G
45	55	23	60	26	61	32	61	5.9	56	276-325	O O
		22	59	25	60	31	60				D
		21	58	24	59	30	60				
		20	57	23	59	29	58				
		19	56	22	58	28	57				
		18	55	21	58	27	57				
		17	55	20	57	26	56				
				19	56	25	55				
				18	55						

GIRLS — SEVEN YEARS (Continued)

PHYSICAL FITNESS ELEMENTS											
POWER		STRENGTH AND ENDURANCE						SPEED		TOTAL PHYSICAL FITNESS	
Standing Broad Jump		Bench Push-ups		Curl-ups		Squat Jump		30-yd. Dash			
Score (In.)	Points	Score (No.)	Points	Score (No.)	Points	Score (No.)	Points	Score (Sec.)	Points	Points	Rating
44	54	16	54	17	54	24	54	6.0	54		
43	53	15	53	16	53	23	53	6.1	53		AVERAGE
42	52	14	52	15	52	22	52	6.2	51		
41	50	13	51	14	52	21	51	6.3	50	225-275	
40	49	12	50	13	51	20	50	6.4	49		
39	47	11	48	12	50	19	49	6.5	46		
38	46	10	46	11	48	18	48	6.6	45		
37	45	9	45	10	47	17	47				
				9	46	16	45				
				8	45						
36	43	8	44	7	43	15	44	6.7	42		BELOW AVERAGE
35	41	7	42	6	41	14	43	6.8	40		
34	40	6	41	5	40	13	42	6.9	39	178-224	
33	39	5	40	4	38	12	40	7.0	37		
32	37	4	38	3	36	11	39	7.1	36		
31	36	3	36			10	38	7.2	35		
						9	37	7.3	35		
						8	35				
30	34	2	32	2	33	7	33	7.4	34		
29	33	1	28	1	29	6	31	7.5	34		
28	31					5	30	7.6	33		
27	30					4	27	7.7	33		
26	29					3	26	7.8	32		
25	28					2	24	7.9	32		
24	27					1	21	8.0	31		
23	26							8.1	30		
22	25							8.2	29		POOR
21	25							8.3	28	177-down	
20	24							8.4	27		
19	23							8.5	25		
18	21							8.6	25		
								8.7	24		
								8.8	23		
								8.9	22		
								9.0	21		
								9.1	20		
								9.2	20		
								9.3	19		
								9.4	18		

GIRLS – EIGHT YEARS

PHYSICAL FITNESS ELEMENTS										
POWER		STRENGTH AND ENDURANCE						SPEED		TOTAL PHYSICAL FITNESS
Standing Broad Jump		Bench Push-ups		Curl-ups		Squat Jump		30-yd. Dash		
Score (In.)	Points	Score (No.)	Points	Score (No.)	Points	Score (No.)	Points	Score (Sec.)	Points	Points	Rating
72	82	50	78	50	74	50	70	3.9	78		
71	80	49	76	49	74	49	68	4.0	77		
70	79	48	76	48	72	48	68	4.1	76		
69	78	47	74	47	72	47	67	4.2	75		
68	77	46	74	46	70	46	67	4.3	74		
67	77	45	73	45	69	45	66	4,4	73		
66	76	44	73	44	69	44	65	4.5	72		S
65	75	43	72	43	68			4.6	70		U
64	74	42	72	42	68			4.7	67		P
63	72	41	70	41	67			4.8	65		E
62	71	40	70	40	67						R
61	70	39	69	39	66						R
60	68	38	69	38	66					325-up	I
59	67	37	68	37	65						O
58	66	36	68	36	65						R
57	66	35	67								
56	65	34	67								
		33	66								
		32	66								
		31	65								
		30	65								
55	64	29	64	35	64	43	64	4.9	64		
54	63	28	63	34	64	42	64	5.0	64		
53	61	27	63	33	63	41	63	5.1	63		
52	60	26	62	32	63	40	63	5.2	60		
51	59	25	62	31	62	39	62	5.3	57		
50	57	24	61	30	62	38	61	5.4	56		
49	56	23	60	29	61	37	61	5.5	55		G
48	55	22	60	28	60	36	60				O
		21	59	27	60	35	60			275-324	O
		20	58	26	59	34	59				D
		19	56	25	59	33	59				
		18	55	24	58	32	58				
				23	57	31	57				
				22	56	30	56				
				21	55	29	55				
				20	55	28	55				

GIRLS – EIGHT YEARS (*Continued*)

PHYSICAL FITNESS ELEMENTS											
POWER		STRENGTH AND ENDURANCE						SPEED		TOTAL PHYSICAL FITNESS	
Standing Broad Jump		Bench Push-ups		Curl-ups		Squat Jump		30-yd. Dash			
Score (In.)	Points	Score (No.)	Points	Score (No.)	Points	Score (No.)	Points	Score (Sec.)	Points	Points	Rating
47	53	17	54	19	53	27	54	5.6	54		
46	52	16	53	18	52	26	53	5.7	53		
45	51	15	52	17	52	25	53	5.8	52		A
44	50	14	51	16	51	24	52	5.9	51		V
43	48	13	50	15	50	23	51	6.0	50	225-	E
42	47	12	49	14	49	22	50	6.1	48	274	R
41	45	11	48	13	48	21	49	6.2	46		A
		10	47	12	47	20	48				G
		9	45	11	46	19	47				E
				10	45	18	46				
						17	45				
40	44	8	44	9	44	16	44	6.3	44		B A
39	43	7	42	8	42	15	43	6.4	42		E V
38	42	6	41	7	41	14	42	6.5	40	175-	L E
37	40	5	40	6	40	13	40	6.6	39	224	O R
36	39	4	37	5	39	12	39	6.7	38		W A
35	37	3	35	4	37	11	38	6.8	37		G
34	35			3	35	10	37	6.9	35		E
						9	35				
33	34	2	32	2	32	8	34	7.0	34		
32	33	1	26	1	28	7	32	7.1	33		
31	31					6	30	7.2	32		
30	30					5	28	7.3	31		
29	28					4	27	7.4	30		
28	27					3	23	7.5	29		
27	26					2	21	7.6	28		
26	25					1	19	7.7	28		
25	25							7.8	27		P
24	23							7.9	26	174-	O
23	22							8.0	25	down	O
22	21							8.1	24		R
21	20							8.2	23		
20	19							8.3	23		
								8.4	22		
								8.5	22		
								8.6	20		
								8.7	20		
								8.8	19		
								8.9	19		

GIRLS — NINE YEARS

PHYSICAL FITNESS ELEMENTS											
POWER		STRENGTH AND ENDURANCE						SPEED		TOTAL PHYSICAL FITNESS	
Standing Broad Jump		Bench Push-ups		Curl-ups		Squat Jump		30-yd. Dash			
Score (In.)	Points	Score (No.)	Points	Score (No.)	Points	Score (No.)	Points	Score (Sec.)	Points	Points	Rating
74	82	50	78	50	74	50	70	3.8	80		
73	82	49	78	49	72	49	69	3.9	79		
72	81	48	76	48	70	48	68	4.0	78		
71	80	47	76	47	69	47	68	4.1	76		
70	79	46	75	46	68	46	66	4.2	75		
69	78	45	74	45	68	45	65	4.3	73		
68	77	44	74	44	67			4.4	72		
67	76	43	73	43	66			4.5	70		S
66	75	42	73	42	66			4.6	67		U
65	74	41	72	41	65			4.7	65		P
64	72	40	72	40	65					325-up	E
63	70	39	71								R
62	69	38	71								I
61	68	37	70								O
60	67	36	70								R
59	66	35	69								
58	65	34	68								
		33	68								
		32	67								
		31	66								
		30	66								
		29	65								
57	63	28	64	39	64	44	64	4.8	61		
56	62	27	64	38	64	43	63	4.9	60		
55	61	26	63	37	63	42	63	5.0	58		
54	60	25	62	36	63	41	62	5.1	56		
53	58	24	62	35	62	40	62	5.2	55		
52	57	23	61	34	62	39	61				
51	56	22	60	33	61	38	61				
50	55	21	60	32	61	37	60				
		20	59	31	60	36	60				G
		19	57	30	59	35	59			275-	O
		18	56	29	59	34	58			324	O
		17	56	28	58	33	57				D
		16	55	27	58	32	57				
				26	57	31	56				
				25	57	30	55				
				24	56						
				23	55						
				22	55						

GIRLS — NINE YEARS (Continued)

PHYSICAL FITNESS ELEMENTS

POWER		STRENGTH AND ENDURANCE						SPEED		TOTAL PHYSICAL FITNESS	
Standing Broad Jump		Bench Push-ups		Curl-ups		Squat Jump		30-yd. Dash			
Score (In.)	Points	Score (No.)	Points	Score (No.)	Points	Score (No.)	Points	Score (Sec.)	Points	Points	Rating
49	53	15	54	21	54	29	54	5.3	53		
48	52	14	53	20	53	28	53	5.4	52		
47	50	13	52	19	52	27	53	5.5	50		
46	49	12	51	18	51	26	52	5.6	49		AVERAGE
45	48	11	50	17	50	25	51	5.7	48	226-274	
44	46	10	48	16	49	24	50	5.8	45		
43	45	9	47	15	49	23	49				
		8	46	14	48	22	49				
				13	47	21	48				
				12	46	20	47				
				11	45	19	45				
42	44	7	44	10	44	18	44	5.9	43		
41	42	6	43	9	42	17	43	6.0	40		
40	41	5	41	8	42	16	42	6.1	39		BELOW
39	40	4	40	7	41	15	41	6.2	38	178-225	AVERAGE
38	38	3	38	6	40	14	40	6.3	37		
37	37			5	38	13	39	6.4	36		
36	35			4	37	12	38	6.5	35		
				3	35	11	37				
						10	35				
35	34	2	33	2	32	9	34	6.6	34		
34	33	1	28	1	28	8	33	6.7	33		
33	32					7	32	6.8	32		
32	30					6	30	6.9	30		
31	29					5	29	7.0	29		
30	28					4	27	7.1	29		
29	27					3	25	7.2	28		
28	25					2	22	7.3	27		
27	24					1	20	7.4	26		
26	23							7.5	25		POOR
25	20							7.6	25	177-down	
24	19							7.7	24		
								7.8	23		
								7.9	23		
								8.0	22		
								8.1	22		
								8.2	21		
								8.3	21		
								8.4	20		
								8.5	20		
								8.6	19		
								8.7	18		

GIRLS – TEN YEARS

PHYSICAL FITNESS ELEMENTS										
POWER		STRENGTH AND ENDURANCE						SPEED		TOTAL PHYSICAL FITNESS
Standing Broad Jump		Bench Push-ups		Curl-ups		Squat Jump		30-yd. Dash		
Score (In.)	Points	Score (No.)	Points	Score (No.)	Points	Score (No.)	Points	Score (Sec.)	Points	Points	Rating
78	80	50	76	50	70	50	72	3.7	82		
77	79	49	76	49	70	49	72	3.8	80		
76	78	48	75	48	68	48	70	3.9	79		
75	77	47	74	47	68	47	68	4.0	78		
74	77	46	74	46	67	46	68	4.1	77		
73	76	45	73	45	66	45	66	4.2	76		
72	76	44	73	44	65	44	65	4.3	75		
71	75	43	72	43	65			4.4	70		S
70	74	42	72					4.5	66		U
69	72	41	71					4.6	65	327-up	P
68	71	40	71					4.7	65		E
67	70	39	70								R
66	69	38	70								I
65	68	37	69								O
64	68	36	69								R
63	66	35	68								
		34	68								
		33	67								
		32	67								
		31	66								
		30	66								
62	64	29	64	42	63	43	64	4.8	60		
61	63	28	64	41	63	42	62	4.9	57		
60	63	27	63	40	62	41	61				
59	61	26	63	39	62	40	61				
58	60	25	62	38	61	39	60				
57	59	24	61	37	61	38	59				
56	58	23	61	36	60	37	58				G
55	56	22	60	35	60	36	58			277-	O
54	55	21	59	34	59	35	57			326	O
		20	58	33	59	34	56				D
		19	57	32	58	33	55				
		18	56	31	58	32	55				
		17	55	30	57						
		16	55	29	57						
				28	56						
				27	56						
				26	55						

GIRLS — TEN YEARS (Continued)

PHYSICAL FITNESS ELEMENTS										
POWER		STRENGTH AND ENDURANCE						SPEED		TOTAL PHYSICAL FITNESS
Standing Broad Jump		Bench Push-ups		Curl-ups		Squat Jump		30-yd. Dash		
Score (In.)	Points	Score (No.)	Points	Score (No.)	Points	Score (No.)	Points	Score (Sec.)	Points	Points	Rating
53	54	15	54	25	54	31	54	5.0	54		
52	53	14	53	24	53	30	53	5.1	53		
51	51	13	53	23	53	29	53	5.2	53		A
50	50	12	52	22	52	28	52	5.3	52		V
49	49	11	50	21	52	27	52	5.4	51	225-	E
48	48	10	48	20	50	26	51	5.5	50	276	R
47	46	9	47	19	49	25	50	5.6	48		A
46	45	8	46	18	48	24	49	5.7	46		G
		7	45	17	48	23	48	5.8	45		E
				16	47	22	47				
				15	46	21	46				
				14	45	20	45				
45	44	6	43	13	44	19	44	5.9	41		B	A
44	43	5	42	12	43	18	43	6.0	38		E	V
43	41	4	40	11	42	17	42	6.1	36		L	E
42	40	3	38	10	41	16	41	6.2	35	175-	O	R
41	38	2	35	9	40	15	40			224	W	A
40	37			8	39	14	38					G
39	35			7	38	13	38					E
				6	37	12	37					
				5	35	11	35					
38	34	1	32	4	34	10	34	6.3	34		
37	33			3	32	9	32	6.4	33		
36	32			2	30	8	31	6.5	32		
35	30			1	28	7	30	6.6	30		
34	29					6	29	6.7	29		
33	28					5	27	6.8	29		
32	27					4	25	6.9	28		
31	26					3	22	7.0	26		
30	25					2	20	7.1	25		
29	25					1	19	7.2	25		P
28	24							7.3	24	174-	O
27	23							7.4	23	down	O
26	22							7.5	23		R
25	21							7.6	22		
								7.7	22		
								7.8	20		
								7.9	20		
								8.0	19		
								8.1	19		
								8.2	18		
								8.3	17		
								8.4	17		

GIRLS – ELEVEN YEARS

PHYSICAL FITNESS ELEMENTS

SUPERIOR (325-up)

POWER		STRENGTH AND ENDURANCE						SPEED		TOTAL PHYSICAL FITNESS	
Standing Broad Jump		Bench Push-ups		Curl-ups		Squat Jump		30-yd. Dash			
Score (In.)	Points	Score (No.)	Points	Score (No.)	Points	Score (No.)	Points	Score (Sec.)	Points	Points	Rating
84	84	50	80	50	70	50	70	3.5	80		
83	82	49	80	49	69	49	70	3.6	79		
82	82	48	78	48	68	48	69	3.7	78		
81	80	47	77	47	67	47	68	3.8	76		
80	78	46	76	46	66	46	67	3.9	74		
79	77	45	75	45	65	45	65	4.0	72		
78	76	44	75	44	65			4.1	70		
77	76	43	74					4.2	68		
76	74	42	73					4.3	65		
75	72	41	72								
74	71	40	71							325-up	SUPERIOR
73	71	39	71								
72	70	38	70								
71	69	37	70								
70	68	36	69								
69	67	35	69								
68	66	34	68								
67	65	33	68								
		32	67								
		31	66								
		30	66								
		29	65								

GOOD (275-324)

Standing Broad Jump		Bench Push-ups		Curl-ups		Squat Jump		30-yd. Dash		TOTAL	
Score (In.)	Points	Score (No.)	Points	Score (No.)	Points	Score (No.)	Points	Score (Sec.)	Points	Points	Rating
66	64	28	64	43	64	44	64	4.4	63		
65	63	27	64	42	63	43	63	4.5	62		
64	62	26	63	41	63	42	61	4,6	59		
63	61	25	63	40	62	41	60	4.7	57		
62	60	24	62	39	62	40	59	4.8	56		
61	58	23	61	38	60	39	58	4.9	55		
60	57	22	60	37	60	38	57				
59	56	21	60	36	59	37	57			275-324	GOOD
58	55	20	59	35	59	36	56				
		19	58	34	58	35	56				
		18	57	33	58	34	55				
		17	56	32	57						
		16	56	31	57						
		15	55	30	56						
				29	55						
				28	55						

GIRLS — ELEVEN YEARS *(Continued)*

PHYSICAL FITNESS ELEMENTS							
POWER	STRENGTH AND ENDURANCE				SPEED	TOTAL PHYSICAL FITNESS	
Standing Broad Jump	Bench Push-ups		Curl-ups	Squat Jump	30-yd. Dash		
Score Points (In.)	Score Points (No.)		Score Points (No.)	Score Points (No.)	Score Points (Sec.)	Points	Rating
57 54	14 54		27 54	33 54	5.0 54		
56 53	13 53		26 54	32 53	5.1 52		
55 52	12 52		25 53	31 53	5.2 50		
54 51	11 51		24 52	30 52	5.3 49		A
53 50	10 50		23 51	29 51	5.4 48		V
52 48	9 48		22 50	28 50		228-	E
51 47	8 47		21 49	27 49		274	R
50 46	7 46		20 48	26 49			A
49 45			19 47	25 48			G
			18 46	24 47			E
			17 46	23 46			
			16 45	22 46			
				21 45			
48 44	6 44		15 44	20 44	5.5 44		
47 42	5 43		14 44	19 43	5.6 42		B A
46 41	4 41		13 43	18 42	5.7 42		E V
45 40	3 38		12 42	17 41	5.8 39		L E
44 39			11 41	16 40	5.9 37	180-	O R
43 38			10 40	15 39		227	W A
42 37			9 38	14 38			G
41 36			8 37	13 38			E
40 35			7 36	12 37			
			6 35	11 36			
				10 35			
39 34	2 34		5 34	9 34	6.0 34		
38 33	1 33		4 33	8 33	6.1 33		
37 32			3 31	7 31	6.2 32		
36 30			2 29	6 30	6.3 31		
35 29			1 25	5 30	6.4 30		
34 28				4 29	6.5 29		
33 27				3 27	6.6 27		
32 27				2 25	6.7 26		
31 26				1 20	6.8 25		P
30 25					6.9 25	179-	O
29 25					7.0 24	down	O
28 24					7.1 24		R
27 23					7.2 23		
26 23					7.3 22		
25 22					7.4 21		
24 20					7.5 21		
					7.6 20		
					7.7 20		
					7.8 19		
					7.9 19		
					8.0 18		

GIRLS — TWELVE YEARS

PHYSICAL FITNESS ELEMENTS											
POWER		STRENGTH AND ENDURANCE						SPEED		TOTAL PHYSICAL FITNESS	
Standing Broad Jump		Bench Push-ups		Curl-ups		Squat Jump		30-yd. Dash			
Score (In.)	Points	Score (No.)	Points	Score (No.)	Points	Score (No.)	Points	Score (Sec.)	Points	Points	Rating
84	84	50	80	50	72	50	70	3.5	80		
83	82	49	78	49	71	49	69	3.6	79		
82	80	48	76	48	70	48	68	3.7	78		
81	78	47	74	47	69	47	66	3.8	78		
80	77	46	74	46	68	46	65	3.9	77		
79	77	45	72	45	67			4.0	76		
78	76	44	72	44	66			4.1	74		
77	75	43	71	43	66			4.2	73		SUPERIOR
76	74	42	71	42	65			4.3	72	326-up	
75	73	41	70					4.4	71		
74	72	40	70					4.5	68		
73	70	39	69					4.6	65		
72	69	38	69								
71	68	37	68								
70	67	36	68								
69	66	35	67								
68	66	34	67								
		33	66								
		32	66								
		31	65								
		30	65								
67	64	29	64	41	64	45	64	4.7	63		
66	63	28	64	40	64	44	62	4.8	62		
65	62	27	63	39	63	43	61	4.9	61		
64	61	26	63	38	62	42	61	5.0	57		
63	60	25	62	37	61	41	60				
62	59	24	62	36	61	40	60				
61	58	23	61	35	60	39	59				
60	57	22	61	34	60	38	59			277-	GOOD
59	56	21	60	33	59	37	58			325	
58	55	20	60	32	58	36	58				
		19	58	31	58	35	57				
		18	58	30	57	34	57				
		17	57	29	57	33	56				
		16	57	28	56	32	56				
		15	56	27	56	31	55				
		14	55	26	55	30	55				

GIRLS — TWELVE YEARS *(Continued)*

POWER		STRENGTH AND ENDURANCE						SPEED		TOTAL PHYSICAL FITNESS	
Standing Broad Jump		Bench Push-ups		Curl-ups		Squat Jump		30-yd. Dash			
Score (In.)	Points	Score (No.)	Points	Score (No.)	Points	Score (No.)	Points	Score (Sec.)	Points	Points	Rating
57	54	13	54	25	54	29	54	5.1	54		
56	54	12	54	24	54	28	53	5.2	52		
55	53	11	53	23	53	27	53	5.3	50		
54	51	10	51	22	53	26	52	5.4	48		
53	50	9	50	21	52	25	52				
52	49	8	49	20	50	24	51			230-276	AVERAGE
51	47	7	47	19	49	23	50				
50	47	6	46	18	48	22	49				
49	45			17	47	21	48				
				16	47	20	47				
				15	46	19	46				
						18	46				
						17	45				
48	44	5	44	14	44	16	44	5.5	44		
47	43	4	42	13	44	15	43	5.6	43		BELOW
46	42	3	41	12	42	14	42	5.7	43		AVERAGE
45	41	2	37	11	41	13	42	5.8	42	178-229	
44	39			10	40	12	41	5.9	40		
43	38			9	39	11	40	6.0	37		
42	37			8	38	10	40	6.1	36		
41	36			7	37	9	38	6.2	35		
				6	35	8	37	6.3	35		
						7	35				
40	34	1	32	5	34	6	34	6.4	34		
39	32			4	34	5	33	6.5	34		
38	31			3	31	4	31	6.6	33		
37	30			2	28	3	38	6.7	32		
36	29			1	27	2	27	6.8	31		
35	28					1	23	6.9	29		POOR
34	24							7.0	27	177-down	
33	22							7.1	26		
32	20							7.2	25		
								7.3	24		
								7.4	23		
								7.5	22		
								7.6	22		
								7.7	20		
								7.8	19		

FOLLOW-UP MATERIALS FOR THE TEACHER

According to a previous definition, physical fitness is the possession of adequate strength and vitality to meet daily life activities and unforeseen emergencies. In its broadest meaning, physical fitness should be considered as a means to an end rather than an end in itself. To illustrate this principle, playing a vigorous game such as basketball or soccer requires a high level of endurance. If a child or class does not possess sufficient muscular and organic endurance to play the game, appropriate remedial measures in the form of longer warm-up periods involving continuous movement therefore should be taken. Adhering to the same principle, a boy who cannot perform the "skin-the-cat" on the horizontal bar may well be in need of additional shoulder girdle strength rather than a change or correction in his motor skill pattern.

On the basis of the principle described in the foregoing paragraph, the norms for boys and girls on the preceding pages were established to show high, medium, and low levels of performance in five key elements of physical fitness. If a child scores average or better on these elements we can assume he possesses adequate physical fitness to perform the motor skills of the games and self-testing activities earmarked for his age level. Equally important to this physical prerequisite is the fact that a high level of physical fitness is usually indicative of optimum physical and mental well-being. In the latter respect, a child possessing abundant physical vitality is, in most cases, organically sound, mentally alert, and socially well-adjusted. For these reasons, classroom teachers should test children in the early part of the school year to determine specific and general areas of weakness, then to select appropriate activities to remove these deficiencies. The procedure and activities described in the following sections will assist teachers in evaluating a class's current level of physical fitness and selecting appropriate physical activities to meet individual and group needs.

Determining Areas of Need

During the first few weeks of the school year, each class should be given the physical fitness test. Once the scores and ratings for each test item and the total physical fitness score are recorded on the class score sheet, a general diagnosis of the class can be made. In the diagrammatic illustration below, both boys and girls scored well above average on the standing broad jump and the thirty-yard dash tests. On this basis, little additional emphasis need be given to activities that will enhance the level of performance involving power or speed.

On the other hand, a brief glance at the middle three test items involving strength and endurance reveals a general area of need on the part of both sexes. The high percentage of below average scores in each of these items indicates a definite need for activities that will increase the strength

CLASS SCORE SHEET

	Power	Strength and Endurance			Speed	Total
	Standing Broad Jump	Bench Push-ups	Curl-ups	Squat Jumps	30-yd. Dash	Physical Fitness
Boys	70% above average	90% below average	60% below average	90% below average	75% above average	65% below average
Girls	75% above average	92% below average	70% below average	95% below average	80% above average	70% below average

and endurance of the arm and shoulder girdle, abdominal and leg muscles. In the majority of cases where the three middle test items are low, a parallel situation will occur with the total physical fitness score. By increasing the performance within these three items, the total fitness score therefore will also show a proportionate increase.

An individual analysis can also be made on each child to determine specific areas of weakness. Any child who has extremely low scores on all test items should be referred to the school nurse or family doctor for additional diagnosis. Low physical scores, particularly for children who may appear to be healthy, may often indicate that the child may be suffering from nutritional or temporary illnesses. After these low fitness cases are checked by competent medical authorities and the diagnosis is simply lack of adequate exercise, appropriate remedial steps can be taken by the teacher and parents.

Selection of Appropriate Activities

All teachers of physical education are confronted with a multiple purpose of providing vigorous physical activities, teaching motor skills, and providing experiences that will foster intellectual and social development. An analysis of the areas of contribution of physical fitness inherent in each activity shown in the chart on page 648 indicates there is no single activity that can accomplish this task. Furthermore, no single activity can accomplish one or all of the objectives of a well-rounded physical education program. The value of the chart is that it indicates the high and low contributions of each activity with respect to the basic elements of physical fitness.

To illustrate the use of the accompanying chart, let us assume we have tested a fourth grade class in September and found results similar to those shown in the sample score sheet in the preceding section. The class is in definite need of activities that will increase the strength and endurance of arm and shoulder girdle, abdominal and leg muscles. During the first few months of the school year, pleasant weather and student interest are two strong factors that would indicate an outdoor activity would be the most suitable choice. Assuming the teacher decided to begin with a four-week unit on soccer activities, we note in the chart that soccer as a "skill game" is a low contributor to strength and high in the remaining items. Recognizing this inherent weakness of the activity and the need for activities involving strength, the teacher should emphasize within the warm-up period exercises involving strength of the arm and shoulder girdle, abdominal and leg muscles.

ACTIVITIES AND PHYSICAL FITNESS

Type of Activity	Area of Contribution							
	Strength		Endurance		Power		Speed	
	High	Low	High	Low	High	Low	High	Low
Games								
Relays		X	X		X		X	
Tag Games		X	X		X		X	
Skill Games		X	X		X		X	
Scooter Activities		X	X		X		X	
Dance								
Fundamental Skills		X		X		X		X
Singing Games		X		X		X		X
Folk Dances		X		X		X		X
Creative Rhythms		X		X	X		X	
Self-Testing								
Conditioning Exercises	X		X		X			X
Rubber Band Exercises	X		X		X			X
Vaulting Box	X		X		X		X	
Balance Beam		X		X		X	X	
Rope Skipping	X		X			X	X	
Horizontal Bar	X		X		X			X
Climbing Rope	X		X		X			X
Stunts and Tumbling	X		X		X		X	
Swedish Gym	X		X		X			X
Climbing Cube	X		X		X			X
Overhead Ladder	X		X		X			X
Agility Apparatus	X		X		X			X

Other units of instruction involving games, dance or self-testing activities should be analyzed for their potential contribution towards enhancing physical fitness. Once the inherent limitations of the activity are known, supplemental activities can be included in the unit of instruction to meet the physical fitness needs of the class.

There may be situations where a major concern for physical fitness by the teacher, other school authorities, and the general public requires immediate remedial programs. This strong concern has been voiced by the President's Council on Physical Fitness as well as by leading medical authorities and members of the physical education profession. It is the opinion of this writer, as well as of many other physical educators, that we should provide a diversity of physical activities, such as those shown under Self-Testing, rather than develop a daily fifteen or twenty minute vigorous calisthenic program for all grade levels in the elementary school. The logic in the broad based activity program is simply that it not only produces physically fit children but, in addition, develops many useful motor skills and a long range positive attitude toward maintaining an optimum level of physical fitness.

A CUMULATIVE RECORD OF PHYSICAL FITNESS

The cumulative record shown on page 650 is a method of plotting a child's performance on each test item at the beginning and end of each school year.* If all teachers within a school decide to adopt a cumulative record such as the one that will be described, it will produce extremely desirable results for teachers, children, and parents. By plotting a child's performance at the beginning and end of each school year, one gains an insight into the effectiveness of the physical education program as well as a clear understanding of what specific improvements each child has made. Another value inherent in the cumulative record is its diagnostic and predictive ability. This is well illustrated in the six year record of Mark Brown shown on page 650.

In analyzing Mark's performance in relationship to his height and weight gains, it becomes quite evident why he produced a definite decline on all items in the Spring test of his eighth year. In essence, he was simply too heavy for his age and height. However, during the second phase of his ninth year his record shows a significant increase in height coupled with a loss of eighteen pounds. The charts also show a general increase in all items of physical fitness from his ninth through twelfth year. With this type of record, each succeeding teacher could understand Mark's potentialities and set appropriate goals for him to achieve within each respective grade level.

The value of a cumulative record of physical fitness extends beyond the realm of physical education. School nurses and parents can refer to this record for answers relating to sudden changes in height, weight, and physical performance.

---

*The Cumulative Record shown on page 650 was developed by Mr. Larry Merlino, Federal Way Public School District, Federal Way, Washington.

CUMULATIVE PHYSICAL FITNESS RECORD
AGES 6 – 12

Name _____

Address _____

School _____

Grade   Teacher
1 _____
2 _____
3 _____
4 _____
5 _____
6 _____

Age	Ht. In.	Wt. Lbs.	Test No.	Date	Standing Broad Jump			Bench Push-ups			Curl-ups			Squat Jump			30-yd. Dash			Total Physical Fitness	
					S	P	R	S	P	R	S	P	R	S	P	R	S	P	R	P	R
6	48	53	1	Sept. 1960	29	36	4	4	34	5	8	48	3	9	39	4	7.5	37	4	194	4
	49	55	2	May 1961	32	40	4	10	45	3	12	53	3	12	44	4	6.7	47	3	229	3
7	51	59	1	Sept. 1961	38	43	4	14	48	3	15	52	3	16	46	3	6.5	45	3	234	3
	52.5	62	2	May 1962	47	55	2	20	54	3	20	56	2	22	52	3	5.7	57	2	274	3
8	53	63	1	Sept. 1962	57	62	2	27	58	2	30	59	2	33	58	2	5.1	60	2	297	2
	53	85	2	May 1963	43	44	4	11	43	4	14	48	3	9	35	5	6.3	39	4	209	4
9	53.5	86	1	Sept. 1963	44	42	4	12	45	3	16	48	3	11	37	4	6.0	37	4	209	4
	56	68	2	May 1964	50	50	3	20	53	3	23	53	3	24	50	3	5.3	53	3	259	3
10	57	74	1	Sept. 1964	55	52	3	22	54	3	28	53	3	30	51	3	5.0	52	3	262	3
	58	79	2	May 1965	60	58	2	27	57	2	33	57	2	34	54	3	4.9	55	2	281	2
11	58	80	1	Sept. 1965	64	58	2	31	59	2	35	55	2	36	53	3	4.7	56	2	281	2
	59	85	2	May 1966	68	63	2	37	63	2	40	57	2	40	56	2	4.5	60	2	299	2
12	61	90	1	Sept. 1966	72	64	2	39	64	2	43	62	2	42	58	2	4.4	62	2	310	2
	61.5	93	2	May 1967	79	71	1	44	68	1	46	66	1	48	64	2	4.1	68	1	337	1

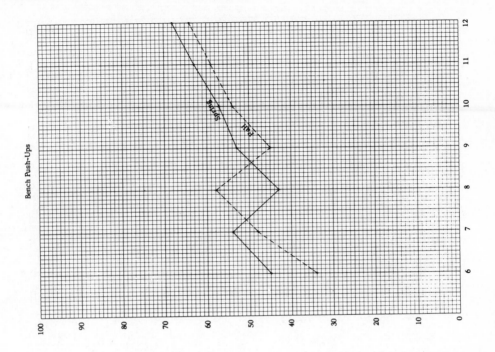

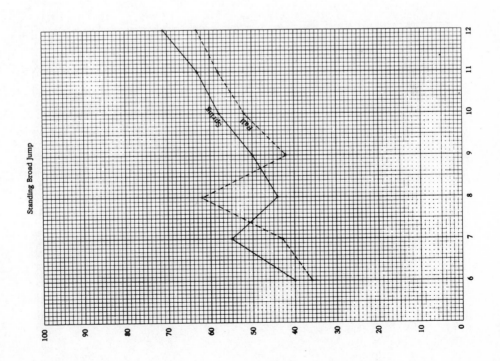

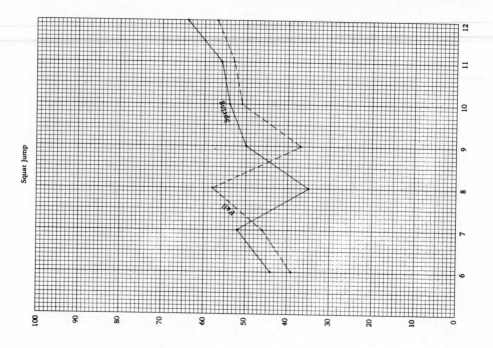

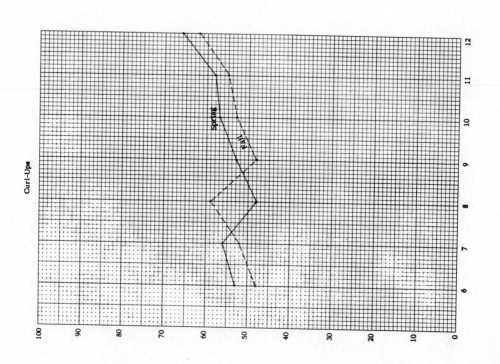

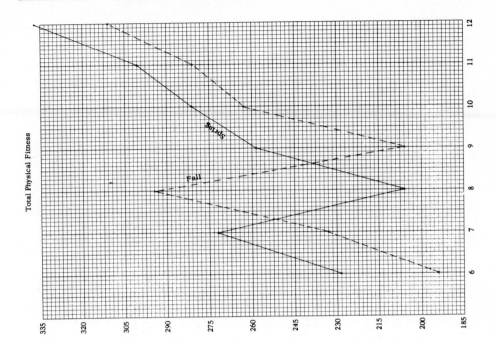

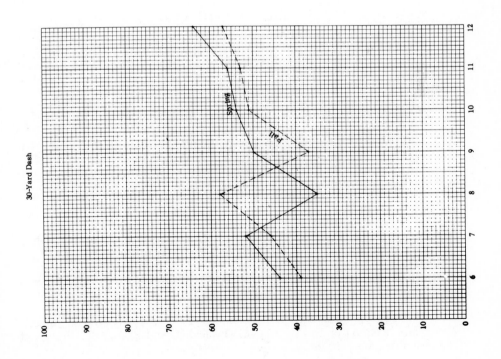

How to Construct a Cumulative Record

Before adopting any cumulative record, a committee composed of teachers, administrators, medical supervisors, and possibly parents should be assigned the responsibility of preparing a form that will include mutually agreed upon items. Other items such as skill performance, attendance, and information relating to social adjustment may also be included on this form. Care should be taken to develop a form that is informative yet simple in its instructions and efficient in its recording. The following suggestions will assist in developing a useful and practical cumulative record.

1. Involve representatives of all personnel who will eventually use the cumulative record.
2. Immediately following each test administration record all pertinent data.
3. Establish a standard procedure for recording and storing records.
4. Establish a procedure for transferring cumulative records to each succeeding teacher.
5. Establish a policy of forwarding complete cumulative record of each sixth grader to his junior high school.
6. Establish a policy of periodic review of the cumulative record and make appropriate additions and changes as dictated by the needs of the program and other pertinent factors.

SELECTED REFERENCES

American Association for Health, Physical Education, and Recreation, *Youth Fitness Test Manual.* Washington, D.C., AAHPER 1966.

California Performance Tests, Bureau of Health Education, Physical Education and Recreation, California State Department of Education, Sacramento, California, 1962.

CLARKE, H. HARRISON, and HAAR, FRANKLIN B. *Health and Physical Education for the Elementary School Classroom Teacher.* Englewood Cliffs, New Jersey: Prentice-Hall, Inc., 1964.

CLARKE, H. H. *Application of Measurement to Health and Physical Education,* 4th Edition. Englewood Cliffs, New Jersey: Prentice-Hall, Inc., 1967.

HUNSICKER, P. *Physical Fitness: What Research Says to the Teacher,* No. 26, Washington, D.C.: Department of Classroom Teachers, N.E.A., 1963.

KRAUS, HANS, and HIRSCHLAND, RUTH P. "Muscular Fitness and Health," *Journal for the American Association for Health, Physical Education and Recreation,* Vol. 24, December, 1963.

National Conference on Fitness of Children of Elementary School Age, "Children and Fitness: A Program for Elementary Schools." Washington, D.C., AAHPER 1959.

President's Council on Youth Fitness, "Youth Physical Fitness: Suggested Elements of a School-Centered Program." Washington, D.C.: U.S. Government Printing Office, 1961.

The New York State Physical Fitness Test for Boys and Girls Grades 4-12, Albany, New York: Division of Health, Physical Education and Recreation, Bureau of Physical Education, 1958.

SUGGESTED FILMS

Title: "The Time of Our Lives"
Details: 16 mm., 28 minutes, sound, color
Distributor: Association Films
Description: For family audiences—designed to encourage interest in physical fitness and emphasize relaxation
Purchase Price: $145.00. Free Loan

Title: "Vigorous Physical Fitness Activities"
Details: 16 mm., 13½ minutes, color, black and white
Distributor: President's Council on Physical Fitness, Washington, D.C.
Description: Shows how to get maximum participation in the physical activity period through proper use of time, equipment, and facilities
Purchase Price: Color $55.00; Black and White $30.00

Title: "Youth Physical Fitness—A Basic School Program"
Details: 16 mm., 13 minutes, color and black and white
Distributor: President's Council on Physical Fitness
Description: Gives overview of an elementary school physical education program and illustrates techniques of physical fitness testing
Purchase Price: Color $65.00; Black and White $30.00

Title: "Youth Physical Fitness, A Report to the Nation"
Details: 16 mm., 28 minutes, color, sound
Distributor: Equitable Life Assurance, 1285 Avenue of Americas, New York
Description: Demonstrates how school and community groups will benefit from a well-rounded physical education program
Free Loan

Appendixes

Inexpensive Equipment

1. Skipping Ropes
2. Horizontal Bar
3. Inner Tube Tires
4. Balance Beam
5. Balance Bench
6. Scooters
7. Wands
8. Vaulting Box
9. Sawhorse
10. Jumping Boxes

1. SKIPPING ROPES

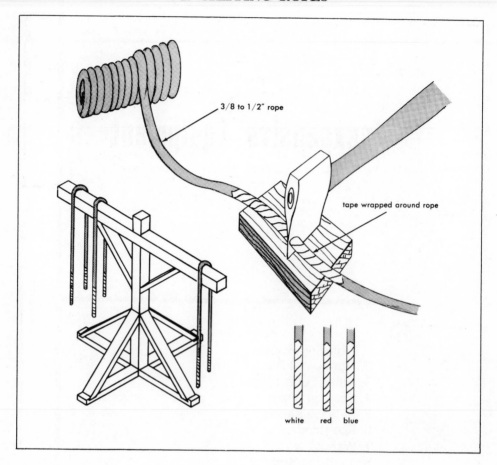

3/8 to 1/2″ rope

tape wrapped around rope

white   red   blue

To Cut Ropes:

1. Measure off the desired length of rope.
2. Wrap five inches above and below the cut mark with tape (plastic preferred; adhesive acceptable).
3. Place rope on small wooden block and cut rope in middle of taped area.

To Store Ropes:

1. Since there may be three or four different lengths of rope, dip the ends of the ropes in different colored paint to represent short, medium, and long lengths. (Dip about six inches.)
2. A simple way to store ropes is across or over a bar as shown above. The standard can be of any design with the top bar about four feet off the floor.

2. HORIZONTAL BAR

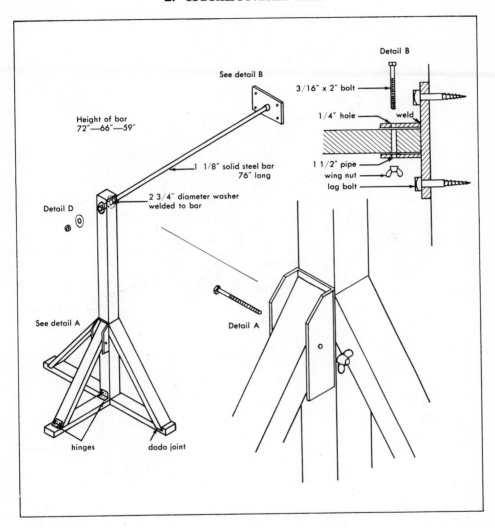

Detail B

3/16" x 2" bolt

1/4" hole — weld

1 1/2" pipe
wing nut
lag bolt

See detail B

Height of bar
72"—66"—59"

1 1/8" solid steel bar
76" long

2 3/4" diameter washer
welded to bar

Detail D

See detail A

Detail A

hinges   dado joint

General Features:

The above horizontal bar can be made at a cost of approximately fifteen to twenty dollars. It is designed for efficient assemblage and storage. The bolt as shown in Detail B prevents the bar from rotating while performing stunts. The bar is held firmly to the upright standard with a fixed 2¾" washer on the inside and a washer and bolt shown in Detail D. For efficient storage, the side support shown in Detail A may be drawn upward.

Designed by Bill Bressler
Drawn by Gary Sciuchetti

3. INNER TUBE TIRES

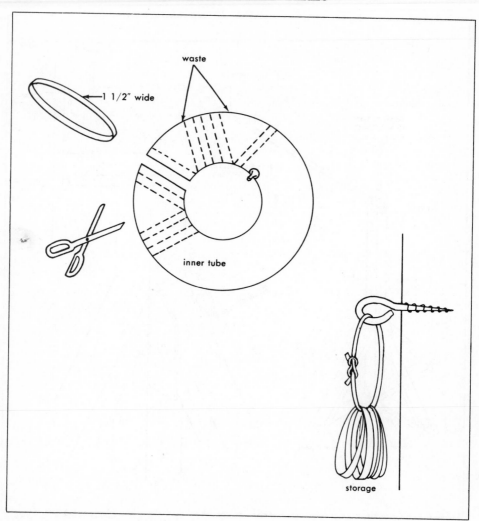

General Features:

The best type of inner tube is the one used in tractor size tires; however, the inner tubes used in most automobile tires are quite acceptable. With ordinary scissors, cut across the tube, then cut three or four bands. At the end of the fourth cut you will have an undesirable angle; cut this piece off (see waste above) and begin the next series of cuts. After cutting the bands, wash them with regular soap and water to remove dirt and powder usually found on the inside surface of the tube. For efficient storage, tie a rope around the bands and hang them in your storage room.

4. BALANCE BEAM

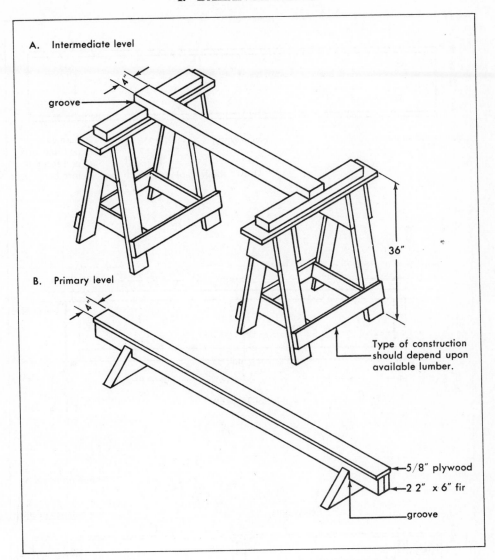

A.   Intermediate level

groove

4″

36″

B.   Primary level

4″

Type of construction
should depend upon
available lumber.

5/8″ plywood

2 2″ x 6″ fir

groove

General Information:

The diagram of the intermediate level balance beam is basically a 12′ ×
4″ beam mounted on two sawhorses. Standard competition height for a beam
is four feet; however, for intermediate level children, the height may range
from 3½′ to a maximum of 4′. It is also desirable to make the grooves for the
low and high balance beams the same in order to mount the same beam on
both standards.

5. BALANCE BENCH

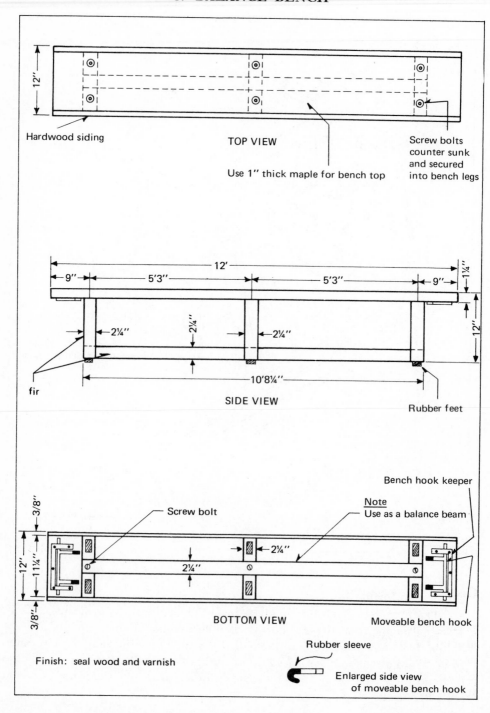

Hardwood siding

TOP VIEW

Use 1" thick maple for bench top

Screw bolts counter sunk and secured into bench legs

fir

SIDE VIEW

Rubber feet

Bench hook keeper

Screw bolt

<u>Note</u>
Use as a balance beam

BOTTOM VIEW

Moveable bench hook

Rubber sleeve

Enlarged side view of moveable bench hook

Finish: seal wood and varnish

6. SCOOTERS

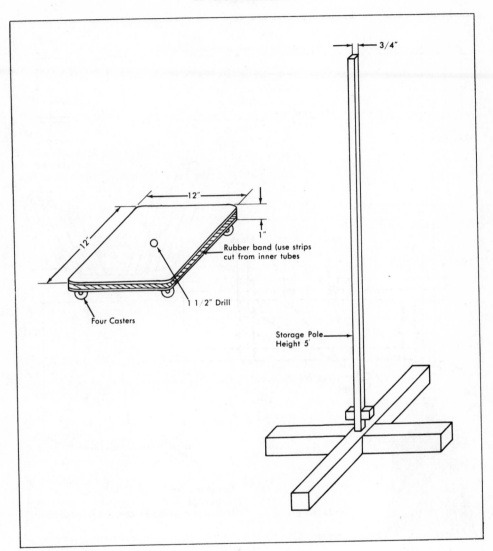

General Information:

An inexpensive set of floor scooters may be made from ¾" plywood and plastic casters. Cut 12" squares, round the edges and attach a strip of rubber around the outside edge. The latter strip prevents the edges from splintering as well as lessens the noise when scooters hit. A simple way to store scooters is illustrated above. The pole should be at least ¾" thick and firmly attached to the base.

7. WANDS

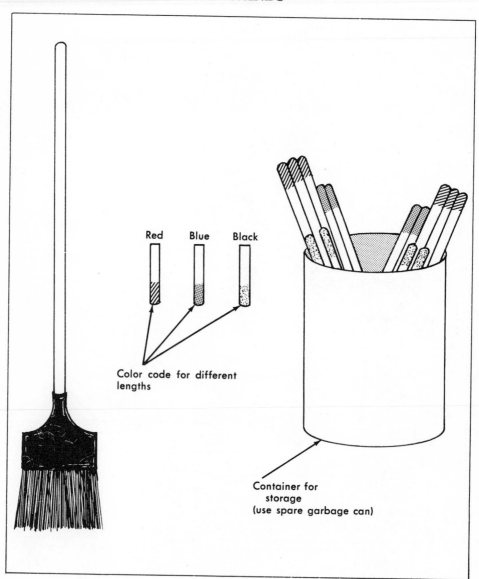

Red   Blue   Black

Color code for different
lengths

Container for
storage
(use spare garbage can)

General Information:

A set of wands (see Chapter 5 for appropriate lengths) may be made from old broom handles. Cut each broom handle off at the desired length and round both ends. Dip the end of each set of wands in different colored paint to facilitate each selection.

8. VAULTING BOX

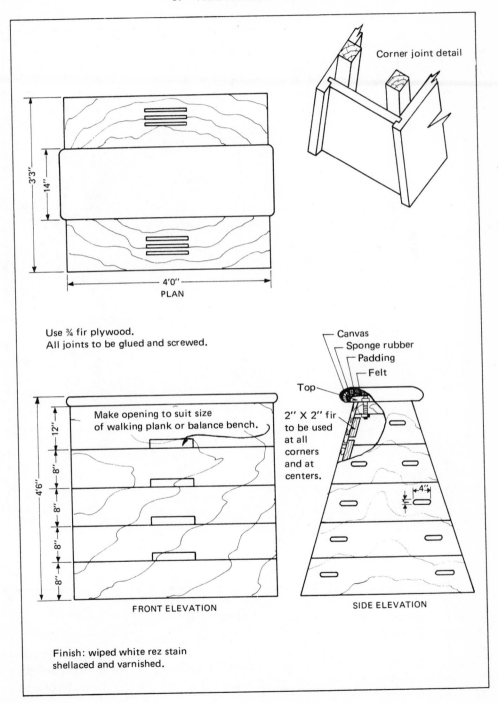

Corner joint detail

3'3"
14"
4'0"
PLAN

Use ¾ fir plywood.
All joints to be glued and screwed.

Canvas
Sponge rubber
Padding
Felt
Top

Make opening to suit size
of walking plank or balance bench.

2" X 2" fir
to be used
at all
corners
and at
centers.

12"
8"
8"
8"
4'6"
4"

FRONT ELEVATION

SIDE ELEVATION

Finish: wiped white rez stain
shellaced and varnished.

9. SAWHORSE

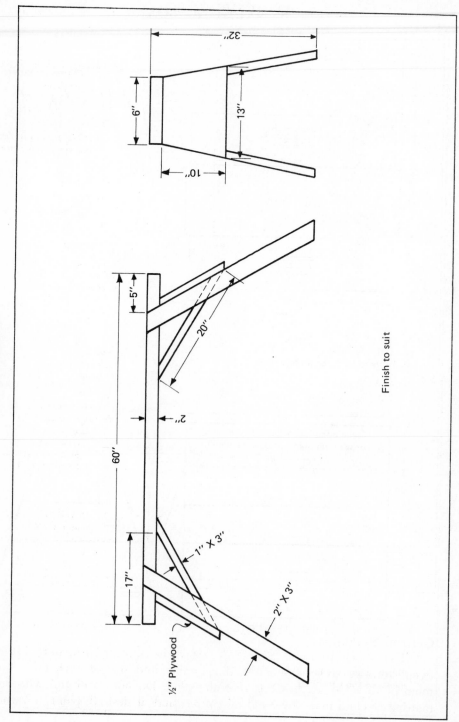

Finish to suit

10. JUMPING BOXES

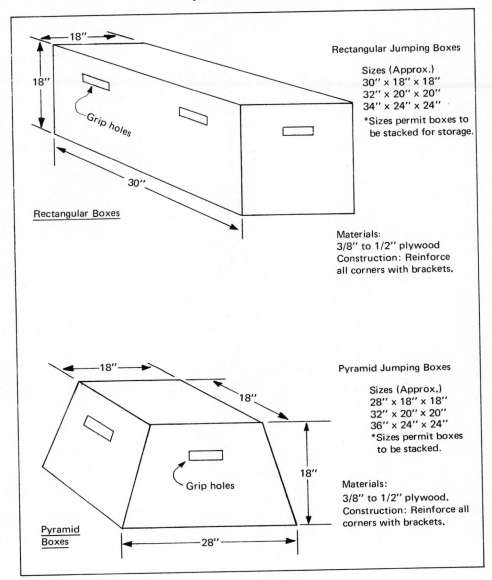

Rectangular Jumping Boxes

Sizes (Approx.)
30" x 18" x 18"
32" x 20" x 20"
34" x 24" x 24"
*Sizes permit boxes to
be stacked for storage.

Grip holes

30"

Rectangular Boxes

Materials:
3/8" to 1/2" plywood
Construction: Reinforce
all corners with brackets.

18"

18"

18"

Pyramid Jumping Boxes

Sizes (Approx.)
28" x 18" x 18"
32" x 20" x 20"
36" x 24" x 24"
*Sizes permit boxes
to be stacked.

18"

Grip holes

18"

Materials:
3/8" to 1/2" plywood.
Construction: Reinforce all
corners with brackets.

Pyramid
Boxes

28"

General Features:

The above Jumping Boxes can be made for approximately fifteen to twenty dollars, depending upon the number and size of each box. A minimum of three for each set is recommended. Do not cover top with rubber matting or cloth material. Sand all corners and, if desired, paint or varnish.

Index

Index